The Essential Internet Information Guide

The Essential Internet Information Guide

Jason J. Manger

McGRAW-HILL BOOK COMPANY

London · New York · St Louis · San Francisco · Auckland · Bogotá · Caracas
Lisbon · Madrid · Mexico · Milan · Montreal · New Delhi · Panama · Paris
San Juan · São Paulo · Singapore · Sydney · Tokyo · Toronto

Published by
McGRAW-HILL Book Company Europe
Shoppenhangers Road, Maidenhead, Berkshire, SL6 2QL, England
Telephone 0628 23432
Fax 0628 770224

British Library Cataloguing in Publication Data

Manger, Jason J.
  Essential Internet Information Guide
  I. Title
  004.6
  ISBN 0–07–707905–1

Library of Congress Cataloging-in-Publication Data

Manger, Jason
  The essential internet information guide / Jason Manger
      p.   cm.
  Includes index.
  ISBN 0–07–707905–1
  1. Internet (Computer network)   I. Title.
  TK5105.875.I57M364   1994
  005.7′ 13- -dc20   94–157082
                                                                           CIP

12345 BL 98765

Typeset by Alden Multimedia, Northampton
and printed and bound in Great Britain by Biddles Ltd, Guildford, Surrey.

Contents

Appendix D   The A–Z Internet resource guide   373
Appendix E   A–Z anonymous FTP listings   441
Appendix F   Internet domains: country codes and hostname details   452
Appendix G   A–Z USENET group listings   457
Index   509

Acknowledgements

Many thanks to Grahame Davies of Demon Internet Systems UK, who gave me unlimited access to their Internet system while this book was being written. Thanks also to Adrian Hall of the IBM PC User Group, who gave me a free trial period of their system. Both Demon's and the IBMPCUG system were a pleasure to use and I recommend them highly to all potential UK Internet users. My thanks also to Jane Waters, Rupert Knight and Jenny Ertle of publishers McGraw-Hill UK for their comments and much-welcomed feedback during the writing of this book, and a note of gratitude to Eric Munson of McGraw-Hill US, who originally put me in touch with the publishing division in the UK and thus started this project (it's all a bit complicated really). Finally, thanks to my cat, Minou, who kept me company throughout those long and arduous keyboard sessions, and to all the users of the Cyberspace who gave me details on their systems for inclusion in this book.

1
Introduction

1.1 Introduction to the Internet

In many ways the Internet exhibits features similar to that of our own universe: seemingly endless and vastly unexplored. What we can conclude, however, is that the Internet is the world's largest computer network and information resource. From its inception well over twenty years ago, the Internet has grown from just a few computers into a vast network of many tens of thousands of machines which currently serve many millions of users worldwide. Future estimates for the 21st century predict that one billion nodes will carry Internet traffic, and that in excess of 20 million people will have on-line access to the network.

THE INTERNET AND TCP/IP

One of the most important observations that we can make about the Internet is that it uses a suite of standard protocols, namely TCP/IP (Transmission Control Protocol/Internet Protocol), and that the protocol is very robust. For all intents and purposes the TCP/IP protocol *is* the Internet. In computing terms, standardization is a very difficult task to achieve although the Internet is one glaring exception with respect to TCP/IP. The TCP/IP protocol can also be implemented independently of any machine-platform, so it doesn't matter if you are using the Internet from a PC, an Atari ST or even a VAX 11/785 super minicomputer; just as long as all hosts are running TCP/IP, they can communicate – hence the massive expansion in the network between different hardware platforms.

THE INTERNET'S GENESIS

The Internet itself grew out of a military experiment that was undertaken in the 1970s by the US Defense Department (also known as DARPA). In those days the 'Internet', as it is known today, was referred to as the ARPAnet and the system was very much in the experimental stage. In essence, DARPA wanted to build a network that was disaster-proof, principally during the time of war, and they succeeded, as was to be proven two decades later. Back to the 1990s, and DARPA's research was being put to the test during the Gulf conflict. At the time, Iraq was in posession of TCP/IP routers to join together computers in order to facilitate its chain-of-command. Western attempts to destroy portions of the Iraqi network to cut these vital information links were made extremely difficult by the fact that the robust TCP/IP protocol simply bypassed those nodes that had been put out of action in order to reconnect the network. The reader may also be interested to know that the Internet Relay Chat service (see Chapter 10) was used extensively during the Gulf conflict to convey events in real time, i.e. 'events as they happened'. Many war experts were quoted on IRC channels around the world at the time of the conflict and the actual conversations are available on the network to examine.

Of course, the Internet is not a new system. You may therefore have been surprised to hear about the existence of this vast resource in the computer media over recent years. This has been due to a combination of factors. Becoming part of the network was, until recently, very difficult. The Internet has always been feared in many respects, the network being seen as solely an environment for technical denizens and academics. Such a belief is clearly total nonsense even though such users do, of course, inhabit the network. The key point is that they are not the only users. Internet services have also been described as being very esoteric and following only very specialized channels of information. There is a certain amount of truth in this statement, although this is easily outweighed by the sheer size of the Internet's user-population and its ability to adapt to new informational needs very quickly. Esoteric services exist because the Internet is a global resource; people will use the resource to advertise and promote their local services, just as we might advertise a local fund-raising event in our own home town, for example.

As well as being a very public resource, the Internet is also a very private resource. You can tap away in the privacy of your own home while experimenting with various services without any external distractions. There are also very few concrete rules regarding use of the system ('rules' are mainly formulated by the network users themselves and are referred to aptly as netiquette – most rules therefore tend to be based around the individual rather than the network). This particular aspect of the network makes it a joy to use since you no longer have to belong to a college or university to gain access to the system. Put quite simply, the Internet is information for the masses.

The open-access aspect of the Internet has been causing much concern in recent months. Stories about malicious hackers roaming the Internet are undoubtedly true, and there are additional problems, such as the passing of illegal or 'pirated' software between computers – a task made easier through global computer networks. Many companies are placing firewalls (buffers and data filters) between themselves and the network in a bid to stop unauthorized access to their resources, or to allow only verified data to pass through their network. This is a great shame because the Internet's ultimate strength lies in its flexible and undiscriminating accessibility. All of these problems can't be that worrying, however, since the queue of people wanting access to the network grows ever longer, and new resources become available on a daily basis.

Because the Internet has undergone a technical evolution it does tend to appeal to the more established computer user, in whatever capacity. The Internet has developed very quickly owing to the interest and input generated by other computer users. In saying this, however, the newly established home computer user (HCU) can get up-and-running without any extensive knowledge of computers, or indeed of the Internet. Some knowlege of your computer's operating system and a modem device (plus this book by your side) will quickly allow you to dial into a whole new world of information. Another important point regarding the success of the Internet among HCUs has been the willingess of commercial service-providers to supply the public with cheap access to the network. This has boosted interest in the Internet almost exponentially, and has led to much of the media coverage. Probably the most important point regarding the Internet from your own viewpoint is that it is here, now.

1.2   Readership

You do not have to understand the intricacies of the TCP/IP protocol in order to use the Internet. Indeed, the operation of the underlying protocol is transparent to the end-user. It is, however, assumed that you have used some sort of computer at one time or another. The majority of examples given in this book are for a system called Unix, although you do not have to understand Unix in order to use the Internet. As with all things, you can get by with just a little bit of knowledge and then expand upon this as the need arises. Both Unix and the Internet are closely related; many of the standard Internet tools in existence have stemmed from the Unix operating system (notably the `mail`, `ftp` and `telnet` programs). Unix is used extensively in academic environments – its birthplace – although if you are a home computer user then you will probably have access to a personal computer (PC) running an operating system such as DOS, rather than an expensive Sun workstation running Unix.

THE UNIX MYTH

As mentioned earlier, much of the development behind the Internet has been carried out on Unix-based systems. In reality, however, you need not be a Unix expert in order to use the Internet; commands from Unix systems can be translated into an equivalent command on most other systems without too much fuss. In theory, any computer can connect to the Internet – DOS, UNIX, VMS, Amiga, Apple, and even Atari-based machines have their own place on the network and have been accessing the network for many years.

1.3   Why would I want to use the Internet?

In summary, any person with an informational requirement may want to use the Internet. It is very easy to get bogged down into categorizing different groups of people who may or may not have an interest in the network. All that I am going to say on this matter is that the system will appeal to all users, whatever their background.

If you are already a computer user, the Internet is an almost endless source of technical information and software (freeware and shareware software databases are abundant), and the system is updated minute-by-minute. The Internet is also a great place to chat with other users on any subject or topic. USENET is the Internet's 'news' network; its size and subject coverage is truly overwhelming and it would be impossible to read all of the news available. Instead, people subscribe to a handful of groups and read the news in these to keep abreast of developments in their chosen areas. If you are fed up being a MSDOS user, you don't have to be any more; you can use your computer to access a Unix machine instead. Appendix D (the A–Z resource guide) lists many of the services you can access on the network – although be warned, the Internet is highly addictive, and just browsing to see what is available can be a good enough reason to join up. Students invariably require access to all sorts of information during their studies, and the Internet can be used for just this purpose; students may want to use the network to browse on-line databases, or to search library OPACs for a book or other published works. The Internet also breaks down campus boundaries and allows students access to other academic institutions and their research.

Business users will not know what they have been missing. A global network which can reach potential customers and audiences in seconds. A network with an abundance of free material on news and business-related subject areas are available on systems such as Clarinet, a branch of the USENET news network which specializes in news from all over the world; other USENET hierarchies, such as the `biz.*` groups, carry advertisements and other market information for businesses. The Internet is also a great way for companies to keep in touch. Electronic mail (and electronic conferencing) between geographically separated offices will be one immediate help with respect to intercompany communications. Electronic mail is now placed alongside the ubiquitous facsimile and telephone, and it almost seems strange for a company to advertise without an email address. Some of the largest companies in the world have been using the Internet for years, including 3-COM, Apple, AT&T, Boeing, DEC, Dell, Honeywell, IBM, Intel, Samsung, Siemens, Sony, Unisys, and Xerox, as well as many dozens of other small and medium-sized businesses.

The one thing that Internet does best is to put people in touch with one another. Electronic mail and real-time chat facilities are among the most popular services that currently exist on the network. The ability to share information is one of the cornerstone principles of the Internet. Remember, information on the Internet covers many general topics, not just computing – as is widely believed – so the Internet will appeal to the majority of people either in a professional, academic or leisurely capacity.

1.4 System requirements and purchasing advice

If you are a student or academic user with access to a computer that is already connected to the Internet you clearly do not need any additional equipment. You can therefore delve straight in at your own pace. Home computer users will, however, require the following:

- Your own telephone line (you probably have this already)
- A modem device (this will allow your telephone to communicate with a remote computer via the telephone-network)
- A computer (a personal computer, such as an IBM PC or clone, etc. is probably the cheapest piece of equipment available)
- An Internet account provided by a local service-provider.

If you are purchasing a modem device ensure that it is capable of at least 2400 baud (or the V22bis standard), although we strongly advise that you purchase a 9600 baud or even a 14 400 baud modem, now that prices have dropped significantly for this type of equipment. Most service-providers do not support speeds less than 2400 baud. We also advise you to check with your service-provider before purchasing any equipment; check with them to see which computers they support, since most will provide you with some specially configured software that you must use with their system (this runs something like the TCP/IP protocol on your PC, etc., TCP/IP being the fundamental communications protocol used over the entire Internet network). Dial-up access is the most common way of gaining entry into a service-provider's machine (this in turn allows access to the Internet network via a dedicated line from their machine). A variety of systems are in use: in some cases you may dial up a provider and gain access to a Unix account or other interface. Other systems may provide an interface via a software program on your own computer which facilitates the entry of commands to access the Internet's services. Appendix B details many of the service-providers that provide Internet access; information on choosing a provider and the system features to look for are also documented in this appendix, so read carefully before you pay any subscription.

A personal computer (PC) will be completely satisfactory for all of your requirements; a monochrome screen-based system can be used if you are on a budget, but ensure the machine has a hard disk (or hard card) so that you can store the information you download. Conventional floppy-disk-only systems will not have the capacity to store both the communications software and the information that you want to download. Your system will also be very slow to operate with just a floppy-disk-based computer, mainly since floppy disks are much slower to read and write from than hard disks. You may also consider getting hold of a printer, since you will be accumulating a lot of information that you may want to refer to later on paper. Don't get it wrong – computers will not replace books for a long while yet, if ever.

1.5 Notation conventions

Internet hostnames (i.e. names of computer sites), interactive commands and filenames are all set in Courier, e.g. 'Access ftp.uu.net and get hold of the file in directory /pub/pc/graphics called gws.zip'. All example program output is also given in the Courier font. Commands that require a carriage return to be pressed after them are followed by the symbol ↵. Special keyboard keys are enclosed in square-brackets, for example [Return], [Tab], [Space], etc. For commands that require compulsory arguments (an option, file, etc. that must be given) the argument will be enclosed in chevrons, e.g. whois <person>; optional arguments are enclosed in square-brackets, e.g. telnet [hostname]. Commands that take multiple arguments, such as filenames, are denoted using the <arg-1..arg-n> notation, for example, the command mget <file-1,..file-n> specifies that the mget command can be used with multiple filenames, where the actual filename(s) are themselves compulsory.

Most of the interactive examples assume that they have been typed on a Unix system. Unix is an interactive system, just like MSDOS, VMS, etc., and the command prompt is commonly a $ or %. On MSDOS this would be a C:\>, or something very similar at least. Only local commands, i.e. local to your own operating system (or local to your communications software package) will be different. Whether your system prompt is a $, % or C:\>, the actual commands you type will essentially be the same, whatever system is in use.

1.6 What subject areas does this book cover?

The Internet is a vast resource, and yet only three basic tools are ever required in order to use it, namely: (i) FTP (File Transfer Protocol) – to download files from remote Internet hosts; (ii) TELNET (the virtual terminal protocol) used to access real-time systems and databases interactively; and (iii) email (electronic mail) – used to send and receive messages from other users and to post messages to USENET. In addition, you may need to learn how to use a newsreader in order to browse USENET articles that interest you (although as you will come to see, this is not compulsory). As well as covering the core tools such as FTP and TELNET, some new areas are also dealt with, including image processing and file compression, as well as the world of Internet Relay Chat (IRC).

Our emphasis in this book has not been placed on network technicalities (such as the TCP/IP protocol, etc.) but has instead been based upon end-user applications and tangible public services that the Internet offers. An abundance of literature on the Internet's TCP/IP protocol is available if required; a good reference to start with is *TCP/IP and Related Protocols,* McGraw-Hill, England.

As for this book, you can expect the following: Chapter 2 examines the USENET system, the world's largest 'bulletin-board' network. USENET has many thousands of discussion groups on nearly every subject you can think of. In this chapter we examine the standard Unix newsreaders such as nn and rn, and examine the internal structure of USENET messages. We also discuss how to send messages to USENET and to deal with binary files such as images and compressed files. Chapter 3 is all about FTP, the Internet's main file downloading tool. FTP allows you to access hundreds of remote machines that offer public information in the form of documents, user guides, images, sounds, and computer source code. We examine the FTP commands and how to browse remote file systems for the information you require. Services such as FTPmail are also discussed for users without access to an FTP program. Chapter 4 follows on from FTP and discusses the Archie service. Archie is a file-archiving program and allows you to search for files stored on anonymous FTP sites all over the world. Archie is used in conjunction with FTP to find the file(s) you require.

Chapter 5 discusses one of the core Internet commands, TELNET. This tool allows you to use a remote computer interactively. Many on-line services are publically available to the user. TELNET allows you to do such things as use a remote Unix machine from your own computer, or log in to a medical database to find information on a certain disease. TELNET must be learnt since it also allows access to services such as Archie. Chapter 6 explores Unix in a little more detail, and explains how it has provided many of the standard Internet-related commands. We examine tools such as UUCP, the first remote file-copying utility, now superseded by FTP, the r* programs such as rlogin, rsh and rdist, and other communication tools tip and cu, as well as old Unix favourites such as talk. An in-depth treatment is given to the configuration of such utilities in this chapter.

In Chapter 7 the topic of data compression is examined. The Internet employs data compression to save on disk resources and file transmission times. The whole area of compression has become very complex because of the lack of a single compression standard. We show you what formats to expect, what tools to use and get hold of, and where you can find them. A range of machine platforms are considered, including DOS (PC), Unix, Amiga, Atari and the NeXT hardware platform. Chapter 8 examines how images are transferred and accessed over the Internet, covering such subject areas as image formats, viewing utilities and the whereabouts (via FTP) of the best image freeware and shareware programs. A variety of machine platforms are again considered, taking into account DOS (PC), Unix, Amiga, Atari, Apple and the NeXT systems. USENET and FTP is explored in more detail to show how to access images, and the problem of image corruption and a series of remedies are all also explored in this extensive chapter.

Accessing textual information is the principle concern for most people on the Internet. In Chapter 9 the main information-retrieval tools are examined, including WAIS (Wide Area Information Server), Gopher and Veronica, and the World-Wide-Web (WWW) services. Dozens of examples are provided taking you step-by-step through each system. Whatever information you require, a tool for the task can be found in this chapter. Another area taking the Internet by storm is Internet Relay Chat (IRC), which allows users all over the world to communicate simultaneously. In Chapter 10 we examine the most common IRC client program and commands, and an extensive series of examples are provided in order to get you up-and-running. Finally, Chapter 11 looks at electronic mail, the most popular resource currently used on the Internet. The focus in this final chapter is on the Unix mail program, although all electronic mail programs are very similar to one another.

1.7   Hints and tips

Be on the lookout for hints and tips on each subject; these are scattered throughout each chapter and will provide you with shortcut solutions to many problems, as well as pointing you in the right direction for many other related tools and utilities. An extensive set of appendices are also provided, including: (i) a list of Internet service providers (a requirement if you are considering becoming a member of the Internet); (ii) commonly asked questions and answers (a series of Q&As dealing with the most common Internet problems); (iii) an extensive A–Z glossary of terms and acronyms; (iv) an A–Z resource guide to various Internet services available via the FTP, WAIS, Gopher,

WWW, TELNET, etc.; (v) an A–Z guide to well-known anonymous FTP sites and popular public software; (vi) an A–Z listing of all the main USENET newsgroups that are currently in existence; and (vii) a list of Internet country codes and details on how Internet hostnames are structured.

2

USENET – the global bulletin board system

2.1 Introduction to USENET

USENET (USErs NETwork) is the world's largest bulletin board system (BBS) and is made up solely of electronic mail messages. A recent survey of the USENET system found that around 20 000 articles arrive daily onto USENET and that the number of people accessing the system is approaching 2 million. The concept behind USENET is to provide the user with a vast range of subject areas, each of which is referred to as a newsgroup. Many thousands of newsgroups exist, covering nearly every subject you could care to think of. Although USENET cannot escape the technical bias that is inherent on nearly every part of the Internet (around 30 per cent of USENET is related to computing in one way or another) you will still find many hundreds of newsgroups covering non-Internet topics such as the arts and science-related subjects. In summary, USENET is a great place in which to read articles, express your own opinions and more importantly, to make new friends on the network.

All of the messages posted to USENET are ASCII, that is to say they are plain-text messages. In saying this, however, a number of binary forums also exist, and it is quite possible to download images, sounds, and even entire computer applications (via an ASCII-to-binary conversion). Users from all over the world post many thousands of messages to USENET on a daily basis; messages are uploaded to the newsgroup of your choice via electronic mail (needless to say, a variety of systems are available to post messages) and in the case of a rhetorical message, you can simply await responses from the people who read your posting and then decide to contact you. Some newsgroups act as repositories for complete computer applications freeware and shareware. All in all, USENET is a vast and somewhat anarchic system, kept alive solely by the fact that people want to share information. USENET contains well over 5000 individual newsgroups which can be accessed. In this chapter you will learn how to:

- Access USENET through your computer
- Understand how USENET is organized hierarchically
- Use an NNTP news-server to read and post messages
- Use the Unix-based newsreaders such as nn and rn
- Decode binary messages such as images, sounds and programs
- Access USENET without an email system
- Use an FTP-mail server to retrieve messages
- Subscribe to mailing lists in order to keep up-to-date with your chosen subject area

NOTES FOR NEW USENET USERS

The USENET system is continually changing. In order to get a list of the current newsgroups you are advised to use a newsreader and examine the news.lists newsgroup. Alternatively you can use an NNTP news-server to browse which newsgroups are available. If you are a first-time USENET user and you have access to the Unix nn newsreader, run nn and then exit with the Q command immediately. The file .newsrc will then have a list of all USENET newsgroups which you can print to examine. You may also want to keep abreast of new groups by looking at the newsgroup news.announce.newgroups. New users should also examine the group news.announce.newusers. Users without access to a Unix newsreader such as nn and rn will have to use their own systems – these will be extremely similar to, if not clones of, the most popular Unix newsreaders.

2.2 An introduction to the USENET system and its terminology

This section examines the USENET system in more detail, and describes how USENET is organized and distributed over the Internet.

THE USENET HIERARCHIES

Individual newsgroups are broken down into hierarchies which are distributed to Internet sites worldwide. Hierarchies are made up of a number of word-verbs which describe each newsgroup in question. A special newsgroup prefix is first allocated; these determine which hierarchies are available. Each prefix is then followed by one or more suffixes which break down the hierarchy into its respective subject areas (each suffix and prefix combination is separated by a period, .). An example hierarchy prefix is sci for science-related messages; a prefix for this hierarchy could be astro for astronomy-related messages so a USENET group entitled sci.astro.hubble deals with events concerning the Hubble space telescope. The most important USENET hierarchies include those in Table 2.1.

In addition to the hierarchies listed in Table 2.1, additional prefixes for individual companies also exist, for example 'u3b' for AT&T 3B computers, and 'vmsnet' for the DEC/VAX range of computers that run the VMS operating system. Refer to the newsgroup news.lists for up-to-date USENET group and hierarchy details, since the network changes so rapidly. Groups in the alt hierarchy change very frequently, mainly because the procedure for starting a new newsgroup in this hierarchy is more lenient; other USENET hierarchies tend to be more permanently situated. In addition to the hierarchies mentioned you may find you have access to country-specific hierarchies. Germany, for example, uses hierarchy names beginning with 'de.', and many others exist. You should also be aware that some news-servers carry local newsgroups; these are used by local machines for passing on news and specific information local to a particular computer network, campus, etc. These could be passed to external news-servers, although it is unlikely unless they have a broad appeal (the alt.* hierarchy is a good example which has grown from a local newsgroup into a global newsgroup).

Table 2.1   USENET hierarchies (prefix names)

Prefix	Meaning
alt	The alternative hierarchy. Contains many hundreds of subject areas such as television, sex and religion
bionet	Biology-related subject areas
bit	BITNET newsgroups (because-it's-time network). Bitnet newsgroups are mainly implemented as mailing lists
biz	Business, marketing and advertisement related
comp	Computer related. These are mainly broken down into their respective areas, e.g. comp.os for operating systems, comp.protocols for computer protocols, etc.
gnu	Messages for the Free Software Foundation (GNU project)
ieee	Institute of Electrical and Electronics Engineers. This standard-setting body has its own hierarchy
k12	Children's hierarchy (kindergarten to high school)
misc	Miscellaneous hierarchy. This is used mainly as an overspill and contains groups concerning such subject matters as jobs, items for sale, etc.
news	All matters concerning USENET itself. Articles about newsreading software and general USENET developments are sent here
rec	Recreational hierarchy. Arts, hobbies and other recreational pursuits are covered here
sci	Science-related hierarchy
soc	Social issues hierarchy
talk	A hierarchy dedicated to the world's more controversial and political subjects areas, e.g. abortion, philosophy, the environment, etc.

NEWS DISTRIBUTION

USENET itself is referred to using many different names, although the terms 'NetNews' and 'The News' seem to be most common. In fact, USENET does not carry that much real 'news'; the Clarinet (clari.*) newsgroups are probably the best for real-life news stories since it is a privately run organization that carries news-wires on many important topics. Your systems administrator may have already organized a news-feed to the Clarinet USENET hierarchy, so check to make sure (see Appendix G for a full list of such newsgroups). The actual articles that are posted to USENET are referred to simply as 'articles' or 'postings'. The term postings has derived out of the fact that USENET is composed solely of electronic mail messages and these are posted between users over the network. Figure 2.1 illustrates how the USENET system is implemented, and how news-feeds are established with other sites. News propagates from one site to the next depending on how two adminis-

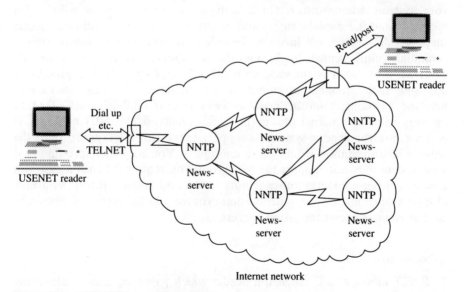

Figure 2.1　USENET server illustration

trators agree what news to share with each other. Sites therefore exchange news, and many newsgroups become distributed all over the world in this way.

All articles have an expiry date that will be set by the administrator of the USENET site that you are using. Expiry dates ensure that no messages are stored indefinitely (thus overburdening disk resources). Expiry dates also ensure that the messages you are reading are reasonably up-to-date. You can expect articles to have a life of between one and three weeks in most cases. The concept of collecting messages is quite simple; each USENET site that you contact has its own disk storage and is able to store as many messages as it is able to cope with (messages going back a month and more are sometimes found). When you come to browse these messages you use a newsreader to access the postings that interest you. It may be the case that your site does not actually store the messages locally, but instead you access a remote newsreader (such as an NNTP server – see Section 2.3 for more details). Other systems may actually download messages locally and then pass these on to you when required – this method is common on Unix systems where a special file called .newsrc contains the names of each individual newsgroup that you want to receive messages from. Newsreading software is available in abundance. Systems such as Unix use a standard set of readers such as rn or nn, although non-Unix systems (such as personal computer systems) will employ other alternatives.

News distribution is normally handled by a single dedicated machine commonly referred to as a 'news-server'. It is the duty of this server to provide the necessary disk storage to download all of the necessary USENET messages from each hierarchy. The hierarchies that are supported will be controlled by your systems administrator. On a daily basis the news-server will be fed messages, and these will be stored and then made available to users who access the server. The server machine may be able to be interrogated directly (this is commonly implemented by having the news-server answer on a specific telnet port – such is the case with NNTP news-servers). The process of accessing such messages is known as a 'news-feed'. A single news-server machine may contact another news-server in order to establish a news-feed. In this way all of the Internet sites in the world can access USENET messages. It is quite rare for a news-system to support every USENET group since the volume of information would be so enormous. You may therefore find that your system may not support the newsgroup you require (in such a case you can, of course, contact another remote server and enquire there). You may also be able to make your systems administrator add the necessary news-feed so that you can access the group concerned.

MESSAGE STRUCTURE

USENET messages are assigned a header which tells recipients all about the message. Your system will also include information such as the subject of the message, and even the number of lines that make up the posting. A typical header for a message can be seen in Fig. 2.2 (this header would be seen when you used a newsreader to read such messages – see Section 2.3 for examples with NNTP news-servers). All messages that are posted to USENET are assigned a unique identification code (the message-ID) and your news-server will use a unique numbering system for each USENET hierarchy in the case that messages are stored locally. Message identification codes are used by some newsreaders to keep track of what you have read, so that identical messages are not downloaded to your account. Different servers will allocate different

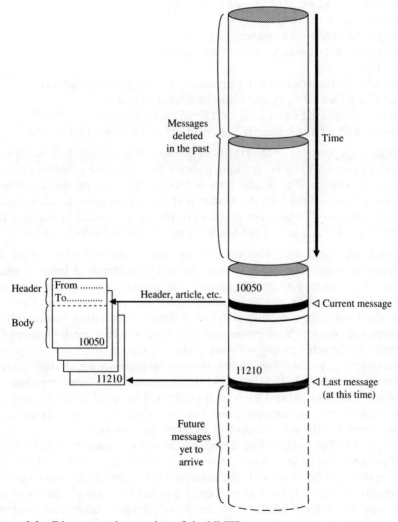

Figure 2.2 Diagrammatic overview of the NNTP news-server

IDs, and most will incorporate a time and date for part of the ID to indicate when the message was received. A typical header and message for a USENET posting could resemble that shown below:

```
From: jason@wombat.demon.co.uk (Jason Manger)
Newsgroups: comp.graphics
Subject: Graphics Workshop?
Summary:
Keywords: GWS
Message-ID: <1993Dec20.093901.868@demon.co.uk>
Date: Mon, 20 Dec 1993 09:39:01 GMT
Distribution: world
Sender: jason@news.demon.co.uk
Organization: Demon Computer Systems UK
Lines: 6
Does anyone know where I can obtain a copy of Graphics
Workshop via FTP?. Many thanks in advance.
>> Demon – Cost Effective UK Internet Access    <<
>> email internet@demon.co.uk for more details <<
```

This message was sent to the USENET group comp.graphics (computer graphics newsgroup) and is an enquiry about the shareware graphics package Graphics Workshop. The header lines in this message occupy the first eleven lines; the Lines: field tells the reader that the actual message occupies six lines (the last two of which are a signature file – as contained in the user file .signature). Each line of the header is now examined in more detail:

- From: This identifies who the message was from, i.e. who posted the original message. The name in this line will be a standard Internet email name of the form: person@domain. The person's full name is normally taken from the Unix password description file /etc/passwd. You can use the Unix chfn command (change finger information command) to change such details. Your name may also be stored in a special control file specific to the newsreading software you are using.
- Newsgroups: This line shows the newsgroups to which the current message was posted. It is possible for newsreaders to send messages to multiple newsgroups, and each such group will be listed in such a case. In the context of our example, we can see that the comp.graphics newsgroup was the only group that received the message.
- Subject: The subject line describes the subject matter of the article. Subject lines can be specified from within your mailing system (on Unix, the –s option can be used with the standard mail program – most systems normally ask for a subject in any case). Subject lines allow readers of the message to quickly identify its contents. Subject fields are used by newsreading programs for message summaries, etc.

- Summary: In long messages, summary lines can be a useful addition in order to provide some extra information that goes beyond the normal subject line.
- Keywords: Some systems allow keywords to be added in order to allow a newsreader to scan for specific keywords. In the example header, the keyword GWS was used. Again, these are of use in long articles to aid searching for relevant material.
- Message-Id: This line is provided automatically by your news-server and contains the time and date that the message was received, along with the name of the news-server which received the message.
- Distribution: This line determines which USENET sites will receive the message. The keyword 'world' therefore refers to all USENET sites in existence, although it is at the discretion of the systems administrator which newsgroups are maintained. Your news-server or newsreading software will examine this line to see whether or not to allow the message to be processed.
- Sender: The sender of the message is normally the name of the news-server machine that posted the message to the USENET network. The userid of the machine is commonly called 'news'.
- Organization: This will be the name of the institution or company which originally sent the message. This name can be changed by the sender via their own system (commonly through alteration of an option on their newsreading software).
- Lines: This shows the number of lines in the article, excluding the header, but including the signature file. Signature files are small textual messages which are appended to all messages a user posts. They commonly quote the user's mail and/or phone number for contact purposes, although the exact message can differ. Many carry jokes and quotes from the famous (Dan Quayle quotes are common). Signature files are maintained on Unix systems through use of the dot file .signature (placed in your home directory).

TIP

Signature files are normally restricted to four lines, and if exceeded your news software may cut away any additional lines.

Depending on your newsreading software, not all of the header lines described above may be used. The only compulsory fields that are common to all messages are the From, To, Subject, Lines, Newgroups, Message-ID and date fields; all others are really superfluous as far as distributing the news is concerned.

2.3   Using an NNTP news-server via `telnet`

A variety of newsreaders exist in order to access the messages that are posted to the USENET system, and the application you eventually use will depend on what has actually been installed on your system. An excellent alternative to a specific newsreader is to use an NNTP news-server. These systems have sprung up all over the Internet, and they can be accessed via `telnet`, the virtual terminal protocol. Using `telnet` it is possible to access a remote news-server and then instruct it to load the newsgroup of your choice. Many service providers run NNTP servers that answer on a specific `telnet` port (commonly port 119). Such news-servers allow you to directly interrogate many USENET hierarchies. In the case that a news-server does not have the group you request, simply `telnet` to an alternative server. Table 2.2 illustrates the main NNTP news-servers that are available on the Internet. Appendix D also documents some other servers. If you are not proficient with the `telnet` program please refer to Chapter 5 for a more in-depth treatment of the `telnet` system.

One could therefore use `telnet` with the name of the NNTP server that you want to contact, for example one could type:

```
$ telnet news.fu-berlin.de 119↵
```

and the system would respond with a dialogue informing you that the system is calling the address (the systems numeric IP address will be shown by the `telnet` program), along with the message 'Connected' which will be displayed when connection has finally been established, for example:

```
Trying 130.133.4.250 119 .... Connected
NNTP news-server version 1.01 (posting disabled). Ready.
```

It makes sense to use the nearest NNTP server to increase performance and data throughput. After a few seconds the NNTP server will identify itself and tell you if posting is available. The abilty to post messages to USENET using an NNTP server depends on whether or not you are a registered user of that particular system. If you are calling a local NNTP server that is part of your own system (on which you are a registered user) posting should be enabled. If

Table 2.2   NNTP news-servers available via telnet

Server name	Location
news.demon.co.uk 119	United Kingdom, Demon
news.ibmpcug.co.uk 119	United Kingdom, IBMPCUG
sol.ctr.columbia.edu 119	US, Columbia University
rusmv1.rus-uni-stuttgart.de 119	Germany, Stuttgart University
news.fu-berlin.de 119	Germany, Berlin

posting is not available you will only be able to read USENET messages. Make sure that your host software can record your session into a file, especially in the case that you are downloading binary files for later storage and viewing.

TIP

Use the NNTP GROUP command to list all of the available USENET groups. Make sure you capture the output into a file, and be warned that the list is very long.

NNTP servers accept a standard set of commands which control which messages are displayed and the loading of newsgroups, etc. Table 2.3 illustrates the most common NNTP news-server commands. Optional parts of various commands are denoted using the <arg> notation.

TIP

For MSDOS users who use a DOS-interface to the Internet: when browsing a large newsgroup make a note of the message number given by the NNTP server so that you can use the HEAD command with that number next time, to save using multiple NEXT commands to get back to the message. If you use DOS to access an NNTP server, you can program the PROMPT command to define a series of control-keys for the NEXT and LAST commands, etc. to make things faster, e.g. [Alt-N] for NEXT using a command of the form:

PROMPT $e[0;49;'next';13p

Make as many additions to this one command as you need (add other $e... definitions onto this; finally, place the whole in a batch file which can be run at your convenience, i.e. when you start your Internet software from your PC, etc.

NNTP servers are not very verbose – most do not even have a prompt, even though the system is interactive. One of the first commands you will want to use is the group command, since this loads a USENET group for you to browse. Refer to Appendix G for a list of USENET groups. For example you could type

group clari.biz.market ↵

and the system would respond with a reply similar to

Group: clari.biz.market 001456 002140
<1993Dec20.04601.561@somewhere.com>

Table 2.3 Common NNTP news-server commands

NNTP command	Action
group <group-name>	Loads the newsgroup specified by argument <group-name>. The first message stored is then loaded and displayed. A short one-line description of the newsgroup will be given including the number of messages that are available, etc. This command must be used first in order to navigate the list of available messages
head <number>	Shows the header for the current message. In order to jump to a message, simply type the message number. You should note that message numbers are not always sequentially ordered, and that numbers may jump depending on the messages that have been stored on your NNTP server
article	Shows the actual message, or article. The message header will be included
next	Move to the next message. The system will tell you when you have reached the last available message with the message 'No next article to retrieve'
last	Move back to the previous message
quit	Quit from the NNTP server

which basically means that you are on message number 000128 (128) and that there are 439 messages in this group (so you have 311 yet to read). The text after this is normally the message's unique identification code and the sender's name and/or hostname. Remember to keep a note of the first message number so that when you leave the NNTP server you can rejoin the group at that point to start reading again – this way you won't miss any messages. If you try to load a newsgroup that does not exist on your server (either you have spelt the name incorrectly or your NNTP server doesn't carry this particular group) you will see a message along the lines of

Newsgroup not in current list

and you will have to retype the group command with a valid group (none of NNTP's message browsing commands will work until you have joined a group). When you have selected a valid group you have a number of commands that are open to you. When you initially enter a NNTP server the first message number will not always be 000001 (it hardly ever is). This is because news arrives and goes out-of-date very quickly. Many servers only hold messages for around a week or so, and as new messages arrive, older (earlier) messages get pushed off the server, i.e. they are deleted (however, some FTP sites do keep such messages archived).

When browsing messages it is best not to display a message until you have seen how long it is – some messages can be many hundreds of lines in length, and NNTP servers don't all respond to the [Ctrl-C] interrupt key (in fact, I have not yet found one such server). Use the `head` command to display the current messages header, and look at the very last line – this will be the `Line:` field which tells you how many lines are in the message. Also look at the `Subject:` field to see if this message is actually useful to you.

TIP

Not all NNTP servers carry all the USENET groups. Try to `telnet` to another NNTP server to see if they carry the group you require.

If a message does interest you, type `article`, and the message body (and normally the header) will be displayed on the screen. NNTP servers don't have screen pause facilities, although your own terminal may have such a facility. For this reason, it is best to capture your NNTP session to disk. This can be done on Unix using the `script` command (output goes to a file named `typescript`); on other systems, such as MS-DOS, it will be up to your communications software to provide a session-capture facility (systems such as Odyssey and ProComm have this as standard). Here is a typical session using the commands we have mentioned so far:

```
$ telnet news.fu-berlin.de 119↵
Trying 130.133.4.250 119 .... Connected
NNTP news-server version 1.01 (posting disabled). Ready.
group comp.graphics↵
comp.graphics 001456 002140
<1993Dec20.093901.868@demon.co.uk>
head↵
From: jason@wombat (Jason Manger)
Newsgroups: comp.graphics
Subject: Graphics Workshop?
Summary:
Keywords: GWS
Message-ID: <1993Dec20.093901.868@demon.co.uk>
Date: Mon, 20 Dec 1993 09:39:01 GMT
Distribution: world
Sender: jason@news.demon.co.uk
Organization: Demon Computer Systems UK
Lines: 6
article↵
Does anyone know where I can obtain a copy of Graphics
Workshop via FTP?. Many thanks in advance.
>> Demon - Cost Effective Internet Access <<
>> email internet@demon.co.uk for more details <<
```

From the session above we can see that we have joined the `comp.graphics` USENET forum, and that we have viewed the header of the first message. The number of lines in the message totals six, and the `Subject:` field interest us, so we type the `article` command to view the posting. After the message has been displayed the NNTP server simply awaits our next command – note the absence of any system prompt.

TIP

The NNTP `HEAD` command accepts an article-number argument; use this to get back to the last message you read in a previous session, rather than using multiple `NEXT` commands!

You can move back and forth between messages using the `next` and `last` commands, for example in the above context we would type `next` and then receive the dialogue:

```
next↵
comp.graphics 001457 002140
<1993Dec20.093904.868@demon.co.uk>
```

There will be a short delay after you type the `next/last` command as the message is retrieved on the remote host and then sent to you. Notice how the message number has increased by one, to 1457. The `message-Id` and sender's address may also be shown. When you issue enough `next` commands to make both numbers match, you will have reached the end of the message list and will receive a message similar to

```
No next message to show
```

The exact messages displayed from system-to-system may change slightly, although the essence and meaning will be the same. One other command you may want to learn is `help`, which will show you all of the commands your NNTP server obeys. Finally, you will want to issue a `quit` command to exit the NNTP/`telnet` session. Figure 2.2 illustrates the NNTP server diagramatically.

2.4 Using the Unix nn and rn newsreaders

The newsreading software programs nn ('no news is good news') and rn ('read news') are among the most common for the Unix platform. Both programs allow you to browse the USENET hierarchies for the messages that interest you. The rn program differs from nn in that it will display a screenful of articles at a time (nn shows you the subject lines of each article in a newsgroup and then allows you to mark the articles you want to read).

Many people miss out the subject lines in their messages, so rn is better in this respect.

CREATING A .newsrc FILE

The .newsrc (news run-commands file) is an ASCII file that contains the names of each newsgroup you want to examine when you run your news-reader. Without a .newsrc file your newsreading software will simply plough through all of the available newsgroups, which will be extremely time-consuming to say the least. The .newsrc file is used to keep track of the articles you have read, and those you have not. If you do not have a .newsrc installed in your home directory, nn and rn (or any other news-reader) will detect this, and you will therefore not be subscribed to any particular group. An empty .newsrc will normally be created for you in such cases, and it is up to you to maintain this file in the future. Both nn and rn will modify the file for you if you require, although any ASCII editor (such as vi or ex on Unix systems) can be used. Manually editing the .newsrc before you use your newsreader is the best approach to follow, since you will be able to deal with a subset of the available USENET groups that you have specifically chosen.

Software rn is normally shipped with a utility called newsetup. Run newsetup and you will be able to configure the newsgroups you wish to subscribe to. If you are using nn (or another newsreader) you will have to create the .newsrc file manually using a text editor of your choice. The structure of the .newsrc file is basically a list of newsgroups delimited by either a colon (:) or an exclamation mark (!), followed by the number(s) of each article that you have yet to read (these will be empty if you are starting from scratch), for example:

```
misc.books.technical:
news.software.nn:
```

The above hypothetical .newsrc file contains the names of just two groups, namely the USENET group news.software.nn, and the miscellaneous newsgroup misc.books.technical (latest technical book reviews). The colons at the end of the newsgroups indicate that we want messages to be retrieved from these particular groups (only). Alternatively, a group can be excluded by placing an exclamation mark instead of a colon at the end of the group name.

TIP

To create a custom .newsrc automatically, run nn and then press Q (to quit). Then edit the resulting .newsrc file and change all colons (:) to exclamation marks (!) to exclude all groups at first. Then replace the !s with :s for the groups you want included. In an editor such as vi or ex use a command of the form: 1,$s/:/!g (note that in vi you should press : to get into ex mode). If you hate vi, etc. use sed (Unix stream editor) using the Unix commands:
$ sed -e 's/:/!/' .newsrc > .newsrc2↵
$ mv .newsrc2 .newsrc↵
$ rm .newsrc2↵

You are now free to start your newsreader with your newly created .newsrc file. Your newsreading software will update .newsrc with the article numbers that you have read from each group automatically. A typical .newsrc file may resemble the following after you have started to read some articles:

```
misc.books.technical: 1-4531
news.software.nn: 1-68, 73
```

In the above .newsrc file we can see that articles 1 to 4531 of newsgroup misc.books.technical have been read, as have articles 1 to 68 and 73 of news.software.nn (the number 73 by itself indicates a single message that has been read; the person who read this group missed out on reading articles 69 to 72 in this particular case).

TIP

Your .newsrc file will dicate the order in which your groups are examined. Rearrange the order of groups to ensure you read the most important first (especially job vacancies!).

Other configuration files

Newsreader nn also uses another configuration file called .nn/init. This file is used to set up a series of configuation variables, as well as playing a similar role to .newsrc in defining which groups you are interested in. A typical .nn/init file could resemble that shown opposite:

```
sequence
alt.binaries.pictures.multimedia
!comp
!news.software.nn
```

The first line in the .nn/init file must be the word sequence. This is then followed by a list of newsgroups that you are interested in. Notice the ! sign on the front of the comp hierarchy–this means that we are not interested in this hierarchy at all. You could exclude a single newsgroup by placing an exclamation mark in front of the group in question, as shown in the last line of the above file which excludes the group news.software.nn but not any other groups in the news.* hierarchy.

THE nn NEWSREADER

Newsreader nn is rather a strange program in many respects. It is by far one of the most complex newsreading programs in respect of its customization, and yet it is very simple to get up-and-running from scratch in the case that you don't want to get involved with all of its many other features. Starting nn requires that you simply enter nn at the Unix prompt (nn clone programs will have an equivalent command), and press [Return], for example:

```
$ nn↵
```

If you have already created a .newsrc file you will see a list of articles for the first newsgroup that has been specified. At this stage you can read the article, save it to another file, reply to the person who sent the article, make a follow-up article, and so on and so forth. The options for article manipulation are very extensive, and one of the first commands that you should therefore learn is ?, the help command. All of nn's commands are letters and/or numbers that represent an action (or in the case of a number an actual article). Only unread articles are shown in the first screen that is shown. The first screen could therefore resemble that shown on page 27 (your screen will obviously be different, according to the groups you have in your own .newsrc file).

Command line options for nn

The nn program accepts a range of command-line options which affect its overall behaviour upon startup. The syntax for the nn program itself is:

```
nn [-grmxX] [group1,..group n]
```

The optional arguments shown in the syntax description are summarized in Table 2.4. Program nn can be started automatically to read a specified newsgroup (or groups); from the syntax description we can see that the group name(s) are specified on the command line–each group should be separated

Table 2.4   nn command-line options

Option	Description
-g	Make nn ask you which newsgroup to use upon startup: nn will quit after you have read all the required articles from the group which you enter when the program starts
-r	Repeat option. This option makes nn continually ask for newsgroups when you have read all the articles in a single group. This option can be used with the -g option e.g. -rg will make nn continually ask for new group names until you quit with the Q option
-m	Merge all articles in a newsgroup to construct a 'meta-group'. This option is useful when you are searching a newsgroup for a particular pattern using the -s option (search option). This option merges all articles from the group(s) specified to create one large group that can then be scanned. Useful if you don't know what group a particular article is in
-X	Scan all newsgroups that are subscribed and unsubscribed (e.g. ! and : groups)
-x	Similar to -X, except that this option makes nn scan for read and unread articles
-s\<pattern\>	Search a newsgroup for the pattern specified in \<pattern\>. Only the articles with \<pattern\> in them are returned
-a0	Catch-up option. This option invokes nn's catch-up menu allowing you to purge groups and catch up on new messages. See Section 2.7 for more details
-i	Makes the searches using the nn, -n and -s options case sensitive. By default case is ignored in such commands

by one or more spaces. For example, to start nn reading the news.software.nn newsgroup one could type:

$ nn news.software.nn↵

Command-line options can be combined on the command-line, if required, so, for example, it would be possible to form a command of the form:

$ nn -rgx news.software.nn↵

As a further example, we could make nn search all of the articles that have the word 'usenet' in them using a command of the form:

$ nn -mx -susenet↵

The -mx options specify that we should search all articles (as in the groups specified in .newsrc) and then create a meta-file of all the articles found with the word usenet in them (the matching is case-insensitive). Program nn will then allow us to browse through the articles retrieved. Note that the -X (upper case) option has not been used, so nn will only search those newsgroups in the current `.newsrc` file. Specifying the special term 'all' in a newsgroup name allows specific USENET hierarchies to be searched, for example:

`$ nn -mxX -susenet news.all↵`

This command will search for the word usenet in the news hierachy. The `-X` option ensures that we search both subscribed and un subscribed newsgroups in the news hierarchy. To make nn search a group of your choice, use the `-g` option, for example we could enter:

`$ nn -mxg -susenet↵`

Such a command would result in nn asking us for the group we require, and then searching for the term 'usenet' in all read and unread articles (note, however, that we will not search all newsgroups – no `-X` option has been specified).

The nn *opening screen*

Program nn arranges articles into 'threads', an individual thread representing all articles which share the same subject field. A sample screen could resemble that shown below:

```
Newsgroup: news.software.nn   Articles: 50 of 100/7 NEW

a.J. Frederick        5    How do you use nn's -g option?
b.John Duncan        10    >
c.Steve              12    >
d Mark Stephens      11    New nn source at funet.fi via FTP
e.Jenny Williams      8    >
f*F. Lane            15    >> New release of nn imminent
g*M. Jackson         58    >
h.H. Marks           32    New NNTP server at etl.go.jp
i.J. Lawson          87    nn
j.Samuel Brown       14    -
k.Mark Stephens      10    Re: nn source
l.Dominick Westlow   16    >
m*Susan West         14    Wanted: good book on nn and rn
n.J. Manger          21    New nntp server at demon.co.uk
o F. Jacobs           9    >
p bob                 3    Wanted: nn source
q H. Stone           15    >
r Paul Smith         27    >
s*John Taylor         6

-- 12:07 -- SELECT -- help:? -----Top 50%-----
```

As can be seen from the example screen, nn divides its default screen (other screen layouts are available by pressing the ʺ key) into three main columns, namely:

- Sender's name. This field is flagged with an article identification code – in our example these are the letters 'a' to 's' (0–9 can also be used if your VDU supports more lines). This identificaction character is followed by an article attribute character, which can be any one of those shown in Table 2.5.

  It should be noted that a space indicates an article that is unread, as in the cases of articles d, and o, p, q and r. Articles that have been flagged in our example include articles f, g, m and s. Articles that have already been read include a, b, c, e, h, i, j, k, l and n.

- Line count. The second column of information is a simple line count of the article in question. We can quickly see from the example that article i is the largest, whereas article 'a' is the smallest in terms of the number of lines that make up the article's message part.

- Subject field. The third column represents the message's subject field, as taken from the original message when it was composed by the user with their email/news software.

The number of new articles awaiting our attention is shown in the top right-hand corner of the screen, along with the current message number (at the cursor position) and the total number of messages that exist in the current newsgroup (in this case the group news.software.nn). Along the bottom of the screen we can see that the time is shown, along with a message telling us what mode we are in; select mode, as the name suggests, allows us to highlight the messages we want to read. Program nn also shows a percentage indicator that tells us how far into the message list we are. Depending on the capabilities of your computer screen nn may use all manner of screen effects such as embolding and reverse video to mark your selected articles.

Table 2.5   Attribute characters

>	A right-facing chevron indicates an article which has been followed-up. Follow-up articles contain an original article which has been taken up by another user and re-posted back to the newsgroup for further discussion. Follow-up articles have the characters re: (regarding) at the start of the subject field
>>	Two right-facing chevrons indicate a follow-up to a follow-up article (see above)
*	An asterisk denotes a selected item. Selected items are those which you want to read (more on this later)
–	A hyphen indicates article(s) with the same subject field but without the 're:' string in the subject field. Article 'j' shows an example of this
.	A period indicates an article that has already been read

The nn *command set*

Program nn is rich in commands, but it is not necessary to learn the entire set in order to use the program; learning a small subset will be more than sufficient. Table 2.6 illustrates the most common nn commands. All of the commands shown are available from nn in all modes. Some commands are control-code commands, and these are denoted with a ^ sign. For example ^G means 'press the [Ctrl] key, and while holding it down press G'. Compulsory command arguments are denoted using the <arg> notation. Actual keyboard keys are denoted using the notation [key], for example [spacebar]. The operation of nn is not far different from the Unix editors such as ex and ed, indeed, you may notice some features which are actually implemented in the same way as these editors (notably the shell escape commands).

Quitting from nn

Quitting nn is performed using the Q command. This will result in you being returned to the previous program that invoked nn (normally this will be the shell itself).

Shell features

Shell escape features are performed using the ! construct (carried on from the Unix editors). Used by itself, the ! command will invoke a shell – the shell

Table 2.6 Common nn commands

nn *command*	*Description*
Q	Quit nn back to previous program, e.g. shell
G	Go to a new newsgroup (in sequence of .newsrc)
U	Unsubscribe/subscribe from a newsgroup (toggle)
Y	Show an overview of all the newgroups that have unread articles in them
?	Help function. Shows all available commands
!	Run a shell (Unix, etc.)
! <cmd>	Runs a temporary shell (press ^D to exit)
:post	Posts a new article to current newsgroup
:man	Invokes manual page from Unix on-line manual for the nn program
:help	Help command. Same as the ? command
[spacebar]	When SELECTING articles this key will move you on to the next article. When you reach the last article [spacebar] will move you on to read the article(s) you have chosen (you can then move through each article using [spacebar]). In all commands, [spacebar] will also choose the default option – these are shown sometimes in brackets next to the command in question
>	Move on to the next screen (if available)
<	Move back to the previous screen

invoked will be the one you have defined in the last field of the /etc/ passwd file. Use the chfn command (Berkeley Unix), or chsh (System V) to change shells. Common shells are /bin/sh (Bourne Shell), /bin/csh (C Shell), and /bin/ksh (Korn Shell).

Changing newsgroups

You can jump to a new newsgroup (any sequence) using the G command; this will result in a prompt of the form:

Group or Folder (+./%=sneN)

Typing the name of a valid newsgroup and pressing return (↵) will make nn change to that group, as shown below with the group news.software.readers.

Group or Folder (+./%=sneN) news.software.readers↵

You will then be shown the message below, whereupon you should press 'a' (or [spacebar] for the default – the default is shown in the brackets).

Group or Folder (+./%=sneN) news.software.readers↵
Number of articles (uasne) (a) a↵

Selecting articles for reading

Article selection is performed in a number of ways. The easiest way of selecting an article for reading is to type the identification letter/number. Program nn will then mark the article with an asterisk (*), and it may highlight the entry for you with a reversed-video effect, depending on your screen's capabilities. You can unselect an article in the same way, so this action acts as a toggle between selection and de-selection. It is also possible to select a range of articles. To do this type the starting article identifier followed by a hyphen (-), followed by the final identifier, i.e. so as to construct a range of articles (a-d to select articles a, b, c, and d). Thread selection (selecting articles with the same subject) is possible by using an asterisk after the article in question, for example, typing b* would select all articles that have the same subject as article b. Pressing the [spacebar] on an article will also select that message in most cases.

Finally, it should also be possible to use the keyboard cursor keys to navigate between articles. For example, [↑] and [↓] to move up and down. The ability to use this feature will depend on your screen's capabilities. Some dumb terminals do not support such luxuries; in this case you can use the [.] and [/] keys to move up and down instead. Table 2.7 illustrates all of the article selection commands.

Table 2.7   nn article selection keys (. . denotes a range)

nn *command*	*Description*
a..z, 0..9	Select/unselect the article with the identifier supplied by the user
a-z, 0-9	Select/unselect a range of articles
a..z*, 0..9*	Select/unselect articles in the same thread as the identifier supplied by the user
/	Move up to article above
.	Move down to article below (if last article, nn will start reading the article(s) selected)
and	Cursor key movement (up and down) – as above
@	Reverse all selections made on current screen
*	Select/unselect article with same subjects as the currently selected article
=.[Return]	Selects all articles in current newsgroup
	De-selects all articles in current newsgroup
[space]	Move on to next screen (unselected articles will be marked as read by the user). If on last screen, nn will start to read the article(s)
>	Go to next screen of articles
<	Go to previous screen of articles
"	Change article display layout (various modes)
^	Jump to first screen of articles
$	Jump to last screen of articles
X	Start reading article(s) at this point: nn will move to next newsgroup when all articles have been read
Z	Start reading article(s) at this point: nn will return to current newsgroup when all articles have been read
P	Moves back to the previous logical group
N	Moves forward to the next logical group

TIP

Cursor movement between articles requires a terminal that can support screen escape codes such as the VT100 and ANSI emulations; examine the Unix TERM variable (or your comms. software) to see what emulation you are using.

Reading articles

In reading mode the [spacebar] can be used to move through each article that has been selected. If an article is longer than the current screen, the output will be paused and you can use the [Return] key to advance the screen a line at a time (the [spacebar] may be used to advance an entire screen). The [backspace] key can be used to move back one page, in addition. Table 2.8 illustrates all of the available commands in reading mode.

Table 2.8   nn article reading keys

nn *command*	*Description*
Commands within articles	
h	Display current article with its full header
c	Display current article in 'compressed' mode (removes all multiple tabs and spaces)
[tab]	Display all follow-up articles at this point
[spacebar]	Move forward one screen at a time
[Return]	Move forward one screen at a time
d	Move forward one half-screen at a time
$	Move forward to last screen
[Backspace]	Move backward one screen at a time
u	Move backward one half-screen
^	Move backward to the first screen
/<pattern>	Search for <pattern> text in an article: nn searches forward for the pattern
.	Repeats the most recent search (using /)
Replying to an article	
r	Reply to sender of current article
f	Create a follow-up article to be posted back to the sender of the current article
Moving to other articles within a newsgroup	
[spacebar]	Move to next article (when on last screen)
n	Go to next article (as on selection screen)
k	Kill command. Marks all article threads as being read by the user
p	Go to the previous article (as on selection screen)
*	Go to next article with the same subject (or to next article in the current thread)
Miscellaneous commands	
Q	Quits from the nn program. Updates messages
s	Saves an article to a file
D	Decode an article in the Rot 13 code. Refer to Section 2.8 for a discussion of Rot 13

Posting articles

The :post command can be used to post articles to users from scratch, although you may have access to the nnpost program on your system which can also be used (nn is one of a number of programs in a family of news-reading-related programs). Posting an article requires that you compose the message with an editor of your choice (Unix users can alter the $EDITOR variable to change the editor they require, e.g. EDITOR=vi for the vi screen editor or EDITOR=ex for the line-based ex editor). Such customization commands should be placed in your auto-login file, such as .cshrc for the C-Shell or .login for the Bourne Shell. You will also have to mention the name of the newsgroups/recipients you want the message sent to, along with any other details such as a subject line, etc. All such questions will be asked during your session. Enter the details and press [Return] after each response you provide. Program nnpost operates in exactly the same way had you entered the :post command from within the nn program itself. The example below shows the :post command in action:

```
post↵
POST to group: news.software.readers↵
Subject: help with nn↵
Keywords: help↵
Summary: ↵
Distribution: (default 'world')↵
```

The Subject, Keywords, Summary and Distribution fields are placed in the header of your message and are mainly used by newsreading programs to conduct searches, etc. If you want to leave a field empty simply press the [Return] key, as indicated above with Summary: field. The only field that must be supplied, even by default, is the Distribution field. This field is used to instruct USENET how far the message should be passed down the line, although there is no assurance that such a distribution will be guaranteed. Local groups distribution seem to be the major problem when it comes to specifying a distribution area; it is up to a news-administrator to control the propagation of site messages to other locations. Some common distributions in everyday use are shown in Table 2.9.

After setting up the subject and summary details you will have to compose the message. Program nn normally invokes the vi editor at this stage (although you may be able to configure which editor is used via the EDITOR variable).

Replying to articles

This can be done in a number of ways. When reading a message you can use the r command to reply via email to the original author of the message. Remember to distinguish between using email to post a message to a person,

Table 2.9   Common distributions

Name	Distribution
world	The default. News is passed to all sites worldwide
eunet	European sites only
na	North America. Use N (New York), FL (Florida), etc. for specific US states
can	Canada

or using email to post a message to USENET. A follow-up article is not a message to an individual, rather it is a message back to the same newsgroup Use the f command to create a follow-up message. If you use the r command nn will ask you if you want the original author's message included: nn will then invoke an editor (vi by default) to allow you to edit your reply (it will also provide a minimal mail-header automatically). After you have saved your message (if using vi use the command: ZZ) nn will ask you whether or not to post it, along with some other options. You should see the message:

```
a)bort e)dit h)old m)ail r)eedit s)end v)iew w)rite
Action: (send letter) s↵
```

Most of these commands are self-explanatory. Use the s command to send the message, or a to abort it. The h (hold) command is useful to save your message in a file for later posting, rather than sending it now. The default option is s, to send the message, as indicated in the brackets. Pressing [Return] will invoke the default send option. If you notice a mistake in your message, simply use the r command to re-edit it.

THE rn NEWSREADER

Program rn is in many ways very similar to nn although it has a slightly different way of presenting its information. When starting rn the program will scan your .newsrc file for the groups you want to examine. It will then display which groups have unread news, that is, new messages that are await- ing your attention. For example:

```
$ rn↵
Scanning .newsrc ...
Unread news in news.software.nn          14 articles
Unread news in news.software.readers     12 articles
Unread news in uk.jobs                    1 article
...
```

TIP

rn comes with the newsetup program which will create a new .newsrc file for you with the minimum of fuss.

---

rn then examines a master newsgroup list and scans those which are not in your .newsrc file (this is bound to be quite a large list), and it will ask you whether or not you want to subscribe to the group(s) concerned, i.e. add them to your .newsrc file, for example:

```
$ rn⏎
Scanning .newsrc ...
Unread news in news.software.nn              14 articles
Unread news in news.software.readers         12 articles
Unread news in uk.jobs                        1 article
Newsgroup alt.3d not in .newsrc--subscribe? [YnNn]
...
```

This process can go on for some time, so you may want to use the command-line option −q which makes rn start in its 'quiet' mode – this will make the program stop searching for new groups for you to subscribe to, and you will be asked to read the message(s) that await you in your selected groups (as in .newsrc), for example:

```
$ rn -q⏎
Scanning .newsrc ...
Unread news in news.software.nn              14 articles
Unread news in news.software.readers         12 articles
Unread news in uk.jobs                        1 article
******** 14 unread articles in news.software.nn--read now? [ynq]
...
```

All the available options are shown in the square brackets, e.g. [ynq] refers to the options yes, no and quit in the example above. Answering y (yes) in the example above would result in rn displaying the messages one-by-one. We could then read or skip these as we like, and then eventually move through the unread messages in each group until we had finished. The h command can also be used at any point in the program; this calls up some on-line help – basically a list of commands that can be used. Program rn's prompts can be a bit confusing, since many more commands are available than the default commands that are shown.

The rn command set

Working with rn you become accustomed to working in three modes, namely:

- Newsgroup selection mode
- Article selection mode
- Reading mode

Newsgroup selection mode

Selecting a newsgroup can be performed quite easily using the g option. This option is used in conjunction with the name of the group you want to select and then pressing [Return], for example:

```
g alt.binaries.multimedia⏎
```

The group `alt.binaries.multimedia` will then be loaded and you can scan through the articles as required. Because there are so many newsgroups a search capability is invaluable. As in nn, the search command is /, followed by the pattern to search, for example:

```
/greek↵
Searching ...
******** 3 unread articles in soc.culture.greek--read now? [ynq]
```

As can be seen, `rn` locates the newsgroup `soc.culture.greek`, and then gives us the option of loading it to scan for any unread articles. Use the / command by itself to scan for the same string again. Program `rn` will tell you if any further matches are found. Table 2.10 illustrates all of the newsgroup selection commands that are available.

Table 2.10   `rn` newsgroup selection commands (from `[ynq]` prompt)

`rn` command	Description
Basic commands	
c	Catch up – marks all articles in the current newsgroup as being read
h	Displays help information to the user
q	Quits the `rn` program
u	Unsubscribe from newsgroup
y	Yes option. Read the newsgroup articles
n	No option. Skip this newsgroup and move on to the next (if it exists, else quit)
`[spacebar]`	Default option. This will be the y (yes) option (read group articles)
Group commands	
p	Go to previous newsgroup: unread articles
$	Go to the end of the newsgroup list
^	Go to the first newsgroup: unread articles
`l<pattern>`	List unsubscribed groups containing `<pattern>`
L	Show `.newsrc` file groups
`g <group>`	Go to the newsgroup specified in `<group>`
Pattern searching commands	
`/<pattern>`	Search for pattern `<pattern>` in article
/	Search for previous pattern again
`?<pattern>`	Search backwards for `<pattern>`
?	Search backwards for `<pattern>` again
Shell commands	
`!<command>`	Run command `<command>` and return to `rn`
!	Run a shell. Leave `rn` temporarily. Press ^D to return to the `rn` program

Article selection mode

Once you have chosen to read a newsgroup with the y (yes) option, the system enters a new mode of operation, namely article selection mode. The commands in this mode behave slightly differently since we are now working with individual articles, rather than newsgroups. Even so, the principles stay very much the same. Articles in r n are stored as 'threads', as in the nn system described earlier – a thread being a list of articles with the same subject field. In order to read an individual thread you should use the keystroke ^N (Ctrl-N). This will move you on to the next article with the same subject matter. In order to see a summary of the articles in a thread use the = command. Finally you can use the k (kill) command if you want to discard all of the articles in the current thread (effectively removing you from this newsgroup to another of your choice). Table 2.11 illustrates all of the article selection commands which are available once you have joined a newsgroup. Program r n is supplied with a news-posting program called PNEWS; this can be invoked from within r n using the appropriate option (refer to the table of commands).

Reading mode

When an article is very long r n will allow you to browse though the article a piece at a time (refer to the paging commands section of Table 2.11). Reading mode is similar to the Unix more program in many respects (this program delays the output of a text file to the screen, allowing you to advance when you have read the necessary information).

pnews – THE r n NEWS-POSTING UTILITY

pnews is a program supplied with the r n newsreader to facilitate the posting of messages to the USENET system. From the command line it has the following syntax:

pnews [newsgroup [subject]]

For example, you could start pnews with the command-line

$ pnews news.software.readers NNTP↵

which will start pnews with the group news.software.readers (pnews will use this as the group you wish to post to), and with the subject 'NNTP' (if your subject field has more than one word enclose the entire string in quotes, e.g. 'The NNTP news-server' (both arguments to pnews are optional since it will ask you for both of them if they are omitted from the command-line). pnews will then allow you to compose your message with your favourite editor, and the message can then be sent.

Table 2.11   rn article selection commands

rn *command*	*Description*
Basic commands	
c	Catch up – marks all articles in the current group as being read
h	Displays help information to the user
q	Quits the newsgroup, rn asks for a new group
u	Unsubscribe from newsgroup
f	Move forward to the next article in the group
=	Display a summary of all the unread articles
^N	Move forward to next unread article in thread
^R	Re-display the current article. Useful if the article is long and you missed a part
v	Verbose option: display article (and header)
b	Go back one screen of information
Article commands	
–	Re-display the most previous article
$	Go to the end of the last article
^	Go to the first unread article
N	Go forward to the next article (read/unread)
P	Go backward to the next article (read/unread)
^P	Go backward to the previous article in thread
p	Go backward to previous article
Reply commands	
r	Reply to author of article via email
R	Reply to author article (include message)
F	Create a follow-up article to this article including original article (runs pnews)
f	Create a follow-up article (runs pnews)

continues

2.5   Anonymous postings

Many USENET articles arrive from anonymous addresses, for example you may see a message with the sender's name as: an6563@anon.penet.fi. Anonymous servers are starting to appear in ever increasing numbers on the Internet; the site anon.penet.fi seems to dominate the majority of anonymous postings, however. Some of the USENET newsgroups cover sensitive areas such as rape and physical abuse, and anonymous servers allow users to post their messages to such forums without identifying themselves. Other controversial USENET groups include the erotica forums, such as alt.binaries.pictures.erotica which deal solely in adult imagery which is nearly always X/R-rated. If you subscribe to such a group you may find that a high degree of articles arrive from anonymous users. The majority of postings arrive from universities, and it follows that many people would not like to be identified, for obvious reasons (I don't think a BSc in erotica exists, does it?).

If you want more information on obtaining an anonymous id, simply email

Table 2.11 – *continued*

rn *command*	*Description*
Save article commands	
w <file>	Write a file to disk under filename <file> excluding message header
s <file>	Write a file to disk under filename <file> and include header of message
	Note: typing the article number will move to that article.
Pattern searching commands	
/<pattern>	Search for pattern <pattern> in subject
/	Search for previous pattern again
?<pattern>	Search backwards for <pattern> in subject
?	Search backwards for <pattern> again
Reading an article	
[Tab]	Examine follow-up articles
[spacebar]	Display the next screen of the article
b	Move back one screen
d	Move forward half a screen
h	Display help screen (list of valid commands)
j	Junk article: mark article as read at this point and continue to next article
g <pattern>	Search forward for pattern <pattern> (within the current article – do not use / for this)
G	Repeat the previous search
Shell commands	
! <command>	Run command <command> and return to rn
!	Run a shell. Leave rn temporarily. Press ^D to return to the program

postmaster@anon.penet.fi and in a few days your own id will be posted back to you. The concept of the system is quite simple. You mail your messages not to USENET directly, but instead to the site anon.penet.fi. This then examines your header for the sender's name, and assigns your id on to a new message header along with the original message, which is then sent on to USENET and placed in the appropriate newsgroup. For people wishing to respond to anonymous individuals, simply email your anonymous id at anon.penet.fi and this is decoded into your real mail name and sent on to you as normal. This system is known as a 'double-blind' mode of operation.

2.6 Manipulating binary files over USENET

Binary files are regularly passed over USENET on a daily basis. Many binary forums exist and are posted images, sounds and even complete programs for a wide variety of computing platforms (e.g. DOS/UNIX/Amiga/Atari). Table 2.12 lists some of the most popular binary USENET forums. When reading

Table 2.12   Binary USENET forums

Group type and name	Description
Imagery	
alt.binaries.pictures.misc	Miscellaneous pictures
alt.binaries.pictures.erotica	General erotic pictures
alt.binaries.pictures.erotica.female	Female erotic pictures
alt.binaries.pictures.erotica.male	Male erotic pictures
alt.binaries.pictures.fractals	Fractal images
alt.binaries.pictures.fine-art.digitized	Digitized pictures
alt.binaries.pictures.fine-art.graphics	Graphics pictures
alt.binaries.pictures.tasteless	Tasteless pictures!
alt.sex.pictures	Erotic imagery
Computer Applications	
comp.binaries.acorn	Acorn machines, BBC, etc.
comp.binaries.amiga	Amiga machines
comp.binaries.apple2	Apple machines
comp.binaries.atari.st	Atari ST machine
comp.binaries.ibm.pc	IBM PC and 100% clones
comp.binaries.mac	Macintosh machines
comp.binaries.os2	OS/2 ABI binaries
Sounds	
alt.binaries.sounds.misc	Miscellaneous sounds
alt.binaries.sounds.erotica	Erotic sounds

articles on USENET you may see people referring to groups using an acronym, for example a.b.p.e. for alt.binaries.pictures.erotica, etc. (after all, it takes too long to keep typing in all of these names).

In addition to the forums in Table 2.12 many country-specific sites offer their own image forums – you will have to get hold of the master USENET list from group news.lists or make an enquiry through an NNTP server (see Section 2.3).

TIPS

Look out for the groups that end with .d, since these are the discussion groups for the newsgroup in question. It is these groups that you should post 'text' messages, such as enquiries, if you encounter a problem. An example is the group alt.binaries.pictures.fine-art.d. Not all newsgroups have a .d group associated with them (only binaries mainly).

As a rule of thumb, don't start a textual discussion in a binary forum. USE THE BINARY FORUMS FOR BINARY FILES ONLY! Everyone still does the contrary, however.

Binary files are transmitted as ASCII files via a technique known as UU-encoding. A UU-encoded file is a binary file that is converted into a series of ASCII characters. This facilitates transmission over USENET and email, which are both ASCII-based messaging services (unlike FTP which can handle binary files with ease). In order to send binary files over the Internet you will therefore have to get hold of a UU-encoder/decoder. Such programs are widely available as freeware and shareware. Contact a group such as `alt.graphics.pixutils` which deals solely in graphics questions and answers in order to make some enquiries. Many binary programs are posted to the binary forums as new releases become available; if requests are large someone will probably email one to the newsgroup. Someone may even email you a personal copy. Be warned that many binary files, because of their size, are sometimes compressed at source and then UU-encoded before being mailed. Read Chapter 8 for an in-depth treatment of the graphics formats and utilities that are used on the Internet. You must have access to the correct software before you start. The steps required in order to process a UU-encoded file can be briefly summarized as:

- Save your message(s) into separate files (probably using the `s` command on your mail/newsreading software).
- If there are segments that make up one large file, join all the files together, remembering to remove all mail headers and other information Except the data between the `begin` and `end` lines (leave these lines in as well). Make sure there are no blank lines in your UU-file, amd that `begin` is the first line and `end` is the last.
- Run UUdecode on the file you have just edited to produce the binary file (this may be an image, e.g. a `.GIF`, or a compressed file such as a `.ZIP` archive, or a `.JPG` compressed image etc.).
- Process the binary file as required, i.e. if it is a compressed file, uncompress it, etc. (see Chapter 7).

TIP

Some 'smart' newsreaders can decode UU-files using a special option. Read Chapter 8 for more information on smart UU-decoders and Unix shell utilities that do the same job.

The other alternative to USENET for your images and utilities is FTP (file transfer protocol). Anonymous FTP sites that deal solely in graphics software (and even images and sounds) are widely available on the Internet. Get hold of one of the image FAQs that are posted to the binary forums for more details, or, if you can't wait any longer, just turn to Chapters 3 and 8 now. Chapter 2 examines the FTP program in more detail.

2.7 Catching up on USENET news

News messages arrive in copious quantities on a daily basis, so being away from USENET for a week will result in a massive backlog of messages. To deal specifically with this problem nn provides the catch-up option. Entering the command

```
$ nn -a0↵
```

results in a menu display similar to that shown below:

```
Release 6.3.1
Catch-up on 868 unread articles ?
(auto)matically (i)nteractive: i↵
y-mark all articles as read in current group
n-do not update group
r-read the group now
U-unsubscribe the current group
?-this message
q-quit
Update alt.binaries.multimedia (8)? (ynrU?q): y↵
...
```

The first response we must supply is the reply auto (automatic catch-up) or i (interactive catch-up). An automatic catch-up removes the need to answer questions interactively for each group. In the example we have typed i for an interactive session. Program nn then displays each group in which new messages have arrived since we have been away (the number of actual messages are shown in the brackets by nn) after the group name. Each group will be displayed, as mentioned in the .newsrc (and .nn/init files), and we are offered a choice of options at each stage. The y (yes) command will mark all messages as read, thus you will not be bothered with these again, while the n command does not update the groups, therefore leaving them to be read at a later date. Command U unsubscribes you from a group, thus altering the .newsrc and .nn/init files accordingly, while the r command will give you the chance to read the messages waiting for you. You can use the ? command to redisplay all of these options as the screen advances.

2.8 The Rot 13 code

Some messages posted to USENET are encrypted using a code called Rot 13. Encrypted messages can easily be deciphered by newsreaders (nn uses the D command in reading mode); the intention is not to make the message secret, but is instead done to ensure that the article is not read accidentally. Some articles are of a sensitive, and maybe offensive nature (for example, some jokes in alt.tasteless.jokes) and the Rot encoding scheme allows potentially offensive messages to be avoided while the user is casually reading. Rot 13 messages are shown on the message selection line, for example in nn one may see an entry of the form:

b The Riddler   12   Joke: offensive nature?

Reading this posting would yield an encrypted message, and you would have to invoke the necessary command (nn uses D) to decrypt the message. Rot 13 articles use a rotating-alphabet code (rather like the Romans did some years back, although a little more sophisticated). A rotation unit of 13 is used so that the letter 'a' maps to the letter 'n', 'b' to the letter 'o' and so on. Numbers and other punctuative symbols remain the same for the sakes of simplicity.

2.9 The USENET user database

A service which you may find useful is known as the USENET user database. It is run by MIT (Massachusetts Institute of Technology) in the US, and contains the names and addresses of all people that have posted USENET articles into MIT (this includes all their newsfeeds also). It is therefore possible to browse this database in order to search for a person that posted a message of interest to you (perhaps you want to get hold of some software or information that was posted). The service is run via an email interface, so all enquiries must be posted to MIT at the address: mail-server@pit-manager.mit.edu. Messages must adhere to the format:

send usenet-addresses/<search string>

where <search-string> is a pattern that will be matched from the many From: lines in a messages header. Any part of the header will be matched, so you may want to place a username or a person's full-name in the field (or at least a part of it such as a surname). For example, we could mail the message:

send usenet-addresses/mjackson

if user mjackson is found in a From: field in the MIT database, you will see an entry for that user in your mail message that is returned; for example, you may see

```
Date: Sun, 1 Aug 93 12:19:45
From: Mr Background <daemon@pit-manager.mit.edu>
Subject: reply from mserv re: send usenet-addresses/mjackson
Reply-To: mail-server@pit-manager.mit.edu
X-Problems-To: postmaster@pit-manager.mit.edu
Precedence: bulk
To: fred@somewhere.com
mjackson@aber.ac.uk (Michael Jackson) (Jul 20 93)
```

which tells you that user mjackson posted his last message to USENET on
20 July (unfortunately the service does not tell you which newsgroup he posted
his message to). The person's full-name in brackets is not always used by some
users; indeed some use aliases, and in such cases you may have to rely on a
username rather than a person's real name. In the case that the person you
specified was not found, you will see an appropriate message, for example:

```
No matches for "mjackson"
```

2.10   Posting messages to USENET – NewsMail server at cs.utexas.edu

Users without access to a newsreader to post messages can use the mail-server
cs.utexas.edu. This mail-server takes a mail message the username of
which is the actual newsgroup, for example you could post a message to the
alias:

```
alt.save.the.earth@cs.utexas.edu
```

which would send your mail message onto USENET via the mail-server
specified in the hostname. The server extracts the USENET group when it
arrives, and then passes it on accordingly. Users without a USENET posting
program may also want to examine their system to see if it accepts a username
alias (such as mail2news which redirects their messages to USENET rather
than to an individual recipient; a header in your message is normally required,
e.g. Newsgroups: alt.bbs in order that the system knows which
USENET group to post the message, here alt.bbs, for example).

3

Downloading information from the Internet – using FTP

3.1 Introduction to FTP

FTP, or file transfer protocol, is probably the second most popular tool used on the Internet today (email taking first place); it is the principal Internet tool for moving files around the Internet. The Internet has many thousands of FTP sites located worldwide, and a variety of information is available in the form of software, imagery and textual data on a vast array of subjects (FTP is also the principal method for software distribution on the Internet). FTP is a very easy program to use. The concept behind its use can be summarized in the following steps:

- Locate the FTP host you require (done via using Archie, etc.)
- Create an FTP session between that host and your own machine
- Browse the remote host's file system to locate the file(s) you require
- Download the file(s) to your own machine
- Exit from the remote host

All of the examples in this chapter assume you have access to an FTP program. In the examples of this chapter, we have used the $ to refer to the Unix prompt, although this is irrelevant just as long as you know how to call up your own particular FTP program. In this chapter you will learn how to:

- Use the FTP program to browse remote Internet hosts' file systems
- Download and upload files of information between hosts
- Use FTP's interactive commands
- Understand how security is implemented for systems files

Because so many FTP sites exist, some of which specialize in particular programs and information, we direct readers to the appendices which contain a list of the most popular FTP sites currently in existence. If you do not have access to the interactive FTP program, refer to Section 3.5 where we discuss FTPmail, a method of accessing FTP via email (we assume you have access to email).

TIP

If you want, you can access FTP through the Gopher program instead. For the novice user this may be better, since the approach is totally menu based. See Chapter 9 for details on the Gopher program.

3.2 Starting FTP

FTP is an interactive program that accepts commands from a prompt in much the same way as Unix or MSDOS does. Once you have connected to the remote FTP host you can navigate its file system (i.e. its directories) just as you would on your own machine in order to find the files you require. The syntax of the FTP command is:

```
ftp [hostname]
```

where [hostname] is either the name of an FTP host, for example the name ajk.tele.fi (a site in Finland) or an IP (Internet Protocol) address for that site (in this case ajk.tele.fi has the IP address 131.177.5.20). IP numeric addresses are equivalent to the dotted notation used in character-based names – IP addresses are slightly faster to use since they do not have to be resolved (resolving is carried out automatically when you enter a non-IP address). An example command could therefore be (from the Unix prompt)

```
$ ftp ajk.tele.fi↵
```

Since the IP address is equivalent, we could also use a command of the form:

```
$ ftp 131.177.5.20↵
```

You will also notice that the [hostname] argument of the FTP command is optional, it is possible just to type ftp by itself. In such a case this would invoke FTP's command-line mode directly whereupon you would have to use a further command to make the necessary host connection. You may come across the terms FTP-client and FTP-server in your travels; these terms are used because FTP is really a symmetrical protocol, i.e. both the local and remote systems are FTP programs and they behave in an inverse fashion –

either one acts as a server to send back files, or one acts as a client to inter-rogate another machine, and vice versa.

The Archie service can display a list of all the world's FTP servers including their IP addresses. Refer to Chapter 4 for more information on Archie.

Starting `ftp` without the `[hostname]` argument simply places you into FTP's interactive mode directly, i.e. without calling the host. In order to call a host from this mode you must use the `open` command along with the name of the host in question (refer to Table 3.1 for a list of FTP commands), for example:

```
$ ftp↵
ftp> open ajk.tele.fi↵
... etc ...
```

LOGGING IN TO A REMOTE FTP HOST

In order to make a connection with a remote FTP host you can do one of two things, namely:

- Log in as a registered user
- Log in as an anonymous user

A registered user is simply a user who has an account on the machine in question. Logging in to a host as a registered user does not alter FTP's beha-viour in any way, other than giving you a different priority level to access certain files, i.e. your own files in this case, perhaps. It should be noted that Unix is a multi-user system and enforces its own security in the form of file ownership. No casual user has access to all the files on an FTP site; only the systems administrator, or superuser, has such access.

Anonymous users

It would be impractical (although not impossible) for one person to be a registered user on all of the FTP sites in the world, so the concept of an anonymous user is implemented by FTP for those people who do not have an account on the machine they are contacting. Anonymous FTP sites are abun-dant on the Internet and the special username `anonymous` should be supplied, along with a password that is simply your email address, e.g. `fred@somewhere.co.uk`. An example anonymous log-in session is illu-strated step-by-step in three phases. All user input is denoted by the sign ↵ which signifies the pressing of the [Return] key by the user:

Step 1: Call the machine in question

```
$ ftp ajk.tele.fi↵
Trying 131.177.5.20.... Connected
Connected to ajk.tele.fi
220 ajk.tele.FI FTP Server (Version 4.2 Mon Dec 20 12:07:34 1993)
Name (ajk.tele.fi):
```

After you have called the machine in question you should see your FTP program issue a message saying that it is trying to contact the host you require. The remote host's IP address should be shown in this display. Eventually the remote machine will answer (this can take as little as 5 seconds and as long as half a minute for distant hosts). You will then see a short welcome message and the remote server will identify itself and ask you to log in.

TIP

If you are contacting an FTP server that exists on your own computer network the shortcut command:

```
$ ftp ftp↵
```

will call the local machine, assuming its first name is ftp, e.g. as in the name ftp.demon.co.uk. This works for most applications that require hostnames, e.g. telnet.

Step 2: Identify yourself to the remote machine (log-in)

```
$ ftp ajk.tele.fi↵
Trying 131.177.5.20.... Connected
Connected to ajk.tele.fi
220 ajk.tele.FI FTP Server (Version 4.2 Mon Dec 20 12:07:34 1993)
Name (ajk.tele.fi): anonymous↵
331 Guest login ok, send ident as password
Password (ajk.tele.fi:anonymous):
fred@somewhere.co.uk↵
```

For an an anonymous user the name anonymous (in lower case) should be entered. Press [Return] to send the name back to the server. In a few moments the system will ask you for a password, whereupon you should enter your full electronic mail address, as shown in the hypothetical example above. FTP's responses are easily seen since they are nearly always start with a numeric code, e.g. 331 for 'Guest login ok' above.

After a valid username and password have been entered, the system will respond by welcoming you to the system by telling you that your credentials are all in order.

Step 3: Gain access to the system

```
$ ftp ajk.tele.fi↵
Trying 131.177.5.20.... Connected
Connected to ajk.tele.fi
220 ajk.tele.FI FTP Server (Version 4.2 Mon Dec 20 12:07:34 1993)
Name (ajk.tele.fi): anonymous↵
331 Guest login ok, send ident as password
Password (ajk.tele.fi:anonymous): fred@somewhere.co.uk↵
230 Guest login ok, access restrictions apply
ftp>
```

Message 230 is interesting (access restrictions apply). As mentioned before, the vast majority of FTP hosts are Unix based, so security will be enforced. Such security is implemented at the log-in stage, and is also administered at the file-level stage; individual files have access codes which dictate whether or not you can access that particular file (this restriction applies to directories also, so some parts of the file system may not be accessible to anonymous users). Also notice the ftp> prompt in the last phase above. As we mentioned, FTP is an interactive system so you will need to learn some commands to get started.

FAILED LOG IN?

If you misspell your username and/or password (or both) you will not be logged in. Instead FTP will leave you at the ftp> prompt awaiting your next instruction (FTP does not disconnect until you type quit or close (see the command-set in Table 3.1 for more details of these two commands). To try to log in again you will need to enter the user command at the ftp> prompt. This command will allow you to identify yourself to the remote system whereupon you can again enter your username and password. The example session below illustrates the use of this command in the case where we misspelled anonymous:

Using the user command after a failed log in

```
$ ftp ajk.tele.fi↵
Trying 131.177.5.20.... Connected
Connected to ajk.tele.fi
220 ajk.tele.FI FTP Server (Version 4.2 Mon Dec 20 12:07:34 1993)
Name (ajk.tele.fi): anonyous↵
333 login ok, send ident as password
Password (ajk.tele.fi:anonyous): fred@somewhere.co.uk↵
440 Access denied
ftp> user↵
Name (ajk.tele.fi): anonymous↵
331 Guest login ok, send ident as password
Password (ajk.tele.fi:anonymous): fred@somewhere.co.uk↵
230 Guest login ok, access restrictions apply
ftp>
```

The key message to look out for is the Guest login ok which tells us we have access. Unfortunately Unix does not validate usernames at the point of entry; any username will generate a response from the server, and both the username and password must be valid. A shortcut way of entering the username and password is to use the syntax: user <user> <pass>, for example:

```
...
ftp> user anonymous fred@somewhere.co.uk↵
230 Guest login ok, access restrictions apply
ftp>
```

TIP

If you use one anonymous FTP site on a regular basis, you may consider creating a `.netrc` file. This file must reside in your file's home directory; it contains three line entries of the form (each entry separated by a blank line):

```
machine      ftp.demon.co.uk
login        anonymous
password     fred@somehere.com
```

When you call a machine with FTP from the command-line, the FTP program will do the rest for you. Do not provide passwords for registered FTP (non-anonymous servers) since they are the same as for your own account; plain text passwords can be read by anyone who has access to your `.netrc` file *unless* you protect it using the exact Unix command:

```
$ chmod u+rwx,o-rwx,g-rwx .netrc
```

This will allow you to place registered FTP sites in your file.

3.3   The FTP command set

Table 3.1 illustrates the most common FTP commands that are supported (compulsory command arguments denoted `<arg>`, mandatory arguments denoted as `[arg]`). Make sure you learn the `ls`, `cd`, `get`, `binary` and `quit` commands since these are all a casual user will ever need. Navigation is performed using the `cd` (change directory) command; you move down into the file system by moving into lower directories – all FTP sites are organized into a hierarchy of directories (similar to your computer's hard disk perhaps). The top level directory is aptly named the root directory, and this is where you are initially placed when you log in to your FTP host. Files can be downloaded from a host using the `get` and `mget` commands (`mget` is used for multiple file downloads, `get` for single files). The `put` and `mput` commands are analogous to `get` and `mget` when uploading files to a host, i.e. placing a file onto a remote host.

TIPS

Binary files (applications, images, compressed files, etc.) *must* be downloaded using the `BINARY` command. Enter this command before downloading a binary file. ASCII files can in most cases be downloaded with binary mode enabled, although the ASCII command is sometimes provided.

Make sure you are in the correct mode before downloading (or indeed uploading files). FTP starts in ASCII mode by default. FTP uses the messages:

200 Type set to A. → for ASCII mode
200 Type set to I. → for binary 'image' mode

The binary command is replaced by the command tenex on some FTP
servers.

Table 3.1   FTP command set

Command	Action
quit	Close connection to remote host and quit the FTP program
help [command]	Shows help for the command [command] or displays a list of available commands if [command] is omitted
?	Same as help command above
! [cmd]	Run shell command [cmd]. Used by itself the ! command temporarily leaves FTP to run a shell
open <host>	Establish a connection with the host named in <host>. <host> can also be a numeric IP address. This command is useful when using the close command to call another host after the previous one, since you do not have to restart the FTP program
close	Closes connection with remote host and leaves user in the FTP program
user [username [pass]]	Provides a username and password to the remote host. Useful if you have made an incorrect log in
cd <directory>	Change directory to directory named <directory>. The special name '..' refers to the parent directory (the directory immediately above you), and should be used to move upwards towards the root directory. Any valid name will be accepted to cut down using too many cd commands
cdup	Same as a cd .. command. Changes directory to the parent directory
lcd <directory>	Change the local directory. Useful when using put/mput so that you can find the correct files to upload. Also useful to allow downloads to be made into a specific directory
dir [[directory] [file]]	Lists the files in the current directory. The optional [directory] argument allows any valid directory to be listed. The [file] argument is used to save the listing in a local file named in [file]. Dir uses a different format to ls

Continues

Table 3.1 – *continued*

Command	Action
ls	Lists the files in the current directory (short format)
pwd	Prints the current working directory on the screen, thus telling you where you are in the system
get <<rfile> [lfile]>	Download a file from the host. The <rfile> argument is the remote file to download; [lfile] is an optional name for the file which is to be used by the local system. Unix names differ from DOS names so the [lfile] argument may be required
mget <rfile1 .. n>	Download multiple files from the host. Use this with the wildcards (see below); the server will ask you to confirm each download by default, unless the prompt command has disabled this. Multiple files are specified one-by-one on the command-line separated by spaces, or by using wildcards (* and ?)
put <lfile>	Upload the local file <lfile> on to the remote host. Ensure that you are in the correct remote directory
mput <lfile1 .. n>	Places multiple files on a host. The filenames can be separated by a space, or a wildcarded expression can be used (e.g. file*.zip)
binary	Enable binary mode (up/downloads)
ascii	Enable ASCII mode (up/downloads)
hash	Display a hash (#) for every block of data up/downloaded. A block may be 1024 bytes or more
prompt	Toggles on/off interactive mode for multiple downloads

Notes
Local filenames [lfile] can sometimes be given the – (hyphen) to make the FTP server display the file on your screen rather than downloading it. Useful for documentation (README) files, etc.
Wildcards: * for one or more characters, or ? for a single character. Both match white space, i.e. nothing. The wildcard [.-.] can also be used, for example, faq_part[1-8] to match the filenames faq_part1, faq_part2 .. faq_part8 (Unix FTP only). Deletion functions: some FTP servers allow the deletion of remote files using the delete <rfile> command.

FILE-SYSTEM NAVIGATION COMMANDS

The cd command is the principal command for file-system navigation. It is used with the name of the directory you want to move to; this name can be

fully or partly qualified (fully qualified pathnames start from the root directory – a pathname is a route from the root directory to the file or directory you
require). Apart from literal directory names, some special notation can be
used, notably: / (root directory), and .. (the parent directory). Some examples are given below.

Example 3.1

Changing directory using a fully-qualified pathname:

```
ftp> cd /uploads/files/source/c↵
250 CWD successful
ftp>
```

In Example 3.1 we have used the directory name /uploads/files
/source/c. This is a fully qualified pathname because we can see the /
character (the root directory) in the left column of the pathname. This type of
command can be used to move you to any directory in the file system rather
than issuing multiple cd commands to move up and down to the appropriate
directory. Notice the FTP message 250 CWD successful—CWD is an
acronym for change working directory, and the successful message indicates the directory was valid. Incorrectly named directories will result in an
error message to that effect.

Example 3.2

Changing directory using a partially qualified pathname:

```
ftp> cd /uploads↵
250 CWD successful
ftp> cd files/source/c↵
250 CWD successful
ftp>
```

In Example 3.2 we have first changed directory to the /uploads directory
(a fully qualified pathname was used here). The second command, however,
uses a partially qualified name (a pathname in which the root directory does
not begin the pathname). Since we are already in the /uploads directory at
this stage, we do not have to issue a longer pathname to reach the directory we
require; instead we can quote the name of the subordinate directory (files
/source/c) and move there using a smaller pathname. Note that Examples
3.1 and 3.2 are equivalent in terms of the end result.

TIP

Many FTP servers will invoke the display of a small text file when you use the cd command with a particular directory. This will sometimes contain instructions and/or help with that directory's contents. Read all such details carefully in case you miss something important.

Example 3.3

Changing to the root directory:

```
ftp> cd /↵
250 CWD successful
ftp>
```

It is often the case that we want to move to the root directory, since this is the top-level directory and is normally organized into separate areas of interest e.g. categories of machine platforms, etc. Example 3.3 shows how the name / was used to achieve this with the minimum of fuss, and in just one command.

Example 3.4

Changing to the parent directory:

```
ftp> pwd↵
/uploads/files/source/c
ftp> cd ..↵
250 CWD successful
ftp> pwd↵
/uploads/files/source
ftp>
```

Example 3.4 demonstrates how the .. notation can be used to move to the immediate parent directory. The pwd (print working directory) command has first been used to show the user in which directory they reside; we then use the cd .. command, and invoke pwd again to prove that we have indeed moved up one directory level (individual directory 'levels' are represented by individual / signs; this is the reason why the root directory is called /). Local directories can also be changed using the FTP lcd command. You may have to change your local directory in order to retrieve the correct file when making an upload, etc. On the other hand, you may want a download to occur in a particular directory of your choice.

TIP

Rather than typing cd .. to change to the parent directory use the cdup
command instead. This command has to be used on VMS systems

FILE LISTING COMMANDS

Aside from file-system navigation, FTP also provides us with two commands
for the listing of files in a directory. The ls command (as on Unix) is impl-
mented on all FTP servers. The ls command has an abundance of options
which include −l to display a long listing – long listings include file ownership
details among other things. The dir command may also be available on your
system; this command is roughly equivalent to an ls −l command. Example
3.5a illustrates a typical ls −l listing, while Example 3.5b shows the ls
command in use without the −l option. The ls −R option is also useful, since it
runs a recursive list of all the files in a particular directory; run from the root
directory, or with the / argument, ls −R will list all files in the entire file
system – hence the index file ls−lR that resides on many sites acts as an index.

Example 3.5a

An ls −l listing (long listing):

```
ftp> ls -l↵
150 Opening ASCII mode transfer for /bin/ls.
-rw-rw-r-- 1    ftp       8976    Dec 10  12:07  file1
drw-rw-r-- 7    ftp      98654    Dec 08  11:01  dir1
ftp> cd ..↵
250 CWD successful
```

Example 3.5a illustrates two files, one of which is termed an ordinary file,
the other a directory file. Ordinary files are files such as documents, programs,
images and so on. An ordinary file can be identified by the hyphen (−) in the
leftmost column. Directory files are repositories for further files (ordinary and
directory) and are used to implement the hierarchical nature of the file system;
these files have a d (for directory) in the leftmost column. The next nine characters are the files permission codes. These nine characters are broken into
three groups (three characters each) for the USER, GROUP and OTHER
users (Unix parlance). Unix security at the file level is implemented by assigning a code to each class of user on the system for every file. The permissions R,

W, X (read, write and execute) may be used. From Example 3.5a we can therefore see that the ordinary file named file1 has read and write permission
enabled for the USER and GROUP class of users, whereas only read permission is enabled for the OTHER class of user. The actual owner of the file is
named ftp – as shown in the third column of the listing.

TIP

The dir and ls commands take wildcarded expressions. Some listings may
be gigantic so you can cut down the length of a listing using a wildcard, for
example:

```
ftp> dir RFC*
```

to show all files beginning with the characters 'RFC' (and this will also match
'RFC' by itself).

Save your ls -1R commands, etc., into a local file using the FTP command
below (in order to read the list later):

```
ftp> ls -1R filelist
```

where filelist is a local file that stores the output of the ls -1R
command. You can also use this format with the dir command in most
instances.

The second column in Example 3.5a represents the number of links to the
file (directory files have a figure representing the number of files in the directory, 7 in our example). The Unix ln (link) command is used to link files
together so that it is possible for one file to appear in more than one directory – a useful shortcut approach to file location. Column 3 is the owner of the
file (you will find all such users in the Unix file named /etc/passwd), while
column 4 is the size of the file in bytes. Columns 5, 6 and 7 represent the time
and date of modification of the file (or creation if the file is newly created) and
the last column, column 8, is the actual name of the file.

Example 3.5b

An ls listing (short listing):

```
ftp> ls↵
150 Opening ASCII mode transfer for /bin/ls.
file1
file2
ftp>
```

Notice how the listing in Example 3.5b is much shorter in content. This command should work faster than `ls -l` (or `dir`) since less information has to be transferred.

Anonymous users probably fall into the OTHER class of user since they do not own any files on the system, and they do not belong with any other users in a particular group (that would be a bit dangerous), so they can only read the file named `file1` in the example (i.e. examine its contents, download it, etc.). If write permission were available we could potentially delete the file or alter its contents (FTP normally denies such features anyway although some FTP servers are in existence which do have deletion facilities). File grouping allows users in the same group to share files. For example, we can see that the GROUP users for the file `file1` can write to (or modify) the file. The group users will themselves be defined in the `/etc/group` file and will be listed alongside the user named `ftp`, for example you may have a `/etc/group` entry structured as:

`ftpusers:3:30:ftp,john,fred,jim`

which means that users `john`, `fred` and `jim` are in the same group as user `ftp`, and therefore the GROUP permission codes for ftp's files will allow the other users in that group to access them as set by the owner (`user ftp`), for example, users `fred`, `john` and `jim` can all read and write the file named `file1`. Since the user anonymous is not mentioned here, that user does not have the associated GROUP permissions of the other users. The owner of the file assigns persmissions using the Unix command `chmod` (change mode). Users in the OTHER group represent all other users of the system who are not group users (and who are clearly not the owner of the file).

FILE DOWNLOADING COMMANDS

FTP essentially is about the downloading of files. Two alternative commands are provided here, namely `get` and `mget`. The `get` command is used to download individual files whereas `mget` is used for multiple file downloads. The `get` command is very simple to use, as Example 3.6 shows.

Example 3.6

A typical get operation (file download):

```
ftp> hash↵
ftp> binary↵
200 Type set to I.
ftp> cd /graphics/msdos/gws↵
250 CWD successful
ftp> ls gws.zip↵
150 Opening ASCII mode transfer for /bin/ls.
-rw-rw-r-- 1 ftp        105553  Jun 05  09:11  gws.zip
ftp> get gws.zip↵
200 PORT command successful
150 Opening binary mode data connection for gws.zip (105553 bytes)
####################################################
#### #### #### #### #### ###
226 Transfer complete
ftp>
```

Example 3.6 starts by enabling the hash command to show the progress of our download. The user then enables binary mode, anticipating the fact that they are going to download a .ZIP file (these are compressed files created with the PKZIP utility – see Chapter 7 for further details). The cd command is then entered along with the directory in which the file required resides; the ls command has been used in the example with a filename argument to list the details of the file we want to download. We can see that the file is called GWS.ZIP and it is 105Kb in size. Next, the user issues the get command followed by the filename GWS.ZIP. FTP then initiates the download, printing a hash for every 1024 bytes downloaded (this may differ between systems). The Transfer complete message indicates the file was downloaded to your local machine.

TIP

Unix filenames are sometimes too long to be accepted by MSDOS machines. If this is the case, you can use a local filename with the get command, for example

```
ftp> get example_file.txt example.txt
```

will allow you to get the file example_file.txt and store it as example.txt (valid DOS filename) on your local system.

A local filename of just - (hyphen) will make the get command display a file on the screen, rather than down-loading it, e.g. get file -. This works on Unix machines but DOS machines may create a file called - so watch out if you are expecting a printout. This facility will differ between FTP servers.

Example 3.7

A typical get operation (multiple file download):

```
ftp> binary↵
200 Type set to I.
ftp> cd /graphics/msdos/gws↵
250 CWD successful
ftp> ls↵
150 Opening ASCII mode transfer for /bin/ls.
-rw-rw-r-- 1 ftp        105553  Jun 05  09:11  gws.zip
-rw-rw-r-- 1 ftp         12004  Jun 05  09:25  readme.gws
ftp> mget gws.zip readme.gws↵
mget gws.zip: ? y↵
200 PORT command successful
150 Opening binary mode data connection for gws.zip (105553 bytes)
226 Transfer complete
105553 bytes received in 58.1 seconds
mget readme.gws: ? y↵
200 PORT command successful
150 Opening binary mode data connection for readme.gws (12004 bytes)
226 Transfer complete
9876 bytes received in 6.2 seconds
ftp>
```

Example 3.7 demonstrates the mget command in operation. Mget is interactive, that is to say it will ask you which files to download out of those that have been supplied in the command (the only exception here is when you use the prompt command to disable interactive mode – this will make mget retrieve all of the files named). In the example we can see that two files are being retrieved (namely GWS.ZIP and README.GWS). Mget asks us whether we want to download each file, and the response should be y or n (yes or no – all other keys supply negative responses on most servers). After each transfer is complete FTP tells us this is the case and displays the size of the file downloaded, along with the time it took to download the file.

The actual statistics shown vary from server to server. The hash command has not been used in this example so no progress monitoring is shown to the user.

TIP

The interrupt key ^C (Ctrl-C) will interrupt a download that is in progress, if you want to abort such a task.

Mget can also be used with wildcarded filenames. The wildcards ? and * can be used: ? matches a single character (or nothing), and * matches one or more characters (or nothing) as demonstrated in Example 3.8.

Example 3.8

A typical get operation (multiple file wildcard download):

```
ftp> binary↵
200 Type set to I.
ftp> cd /graphics/msdos/gws/v21↵
250 CWD successful
ftp> ls↵
150 Opening ASCII mode transfer for /bin/ls.
-rw-rw-r-- 1 ftp      105553  Jun 05  09:11  gws.zip
-rw-rw-r-- 1 ftp       12004  Jun 05  09:25  gws.txt
ftp> mget gws.*↵
mget gws.zip: ? y↵
200 PORT command successful
150 Opening binary mode data connection for gws.zip (105553 bytes)
226 Transfer complete
105553 bytes received in 58.1 seconds
mget readme.gws: ? y↵
200 PORT command successful
150 Opening binary mode data connection for gws.txt (12004 bytes)
226 Transfer complete
9876 bytes received in 6.2 seconds
ftp>
```

In Example 3.8, the user has used a wildcarded filename expression to match all files that begin with gws irrespective of their filename extension; such an

expression in this context would match GWS.ZIP and GWS.TXT, the * wildcard matching the TXT and ZIP extensions of the files. The download then
continues as normal. The interactive nature of mget can be disabled using the
prompt command, as Example 3.9 demonstrates.

Example 3.9

A typical get operation (multiple file wildcard download) with interactive
mode disabled:

```
ftp> prompt↵
ftp> binary↵
200 Type set to I.
ftp> cd /graphics/msdos/gws/v21↵
250 CWD successful
ftp> ls↵
150 Opening ASCII mode transfer for /bin/ls.
-rw-rw-r-- 1 ftp      105553  Jun 05  09:11  gws.zip
-rw-rw-r-- 1 ftp      12004   Jun 05  09:25  gws.txt
ftp> mget gws.*↵
200 PORT command successful
150 Opening binary mode data connection for gws.zip (105553 bytes)
226 Transfer complete
105553 bytes received in 58.1 seconds
150 Opening binary mode data connection for gws.txt (12004 bytes)
226 Transfer complete
9876 bytes received in 6.2 seconds
ftp> quit↵
221 Goodbye
$
```

Example 3.9 is exactly the same as shown earlier in Example 3.8 except for
the inclusion of the prompt command, which as can be seen, disables all
input responses and thus mget downloads all of the files specified (useful if
you want all of the files in a directory). Selecting all of the files in a given
directory could be done using the command: mget *.*.

TIPS

Many FTP hosts have a file called `ls-1R.z` (or just `ls-1R` for non compressed files – `.z` refers to Unix compressed program files) which is basically an index to that FTP site's files. It may be worth getting hold of this file if you haven't a clue where to begin your search. Note that `.z` files are binary files, so use the `BINARY` command.

Archie, the file archive service, is an excellent partner program for FTP. Archie can locate files from all of the main anonymous FTP hosts (see Chapter 4).

Moving directory files

Unfortunately, FTP cannot (yet) download complete directories, although you could get at all the files in a directory using an `mget` command with the wild-card `*` (match all files). If you wanted to download part of a file system that, for example, contained three or four subdirectories, you would have to issue separate `mget` commands for each directory – a bit long winded to say the least. The only other way of getting at a whole directory of files depends on whether or not the administrator of a site uses a command called `tar`. Tar is the Unix tape-archive command; it is not a compression program as such (hence it is used with `compress` to form `.tar.z` files), but instead it backs up entire directories and stores them in a compacted form in a file. You cannot access the `tar` command from an FTP server, so the possibility of getting hold of a complete `tar` file for an entire directory will depend on whether or not the administrator of this site implements this facility.

TIP

Very large tape archive files are split into a number of smaller files; these are numbered 01 upwards, for example `file.tar.z.01`, `file.tar.z.02`, etc. To process such files you must join all the files together to form one file and then de-tar the file. The Unix command below will do this:

```
$ cat file.tar.z.* > large_file.tar.z↵
```

On DOS this would be (assuming all files are `tar.z` files):

```
C:> copy file.01 + file.02 bigfile.tar↵
```

You can, of course, make your own `tar` archives and make these available to people via FTP. The `tar` command has many options, the most basic of which are `-c` (create a new file), `-r` (append new files into file), `-x` (extract files from an archive), and `-f` (specify tar filename). Using these options we can see that the command

```
$ tar -cf graphics.tar /pub/graphics↵
```

will create a tar file called graphics.tar which contains all of the files in the directory /pub/graphics (and its subdirectories). The resulting file graphics.tar will be very large in its uncompressed form; for this reason many administrators employ the Unix compress command on the file using a command of the form:

```
$ compress graphics.tar↵
graphics.tar: Compression 49.1% -- replaced with graphics.tar.z
$
```

The file graphics.tar has been replaced with graphics.tar.z, its compressed equivalent. Anybody downloading this file must now, of course, have access to both the Unix tar and decompress utilities, or suitable equivalents for their machine platform (Chapter 7 deals with this topic in more detail). Notice also from the example how compress tells you the compression ratio; in the context of the example, we have saved nearly half of the original disk space that the file graphics.tar consumed.

TIP

Make sure you decompress your files in the correct order: a tar.z file needs decompressing first with a utility such as decompress (on Unix) and then de-tarring with a utility e.g. tar -x on Unix (tar is used to store and recover commands, rather like DOS's BACKUP/RESTORE tools).

Some DOS/FTP sites are using BACKUP/RESTORE archives to save multiple directories. Make sure your users have the the corrrect version of DOS when restoring, or an error may occur, disallowing the restoration.

Finally it may be useful if you know how to extract tar files. The command to extract a tar.z file is (you will only need the second command here if the file is not compressed)

```
$ uncompress file.tar.z↵
$ tar xf file.tar↵
```

FILE UPLOADING

As well as downloading files, uploading a file to a remote host is also possible using the FTP put command. This command is similar in operation to the get command in reverse, although some discussion of the problems of file uploading should first be made. Uploading files is technically more tricky than downloading since the remote file system you are accessing will have storage quotas in place. Security considerations must also be taken into account. File access permissions on certain directories may mean that file uploading cannot be performed. On a Unix system the directory you upload into must have write permission for the anonymous FTP user. As mentioned earlier, the anonymous FTP user will not have that many privileges, indeed not many registered users can create files in system directories. Many FTP administrators overcome this problem by providing an upload area, a directory in which the anonymous user has write permission. Using FTP we could examine such a directory, assuming one exists (of course, any directory with the necessary write permission can be used, even if this was not the original purpose). Example 3.10 illustrates how we can use FTP to check for a publicly writable directory. Bear in mind that the 'anonymous' user is commonly placed in with the OTHER user group, that is, people who are not the owner or even group users.

Example 3.10

Using ls to search for a publicly writable directory:

```
ftp> cd /↵
250 CWD successful
ftp> ls↵
150 Opening ASCII mode transfer for /bin/ls.
drwxrwxrwx 1    ftp    653213  Jun 05  09:11  uploads
drwxrwxr-- 1    ftp    45424   Jun 05  09:25  misc
drwxrwxr-- 4    ftp    12356   Jun 06  09:30  source
drwxrwxrwx 15   ftp    8094    Jun 07  09:36  public
ftp>
```

Example 3.10 illustrates the ls command in action within the root directory. In Example 3.10, four directory files have been found. Names to look for include pub, public or uploads, which indicate freely writable directory areas where files can be uploaded for the administrator (users can contribute files in this way). We can see that the only writable directories for the OTHER user group (of which anonymous is a member) are the /uploads and / public directories. We could therefore issue a cd command to move into one of these and try out an upload task, as in Example 3.11. Assume the file to be uploaded is an ASCII file called upload.txt; this file will reside on our local hard disk. (FTP will look in your local machine's current working directory for the file to be uploaded.)

Example 3.11

Uploading a file:

```
ftp> cd /uploads↵
250 CWD successful
ftp> put upload.txt↵
200 PORT command successful
150 Opening binary mode data connection for upload.txt (48050 bytes)
226 Transfer complete
48050 bytes sent in 17.1 seconds
ftp>
```

As can be seen from Example 3.11, FTP sends the file to the host and informs you when it has completed the task. But what would happen if we tried to upload a file into a directory that did not have write permission (remembering that we must have write permission on the directory into which we want to upload a file)? In such a case FTP would respond with an error such as that shown in Example 3.12.

Example 3.12

Uploading a file: write permission denied:

```
...
ftp> put upload.txt↵
345 Access denied
ftp>
```

FTP's message is minimal, but straight to the point. We are simply denied access to upload the file. Another curious point regarding directories and permission settings is execute permission. When this is denied from a directory file, the system will not allow us to cd (change directory) into that area, and FTP will respond in much the same way as in Example 3.12, for example as shown in Example 3.13.

Example 3.13

Access denied from directory (execute access disabled):

```
ftp> cd /↵
250 CWD successful
ftp> ls↵
150 Opening ASCII mode transfer for /bin/ls.
drwxrwxrw- 1    ftp       546211  Jun 05  08:12  admin
drwxrw-rw- 1    ftp       11233   Jul 06  08:15  tempfile
drwxrw-r-- 4    ftp       14310   Jul 07  09:01  system
drwxrwxrwx 15   ftp       4096    Jul 15  10:22  execs
ftp> cd admin↵
345 Access denied
ftp>
```

In Example 3.13 we are denied access to the /admin directory because its execute permission (x) is disabled for the OTHER user group (note the rw- at the end of the permission settings). Only the USER (owner) and GROUP users have access to the /admin directory. The only other directory in the example we can actually access is the last directory, /execs, which has the necessary execute permission.

TIPS

If you find a public upload area, mail the user called postmaster at that site's address and ask them if it is okay to upload some files, or to store some files on a temporary basis, etc. This will ensure that the files are not removed before a friend has accessed them, etc. Many upload areas are being closed down because users abuse the facilities provided. Postmaster is an email alias that is commonly the administrator on that site.

The vast majority of FTP servers do not have 'sensitive' commands such as rm or rmdir (remove files and directories) for obvious reasons. The site sun.nsf.ac.uk has a guest FTP service (use username and password of guestftp to access); You must telnet to this site in order to use the service, which has access to some directory creation and deletion functions to allow you to create and remove your own files. Note though that logging in as anonymous means that any one can delete the files that you create.

Multiple files can be uploaded using the mput command. This command takes the name of each file to be sent (either separate filenames or a wildcarded expression can be used) and then sends them across to the remote site, as

Example 3.14 demonstrates with the two ASCII files file1 and file2. If the files were binary we would have to issue a binary command first. The ASCII command has been used in Example 3.11 – useful to remember if you have just sent some binary files and are now dealing with ASCII files.

Example 3.14

Uploading multiple files:

```
ftp> ascii↵
200 Type set to A.
ftp> mput file1 file2↵
200 PORT command successful
150 Opening ASCII data connection for file1.
226 Transfer complete
12091 bytes sent in 4.2 seconds
150 Opening ASCII data connection for file2.
226 Transfer complete
14516 bytes sent in 5.1 seconds
ftp>
```

3.4   FTP programs on different operating systems

All of the FTP examples up to the present have been given for Unix machines, simply because 99 per cent of the FTP servers you find will be Unix based. However, now and again you may run into a different FTP environment, perhaps an FTP server running under MSDOS or VMS (DEC/VAX systems). It is worth while knowing about such systems because the interface may change, albeit to a very small degree. Some operating systems also have minor anomalies which are different from Unix systems, especially in relation to how the file system is structured. Most FTP servers will tell what operating system they are running when you initially log in, for example a DOS-based session may resemble:

```
$ ftp server.ugap.edu↵
Calling 128.19.7.88... Connected
220-Welcome to the FTP server at server.ugap.edu running PC/TCP 2.1
220-Public files are in D:\PUBLIC and its subdirectories
Name (server.ugap.edu): anonymous↵
300 User Ok, send password as ident.
Password: fred@somehere.com↵
230 anonymous logged in
Remote system type is MSDOS
```

the last line here informing us that we are indeed using an MSDOS system (which is, basically, running TCP/IP on a PC).

MSDOS-BASED FTP SYSTEMS

MSDOS (and PCDOS) implement a hierarchical filing system similar to that found on Unix. Files are grouped into directories and subdirectories on different disk drives. Disk drives under DOS are identified by a single letter from C up to Z (A and B are reserved for floppy-disk drives). Drive letters are always followed by a colon (:), so that the drive can be distinguished from an actual file.

The notable difference between DOS and a system such as Unix, is the absence of any file-protection mechanism. While all of the FTP commands you have learnt in earlier sections will still be valid, the file-listing and navigation commands may change slightly in order to take into account the drive identifiers that were mentioned. Unlike Unix, DOS directories are not normally mounted onto one large file system. Instead, they are disk specific, that is to say that a particular part of the file system, may reside on a different disk (this is true of Unix also, except that Unix 'grafts' these parts of the file system onto its main file system allowing the user transparent access to such files). Under DOS it would therefore be valid to issue a cd (change directory) command of the form:

```
ftp> pwd↵
Current working directory is C:\HOME\FTPUSER
ftp> cd s:\unix↵
200 OK
```

Of course, it will also be possible to change directory within the same disk using a command without the drive letter, for example:

```
ftp> cd \source\unix\c↵
200 OK
```

Another quirk of DOS lies in its filenames; files under DOS can only have a maximum of 12 letters, three of which are used as an extension; a filename and extension are separated by a period (.). This naming convention is also used under Unix, although the naming is not strictly implemented. Also, files under Unix can be of an arbitrary length, commonly up to 255 characters on a BSD (Berkeley Distribution System) version of Unix – and they do not have to have extensions. In the example above we have changed directory from C:\HOME\FTPUSERS to S:\UNIX, a change of directory and physical disk drive. In the majority of cases you may not be able to change disk, simply because the disk is not mounted, or because the disk simply does not exist. The drive you may be accessing could be a hard disk, a CD-ROM or may be a part

of the memory of the computer configured as a disk drive. Also note how the
directory-separator character is now a \, rather than a /. This is because DOS
uses \ instead, just to be awkward.

Directory separators in DOS-based systems are \, while in Unix the / is used.
Some 'intelligent' DOS-based FTP servers normally allow both characters to
be used for flexibility (albeit very few machines). Remember: \ → DOS, / →
Unix just in case.

Filenames are case-insensitive on DOS. On Unix they are *not*; The files: 'Unix'
and 'UNIX' are different files on a Unix system.

As has already been mentioned, the file-listing commands also differ
slightly. A typical DIR command could display the following hypothetical list
of files:

```
ftp> dir↵
200 Port OK
150 Opening data connection
      105553     GWS.ZIP      Wed Dec 20  15:12:09  1992
        1045     READ.TXT     Wed Dec 20  14:18:01  1992
<dir>             VERSION2     Fri Nov 05  12:00:45  1992
226 Transfer successful. Closing data connection
ftp>
```

This example shows a directory listing containing three files, two ordinary files
and one directory file (the <dir> string flags all directories on DOS-based
machines); the file named GWS.ZIP is a PKZIP compressed file, a binary file,
whereas READ.TXT looks like an ASCII file. VERSION2 is a directory in
which further files may be stored, perhaps for a newer version of some software, for example.

DOS-based servers use data compression formats that are mostly DOS based,
e.g. .ZIP (PKZIP), .ARC (ARC), etc. Refer to Chapter 7 for more information
on decompressing and processing DOS archives and compressed files.

All of the other FTP commands should work as normal; any differences
should be very minor. Remember to use the help (or ?) command to see just
what commands are available. Another point to note regarding DOS-based
FTP servers are the wildcard characters: DOS allows * and ?, but not more

complex combinations such as `file[1-3]` to match `file1`, `file2` and `file3`, etc.

VMS-BASED MACHINES (DEC/VAX)

There are quite a few **VAX** (Virtual Address eXtension) machines on the Internet that offer the anonymous-FTP service. VAX machines also implement a hierarchical filing system, although the method of changing directories can be a real pain.

Logging in to a VMS FTP-server should yield a welcome message similar to any other server, although look out for the welcome message telling you the remote system type, for example

`Remote system type is VMS`

Under **VMS** a directory is referred to using the notation `HDSC$DUA0:[SYSTEM]` where `HDSC$DUA0` is the disk name (rather like `C:` in **MSDOS**) and `[SYSTEM]` is the name of the current working directory. Directories, and their subdirectories are separated by periods (`.`), for example a subdirectory of `HDSC$DUA0:[SYSTEM]` called FTP would be called: `HDSC$DUA0:[SYSTEM.FTP]`, and so on. This is analogous to `C:\SYSTEM\FTP` on **MSDOS**, or `/system/ftp` on Unix. A typical directory listing on a VMS machine would therefore resemble the following:

```
ftp> dir↵
200 Port Command OK
135 File transfer started
Directory: HDSC$DUA0:[SYSTEM.FTP]
README.TXT;15    20-DEC-1992 12:11:02    24/1  (RWED,RE,,R)
GWS.LZH;1        21-DEC-1992 01:56:15  103/3   (RWED,RE,,R)
VERSION2.DIR;1  22-DEC-1992 03:01:09 1024/1   (RWED,RE,,RE)
Total of 3 files, 1151 blocks.
226 File transfer completed OK
ftp>
```

The salient features of this listing are the file filename version numbers (indicated by ; and then a number), the file sizes, and the permission attributes. VMS employs a version number system whereby each file has at least three versions, one for each period of modification. Every time a file is modified, the system updates the versions accordingly. Users on a VMS system have the PURGE (or PU) command to delete all but the most recent versions. In the example we can see the file README.TXT which has been modified 15 times. FTP will always access the most recent version of the file. The file sizes are given as blocks (not bytes) in column 4, whereas the file-permission codes are stated for four different classes of user. Once again, VMS has taken the Unix route in file permission and both systems are roughly equivalent for the purposes of understanding.

Directory files under VMS have the extension .DIR, for example the file called VERSION2.DIR in the example. Directory files cause most of the problems on VMS systems since the cd (change directory) command has a rather mixed meaning on such systems. For a start, most VMS FTP users have to use the directory format [dir1.dir2.dir3] instead of /dir1/dir2 /dir3; secondly, changing to a parent directory will not work using the ubiquitous cd .. command – you *must* use CDUP instead. In saying this, however, I have known some VMS FTP servers allow the / directory separator, so check yours to see. A typical file download would therefore resemble:

```
ftp> dir↵
200 Port Command OK
135 File transfer started
Directory: HDSC$DUA0:[SYSTEM.FTP]
README.TXT;15      20-DEC-1992 12:11:02    24/1  (RWED,RE,,R)
GWS.LZH;1          21-DEC-1992 01:56:15 103/35  (RWED,RE,,R)
VERSION2.DIR;1    22-DEC-1992 03:01:09 1024/1   (RWED,RE,,RE)
Total of 3 files, 1151 blocks.
226 File transfer completed OK
ftp> cd [VERSION2]↵
200 Working directory changed to HDSC$DUA0:[SYSTEM.FTP.VERSION2]
```

```
ftp> get V2.TXT↵
200 Port command OK
125 ASCII transfer started for HDSC$DUA0:[SYSTEM.FTP.VERSION2];V2.TXT
226 File transfer completed OK
1876 bytes received in 0.60 seconds (6 Kbytes/s)
ftp>
```

In this example we can see that the dir command has revealed three files, one of which is a directory. The cd command is then used with the argument [VERSION2] which changes our current working directory to [SYSTEM.FTP.VERSION2], remembering that we were already located within the [SYSTEM.FTP] directory to start with (this saved us typing in the entire, or fully qualified pathname). All in all, VMS systems are not that difficult to use, just as long as you remember to note how file and subdirectory names are constructed.

TIP

You can normally download a particular version of a file when using FTP's get command on a VMS server by specifically typing the version number, for example the command

ftp> get FILE.TXT;3↵

will retrieve version 3 of the file named FILE.TXT. Version 1 is the most up-to-date remember. Omitting the version number will make FTP search for version 1 by default.

MACINTOSH-BASED MACHINES

If you ever access a Macintosh FTP server the only differences between a Unix-based system are the file and directory names. Macintosh files can be of an arbitrary length, and can even contain spaces. It is therefore important to quote your filenames so that the relevant command understands you are not after a series of filenames. A typical directory listing could therefore yield a list resembling that shown below:

```
ftp> dir↵
Gopher servers/
Hypercard
Hypercard Documentation
Hytelnet-service/
ftp>
```

As can be seen, filenames are of an arbitrary length, and can contain spaces. Notice too, how some files are delimited with a / character. These files are directories, or 'folders' in Macintosh parlance. A typical change-directory command for a filename with embedded spaces would take the form:

```
ftp> cd "Gopher servers"↵
```

whereas a single directory would not require the quotes, for example

```
ftp> cd Hytelnet-service↵
```

Multiple directories (a complete path) can also be specified, for example the directory Hytelnet-service may have the subdirectory Europe, in which case we would type a more familar command, for example

```
ftp> cd Hytelnet-service/Europe↵
```

Downloading operations should take into account the naming convention of Macintosh files; a file called Hypercard Documentation would therefore require a command of the form:

```
ftp> get "Hypercard Documentation" ↵
```

TIP

VMS filenames are categorized into the common following types, according to their extension (note that this is not a full list):

.DIR   ⟶ A directory file (subdirectory)
.TXT, .DOC, etc. ⟶ An ASCII file/document
.EXE   ⟶ An executable program/binary
.COM   ⟶ A DCL (digital command language) file; analogous to a .BAT file in the MSDOS system.

3.5   FTP via electronic mail

It may be the case that you do not have access to the FTP program. All is not lost, however, since users without FTP that have access to electronic mail (email) can access an FTPmail server. FTPmail is as the name suggests, FTP via email, that is to say that you send FTP commands in a mail-message to an FTPmail server machine. The FTPmail server then processes your request, downloads the file you require, and then posts it back to you. FTPmail commands are similar to the standard commands found with any FTP system although there are some minor differences, depending on which server you choose. The main FTPmail servers are shown in Table 3.2.

The main FTPmail commands are illustrated in Table 3.3. Use these in your mail-message when sending it to the appropriate server. Remember that using FTPmail requires that you know where the file(s) you require are, e.g. both the host and directory. Use the Archie service (Chapter 4) to do this if you do not know where the file(s) you require are located. Binary files are by default encoded into ASCII using the Unix command `btoa` (binary to ASCII). If you do not have this utility, or if you are not using a Unix machine, use the `uuencode` command (UU-decoders are easier to come by in any event – see Chapter 8 for FTP locations).

Notice that no multiple `get/put` commands such as `mget` and `mput` are

Table 3.2 Main FTPmail servers

Server name	Optional message-body contents
`ftpmail@decwrl.dec.com` `bitftp@pucc.princeton.edu`	`help` – for help with service `list` – for list of FTP sites `help` – for help with service

Table 3.3 FTPmail command set for most servers

Command	Action
`connect <host> <log> <pass>`	Establishes a connection with the FTPmail server. The `<host>` argument is the name of the anonymous FTP site to use for a file transfer. The compulsory `<log>` and `<pass>` arguments will allow a log-in name and password to be specified
`binary`	Enable binary mode for transfer. FTPmail uses `btoa` format by default. See UUencode
`ascii`	Enable ASCII mode for transfer
`uuencode`	UUencode the file before transmisson. See Chapter 8 for more information on UUen-coding
`compress`	Uses the Unix compress (the `.z` format) to compress the file before sending it
`chdir <directory>`	Changes to the directory named as `<directory>`. You must `cd` into the directory where the file you require is located before downloading it (or the download will fail)
`dir [directory]`	List files. The `[directory]` argument (optional) allows a specific directory to be listed
`get <filename>`	Downloads the file `<filename>` from the remote host
`quit`	Quit from the FTPmail server

supported. The `cd` command is often changed to `chdir` as well. A typical email message could therefore take the form:

```
connect ftp.uu.net anonymous fred@somewhere.com
chdir /pub/graphics/pc/msdos
binary
get gws.zip
quit
```

and will connect us to the anonymous FTP machine `ftp.uu.net`, and will change directory to `/pub/graphics/pc/msdos` (which is where we assume our file will be found). We then change to binary mode, since the file we require is a `.ZIP` compressed archive, and we grab the file using the `get` command. The final quit command makes FTPmail process the request, and the file will be mailed back to you as soon as possible.

TIP

If you want more than one file, possibly from a series of different hosts, use as many `connect` and `get` commands, etc. as you require, rather than using multiple mail-messages. Remember to use the `binary/ascii/uuencode` commands as required also.

You can send your FTPmail message using any mailer you like. A Unix command to send the above mail message could be as simple as

```
$ mail ftpmail@decwrl.dec.com < ftp.mail↵
```

where the file `ftp.mail` holds the FTPmail commands to be sent. You will have to use an editor to create the file such as `vi` on Unix, unless you use a Unix command of the form:

```
$ mail bitftp@pucc.princeton.edu < 'cat'↵
```

which uses the Unix `cat` (concatenate) command to read from the keyboard, allowing you to enter the file by hand (any mistakes – use [Ctrl-C] and start again I'm afraid).

4
Software searching – using Archie

4.1 Introduction to the Archie program

The Internet is such a large network that it can become become a real chore locating the information you require. Before continuing to explain the merits of the Archie system, it should be said that Archie is a file location tool and not a file downloading tool. Conventional tools such as FTP must be employed to access the files that Archie finds for you. Alternatively, you can use an FTPmail server. Chapter 2 covers the FTP program in more depth. Archie is an interactive program, accepting various commands which configure its searching behaviour. The steps one must follow in order to use Archie and then retrieve a file are as follows:

- Log into an Archie server via `telnet` (or use an Archie client program that is installed on your machine).
- Tell Archie what file(s) you require and make it search for the file(s). Make a note of the files that interest you by saving the list Archie provides (more on how to do this later).
- Exit the Archie server back to your local host.
- FTP to the site(s) found and download the file(s) you require; alternatively use an FTPmail server to get the file(s). Read Chapter 2 on the anonymous FTP service for more details.

In this chapter you will learn how to:

- Use Archie's command-set to browse remote anonymous FTP sites
- Use Archie's software description database (SDD) to locate software and other files

- How to email the Archie server for information, rather than using it interactively
- Search for specific file types, e.g. images, compressed files, and public upload areas

Each Archie server maintains a list of anonymous FTP sites, each of which is contacted on a regular basis, normally once a month at least. The Archie server then uses FTP to download a list of the public files on that machine and this is then merged into one large database on the main Archie server machine. Archie servers maintain many hundreds of thousands of files in this way, and most Archie servers keep track of well over 1000 anonymous FTP sites. Archie servers can be accessed both on an interactive and non-interactive basis; interactive access is achieved using a program such as `telnet` to access an Archie server, while non-interactive access is made available via emailing the Archie server with a number of commands placed in the body of the message. The search results are then mailed back to you.

TIP

The Archie system can be accessed though the Gopher program if you prefer using menus to access FTP sites and files. See Chapter 9 for more details on the Gopher system.

4.2   Logging into an Archie server via `telnet`

By far the easiest way of accessing Archie is to use the `telnet` program to call a remote Archie server. Many such servers are now in existence all over the world, and more continue to appear as sites start their own Archie services. Table 4.1 illustrates a selection of Archie servers that can be accesed via `telnet`.

Table 4.1   Archie servers accessible via `telnet`

Server name	Location and IP address
`archie.doc.ic.ac.uk`	UK, Imperial College London (146.169.11.3)
`archie.au`	Australia (139.130.4.6)
`archie.sura.net`	US (128.167.254.179)
`archie.unl.edu`	US (129.93.1.14)
`archie.ans.net`	US (147.225.1.2)
`archie.rutgers.edu`	US (128.6.18.15)
`archie.kuis.kyoto-u.ac.jp`	Japan (130.54.20.1)
`archie.nz`	New Zealand (130.195.9.4)
`archie.th-darmstadt.de`	Germany (130.83.128.111)
`archie.cs.huji.ac.il`	Israel (132.65.6.15)

All Archie servers respond to the log-in name archie; a password is not required. Once you have logged in, the Archie server will display a short welcome message and will normally display a list of other Archie servers, such as those illustrated in Table 4.1. You may want to examine the Archie server's command which gives you an up-to-date list of servers. Example 4.1 illustrates a typical log-in session with an Archie server:

Example 4.1

A typical log-in session with an Archie server:

```
$ telnet archie.doc.ic.ac.uk↵
Trying 146.169.11.3... Connected
login: archie↵
Last login: Thu 19 Aug 15:53:01 from acsc.com
SunOS Release 4.1 (Archie): Thu 19 Aug 16:01:19 GMT 1993
Welcome to the Archie server at Imperial College London.
archie>
```

As can be seen from Example 4.1, we use telnet to call the Archie server at Imperial College London (it clearly makes sense to use the nearest Archie server to yourself in order to improve performance). We then receive a login: prompt which means that we have to identify ourselves to the system. The username archie is standardized across all Archie servers, and this is typed next to the login: prompt. No password is required and we are logged in automatically. Next, the system displays some system information including the time and date the service was last used, and the version details of the software being used – nearly all Archie servers are Unix-based machines. A greeting message is then shown, and we are placed at the archie> prompt.

THE ARCHIE COMMAND SET

Table 4.2 illustrates the Archie command set. Searching for a file is performed using the prog command, along with the name of the file you require. Archie assumes that you know the name of the file(s) you want to find, but in the case that you do not know, Archie provides the whatis command. The whatis command allows you to search Archie's software description database (SDD). This is a database of common software programs and keywords which identifies many of the files that Archie has access to. More on the SDD facility later.

Table 4.2　The Archie command set

Archie command	Description
help [command]	Display help information; use optional [command] argument to be more specific
quit	Quit the Archie system
set <variable> [value]	Set an Archie variable. Some variables accept a [value] argument, others are logical values (on/off toggle settings)
unset <variable>	Unset a variable (or reset its default)
show	Display all variable values
list [string]	Show a list of FTP sites. The [string] argument can be used to find specific sites; wildcards (* and ?) are sometimes accepted also. If [string] is omitted all sites are shown
mail [address1 .. n]	Mail search results to the recipients specified in the [address] arguments
site [sitename]	Shows the files available at FTP site named in the [sitename] argument
servers	Shows a list of all the currently known server machines
prog [pattern]	Initiate a search for the file(s) that contain the pattern in [pattern]
whatis [pattern]	Search software description database for a file/utility, e.g. compress for a list of compression programs/utilities, etc.
compress	Compresses your emailed reports and uuencodes them. The Unix compress command is used for compression, as is the Unix uuencode program. Use this command when you are using the mail command, and when you think a mail message may exceed 45K

4.3　Starting a search

Initiating a search could be performed immediately using the prog command as shown in Table 4.2, however, this may not be the optimal solution. Archie's searches should be refined as much as possible so that the search pattern is accurate, and such that the number of items actually displayed is quite small. Unfortunately, Archie does not take care of file duplication, and nor should it. If a particular file exists on 100 sites then all 100 sites will be shown unless you instruct Archie to show only the first 10. It may be the case that a site is unavailable due to a line failure, etc., so always make sure that you look at half a dozen or so sites and not just the first.

TIP

Archie can be used to find both ordinary and directory files. Searching for a directory may yield the file(s) you are looking for. Archie's what is command will also pick up a person's name, in fact anything that is stored in the what is database.

Archie uses a command called set to alter its searching behaviour. This command will allow you to make substring searches and limit the number of hits (or files displayed), among other things. It may be the case that you don't have the complete filename you require and you will therefore need to make Archie search for part of a filename. In all such cases the set command will yield the solution required. Table 4.3 illustrates the various Archie variables that can be used; the left-hand column shows the variable name, while the middle column shows the keywords that configure the variable; the final column explains the meaning behind each variable.

You should use the set command along with the required keyword in order to refine your searches; Example 4.2 below demonstrates the process.

Example 4.2

Enabling a subcase search with hostname sorting:

```
archie> set sort hostname↵
archie> set search subcase↵
archie>
```

Finally, we can actually search for the file or utility that interests us. Assume we wanted to search for the image viewing utility Graphics Workshop and we knew the utility had the string gws in the filename. We would use the prog command to initiate a search as shown in Example 4.3.

Example 4.3

Searching for a file with the string gws (subcase):

```
archie> set sort hostname↵
archie> set search subcase↵
archie> set maxhits 3↵
archie> prog gws↵
Sorting by hostname
# matches / % database searched: 3 / 100%
Host ccb.ucsf.edu (128.218.1.13)
Last updated 12:45 9 Dec 1993
```

```
Location: /pub/graphics/msdos
  FILE    rw-r--r--    105553  Jun 05  1993    gws.zip
Location: /pub/graphics/msdos
  FILE    rw-r--r--    121319  Aug 08  1993    gwsv21.zip
Host du9ds3.uni-duisberg.de (134.91.4.130)
Last updated 09:15 1 Dec 1993
  Location: /pub/msdos/graph
  FILE    rw-r--r--    105553  Jun 05  1993    gws.zip
archie>
```

Table 4.3 Archie variables

Set variable	Keyword	Action
Alter search criterion		
search →	regex	Regular expression search allowing wildcards to be used in patterns, e.g. *, ?, etc. This is the default search method used by Archie
	sub	Substring search allows strings within a pattern to be matched, e.g. ix matches unix, etc. The case of patterns will be ignored in this case
	subcase	Substring search with full case checking. This will be faster than the above search type
	exact	The fastest search; will match string patterns exactly as typed
Sort output display		
sortby →	none	The output report will not be sorted in any way
	hostname	Reports will be sorted by Internet FTP hostname (A–Z order)
	rhostname	Reports will be sorted by Internet FTP hostname (Z–A order)
	time	Reports will be sorted in file creation/modification timestamp (ascending order of time)
	rtime	Reports will be sorted in file creation/modification timestamp (descending order of time)
	size	Reports will be sorted in terms of file size (largest to smallest)
	rsize	Reports will be sorted in terms of file size (smallest to largest)
	filename	Reports will be sorted in terms of the filename (ascending order A–Z)
	rfilename	Reports will be sorted in terms of the filename (reverse order Z–A)

Table 4.3 – *continued*

Set variable	Keyword	Action
Configure terminal		
term ⟶	<term> [r] [c]	Set up terminal <term>; [r] and [c] represent the rows and columns of the terminal screen, e.g. set term vt100 24 79. The <term> argument can be found in the /etc/termcap file on a Unix system
Auto logout mode		
autologout ⟶	<minutes>	The number of minutes that Archie will wait before logging you out when no commands have arrived in that time
Pager function		
pager ⟶		'Pager' decides whether or not a pager is used to slow down output. The Unix variable PAGER holds the name of a pager such as less, more, etc.
Mailing functions		
mailto ⟶	<Person@host>	Specifies that user wants results of search mailed to the user <Person@host> for example fred@abcd.com
Progress monitoring		
status ⟶		Specifies that user wants a progress check made. A percentage and number of hits display is given. Toggle this function on and off using the same command
Located files		
maxhits ⟶	<number>	Makes Archie show only <number> matches, after which it stops

---

TIP

Many programs on FTP sites are compressed to save space. You must have an understanding of the utilities that are used to compress and decompress files. Please read Chapter 7 for an insight into this topic. The most common compression types are as follows (as per file-extension):

.Z   ⟶ A Unix compressed file (use decompress on Unix)

.z   ⟶ A Unix packed file (use unpack to decompress)

.ZIP   ⟶ A PKZIP archie; widely used on DOS. Get Unzip, etc.

.zoo   ⟶ A zoo archive (use zoo210 on Unix to uncompress).

.tar.Z ⟶ A Unix tar file (compressed as a .Z file. Use tar command on
        Unix: tar -x, then decompress.

Example 4.3 shows how Archie has been used to find the file gws.zip (a PKZIP archive of the GWS program that we required). The listing from the Archie program is similar to that provided by the Unix ls command. In Example 4.3, three matches have been found. The lines beginning with FILE show the file(s) details. It is possible that a single host may hold more than one copy of the file required, so all matches will be shown in such cases, as in the example of the host ccb.ucsf.edu which has two copies of a filename that match our search criterion. Archie has been made to stop its search after three matches using the command set maxhits 3; this is a useful command to get into the habit of using since Archie will churn out endless lists of information from all hosts that match the filename pattern. The most important piece of information in the listing is the FTP host on which the file resides; the directory in which the file resides should also be noted to avoid lengthy searches (remember, you must FTP in order to access these files – see Chapter 2).

TIP

The interrupt key ^C (Ctrl-C) can be used to halt an Archie search (in most cases), so if you tire of waiting for a long listing to end, this is the keystroke to use!

As Archie finds the file(s) you require it keeps you up-to-date with its progress using a small indicator display as shown below. The number of 'hits' (pattern matches) and a percentage display of the amount of the database that Archie has searched are given. Both numbers will increase as matches are found. A hit count of 0 and a 100 per cent search clearly indicate that the pattern you specified was not found.

matches / % database searched: 3 / 100%

The display indicator can be disabled using the Archie command set status (on/off toggle command).

Use `set search subcase` to locate different file types by their filename extensions, e.g. `prog.gif` for a `.GIF` image, `prog.c` for a C program, etc.

In the case that a listing is too long, the `set pager` command can be used. By setting the PAGER variable on your Unix system to the name of a program such as `more`, you can pause your screen searches accordingly. Many filter programs such as `more` come with Unix; examples are `less` and `tail`. If you are using a non-Unix machine the pager option may not be available. Some Archie servers pause output every 25 lines (a full screen of data) by default. On a Unix machine, the PAGER variable can be set up from an auto-login file such as `.login` or `.cshrc`, or directly from the prompt, as shown in Example 4.4. Note that the `set pager` command is a Boolean (logical) command and therefore does not require a specific value to be configured – toggle the function on and off accordingly using the same command.

Example 4.4

Using the pager function (Unix):

```
$ set PAGER=/bin/more↵
$ telnet archie.ans.net↵
... etc ...
archie> set pager↵
archie> prog gws↵
Sorting by hostname
# matches / % database searched: 3 / 100%
Host ccb.ucsf.edu (128.218.1.13)
Last updated 12:45 9 Dec 1993
  Location: /pub/graphics/msdos
    FILE   rw-r--r--   105553 Jun 05  1993    gws.zip
  Location: /pub/graphics/msdos
    FILE   rw-r--r--   121319 Aug 08  1993    gwsv21.zip
Host du9ds3.uni-duisberg.de (134.91.4.130)
Last updated 09:15 1 Dec 1993
  Location: /pub/msdos/graph
    FILE   rw-r--r--   105553 Jun 05  1993    gws.zip
Host entergo.co.ca (128.16.4.101)
Last updated 10:11 1 Dec 1993
  Location: /utils/graphics/pc
```

```
FILE    rw-r--r--    105553  Jun 05  1993    gws.zip
---More 10%---
```

Notice in Example 4.4 how the `more` program has been specified. The Unix `set` command can be used to modify the contents of shell variables, and has been used in the example to set the `PAGER` variable to use the `more` filter; the full pathname of the utility has been used just in case your Unix `PATH` variable does include the `/bin` (system binaries) directory – this will ensure the `more` program is found (configure your own path accordingly). When the `more` program encounters more than a full page of information it pauses allowing you to read what is on the screen. You can then advance the screen using [`Return`] for a line of information, or [`spacebar`] for a full screen. If you are using a Berkeley Unix system, the `setenv` command can be used instead of `set`, if the `set` command is not available.

TIP

You can use Archie to locate public upload areas on sites by specifying the name of a directory, rather than an ordinary file, for example: `prog upload` (use a subcase search in order to guarantee the search more chance of finding the directory).

Quitting the Archie system

When you have finally finished your searching you can quit Archie using the command `quit` by itself. FTP then says `Goodbye`, for example:

```
archie> quit
221 Goodbye.
```

Refer to Chapter 2 for a discussion on the FTP in order to use Archie's results to actually download the file(s) you require.

TIP

If you are a USENET user, use Archie to search for group names, e.g. `comp.sources`, etc. Many FTP sites hold USENET articles for you to download, and Archie will find them for you.

4.4 Mailing results back to yourself (or another user)

Using Archie's `mailto` variable it is possible to send the output of a search to yourself, or any other user for that matter. The Archie mail command will also take an email-name argument as an alternative method. Example 4.5 shows a typical mailing operation.

Example 4.5

Mailing a report back to yourself (method 1):

```
...
archie> set mailto fred@somewhere.com↵
archie> prog gws↵
... etc ...
archie> mail↵
archie>
```

Note that `set mailto` does not initiate the mailing, rather it sets up the recipient to receive the mail. The `mail` command then performs the actual task of sending the report on. Another alternative would be to use the `mail` command with the recipient name directly, as shown in Example 4.6. I have known some Archie servers to ommit the output generated by a report when the `set mailto` command is used – watch out for this and use the Archie command `unset` to remove the email name to overcome this problem, e.g. `unset mailto`. Using the `mail` command with the recipient name is a much better way of mailing reports.

Example 4.6

Mailing a report back to yourself (method 2):

```
...
archie> prog gws↵
... etc ...
archie> mail fred@somewhere.com↵
archie>
```

In both instances the search report will be mailed back to you using conventional email. The time it takes for a report to reach you can vary, depending on how busy the Archie server is. Expect results back in no longer than a couple of hours (a day at the most).

TIP

The `mail` command works in the background, so you can still continue your search while a report is being mailed to you.

USING THE COMPRESS COMMAND

If you are mailing reports and anticipate that the length of such reports will be large (typically larger than 40 Kb) you can use the Archie compress command, which as the name suggests will compress the file and mail it to you. Compressed files are binary files and cannot be handled by the email network. The compress command therefore uuencodes the file to convert it into ASCII. When you receive the file you should strip away all of the header leaving just the begin and end lines and everything in between. The file should then be passed through the uudecode utility, whereupon the ASCII Archie report will be created. For an in-depth discussion of the uuencode utility please refer to Chapters 7 and 8. If you are using a non-Unix machine you will have to acquire a Unix .Z file decompress utility, and an appropriate uudecoder for your machine (refer to Chapter 7 on file compression for more details).

TIPS

If you don't want to use an editor such as vi to strip out the header from your uuencoded mail message, simply use the Unix command below which will do this automatically (note that you will have to save the mail-message into an external file, and this is normally done using the s (save) command, along with a filename of your choice, e.g. file.uue, as below):

```
$ cat file.uue | sed '/^END/, /^BEGIN/d' | uudecode
```

Read Chapter 8 for more Unix scripts and details regarding uuencoded files.

4.5   Mailing an Archie server directly

If you don't have time to get involved in an interactive discussion with an Archie server, you may want to consider emailing it instead. All Archie servers accept email requests which are processed just as if you had used the server interactively in real time. A typical mail-message will contain all of the Archie commands that you need to conduct your search, i.e. the sorting options and search criteria. Archie uses the From: line in your email header to send back the details, so no mail command or mailto variable needs to be set up. A typical Archie mail-message could resemble that shown in Example 4.7a. The quit command is important in a mail-message because some people use signature files; these are appended to the bottom of every mail-message sent, and whatever text is sent may cause Archie some problems when it comes to deciphering them.

Example 4.7a

A typical Archie mail-message body:

```
set maxhits 2
set search subcase
set sort hostname
prog gws
quit
```

All mail-messages should be sent to the special username `archie` at the address of the server you want to use, for example you could type

```
$ mail archie@archie.ans.net < archie.msg↵
```

which would send a file of Archie commands (assumed to be in the file `archie.msg`) to the archie server at `archie.ans.net`. If you don't want to get involved in creating files (scared of `vi`, perhaps?) you can use the Unix command

```
$ mail archie@archie.ans.net <`cat`↵
```

which will invoke the Unix `cat` command; by default this reads from the standard input, so you can type `archie` commands and then press `^D` (Ctrl-D) to send the input to the mail address specified. Note though that your input must be accurate, as there will be no scope to make corrections as if you were using an editor – mistakes will be ignored by Archie just as if you had typed them in wrongly at its interactive mode (a small error message will be displayed in such cases). Enclosing the `cat` command in grave accents (` ` `) makes Unix perform command substitution, i.e. the `cat` commands input will used as a mail-message rather than a file. A typical reply from an Archie server is shown (in the context of Example 4.7a) in Example 4.7b.

Example 4.7b

A typical reply from Archie (in the context of Example 4.7a):

```
From: archie@archie.ans.net
Received: from ans.net from somewhere.com (SMTP)
Date: Mon, 15 Jul 93 14:23:46 EST
 Message-Id: <87232232.JM76541@ans.net>
From: archie@archie.ans.net
To: Fred <fred@somewhere.com>
Subject: archie reply: prog gws
Status: R
```

```
Sorting by hostname
Search request for 'gws'
Host ccb.ucsf.edu (128.218.1.13)
Last updated 12:45 9 Dec 1993
  Location: /pub/graphics/msdos
    FILE    rw-r--r--    105553 Jun 05 1993    gws.zip
  Location: /pub/graphics/msdos
    FILE    rw-r--r--    121319 Aug 08 1993    gwsv21.zip
Host du9ds3.uni-duisberg.de (134.91.4.130)
Last updated 09:15 1 Dec 1993
  Location: /pub/msdos/graph
    FILE    rw-r--r--    105553 Jun 05 1993    gws.zip
```

4.6   Archie's software description database

One problem with the Archie system is the assumption that users know what
the file they require is called. Filenames can be very cryptic, especially under
the Unix operating system, so Archie provides a command called whatis.
The whatis command uses a keyword supplied by the user and then uses this
to access its software description database (SDD). The SDD is a list of the
most popular software utilities and programs that have arrived onto the
Internet; it currently has over 3000 entries, and is continually growing. I
personally find the SDD a bit cumbersome to use, mainly since you still have
to know a filename or keyword which describes the utility you want to find.
The majority of descriptions in the SDD come from the USENET groups such
as alt.sources and comp.sources, and many are submitted by authors
when their utility has been accepted onto the network. Example 4.8 illustrates
a typical search of the SDD using the whatis keyword curses (curses is
a library of cursor-related control sequences under Unix):

Example 4.8

Typical SDD enquiry (keyword: curses):

```
archie> whatis curses↵
chemtab        Visual period table using curses
clock          Curses-driven digital clock for ASCII
               terminals
kiface         Key mapping library for curses type appli-
               cations
pcurses        Terminfo/curses
uustatus       Curses orientated uustat for UUCP
archie>
```

As can be seen, Archie lists each file in the first column, while the descriptions of each file/utility then follow. As well as specific names of systems such as curses, general purpose names such as compression, sound, word-perfect, etc. can also be used. You may even be able to get hold of the actual SDD file itself; mail the postmaster at one of the Archie sites shown, and enquire there.

4.7 Site information

For real FTP enthusiasts there is nothing better to do on a long winter's night than explore the FTP sites that Archie maintains. Archie's list command is very useful; supply it with a wildcarded expression and it will show you all the sites that match that expression. This can be useful for finding all sites in a particular country for example. Another good feature of the command is its ability to list all the sites it maintains. Some are shown in Example 4.9.

Example 4.9

Using the list command with a wildcarded expression to match all Japanese FTP sites:

```
archie> site *.jp↵
akiu.gw.tohoku.jp       130.34.8.9        19:58 10 Dec 1993
ascwide.ascii.co.jp     133.152.32.11     19:59 10 Dec 1993
dclwide.dcl.co.jp       133.243.1.1       20:05 10 Dec 1993
etlport.etl.go.jp       192.31.197.99     20:45 10 Dec 1993
... etc ...
```

Example 4.9 shows the site command in action. Notice how the wild-carded expression '*.jp' has been used to match all Japanese sites. If you were searching for some Japanese software then these sites may be good places to look first. The first column represents the name of the site; the second is the site's numeric IP address; the final column represents the time and date that Archie extracted that particular site's details for its own master database, thus telling you how up-to-date the details for that site are. For a full list of country codes, please refer to Appendix F.

4.8 Terminal configuration

The Archie command set term allows you to configure the terminal you are using. In order to use the command you must know which terminal type or emulation that you are using. If you are using a communications package to access the network, this should already have a number of modes that can be selected, for example ANSI, VT100, etc. A keyword is used by the set term command which in turn ensures that the correct screen escape codes are used. Archie has some facilities, such as its progress indicator, which require cursor movement commands to be used to update the display. Screen corruption can occur in some instances where the terminal type or emulation does not match what you are currently using yourself in order to access Archie. Many keywords can be used with the set term command; we advise that you look at the Unix file /etc/termcap (terminal capabilities file) for a list of these – they will be situated in the first column of the file. Common examples include: vt100, vt152, ansi, vi (after the editor), ibmpc, xterm (X Terminal window, perhaps) and dumb. dumb is the name of a screen emulation without any special screen features (such as video effects); this is referred to sometimes as an ASCII terminal.

If you are unsure about the emulation you are using on a Unix machine, the environmental variable TERM may hold the answer. The file .login or .cshrc (auto login files for the Bourne and C-Shells) may set up your terminal for you automatically – examine them to see – for example:

```
$ echo $TERM↵
ansi
$ cat .login↵
# Auto login file .login
set TERM =`qterm`
set PATH = /usr/bin
set USER = `whoami`
$
```

This example Unix session contains two user commands. In the first command we have used the Unix echo command to display the name of the TERM variable; an ANSI emulation seems to be in effect, so using the Archie command below would seem appropriate:

```
archie> set term ansi↵
```

In the second command we have used the Unix cat program to display the contents of the auto-login file .login (assuming we are using the Bourne shell /bin/sh). Three commands have been used in .login, namely three set commands to set up various variables for the terminal, path and user-name. Notice how the TERM variable has been set up using command substitution; the utility qterm has been enclosed in grave-accents (`) and therefore the value it returns will be assigned to the TERM variable. Qterm is a non-standard 'Quiz Terminal' utility that examines the current emulation and returns an educated guess as to its type, e.g. it will have returned 'ansi' in our example. You can find your terminal's entry in the Unix /etc/termcap file using the command below (assuming the $TERM variable is defined):

```
$ grep $TERM /etc/termcap⏎
```

Note that on some systems, such as System V based Unix machines, the /etc/terminfo file is used instead of /etc/termcap.

4.9   Archie client programs

An alternative to using Archie via telnet is to use an Archie client program. If you have one of these installed on your system, the operation is essentially the same as using the system via telnet, except for the fact that a number of command-line options must be used since there is no interactive mode. Table 4.4 illustrates the main Archie client command-mode options that are commonly available. The syntax for an Archie client is thus:

```
archie -1cers -h<name> -m<n> <search-pattern>
```

Table 4.4   Archie client command-line options

Archie option	Description
-c	Substring match search. Upper and lower < search-pattern > will match exactly
-e	Exact search. No substrings; upper and lower case match exactly. Fastest search
-r	Use a regular expression (wildcarded), for example: *, ?, [. . .], etc.
-s	Substring search; case ignored
-1	Reformats output into columns suitable for a filtering program
-h<name>	Uses the Archie server specified in the argument < name >. Examine the variable ARCHIE_HOST for the default
-m<n>	Instructs Archie not to return more than <n> matches. Same as set maxhits command.

Notes:
The Archie command yet performs commands such as: whatis, list and sites. Use a telnet-based server to perform such checks.

Some hypothetical examples of various Archie client commands are given below:

Example 4.10

Subcase search for uudecode; 1 hit only; FTP file:

```
$ archie -s -m1 uudecode⏎
Host ccb.ucsf.edu (128.218.1.13)
  Location: /pub/dos/graphics/uu
    FILE   rw-r--r--   28976 Jul 09 1992   uudecode.Z
```

```
$ ftp ccb.ucsf.edu↵
Trying 128.218.1.13.... Connected
220 ccb,ucsf.edu FTP Server (version 6.2 Jan 30 1990) ready.
Name (ccb.ucsf.edu): anonymous↵
331 Guest login ok, send e-mail address as password.
Password: fred@somewhere.com↵
230 Guest login ok, access restrictions apply.
ftp> cd /pub/dos/graphics/uu↵
250 CWD command successful
ftp> binary↵
200 Type Set to I.
ftp> hash↵
ftp> get uudecode.Z↵
200 PORT command successful
150 Opening Binary mode data connection for uudecode.Z (28976 bytes)
############################
226 Transfer complete.
28976 bytes received in 3.1 seconds (9.2 Kbytes/s)
ftp> quit↵
221 Goodbye.
```

Example 4.10 uses the −s option to conduct a substring search of the pattern 'uudecode'. The −m1 option ensures only one hit, i.e. the first file found is displayed. Archie, in this example, finds the file uudecode.Z (this is a Unix compressed file) on the host named ccb.ecsf.edu. The example then continues to use FTP (see Chapter 3 for an in-depth coverage) to actually download the file to our machine. .Z files are compressed by the Unix compress command. How did I know this you are asking? Well I read Chapter 7, of course.

TIP

If you are a Unix user, you can make Archie conduct a search in the background, thus freeing up your terminal for other tasks. Use the & (ampersand) after the Archie command to do this, and redirect the output into a file, for example:

$ archie −s uudecode > archie.1 &

When Archie has completed the command you can examine the file archie.1 for the results. Use the Unix ps command to see when the command is finished.

Another useful option available in most Archie clients is -1 (that's the number one). This option returns a series of filename definitions in the format:

```
Timestamp, File Size, Host name, Filename
```

The output when using this option can be saved into a file using the Unix > redirection operator, for example:

```
$ archie -s uuencode -m2 > archie.uu⏎
```

A typical listing could resemble the following:

```
1992090711100Z   28976   ccb.ucsf.edu /pub/dos/graphics/uu/uudecode.zip
1992080409000Z    512    wuarchive.wustl.edu /mirrors/dos/graphics/uudecode/
```

Files and directories can be determined by looking at the final field. We can see the file uudecode.zip is a file in its own right (because the final character is not /); the other file is a directory because of the tell-tale / sign. We can also see that one file is 512 bytes in length (the directory) while the uudecode.zip file is 28976 bytes in length. If you play about with the Unix commands you can manipulate this output as you wish. For example, we could write shell-script to show us all files that are directories (assuming the -1 listing is saved to the file archie.list):

```
$ grep '/$' archie.list⏎
```

The $ wildcard matches characters at the end of a line. We could use grep to reverse the search to exclude all directories using its $-v$ option, for example:

```
$ grep -v '/$' archie.list⏎
```

Other Unix commands for field processing can also be used. The awk command (and language) could be used to examine a listing from archie and extract only certain fields, for example this awk script finds all entries whose file size exceeds 10 000 bytes (place this script in a file using your favourite editor if you like, but make it executable using the chmod +x command before using it; you can type this on one line if you prefer):

```
# Program 1: List files that exceed 10000 bytes. Uses   archie.list
# file for all processing
awk 'BEGIN {n=0}
   { if ($2 > 10000)
     n++
   } END
{ printf ("Number of entries exceeding 10000 bytes:   %2d",n)
}' archie.list
```

In this first awk example, the $2 matches the second field in our Archie file archie.list. Awk's printf is similar to that found in C; the %2d allows the number of entries found to be displayed (as a decimal number – note the %2d, with two decimal places). The n++ statement keeps track of the number of entries found – notice it is only incremented when $2 is greater (>) than 10000. Notice also that variable n is initialized to 0 at the start of the main program loop. The BEGIN and END constructs show where the main program loop starts and finishes. Awk works its way through every line in a file until the last line is read. If we named this awk script counter, made it executable, and then ran it, for example

```
$ vi counter↵
... edit/enter the file as above ...
$ chmod +x counter↵
$ counter↵
```

we could expect the output (in the context of the example file with two entries shown earlier):

```
Number of entries exceeding 10000 bytes: 1
```

We could modify our utility quite simply. We could make it show us the names and sites of all files that exceed a certain size, rather than having it check for the fixed (hard-coded) 10000 byte limit, for example:

```
# Program 2: List files that exceed a certain size. Uses the file #
archie.list for all processing
echo -n "Enter file-size: "
read fsize
awk 'BEGIN {n=0}
   { if ($2 > $fsize)
     printf (" [%2d] Site: %s Filename: %s", n, $3, $4)
     n++
   }
   END { printf ("Number of entries exceeding %n5 bytes: %2d",fsize,n)
}' archie.list
```

The above awk script would take input from the user in the form of a numeric value representing the size of a file (notice the read statement). Our new utility would run as follows (assume name is counter 2):

```
$ counter2↵
Enter file-size: 10000↵
[1] Site: ccb.ucsf.edu   Filename: /pub/dos/graphics/uu/uudecode.zip
Number of entries exceeding 10000 bytes: 1
```

The list would clearly be larger, depending on the entries for files in our hypo-thetical archie.list file, for example we may see four entries:

```
$ counter2↵
Enter file-size: 5000↵
[1] Site: ccb.ucsf.edu      Filename: /pub/dos/graphics/uu/uudecode.zip
[2] Site: dll.site.com      Filename: /pub/graphics/uu/uudecode
[3] Site: ern.cc.eec.edu    Filename: /dos/graphics/uu/uudecode.arc
[4] Site: demon.co.uk       Filename: /pub/ftp/uudecode
Number of entries exceeding 5000 bytes: 4
```

It makes sense to make all values and filenames variable, so that they can be entered from the command-line. Our two earlier programs use the file archie.list for processing; perhaps we should alter our program to use Archie directly to create the file after asking for a search pattern from the user:

```
# Program 3: List files that exceed a certain size. This program
# Archie automatically to create the neccessary files. Program
# also asks for the search pattern:
echo -n "Enter file-size: "
read fsize
echo -n "Enter search pattern for archie: "
read pattern
archie -1 -s $pattern > archie.tmp
awk 'BEGIN {n=0}
  { if ($2 > $fsize)
    printf (" [%2d] Site: %s Filename: %s", n, $3, $4)
    n++
  }
  END { printf ("Number of entries exceeding %n5 bytes:  %2d",fsize,n)
}' archie.list
rm archie.tmp
```

Notice how the file archie.tmp is created, and then deleted when no longer required (the rm command removes the file). A hypothetical program run, assuming our utility was called counter3, would be

```
$ counter3↵
Enter file-size: 5000↵
Enter search pattern for archie: uudecode↵
[1] Site: ccb.ucsf.edu      Filename: /pub/dos/graphics/uu/uudecode.zip
[2] Site: dll.site.com      Filename: /pub/graphics/uu/uudecode
[3] Site: ern.cc.eec.edu    Filename: /dos/graphics/uu/uudecode.arc
Number of entries exceeding 5000 bytes: 3
```

As you would imagine, the possibilities for manipulating files under Unix are quite vast. If you want to understand how to write your own programs in the language of the shell, or perhaps using awk, refer to your Unix manual for awk and csh (C-Shell – or whatever shell you use). My book on Unix, *Unix – The Complete Book*, has many examples, and covers the Unix awk, sed, and xargs tools that can be used for programming many different types of utilities.

5

Interactive Internet services – `telnet`

5.1 Introduction to `telnet`

`Telnet` is the Internet's virtual terminal protocol, allowing you to log in to a remote machine and use it interactively in real time, just as if you were using that machine locally. A vast amount of resources are available to you via `telnet` including such things as remote databases, information servers and on-line OPACs. `Telnet` is one of the Internet's basic tools-of-the-trade. Once mastered, you will be able to access many other standard network services such as Gopher, WAIS, the World-Wide-Web, Archie and numerous other on-line resources (Chapter 9 covers these core services in more detail). `Telnet` can also be used to conduct interactive sessions with a Unix machine (or any other machine in theory). Among the core services that you will use `telnet` to access are:

- Archie, the file archiving system (see Chapter 4)
- Gopher, WAIS and the World-Wide-Web (see Chapter 9)
- USENET – NNTP servers (see Chapter 2)
- Gateway machines (network-to-network systems, e.g. Internet JANET)
- On-line OPACs (on-line public access catalogues, e.g. at libraries)
- On-line bulletin boards (e.g. BUBL and NISS – see Appendix D)
- Interactive Unix
- IRC – Internet Relay Chat

`Telnet` works by establishing a TCP/IP connection with a login server on a remote machine (`login` is the name of the Unix program that identifies a user and allows them access upon supplying a valid username and password). `Telnet` then allows keystrokes from one machine to the other, for example when you type your password `telnet` copies the characters to the remote

machine for checking against its password database (/etc/passwd). One
beauty of the telnet system lies in its ease-of-use.

TIP

Appendix D, the A–Z resource guide, documents many Telnet-based services,
such as those mentioned above.

As you will come to see, it is not telnet that is difficult to use, rather it is
the service you eventually access that you will need to spend time actually
learning about. Telnet offers a standard interface into any on-line service.
The on-line services themselves will differ enormously; some services will be
menu based, and others will not; some will require a specific terminal emulation, e.g. a VT100, while others will require just a dumb emulation e.g. a
simple ASCII display (or TTY emulation). All this, and more, will be
explained in this chapter.

TIP

The Gopher system allows menu-access to many Telnet-based resources
(completely menu-driven for ease of use). You can also search for specific
Telnet services using Gopher. See Chapter 9 for more information on Gopher.

5.2   A sample telnet session

The simplest way of invoking telnet is via the command telnet; the
command-line syntax of the program is

telnet [hostname]

where the optional [hostname] argument is the name, or numeric IP
address, of an Internet host you want to contact. For example one could type
the following command to access the Archie file-archiving service located at
Imperial College UK:

telnet archie.doc.ic.ac.uk↵

or one could also type the equivalent command:

telnet 146.169.11.3↵

After invoking telnet with the service required you should shortly see a
welcoming screen for that service. It should perhaps be mentioned that some
services require you to identify yourself (providing perhaps a username and/or
password combination) while others will log you in automatically. It all
depends on which service you are contacting. Invoked without the
[hostname] argument, telnet drops into command mode and displays a

telnet> prompt allowing you to input commands directly. Telnet is an interactive program, and its commands are discussed in Section 5.4. Telnet's command mode interface looks simply like this:

telnet↵
telnet>

The ability to invoke telnet in this way depends on whether or not you are using a telnet client program. On Unix this will be the case, although some systems will not allow telnet to be invoked without a [hostname] argument (these include non-Unix systems where telnet has been implemented slightly differently).

TIP

If you are an academic Internet user you can use telnet to access your academic account in order to log in and use the system from an external computer.

TELNET PROBLEMS

In some cases the system you are calling may be unavailable, or may be simply too full to cope with any additional users. If this is the case the system being contacted should display a message to that effect. In the case that a host is unavailable due to technical problems you will normally see a message

Telnet: Unavailable to connect to remote host.

or, similarly

Telnet: Connection timed-out

In these cases you will simply have to wait for the service to come back on-line again. Try emailing the postmaster alias at the host you are trying to contact and ask them what is happening (assuming their line-connection is not down, in which case email won't of course get through either).

5.3   Terminal emulations

TIP

Always have a VT (video terminal) emulation enabled when calling menu-based services. This will save your screen from being corrupted when the service starts. If you are using a communciations package (i.e. from DOS, etc.) ensure it is using the same emulation as you. On Unix you must alter the TERM variable, as described below.

Depending on the service you access, the system you interact with may require a particular terminal emulation in order to function properly. For example, a system may use a series of special screen escape codes to draw a menu on your terminal; if your terminal cannot mimic such an emulation, your local display is not going to function correctly and you may experience some screen corruption. In the worst cases your whole session may grind to a halt. Some services require only a dumb terminal emulation, simply because their display will be simple ASCII text, shown perhaps a line at a time, and without any fancy screen facilities such as menu bars, cursor navigation, etc. When you are required to supply a terminal emulation to use during your session, you will commonly see a message similar to

TERM = (vt100):

TERM is in fact a special Unix variable which is used to store the name of a terminal or emulation, for example the common VT100 mode (this allows for screen clearing, cursor movement and video effects such as bold, underline, blinking text, etc.). A default emulation may be provided for you – notice the 'vt100' sign in brackets. You can accept a default emulation by pressing the [Return] key although be warned that if your screen is not expecting a VT100 emulation you will experience problems, notably a mass of gibberish on the screen. In order to know which emulation you are running you will have to ascertain one of the following:

- Have I loaded an emulation driver already? This may be the ANSI.SYS driver under MSDOS in the CONFIG.SYS file. On Unix, you may have set the TERM variable already – in this case you can override this by using a new value when the remote program asks you (as in the previous example).
- Have I run an emulation program? These vary. A specific program to make the screen handle VT requests could be loaded; one example is the vt102.exe program for DOS; numerous others exist such as the screen program under some Unix systems. Your service-provider may be able to help with a utility to handle screen emulations; many shareware and freeware programs do, of course, exist.
- Is my communications software using a specific emulation? The majority of communications programs, e.g. Odyssey, Procomm, etc. support specific emulations, e.g. VT100, VT52, ANSI, etc. You must ensure this emulation matches the remote system. You may be able to correct the emulation while actually on-line, i.e. to save hanging-up the connection and re-telnetting to your host.

On Unix, common TERM values can be found in the /etc/termcap file. Copy or print out this file to get an idea of which terminal emulations are available. Common values include:

dumb   → A dumb (ASCII) terminal emulation (also tty or ascii in some cases)

ansi   → A terminal that accepts ANSI escape codes

vt100   → A VT100 terminal emulation ('vt102' may be ok)

vt52   → A VT52 terminal emulation

vi   → A terminal that accepts the vi editor keys

ibmpc   → An emulation for the IBM PC used on some systems

NB: these are not standard names, although they are common on many Unix-based systems.

If a service offers a default emulation check that is supported on your system using the Unix command:

$ grep default /etc/termcap

where default is the name of the default emulation shown. The value returned by the grep command should be used in your TERM variable.

If the worst happens and your screen is so badly corrupted that you cannot exit, simply press the [Control] key and] together. This will interrupt telnet, and you can type close to hang-up the session (more on these commands in Section 5.4). In some cases a default emulation will not be given (some systems even start without telling you what emulation is in use!). You may even be able to cycle through a series of emulations on your communications software program (if you are using Unix, you may have to exit and restart with a different emulation until you get the right one–or at least one with the minimum of screen corruption).

Most Unix-based services such as Archie and Gopher require a series of standard emulations, which are:

Archie → tty or dumb (vt100 or ANSI is better since some Archie progress displays use cursor movement and may corrupt the screen in some cases).

Gopher → Requires a vt100 or ANSI emulation at least so that you can get screen effects such as bold, reverse screen, and of course cursor movement

WAIS $\longrightarrow$ Requires at least a vt100 or ansi emulation for on-screen navigation, screen updates, etc.

WWW $\longrightarrow$ The World-Wide-Web can be run in dumb or tty mode, since its screens are not complicated.

IRC $\longrightarrow$ Internet Chat requires an ansi or vt100 at least. See Chapter 10 for more on IRCs.

NB: Services such as ftp, telnet, etc. are all text based, and do not require special emulations. Unix tools such as talk will require screen cursor movement, so a vt100 emulation should be used in such cases.

A typical /etc/termcap entry can be seen below. This entry is for an IBM PC emulating a VT100 terminal (explanations below):

```
# Partial /etc/termcap entry for an IBM PC/VT100
ib|ibmpc|vt100:\
    :ce=\E[B:\
    :cl=\E[2J\E[H:\
    :co#80:\
    :li#23:\
    :cr=^M:\
    :dc=^H:\
    :dl=\EM:\
    :do=\E[%B:\
    :ho=\E[H:\
    ... etc ...
```

The /etc/termcap file may at first seem confusing–after all it is. By looking at the first line, we can see three names each separated by a | (pipe) sign; these are the names of the terminal emulations in question–it is these names that are placed in the TERM variable. After this line we can see that there are a number of special keywords which configure the emulation. A screen escape code has the characters \E in front of it, for example the cl=\E[2J\E[H line tells the system how to clear its screen; the lines with #'s in them are fixed constants, for example co#80 sets up 80 screen columns whereas li#23 sets up 23 lines–a typical PC screen setup. Control codes are flagged with the ^ prefix, so we can see that a carriage return (cr) is set to ^M (Ctrl-M–try it on your PC now), whereas ^H (Ctrl-H) will delete a character to the left (try this also). Look at your Unix manual page using the command man termcap for more information on the terminal descriptions database. In order to create your own termcap entries you will need access to a map of the screen escape codes that your screen emulation supports–you may want to set up a simple ANSI entry since you can find the ANSI escape codes in most computer manuals, e.g. the DOS manual for PCs.

TIP

If your terminal does not understand the DELETE key, try using the Unix stty (set terminal settings) program using the command:

$ stty erase " ^H "

Log onto a Unix machine via FTP and get hold of a largish /etc/termcap (or /etc/terminfo) file and then jot down the various settings and emulation names in your own time. The next time you log in your task should be easier. Of course, you could note down the emulations from the machine at which you are accessing a particular service, so as to ensure that service accepts the emulation name you type when required.

IBM MAINFRAME EMULATIONS

Some machines on the Internet are IBM mainframes running operating systems such as MVS (look out for the string vm in the hostname for such hosts). These systems can be quite fussy about the emulation you use, and in order to remedy screen problems, Unix systems use a version of telnet called tn3270. This is a version of the telnet program that has been designed to work with IBM 3270 based mainframes. Some versions of telnet even have a tn3270 option built in, although this is rarely found.

5.4 The telnet command set

Telnet's command-mode interface is very easy to master; the user need only know half-a-dozen commands to get by. Telnet programs can differ in the features they offer so you are advised to use the ? (help) command to see just what facilities are available. The core commands suported by nearly all telnet programs are illustrated in Table 5.1. Compulsory keywords are shown using the <keyword> argument.

A typical telnet session to a Unix machine could therefore be as follows:

```
$ telnet↵
telnet> open tracey.ibmpcug.co.uk
Trying...
Connected to tracey.ibmpcug.co.uk
Escape character is ^]
SunOS UNIX (tracey)
login: fred↵
Password: <freds-password>↵
Last login: Fri Dec 11 15:31:03 from demon.co.uk
SunOS Release 4.1 (GENERIC) #1: Sat Dec 12 18:55:17 GMT  1993
$
```

Table 5.1 Core `telnet` command set

Telnet *command*	*Description*
?	Help command. Makes `telnet` display all valid commands, such as those below
open <hostname>	Establishes a connection with a remote `telnet` server. The <hostname> argument is the name of an Internet host, or an equivalent numeric IP address. The <hostname> argument can also be given at the command-line stage
close	Terminates your `telnet` connection. If you used a hostname argument on the command-line you will be exited from the program. This command is useful when used with the open command to allow multiple connections (one after another) without quitting the program
set <variable>	Allows the user to set various `telnet` variables. Use the ? argument to see a list of such variables that are valid. Variables control `telnet`'s behaviour
z	Suspends `telnet` into a shell environment to allow local commands. This command is system specific, and if not available you can use `Ctrl-]` and type in the name of a shell, e.g. `csh` for the C-Shell (press `Ctrl-D` to leave shell)
quit	Quit from the `telnet` program
[Return]	From a blank line, this keystroke will return you temporarily back to the remote machine session, i.e. the session which invoked `telnet`
^] (Ctrl-])	Escape session into `telnet` command-mode

The example above shows how we can log in to an Internet host to run a Unix session. You must have a registered account in order to carry out such a session. Alternatively, you access a public Unix account (see the resource A–Z guide for details under Public Access UNIX Systems). If we now pressed `Ctrl-]` we could escape back to the `telnet>` prompt. This would be useful if our `telnet` session became locked-up for any reason. For example:

```
...
Last login: Fri Dec 11 15:31:03 from demon.co.uk
SunOS Release 4.1 (GENERIC) #1: Sat Dec 12 18:55:17 GMT 1993
$ <Ctrl-]>
telnet> close↵
Connection closed. Press any key.
```

The escape character for interrupting a `telnet` session is always `^]`. You can, however, change this using the `telnet set` command if you wish.

USING THE SET COMMAND

Telnet can be configured manually using the set command. This command can be used with a number of variables. To find out which variables are valid on your system issue a set command of the form:

```
telnet> set ?↵
```

and all of the variables that can be modified will be shown. The most common variables which you need to alter are the echo and escape variables, the former controlling echoing of characters during a session, and the latter controlling which escape character is used (by default this is ^], although it can be changed to any control-key combination – useful if this key is duplicated in a program to provide another function). When entering the set command the telnet program will exit you back to your main session. Press the [Return] key once to return to your telnet session in all such instances. An example of the set command is given below in which we change the ^] escape character to ^E instead:

```
telnet> set escape ^E
Escape character is ^E
telnet>
```

5.5 Telnetting to specific ports

Some telnet sites ask you to connect to a specific port. An example is an NNTP news-server which answers on port number 119. Port numbers are used extensively on the network in order to provide multiple services from a single telnetable hostname. In order to connect to a service on a specific port simply mention the port number after the hostname. Issuing the port number allows you to bypass the normal log-in stage for that computer and you will instead be placed within the interactive application you require (many telnet servers still do this without a port number, however). In the case that a port number must be supplied, simply type it in after the hostname, for example:

```
$ telnet news.ibmpcug.co.uk 119↵
```

If you missed out the port number the remote machine would assume that you were going to log in as normal. In that case you would see a login: prompt (press Ctrl-] and type close to shut down this session and start again if you get stuck). In the future, be on your lookout for port numbers on servers which offer services such as IRC (Internet Relay Chat – see Chapter 10), Games, and NNTP USENET servers (Chapter 2). The A–Z Resource Guide (Appendix D) quotes all port numbers for each service, when required.

6
Unix-related Internet tools

6.1 Introduction

Unix has been the system on which the vast majority of Internet development has taken place. Unix encourages the development of software tools to a level that is unparalleled in any other operating system. It is therefore not surprising to find that most of the standard Internet tools are found on Unix systems. Examples include the `telnet`, `ftp` and electronic mail programs. An abundance of other tools have yet to be covered in any detail. This chapter provides an in-depth coverage of Unix tools such as UUCP (Unix-to-Unix copy program), `whois` and `finger` (user lookup programs), and the Unix `r*` programs (such as `rsh`, `rlogin`, etc.).

6.2 UUCP – Unix-to-Unix copy program

UUCP, or Unix-to-Unix copy program combines a whole suite of programs which allow Unix machines to copy files among each other over a network. UUCP's operation can therefore roughly be compared to FTP (see Chapter 3) in this respect, however, UUCP goes much further. It is also a file maintenance system; it can also run remote applications, and it can batch various tasks for execution at various periods. On its own, UUCP cannot achieve much. It is when UUCP is coupled with programs such as `mail` and `cron` (the Clock daemon) that it really comes into its own. More importantly, UUCP works. It is an old program and its roots lie at the very foundation of the Unix operating system. UUCP is large system and has acquired many new utilities and 'add-ons' as time has passed. The text in this section should act as a useful introduction to the UUCP tools, but it is by no means a complete study of the subject.

UUCP programs are ubiquitous on Unix systems, although implementations for other machine platforms are also available, e.g. MSDOS on the PC.

The Internet is made up of many different types of computers and networks. UUCP sites make up a considerable portion of the active network, and many sites rely on UUCP, such things as USENET news and email. Using UUCP, it is possible to build a network in which inexpensive modem devices can be used for all network links. In this way it is possible for UUCP hosts to connect to Internet hosts and then exchange information (and vice versa). We suggest that you check your Unix manual page for your own UUCP system since some cannot handle multiple machine paths (also known as 'bang-paths' of the form machine1!machine2, etc.). Only the later versions of the UUCP program have the capability to address a machine that lies several 'hops' away. UUCP can communicate across many mediums; the Internet (via TCP/IP) is one medium, phone lines and PABX lines are another; dedicated land lines are yet another. In some cases a remote site may not have any means of connection with the caller; in such cases the remote site will only 'wake-up' and start its requests when the remote site has established a network connection.

THE BASIC UUCP PROGRAMS – uucpm, uux, uucico

The UUCP system gains its name from the uucp utility of the same name. The uucp program is the most basic tool in the UUCP suite; it requests that a file be sent from one site to another. The next most fundamental program is probably uux, which requests that a command be executed on a machine. In most cases the machine will be a remote UUCP/Internet host. All of UUCP's commands run in batch mode. The exact time at which a command will be completed will depend on how the system has been configured by the UUCP administrator.

Spooled requests are commonly stored in the Unix file /usr/spool/uucp. This file is a directory and contains control information, as well as the data to be transmitted. Control information normally takes the form of a filename which is to be copied to a host (a fully qualified filename). Other control information also takes the form of a series of one or more subdirectories in the /usr/spool/uucp directory; these are named after the hosts which they will be connected to in order to carry out the necessary file transfer (this implementation is common on Berkeley BSD Unix systems). UUCP then invokes a program called uucico (Unix-to-Unix copy in copy out). It is the duty of uucico to perform the file transfer between the local and remote UUCP hosts. The cron utility normally invokes uucico from a control file in order to achieve this, although direct transfers can be initiated at any time using the uucico command (problems such as a file transfer failure will be handled when cron next invokes uucp in most cases).

THE UUCP L.sys (Systems) FILE

The actual file transfer method will be determined by a control file. This is most commonly called L.sys and is located in the directory named /usr/lib/uucp. The file L-devices stores the names of a series of communications devices, commonly modem devices, and this is then used in conjunction with a file called L.sys (or Systems on older UUCP systems) to establish a connection, i.e. a modem number may be used to establish a dial-up connection – this is the most common connection method. In the case of an Internet connection the appropriate TCP/IP request is made to obtain a connection (an inter-process communication technique known as sockets is used – this is similar to the open() and close() routines found in Unix's file-processing commands). The L-dialers file, as the name suggests, contains phone-number information for modems, etc.; it also may contain a series of control characters in order to carry out other tasks, e.g. waking up a remote system using the [Esc] or [Return] keys. After connection has been established both machines run uucico, and identify themselves to each other. This sequence is rather like the standard Unix login sequence.

The L.sys file contains the username and passwords for this interaction, for example you may see an entry resembling that below located near the right-hand side of each entry:

... login: uucp Password: wombat

which means that the local uucico will await the remote uucico program to send the string login:; when it sees this the local system will send uucp back to log in with. This type of entry is not common, for reasons yet to be discussed – see later for more details on login details. The remote system then sends the password: prompt and when the local system sees this it sends back wombat as a password. Log-in completed. Logging in may be made easier by having the /etc/passwd file contain the special username uucp. You may see the /etc/passwd entry for this user:

uucp::66:66:UU copy:/usr/spool/uucppublic:/usr/lib/uucp/uucico

The above entry is provided for the UUCP user. No password is required to log in under this account. Notice the shell the user is provided with; it is not an interactive shell, such as csh or sh, but is instead the uucico program. Uucico will therefore be run if the user uucp logs into this machine (by whatever means, dial-up, etc.). Notice also the home directory for the UUCP user in the /etc/passwd entry, which is nearly always the directory /usr/spool/uucppublic.

Different UUCP systems have different ways of answering a connection request. UUCP can only be set up between cooperating administrators, so each must find out how their system responds to a request for a UUCP file transfer. Most commonly, it will be done using the method above using the special username uucp. This will require that your L.sys file (discussed in the next section) contains a field to send the username uucp to the remote host.

SETTING UP A UUCP SYSTEM

The L.sys *File*

The L.sys file contains all of the information pertaining to a remote UUCP system that we are in communication with on a regular basis. Each line of the L.sys file relates to one remote system. Older systems still refer to the file as Systems, although your own system may refer to the file as L.sys. The L.sys file is used to establish a connection with a remote host, and if a failure to establish a connection occurs, UUCP will work its way though the L.sys file until it finds a route to the host. Each line in this file must adhere to the following format:

System   Times   Device   Class   Number   Log-in details
name

                                                                   └→Log-in
                                                                     details, i.e.
                                                                     usernames
                                                                     and login
                                                                     strings (arbi-
                                                                     trary length)

                                                      └→A telephone number of a
                                                        remote system (modem)
                                                        (and/or area name)

                                        └→Line speed, most commonly (ttys,
                                          PABXs, direct lines) although '-' for
                                          TCP

                          └→Type of connecting device. Can be: TCP, or a built-
                            in device name, e.g. Sytek. May be held in the L-
                            devices file

            └→Times and dates when this remote system may be used by the
              local system

└→The name of the system being called.

Each of these entries are now examined in more detail, in which we will build up a hypothetical entry for the `L.sys` file at each stage.

System name (field 1)

The system name is a simple character string representing the literal name of the system to be contacted. Some versions of the UUCP system, notably the older versions, may allow for a maximum of only seven characters. Ensure that if name truncation takes place between systems, that the system name is still the same i.e. keep it on or under seven characters if possible, to avoid potential incompatibility problems. A typical system name would be 'vax1', for a DEC/VAX machine, 'sun' for a Sun machine, etc.; for example we could enter 'sun' as the device name in our file; our systems file would therefore start as follows:

```
sun
```

Operating times (field 2)

The second field of the `L.sys` file contains a list of valid times when the remote system in this entry can be called. Times are broken down into hours and days. Hours are represented on a 24-hour clock in the range 0000–2359. if no hour-range is given, all hours are assumed valid. The hyphen (–) must be used to separate a given period of time. Days are represented using just two characters, the first of which must always be capitalized, for example: Sa, Su, Mo, Tu, We, Th, Fr (Saturday–Friday). The special keyword 'Any' can be used to stand for all days, and 'Wk' can be used for any valid weekday (e.g. MoTuWeThFr). Finally, a numeric field representing the time to wait before a retry (in the event of a connection failure) can be specified using a semi-colon (;) followed by the time, which is always given in minutes of time. In the case that individual days are stored, use a comma (,) to separate the entries (use commas to separate all such fields); valid entries could therefore take the form:

`SaSu,1100-1300`	Saturdays and Sundays only, between the hours of 11 am and 1 pm
`Any`	All hours and all days
`Any;5`	All hours and all days. Establish a reconnection after 5 minutes in the case of a failed connection
`Wk`	All weekdays only. Any time

Our hypothetical `L.sys` file entry could now resemble (assuming all weekdays only between the hours of 4 and 7.30 pm – the retry time for a failed connection will be the default `uucico` uses – commonly around a minute):

```
sun SaSu,1600-1930
```

Device names (field 3)

A device name is the literal name of the connecting device. Such names are varied, 'TCP' being used if the local machine is making an Internet connection via TCP/IP, 'ACU' if an automatic calling unit is being used. An ACU could be an autodial modem in this context. Alternatively, a built-in name may be specified – Micom and Sytek are examples although these are system specific. Check your system documentation to see how your connecting device should be named and configured. In particular check the L-devices file for a list of all the valid devices connected to your system. In summary this field is used to locate entries in the L-devices file. The L-devices file is covered in more detail in a moment. Our hypothetical L.sys file could now resemble:

```
sun SaSu,1600-1930 ACU
```

If a TCP/Internet connection is being used the device name can be suffixed with a protocol code, for example:

```
uucphost SaSu,1000-1200 TCP,e
```

The optional protocol code e is built into the UUCP system (it could be called the UUCP-protocol). Other protocols are available including: X25 (x), Telnet (f), DataKit (d), TCP/IP (t). Such protocols are site specific so it is impossible to name all of those in existence. The protocol in use will depend on the conditions required for the transfer. The e protocol used in our examples stands for 'error-free'; a simple protocol which sends the number of bytes sent in a trransmission and then the data – allowing error-checking to be handled by other services, such as by TCP/IP itself which has such error checks built in as standard. The protocol specified in the L.sys file allows the local host to choose a protocol for the transfer. The remote host will instruct the local host just what protocols it supports after the log-in stage has been completed. Hopefully, the preference stated in the L.sys file can be selected. If not, an arbitrary choice is made which is supported by both systems.

The L-devices file

The L-devices file, as the name suggests, holds the names of each device along with some additional details such as its speed and type. The file has the following structure:

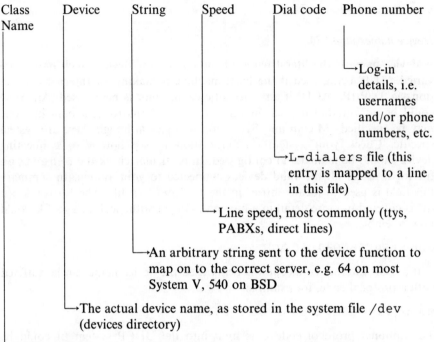

Class Device   String   Speed   Dial code   Phone number
Name

  →Log-in details, i.e. usernames and/or phone numbers, etc.

  →L-dialers file (this entry is mapped to a line in this file)

  →Line speed, most commonly (ttys, PABXs, direct lines)

  →An arbitrary string sent to the device function to map on to the correct server, e.g. 64 on most System V, 540 on BSD

  →The actual device name, as stored in the system file /dev (devices directory)

  →TCP, ACU (modem) or a specific device name, e.g. Develcon

The first field of the L-devices file is the class name. Classes such as TCP (direct TCP/Internet connection), ACU (for a dial-up modem) are valid, as is the name of a device taken from the third field of the L.sys file . Remember, the third field of the L.sys file is used solely to locate entries in the L-devices file. A typical L-devices file entry for a system with three tty lines connected to a data switch called gandalf, three lines connected to a series of auto-dial modems, and a single TCP connection for UUCP would lead to a L-devices file structured as below:

```
ACU tty04 - 2400 hayespro
ACU tty05 - Any linnet
Gandalf tty01 - Any gandalf \D
Gandalf tty02 - Any gandalf \D
Gandalf tty03 - Any gandalf \D
TCP TCP 540 uucp TCP \D
```

Field 2 of the L-devices file is the device name allocated to the modem, data switch, etc. (as in the Unix device directory /dev); the keyword TCP can be specified for TCP/Internet connections. The third field contains an arbitrary string which is sent to the device; this identifies the appropriate server on the remote machine (64 on most non-System V Unix systems, 540 on most others, e.g. Berkeley BSD Unix). This field, if not required, as in the case of autodial modems, etc., can be nulled with a hyphen (−). Line speeds are placed in field 4 of the L-devices file; the baud rate of a tty line can be entered directly, e.g. 1200, or the special word Any can be used to represent all speeds; the keyword uucp can be used in the case of TCP/Internet connections, as shown above. Field 5 is always a string; it matches the L-dialers file to perform any device-specific tasks on this entry. The final field, field 6, is sent directly to the device in question, and may be an address or phone-number string which is taken from the fifth field of the L.sys file. The \D entry relates to Table 6.1 to ensure the correct phone number is translated (a \T would use the L-dialcodes file to recover an area code, for example, whereas \D would use the untranslated phone number directly from the L.sys file).

The L-dialers *(*dialers*) file*

In addition to the L-devices file, a file called L-dialers also exists. The L-dialers file instructs UUCP how to communicate with a device located in the L-devices file, i.e. how to make a modem dial a specific number mentioned in the L.sys (and L-dialcodes file, if required). The L-dialers file consists of a separate line for each device; the format resembles that shown below:

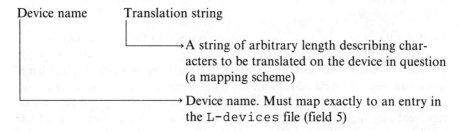

Device name   Translation string

                                    → A string of arbitrary length describing characters to be translated on the device in question (a mapping scheme)

                     → Device name. Must map exactly to an entry in the L-devices file (field 5)

Field 1 is self-explanatory. Field 2 is a string of arbitrary length which is used to send commands to the device in response to that device's feedback. A number of tokens are placed side-by-side, the first representing the response from the remote host, the next sending back a string in response to that information. The operation is therefore the same as in the last field of the L.sys file. The L-dialers file can be used for codes such as the Hayes command set to tell UUCP how to dial the number in the L.sys file. Responses from a device such as a modem must therefore be provided. A typical Hayes command could use the ATDT (attention, dial tone) to dial a number using tone dialling. Alternatively, pulse dialling (ATPD) could be used. A typical entry for the L-dialers file for a Hayes-compatible modem could therefore resemble:

`hayespro =ATDW-ATD, " " ATZ OK ATDTMO`

Notice how the name `hayespro` was defined in our earlier `L-devices` file example. The first string in this file tells the device what command(s) are used to implement a wait for dial-tone and pause facility (represented by the = and – characters, respectively). My modem uses the Hayes command `ATDW` for dial-tone waiting, while it uses `ATD`, for pause control. The next string is entered as " " – this matches a null response from the modem (since no command has yet been entered). We then send the Hayes command `ATZ` to bring the modem to life, and await the response `OK` (some modems respond using numbers – make sure you check for the correct response although the character replies are used by default on most modems). When the `OK` response has been received we tell UUCP what command to use in order to dial the number in the `L.sys` file. The command `ATDT` dials the number using tone dialling, while `MO` turns off the speaker on the modem.

Bear in mind that the `L-dialers` file does not have any phone-number details. The `L.sys` and `L-devices` files will control which number is used (and the `L-dialcodes` file is used to hold any special numbers such as external lines or area codes, and the `\D` or `\T` in the `L-devices` file will determine whether or not the `L-dialcodes` file is used). Refer to Table 6.1 for a list of special codes that can be used in the `L-devices` file (this includes details regarding the use of delays and other codes).

Class type (field 4)

Field 4 is the class type used by the remote system. In the case of devices such as ACUs, PABXs and direct-line systems the line speed should be used. Typical line speeds are given as a baud rate (bits per second). Typical baud speeds include 300, 1200, 2400 and 9600. In the case of TCP connections, the hyphen (–) should be used. In addition, the special word `Any` can be used to represent any speed. Assuming our connection was a dial-up line with a 1200 baud speed we would use

`sun SaSu,1600-1930 ACU 1200`

Phone numbers and addresses (field 5)

The penultimate field of the `L.sys` file contains the phone number or more importantly, the address of the remote system which will be used for connection purposes. In the case of a direct Internet connection via TCP you will not require a phone number since the Internet's hostname can be used (e.g. `vax.ftp1.com`). PABX lines should also use a valid name which applies to the system concerned. Telephone numbers can be alphanumeric in content; an alphabetic prefix can be used to represent an area code for a phone number – this alphabetic code must be used in conjunction with the UUCP L-

`dialcodes` file. If not used, the alphabetic prefix should simply be omitted and the full phone number used instead. Assume we wanted to connect to a UUCP site in Japan; the Japanese dialling code could be included in the number using the keyword `japan` (this must be defined in the `L-dialcodes` file accordingy). Our `L.sys` file now looks like:

`sun SaSu,1600-1930 ACU 1200 japan09897654`

The `L-dialcodes` file is a simple ASCII file containing two entries per line, namely the area-code name, e.g. `japan`, and the actual numeric phone number area code, for example we may have the `L-dialcodes` entry:

`japan 01081`

You could do away with the `L-dialcodes` file entirely if you were to use the complete phone number, i.e. `0108109897654` in our example.

TIP

Remember to place a 9 in front of your number if you want to get an outside line. This can be done from either the `L-dialcodes` file, or directly in the phone number itself.

Log-in details (field 6)

The final field in the `L.sys` file stores the log-in details of the remote machine. You should note that this field can be of an arbitrary length and it can contain the names of special control characters which are used in the log-in sequence (an example is `\r` for a carriage return). Table 6.1 shows a list of control characters that can be used in the log-in sequence. When entering control characters think carefully how you would log in to the remote system manually, i.e. what exact keys would you press in order to facilitate a log-in. Some systems have to be woken-up, that is to say that a few carriage returns (ASCII 13) have to be sent to the system before it responds with a `login:` prompt, etc. All such details must be known about the remote system, and a trial-and-error approach may be the only answer to obtain the required details.

An Internet connection with the username `uucp` may allow the system to log in directly without a password – the remote system will probably run `uucico` (as shown in an earlier `/etc/passwd` example if you can recall). Then again, some UUCP hosts require usernames and no passwords; others may require both. It all depends on how the remote system answers your connection request. It should also be noted that the character strings in this final field represent local and remote responses, for example if you placed the characters:

`ogin uucp word wombat`

Table 6.1   Control codes that can be used in the login string of the UUCP L.sys files (and the L-devices file)

Control code	Description
" "	Nothing. Sends carriage return
BREAK	Sends a break code
\c	Do not add the normal carriage return which is added to all strings
\d	Pause for 2 seconds
\e	Turns off echo checking
\n	Sends a newline code
\p	Pauses for 0.5 seconds
\r	Sends a carriage-return code
\s	Sends a single space
\t	Sends a TAB code
\\	Sends a \ character
\N	Sends a NULL code (0)
\T	Sends a translated phone number when used in the L-dialers file. A null string will be sent when used in the L.sys file
\D	Sends the untranslated phone number when using the L-dialers file (else null)
\E	Turn on echo checking (for slow devices)

into the final field, our local system would send uucp when the words ogin (for login:) have been matched from the remote system, i.e. sent back by the remote system. Likewise, the password wombat will be sent when the string word of Password: has been sent back, and so on. You may find it strange why only parts of names are used, e.g. ogin for login:. This is done because the characters must match exactly. If a system was expecting login: and instead received Login: we would never gain access!

For example, assume that our remote system requires the user to press the [Return] key (or carriage-return key) in order to obtain a login: prompt. From Table 6.1 we can see that the " " combination expects or sends nothing. Since our remote system does nothing when contacted we will expect nothing, hence the use of the " " code first. We must now wake-up the remote system with a single carriage return, so we place another " " string in the field to send back to the system. The next thing we should receive back is a login: prompt, so we should type something along the lines of ogin: to match this prompt. In order to respond to the login: prompt we can assume our system requires the username uucp, so this will go in the field next. All such strings are assumed to have a carriage return at the end of them so there is no need to add further \rs. Our completed L.sys file for a simple uucp log-in now resembles:

sun SaSu,1600-1930 ACU 1200 japan09897654 " " " " ogin: uucp

If your remote system has a more complex way of logging in you will have to code the responses as required. Table 6.1 illustrates a number of useful control codes which include, among other things, the ability to build delays into the log-in sequence. In most cases the remote system will answer with just a `login:` prompt. A `L.sys` file with an entry such as that shown below will suffice (assuming that the remote machine has an `/etc/passwd` entry for the user `uucp`):

```
sun SaSu,1600-1930 ACU 1200 japan09897654 ogin: uucp
```

COMMAND-LINE OPTIONS FOR THE UUCP PROGRAM SUITE

This section examines all of the main UUCP program's command-line interfaces. Programs examined in this section include: `uucp`, `uux`, `uucico`, `uuname`, `uuxqt`, `uulog`, `uustat`, `uusched`, `uucheck` and `uuencode/uudecode` (see Chapters 7 and 8 for more information on `uuencode` and `uudecode`).

The uucp *program*

The `uucp` utility is the most fundamental command in the UUCP suite of programs. It supports a number of command-line arguments to control which file(s) will be copied to a remote host. The syntax of the `uucp` command is as shown below, following which, we examine each of the options in more detail:

```
uucp [options] <source-file> <destination-file>
```

where `<source-file>` is the file (or files) to copy to a remote host, and `<destination-file>` is the remote file name to be used for the copy. If the `<destination-file>` is prefixed with a `~` (tilde) the `~` will be expanded into the name of the UUCP public directory on the remote machine – this is usually the directory `/usr/spool/uucppublic`. If the `<destination-file>` is prefixed with a `username` argument, where `username` is a valid username on the remote system, the `username` argument will expand into the full pathname of that user's home (or log-in) directory – useful if you don't want to upload a file into the `uucppublic` directory. For example, we could initiate a UUCP request to copy the file `/usr/section2/paul/report.txt` to the file `/usr/spool/uucppublic/pub/report.txt` using the command

```
$ uucp -r /usr/section2/paul/report.txt sun!/pub/report.txt↵
```

This command would send the file named to the computer named `sun`. Similary, we could use the following command to upload the same file into a friend's home-directory; assume this person's username is `john`:

```
$ uucp -r /usr/section2/paul/report.txt sun!john↵
```

This time the file is sent to user john, but is uploaded to his home-directory which could be /usr/users/john. The -r options in these examples stop uucico from processing the transfer, effectively suspending the job until a daemon such as cron picks it up later.

The uucp *options*

The options available to the uucp program are as shown in Table 6.2. It should be noted that without the -r option uucp immediately invokes uucico to process the file transfer. Uucico is normally only run directly for debugging purposes.

The uux *options*

The options available to the uux program are as shown in Table 6.3.

The uucico *options*

The options available to the uucico program are as shown in Table 6.4.

The uuxqt *options*

uuxqt is a UUCP command that is executed by commands such as uux and uucico after file transfer has taken place (i.e. after the connection has

Table 6.2   Command-line options for uucp

Option	Description
-f	Stops uucp from making intermediate directories for the file copy
-g<grade>	Controls priority level. <grade> can be a letter or number. The higher the ASCII value the greater the send priority. The uux defaults to A; file is usually sent at priority C
-j	Will make uucp add a job-identifier code on the screen (a job PID in most cases). This can be used for examination tasks, or to kill off the request
-m	Makes uucp send a mail-message to you when the file has been sent
-n<username>	Makes uucp send notification via email to the remote user when a file has been transferred, e.g. -nfred!sun
-r	Stops UUCP from running the uucico program after spooling your request. This queues the job for a daemon such as cron
-s<filename>	Writes a report to the file <filename> after uucp has performed a request
-x<n>	Sets the debugging level of the uucp system. Range is 0–9
-C	Makes uucp take a copy of the file you have specified and use that to transmit (file is copied to /spool/uucppublic)
-d	Makes all of the necessary directories specified in the copy operation (default)

Table 6.3 Command-line options for uux

Option	Description
-a\<name\>	Uses the program \<name\> for the program that runs uux for user notification. A handy option to use when uux is run by a setuid program and the true owner must be preserved
-b	Exits the uux program with a non-zero status level, and redirects all program output to the user
-c	Copies any files to the spool area used by UUCP, and uses these rather than the actual files specified on the command-line by the user
-g\<grade\>	Sets the priority level. The higher the ASCII value the higher the priority
-n	Does not notify the user in the case of a program failure
-r	Prevents uux from invoking uucico after the request is spooled

Table 6.4 Command-line options for uucico

Option	Description
-d\<directory\>	Uses \<directory\> as the spool directory rather than /usr/spool/uucpp which is the default
-r\<n\>	Makes uucico start in the master or slave role: 1 = master, 0 = slave
-s\<name\>	Names a master system for uucico
-x\<n\>	Sets the debugging level of the uucico progam. Range normally 0–9

ceased). Uuxqt examines the UUCP spooling directories, such as the area /usr/spool/uucp and searches for executable control files (these have the prefix X) and then runs them accordingly. This command is used in conjunction with the permissions file in order to determine which files can be accessed by the remote system. The options available to the uuxqt program are as shown in Table 6.5.

The uulog options

uulog is a UUCP command that maintains a series of log (audit) files for all UUCP requests. Such log files are created in a spooling directory called /usr/spool/uucp/.Log. The .Log directory contains a series of further

Table 6.5 Command-line options for uuxqt

Option	Description
-s\<system\>	Looks for files to be executed using the system \<system\>
-x\<n\>	Debugging level \<n\>. Range 0–9

subdirectories for uucp, uux, uuxqt and uucico. It is in these subdirectories that a file is maintained for each remote system (as mentioned in the
L.sys file). The command-line options for uulog, if omitted, will make it
display all of the log files for the uucico program. Table 6.6 illustrates the
main uulog command-line options.

The uustat *options*

uustat is a UUCP command that monitors UUCP spool requests (i.e.
queues of requests), and connection periods, in order to gather statistics and
remove pending requests. Table 6.7 illustrates the main command-line options
that can be used with the uustat program.

Table 6.6   Command-line options for uulog

Option	Description
-x	Makes uulog display the log files for the uuxqt program (rather than uucico)
-s<system1 ..n>	Looks for specific system files. A number of -s commands can be used, one for each specific system file
-f	Allows uulog to slow down the output of a log file display, by invoking a tail -f command (end of file → front of file). The <system> system log will be used by uulog for the -s <system> specified

Table 6.7   Command-line options for uustat

Option	Description
-a	Lists all queued requests that have yet to be processed
-m	Reports the outcome of the last connection to each UUCP site contacted and also gives a brief status report of pending jobs
-p	Runs the ps (processor status) command to show the ids of all UUCP processes (and to specifically show those which have created a lock-file)
-q	Lists the requests pending for each host and shows the number of control and execute files (X.*) along with their status (connected, trying, etc.), number of reconnection attempts, etc.
-k<id>	Kill option. Removes the job with <id> from the queue. Use the -p or -q to show the specific <id> of individual jobs
-s<system>	Reports the status for requests on the system called <system>
-u<user>	Gives a report for the status of all the requests issued by the user with username <user>

The uuname *options*

uuname is a UUCP command that lists the remote systems in the L.sys file
(or Systems on some older UUCP systems). The L.sys file does not
normally have read access for casual users; setting the setuid bit using the
command chmod +s uuname while you re-log in as uucp (or root, and
then issuing a chown uuname uucp command) will allow the uucp user to
read this file. Table 6.8 lists the command-line options for uuname.

The uusched *options*

uusched is a UUCP command that invokes uucico for each remote system
for which requests are pending. The most common options are -x<n> to
provide debugging information; <n> ranges from 0–9 (9 is most verbose).
Some systems have a -u option which simply sends a -x to the uucico
program automatically.

The uucheck *options*

The uucheck program is a tool for the UUCP administrator: uucheck, as
the name suggests, checks the entire UUCP system, checking for the correct files
and subdirectories which must be present on the system for UUCP to function
correctly. Command-line options for uucheck are given in Table 6.9.

The uucleanup *options*

The uucleanup program can be used to automate a UUCP system. This
tool scans the UUCP spooling directory cleaning away orphaned files
(requests that have expired – normal default expiry time is seven days for

Table 6.8   Command-line options for uuname

Option	Description
-1	Print the local system name only. If -1 is not specified all systems are displayed

Table 6.9   Command-line options for uucheck

Option	Description
-v	Makes uucheck examine the permissions file in more detail. The permissions file dictates which commands and files can be accessed by a remote system
-x<n>	Set debugging level; range 0–9 (9 is most verbose level)

command and data files; two days for execute files). Mail-messages warning users of problems with their requests can be sent using elecronic mail. The options for use with uucleanup are as summarized in Table 6.10.

Files uudecode and uuencode

These files allow binary files to be encoded into their ASCII equivalents: uuencode is used to convert a file from ASCII to binary, whereas uudecode is used to perform the reverse operation. Files are normally broken into segments of around 60K in length; this is because some email gateways do not allow files larger than this size to be processed. Command-line arguments such as -s<n> allow the user to specify the size of the segment generated (a single file may therefore contain many segments, i.e. file1.uue, file2.uue, etc.). Check your documentation to see which command-line arguments are available since they differ from system to system. Files uuencode and decode were originally required before UUCP could transmit files over multiple hops, that is to a machine using a path such as machine1!machine2!remotefile. Most UUCP implementations now work on a system such as the mail program which has the multiple hop capability. A multiple path such as that shown would invoke the uux utility on each system in the path until the destination is reached.

DAEMONS AND CRON FILES

Daemons are processes (executing programs) that run as background tasks. In the context of UUCP, one of the most important daemons is cron, the clock

Table 6.10   Command-line options for uucleanup

Option	Description
-C<days>	Determine how many days to delete command files that have not been used from the spooling area. Command files have a C.* prefix normally
-D<days>	Determine how many days to delete data files that have not been used from the spooling area. Data files have a D.* prefix normally
-X<days>	Determine how many days to delete control files that have not been used from the spooling area. Execute files have a X.* prefix normally
-o<days>	Determine how many days to delete all other UUCP files
-W<days>	Number of days after which to send warning messages to users regarding their files. This should be less than deletion time to give them a chance to resend the file
-m<string>	Used in mail messages to include the string <string> in the message. Any textual message can go in here to help users. UUCPs warning messages are not that user-friendly

daemon. This program executes commands from a control file on a regular basis. The file /usr/lib/crontab holds the commands that are run by the cron program; each line of the crontab file is broken up into a number of fields that dictate the command to run, and the time that the particular command will be run. You can expect to see a number of UUCP entries in your crontab file. The format of the /usr/lib/crontab file is as follows:

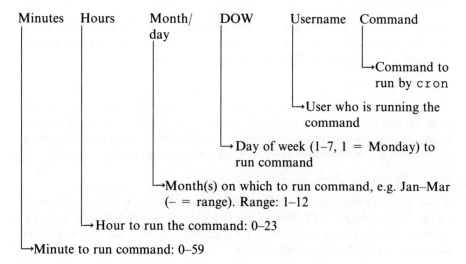

Minutes   Hours   Month/   DOW   Username   Command
                  day

↳Command to
   run by cron

↳User who is running the
   command

↳ Day of week (1–7, 1 = Monday) to
   run command

↳Month(s) on which to run command, e.g. Jan–Mar
   (– = range). Range: 1–12

↳ Hour to run the command: 0–23

↳Minute to run command: 0–59

A crontab entry of * (asterisk) indicates any valid value. cron examines the crontab file every minute to see if a command needs to be a run. A typical crontab entry could resemble the following:

```
5 14 1 * * root /usr/adm/utils/cronscripts/monthly
```

This entry would run the executable shell script (this is how multiple commands are run from a single file monthly. This file could have administrative commands that need to be run every month for example. We can see from the times that the script is to be run at 2:05 pm (5 14 – 24-hour clock) on the first day of the month (1) on all months (*) and days of the week (*). The command is run by root (the superuser) so the monthly file must have its setuid bit set for root execution. uucp could have a similar entry, for example to run uucico:

```
59 * * * * root /usr/adm/utils/cronscripts/uudemon.hour
```

This entry would run the uudemon.hour file (this file would contain uucico, possibly by the uusched program). The file is run every hour on all days and months of the year.

UUCP daemon scripts

The most common executable files (shell scripts) which are used by UUCP are listed below. This is by no means a complete list of such files; you can of course create any script and run it from crontab in reality. Files you may find on your travels include:

uudemon.hour

This file, as the name suggests, is run every hour. It normally contains the uucico command or uusched command (the latter invoking uucico) in order to perform pending UUCP file-transfer requests.

uudemon.admin

This file allows administrative details to be sent to the administrator. You may want to run the uustat program to show the details of pending requests from this file. Notification via email is possible using a uustat command redirected into the email program, for example the command

uustat -a | mail -s UUCP-update root

if run from the uudemon.admin file would make uustat give a listing of all current pending UUCP requests, and would then pipe this into the mail command using a subject field of 'UUCP-update', making the recipient root, the superuser (or UUCP administrator).

uudemon.cleanup

This file is normally used to perform housekeeping tasks such as deleting outdated versions of files. The uucleanup program is normally called from this file on a weekly basis, as set by the crontab file (discussed earlier).

THE permissions FILE

The security of UUCP is of prime importance to any Unix administrator. UUCP maintains a file called Permissions (also known by the name USERFILE on some systems), used to control which files and commands can be executed by a remote system. Log-in permissions are also dealt with using this file. Each entry in the Permissions file contains a number of keywords which are used to implement the various permission settings. Keywords can be separated by one or more spaces (or a tab). Comments start with a hash (#) sign in the file. A keyword and value are separated by an equals sign (=). The \ character can be used to start a new line as an extension of the previous, and additional arguments should be added after a colon (:). A typical file could resemble:

```
LOGNAME=uucp READ=/ NOREAD=/usr/admin:/etc \
         WRITE=/usr/spool/uucppublic \
         SENDFILES=no REQUEST=yes \
         MACHINE=unixa:unixb:unixc
```

An explanation of the above `Permissions` file is given in the following sections under their respective keyword entries.

LOGNAME

This keyword identifies the name of the `uucp` login-identifier, as in the `/etc/passwd` file in most instances. When installing UUCP the system will often look for `/etc/passwd` entries where `uucico` is the login shell; a sample `Permissions` file is then created with all the LOGNAMEs required (in the case that there is more than one `/etc/passwd` entry for uucp). For example:

`LOGNAME=uucp`

would set up the machine to respond to 'uucp'; this could correspond to the `/etc/passwd` entry:

`uucp::66:66:UU copy:/usr/spool/uucppublic:/usr/lib/uucp/uucico`

LOGNAME also accepts multiple arguments, if separated by a colon (`:`), for example:

`LOGNAME=uucp:uucppub:uu`

MACHINE

The `MACHINE` keyword identifies a set of commands to be used when a remote UUCP host contacts a local UUCP host (or when the `uuxqt` program is running commands on behalf of the remote UUCP host). `MACHINE` may be used on the same line as LOGNAME if you wish; do this in the case that both share common values when being called by a remote UUCP host. For example:

`MACHINE=unixa`

could be used on its own, while it would also be possible to use

`LOGNAME=uucp MACHINE=unixa`

REQUEST

This keyword is used in conjunction with the `MACHINE` or `LOGNAME` keywords, as described earlier. The value assigned to `REQUEST` is either `yes` or no. A yes value will indicate whether a remote UUCP host may request files to be sent to it from the local UUCP host, for example:

REQUEST=yes

would allow such transfers to take place. We could also have the entry

LOGNAME=uucp MACHINE=unixa REQUEST=yes

READ and NOREAD

Files which can be read using the REQUEST keyword are normally stored in a default location such as /usr/spool/uucppublic. You can control which directories can be accessed in this way. READ can be appended onto the LOGNAME line if required, for example:

READ=/usr/spool/uucppublic

or, the continuation:

LOGNAME=uucp MACHINE=unixa REQUEST=yes READ=/usr/spool/uucppublic

The NOREAD keyword, as the name suggests, mentions the names of all directories which cannot be read, to provide exceptions to some directories. For example, a keyword setting such as READ=/ would allow an entire file system to be read, so you may want to add additional NOREAD settings to deny certain areas (directories), for example:

NOREAD=/usr/admin

or, the continuation:

LOGNAME=uucp MACHINE=unixa REQUEST=yes READ=/ NOREAD=/usr/admin:/etc

The last entry here would allow a log-in of uucp to access files in the entire file system except the /etc and /usr/admin directories. Notice the colon (:) to separate the two directories mentioned.

WRITE and NOWRITE

Similar to READ, the WRITE keyword identifies all directories that can be written to by a remote UUCP host, for example:

WRITE=/usr/spool/uucppublic /usr/users/john

should always be available (which is the default, coincidentally). You can make as many directories writable to allow UUCP to upload files into these areas. The WRITE command can be appended to the LOGNAME line if you require. The

NOWRITE keyword is self-explanatory; it simply allows you to supply the names of directories to which people cannot upload files, for example:

NOWRITE=/bin /usr/bin

disallows uploading to /bin and /usr/bin. The directories you specify will normally be subdirectories of those in the WRITE statement, although any valid directory name is normally allowed.

SENDFILES

Determines whether or not a file or file(s) queued for a remote UUCP transfer will be sent if that system decides to call your host beforehand. Valid values are yes and no only, for example:

SENDFILES=no

will not allow the transfer to take place if the remote system calls you first and asks for such transfer. SENDFILES applies to outgoing file transfers only. You can append SENDFILES to the LOGNAME keyword if you require.

COMMANDS

This entry is normally used after the MACHINE keyword to specify a series of commands that the remote UUCP host may execute on the local UUCP host. All commands must be valid Unix commands, and should be fully qualified pathnames to ensure the commands can be found; if you do not know the pathnames exclude them and the system should still find them; for example:

MACHINE=unixa COMMANDS=/bin/ls /usr/bin/who

If you use the special name ALL, all commands in the local machines PATH variable can be executed (this normally includes commands in: /bin, /usr/bin, etc.).

VALIDATE

The VALIDATE keyword is used in conjunction with a LOGNAME entry to allow a machine name to be associated with a log-in name, thus ensuring that a particular log-in uses a specific machine of the administrator's choice, for example:

LOGNAME=uucp VALIDATE=systema

PUBDIR

The PUBDIR keyword identifies a public directory where all users of a system have write permission to create files. This keyword can be used on the LOGNAME line if required. The default is commonly

LOGNAME=uucp MACHINE=OTHER PUBDIR=/usr/spool/uucppublic

A special keyword called OTHER has been used in this example to specify that all machines not listed in earlier MACHINE keywords be used.

MYNAME

MYNAME is mainly used for debugging purposes. It holds the name of a machine associated with the MACHINE or LOGNAME entry therefore telling the local UUCP system to identify itself using an alias. It would therefore be possible for a local UUCP host to call itself and run UUCP for test purposes. For example

LOGNAME=test MYNAME=uucptest

would make the local UUCP host identify itself as 'test' to remote hosts that log in as uucptest.

6.3   The finger command

The finger command is a user lookup program found on many Unix machines. Its origins came from Berkeley Unix although with the new release of SVR4, finger should be widely available. Finger examines the /etc/ passwd file to match a username supplied by the user. If the user specifies a user on a remote machine, using the name@host format, finger looks to that machine for the relevant information. Used without any <username> argument, finger will display a list of all the users on the system at the current time. The syntax of the finger command is:

finger [options] <username>

where <username> is a local username, e.g. john, or a remote username of the form name@host, e.g. john@dro.org.com, etc. Options that can be used with finger vary between systems, although the -i (show idle time) is nearly always available. When finger locates a user it examines /etc/ passwd entry for that user and prints out some details on the screen, for example:

```
$ finger john
Login name: john              In real life: John Williams
Directory: /usr/users/john   Shell: /bin/csh
Last login: Wed 28 Aug 1993, on tty03 from unixa
No Plan.
```

This finger command has been used with the local name john. finger has found that the real name of this person is John Williams and that his home directory is /usr/users/john. We can also see the time he last used this account, and we are also told the terminal that he logged in to. Finger also tells us the shell he uses (the C-Shell in this case). All of this information (apart from the log-in time – which is taken from /etc/wtmp which is a common system accounting file) is gleaned from the fields of the /etc/passwd file and presented in a more readable form to the user. Used without an option, finger displays output similar to

```
$ finger↵
Login       TTY         When
John        *tty01      Mon Jul 4 11:02
Fred        tty03       Mon Jul 4 12:45
Susan       tty08       Mon Jul 4 09:05
```

which is basically a list of users and log-in times. The * next to the entry for user John indicates that this terminal is write protected, that is to say another user cannot use the write or talk commands with this user/terminal. The Unix mesg command is used to control this facility. Used with the –i (idle) option it is possible to ascertain the idle times for each user (this is the period of time that elapsed since a command was last typed by the user), for example:

```
$ finger -i↵
Login       TTY         When                Idle
John        *tty01      Mon Jul 4 11:02     45 minutes
Fred        tty03       Mon Jul 4 12:45
Susan       tty08       Mon Jul 4 09:05     1 hour 10 minutes
```

In the above listing we can see that user John has been idle for 45 minutes, while user Susan has been idle for over an hour. User Fred does not have an idle time, therefore he is still issuing commands from his terminal at the current moment in time.

Fingering a remote user takes a little more time since the finger server on that machine has to respond to the local machine, i.e. it must search its /etc/passwd file and send back the results. Users may be registered on more than one machine on a network so you may have to poke around a bit to find some individuals. For example we could type

```
$ finger mark@unixa.cs.ac.uk↵
Trying 128.16.1.44 ...
Login name: mark              In real life: Mark Johnson
Directory: /u1/mnt/mark       Shell: /bin/ksh
Last login: Mon 20 Jul 1991, on ttyp03 from unixa
No Plan.
```

which shows us that user mark does indeed exist on the host in question, although it seems it was a long while ago since he logged in (perhaps his account is not in use anymore). In the case that a user was not found you would see a message along the lines of No such user, for example:

```
$ finger mark@unixa.cs.ac.uk↵
Trying 128.16.1.44 ...
No such user.
```

which indicates that a finger server has answered your request, but that no user has been found with the username specified. In some cases you may also see a Connection refused message, for example:

```
$ finger laurel@hardy.com↵
Trying 128.33.5.12 ...
connect: Conection refused.
```

This message means that a finger server is not running on the remote machine, so there is no way you can enquire about users on this system, apart from FTPing to the machine and trying to grab a copy of its /etc/passwd file, or, of course, mailing the postmaster alias to contact the administrator of the site concerned.

TIP

If you want to know if a particular user exists on a site, mail the postmaster and ask them to help you. Postmaster is an alias for the person charged with the responsibility over email names and the general email system.

FINGER – PLANS AND PROJECTS

You may have noticed the No Plan message at the end of some finger listings. This relates to the file .plan (stored in the user's home directory area). This file contains an arbitrary amount of text which can be used to tell users about this user and his plans. Many people user finger for this facility alone, allowing people to finger their username and find out some information (this information may change periodically depending on the service offered). Many people use .plan for phone and contact details.

TIP

If you have the patience it is possible to place a series of screen-escape codes to present a series of screen effects such as scrolling and cursor movement. Try fingering: yanoff@csd4.csd.uwm.edu for a pretty example (you must use an ANSI/VT100 emulation, however, or you may see a mass of gibberish).

Another file called .project can also be used with the finger command. This file should contain a single line of text (for this is all that will be displayed by finger) describing the project the current user is working on (whatever this may be). Here is an example:

```
$ finger fred@somewhere.com↵
Trying 128.19.2.65 ...
Login name: fred             In real life: Fred Smith
Directory: /ul/users/smith   Shell: /bin/sh
Last login: Fri 19 Dec 1992, on tty07 from sun1
Project: Superconductor Technology.
Plan:
My plan in life is to understand 1% of Unix!
```

As can be seen from the above listing, user fred has both a .project and .plan file; his plan file contains the text My plan in life is to understand 1% of Unix! while his project is a more sensible Superconductor Technology (at least he understands the finger command now).

TIP

The finger command may be placed in your systems /etc/passwd file to allow users to see who is logged on. Place the finger command (or a copy) in the shell field to run it. This is common practice with other commands such as who, sync, etc. For example you use an /etc/passwd entry of:

```
finger::93:0:Finger command:/tmp:/usr/ucb/finger
```

6.4   Whois – who is this person?

Another useful utility from the Berkeley Unix tool-set is whois. This command allows an enquiry about another user in much the same way as the finger command does, although whois is more centrally available, and its contents are updated regularly. The military database at nic.ddn.mil is responsible for maintaining the massive whois (75 000 + entries) database of network individuals, most of whom are academic and scientific users. The listing you receive about a user is not as detailed as something from the finger command but is instead a breakdown of a user's name and work address, along with their full email address – useful if you know the name of a user but not their email address. The whois command connects to a well-known whois server for its information (see the A–Z resource guide for a list of Internet whois servers that are available).

---

telnet to nic.ddn.mil to use their central whois server resource. Use
this service if you do not have a whois command on your system.

Whois is known as a white-pages server (white-pages named after the tele-
phone-directory listings); and it is available as both a Unix command and as a
central server resource. To access the server version of whois you must
telnet to nic.ddn.mil (see Chapter 5 for details on telnet). The Unix
whois command has the syntax:

whois <person>

A typical whois command with a username could yield the hypothetical
whois entry:

```
$ whois salter↵
Salter, John (JS90)                salter@sun.lon.ac.uk
    University of London
    Computing Department
    WC1
    +44 (0) 71 333 3432
    Record last updated on 1-Jul-91.
$
```

The period (.) wildcard can be used with whois to make it search for a
portion of a name, for example pa. for patterson, parsons and so on
(note though that this wildcard must apply to a person's surname). Whois will
list as many names as it finds, especially if a special wildcard is used. Multiple
patterns that are found will be shown as separate lines in the format:
[Surname, Christian name, Title], for example:

```
$ whois smi.↵
Smithson, John (JS451)     smithson@hd3.army.mil (615) 290-9801
Smith, Peter (JS066)       peter@suna.cc.lk.edu (504) 657-1101
Smith, Sharon (JS981)      altos1@tracey.vax.com (890) 761-1245
...
```

The Gopher system can look up whois server entries, and CSO white-pages
servers. See Chapter 9.

The code in brackets, e.g. (JS451) is known as a handle; it is a unique code assigned by the whois system. This handle can be used by whois to locate a record directly, for example using the command:

```
$ whois "!js451"↵
. . .
```

The exclamation mark is a code used by whois to tell it to expect a handle rather than a username. This is not a very good choice of codes since the ! may clash with the history command of shells such as csh. The double-quotes can be used to remove the meaning of the ! mark, as can the \ sign, e.g. \!js451. In some cases the whois command may connect to a whois server that has become out-of-date (it probably still uses the older ARPANET address such as was disbanded some years ago). In these instances you will see a message telling you that the service has been relocated – probably to the nic.ddn.mil site. You can override the older server name using the -h (host) option of whois, for example:

```
$ whois -h nic.ddn.mil smi.↵
Smithson, John (JS451)      smithson@hd3.army.mil (615) 290-9801
Smith, Peter (JS066)        peter@suna.cc.lk.edu (504) 657-1101
Smith, Sharon (JS981)       altos1@tracey.vax.com (890) 761-1245
```

TIP

Use Archie to find the whois-server list. This file is a list of all the known whois servers reachable via telnet. Use the Archie commands (or mail them) as follows:

```
archie> set search subcase
archie> prog whois-servers-list↵
```

THE whois MAIL INTERFACE AT nic.ddn.mil

The central whois server at nic.ddn.mil can be queried via email if you do not have access to a whois program or telnet (we assume you have email!) by sending a message to the special alias service@nic.ddn.mil. The body of your message should contain a single line with the word 'whois' followed by a person's name or his or her place of work. For example, a typical message could be

```
whois mjackson
```

or it could refer to an institution or place of work, for example

`whois University of Aberdeen`

The message you receive back from `nic.ddn.mil` will resemble the listings already shown. If your search is pretty specific you may receive just one entry back; if more than one entry was matched you will see a list of names (in which case you send another message back with the person's handle, etc. in order to get their full database record). For example, you may see a mailmessage resembling the following waiting for you:

```
Date: Mon, 10 Jul 93 12:01:56 EST
From: service@nic.ddn.mil (NIC Mail Server)
To: fred@somewhere.com
Subject: re: whois mjackson
Jacson, Mark (MJ87)              mjackson@aber.ac.uk
    University of Aberdeen
    Computing and IT Department
    +44 (0)565 70956
    Record last updated on 8-Mar-92.
```

TIP

The Internet also has the `netfind` program for finding individuals. `Telnet` to a netfind server, as shown in the A–Z resource guide (e.g. `netfind.oc.com`) and type ? for on-line help on how to search for a user.

X.500 RESOURCES–`fred`

X.500 is an ISO standard for directory related services, in this case directories of user-information. X.500 is very much in the development stage although there are tools available on the Internet, notably `fred`, which allow user lookup ('white-pages') services. Fred can currently be reached via `Telnet` at the sites `wp.psi.com` and `wp2.psi.com`. The `fred` system is quite extensive, and its interface has many commands for finding users. Fred can be queried interactively via `Telnet` and via email for off-line enquiries. The most fundamental command is `whois`, which has the syntax

`whois [person] [-org <organisation-name]`

where `[person]` is the name of a person, most commonly a surname, although a christian name can be used also. The optional `-org` option allows an organization (workplace) name to be specified in order to refine your search for a person at a particular location. The * wildcard can be used in both the `[person]` and `<organization name>` arguments so as to match multiple persons and/or organizations; both these arguments accept strings for names such as:

`Wilson`	Finds person with surname: Wilson
`W*`	Finds people starting with: W
`"Rene Wilson"`	Finds the person called: Rene Wilson
`*`	Finds all persons

Organization names can be structured similarly, for example:

`"London University"`	Finds entries for London University
`London*`	Finds a place starting with: 'London'
`*ham`	Finds a place ending in: 'ham'
`*`	Finds all organizations
`intel`	Look up an organization (1 word)

For example, if we wanted find a person with the surname Wilson, and we didn't know which organization this person worked at, we could use the `fred` command:

```
fred> whois wilson -org *⏎
```

This command searches all organizations that fred's X.500 database knows about for persons with the surname Wilson. When fred finds more than one entry for the criteria specified, it displays the entries ordered by their organization, for example:

```
12 matches found.
1. London University        +44 (0) 71 387 7050
2. Aberdeen University      +44 0431 0900 652
... etc ...
```

It is then up to the user to pick an entry from this list using another `whois` command, for example we could look up the first organization here using the `fred` command

```
fred> whois 'London University' -org *⏎
```

which, in turn, would yield a list of details for this organization, such as its address, contact details, etc., i.e.

```
London University (1)
+44 (0) 71 387 7050 (main switchboard)
   aka: ucl
University College London
Gower Street
London WC1E 6BT
UK
... etc ...
```

In order to refine a person search to this organization, we would issue a command of the form:

```
fred> whois wilson -org 'London University'↵
```

Notice the aka: line in the output from the fred command shown earlier. This is an alias that can be used to save you typing in the full name of the oranization in question, so we could save some keying and type instead:

```
fred> whois wilson -org ucl↵
```

The output from this command may resemble the following:

```
Rene Wilson (16)                          rwilson@ucl.ac.uk
Telephone: +44 (0)71 387 7050 (extension 9999)
University College London
Gower Street
London WC1E 6BT
UK
Modified: Mon Dec 20 15:30:09
```

As can be seen, we now have access to this person's email address, as well as an address and phone number for their place of work (note that the exact display may differ slightly between servers).

TIP

Fred can match names phonetically using its soundex feature. Use the command:

```
fred> set soundex on↵
```

This feature is useful in the case that you do not know how to spell a name although you know what it sounds like, e.g. smith matching smythe, smiff, etc.

Fred's email interface

If you are not in a hurry to use fred interactively, or if you do not have access to Telnet (or if you are using UUCP only), fred is accessible via email. Mail should be sent to the alias whitepages at either wp.psi.com or wp2.psi.com, and your messages Subject: line should include the command you want to send, for example on Unix you could use the command

```
$ mail -s`whois wilson -org ucl`↵
[Ctrl-D] or [.]↵
```

Other mailing systems will have their own methods of providing a subject line. Unix mailers commonly use the -s <subject> option, although if this is omitted the `mail` program will normally ask you what the subject line will be automatically. Your message-body can be left empty, so just enter a period (.) or press [Ctrl-D] to send the message.

TIP

Take a look at the KNOWBOT service via `Telnet` at `nri.reston.va.us`. This is similar to `fred` and can access X.500, `finger` and `Whois` servers to locate a person you require. See the A–Z resource guide for more information on KNOWBOT server locations.

6.5 `Write` and `talk`

`Write` and `talk` are two Unix utilities that are used to conduct a real-time communications link between Internet users. Both utilities are commonly used to conduct a terminal session between users on a local network, although the power of these tools, especially `talk`, really come into their own when used between remote Internet users. `Write` is not a very friendly command since it can only be used for a half-duplex communications link, that is to say that both users can communicate, but only one way at a time. `Write` also has the horrible habit of corrupting the recipient's screen when a message arrives. More importantly the `write` command is not designed to send messages to a remote Internet user. We cover it here for the sake of completeness.

THE `write` COMMAND

`Write` is not the best of commands. It tends to annoy some users because it simply writes your message on a recipient's screen without warning. Also, most implementations of `write` cannot send messages to remote hosts. It is probably best to use the `talk` command (see the following section) for proper one-to-one conversations. The `write` command has the simple syntax:

```
write <user> [terminal]
```

where <user> is a valid username, and [terminal] is an optional terminal name (as in the Unix /dev [devices] directory). You conduct a `write` session such as this:

```
$ write john↵
Hello John, Just a reminder that our meeting has been put↵
back an hour to 8.30. See you then.↵
Jason.↵
<Ctrl-D>
```

When write starts it allows a message to be typed from the standard input. Input can continue until you press <Ctrl-D> on a new line; write then sends the message to the user and it will appear on their screen.

TIP

You can stop write messages from appearing on your screen using the mesg n (no messages) command. The mesg y command will enable such messages. The mesg command simply enables/disables write permission on your terminal in the /dev directory. You can also use the who and finger commands to see who is logged in. The finger command will show which users have disabled messages using mesg n (look for the *).

THE talk COMMAND

A much (much) better command than write is called talk. Talk allows two parties to conduct a conversation in separate parts of the screen. The program is 'intelligent' in that it will inform the recipient that someone wants to talk to them (even though some implementations still corrupt the recipient's screen temporarily). The recipient can then confirm that they want to take part in the conversation, and a two-way link is then set up accordingly. The talk command has the syntax

```
talk <user> [terminal]
```

where <user> can be a local user, or a remote user using the format name@host. As with the write command, the optional [terminal] name can be used. Finding out who is using a remote terminal can be tricky unless you have access to a 'remote' who command, such as rwho – see Section 6.6). You can deny access to a user by using the mesg n command (as with the write command); anybody attempting to perform a talk operation with you will then be denied access. A typical talk session is started with a command such as

```
$ talk mark@suna.cc.ac.uk↵
```

The screen then clears into two portions and you see the message

```
[Ringing your party]
```

at the top of the screen. If a recipient is not logged in you will not normally even get this far, and talk will sometimes respond as follows:

```
$ talk mark@suna.cc.ac.uk↵
User mark@suna.cc.ac.uk not currently logged in.
```

TIP

You can always try chatting to yourself to see how the program works in more detail! Make sure that mesg y has been typed to enable messages on your terminal.

In some cases you may see a message on the screen saying

[Your party is not logged in]

If your party has requested to be left alone (i.e. they have used mesg n), you will see the message

[your party is refusing messages]

If logged in and accepting messages, your recipient's screen will resemble the following (note that this will not corrupt the work they are engaged in, for example an editing session – they can press ^L to refresh their screen in most instances):

Message from Talk_Daemon at 11:01
talk: connection requested by john@suna.cc.ac.uk
talk: respond with: talk john@suna.cc.ac.uk

while at the same time you will see the message

[Ringing your party]

In order to set up the link, the recipient must type talk followed by your username, for example:

$ talk john@suna.cc.ac.uk↵

If the recipient waits before responding, talk keeps you informed with messages (along with a little beep) such as

[Ringing your party again]

Assuming your recipient types the necessary command, as previously shown, the screen should clear and two screen portions will be shown. You should also see the message

[Connection established]

in which case both parties are now communicating. Whatever the recipient types will be seen in one screen (normally the upper screen), and whatever you type will be seen in the other. Both users have a full-duplex link so it is possible to type at the same time. Mistakes can normally be corrected using the [Delete] key (make sure you have a stty erase '^h' command in your auto-login file such as .login, etc.). To clear your screen-portion simply press [Return] until you clear it away. Remember to also press [Return] to obtain a new line. If you press [Ctrl-C] (the interrupt key) the session will be terminated and your party will see the message

[Your party has put down the phone]

which is self-explanatory. A more graceful method of terminating the conversation is to use [Ctrl-D] after you both know the conversation has terminated; the message below will be shown in this case:

[Connection closing, exiting]

There are many ways to chat to users over the Internet in this way. The IRC (Internet Relay Chat) facility is available, although this is frowned upon because of all the bandwidth it uses up – see Chapter 10 for an introduction to the world of IRCs. You can also chat to other users using a MUD (multi user dimension/dungeon) server – these are essentially games although users use them to chat to each other as well. The only other way to access something like talk is to use a chat or talk server; see the A–Z resource guide for details. These servers allow telnet access to a program similar to talk, although they are gradually nearing extinction due to the network usage they demand. Oh well, there's always email.

TIPS

Talk requires that you have an appropriate screen or terminal emulation loaded. This is required for cursor handling and character echoing that talk uses to draw the two parties' messages. Examine the TERM variable to ensure an emulation such as VT100 or ANSI is loaded. If the screen is corrupted, exit and alter the TERM variable, and then retry.

Use the ^L key [Ctrl-L] to refresh the screen in the case of any screen corruption.

6.6   The r commands

The r commands, or r* commands as they are sometimes known, are a series of Unix-based programs which can be used to perform remote operations (r standing for 'remote' in this instance). Remote commands commonly refer to external hosts, which in turn implies some connection with the Internet. Typical r* commands include:

• a remote version of the Unix who command
• a remote login program similar to telnet
• a remote copy command similar to the Unix cp

All of these commands can be bypassed if you are happy with utilities such as FTP and `telnet`. It should be said, however, that these latter commands all require user authentication, that is to say that you have to provide some information about yourself before you are allowed to log in, i.e. a username/password combination. The `r*` commands do not require such information to be provided (if properly configured) since the remote system will be configured to allow you access. Proper use of the `r*` command therefore requires that you are in touch with a user or administrator on a remote site who is willing to grant you access to that site. Without this participation, you are not going to gain access.

SECURITY CONSIDERATIONS–`/etc/hosts.equiv` AND `.rhosts`

The `r*` commands pose a considerable security problem, since they can be used for malicious activities in the wrong hands. For this reason Unix provides the file `/etc/hosts.equiv`. This file is basically a list of hosts, i.e. machine names whose users are allowed to perform a remote log-in (`rlogin`) to your machine without supplying a password. A typical `/etc/hosts.equiv` file would be:

```
host1
host2
+@group1
-@group2
```

When a machine name is placed in the `/etc/hosts.equiv` file, such as in the example above with machines `host1` and `host2` this means that anybody logging in a remote machine from the machine `host1` or `host2` is a trusted person. If the user logging in from either of these machines also has an entry in `/etc/passwd` (the password database) that user will be logged in automatically and a password will not be required. In all cases it is the remote machine's `hosts.equiv` file that dictates just what access is granted to outside machines and users. Bear into consideration the following rules that deny `rlogin` access:

- If a user does not have an entry in the remote machine's `/etc/passwd` file but that user's machine (or host name) is specified in the `/etc/hosts.equiv` file, that user *cannot* `rlogin` into the remote machine in question.
- If the user logging into a remote machine does not have an entry in the remote machine's `/etc/passwd` file and there is no entry in the `/etc/hosts.equiv` file for that user's machine, then that user *cannot* `rlogin` into the remote machine in question.

Only the following rules, if followed, allow access to a remote machine via the `rlogin` program:

- If the user logging in to a remote machine has an entry in that machine's `/etc/passwd` file and the user's machine is mentioned in the remote machine's `/etc/hosts.equiv` file, that user *can* `rlogin` on the remote machine in question.
- If the user is in the remote machine's `/etc/passwd` file but the user's machine is not in the `/etc/hosts.equiv` file that user must supply a password to gain access (as in the remote machine's `/etc/passwd` file for the user).

TIP

Make sure you check your `/etc/passwd` file if you are in an administrative capacity. Use the Unix command below to search for empty password entries, and then fix these by entering `*` in the password field (field 2):

$ `grep "^*::" /etc/passwd`

The `::` in the regular expression fed to grep will match the empty password field. An `/etc/passwd` file with an empty password allows the user access to that account, even if a shell has not been allocated, some Unix systems assign a default shell (such as `/bin/sh`, for example).

The special characters `+@` and `-@` can also be used. These are used in the `/etc/hosts.equiv` file to denote that everyone logging in to a remote machine is trusted. The groupname that is added to the `+@` or `+@` is a group as specified in the `/etc/group` file, where `+@` allows such access, and `-@` takes away such access, i.e. trusted and non-trusted user groups. Remember that other `r*` commands, such as `rsh` and `rcp`, are also bound by the same rules as `rlogin`. The order of checking is normally sequenced as: (i) you attempt to `rlogin` (or `rcp`, `rsh`, etc.) to a remote machine; (ii) the remote system checks its `/etc/passwd` file for your name; (iii) if your username is found the remote system then checks for your machine name (hostname) in `/etc/hosts.equiv`, and if found you are given access, otherwise you receive a `Permission denied` message and are halted from logging in; (iv) if no `hosts.equiv` entry for your machine is found the local `.rhosts` file is checked, and if this contains your machine you gain access.

In all cases you can always rlogin to a machine if you have a `/etc/passwd` entry on it (i.e. without a `.rhosts` or `/etc/hosts.equiv` entry) although you cannot perform commands such as `rcp` (file transfer), or `rsh` (remote command execution). For example, assume we had the `/etc/hosts.equiv` entry:

```
laurel
hardy
```

These entries would allow the machines named laurel and hardy to access your machine via rlogin without a password. In addition, users on the above machines can also use a rsh or rcp command if they have a password entry in the remote machine's /etc/passwd file. Security can be improved further by using the .rhosts file; this file allows only certain users access, rather than all users of a particular host (as with hosts.equiv).

The .rhosts file

The .rhosts file is provided to allow local users to grant access rights to external (remote) users. Access rights in this context means access to a user's directory, etc. The structure of the .rhosts file is not the same as the /etc/hosts.equiv file previously discussed. An optional username can be specified next to a machine name to allow only that user to gain access. The .rhosts file is used in addition to /etc/hosts.equiv for permission checking when a user is trying to rlogin (or perform a rsh) to a particular user's account on a remote machine. Whenever rlogin, or rsh, is used the .rhosts file in the remote machine's home directory is as normally appended to the main file /etc/hosts.equiv for additional security checks.

TIP

The /etc/hosts.equiv and .rhosts files are sensitive to a trailing space character. If a space is included at the end of an entry in either of these files it will be invalid. In order to see if there is a space at the end of the line use the cat command with the −e option, or use the vi editor with the command :set list (these methods will show a $ at the end of each line and you can therefore see if a space is present).

If the /etc/hosts.equiv file denies you access because you are in a −@ group, even though your machine may still be mentioned in the local .rhosts file, you will still be able to access to the remote machine (using rlogin, rsh, etc.). In summary we can say that the .rhosts file is used to allow only certain users access to your machine. In most cases a machine's hostname will not be placed in this file; instead the machine name will be placed in the .rhosts file for each user's home directory that remote users wish to access (make sure that the owner of this .rhosts file is the real owner or root). For example, if a user called joe on host sun1.example.edu created a .rhosts file in his home directory containing

```
sun2.example.edu fred
```

this would allow user fred on host sun2.example.edu to access joe's account on his machine. Similar lines for other users could be provided for as many users as you like. `.rhosts` files are not welcomed by administrators for obvious reasons. A user gaining unauthorized access to an account could create a `.rhosts` file granting them access, thus creating a security loop-hole for future use. It is not hard to find `/etc/passwd` files with accounts that are left open, especially in academic institutions where accounts are set up and changed on a daily basis. Administrators beware. It is not hard to write a small shell-script to try hundreds of hosts with different usernames in this way.

TIP

Making `root` the owner of the `/.rhosts` file is very sensible, since this will not allow anybody but `root` (the superuser) to modify the file and therefore compromise security. Only `root` can, of course, become the owner of the file by making themselves the owner, i.e. you cannot make a user an owner of a file by a direct command (ask your administrator to do this for you after you have decided what users will be in your `/.rhosts` file).

---

rlogin—remote login program

The program `rlogin` allows you to log in to a remote Internet host. Its operation is rather like `telnet` in many respects. If the remote host does not have an appropriate `/etc/hosts.equiv` entry for you, or if a local user has not granted you access, you will have to provide some identification in order to gain access. Access will be granted at the Unix shell level when you gain entry. For example, password-free access would resemble:

```
$ hostname↵
unixa
$ rlogin panda.zoo.ac.edu↵
$ hostname↵
panda
$
```

The `hostname` commands in the above example have been used to indicate that we have indeed changed systems. You will also notice that no username or password was required as with the `telnet` program (the `login` program has been bypassed completely). In the case where you were not granted pass-word-free access, i.e. a `.rhosts` file without an entry for you was used) you would be prompted with a `Password:` prompt, for example:

```
$ rlogin panda.zoo.ac.edu↵
Password: <your password>↵
Last login: Wed Aug 21 12:09:40 from tty06
$
```

If you wanted to log in under a different username then the user granting you access must have an appropriate .rhosts file in their home directory, i.e. an entry with your own username next to your calling machine. You could then use the -l option, as follows:

```
$ rlogin panda.zoo.ac.edu -l mark↵
```

A password would be required if your own username was not mentioned in user mark's .rhosts file. If it is mentioned, you will be given access immediately, and you will also gain a new identity in the process, for example:

```
$ whoami
joe
$ rlogin panda.zoo.ac.edu -l mark↵
$ whoami
mark
$
```

In order for the above to work, user mark must have a .rhosts entry which matches

```
sun2.example.edu joe
```

assuming that you are user joe and that you reside on the host called sun2.example.edu. No other users from this site can gain access without a password. Remember how the .rhosts and /etc/hosts.equiv files work; the former is to facilitate the using of an account, while the latter is used to determine which remote sites can use r* commands to query the current site (query in this case would refer to the use of any valid r* command).

rwho – remote who command

The command rwho emulates the Unix who command, except for the fact that it can be used to list remote users that are logged in on your computer: rwho has the simple syntax

```
rwho [-a]
```

A sample output of the rwho command could resemble the following:

```
$ rwho↵
Fred       suna:tty01        May 7 10:54
John       suna:tty09        May 7 15:04
Jim        suna:tty07        May 7 09:15 :14
Mike       vax1:ttyp02       May 7 11:15
$
```

From this listing we can see that there are currently four users accessing the system, three of which are using the host suna, while one is using another host called `vax1`. The various times and dates that are shown represent the time/date that each one logged in. Without any options, `rwho` also shows the idle times (as does the `finger` command) for users – although for this to be shown the user must not have been idle for more than an hour. In the example above, the user `Jim` has been idle for 14 minutes; all other users are using their terminals interactively. The `-a` (all) option will make `rwho` display users who have been idle for longer than an hour, for example:

```
$ rwho↵
Fred      suna:tty01      May 7 10:54
John      suna:tty09      May 7 15:04
Jim       suna:tty07      May 7 09:15 :14
Mike      vax:ttyp02      May 7 11:15
Tim       suna:tty06      May 7 12:02 1:14
$
```

We can now see that user `Tim` has appeared and that his idle time is 1 hour, 14 minutes (1:14). It should be noted that `rwho` cannot be used to enquire about remote systems, for example using a `host@name` argument. It is not possible therefore to find out who is using a system unless you `rlogin` or `telnet` to the machine in question and then issue a `who` command, or better still, if you perform a `rsh` command with the `who` program.

rcp – remote copy program

Program `rcp` is like the Unix `cp` (copy file) program, except that it copies file(s) between remote hosts (rather like FTP). Rcp is more powerful in many respects: it can copy files from your own machine to another, and it can even copy files from one remote machine to another remote machine. The syntax of the `rcp` command is

```
rcp [-r] <source-file> <destination-file>
```

where `<source-file>` is the local file to be copied, and `<destination-file>` is the name of a directory and/or filename to store the copy. In addition both arguments can also specify a computer name, so that file movements can be performed across networks; in this case use `machine:filename` as the name of the file, where `machine` is the name of the machine which the file is to be copied from or placed on (files without this notation are assumed to be stored locally, i.e. on the current machine). Security is again implemented using the `.rhosts` file, so copying operations will require a password if you try to copy a file to a `machine` that does not know about you. The `-r` option allows recursive copying of complete subdirectories – more on this later. For example, the command

```
$ rcp file1 sun2:file1↵
```

would copy the local file named `file1` to the system named `sun2` using the same filename. The location of the file will be determined by the `.rhosts` file, so in this case the user allowing us to `rcp` the file will have that file stored in their home directory. For example the person transferring the file above was called `joe` and he was calling from host `sun1.cc.com`. Also assume the person granting us access was called `mark` and his `.rhosts` entry was:

`sun1.cc.com joe`

this would allow user `joe` to upload a file using `rcp` to user `mark`'s home directory, as shown in the above `rcp` example. Also note that in the case that we mention only the first part of a hostname, e.g. the `sun1` of `sun1.cc.com` we are referring to a machine on the same network portion to our own (this could be considered a 'remote' machine, although not remote in terms of another Internet host elsewhere). Autonomous Internet hosts must have their full hostname specified, e.g. `vax.cc.t1.edu`, etc.

Transferring a file from the remote system to the local system can be done in a number of ways. For example we could type

`$ rcp remote:rfile lfile↵`

which would transfer the remote file called `rfile` onto our local machine with the new name `lfile`. It is assumed that all files will be stored in the home directory of each user, as in the `.rhosts` file. `rcp` knows that the file `lfile` is the local name since no machine name is specified with it. In the case that a host stored a file which was in another subdirectory, we would give the name of the directory in the `<source-file>` name, for example

`$ rcp remote:dir1/rfile lfile↵`

would copy the file `lfile` that exists in the directory `dir1`, to our local machine. The file `lfile` will be created in the local user's home directory, i.e. the user that issued the `rcp` request. Fully qualified pathnames can also be used, for example we could say

`$ rcp report.txt remote:/usr/users/joe/reports/report.txt↵`

which would copy the file `report.txt` to the machine remote, storing it not in the home directory of user `joe` but instead saving it in a subdirectory `report`. Of course, you must have write permission to write files into this directory, as set by the owner.

Of course, it is also possible to copy files between systems which are not part of the local system, for example

`$ rcp remote:file1 ftp.sun.edu:file1↵`

will copy the file on the system remote called `file1` to the Internet host `ftp.sun.edu`, using the same filename. The host `ftp.sun.edu` to which we are copying this file must have the appropriate `/etc/hosts.equiv` and

.rhosts files before the transfer can take place. Also note that we have given the full hostname for the <destination-file> argument – this denotes another Internet host which is not reachable on our local machine's network. In all the examples shown Unix will enforce any file permissions in force, so for example it would not be possible for you to copy a file without the appropriate read permission.

TIP

If possible ask your administrator to place users who regularly copy files into the same group (as in /etc/group) so that file copying and permission setting can be made easier, and more logical.

And now what you have all been waiting for: the ability to transfer a complete directory, something that FTP cannot yet accomplish. Copying a directory requires use of the -r option. In this case the <source-file> would be a directory and the destination another directory in which to hold the files, for example

```
$ rcp -r newfiles ftp.sun.edu:files/new↵
```

would copy the entire directory called newfiles, i.e. all the files in this directory, into the directory files/new in the home directory on the remote machine ftp.sun.edu.

rdist

The program rdist is a file/software distribution program. It uses a control file to list a series of files that are to be copied to specific hosts. A typical control file takes the form:

```
( <files to move, ..> ) ->
( <hostname destinations, ..> )
notify <person>
```

For example, assume that we wanted to distribute the files update.txt and update.Z (an ASCII and compressed version of a weekly report) to the hosts ftp.sub.cc.edu, vax1.sol.edu and etl.ftp.com. The rdist control file to perform this task would look like

```
(update.txt update.Z) ->
(ftp.sub.cc.edu vax1.sol.edu etl.ftp.com)
notify postmaster ;
```

The necessary command to transfer the files depends on whether or not a control file is being used to house the instructions. Some rdists read from the standard input, whereupon you can type in the control file directly. In the case of an external control file, such as the one created above with an editor, you would use the −f <file> option of the rdist command. Also note the final semicolon (;) which terminates the control file, and the −> string which separates the filenames from the hostnames. In addition, all filenames and hostnames must be enclosed in brackets. A command to invoke the above control file (assuming it was named control.file) would require the following rdist command:

```
$ rdist −f control.file↵
```

The files are then transferred via rcp to their respective hosts. You will, of course, have to ensure that the .rhosts file on each host has the necessary details, i.e. your login name and machine name, as well as a directory that has the necessary write permission to store the files. The notify statement in the control simpy instructs rdist to send an email message to the person named (here the alias postmaster) when the file transfer has been completed. Postmaster is an alias that will allow the site administrator to be contacted. Notice that mail is sent to all hosts. The previous rdist command would yield the following program output:

```
$ rdist −f control.file↵
updating host: ftp.sub.cc.edu
updating: update.txt
updating: update.Z
notify @ftp.sub.cc.edu ( postmaster )
updating host: vax.sol.edu
updating: update.txt
updating: update.Z
notify @vax.sol.edu ( postmaster )
updating host: etl.ftp.com
updating: update.txt
updating: update.Z
notify @etl.ftp.com ( postmaster )
$
```

TIP

If you are an administrator, you may consider using the cron utilty to control rdist file transfers so that they can be carried out automatically at a time of your choosing e.g. weekly.

---

rsh – remote shell utility

This utility can be used to run a Unix command on a remote computer, thus temporarily logging you in with a shell and then executing a command. As with all `r*` commands, the remote systems `.rhosts` file must be configured accordingly. The syntax of `rsh` (check your manual page for specific options) is

```
rsh <hostname> <Unix-command>
```

For example, we could run the Unix `who` command on the remote system `mercury.tn.edu` using the command:

```
$ rsh mercury.tn.edu who↵
```

The `who` command is executed on the machine specified and the results are echoed back on your machine.

It is also possible to run a shell in this way, effectively leaving you logged-in on the remote computer until you exit (using `logout` or `^D` keystroke). For example, we could run the C-Shell on the remote machine

```
$ rsh mercury.tn.edu /bin/csh↵
```

noticing that we used the full pathname of the `csh` program. Our `PATH` command may not be valid on the remote machine because the file-system may be structured differently (quoting `/bin` will find the standard Unix binaries directory (which exists on all Unix systems).

6.7 `tip` – terminal emulator program

The program `tip` is a Unix command that is used to engage in a connection with a remote Unix host, principally for a `login` session (in the same way as the `rlogin` and `telnet` programs described already). `tip` attempts to engage in a full-duplex connection with its host (communication in both directions at the same time), and then connects to the `login` program on the remote machine in order that the user can then identify him or herself and then conduct a normal Unix session. Unix users may also want to look out for sections on the older `cu` (call unix) command which has many simililarities with `tip`. The `tip` command has the syntax

```
tip [-v] [-speed] [<hostname> | <phone-number>]
```

The `-v` option causes `tip` to display the contents of the run-command file `.tiprc` – this file can contain various commands to be used when the program starts up. The `-speed` argument allows a line-speed (or baud rate) to be specified for the connection. Line-speeds that are available to you will depend on the equipment you have, as configured in the file called `remote`, which is used to summarize each remote system and the line-speed to use.

TIP

The REMOTE variable defines where the remote file is stored. Normally, this is /etc/remote by default although the location, and even the name, can be changed using this variable.

A <hostname> or <phone-number> argument is then used (mutually exclusive options) in order to start the session. Each host has a default baud rate for the connection, although this can be overridden with the -s argument, -s9600 for example. When a <phone-number> is specified, tip looks at the remote file for an entry which will tell it what system to call and the line-speed to use. Such entries could resemble

```
tip-300:tc=label1
tip-1200:tc=label2
unix1:dv=/dev/tty15:br#9600:cm=^M^Mcall uk.ac.janet.news^M
```

where tip-300 is a 300 baud line, and tip-1200 is a 1200 baud line. The line-speeds are hypothetical and can, of course, be any valid speed, although 300–9600 baud is common. The :tc=300 part is known as a 'continue capability' code, it tells tip (in this case) to use the settings indicated in label1, where label1 is a line further down in the remote file that contains all the details required in order to dial the remote host's modem number. So, for example, if we entered the command

```
$ tip -300↵
```

the system would look for the tip-300 line, and so on. As we will see later, a series of 'labels' are used to point various line-speed entries to a phone number that will actually be dialled – for example, the entry for tip-300 points to a line called label1 (which has not been included in the example). In the case that an entry is not found an error message will be generated and the system will stop. The remote file will have many entries, as we will see in later examples of this file. The unix1 line in the file is in fact a hostname entry, connected to a dedicated line. We will start by examining these type of entries in the next section.

TIP

Here's a tip about tip. Some users may remember the ancient (v7 Unix) cu (call Unix) command. This is still available on some Unix boxes and this command can use the remote file to call a host. Simply place an entry of the form:

```
cu<speed>:tc=<label>
```

in the remote file, where <speed> is a line-speed such as 1200, and <label> is a label for a further entry in the remote file for all the details (as with the tip command described above).

SPECIFYING A HOSTNAME WITH tip

An optional <hostname> argument can also be used. The remote file can have the names of hosts that can be connected by standard commands via a standard tty connection, rather than a telephone line, i.e. via TCP/IP. When a hostname is specified, the system will not search for a tip line; instead tip will look for a hostname entry that matches the user's input (tip will distinguish a speed entry from a hostname by the absence of the hyphen in the argument (-). After a hostname entry is located, a tty line will be used (as specified in the remote file entry for this host) and this will be used to contact the remote host. The remote host may be running Unix, in which case the login system will be called directly. In other cases tip may call a software interface such as a PAD, in which case this will need to be 'woken up' and a command executed to call the necessary Unix machine.

The remote file can include as many command(s) strings and control codes as are required in order to get to the machine you want to log in to.

TIP

tip, contrary to the definition, does not have to provide a means of logging in to a Unix machine. It could be used to call up any service you like, as long as the system is up-and-running and is contactable i.e. it resides at the end of a tty line. This feature is used in many academic institutions where a PAD is called in order to get at a service.

THE remote FILE

At a first glance the remote file looks as if it will require many hours of understanding. Not true; an hour at least. The format of the file is either one of the following, depending on whether or not you want to call a host via <telephone-number>, or whether or not you are calling a host directly using a <hostname> argument:

```
<hostname>:dv=<tty>:br#<baud-rate>:cm=<connection-string>:

tip-<speed>:du:at=<ACU>:br#<baud>:tc=<label>: pn=<phone-number>:
<label>:dv=<tty>br#<baud-rate>:cm=<connection-string>
```

Hostname entries

In the case of the `tip` command being used with a `<hostname>` argument a `remote` file entry consists of the hostname's name, a `tty` line, the baud-rate, and a connection string. The connection string is a sequence of characters which tell `tip` how to talk to the remote system, i.e. how to wake it up by providing some keystrokes or additional commands (a PAD device may need a call command to call a particular Unix machine – the actual commands and keystrokes required will depend on the hardware you are using). If your `tty` line led directly to a Unix box you may want to insert a carriage-return code to wake up the login program. A typical remote entry for a hostname argument could be a simple entry consisting of

```
unix1:dv=/dev/tty15:br#9600:cm=^M:
```

where `unix1` is the host to be contacted, `/dev/tty15` is the terminal line that connects it to you, and 9600 is the baud rate. This example assumes that the remote machine will answer us with the `login` program, although you may want to place additional commands in here to do this, as we will discuss very shortly. You will have noticed the various two-character codes in the examples and syntax descriptions. These instruct `tip` what each field value actually represents, so the ordering of fields is not important. Table 6.11 illustrates all of these codes and their respective meanings for the `tip` program.

Table 6.11   Field identification codes for use with the `tip` program

Field code	Description
cm	Call machine field. Used to feed commands and keystrokes to the remote machine in order to wake it up. The ^ character allows control codes to be generated, the most useful of which is ^M (the carriage-return code) which should be used to send commands. For example: `:cm=^Mcall unixa.fred.cc.com:`
dv	Device to use for `tty` line. For example: `:dv=/dev/tty15:`
el	EOL (end of line) marks – default null. The escape/control codes used to mark an end-of-line
du	Dial up command. Makes a call via an ACU. All telephone-number entries should have one of these by itself in a field
pn	Phone-number field. This can contain an explicit phone number, or if a @ is used, `tip` uses the phones database (as defined in the PHONES variable) to make a call
at	ACU name (manufacturer's name, e.g. Ventel)
br	Baud rate. Takes the form `br#` then the baud rate in question, e.g. `:br#9600:`
tc	To continue a capability. Used to allow a label to be named. Labels are names that identify an entry elsewhere in the remote file (used for breaking up entries into separate parts in the remote file)

Check your Unix manual for `tip`, as many other variables may be available in later releases.

If our tty line connected to a device such as a PAD (PADs are often used as a means of an external-connection capability, while allowing users to call up different network services, perhaps using entirely different protocols) we would have to modify the :cm= (call machine) field to wake-up the correct machine, for example we would need an entry consisting of

```
unix1:dv=/dev/tty15:br#9600:cm=^M^Mcall uk.ac.janet.news^M
```

where the command call uk.ac.janet.news (janet news machine) is the PAD command we require in order to call up the remote system we require. I can tell you that in the example, the host uk.ac.janet.news will not call up an Internet host, but instead a janet host. Clearly, you can substitute any name of your own choosing, depending on which hostname you want to call. Remember that dial-up PADs are also in existence, so you may want to read the section on constructing phone-number entries a bit later. The ^M code will generate a carriage return (ASCII 13, or [Ctrl-M] – try it on your keyboard) so that we wake-up the system as well as committing the call command. Without the final ^M keystroke the command would not be executed, just as if you had typed it at the PAD interface and didn't press [Return]. Coincidentally, pad is a command found in some versions of Unix – check your system documentation to see if it is supported on your system.

The tip command to invoke the above entry would therefore be as simple as the following, after which the machine uk.ac.janet.news should answer:

```
$ tip unix1↵
[connected]
Welcome to the JANET news machine on August 29th 1993
... etc ...
```

When you quit the service (or log-in session) on the remote machine you will be returned to the Unix prompt from where you came.

TIP

Remember that you must include all keystrokes in the :cm=: field, just as if you were using the remote machine directly from the keyboard (in fact you may want to do this to find out what keystrokes are actually required).

Fields must be separated with a colon (:), and you can use the \ character to continue an entry on to the next line, although be sure to start the new line with a colon (the previous line should ideally end as :\ to end the previous field definition). It is not possible to send conditional input from tips remote

file since the cm field sends a complete string of characters at once, not waiting
for any response from the remote system.

TIP

The HOST variable, if set, makes t ip connect to a default hostname. For
example the variable could be set to HOST=unixa.cc.edu for example.
Control codes (such as ^M) are implied at the end of the host named, although
explicit control codes may also be included with most tip versions.

Phone-number entries

These are slightly more tricky to set up, although the principle is the same as
for the hostname entries. The main exception here is that two entries are
normally required in the remote file: (i) a line-speed entry; and (ii) a device-line
entry. Apart from these two requirements, a phone-number entry uses some
different field codes to set up a series of additional values that are required (see
Table 6.11 for code meanings). All that we need to do then is provide some
labels that define how t ip is to dial the number (of course, we will need the
actual number as well), and use the :tc= field to make t ip find the correct
label once it has found the line-speed entry. A typical remote file entry for a
phone-number entry would thus resemble (look to the earlier syntax for the
layout – although any field order is valid):

```
tip-9600:tc=UNIX-1200
UNIX-1200:du:at=Ventel:br#1200:tc=dial:
dial:dv=/dev/cual:pn=0913851000:
```

The t ip-9600 entry would therefore relate to a -9600 option on the
command-line (i.e. for the [-speed] argument of the t ip command), while
du specifies that this is a dial-up line; br defines the baud-rate (or line-speed),
and the pn entry defines the phone number that is actually dialled by the t ip
program. The tc code allows us to use a label to jump down to the entry for
dial; this sets up the device (modem or automatic call-up unit) to contact the
system required; it specifies the name of the ACU/modem device, in this case a
'Ventel' (call and answer modem devices) – the inclusion of this option may be
optional. In theory, we don't have to use any tc label names since all codes
can be included on a single line. However, it does make sense to break up
entries in this way to separate the dial-up systems from the hostname systems.
Of course, you could have multiple line-speed devices referring to one tty line,
and so forth.

Since the line-speed option is optional, a phone number can be specified
on the command-line directly. In such cases your remote file must have a
tip0 entry in the file – this is a default line-speed for the phone-number

connection you require, for example, placing this in our previous remote file we now have

```
tip0:tc=UNIX-9600
tip-9600:tc=UNIX-9600
UNIX-9600:du:at=Ventel:br#9600:tc=dial:
dial:dv=/dev/cua1:pn=0913851000:
```

If an entry for tip0 is missing and you only specify a phone number on the command-line an error message will be generated. A typical command used with a phone number could be:

```
$ tip 90713218765↵
```

This command would use the tip0 entry to set a default line-speed. We could of course choose a line-speed for a particular device using a command such as

```
$ tip -9600 90713218765↵
```

which in this case would make tip use a 9600 baud connection. Other devices with different speeds will clearly require their own lines in the remote file. Since our tip0 entry in the example also points to the same 9600 baud modem entry the commands above are, in fact, equivalent.

TIP

tip supports Hayes modems so you may want to include AT commands in some cases, i.e. to set up various modem settings. Modem commands can normally be stored in with the pn field, or in the phone-number file, as set by the PHONES variable. Check your manual for specific details.

Phone numbers can also be stored in a phone file. The variable PHONES defines where this file is stored (you could have your auto-login file such as .login or .cshrc have a PHONES=/usr/users/jim/phone. numbers type entry, in this case setting up the file phone.numbers to store your numbers. The default file is called /etc/phones. The phone file contains two entries per line, simply an identifier, then a space or [Tab] and then the phone number itself. You would have to modify the pn field to point to the number required using the @ character:

```
dial:dv=/dev/cua1:pn=@:
```

would make tip examine the phones file and establish a connection with the first system mentioned. If a connection is not established, tip will cycle through each entry until a connection is made. Check your system to see if you can provide the name of a system to call rather than have t ip cycle through entries in this way (for example @id, where id is the name of a system as mentioned in the first column of the phones file).

TILDE ESCAPE COMMANDS FOR USE WITH t ip

t ip obeys a number of additional functions from the user in the form of tilde commands. The tilde character (˜), if typed, makes the remote system perform a function depending on the next character (or code) typed. Table 6.12 indicates the main t ip functions that are commonly available. In all cases type a tilde first, then follow this immediately by the character, code, etc. Control codes are prefixed with the ˆ character, e.g. ˆD means press [Ctrl] and D. Refer to the later examples of t ip's tilde commands for example sessions between local and remote systems.

The most useful tilde commands available are those used to transfer files. Remember that all commands are executed on the system you are calling from, since this has been left temporarily to access the remote system that you are currently communicating with. To execute commands back on the local system can also be done using the ! tilde command to execute a sub-shell back on the local system (you are of course already running a shell on the remote system, so exiting this will return you to the remote system). You may want to look up your Unix manual entry for t ip to see just what tilde commands are available, or alternatively use the ? command.

Table 6.12   Common tilde escape commands for use with tip

Tilde command	Description
?	Show all tilde commands available
ˆD	Drop the connection, and end the t ip session with the remote computer
.	Same as above (line drop)
c [name]	Changes directory on the remote system. The [name] argument specifies the name of the directory to change to. Without the [name] argument t ip changes to the home directory, as in the HOME variable
!	Escape to a shell
!<cmd>	Run shell command <cmd> on local system.
>	Copy a file from local system to remote system (or use p <file> to send a file)
<	Copy a file from remote system to local system (or use t <file> to take a file)
|	Pipes the output from a remote command to a local process
$	Pipes the output from a local command to the remote host
s <boolean> <var=value>	Allows t ip's internal variables to be set or viewed

File transfer

A file transfer task to send a file from the local system to the remote system we are currently connected to would proceed as follows:

```
$ tip unixa↵
[connected]
login: fred↵
password: <freds-password>↵
Last login: Wed Aug 21 12:09:40 from tty06
$ cat > send_file.txt↵
˜>
Filename: send_file.txt↵
78 lines transferred in 2 minutes 18 seconds
$
```

TIP

tip sends and receives text files only, i.e. ASCII files. Use the uuencode program to convert binary files into ASCII prior to transmittal.

In the above example we log in to the remote host unixa. We then issue the Unix cat (concatenate) command to start it reading from the standard input. The ˜> on its own signifies the pressing of the [CTRL] and > keys together. If you are not a Unix user, I will explain: the cat command is used to output the contents of a file (like the MSDOS TYPE command); if the cat command is typed by itself, however, it reads input from the keyboard directly (this would simply output everything you typed), and this is known as reading from the standard input. In the example, we start the cat command and then tell it to send all output into the file send_file.txt; this filename will be used on the remote system to store the local file (you could use any filename, although we have used the same name on both systems for the sake of simplicity).

Now, when we issue the tilde command (˜>) tip asks us what file we want to send (see the Filename: prompt) to which we respond send_file.txt, and then press [Return]. The file send_file.txt is a file that exists on our local machine that we want to send. Tip then sends the file across and it is captured by the cat command that we previously started. When the end of the file is reached, cat stops and we are returned to the Unix prompt. The file send_file.txt has then been transmitted. Notice how tip also tells us how long the transfer took.

The opposite can also be carried out, i.e. we can send a file on the remote system to our local system. In this case, however, we do not start the cat command as in the previous example (with ˜>) since tip will ask us for the actual command to use in order to send the file, for example:

```
$ tip unixa↵
[connected]
login: fred↵
password: <freds-password>↵
Last login: Wed Aug 21 12:09:40 from tty06
$
~<
Filename: new_file.txt↵
List command for remote host: cat new_file.txt↵
39 lines transferred in 1 minute 10 seconds
$
```

In this session we invoke the tilde command `~<` first. We then give `tip` the file we want transferred from the current directory on the remote machine (`new_file.txt` in this case). Then `tip` asks us for the command to print out the file (at this moment the local system is awaiting the file with a similar `cat` command to capture the file) and we type `cat new_file.txt` and press [Return]. The transfer then takes place and the local system grabs the file as it is sent across.

TIP

Use the ? command to show all of the tilde commands available on your system. Useful if you get stuck.

THE p (put) AND t (take) FILE COMMANDS

As you may have seen from Table 6.12 you can also use the p (put a file on local system) and t (take a file from local system) instead of `~>` and `~<`. These commands are essentially the same as the `~>` and `~<` commands already discussed, except that they do not require the `cat` command to be specified, for example you could simply type

```
$
~p put_file.txt↵
```

and the file `put_file.txt` would be taken from the local system and placed on the current, i.e. the remote system currently being used. Similarly

```
$
~t take_file.txt↵
```

would take the file `take_file.txt` which exists in the current directory of the remote machine you are using and send it back to the local system. I find these commands a lot easier to use. Try them to see if they are available on your `tip` implementation.

TIP

In order to get at local files that exist in other directories use the tilde command ~c <name> where <name> is the directory to change to. Press [Return] after you have typed in the name.

Printing files

You may often want to access a remote file and print it out on a local printer where you are currently based. This can be done using tip and the normal Unix print command such as lpr in conjunction with the tilde command ~|, which sends the remote commands output to a local process. The remote command in this case will be the cat command to print out the file, and the local process (also a command since 'processes' are really only executing programs) will be a command to print the file on a local printer (using the Unix lpr command). Assuming we were connected to a remote computer with access to the file we want to print back on the local printer, we would use the following commands:

```
$
~|
Local command: lpr print_file.txt↵
List command for remote host: cat print_file.txt↵
```

In this session we type ~| to make tip process a remote command on the local host. Tip asks us for the local command, in which case we give it a command to print the file we require (here the file print_file.txt which exists in our current working directory). The lpr makes Unix print the file. We now have to send the local system the file so it can actually print it. We therefore provide tip with the command cat print_file.txt which basically outputs the file so it can be captured by the local system. Instead of the local storing the file, tip instead feeds it straight into the lpr command, and it is thus printed. If you want to see the status of the file on the local system, use the Unix lpq (line printer queue status) command, but remember to issue a $ tilde command (not ~|) to send local output to you at the remote site where you are currently situated, for example

```
$
~$
List command for local host: lpq↵
Filename              Owner        Status
wombat.c              mark         Printing ...
print_file.txt        fred         waiting
```

where we can see that our file is second-in-line to be printed.

TIP

Any Unix command can be used with the $ tilde command in order to query the local host. Good commands to use include lpq (print status), who (who's using the system), lpr (print a remote file locally), ps (process status), ls (list files). One command not to use, however, is logout since this would be like committing Unix suicide, i.e. you would log yourself out on the local host, thus cutting your connection to the remote machine. Ouch!

---

cu–CALL-UP-UNIX COMMAND

cu (call up Unix) is an older version 7 Unix command which gave rise to the tip command described earlier: cu is used in much the same way as tip; it monitors the standard input and output channels allowing text files to be sent between systems, as well as allowing a shell environment to be used. Tilde commands such as ~!, < ~<file>, > ~<file>, ~$, etc. are all supported. Command-line options to search for a ACU device and tty line are provided by the −a <ACU> and −l<line> options. The line-speed (baud rate) can be set by the common −s <speed> option–values of 300 and 1200 are common. Some versions of cu can use the files maintained by tip in order to dial up specific hosts. The ability to dial-up terminal devices is provided with the −t option.

7
Manipulating compressed files on the Internet

7.1 Introduction

Transferring files over the Internet is a fairly straightforward process, although you may have noticed the ever-increasing use of data compression in order to reduce file sizes, and thus to maximize disk resources and transfer times. There are now so many compression schemes available that it can really be quite difficult to keep abreast of developments, bearing in mind also that there is no single data compression standard. Finding that elusive decompression utility for a particular machine can also be a problem, so this chapter tackles the problem of file compression from the viewpoint of each particular compression format, and the various utilities that can be used with each type of format. In this chapter you will learn:

- The different compression formats that exist
- Dealing with common decompression problems
- How to locate compression/decompression utilities
- The tools that are required to decompress files on a variety of machine platforms

AN INTRODUCTION TO COMPRESSION FORMATS

Data compression is commonly employed on files stored on disk in order to save disk space. Many of the anonymous FTP sites that you will come in contact with most definitely use compression on some files that are stored. Compression is also beneficial to you, the user, since reduced download times will also be evident. Many dozens of different compression formats exist, and a utility exists for each type. Decompressing files between different machine platforms can be made easier by reading the later sections of this chapter to ascertain which utility should be used with a particular compression format, and then discovering where that particular utility resides.

Note the utility name next to each format to look up details later on in this chapter. Each different compression utility that is used to compress a file can be identified by its filename extension, for example .ZIP is a PKZIP archive and will require the utility PKUNZIP.EXE under MSDOS. Each common machine platform is considered in turn, and the DOS, Atari, Mac, Amiga, VMS, NeXT, Unix, and OS/2 machines are all examined. In many instances the utility shown will compress files as well as decompressing them. You should keep up with the gossip on USENET forums such as comp.compression, especially on news of new utilities and versions. Keeping up-to-date with the latest versions of various compression utilities is sensible, bearing in mind that many sites will start the changeover and you may be left with a redundant utility in the process.

TIP

When coming to download a particular compression utility make sure that it is not compressed itself! If it is compressed and you have the necessary decompressor, this problem will not arise. Many archives deal in uncompressed files for this very reason.

UNKNOWN UTILITIES

Some compression utilities could not be found at the time of writing. These have 'None known' marked by the side of them, although this does not mean that the decompression is impossible. If you can get hold of the file on disk (or you can send it via electronic mail to another computer on which you can copy it over to a floppy disk) you may be able to process the file on another platform. In most cases platform-to-platform conversions will not be a problem, since most compression formats follow a particular machine, e.g. .HQX for the Apple Macintosh platform, and a suitable decompressor will always be available. In the case that you find a file that you want to decompress on to another machine, try to decompress that file where it presently resides before moving it to another machine, since chances are the decompression utility will also be located on the source machine (you will, of course, need permission to use the host machine's disk to decompress the file – on Unix you can do this in the /tmp directory).

In the following tables some formats are marked 'Not possible'; in such cases this means that decompression is impossible, for example a DOS .EXE, a self-extracting executable file, could not be run on an Amiga machine (yet). Things are changing though. Apple's new range of computers actually have DOS/Mac compatibility (via a 486SX chip on the motherboard inside the

Mac), so cross-platform decompression is gradually becoming easier. A question mark (?) by the side of some filename extensions simply means that the name in question is not always used, and that slight variations in the name can sometimes be in use. You may also find that some file extensions may not be acceptable on your system, for example .LZARI is not valid on MSDOS, although .LZA is. In such cases your operating system may truncate the filename (DOS will), although Unix leaves the filename intact if you transfer it via FTP, etc. Make sure you know what a particular decompression utility expects as a filename extension, since some can be fussy.

PERSONAL COMPUTERS (PC)–DOS MACHINES

As you would expect, DOS is very well served and many compression formats are supported, making cross-machine conversions much more flexible for the user (see Table 7.1).

APPLE MACINTOSH MACHINES

All of the main compression formats are supported on the Macintosh II platform so no major conversion problems are evident (see Table 7.2).

UNIX MACHINES

Unix has many available utilities for all of the most common compression formats that are in existence, especially .Z (compress format), and .UUE (uuencode format) (see Table 7.3).

AMIGA MACHINES

Keep subscribed to the USENET group comp.sys.amiga.* for the latest news and Amiga developments in data compression (see Table 7.4).

DEC VAX/VMS MACHINES

The VMS platform is poorly supported when it comes to decompression utilities, although .ZIPs and .ARJs are supported (see Table 7.5). Development continues in the VMS area at a continuing pace. Keep subscribed to the USENET group comp.sys.dec.* groups for news.

APPLE II MACHINES

(see Table 7.6)

ATARI MACHINES

The Atari platfrom is lacking quite badly in decompression utilities (see Table 7.7), although there is support for the popular .ARC and .ARJ formats as well as .LZH and the Unix compress (.Z) format.

Table 7.1 DOS compression utilities

Filename extension	Compression type	Example decompressor
.AP	Whap archive	None known
.ARC	LH(ARC) archive	Arc602.exe
.ARJ	ARJ archive	Arj230/arj.exe
.AVI	Audio/visual interleave	Windows 3.1 multimedia player
.HQX	BinHex archive	Xbin23.zip
.BOO	BOO archive	Msbpct/msbmbk.exe
.BNDL	Bundle archive	None known
.C	Compact archive	None known
.CPT	Tor archive	None known
.COM	• COMT archive	Comt010d.zip
	• Scrunch archive	Scrnch.arc
.DD	Disk doubler archive	None known
.DMS	Disk-masher archive	None known
.EXE	• Self-extracting	None required
	• LZEXE archive	Lzexe91.zip
	• PKLite archive	Pkltel15.exe
.DWC	DWC archive	Dwc-a501.exe
.HPK	HPACK archive	Hpack78.zip
.HYP	HYPER archive	Hyper25.zip
.ISH	Ish archive	Ish200.lzh
.LZH	• LHA archive	Lha213.exe
	• LHarc archive	Lh113c.exe
.LZW	LHWarp archive	None known
.LBR	LU/LAR archive	Lue220.arc
.LZSS	LZSS archive	None known
.MD	MDCD archive	Mdcd10.arc
.PIT	PACKIT archive	Unpackit.exe
.PAK	PAK archive	Pak251.exe
.PP	PowerPacker archive	None known
.SHAR	SharkShell archive	Toadshr1.arc
.SHK	ShrinkIt archive	None known
.STF	ToFit archive	None known
.XQX	Squeeze archive	Sqpc131.arc
.SIT	StuffIt archive	Unsit30.zip
.TAR	Tape archive (Unix)	Tar/Tarread/Ltarv1 and Extar10.zip
.UUE	UU-encoded file	Toaduu20.zip
.WRP	WARP archive	None known
.XXE	XX-encoded file	Ncdc150.zip
.Y	Yabba archive	None known
.Z	Unix compress file	u16.zip
.ZIP	PKZIP archive	Pkz204g.exe
.ZOO	ZOO archive	Zoo210.exe

Table 7.2   Apple Macintosh compression utilities

Filename extension	Compression type	Example decompressor
.AP	Whap archive	None known
.ARC	LH(ARC) archive	ArcMac1.3c
.ARJ	ARJ archive	None known
.HQX	BinHex archive	BinHex4.0
.BOO	BOO archive	None known
.BNDL	Bundle archive	Bundle
.C	Compact archive	None known
.CPT	Tor archive	Compactor1.21 CompactorPro1.33
.COM	• COMT archive	None known
	• Scrunch archive	None known
.DD	Disk doubler archive	DiskDoubler3.7
.DMS	Disk-masher archive	None known
.EXE	• Self-extracting	Not possible on Mac
	• LZEXE archive	None known
	• PKLite archive	
.DWC	DWC archive	None known
.HPK	HPACK archive	None known
.HYP	HYPER archive	None known
.ISH	Ish archive	Ishmac-06
.LZH	• LHA archive	None known
	• LHarc archive	MacLHarc0.41
.LZW	LHWarp archive	None known
.LZARI (?)	LZAri archive	MacLZAri
.LBR	LU/LAR archive	None known
.LZSS (?)	LZSS archive	LZSS 2.0b5
.MD	MDCD archive	None known
.PIT	PACKIT archive	PackIt3.1.3
.PAK	PAK archive	None known
.PP	PowerPacker archive	None known
.SHAR	SharkShell archive	None known
.SHK	ShrinkIt archive	None known
.STF	ToFit archive	STF1.2
.XQX	Squeeze archive	None known
.SIT	StuffIt archive	StuffItLite
.TAR	Tape archive (Unix)	UnTar 2.0
.UUE	UU-encoded file	Uutool2.0.3
.WRP	WARP archive	None known
.XXE	XX-encoded file	None known
.Y	Yabba archive	None known
.Z	Unix compress file	MacCompress3.2A
.ZOO	ZOO archive	MacBooz2.1, maczoo.sit.hqx
.ZIP	PKZIP archive	UnZip1.1

Table 7.3 Unix compression utilities

Filename extension	Compression type	Example decompressor
.AP	Whap archive	yabbawhap
.ARC	LH(ARC) archive	arc521
.ARJ	ARJ archive	unarj230
.HQX	BinHex archive	Mcvert
.BOO	BOO archive	None known
.BNDL	Bundle archive	Unbundle
.BTOA (?)	BTOA (Binary to Ascii)	btoa, atob
.C	Compact archive	uncompact
.CPIO (?)	Unix CPIO archive	cpio
.CPT	Tor archive	None known
.COM	● COMT archive	None known
	● Scrunch archive	None known
.DD	Disk doubler archive	None known
.DMS	Disk-masher archive	None known
.EXE	● Self extracting	Not possible on Unix
	● LZEXE archive	
	● PKLite archive	
.DWC	DWC archive	None known
.F	Freeze for Unix	freeze-2.3.4.tar.Z
.ISH	Ish archive	None known
.LZH	● LHA archive	lha1.00
	● LHarc archive	lharc102
.LZW	LHWarp archive	None known
.LZARI (?)	LZAri archive	None known
.LBR	LU/LAR archive	lar
.LZSS	LZSS archive	None known
.MD	MDCD archive	None known
.PIT	PACKIT archive	Unpit
.PAK	PAK archive	arc521
.PP	PowerPacker archive	None known
.SHAR	SharkShell archive	Unhshar
.SHK	ShrinkIt archive	None known
.STF	ToFit archive	None known
.XQX	Squeeze archive	None known
.SIT	StuffIt archive	Unsit
.TAR	Tape archive (Unix)	tar
.UUE *	UU-encoded file	uudecode
.WRP	WARP archive	None known
.XXE	XX-encoded file	xxdecode
.Y (see .AP)	Yabba archive	yabbawhap
.z	Unix packed file	unpack
.Z	Unix compressed file	compress
.ZOO	ZOO archive	zoo210
.ZIP	PKZIP archive	Unzip50

*Unix also has another binary to ASCII convertor called btoa (binary to ASCII), a utility in its own right. The filename extension of btoa files have many variations, although .btoa is common. The utilities atob and btoa exist for compression and decompression purposes.

Table 7.4   Amiga compression utilities

Filename extension	Compression type	Example decompressor
.AP	Whap archive	yabbawhap
.ARC	LH(ARC) archive	Arc 0.23
.ARJ	ARJ archive	None known
.HQX	BinHex archive	None known
.BOO	BOO archive	None known
.BNDL	Bundle archive	None known
.BTOA (?)	Unix BTOA	compress
.C	Compact archive	None known
.CPIO (?)	Unix CPIO archive	None known
.CPT	Tor archive	None known
.COM	• COMT archive	None known
	• Scrunch archive	
.DD	Disk Doubler archive	None known
.DMS	Disk-Masher archive	dms-102
.EXE	• Self-extracting	Not possible
	• LZEXE archive	
	• PKLite archive	
.DWC	DWC archive	None known
.HPK	HPACK archive	None known
.HYP	HYPER archive	None known
.IMP (?)	Imploder archive	Imploder 1.3
.ISH	Ish archive	None known
.LZH	• LHA archive	None known
	• LHarc archive	
.LZW	LHWarp archive	Lhwarp
.LZARI (?)	LZAri archive	None known
.LBR	LU/LAR archive	None known
.LZSS	LZSS archive	None known
.MD	MDCD archive	None known
.PIT	PACKIT archive	None known
.PAK	PAK archive	None known
.PP	PowerPacker archive	PowerPacker
		PPLib.lha
.SHAR	SharkShell archive	UnShar
.SHK	ShrinkIt archive	None known
.STF	ToFit archive	None known
.SIT	StuffIt archive	None known
.TAR	Tape archive (Unix)	TarSplit
.UUE	UU-encoded file	uudecode
.WRP	WARP archive	WarpUtil
.XQX	Squeeze archive	Sq.Usq
.XXE	XX-encoded file	None known
.Y (see .AP)	Yabba archive	yabbawhap
.z	Unix packed file	None known
.Z	Unix compress file	compress
.ZOO	ZOO archive	amigazoo
.ZIP	PKZIP archive	PKAzip

Table 7.5   VAX/VMS compression utilities

Filename extension	Compression type	Example decompressor
.AP	Whap archive	None known
.ARC	LH(ARC) archive	arcvms.uue
.ARJ	ARJ archive	unarj200
.HQX	BinHex archive	None known
.BOO	BOO archive	None known
.BNDL	Bundle archive	None known
.BTOA (?)	Unix BTOA	None known
.C	Compact archive	None known
.CPIO	Unix CPIO archive	None known
.CPT	Tor archive	None known
.COM	• COMT archive	None known
	• Scrunch archive	
.DD	Disk Doubler archive	None known
.DMS	Disk-Masher archive	None known
.EXE	• Self-extracting	None known
	• LZEXE archive	If DOS, not possible
	• PKLite archive	
.DWC	DWC archive	None known
.HPK	HPACK archive	None known
.HYP	HYPER archive	None known
.IMP (?)	Imploder archive	None known
.ISH	Ish archive	None known
.LZH	• LHA archive	None known
	• LHarc archive	
.LZW	LHWarp archive	None known
.LZARI (?)	LZAri archive	None known
.LBR	LU/LAR archive	vmssweep
.LZSS	LZSS archive	None known
.MD	MDCD archive	None known
.PIT	PACKIT archive	None known
.PAK	PAK archive	None known
.PP	PowerPacker archive	None known
.SHAR	SharkShell archive	None known
.SHK	ShrinkIt archive	None known
.STF	ToFit archive	None known
.SIT	StuffIt archive	None known
.TAR	Tape archive (Unix)	vmstar, tar.exe
.TAR-Z	Tape archive (VMS)	vmstar, tar.exe
.UUE	UU-encoded file	None known
.WRP	WARP archive	uudeode2.vms
.XQX	Squeeze archive	vmsusq.pas
.XXE	XX-encoded file	None known
.Y (see .AP)	Yabba archive	None known
.z	Unix packed file	None known
.Z	Unix compress file	lzcomp
.ZOO	ZOO archive	ZOO210.TAR-Z
.ZIP	PKZIP archive	unzip4.1

Table 7.6   Apple II compression utilities

Filename extension	Compression type	Example decompressor
.AP	Whap archive	None known
.ARC	LH(ARC) archive	dearc.bsq.Z
.ARJ	ARJ archive	None known
.HQX	BinHex archive	None known
.bin (?)	BinAscii archive	binascii.exe
.BOO	BOO archive	None known
.BNDL	Bundle archive	None known
.BTOA (?)	Unix BTOA	None known
.C	Compact archive	None known
.CPIO (?)	Unix CPIO archive	None known
.CPT	Tor archive	None known
.COM	• COMT	None known
	• Scrunch	
.DD	Disk doubler archive	None known
.DMS	Disk-masher archive	None known
.EXE	• Self-extracting	Not possible
	• LZEXE archive	
	• PKLite archive	
.DWC	DWC archive	None known
.HPK	HPACK archive	None known
.HYP	HYPER archive	None known
.IMP (?)	Imploder archive	None known
.ISH	Ish archive	None known
.LZH	• LHA archive	None known
	• LHarc archive	
.LZW	LHWarp archive	None known
.LZARI (?)	LZAri archive	None known
.LBR	LU/LAR archive	None known
.LZSS	LZSS archive	None known
.MD	MDCD archive	None known
.nupack (?)	NuPack archive	nupack
.PIT	PACKIT archive	None known
.PAK	PAK archive	None known
.PP	PowerPacker archive	None known
.SHAR	SharkShell archive	unshar.shk
.SHK	ShrinkIt archive	None known
.STF	ToFit archive	None known
.SIT	StuffIt archive	None known
.TAR	Tape archive (Unix)	None known
.UUE	UU-encoded file	uu.en.decode
.WRP	WARP archive	None known
.XQX	Squeeze archive	None known
.XXE	XX-encoded file	None known
.Y (see .AP)	Yabba archive	None known
.z	Unix packed file	None known
.Z	Unix compress file	compress.shk
.ZOO	ZOO archive	None known
.ZIP	PKZIP archive	None known

Table 7.7   Atari compression utilities

Filename extension	Compression type	Example decompressor
.AP	Whap archive	None known
.ARC	• LH(ARC) archive	arc521b.arc
	• PKPAK	pkunarc.arc
.ARJ	ARJ archive	None known
.HQX	BinHex archive	None known
.BOO	BOO archive	None known
.BNDL	Bundle archive	None known
.BTOA (?)	Unix BTOA	None known
.C	Compact archive	None known
.CPIO (?)	Unix CPIO archive	None known
.CPT	Tor archive	None known
.COM	• COMT	None known
	• Scrunch	
.DD	Disk doubler archive	None known
.DMS	Disk-masher archive	None known
.EXE	• Self extracting	Not possible
	• LZEXE archive	
	• PKLite archive	
.DWC	DWC archive	None known
.HPK	HPACK archive	None known
.HYP	HYPER archive	None known
.IMP (?)	Imploder archive	None known
.ISH	Ish archive	None known
.LZH	• LHA archive	None known
	• LHarc archive	lharc113.arc
.LZW	LHWarp archive	None known
.LZARI (?)	LZAri archive	None known
.LBR	LU/LAR archive	None known
.LZSS	LZSS archive	None known
.MD	MDCD archive	None known
.nupack (?)	NuPack archive	None known
.PIT	PACKIT archive	None known
.PAK	PAK archive	None known
.PP	PowerPacker archive	None known
.SHAR	SharkShell archive	ahar.arc
.SHK	ShrinkIt archive	None known
.STF	ToFit archive	None known
.SIT	StuffIt archive	None known
.TAR	Tape archive (Unix)	sttar.arc
.UUE	UU-encoded file	None known
.WRP	WARP archive	None known
.XQX	Squeeze archive	ezsqueeze.arc
.XXE	XX-encoded file	None known
.Y (see .AP)	Yabba archive	None known
.z	Unix packed file	None known
.Z	Unix compress file	compress.arc
.ZIP	PKZIP archive	STZIP1.1
.ZOO	ZOO archive	booz.arc

OS/2 MACHINES

OS/2 has a few utilities, although a large amount of the more popular formats are not supported (see Table 7.8). You may want to try the DOS archives also since these have OS/2 repositories, bearing in mind that both systems run on personal computers (alternatively, use Archie with an OS2 keyword).

7.2 Locating the utility you require

This section lists each utility in order of its name (A–Z), and according to the platform on which the utility can be found. Table 7.9 illustrates each utility along with the platform machine it is available on, together with the FTP site that it can be downloaded to. We start with a discussion of the various formats.

DOS (PC) UTILITIES

The majority of utilities for the DOS platform can be found on the anonymous FTP site ftp.cso.uiuc.edu (128.174.5.59) in /pc/exec-pc and at the anonymous FTP site wuarchive.wustl.edu (128.152.135.4) in the directory /mirrors/msdos/arc-lbr. Various subdirectories hold the actual tools. Other sites may also be mentioned. Some utilities are posted to the binary USENET forums and these are mirrored on disk at many FTP sites, notably the sites ftp.uu.net and wuarchive.wustl.edu, both in the /usenet directory. The most common formats used for DOS machines are the: .ARC, .ARJ, .LHA, .LZH, .PAK and .ZIP formats.

AMIGA UTILITIES

The Amiga platform is very well supported, the main site for decompression utilities being ftp.cso.uiuc.edu. Support for Unix compressed files, .ARCs, .ZIPS, Shar's, and Tar's are all evident. The most common formats used on the Amiga include: .ARC, .ARJ, .LHA, .PP, .SIT, .ZIP and .ZOO formats.

ATARI UTILITIES

The anonymous FTP archive atari.archive.umich.edu is continuing to grow. Many common archive formats are supported including .ZIPs, Unix .Z compressed files, and .ARC archives.

APPLE II UTILITIES

A poorly supported platform. A few decompressors are available, mainly from sites such as wuarchive.wustl.edu. Support for Unix compressed files, (.Z's), Shar's (Shark archives), .ARCs, and UU-encoded files are available,

Table 7.8 OS/2 compression utilities

Filename extension	Compression type	Example decompressor
.AP	Whap archive	None known
.ARC	LH(ARC) archive	arc2.arc
.ARJ	ARJ archive	None known
.HQX	BinHex archive	None known
.BOO	BOO archive	None known
.BNDL	Bundle archive	None known
.BTOA (?)	Unix BTOA	None known
.C	Compact archive	None known
.CPIO (?)	Unix CPIO archive	None known
.CPT	Tor archive	None known
.COM	● COMT	None known
	● Scrunch	
.DD	Disk doubler archive	None known
.DMS	Disk-masher archive	None known
.EXE	● Self-extracting	None known
	● LZEXE archive	
	● PKLite archive	
.DWC	DWC archive	None known
.HPK	HPACK archive	None known
.HYP	HYPER archive	None known
.IMP (?)	Imploder archive	None known
.ISH	Ish archive	None known
.LZH	● LHA archive	lha214_2
	● LHarc archive	clhar103
.LZW	LHWarp archive	None known
.LZARI (?)	LZAri archive	None known
.LBR	LU/LAR archive	None known
.LZSS	LZSS archive	None known
.MD	MDCD archive	None known
.nupack (?)	NuPack archive	None known
.PIT	PACKIT archive	None known
.PAK	PAK archive	None known
.PP	PowerPacker archive	None known
.SHAR	SharkShell archive	None known
.SHK	ShrinkIt archive	None known
.STF	ToFit archive	None known
.SIT	StuffIt archive	None known
.TAR	Tape archive (Unix)	None known
.UUE	UU-encoded file	None known
.WRP	WARP archive	None known
.XQX	Squeeze archive	None known
.XXE	XX-encoded file	None known
.Y (see .AP)	Yabba archive	None known
.z	Unix packed file	None known
.Z	Unix compress file	None known
.ZOO	ZOO archive	booz.exe
.ZIP	PKZIP archive	pkz101-2.exe

however. You may want to use the Archie service to locate Apple II related files/subdirectories for further additions.

OS/2 UTILITIES

The OS/2 system is another poorly supported platform for compression utilities. Compression types supported do, however, include .ARCs, .LHAs and .ZIPs, which are all commonly found. One omission is a UU-decoder (for .UUE files) and a Unix compress decompressor, both of which are heavily used compression formats on the Internet. The main sites for OS/2 compression utilities are mtsg.ubc.ca and the site ftp.cso.uiuc.edu. Use the Archie service to locate utilities that must undoubtedly exist. The most common formats used on the OS/2 platform are currently .ARC and .ZIP, which are also popular on DOS-based systems.

UNIX UTILITIES

Many utilities such as uudecode, tar, shar, compress and unpack are all standard Unix commands in their own right, and as such should be available on most Unix systems. The archive wuarchive.wustl.edu has most of the compression utilities that you will ever need. Unix utilities are scattered all over the Internet, so using Archie may help you once you know the name of the file you require (Archie may find other sites as well). Unix uses many compression formats, although the .tar.Z, .Z and .ZOO are probably the most popular Unix-based formats. Many others are, of course, supported for cross-platform conversions, principally: .ARC, .LZH and .ZIP.

VAX/VMS UTILITIES

The list of utilities is growing gradually, support being available for .ARJ, UU-encoded files, and .ARCs which are commonly found in use on the Internet (especially .UUEs for image-files). The TAR-Z format, if you were wondering, is a .TAR file encoded on a VAX. The .ARC, .LHA., .Y and .ZOO formats are also popular under VMS.

7.3   The A–Z of compression utilities

This section documents a series of compression utilities for the most popular machine platforms. Table 7.9 illustrates each machine platform and the utilities that are available.

All of the above utilities were available at the time of writing, but there will undoubtedly be new utilities on the network as you are reading, so you may want to browse some of the larger FTP sites and get hold of a file index to see just what is available, and what new versions of various utilities have been released.

Table 7.9   A–Z summary of compression utilities

Utility/platform	FTP site and file location
DOS/PC platform:	
abe.exe	comp.binaries.ibm.pc (USENET)
arc602.exe	wuarchive.wustl.edu
arj230ng.exe	wuarchive.wustl.edu
xbin23.zip	wuarchive.wustl.edu
msbpct/msbmbk.exe	wuarchive.wustl.edu
u16.zip	ftp.cso.uiuc.edu
comp430d.zip	wuarchive.wustl.edu
	garbo.uwasa.fi (/pc/Unix)
comt010d.zip	wuarchive.wustl.edu
dwc-a501.exe	wuarchive.wustl.edu
hpack78.zip	wuarchive.wustl.edu
hyper25.zip	wuarchive.wustl.edu
ish200.lzh	wuarchive.wustl.edu
larc333.zip	wuarchive.wustl.edu
lha213.exe	wuarchive.wustl.edu
lh113c.exe	wsmr-simtel20.army.mil (/pd1)
lue220.arc	wuarchive.wustl.edu
lzexe91.zip	ftp.cso.uiuc.edu
mdcd10.arc	wuarchive.wustl.edu
pak251.exe	wsmr-simtel20.army.mil (/pd1)
pktel15.exe	wuarchive.wustl.edu
pk361.exe	ftp.cso.uiuc.edu
pkz204c.exe	wuarchive.wustl.edu
scrnch.arc	wuarchive.wustl.edu
toadshr1.arc	wuarchive.wustl.edu
squash.arc	wuarchive.wustl.edu
sqpc131.arc	wuarchive.wustl.edu
unsit30.zip	wuarchive.wustl.edu
tar.zip	ftp.cso.uiuc.edu
tarread.arc	pc.usl.edu (/pub/Unix)
extar10.zip	wuarchive.wustl.edu
itarv1.zip	wuarchive.wustl.edu
toaduu20.zip	wuarchive.wustl.edu
ncdc150.zip	wuarchive.wustl.edu
zoo210.exe	ftp.cso.uiuc.edu
MAC platform:	
ArcMac1.3c	ftp.cso.uiuc.edu (/mac)
Binhex4.0	ftp.cso.uiuc.edu (/mac)
Bundle	Various sites
Compactor1.21	sumex-aim.stanford.edu (/info-mac/util)
CompactorPro3.2A	sumex-aim.stanford.edu (/info-mac/util)
MacCompress3.2A	ftp.cso.uiuc.edu (/mac)
DiskDoubler3.7	Commercial product
ishmac-06	isfs.kuis.kyoto-u.ac.jp
	(/ftpmail/ftp.tohoku.jp/pub/mac/tools/archiver)

continues overleaf

Table 7.9 – *continued*

Utility/platform	FTP site and file location
Lzss 2.0b5	Various sites
MacLHarc0.41	sumex-aim.stanford.edu (/info-mac/util)
MacLZAri	Various sites
MacBooz2.1	sumex-aim.stanford.edu (/info-mac/util)
maczoo.sit.hqx	mac.archive.umich.edu (/mac/utilities/compressionapps)
PacIt3.1.3	ftp.cso.uiuc.edu (/mac)
UnZip1.1	tybalt.caltech.edu (/pub/apple2)
UnShar2.0	sumex-aim.stanford.edu (/info-mac/util)
StuffItLite3	sumex-aim.stanford.edu (/info-mac/util)
UnTar2.0	sumex-aim.stanford.edu (/info-mac/util)
uutool2.0.3	sumex-aim.stanford.edu (/info-mac/util)
Unix platform:	
arc521	pc.usl.edu (/pub/Unix)
freeze-2.3.4.tar.Z	ftp.inria.fr (/system/arch-compr)
mcvert	sumex-aim.stanford.edu (/Unix)
btoa	Unix internal command; also on: wuarchive.wustl.edu (/Unix-c/arc-progs)
cpio	Unix internal command; also on: wuarchive.wustl.edu (/Unix-c/arc-progs)
lha1.00	wuarchive.wustl.edu (/usenet/alt.sources)
lharc02	wuarchive.wustl.edu (/usenet/alt.sources) under articles: 2217/2218
lar	Various sites
tar	Unix internal command; also on: wuarchive.wustl.edu (/Unix-c/arc-progs)
unpack	Unix internal command; also on: wuarchive.wustl.edu (/Unix-c/arc-progs)
unpit	Various sites
unbundle	comp.sources.Unix–archives (USENET)
uncompact	Unix internal command; also on: wuarchive.wustl.edu (/Unix-c/arc-progs)
uncompress	Unix internal command; also on: wuarchive.wustl.edu (/Unix-c/arc-progs)
unarj230	wuarchive.wustl.edu (/misc/Unix)
unzip50	wuarchive.wustl.edu (/zip)
unshar	Unix internal command; also on: wuarchive.wustl.edu (/Unix-c/arc-progs)
unsit	sumex-aim.stanford.edu (/Unix)
uudecode	Unix internal command; also on: wuarchive.wustl.edu (/Unix-c/arc-progs)
yabbawhap	wuarchive.wustl.edu (/usenet /comp.sources.Unix)
xxdecode	ftp.cso.uiuc.edu
zoo210	wuarchive.wustl.edu (/mirrors/misc/Unix)

Utility/platform	*FTP site and file location*
Amiga platform:	
amigazoo	ftp.cso.uiuc.edu (/amiga/fish)
Arc0.23	ftp.cso.uiuc.edu (/amiga/fish/ff070)
compress (btoa)	ftp.cso.uiuc.edu (/amiga/fish/ff051)
compress (.Z)	ftp.cso.uiuc.edu (/amiga/fish/ff051)
compress-4.1.lha	ftp.funet.fi (/pub/amiga/utilities/archivers)
dms-102	ab20.larc.nasa.gov (/amiga/utils)
impolder1.3	ab20.larc.nasa.gov (/amiga/utils)
LHarc	ftp.cso.uiuc.edu (/amiga/fish/ff312)
Lhwarp	ftp.cso.uiuc.edu (/amiga/fish/ff305)
PKAX	Various sites
PKAZip	ftp.cso.uiuc.edu (/amiga/fish/ff311)
PowerPacker	ftp.cso.uiuc.edu (/amiga/fish/ff053)
PPLib.lha	ftp.funet.fi (/pub/amiga/fish/501-600/ff561)
UnShar	ftp.cso.uiuc.edu (/amiga/fish/ff345)
Sq.Unsq	ftp.cso.uiuc.edu (/amiga/fish/ff051)
TarSplit	ftp.cso.uiuc.edu (/amiga/fish/ff253)
uudecode	ftp.cso.uiuc.edu (/amiga/fish/ff092)
WarpUtil	ftp.cso.uiuc.edu (/amiga/fish/ff243)
yabbawhap	comp.sources.Unix-archives (USENET)
DEC VAX/VMS platform:	
arcvms.uue	wuarchive.wustl.edu (/misc/vaxvms)
unarj220	wuarchive.wustl.edu (/misc/vaxvms)
lzcomp.exe	kuhub.cc.ukans.edu (/lzw)
vmssweep	wuarchive.wustl.edu (/misc/vaxvms)
unzip41	wuarchive.wustl.edu (/misc/vaxvms)
vmsusq.pas	wuarchive.wustl.edu (/misc/vaxvms)
vmstar	vmsa.oac.uci.edu (/)
tar.exe	wuarchive.wustl.edu (/packages/compression /vax-vms)
uudecode2.vms	wuarchive.wustl.edu (/misc/vaxvms)
ZOO210.TAR-Z	wuarchive.wustl.edu (/misc/vaxvms)
Apple II platform:	
dearc.bsq.Z	wuarchive.wustl.edu (/mirrors/info-mac)
binscii.exe	tybalt.caltech.edu (/pub/apple2)
compress.shk	plains.nodak.edu (/pub/appleII/GS/utils)
nupack	wuarchive.wustl.edu (/mirrors/info-mac)
unshar.shk	plains.nodak.edu (/pub/appleII/GS/utils)
uu.en.code	plains.nodak.edu (/pub/appleII/GS/utils)
OS/2 platform:	
arc2.arc	ftp.cso.uiuc.edu (/Unix-c/arc-progs)
lha214_2	mtsg.ubc.ca (/os2)
clhar103	mtsg.ubc.ca (/os2)
pkz101-2.exe	ftp.cso.uiuc.edu (/zip)
booz.exe	ftp.cso.uiuc.edu (/filutl)

continues overleaf

Table 7.9 – *continued*

Utility/platform	FTP site and file location
Atari/ST platform:	
arc52lb.arc	atari.archive.umich.edu (/atari/archivers)
compress.arc	atari.archive.umich.edu (/atari/archivers)
lharc113.arc	atari.archive.umich.edu (/atari/archivers)
pkunarc.arc	atari.archive.umich.edu (/atari/archivers)
STZIP1.1	atari.archive.umich.edu (/atari/archivers)
shar.arc	atari.archive.umich.edu (/atari/archivers)
esqueeze.arc	atari.archive.umich.edu (/atari/archivers)
sttar.arc	atari.archive.umich.edu (/atari/archivers)
booz.arc	atari.archive.umich.edu (/atari/archivers)

7.4   Common compression topics

This section examines a number of popular data-compression topics, including compression-format problems, tar.Z files, corrupt archives, JPEG and UU-encoded files, and keeping up-to-date with USENET compression forums.

THE 'CHICKEN AND THE EGG' STYLE PROBLEM

Getting hold of the decompression utility you require can be a real nightmare. Sometimes you will find that the utility you require is itself decompressed (the classic 'chicken and egg' problem). For this reason some utilities are left uncompressesd for immediate use as soon as they are downloaded. Tackling the problem of decompresssion is a preventative exercise. Make sure that you have at least half a dozen popular decompression utilities before you even start out–these should include at least: .ARJ, .ARC, .ZIP, .z, .Z (noting the cases of the extension here), .LZH, and .UUE (see Chapters 7 and 8 for more information on UU-encoded files). Clearly, the type of computer you are using will dictate the actual utility that you can employ on a particular file.

FORMAT PROBLEMS

If you are having problems locating a file with a particular compression format, make sure to have a good look around in the same directory for other formats or 'plain' files, that is, files which are not decompressed in any way at all. In the case that a file is compressed into a format which you cannot process (either because the correct utility does not exist, or you know of a tool but not where to acquire it) use a service such as Archie to find all occurrences of the file you require. Archie is discussed in detail in Chapter 4. As a last resort, you can attempt to get hold of the utility you require by mailing a message to the USENET forum `comp.compression` which is commonly used for question and answer sessions on all compression topics. The beauty of the Internet is that someone somewhere is bound to know where to get hold of a particular tool that you need.

`.tar` AND `tar.Z` FILES

Questions about `.tar` and `tar.Z` files frequently appear in the USENET compression forums. `tar` (tape archiver utility) is a utility that originated under Unix many years ago and is a file-backup program allowing files and complete directories to be backed-up to disk or tape. While `tar` is not a compression format in its own right, it is nearly always used with the Unix command compress – mainly because `.tar` files are prime candidates for further compression. Compressing individual files and then processing them with `tar` would be a laborious process; processing a complete `.tar` is much more effective in terms of the compression ratios achieved. You should attempt decompression in order of the filename extension, that is you would first decompress the `.Z` file to produce a `.tar` file, and then unarchive the `.tar` file accordingly. Utilities to handle `.tar` and `.Z` files are widely available for most machine platforms (see the earlier listings).

On the MSDOS platform you can get hold of the tool tarread.exe which is available at the anonymous site `wuarchive.wustl.edu` in the directory `/mirrors/msdos/starter` (as a plain DOS executable). Other utilities are widely available, as previously listed. Under Unix you should have no problem, since `tar` should be a standard command on your system. To de-archive plain `.tar` files on Unix requires a command of the form:

```
$ tar xvf /dev/fp3 /usr/admin↵
```

where the three options xvf tell `tar`: (i) to eXtract the file; (ii) using `tar`s Verbose mode (each filename is shown as it is restored); and (iii) to Force `tar` to restore all files from the media device `/dev/fp3` (a floppy disk for example, although more commonly a tape – check your own documentation to see which device is applicable, or omit this to use a default device). A default disk/tape device will normally be used if the 'f' option is omitted. When tar examines the tape or disk on which the `.tar` file to be restored is kept, it will automatically locate it and start the restoration. The file `/usr/admin` is in fact the name of a directory where all the restored file(s) will be copied into (clearly, you would change this to a directory of your own choice).

The MSDOS user can think of `tar` as being similar to the DOS `RESTORE` command, although `tar` has both a `BACKUP` and `RESTORE` capability built into just one utility, allowing files and complete directory trees to be restored from transportable media to a fixed disk (or tape, etc.). `Tar.Z` files are `.tar` files compressed with the Unix compress command, which is another standard

Unix command coincidentally. On Unix the uncompress utility can be used to decompress the `.Z` file. `.Z` files can be decompressed on Unix using a command of the form:

```
$ uncompress myfile.tar.Z↵
```

where `myfile.tar.Z` is the compressed `.tar` file. When decompressed, the file `myfile.tar.Z` will become `myfile.tar` (noting the omission of the `.Z` extension), and you can use a `tar` command of the form shown below to unarchive the `.tar` file:

```
$ tar -xf myfile.tar↵
```

As you would expect from Unix, there are other ways to process `tar.Z` files. The Unix `zcat` command is useful for displaying the uncompressed contents of `.Z` files. By piping this output into the `tar` command, you can also process such files, for example:

```
$ zcat file.tar.Z | tar xvf -↵
```

And of course, by redirecting the output of `zcat` you could actually decompress a `.Z` file (although not a `tar.Z` file) and keep a copy of it (`zcat` normally only displays the file and does not write it to a file for later processing), for example:

```
$ zcat file.Z > myfile↵
```

A Unix utility called `zmore` also exists on some Unix systems, and has a screen-pausing option (as with the original `more` command). Other users with systems such as MSDOS will have to uncompress their `.Z` file first, and then de-tar the resulting `.tar` file.

TAR-Z files (VMS)

VAX/VMS users may have come across a `.TAR-Z` extension which is baffling them. These files are in the VMS `.tar` format, and were archived by a `tar` command indigenous to a VMS system. Such files should be processed with a utility such as VMSTAR or TAR.EXE (see the earlier file listings for VMS). If you are moving a `.TAR-Z` file to another platform other `.tar` de-archivers, such as `extar10` under MSDOS should work with such `tar` files (try renaming the `.TAR-Z` extension to `.TAR` for non-VMS tools). I have known third-party `tar` de-archivers to work on VMS `tar` files, although this is not guaranteed.

CORRUPT ARCHIVES

When downloading a compressed file from an FTP site always remember to enable binary mode using FTP's `binary` command. If `binary` does not work (as is the case on some VAX FTP servers), use the command `tenex` instead (or even the command `TYPE L 8` – 8-bit transfer is binary, 7-bit is ASCII). File transfers from large machines, such as the VAX machine at the FTP site `wsmr-simtel20.army.mil`, to smaller machines such as a PC can also cause problems because of a difference in transfer modes. Instruct both your host and local machine to use an 8-bit binary mode in all cases (as with the `tenex/binary` commands). Some compressors may also report integrity errors when you actually come to decompress them. Check to see if an integrity checker/fixing utility came with your decompression utility, such as is the case with `PKZIP/PKUNZIP`, which in this case is called `PKZIP-FIX.EXE` and can check and sometimes correct minor integrity errors in `.ZIP` format files, and may allow other `.ZIP` de-archivers to process the file. It goes without saying that it is well worth the effort getting hold of more than one utility to process a particular archive format, and this is especially true in the case where new versions of a compression utility have been released, since incompatibility problems can and do occur.

WHAT DO I DO WITH A .UUE (UU-ENCODED) FILE?

Some files that are transferred over the Internet, especially binary image-files, are compressed using a scheme known as UU-encoding. UU-encoding is not data compression in the real sense, rather it is a form of file-conversion. The UU-encoding process converts a binary file into its ASCII equivalent, in order to allow the file to be posted conveniently via email and USENET (rather than by binary FTP, for example). It is common for some UU-encoded files to produce compressed files which must then be decompressed in the normal way, for example a UU-file may produce a `.ARJ` file which can then be processed under MSDOS by `UNARJ.EXE` etc. You will have to get hold of a UU-decoding utility on your own platform before you can process `.UUE` files, for example `UUDECODE.EXE` for MSDOS. Refer to Chapter 8 for more details on UU-encoding and the tools required for other machine platforms.

A NOTE ON COMPUTER VIRUSES

As a general rule of thumb, all executable files should be checked for viruses before being run on your computer. While the chances of a file being infected are small (the file was most probably checked beforehand at the site from which you acquired it), taking a few minutes to check the file(s) in question is really worth the effort, just in case. When it comes to viruses, prevention is a much better route to take. Many good virus detectors are available for most machines, for example, the Norton AntiVirus and the McAfee systems for DOS. A whole host of freeware and shareware utilities are also available on the Internet via FTP (use Archie with the whatis command using the keyword 'virus'). Be sure to run your virus-detector on executable files only, and not on compressed files; compressed files will be bypassed because their internal format will not be recognizable as an executable program.

As a general rule of thumb you should always try to acquire your files from a reputable source, such as one of the larger FTP archives. Pulling files from public upload areas, where an administrator may not have yet checked files for viruses, is not the best of ideas in the long run.

TIP

Subscribe to the USENET group `comp.virus` for up-to-date information on viruses and anti-viral programs.

JPEG IMAGE COMPRESSION (.JPG FILES)

You may have come across a `.JPG` and wondered what exactly this is. JPEG is, in fact, an image compression standard named after its developers, the Joint Photographic Engineers Group. Many utilities exist to convert JPEG files into `.GIF` images, and to view JPEG files directly. JPEG files are gradually becoming more popular on the Internet since their compression ratio is very high. JPEG works well with dense 24-bit images and is becoming more popular in light of the requirement for higher-quality images. Text compression and image compression are two entirely different matters of course. 'Lossless' compression is a term derived for text and data compression, while 'lossy' compression is a name derived for image and sound files, i.e. binary files.

The majority of JPEG compressions are lossy, since the original image that was compressed cannot be recovered with 100 per cent accuracy. JPEG itself relies on weaknesses in human vision, such as the fact that small areas of colour cannot be distinguished from small light/dark areas. Generally speaking, lossy compression is much more effective than its lossless counterpart.

KEEPING ABREAST OF DEVELOPMENTS VIA USENET

New releases of compression and archiver utilities are constantly released to remove bugs and improve performance. In order to keep abreast of developments subscribe to the USENET group `comp.compression` to hear all the lastest gossip regarding new utilities and version releases. You will find that some of the newer compression utilities will not deal with earlier versions of an archive, so the USENET `comp.compression` forum is essential reading if you experience such problems. Mailing questions to your respective hardware forum on USENET is also a good idea (refer to Appendix G for a list of USENET groups in the `comp.*` hierarchy for such platforms).

8
Manipulating images over the Internet

8.1 Introduction

Computer images are widely available on the Internet and while many remain hidden away on obscure anonymous FTP sites, many hundreds pass over the network daily via USENET (the Internet's public news system – see Chapter 1). This chapter discusses just what images are available and the tools that you will need in order to view them. A wide range of different computing platforms are considered for our discussion, including the PC, Mac, Atari, Amiga, Apple, and Unix systems. In this chapter you will learn:

- The different image formats and encoding schemes that currently exist on the Internet
- What images are available on the USENET system
- The tools that are required to assemble and view images
- How to post your own images to USENET and via email
- Dealing with common image problems
- How to locate image-processing utilities
- Locating FTP image archives

Images are currently found in only two places on the Internet: (i) in the USENET binary newsgroups, for example alt.binaries.pictures.misc; and (ii) via anonymous FTP. USENET is a good place to locate and retrieve images, although it may not always be the most convenient. If you subscribe to a particular newsgroup you may be faced with the problem, depending on your news-reading software, of not being able to control which messages are downloaded; you may have to retrieve dozens of messages, some of which you may not want. Some messages are not even images, of course. On the other hand, many news-reading systems, such as `trn`, allow you to browse through messages picking and saving those which interest you.

A much more convenient way of retrieving images is via the anonymous FTP service. By using FTP you are free to pick and choose the images you require, and indexes are nearly always included for reference purposes. Many hundreds of anonymous FTP archives store image files – you may want to start out by checking out the larger archives such as `wuarchive.wustl.edu`, and the US military site `wsmr-simtel20.army.mil` as a first attempt. Many other smaller sites exist and are documented later on in this chapter.

8.2 Image types – an introduction

A real problem with computer images is the lack of a single format standard. Images come in a variety of types, although the `.GIF` format seems to be the most abundant on the Internet at the time of writing. GIF stands for graphics interchange format, an image format used extensively by the CompuServe system in its quest to develop a device-independent graphics format. In addition to `.GIF` pictures a number of other formats exist. JPEG is a standard for image compression, and was developed by the Joint Photographic Experts Group, hence the name. JPEG is popular because it can compress dense 24 bit images very efficiently. JPEG is really still in the very early stages of development, and has yet to overtake the `.GIF` format in general use, although it is gradually becoming more widely used on the USENET news network.

In addition to static images such as `.GIF` files, a number of image animations formats are also available. Animation files include `.GL`, `.DL`, `.FLI`, `.MPG` and `.AVI` files. All of these files can be very large (200Kb up to 5Mb + is not uncommon) since these files store multiple image 'frames' which are then animated to simulate the effect of movement. The `.MPG` file format was originally devised by the Motion Picture Experts Group (MPEG) and some of these files offer both an audio and visual content. Because of their size, most animation files are nearly always compressed. The PKZIP package for the DOS platform is frequently employed on such files, although other compression formats may also be used, depending on the machine platform being used. You can decompress files on many hardware platforms if you know which software to get hold of, and decompressing between different machine platforms is quite possible. Bear in mind the device-independent images e.g. the `.GIF` format, which can be viewed on virtually any platform given a suitable VDU. Table 8.1 illustrates the most common image types. Those image formats marked with an asterisk (*) are currently the most popular on the network.

The various utilities to process most of the above files are discussed in Section 8.5.

Table 8.1   The main image formats in existence

Type	Image format and comments
.AVI*	Audio visual interleave
.BMP	IBM BitMaP picture file
.DL	Animated picture file
.FLI	Animated picture file
.GIF*	Graphics interchange format
.GL*	Animated picture file; large files
.IFF	Amiga interchangeable file format. May convert to a ILBM (InterLeaved BitMap); HAM (Holf-And-Modify); DHAM (DynaHAM) or a SHAM (Sliced HAM)
.IM8	Sun raster image
.IMG	IMaGe file (could be a GEM picture also)
.JPG*	JPEG image file. May be viewed or converted to other image-types, e.g. GIF
.MAC	Macintosh MacPaint picture file (monochrome)
.PCX	IBM PC Paintbrush file
.PICT	Macintosh QuickDraw PICTure file
.RAW	RGB – 24-bit picture file
.SAM	Animated picture file
.TGA	TrueVision TarGA file picture file
.TIF(F)	Tagged Image Format File – 24-bit image
.UUE*	UU-encoded file – ASCII encoded image file
.WPG	WordPerfect graphics file (bitmapped) (use graphcnv.exe with WP to convert)
.XBM	X-Windows bit map – Unix/X windows picture file

WHAT TOOLS WILL I NEED?

If you are seriously interested in image retrieval you will have to get hold of some basic tools before you start. Essential tools (on any machine platform) include:

- An ASCII word processor. Make sure it can handle large ASCII files
- A UU-decoding utility (an ASCII → binary file decoder)
- An image viewer (.GIF format is essential, others also useful such as .PCX)
- File decompressors. Images are large and are normally stored in compressed form. Many compression formats exist and you are directed to Chapter 7 for more information on the different compression formats that are available

Other tools to consider getting hold of in the future include:

- A .JPG to .GIF convertor. JPEG files are becoming more and more common on the Internet. A .JPG viewer will save you having to convert

.JPGs to .GIFs in order to view the compressed image. Example: ColorView for DOS (PC)
- A posting utility (to send your own images). Email will suffice in most cases, although some 'smart' posters are now available, for example SplitUUE or XmitBin for the Apple platform (see Chapters 2 and 11 for USENET and email, respectively)
- Conversion tools (to convert between image formats). Refer to later sections for lists of these. Example: Graphics Workshop for DOS (PC) is a good choice; many many others exist

---

TIP

JPEG (.JPG) files are compressed using a quality factor ranging from 1–100, 55 being the common default. When sending or receiving .JPG files aim for 55 and above as the image threshold level; below this, image quality gets much worse.

In order to locate the tools mentioned above you can use the Archie service (see Chapter 4), or you can simply read on to the relevant section later in this chapter. If you are new to the network and want to get the most useful tools without any further ado, follow the FTP session below to get the tools you will require (note that some sources may be moved or may no longer exist in which case you will have to use Archie to find the program required, and then FTP it – see Chapter 3 for more details). The example FTP sessions below are given for MSDOS platforms; users of other machine platforms should read the appropriate sections for utilities that are available (noting that the FTP commands will be the same although the FTP hostnames and filenames will clearly be different).

FTP session – Commands to download some common image tools (GWS, UUDECODE and JPG2GIF/GIF2JPG)

```
your-prompt> ftp wuarchive.wustl.edu↵
...
Connected to wuarchive.wustl.edu
220 wuarchive.wustl.edu FTP server (SunOS 4.0) ready.
Name (wuarchive.wustl.edu): anonymous↵
331 Guest login ok, send mail name as password.
Password: <your mail-name>↵
230 Guest login ok, access restrictions apply.
ftp> binary↵
ftp> prompt↵
ftp> cd /msdos/graphics↵
```

```
250 CWD command successful.
ftp> mget grfwk*.zip↵
... etc ...
ftp> close↵
220 Goodbye.
ftp> open oak.oakland.edu↵
Connected to oak.oakland.edu
220 oak.oakland.edu FTP server (SunOS 4.1) ready.
Name (oak.oakland.edu): anonymous↵
331 Guest login ok, send mail name as password.
Password: <your mail-name>↵
230 Guest login ok, access restrictions apply.
ftp> cd /pub/msdos/filutl↵
ftp> prompt↵
ftp> binary↵
ftp> mget uuexe*.zip↵
... etc ...
ftp> close↵
220 Goodbye.
ftp> open msdos.archive.umich.edu↵
Connected to msdos.archive.umich.edu
220 msdos.archive.umich.edu FTP server (SunOS 5.0) ready.
Name (msdos.archive.umich.edu): anonymous↵
331 Guest login ok, send mail name as password.
Password: <your mail-name>↵
230 Guest login ok, access restrictions apply.
ftp> cd /msdos/graphics/gif↵
ftp> binary↵
ftp> prompt↵
ftp> get gif2jpg*.zip↵
... etc ...
ftp> quit↵
your-prompt>
```

Three FTP sessions are conducted in the above session (refer to Chapter 3 if you require more information on FTP). The first session downloads the Graphics Workshop program – this has file viewing and conversion facilities for a wide range of image formats, e.g. .GIF, .PCX, etc. No JPEG support is available in the current version of GWS (the JPEG format is popular on the network for sending compressed .GIF images) so we log in to another site to get hold of the GIF2JPG (this does to/from conversions). A uu-decoder will be essential in order to process USENET images so we also have grabbed the UUDECODER (and encoder) from another FTP site. When you finally come to process these files you will need to get an UNZIP utility, such as PKUNZIP (refer to Chapter 7 on file-compression utilities and get hold of a file to do this – note that you should get a plain executable because at this stage we assume you do not have a decompressor (some executables are self-decompressing so that when you run then they will unarchive themselves)).

The close commands allow you to close a connection without exiting the FTP program (quicker than restarting it again with the next host), while the prompt command turns off the mget commands prompt for downloading a file, i.e. all files with the wildcarded name are downloaded (we have done this since more than one file may be available, and may even be required for the software to function). The binary command must be issued if you are downloading compressed files (.ZIP archives in this case). Note that once the binary and prompt commands have been entered you need not normally retype them; we have done this to simply be more verbose and to remind you of the commands (check your FTP program to see if binary and/or prompt commands need to be reissued when contacting multiple hosts).

TIP

Download your files into a separate directory so that you know what has been downloaded from the host. Do this by using the lcd command (if available on your FTP program, or by changing diectory first, i.e. before you invoke the FTP program). Chapter 3 examines FTP in more detail.

Each file, when downloaded, will then have to be decompressed. For example the file GIF2JPG.ZIP could be unzipped with the DOS command (assuming you are using the PKUNZIP.EXE program)

```
C:\> PKUNZIP GIF2JPG.ZIP↵
... file(s) are then unzipped ...
```

which will leave you with the files JPG2GIF.EXE and GI2JPG.EXE. Note that .ZIP files are archives, so more than one file may be decompressed in the process. System documentation is nearly always provided in a README.TXT file, so be sure to read about any instuctions. Remember too, that shareware programs require payment to the author if found useful; keep shareware alive and pay the small registration fee on all the utilities you use.

TIPS

.ZIP archives can be deleted once you have extracted the files you require. You may want to make a backup first though, just in case you lose the files in the future.

Computer viruses are a reality; make sure you check all executables (`.EXE/`
`.COM/.SYS` on MSDOS) before running a program. Remember to check self-
extracting executables also; checking compressed files will be useless since they
are in a archived format.

8.3 What images are available on USENET?

All tastes are catered for in the image newsgroups. Images are placed in a
hierarchy of the ALTernative USENET newsgroups (see Chapter 2) all of
which contain the word 'binaries' which indicates the nature of the files
content. At the time of writing the most popular USENET image forums are
as follows:

- `alt.binaries.pictures.fractals` (ABP) Miscellaneous pictures and discussion forum.
- `alt.binaries.pictures.fractals` (ABPF) A newsgroup which
  is posted chaos-related images, in this case fractal pictures. You may also
  want to check out `alt.fractals.pictures` in addition to ABPF.
- `alt.binaries.pictures.misc` (ABPM) This newsgroup takes the
  overspill for all the remaining image types (an image miscellany). The group
  `alt.binaries.pictures.d` is a discussion group for this newsgroup.
- `alt.binaries.pictures.erotica` (ABPE) A newsgroup for
  erotic pictures only. A strictly adult newsgroup which is posted a variety
  of adult images. The discussion group for this forum is called
  `alt.binaries.pictures.erotica.d`.
- `alt.binaries.pictures.erotica.female` (ABPEF) An extension of ABPE. This contains adult images of the female gender.
- `alt.binaries.pictures.erotica.male` (ABPEM) An extension of ABPE. This contains adult images of the male gender.
- `alt.binaries.pictures.erotica.blondes` (ABPEM) Another
  extension of ABPE. This contains adult images of the blonde female gender,
  I think.
- `alt.binaries.pictures.tasteless` (ABPT) A newsgroup, as
  the name indicates, for tasteless material. You will find very bizarre images
  posted in this newsgroup (you have been warned).
- `alt.binaries.pictures.fine-art.graphics` (ABPFG) A newsgroup for computer-generated imagery. This consists of original artwork by
  humans using computer imaging programs.
- `alt.binaries.pictures.fine-art.digitized` (ABFD) This
  newsgroup contains original scanned images. Similar to
  `alt.binaries.fine-art.graphics` in this respect. The group
  `alt.binaries.pictures.fine-art.d` is for the discussion of
  most images in ABFD.

- `alt.binaries.pictures.utilities` (ABPU)   A newsgroup that is posted mainly binary programs (executables) for image-related software manipulation. Also posted source code. `Comp.sources.misc` is another good repository for image-utility source code, etc.
- `alt.toon-pics` (ATP)   This newsgroup is posted cartoon pictures once in a while.

Many lesser-known image newsgroups also exist on USENET, and these are normally prefixed with their country of origin, e.g. `de.` for Germany. In addition, many local newsgroups which are not in the mainstream USENET system also carry images. As well as the binary repositories, a number of discussion forums exist which supplement these with technical information. All such discussion forums have the extension `.d`. You may also want to check out the non-binary image forums: `comp.graphics` discusses the actual image formats, while `alt.graphics.pixutils` discusses image-format conversions, utilities, etc. (all good stuff).

8.4   Downloading and processing images – UU-decoding

Images may be retrieved by standard email and news-reading software, or by direct downloading from an anonymous FTP site. Taking email/USENET into consideration, we run in to an immediate problem in that both of these systems deal solely in ASCII, or 'plain-text' messages. You will therefore find that images passed via email or USENET are always converted into ASCII prior to transmission using a scheme known as UU-encoding.

UU-encoding is carried out at source by a tool called UUENCODE (although other encoders – with other names in many instances – also exist). For purposes of simplicity we will refer to UUENCODE and UUDECODE which are the names of the systems found most commonly on the Unix and MSDOS platforms. Both the UUENCODE utility and its counterpart UUDECODE are in fact separate utilities which were originally supplied with the Unix operating system, and they form part of the Unix UUCP (Unix-to-Unix Copy Program) suite of utilities. Versions of UUENCODE exist for nearly all computing platforms including the PC, Mac, Amiga, and Atari machines. UUENCODE is a very clever piece of software in that it converts binary files into their ASCII equivalents, thus allowing them to be transmitted over the Internet via the standard email and USENET services. Processing a UU-encoded image that you receive will depend on the decoding utilities you have access to. The basic UU-encoding scheme breaks up groups of three 8 bit characters (totalling 24 bits) into four 6 bit characters, and then adding an ASCII code 32 (a single space) to each 6 bit character, which in turn maps it onto the character that is finally transmitted (which itself is part of the UU-encoded file). Phew! In the UU-encoding scheme the following characters are used for transmission purposes:

`012356789:;<=>?@ABCDEFGHIJKLMNOPQRSTUVWXYZ[\]^_`!"#$%&'()*+,-./`

You will see many hundreds of lines using these characters in a typical UU-encoded file. Spaces (ASCII 32) can be a real problem, since some transmission systems compress text by removing the spaces. For this reason, spaces are sometimes converted into a grave-accent (`-ASCII 96) by some systems. Nearly all UU-decoders can overcome spaces in files, however, so don't worry about them. Finally, there is an encoding scheme called XX-encoding. XX-encoding is a newer, but less popular method of encoding. It uses a transmission character-set consisting of just the characters:

`0123456789ABCDEFGHIJKLMNOPQRSTUVWXYZabcdefghijklmnopqrstuvwxyz+-`

Some people prefer XX-encoding because the characters are less complex, and are less prone to corruption. Many of the characters used in the UU-encoding method may not get past an EBCDIC to ASCII translation without corruption (EBCDIC is an encoding scheme for characters used on larger mainframe computers, such as IBM mainframes). Some UU-encoding utilities can use both the XX and UU-encoding methods, e.g. the popular UU-encoder by Richard Marks.

FILE SIZES AND MESSAGE SEGMENTATION

Computer images, especially colour images, are always very large in size (100–300K is not uncommon for a `.GIF` file) and many mail-gateways on the Internet restrict the size of individual files that they can process – commonly down to a size of 64Kb (65 535 bytes). For this reason images on USENET commonly arrive as a series of segments. You will clearly have to obtain all the segments of a particular file to complete the entire image (images do sometimes arrive in one segment, although these are normally of a lower-quality, e.g. monochrome images which require less space because of the absence of colour).

TIP

Examine the subject: line for details on the message, i.e. to see whether or not it is an image. When looking at multiple image segments make sure that all segments are available first, i.e. don't download anything until you know all of the image is available!

Decent JPEG files can be transmitted in just a single segment, although in general, the quality will not be much to rave about unless the JPEG is pretty substantial, i.e. more than 50K in size. JPEG images are compressd with an image-quality factor on a scale from 0 to 100, 55 being a common default. If you are downloading JPEGs via FTP, look for files around the 50K size if you want full 640 × 480 VGA resolutions – such files convert to .GIF files of around 200K+ in length. USENET mail-reading software will tell you how many lines a posting consists of, so avoid files with less than 1000 lines if quality is your main consideration. The smaller JPEGs commonly decode into images consisting of 320 × 300 pixels, which is roughly a quarter of a standard VGA screen, so avoid these if you require a full-screen image.

DECODING A UU-ENCODED FILE

The basic steps in reassembling a UU-encoded file are not rigidly defined, although some properly ordered steps must always be undertaken. The eventual method you undertake will depend on the UU-decoding utilities you have access to. Bear in mind the following points:

- You may have to manually edit the UU-files with an ASCII editor and then feed these to your UUDECODE utility. This is the manual method, and is always useful to learn.
- Utilities exist to make decoding simpler, normally to a single phase. Examples include later versions of news-readers such as nn and rn which extract the relevant UU-text by stripping any header information and constructing one large file from all segments, and then processing these accordingly.

MANUALLY ASSEMBLING A UU-ENCODED FILE

The manual editing of a UU-encoded file is basically a four-stage process and requires that you have access to an ASCII word processor with cut-and-paste facilities and/or the ability to concatenate files at the operating system level. A suitable UU-decoding utility will also be required:

- Save each UU-encoded mail-message or news-message into a separate ASCII file. Name the file sensibly, e.g. PT1OF4 for image-part 1 of 4 so that it can be be referred to easily. Newsreading tools such as nn have an option to save a message to an ASCII file (option s in this case). UU-segments are given a tag indicating the image-part they represent, e.g. part one of a four part image is tagged with '1/4', etc. Tags may be listed in Subject: fields, or in the message-body itself.
- Edit each file you have previously stored to strip out mail-message headers to leave just the UU-text.
- Join (concatenate) together each of the files so that they form one large file. Name this appropriately, e.g. MYIMAGE.UUE (the .UUE extension is

commonly used, and may be required by your UUDECODE utility). Ensure that all pieces are joined together correctly and that there are no blank lines.

- Feed this file to your UUDECODE utility to produce the resulting image. The resulting file that is created may be a .GIF, but it may also be a compressed file. Compressed files are commonly UU-encoded first in order to reduce transmission times. Depending on the resulting file that is produced, you may have to get hold of a utility to process that file further. For example a UU-decoder may produce a file called IMAGE.ZIP which is a PKZIP compressed archive, and requires PKUNZIP to decompress and produce the final image. Refer to Chapter 7 for more information on compression formats and utilities.

The structure of a UU-encoded file consists of a header, the actual ASCII image-data, and then a footer, for example:

```
... mail header etc ...
----- CUT HERE ------------------------------------------
begin 640 image.gif
M1TE&.#==A=A=A=A=A< `"".?CefcM.8B""M%)Z.;9Y107E=4?.>>44T+..2;7T@+!`,&+9U42`@`**&;8:""9=.2:4E%.)YI
M<:)E46DDDD)Y;>=Y78)11<]Y7;YQ7?.FCEUM8::>DA`("+J&84TP),>2<7EA
M@K9=36U)05DKKK#(%TL,-M59)=13!-.,]151:9M4:)=1>=]:<=I5;YU8>]U
M69:6CM=U5:YM7:XP/$$SZHH((??>8>O,*9;Z""8>**9;Z`<&-.:@L-M4M9M59(D,!@4$*8H
M-+II400,28:&?7%=1>,H.)!16TX4,HP3<L.Ll+:.<7u)/*8P.#0<),-=3?<X
M2;XL.&$\.,LTL6%-/"$X,#0T40P8&."`F>7EYY4Tp*+Y]7>`""?5$$X,*2>AC`D
M(+JFFI)E31R""9=>*9,*"";;YYY78YZ>YETl3>.><=+];8II54TP,..FAETP*,,MY
... etc ...
`
end
----- CUT HERE ------------------------------------------ 2/4 ---
...
```

The line starting with begin is a keyword telling UUDECODE that the UU-encoded text begins on the next line, and end signifies the end of this segment of image-text. UUDECODE must find these keywords if it is to process your file correctly. The string 640 is used on Unix systems, and is an octal permission code for the current file (this will have no relevance whatsoever once it is posted to a non-Unix machine – DOS for example, has no in-built security features unlike Unix), and the octal code may be zero (0) or even null, i.e. empty. The filename image.gif is the name of the binary image file which is to be created when your decoder extracts the data from the UU-file. In the majority of cases this filename will be a ready-to-use image file, most of which are .GIFs (graphics interchange files). .GIF images are ubiquitous on the

Internet, although bear in mind that many other image formats and even compressed files may be UU-encoded.

To ensure that you are prepared for all eventualities a list of image formats and utilities to process these are discussed later in this chapter. You may have noticed the CUT HERE comments in the UU-encoded file shown earlier. As these lines suggest, they tell the user which parts of the file to cut away and save (for manual extraction purposes mainly – UU-decoders go mostly by the begin and end lines). Never include such lines in with your file when actually decoding, or your decoder will display an error message and halt itself. You should also be aware that some UU-encoded files come with all manner of comments and other material for extraction purposes. Such information is ignored by the smarter UUDECODE systems. In the example UU-encoded file shown previously the image segment number has been labelled 2/4 (part two of four); this segment number will probably be reproduced elsewhere such as in the mail header (principally in the Subject: line). Figure 8.1 illustrates the steps involved in the manual editing of a UU-encoded file.

Another way of manually assembling a UU-encoded file is to use file concatenation techniques. For this method you will still need an ASCII editor, although no cut-and-paste operations of any description will be required. Under DOS a command of the form:

```
C:\> copy file1.uue + file2.uue + file3.uue myfile.uue↵
```

will yield a file called myfile.uue which contains the files file1.uue, file2.uue and file3.uue all joined (concatenated) together. Under Unix you would use a similar command of the form

```
$ cat file1.uue file2.uue file3.uue > myfile.uue↵
```

where cat is the name of the Unix file-concatenation utility, and > is Unix's output redirection symbol which stores all of the UU-encoded segments into just a single file. In both of the methods shown, ensure that all of the mail-headers and comments have first been stripped from the UU-encoded segment(s), and that each file has a carriage return after its last line, otherwise the last line of each file will be concatenated into the first line of the next segment, thus causing a line-length error. Smart UU-decoders exist which ignore all comments and mail headers, and these are discussed in the next section.

'SMART' UTILITIES AND NEWSREADERS

Manual decoding can be a real pain because of all the steps involved. Some newsreading software has a UU-extraction facility which automates all of the steps normally required in manual decoding. Newsreaders with

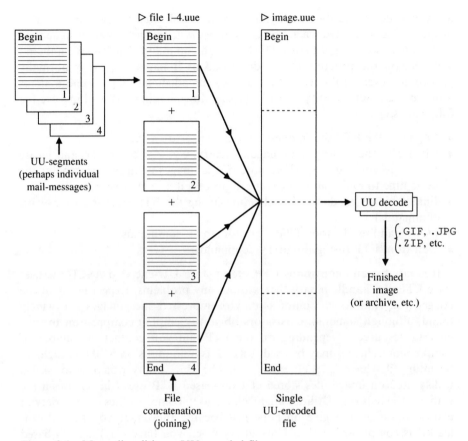

Figure 8.1 Manually editing a UU-encoded file

such a capability include the later versions of nn, rn, unc, and trn (see Chapter 2 for a discussion of nn and rn). With these systems you flag the entries that interest you, and the software sorts through each, stripping the mail and news-headers, and then orders the UU-text using the messages segment label. The file is finally converted into the resulting image file (or compressed file).

8.5 Downloading images from FTP archives

FTP archives store a variety of images which can be downloaded. It is important to remember that both raw and compressed images are binary files (not ASCII files, like their UU-encoded counterparts). You must therefore enable binary mode using FTP's binary or tenex command, and only then attempt to download the file. If you forget to enable binary mode the resulting image will be corrupted when you come to view it. Images can take some time to download so get used to using FTP's hash command. The hash command will tell you the progress of the download as it happens (a # is normally printed for every 1024 bytes that are downloaded, although some systems differ in the exact quantity used). A typical downloading task will involve the following steps:

- Log in to the FTP site in question, e.g. ftp.uu.net.
- Change to the appropriate image directory, e.g. /pub/image and locate the image you require (taking note of the images compression type at the same time to make sure that you can process it at a later stage).
- Enable binary mode for downloading (using the FTP binary or tenex commands).
- Download the file using FTP's get or mget commands.
- Quit from FTP (using the quit command).

It is rare for an anonymous FTP site to store UU-encoded ASCII pictures since FTP can handle binary files without any problems. Expect many of the images you find to be compressed. Uncompressed files images are widely found, although some administrators obviously employ compression to save on disk resources. Depending on the FTP site you contact, a number of compression schemes may be used. PKZIP is ubiquitous on MSDOS archives (resulting files have a .ZIP extension). The Unix utility compress is also widely used on image files stored at Unix-based FTP sites (this creates a file with a .Z extension). Utilities are available to uncompress files on a variety of platforms, so do not give up hope just because the image you have downloaded is compressed with a Unix utility when you have (say) a DOS-based machine. Refer to Chapter 7 for more information on compression utilities. Illustrated below is a typical FTP session to download the image named image.zip from the anonymous FTP site ftp.uu.net:

```
$ ftp ftp.uu.net↵
Trying 137.39.1.9 ....
Connected to ftp.uu.net
220 ftp.uu.net FTP server (SunOS 4.0) ready.
Name (ftp.uu.net): anonymous↵
331 Guest login ok, send mail name as password.
Password: <your mail-name>↵
230 Guest login ok, access restrictions apply.
ftp> binary↵
ftp> hash↵
ftp> cd /pub/msdos/images↵
250 CWD command successful.
```

```
ftp> get image.zip↵
230 Opening binary connection for image.zip (66,987 bytes)
###################################################
######
ftp> quit↵
```

The file `image.zip` can now be processed. From the `.ZIP` extension we can see that we will need to get hold of the decompression utility `PKUNZIP.EXE` (I am assuming a DOS platform is being used in the example). If you are on a Unix platform another `.ZIP` file decompressor will be required (refer to Chapter 7). Decompression of the file can then take place as illustrated in the following example.

```
C:\> PKUNZIP IMAGE.ZIP↵
PKUNZIP (R) FAST! Extract Utility Version 1.1 03-15-90
Copr. 1989-1990 PKWARE Inc. All Rights Reserved. PKUNZIP/h
for help PKUNZIP Reg. U.S. Pat. and Tm. Off.
Searching ZIP: IMAGE.ZIP
Exploding: IMAGE.GIF ....
C:\>
```

Bear in mind also that some images may be compressed more than once, and you will have to decode them in the order that they were originally compressed – starting with the rightmost filename extension and working your way left. An example of this has already been mentioned, namely a UU-encoded file that produces a `.JPG` or `.ZIP` file. While `.JPG` files can be viewed with a special viewing and/or decompression utilities (`CVIEW.EXE` is a very good shareware example under MSDOS) most of the time you will have to uncompress such images first in order to produce a viewable image such as a `.GIF` file. Graphic animation files (`.GL`, `.DL`, `.FLI`, etc.) are nearly always compressed when posted, for example a UU-encoded file may produce a `.ZIP` or `.ARJ` archive, etc. Figure 8.2 illustrates some typical compression sequences that are employed on image files and the steps required to decode and view each image type.

TYPES OF IMAGES AVAILABLE VIA FTP

Images for on just about every taste exist. Clip-art is widely available on all subject areas (people, places, sci-fi, etc.) and much more in the form of computer-generated imagery is also available. Special-interest imagery is also available in copious quantities: astronomical imagery (planets, universes, red-shifts) can be found, as can scientific images, e.g. X-rays, NMR scans, and even DNA sequences. Weather maps and satellite scans are also found in

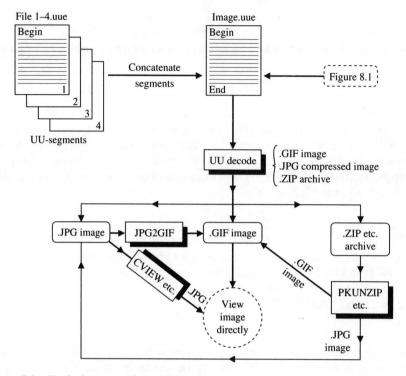

Figure 8.2   Typical compression sequences

abundance. The vast majority of images arrive in the `.GIF` format, so be sure
to have a GIF viewer. Also, be sure to download images in binary mode when
using FTP (this does, of course, apply to compressed files as well).

Controversial images

Much attention has recently been placed on the adult imagery that is available via the Internet. Although actively discouraged on the Internet by most
network providers and academic institutions (although not by the majority
of users I suspect), such material is still widely available for public access
via the erotica USENET feeds–notably those carried in the
`alt.binaries.*` hierarchy). Interesting questions arise for those countries with less stringent controls on adult material, such as Denmark, which
has absolutely no censorship on such material, since they can send in
network traffic directly into USENET via news-feeds propagated from one
site to another. Site administrators could quite easily stop news-feeds to
specified newsgroups although access to this material is now known to be
one of the most popular acivities on the network, and it guarantees more

network subscriptions. The erotica newsgroups cause gigantic increases in bandwidth on portions of the network, such are the size of the images and the time taken to download and process them. Banning access to such images is of course impossible, since the user can telnet through to another news-server that carries the groups required. USENET is not the only carrier for such material, however.

Public upload areas on FTP sites also give rise to increasing numbers of adult erotica material and such areas can be found very easily with powerful Internet tools such as Archie. Even without Archie all Unix users will know of standard directory areas such as /tmp where files can be casually uploaded. System administrators have a hard time monitoring and controlling just what material is uploaded, and of course a filename does not always tell you its contents. Uploading files by mutual agreement cannot be stamped out entirely. Some files arrive on the network in an encrypted format so that only a mutual password will decipher the file. Then of course there are the ubiquitous bulletin board systems (BBSs) that run on stand-alone computers. Complete organizations now run bulletin board systems, and a regular list is posted to the USENET hierarchy alt.bbs.*, some of which are accessible directly via the Internet. Others are run via systems such as UUCP and join up to the Internet indirectly for only short periods of time.

8.6   Image utility sources – anonymous FTP sites

This section explores the main archives where tools and utilities can be downloaded for your own use. The Archie service (see Chapter 4) is the most efficient method of searching for image compression and viewing tools. You may want to use the Archie whatis command along with keywords such as 'compress', 'image', etc. for such purposes; these particular Archie keywords will yield a series of utilities that can be used on many computing platforms. Table 8.2 illustrates the main and well established anonymous FTP sites that

Table 8.2   Some anonymous FTP sites for image software

FTP site name	Directories to look for
bongo.cc.utexas.edu	/uutools, /apple, /ibmpc, /mac, /amiga, /xwindows, /sunview.
export.lcs.mit.edu	Mostly in the /contrib directory.
garbo.uwasa.fi	/pc, /Unix, /win3
hobbes.nmsu.edu	Subdirs of /pub, e.g. /pub/os2.
oak.oakland.edu	Mostly in directory /pub/msdos.
wsmr-simtel-20.army.mil	Mostly in directory /msdos, etc.
wuarchive.wustl.edu	Many: /usenet, /graphics/packages, /msdos, /mirrors/msdos, etc.

house image-related software.

A number of common computer platforms are now considered in turn. Each type of tool is then taken in turn, namely:

- UU-encoding and decoding utilities
- JPEG compression tools
- Image conversion tools
- Compression utilities
- Image viewing utilities
- Animation utilities

TIP

Images and image utilities may be compressed. In order to find out which decompression utilities to get hold of, read Chapter 7 on file compression.

PERSONAL COMPUTERS (DOS)

UU-encoders

The UUENCODE/UUDECODE programs written by Richard Marks are available by FTP from ftp.cica.indiana.edu in the directory /pub/pc/win31/util. These support XX-encoding/decoding as well. A smart UU-decoder called UUEXE (also by Richard Marks) is available from oak.oakland.edu in the public directory named /pub/msdos/filutl as uuexe*.zip, and also at the anonymous FTP site garbo.uwasa.fi in /pc/decode. The larger anonymous FTP sites such as wsmr-simtel-20.army.mil and wuarchive.wustl.edu also have UUEXE. The UUEXE system will strip out mail-headers, etc. and place all UU-segments in the correct order to extract the resulting image. UUEXE is also posted to the binary USENET newsgroup comp.binaries.ibm.pc normally at the beginning of each calendar month. Another similar utility called UUXFER for DOS is available from bongo.cc.utexas.edu in the directory /uutools, or from site oak.oakland.edu in the directory called /pub/msdos/filutl as the .ZIP archive uuxfer.zip.

JPEG compression tools

Two well-known utilities are available for DOS called JPG2GIF.EXE and GIF2JPG.EXE which convert to and from .GIF images respectively. This tool is available from Handmade Software at the FTP site msdos.archive.umich.edu in /msdos/graphics/gif as the file gif2jpg5.zip (and also at the FTP archive wuarchive.wustl.edu. Other DOS-based executable utilities can be obtained from the FTP archives wuarchive.wustl.edu, and wsmr-simtel-20.army.mil in the directory /msdos/graphics/jpeg, and finally on ftp.pitt.edu in directory /users/qralston/jpeg, all stored as .ZIP archives.

JPEG3 is yet another DOS utility for JPEG to GIF image conversions. It is available from wuarchive.wustl.edu in the public directory area called /mirrors/msdos/qraphics as JPEG3.ZIP. Additional files on this site that you may want to get hold of are JPEG3386.ZIP and JPEG3S.ZIP. The anonymous FTP site oak.oakland.edu also has a copy of JPEG3.ZIP.

Image conversion utilities

The PBMPlus toolkit (by Jeff Poskanzer) is available from the FTP site garbo.uwasa.fi in directory /pc/graphics/pbmplus.zoo. It can also be downloaded from the FTP site wuarchive.wustl.edu in the directory called /usenet/comp.binaries.ibm.pc/volume15/ pbmplus. PBMPlus is used widely as a means of converting between different image formats, and has many special effects that can be applied to images.

Another software system called the UtahRaster Tools is also available, and is similar in operation to PBMPlus. The UtahRaster toolset is available from the AFTP site wuarchive.wustl.edu in /graphics/ graphics/packages/urt as urt-*.tar.Z (as a Unix compressed file). A very well-known system which has many features is called Graphics WorkShop (GWS) by Alchemy Mindworks. This excellent shareware program has dozens of special-effect facilities and conversion capabilities (MAC images included), and runs both under Windows and DOS (as two separate applications). GWS can be found on the AFTP site wuarchive.wustl.edu and wsmr-simtel-20.army.mil in the directory called /msdos/ graphics as the files grfwk*.ZIP (DOS version). The anonymous FTP site ftp.cica.indiana.edu has a Windows version of GWS in the directory /ftp/pub/pc/win/win3/desktop as the files gwswin*.ZIP. One particularly nice feature of GWS is its ability to create 'self-displaying' static images, i.e. a .GIF file can have the necessary code to view it built into an .EXE (executable) file along with the image itself.

The site pascal.math.fu-berlin.de (see: /local/pd-soft/ pc/imgsoft) has copies of GWS as well; see the files gws_*.zip. GWS supports many Super-VGA cards for 256 colour images. Alchemy Mindworks also produce the 'Image Alchemy' software, which offers picture conversion between GIF and JPEG, among many others (GWS does not have JPEG conversion, so this could be quite a useful piece of software).

IMDISP is another image-processing utility that has good Super-VGA support. Like GWS it has a number of features for enhancing images. Image support is also a good feature of this utility, since it supports the image formats: FITS, PDS and GIF. Integer binary images are also supported (1–32 bit). IMDISP is available as public domain software from the AFTP site oak.oakland.edu in the directory /pub/msdos/graphics as the file imdisp*.ZIP.

  PaintShop Pro (PSP) is yet another largish utility that has viewing and conversion facilities. It supports many image types including TGA, BMP, GIF and PCX. This shareware product runs under Windows and can be obtained from ftp.cica.indiana.edu in the directory /ftp/pub/pc/win3/ desktop as psp*.ZIP. The larger sites such as wuarchive.wustl.edu also have PSP (see the directory /pub/pc/msdos/win3/pspro101.ZIP). Smaller utilities include GDS which allows for general conversion and the construction of contact-sheet images with pan/zoom capability. GDS can be found on wuarchive.wustl.edu and the site wsmr-simtel-20.army.mil in the directory /msdos/gif/gds*.zip.

Compression utilities

The Unix compress utility is used extensively on the Internet (DOS machines can decompress the .Z files it creates using a suitable utility). You may want to get hold of the files comp*d.ZIP at the anonymous FTP sites wuarchive.wustl.edu or wsmr-simtel-20.army.mil, in the directories called /msdos/sq-usq. PKUNZIPs .ZIP files are ubiquitous on the Internet, so you should get hold of PKUNZIP as a matter of urgency. The larger anonymous FTP sites wuarchive.wustl.edu and wsmr-simtel-20.army.mil also have this utility stored in the directory /msdos/sq-usq/pkunzip*.

Image viewing utilities

Many image conversion tools will also display images, although there are dedicated utilities for viewing images as well. CompuShow for DOS is a good utility to view images from the DOS, Mac (MacPaint), and AMIGA (IFF) machines. FTP this from the site wuarchive.wustl.edu in the directory called /pub/msdos/graphics/gif as cshw*.ZIP, or from bongo.cc.utexas.edu in the directory /ibmpc as cshw*.ZIP. The Finnish archive nic.funet.fi also has CompuShow in the directory /pub/msdos/graphics/gif also as cshw*.ZIP.

  ShowGIF is a viewer, which as the name suggests, displays GIF images. The unusual feature about this program is that it can do this as a file is actually being downloaded. It is available from the anonymous FTP site wsmr-simtel-20.army.mil in /msdos/gif as showgif.ARC. See also ShowBMP under OS/2. A utility called VPIC supports many images and has a few in-built image-effect routines. VPIC can be downloaded from `nic.funet.fi` in the directory `/pub/msdos/graphics/gif` as `vpic*.ZIP`, and from the site `rigel.acs.oakland.edu` in `/pub/ msdos/gif` also as `vpic*.ZIP`. The larger archives have this utility also. WinGIF is a image-viewer that runs under Windows 3.x. It is available from `wuarchive.wustl.edu` in `/msdos/windows3` as the files `wingif*.ZIP`, and from `garbo.uwasa.fi` in the directory named `/win3/gifutil` as `wingif14.ZIP`.

VUIMG is a GIF and TIFF image viewer. You can obtain a copy from the site `wuarchive.wustl.edu` in `/mirrors/msdos/gif` as `vuimg*.ZIP`. Site `ftp.uu.net` (a mirror for simtel 20) also has a copy in the directory called `/systems/ibmpc/msdos/simtel20/gif` also as `vuimg*.ZIP`, as has `garbo.uwasa.fi` in the directory `/pc/gifutil`, again as `vuimg*.ZIP`. Finally, I think a mention of the excellent Naked Eye program should be forthcoming. Naked Eye is a Super-VGA GIF viewer which has all manner of special-effect features built in. It will also play `.VOC` sound files (with SoundBlaster sound support built in), and it supports image modes of 800×600, 640×480 and 1024×768 – you can switch between modes while viewing an image. Naked Eye's autoload facility allows images to be shown in a slide-show manner. Mouse and keyboard support is also provided. Naked Eye is available from the FTP archive `wuarchive.wustl.edu` in `/mirrors4/garbo.uwasa.fi/gifutil` as the file `naked110.zip` (version 1.10 was out at the time of writing).

As you would imagine, there are many other excellent GIF viewers out there. GIFDesk is one notable example, which I cannot find on the net; it allows multiple `.GIF`s to be shown on one screen (and blown-up in full 640×40 VGA, etc.). Ask around for it, or use Archie with the keyword 'gifdesk'.

JPEG viewers are becoming ever more abundant. `ColorView` is a JPEG (and `.GIF`) viewing utility both for DOS and Windows, and should be part of any image-enthusiasts toolbox. It can be obtained from the anonymous FTP site `wuarchive.wustl.edu` in the directory `/mirrors/win3/util/ CVIEW*.ZIP`, or `win3/desktop/CVIEW*.ZIP`. The DOS version of CVIEW will be available in the appropriate DOS directory. `ColorView` is a an excellent tool, since you can view compressed JPEG images without having to expand them first (this saves much hard-disk space in the process, bearing in mind that `.GIF` images are much larger than their `.JPG` counterparts). `ColorView`, if used with a VESA compliant video card, has a mouse-driven interface which makes file viewing much easier (various editing effects are also provided).

Another good JPEG viewer is DVPEG. This system requires at least a 386-based PC with a Super-VGA card. Many features are supported including brightness control, image scaling, etc. This freeware utility is available from the site `ftp.rahul.net` in `/pub/bryanw/pc`, or from wuarchive.wustl.edu in the directory /pub/jpeg/viewers/ dvpeg*.ZIP. HiView is a JPEG viewer which runs under DOS. FTP this from sunee.waterloo.edu in /pub/jpeg/viewers, from wuarchive.wustl.edu in /pub/MSDOS_UPLOADS, or from wsmr-simtel-20.army.mil in /msdos/graphics as the file hv*.ZIP. Another Windows JPEG viewer is called WinJPEG. WinJPEG is a shareware program and is available at the FTP site wuarchive.wustl.edu in /mirrors/msdos/windows3/winjp*.ZIP, and is also in /mirrors/ win3/desktop/winjp*.ZIP. Site ftp.cica.indiana.edu also has a copy of WinJPEG in /pub/pc/win3/util.

Staying on the Windows theme, JView is another alternative. This JPEG viewer can be FTP'd from ftp.cica.indiana.edu in /pub/pc/ win3/desktop as files jview*.ZIP.

Animation utilities

Quite a few of these exist, and take as input .GL, DL and .FLI image files. AAPLAY.EXE is a .FLI viewer, and is available via ftp.rahul.net in the directory /pub/bryanw/pc as aaplay.LZH. The site nic.funet.fi also has a copy in the public directory area /pub/msdos/ graphics/animation as the file aaplay.ZIP. FLIPLAY is another example of an .FLI image-animation utility, and it can be found at the site ftp.rahul.net in the directory /pub/bryanw/pc as fliplay.LZH. Finally, there is WAAPLAY which is an .FLI utility for Windows 3.x; this can be obtained from wuarchive.wustl.edu in the directory /mirrors2/ win3/desktop as file waaplay.ZIP.

DLVIEW, as the name suggests, animates .DL image-files (in colour). You can FTP this utility from aix370.rrz.uni-koeln.de (134.95.80.1) in the directory /msdos/graphics/animation as the file dlview21.ZIP. The site ftp.rahul.net also has a copy stored in the /pub/bryanw/pc directory, under filename dlview.ZIP, as has oak.oakland.edu in /pub/msdos/graphics under the filename dlview*.ZIP. DLVIEW has English/Italian translation and allows images to be speeded up, and slowed down during animation.

GRASPRT is a very well known .GL file animation viewer, and is available from ftp.rahul.net in /pub/bryanw/ps as grasp*.ZOO, or from oak.oakland.edu in /pub/msdos/graphics also as grasp*.ZOO. A .ZIP version of this file can be found at bongo.cc.utexas.edu in the directory /ibmpc/grasp as grasp*.ZIP. Many archives have GRASPRT. A system called PDGRASP.EXE allows .GL files to be created by the user. Support up to EGA resolution (and VGA in later versions, I understand) is also available. Typing grasp as a subcase Archie keyword will yield all manner of copies. A number of fonts and other utilities for picture frame extraction from .GL files are also available, so that you can create your own .GL files (these include GLIB.COM, WHATPIC and WHATCLP.EXE).

MPEG animation viewers (for .MPG files) are still pretty rare, although they are now starting to appear. MPEGXing is an MPEG animation viewer which works under Windows 3.1 (this has Super VGA support). You can obtain a copy from phoenix.oulu.fi in the /pub/mpeg directory as mpegxing.LZH. The site wuarchive.wustl.edu also has a copy stored in the directory called /pub/MSDOS_UPLOADS as the file mpegxing.LZH, and a PKZIP version is available from the site src.doc.ic.ac.uk as mpegxing.zip in the directory called /computing/systems/ibmpc/windows3/desktop. People interested in DOS utilities will be glad to hear about MPEG.EXE (from Xing Technology) which was released in April 1993. Version 1 of this utility processes MPEG files quite well, although later versions will improve quality and also allow .WAV file audio. You can FTP MPEG.EXE (version 2) from site 130.231.240.17 in the directory called /pub/incoming/mpeg2_0, as a plain .EXE file.

MPEG files that have an audio capability normally arrive with a .WAV sound file. These files can be very large and the ability to play them depends on the utility you have access to. The Windows utilities mentioned earlier have audio capabilities, as does the version 2 MPEG.EXE mentioned earlier. If you are interested in the audio aspects of your PC, you may want to get hold of SOUND.EXE which plays .WAV, .AU and .VOC audio files through the PCs internal speaker; this utility can be obtained from the site oak.oakland.edu in the directory /pub/msdos/sound as SOUND.ZIP. The Windows PC sound-driver is available from wuarchive.wustl.edu in the mirrors /win3/sounds directory as speak.exe – install this from Windows using the drivers option in the Control Panel (speak.exe is a self-extracting archive and contains the necessary Windows .DRV and .DLL files). You may want to get hold of this file in order to use Windows 3.1 sound effects. Many other audio utilities are available for the PC and other platforms are also available, including utilities to edit and record sounds, and utilities to play sounds through specialist sound-cards, such as the SoundBlaster. Get hold of the file 00-index.txt (ASCII file) which resides in each directory of the site previously mentioned – this outlines just what each utility is.

New to the world of animation, and the Internet, are .AVI files. These are audio/visual files which require copious amounts of disk space. Viewers are available under Windows, and MicroSoft have designed specific software for AVI (the Multimedia player in Windows 3.1 will play these files). A minute of audio and video will require around 20Mb of disk space, so this format may not appeal to all users; the size of the images can also be quite small to improve quality – typically these are 160×120 pixels. You will also need quite a powerful PC, i.e. 486SX minimum for a decent show.

OS/2

The largest site of OS/2-related material for PCs (over 100Mb of utilities are stored) is available at the anonymous FTP site hobbes.nmsu.edu (IP address 128.123.35.151) in the directory /pub/os2. Get hold of an index before starting to browse, since the directory listings take some while to display. To get an index via the post, email listserv@lekul11.bitnet with a message-body of just the word INDEX.

Image viewing utilities

ShowBMP is a viewer which displays .BMP (Windows Bitmap file) image as it is actually being downloaded. It is available from the anonymous FTP site hobbes.nmsu.edu as showbmp.ZOO. OS/2-GIF is a small utility that displays full-screen GIFs; it can be downloaded from the site hobbes.nmsu.edu as os2gif.ZOO. PMGIF and ViewGIF both display GIF images in a Presentation Manager windows under OS/2. PMGIF and ViewGIF can also be downloaded from hobbes.nmsu.edu as pmgif.ZOO and viewgif1.ZOO, respectively.

Image conversion utilities

Converting GIFs to BMPs can be acheived using the tool GIF2BMP. This is available via AFTP on hobbes.nmsu.edu as a .ZOO archive, and on the site wuarchive.wustl.edu in the directory named /mirrors2/win3/desktop as the file gif2bmp.zip. You will need an UNZIP utility to decompress this .ZIP file. See Chapter 7 for a list of such utilities for the OS/2 platform.

APPLE

UU-encoders

UUlite (written by Jeff Strobel) is probably the best known UU-decoder for the Apple platform. UUlite is a 'smart' decoder, and will concatenate UU-files, order them, and strip out mail and news-headers. You can obtain this utility from the FTP site mac.archive.umich.edu in the /mac/utilities/compressionapps directory as file uulite*.HQX. The FTP site world.std.com also has a copy in the /pub directory. Other UU-decoders include UUCat, a simple decoder which is available from the FTP site sumex-aim.stanford.edu (36.44.0.6) in the directory /info-mac/util as the file uucat-*.HQX, and UUTool, which is available from the same site and directory but as uutool*.HQX.

Compression utilities

Many of these exist for the Apple platform. Most are located at the site `sumex-aim.stanford.edu` in the directory `/info-mac/util`, and these include: `BinHex`, which decompresses `.HQX` files (BinHex*); DeHQX, another `.HQX` decompressor (DeHQX*); CptExpand, a `.CPT` decompressor (CptExpand*), MacCompress, a `.Z` Unix decompressor for files compressed with the Unix `compress` command (MacCompress*); MacLha, `.LZH` decompressor (mac-lha-*.HQX); StuffIt, a decompressor for `.HQX` and `.SIT` files (Stuffit-Expander-*.HQX); StuffIt-Lite; another `.SIT` and `.HQX` decompressor (Stuffit-Lite-*.HQX); UnARJ, a `.ARJ` decompressor (unarj-*.HQX); and finally UnZIP, a `.ZIP` file (PKZIP) decompressor (unzip*-*.HQX).

Image conversion utilities

`GIFConvertor` is a good utility with which to start, and supports many formats including JPEG, TIFF, and PICT (24 bit). GIFConvertor is available from the FTP site `sumex-aim.stanford.edu` in the directory `/info-mac/art/gif` as `gif-convertor-23b2.HQX`. IFFConv is a small utility that will convert from the IFF format. It can be obtained from the site `bongo.cc.utexas.edu` in the directory `/apple/iigs` as `iffconv.SHK` (Shark archive). Imagery is another very useful utility for Unix, ATARI, AMIGA and Apple user's alike. It will convert images from all these machines to either GIF, TIFF, or PICT2; it will also break down `.GL` animation files into their separate image frames. The Imagery system can be obtained from the site `sumex-aim.stanford.edu` in the directory `/info-mac/app` as `imagery-*.HQX`, and from the FTP site called `mac.archive.umich.edu` in the directory `/mac/graphics/graphics.utilities` as the file `imagery*.HQX`.

Finally, there is `PictCompressor`, an impressive program that will import, view and convert the majority of the most popular image formats (JPEG included). It is available on QuickTime 1.0 CD-ROM, and from FTP site `sumex-aim.stanford.edu`, and from the FTP site `mac.archive.umich.edu` in the `/graphics/quicktime` directory.

Image viewing utilities

A good JPEG viewer called `JPEGView` is available from the FTP site `sumex-aim.stanford.edu` in the directory `/info-mac/app` as `jpeg-view-*.HQX`. It requires both System 7 and QuickTime to run. A utility called `PictPixie` handles multiple format files (including JPEG and GIF). It requires QuickTime, and can be downloaded from the archive at `ftp.apple.com` in the directory `/dts/mav/quicktime` as the file pictpixie.HQX. Picture-Decompress is a Macintosh JPEG viewer. Later versions (2.0.1+) support the JFIF format (JPEG derivative), and require 4Mb of memory; you can FTP this utility from sumex-aim.stanford.edu in the directory /info-mac/app as the file picture-decompress-*.HQX.

QuickGIF is a colour GIF viewer for the Mac. It shows thumbnail pieces of multiple images so you can pick and choose. It is available from the site bongo.cc.utexas.edu in /mac under quick-gif.HQX. VisionLAB is a similar utility that works with monochrome files; FTP this from the same site, but under the name visionlab.HQX. IIGIF is an Apple II GIF image viewer, and is also available from bongo.cc.utexas.edu in /apple/ii/iigif. Another GIF viewer, called GIF3200, works on the Apple IIgs and can be obtained from bongo.cc.utexas.edu in /apple/ii/gif3200.SHK. VIEW3200 is another example of the same software (same location).

Image animation utilities

Not many of these are available for the Apple platform at the current time of writing, although the position is bound to change. GLViewer is a animation-utility for .GL files. It is available on the FTP archive mac.archive.umich.edu in the directory /mac/graphics/graphics.utilities as the file called gl-viewer.

UNIX/ULTRIX AND X-WINDOWS

A good source of Unix image-processing software is available on the site uranie.inria.fr. Site export.lcs.mit.edu has some excellent X software. Unix utilities are abundant on the Internet. Archie can help here (keywords for the whatis command include image, X11, and compress). You should note that many sources are distributed as C source-code programs and will have to be recompiled to form an executable program.

UU-encoding utilities

Unix has the original uuencode and uudecode programs, which are part of the UUCP suite of programs. Check your Unix manual entry for more information (type: man uuencode). For starters, Aub is an excellent utility (written by Mark Stantz) which scans news files for UU data; it then intelligently orders and assembles them. The whole utility is written in Perl. Aub is available from liasun3.epfl.ch as /pub/util/aub-1.0, and from ftp.cc.gatech.edu in the directory /pub/Unix as aub.tar.Z, and ftp.rahul.net in /pub/bryanw/Unix. You must have access to Perl in order to use this tool (standard on most Unixes).

Comb is another UU-decoder, available from uranie.inria.fr as
comb.news.Z, and dlhunter is an automated Perl script; this can be
downloaded from the site uranie.inria.fr as /pub/images/
scripts as dlhunter.*. Mcvert is a utility that decodes Macintosh
BinHex files, and is available from the site sumex-aim.stanford.edu in
the directory /info-mac/Unix, and from the site wuarch-
ive.wustl.edu in the directory /mirrors/info-mac/Unix as the
file mcvert-*.tar.Z.

As for intelligent UU-decoders, there is Myuud, which will take care of all
ordering and concatenation tasks. Myuud can be obtained from the FTP site
uranie.inria.fr in directory /pub/images/scripts as myuud.c
(source). Uuxfer is another smart UU-decoder written by Dave Read. You
can obtain it from the site bongo.cc.utexas.edu in the directory
/uutools as uudecode.* (source code and documentation). Uucat is a
similar utility which will strip headers and concatenate files; it should be used
in conjunction with a UUDECODE program that reads files from the standard
input, e.g. you pipe files processed by uucat into your uudecode program.
You can also obtain uucat from the site bongo.cc.utexas.edu in
/uutools/uucat.c.

UUconvert is the final smart decoder to be mentioned here. Written by Jeff
Wiegley, it incorporates uudecode into uucat so that it can complete all
stages of UU-decoding in just one stage. This utility can be used with the rn
newsreader, and again can be obtained from bongo.cc.utexas.edu in the
directory /uutools as uutools.c. One very smart decoder includes the
Viewer utility, which runs under X-Windows. This intelligent utility will view or
archive pictures from your news-server (such as NNTP) without any direct
intervention. It can also open a X-window to show the resulting image; FTP this
from cs.utk.edu in the directory /ftp/pub as the file called viewer.*.

For the posting of images to USENET, etc., there is Splituue, a useful tool
for posting complete binary files automatically as separate UU-segments. Grab a
copy from the site uranie.inria.fr, under filename splituue in the
directory called /pub/images/scripts if sending your own images to
USENET interests you. XmitBin is another example of a image poster, which
has an anonymous mailing capability; this is available from the site
ftp.rahul.net   in   /pub/bryanw/Unix,   and   from
uranie.inria.fr, in the directory called /pub/images/scripts as
xmitBin.tar.Z. Sources and executables for rn and nn derivatives are also
widely available on the network; use Archie to search for appropriate keywords.

Image viewing software

There are quite a few viewers, especially for GIF files. X-Windows also offers
an abundance of tools. For GIF images there is GIF320 which is a viewer for

VT320 terminals (hence the name) which can be obtained from `ftp.maths.tcd.ie` in `/pub/sboyle` as `gif320_*.tar.Z`. Then there is `viewgif`, a SunView GIF viewer, which can be obtained from `bongo.cc.utexas.edu` in the directory `/sunview/viewgif`. ArtShow is a another SunView viewer, written by Alan Sparks. This can also be obtained from `bongo.cc.utexas.edu` in the directory called `/sunview/artshow`. ImageMagick is a multiple 24-bit image viewer – located at `export.lcs.mit.edu` as `ImageMagick.tar.Z`.

X-Windows viewers include: `Xli` (xloadimage), a well-known viewer for X-Windows which supports multiple images formats, especially Unix raster files and the like. It can be found at the site `export.lcs.mit.edu` in `/contrib` as `xli.*`, and at the site `bongo.cc.utexas.edu` in `/xwindows/xloadimage`; `xshowgif`, a GIF viewer for X, is available from `bongo.cc.utexas.edu` in the directory `/xwindows/xshowgif`. Finally there is `Xv`, a multiple image viewer (also including JPEG support) for X. It also writes image files and can convert between images. `Xv` can be obtained from `bongo.cc.utexas.edu` in the directory `/xwindows/xv`, or from `ftp.cis.upenn.edu` in `/pub/xv`, or from `gate-keeper.dec.com` in the `/.1/X11/contrib` directory as `xv-*.tar.Z` (this is version 2.21).

Compression utilities

`Unzip` is a decompression utility that will work with `.ZIP` (`PKZIP`) files, an essential tool for this ubiquitous compression standard. You can FTP this from `wuarchive.wustl.edu` in the directory `/mirrors/misc/Unix` as `unzip*.tar.Z`, or from the site `garbo.uwasa.fi` in `/Unix/arcers` also as `unzip*.tar.Z`. You may have come across some `.LZH` compressed files in your travels. In this case you will need to get hold of `Lharc`, which is a `.LZH` decompressor. `Lharc` can be downloaded from the Japanese FTP site `akiu.gw.tohoku.ac.jp`, in the directory `/pub/Unix/lha` as `lha-*.tar.Z`. `Lharc` can also be obtained from `sun.soe.clarkson.edu` in `/pub/src`, and from `lysator.liu.se` in `/pub/amiga/lhA` as `lha-*.tar.Z`.

Image conversion utilities

`Gif2jpg`, as the name suggests, is a GIF to JPEG convertor. This can be obtained from `bongo.cc.utexas.edu` in the directory `/iris` as `gif2jp.shar.Z`. `FromGIF` and `toGIF` also convert from the GIF format, but to/from the Silicon Graphics IRIS image format; these two utilities can be downloaded from `uranie.inria.fr` in the directory `/iris` as `fromgif.c` and `togif.c` (source code versions).

`Dltogl` is also used for animations, and converts between `.DL` and `.GL` files. This can be used in conjunction with the `XGrasp` utility, and is available from `reseq.regent.e-technik.tu-menchen.de` in the `/pub/local/src` directory as `dltogl.c` (source-code versions). Dltogl is also available from `ftp.rahul.net` in directory `/pub/bryanw` as the file `dltogl.c`.

Image animation utilities

X-Windows is well supported here. `Xanim` is a multi-format viewer and animator (handles `.DL`, `.FLI` and `.GIF`); this can be obtained from the site `ftp.rahul.net` in `/pub/bryanw/Unix` as `xanim.tar.Z`. `Xdl` is another X-Windows `.DL` viewer, and can also be obtained from `ftp.rahul.net` in `/pub/bryanw/Unix` as `xdl.c`. `Xgl` is a handy `.GL` animator which can be FTD'd from `cs.dal.ca` in the directory `/pub/comp.archives`, or from the FTP site `srawgw.sra.co.jp` in the directory `/.a/sranha-bp/arch/comp.archives/graphics/pixutils`. `Xgl` is also available at `aix370.rrz.uni-koeln.de` in the directory called `/pub/usenet/comp.archives/graphics/pixutils` (see also `Xviewgl` below).

   `Xflick`, another animation tool, is used to process `.FLI` animation files. It can be obtained from `ftp.rahul.net` in `/pub/bryanw/Unix` as `xflick.tar.Z`, and from `nic.funet.fi` in `/pub/X11/contrib` also as `xflick.tar.Z`. You may also find it on `ftp.uu.net` in `/pub/window-sys/X/contrib` as `xflick.tar.Z`. XGrasp is another `.GL` (colour) animator. `Xflick` can be FTP'd from `ftp.rahul.net` in `/pub/bryanw/Unix` as the file `xgrasp.tar.Z`. XTango is a complete animation system for X, and can be obtained from `par.cc.gatech.edu` in `/pub` as the file `xtango.tar.Z` (note: DEC and HP users should get hold of the file called `xtangovararg.tar.Z`). Finally, another `.GL` animator called `Xviewgl` can be obtained from `bongo.cc.utexas.edu` in `/xwindows/xviewgl`. Refer to `Image-Magick` in the previous section for details of this system which also has animation facilities. You may also want to look at the X-Windows USENET group `comp.sources.x`.

ATARI

Check out the Atari archive at `atari.archive.umich.edu` (`141.211.164.8`). You can email `atari@atari.archive.umich.edu` to make it send you the file you require, using a message consisting of just the words `send <file>`, e.g. `send /pub/atari/myfile.arc`. You can also get an index by posting just the word `index`. You can also get hold of files in this way using an FTPmail server (see Chapter 2 for more information on FTPmail servers).

Image viewing software

There are an abundance of these, all of which are available from the main Atari archive at `atari.archive.umich.edu`. They include: `Giffer` (monochrome GIF viewer) in `/graphics` under filename `giffer.ARC`; `GifShw2` (a colour GIF and slide-show viewer), in `/graphics` as `gifshw2.ARC`; `MGif`, another monochrome GIF viewer, found in `/graphics` as `mgif37b.ARC`; `QuickGIF`, another slide-show GIF viewer, found in `/graphics` as `quickgif.ARC`; `SPShow`, a Spectrum viewer, in `/graphics` as `specshow.ARC`; `SPSlide`, a slide-show viewer for Spectrum images, found in `/graphics` under the filename `spslidex.ARC`; and finally viewgf a multiple image viewer (including `.GIF`), in `/graphics` as `viewgf12.LZH`.

Compression tools

First, there is `dmjgif` which converts a GIF to Spectrum format. You can obtain this particular utility from the FTP site `atari.archive.umich.edu` in `/graphics` as `jmjgif3.LZH`. GIFSpec is another utility that does the same thing, and is obtainable from the same FTP site, in `/graphics` as `gifspec.ARC`. Another tool, `SpecDec`, converts from the Spectrum format to the Degas image format found on the later Atari machines. This tool can be downloaded from the FTP site `atari.archive.umcih.edu` in the directory `/misc/specdec.LZH`. Finally, JPEG routines for the Atari are available at the atari archive site `atari.archive.umcih.edu` in the directory `/graphics` as `JPEGV3.LZH`.

AMIGA

Image conversion utilities

`AmigaJPEG` is a JPEG convertor (JPEG `<->` PPM, GIF, TGA and GIF. Grab it from the anonymous FTP site `funic.funet.fi` in the directory called `/pub/amiga/graphics/applications/convert` as `AmigaJPEG-*-bin.LHA`. HamLab+ is a multiple image viewer and converter, which also has JPEG support. This shareware system for the Amiga can be downloaded from the FTP site `amiga.physik.unizh.ch` (demonstration version will crop images that are $> 512 \times 512$ pixels) in the directory `/amiga/qfx/hamlab208d.LHA`. The FTP site `wuarchive.wustl.edu` also has a copy in the same directory.

   `GIFMachine` is another multiple image viewer and conversion utility. This can be obtained from `bongo.cc.utexas.edu` in the directory `/amiga` as `GIFMachine.LZH`. The `PBMPlus` system described earlier also runs on the Amiga platform. The executable can be FTP'd from `funic.funet.fi` in the public directory named /pub/amiga/graphics/applications/ convert as file pbmplus. Finally, there is WASP, a quick multiple format convertor, which can be obtained from the AFTP site funic.funet.fi in the public directory called /pub/amiga/graphics/applications/ convert as Wasp-*.LHA.

Image viewing software

HamLab+ (see previous section) will view a variety of images, as will GIFMachine (also described earlier). A system called ViewJPEG can be used to view the older IJG version 2 files and can be obtained from funic.funet.fi in the directory called /pub/amiga/graphics/ applications/display as file ViewJPEG-*.LHA.

Animation utilities

GL1-1 is one such example, although there are not many others in existence (yet). GL1-1, as the name suggests, processes .GL files and can be obtained from bongo.cc.utexas.edu in the directory /amiga as the file gl1-1.LZH.

Subscribe to the USENET group comp.sys.amiga* newsgroups for more information and new software releases.

VAX/VMS

Limited support for VAX computers is available. Keep an eye on the USENET group comp.sys.dec* for up-to-date information.

Image conversion utilities

PBMPlus has VMS support. FTP it from the VAX machine at tgv.com, in the directory [.MAHAN]PBMPLUS.SHAR. If VMS directories confuse you, read Chapter 2 for more information on VMS platforms for FTP.

Image viewing utilities

Xv is an image viewer that runs under X-Windows on DEC machines. It includes JPEG support, and can read and write many different image formats. VMS versions of this software are available at the site acfcluster.nyu.edu in the directory [.VMS]. VMS executables of this system are also available from black.cerritos.edu in the [ANONYMOUS.VMSNET]XV*.BCK_Z. The file called [ANONYMOUS]LZDCMP.EXE is the decompression utility, so get hold of this. A VMS XV.EXE is also available for immediate use from the anonymous FTP site bilbo.imsd.rwth-aachen.de.

NeXT

For information on the NeXT scene, you may want to subscribe to the USENET groups comp.sys.next*.

Image viewing utilities

The PBMPlus kit can be used on NeXT machines, and is available from the site sonata.cc.purdue.edu in the directory /pub/next /2.0release/binaries. NewsGrazer is probably the best utility to use on the NeXT platform. ImageViewer is another example. Both of these public domain utilities are available at AFTP site sonata.cc.purdue.edu. It may be tricky to process UU-files with these utilities; to overcome problems ensure that all UU image segments are in the correct order by control-dragging them on the screen. Once all are in order, select all the parts using the [Shift] key. Click UUDECODE in the [Tools] Menu, and then finally click on the [GIF] icon in the document to process the file.

8.7   Unix scripts for UU-decoding

Unix has an abundance of tools which can be used for the processing of UU-encoded files. These include sed, perl, and awk. You may find that some mail and USENET messages arrive with scripts actually attached to them. If you are running a Unix system you may be able to decode UU-encoded files without manually editing them.

TIP

All Unix scripts must be entered with an ASCII editor, e.g. vi on Unix, and must then be made executable using the chmod (change mode) command, for example

$ chmod +x myfile↵

where +x grants execute permission on the file myfile.

SCRIPTS – FOR UNIX GURUS

This section examines some Unix utilities such as sed, awk and Perl for their role in the processing UU-decoding. The first awk script examines a number of command-line arguments (UU-encoded files), by searching each line of the file (which must be in order) for a line marked begin. When either this or a line of UU-encoded text is found, the line is fed to the uudecode program. The end result is one large UU-encoded file which is then processed into a resulting image.

```
1:    if [ X$1 != X ] ; then cat $* ; else cat <& 0 ; fi
2:    awk '/begin [0-9]/                       {ok = 1}
3:     /^Message/                              {ok = 0;next}
4:     /^M/ && (length == 61 || length == 62)  {ok = 1}
5:     /[cC]ut [hH]ere/                        {ok = 0;next}
6:     /^END-----/                             {ok = 0;next}
7:     /^Path:/                                {ok = 0;next}
8:     /^$/                                    {ok = 0;next}
9:     /^-/                                    {ok = 0;next}
10:    /^_/                                    {ok = 0;next}
11:    {if (ok) print}
12:    /^end/                                  {ok = 0}' $*
13:   (cd $HOME/tmp ; uudecode)
```

The awk script below was written by Nasir Noor and processes UU-encoded files, extracting the resulting binary image in the process. All of the UU-encoded files should be passed to the utility in the correct order, as separate ASCII files. An input file can contain UU-decoded parts of more than one file, and they will still be extracted accordingly. Multiple file names (with wildcards) are also acceptable on the command-line.

```
1:    infunc () {
2:    while (test $curfield -le $fields)
3:    do
4:      myrec=`echo $linenums|nawk '{print $mynum}'
         mynum=$curfield`
5:      nawk '$0 ~ /^begin / && NR > rec {print $0}; $0 ~
               /^M[^a-z]/ && NR > rec {print $0}; NR
               > rec {sl=lr; lr=pr; pr=$0};
               $1 ~ /^end/ && NR > rec
               {print sl; print lr; print pr; exit}'
               rec=$myrec $binfile | uudecode
6:      curfield=`expr $curfield + 1`
7:    done
8:    }
9:
10:   for binfile in $*
11:   do
12:     linenums=`nawk '$0 ~ /^begin / {myrec = (NR-1);
               print myrec}' $binfile`
13:     fields=`echo $linenums|nawk '{print NF}'`
14:     curfield=1
15:     if (test $fields -ge 1)
16:        then infunc
```

```
17:    fi
18:  done
19:  exit
```

Note that some statements have been forced on to separate lines because of space restrictions. Ensure that all statements in a script are in fact placed on single lines where indicated, for example line 5 in the previous script should appear on a single line.

SED SCRIPTS

Sed (the Unix stream editor) is another useful Unix utility which searches its input (here a list of UU-encoded files, in order), and then copies the text between the BEGIN and END keywords to the uudecode program. A neat command from Alan Sparks (asparks@viewlogic.com) is shown below, which concatenates UU-encoded files taken from the command-line:

```
cat $* | sed '/^END/, /^BEGIN/d' | uudecode
```

It should be said that this sed script will not work on files with BEGIN and END lines which form part of a CUT HERE line that have been added by the sender (these are added by the UU-encoder at source).

PERL SCRIPTS

The first Perl script below was written by Dave Mack (csu@alembic.acs.com) and combines split UU-encoded files into a single data stream with email garbage removed; it then pipes this into uudecode. The UU-encoded files must all be in the correct order on the command line – in particular the first file must contain the begin line and the last file must contain the end line. This code relies on uuencode putting out all lines of the form M[61 ASCII characters]\n for every line of the file except the last few before the end line. If you come across a UU-encoded file that does not do this, you will need to modify the code to handle it. Name the following file uumerge and use it on the command-line with the names of the UU-encoded files you want to process.

```
1:    if ($#ARGV < 0 ) {
2:        print "Usage: uumerge filename [file
            name...]\n";
3:        exit 1;
4:    }
5:    $| = 1;
6:    # Open a pipe into uudecode...
7:    open(DECO, "|uudecode") || die "Can't pipe into
          uudecode\n";
8:    # if only 1 file, place it straight into uudecode and
          die
```

```
9:    if ( $#ARGV == 0 ) {
10:       open(FIRST,"<$ARGV[0]") || die "Can't open
          $ARGV[0]!\n";
11:       while ( <FIRST> ) {
12:              # skip past everything before the "begin"
                 line
13:              next unless /^begin [0-9]/;
14:              last;
15:       }
16:    die "$ARGV[0] doesn't contain \"begin\"\n" if
       eof(FIRST);
17:    print DECO $_; # the "begin" line
18:    while ( <FIRST> ) {
19:           print DECO $_ unless /^end/;
20:           if ( /^end/ ) {
21:             print DECO $_;
22:             last;
23:             }
24:           die "$ARGV[0] doesn't contain \"end\"\n" if
                 eof(FIRST);
25:
26:    }
27:    # done with this file...
28:    close(FIRST);
29:    exit 0;
30:    }
31:    # process the first file - make sure we have a "begin"
       line:
32:
33:    open(FIRST,"<$ARGV[0]") || die "Can't open
       $ARGV[0] for input\n";
34:    while ( <FIRST> ) {
35:           # skip past everything before the "begin" line
36:           next unless /^begin [0-9]/;
37:           last;
38:    }
39:    die "First file doesn't contain \"begin\"\n" if
       eof(FIRST);
40:    print DECO $_; # the "begin" line
41:
42:    # Remaining "real" uu-lines in file should begin
       with "M"
43:    while ( <FIRST> ) {
```

```perl
44:     if ( /^M/ ) {
45:         print DECO $_;
46:     }
47:     else {
48:             last;
49:     }
50: }
51:
52: # done with the first file...
53: close(FIRST);
54:
55: # Do all except the last file...
56: $maxindex = $#ARGV;
57: $curr = 1;
58: while ($curr < $maxindex) {
59:         open(CURR, "<$ARGV[$curr]") || die "Can't
                open $ARGV[$curr]\n";
60:     # skip the header junk
61:     while ( <CURR> ) {
62:             next unless /^$/;
63:             last;
64:     }
65: # at the body of the message -- start looking for /^M/
66: while ( <CURR> ) {
67:         next unless /^M/;
68:         last;
69: }
70: die "$ARGV[$curr] isn't a uuencoded file\n" if
        eof(CURR);
71: # OK, we're at the start of the good stuff
        (probably)...
72: print DECO $_;
73: while ( <CURR> ) {
74:         if (/^M/) {
75:             print DECO $_;
76:         }
77:         else {
78:                 last;
79:         }
80: }
81: # Finished with current file ...
82: close(CURR);
83: $curr++;
```

```
84:   }
85:
86:   # Time to process the last file in the set...
87:   $curr = $maxindex;
88:   open(CURR,"<$ARGV[$curr]") || die "Can't open
         89:$ARGV[$curr]\n";
90:   # skip the header junk...
91:   while ( <CURR> ) {
92:          next unless /^$/;
93:          last;
94:   }
95:   # We're at the body of the message - start looking for
         /^M/
96:   while ( <CURR> ) {
97:          next unless /^M/;
98:          last;
99:   }
100: # OK, we're at the start of the good stuff (probably)
         ...
101: print DECO $_;
102:
103: while ( <CURR> ) {
104:          print DECO $_ unless /^end/;
105:          if ( /^end/ ) {
106:             print DECO $_;
107:             last;
108:          }
109:          die "Last file on command line doesn't
                contain \"end\"\n"
110:          if eof(CURR);
111: }
112: close(CURR);
113: # Close the pipe to uudecode and exit...
114: close(DECO);
115: exit(0);
```

Here is another Perl script, this one written by Randal Schwartz (merlyn@iwarp.intel.com). This script is similar to the previous, in that it performs a decoding process on UU-encoded files taking arguments from the standard input or from the Unix command-line.

```
1:    while (<>) {
2:           last if ($mode,$file) =
              /^begin\s*(\d*)\s*(\S*)/;
```

```
 3:    }
 4:    die "missing begin keyword" unless $_;
 5:    open(OUT, "> $file") if $file ne "";
 6:    while (<>) {
 7:           last if /^end/;
 8:           s/[a-z]+$//; # handle trailing lowercase
                  letters ...
 9:           next if /[a-z]/;
10:           next unless int((((ord() - 32) & 077) + 2) / 3)
                  == int(length() / 4);
11:           print OUT unpack("u", $_);
12:    }
13:    die "missing end keyword" unless $_;
14:    chmod oct($mode), $file;
15:    exit 0;
```

Many of the the above scripts, and their variants, can be found attached to standard UU-encoded messages when they arrive from USENET.

8.8   Posting your own images to USENET

At some time or another you may want to post your own images to USENET, or to an individual recipient. A number of special posting utilities exist which will UU-encode your image for you and send it out in segments, although you can, of course, do this manually by uuencoding the image into one large segment and breaking it up in 60 000 byte (typically) pieces. It can then be mailed accordingly. You may want to add CUT HERE lines to the relevant areas, i.e. immediately before the begin line, and immediately after the end line (the begin/end keywords will be added by your UUENCODE utility) to make manual editing easier for those users who do not have smart UU-decoders.

You can also use a compression tool to reduce the size of an image before UU-encoding it, although do not do this for .GIF images since they are already compressed by default. Animation files such as .GLs are good candidates for compression, although .DL animations do not compress as well. Remember to compress your image first (using PKZIP/ARJ, etc.) and only then UU-encode it (not the other way around). Including some information regarding the image's size when compressed and/or decompressed is also a good idea. Some UU-encoders and compressors give statistics which can be incorporated in with the text of your posting.

MESSAGE SUBJECT: LINES

Some conventions have arisen for subject lines when you finally come to post your own images to USENET. Information pertaining to the image type, its dimensions, segment number, and actual content should all be included, plus a description of the image – you may consider posting an initial message telling everyone about the image (making this message's segment number 0 – this is becoming common on many USENET image-forums). The typical structure of a subject line in your outgoing post to USENET should take the following form:

`- filename.ext (part/total) {label} ^REPOST^ [sh] "Full Title"`

The hyphen (–) in the left-most column represents whether or not this image is a first-time post, or whether it is a follow up (use a hyphen for a first-time posting, and omit if this is a repost). Secondly we have the image's file-name, which should also be present in the first segment of your UU-encoded file, an example being `mypic.gif`. Filenames will differ between operating systems, so try standardizing to filenames with 12 characters, including a 3 character filename extension in order to allow your filenames to be acceptable under systems such as Unix and the ubiquitous MSDOS platform. Filename extensions are very important and must be included to tell the recipient just what this file will turn out to be, and, of course, what tool should be used to process or view the file. The (`part/total`) label represents the segment number, e.g. part 2 of 4 is (2/4), noting brackets. A label telling the recipient what this image actually contains will also be useful to say the least, so get in the habit of placing a label including the subject of the image.

The keyword `^REPOST^` indicates that this posting was made earlier, but it went wrong and is now being reposted (messages may, of course, be reposted due to demand) and the [sh] keyword denotes that this posting uses script-wrappers (note the square brackets), an optional label. Finally there is a further descriptive label enclosed in double-quotes. Use this notation to inform people about the image resolution, e.g. the number of colours and pixel dimensions. A typical subject line could therefore resemble:

`- FRACTAL.GIF (2/3) {mandelbrot} "Fractal: 800×600×256"`

noting that this is a first-time posting, and is a 800×600 pixel 256 colour (therefore needs SuperVGA) image of a Mandelbrot fractal. Not everyone adheres to this format for Subject: lines (in fact each person has their own method) although it does make sense to standardize at some point, so why not now?

MESSAGE HEADER STRUCTURES

The header structure of a typical image-segment that is posted on USENET is illustrated in Example 8.1. The Newsgroups: line indicates which USENET groups have received this image-segment, indicating whether or not the posting was made to more than one group, which we can see is the case from the example header. UUCP machines use a 'bang-path' for mailing-purposes of the form machine1!machine2!username (see Chapter 6 for more information on UUCP) and this is indicated in the Path: line. Recipient names are always quoted in the From: line. In the example we can see that an anonymous person posted this message (an9999 is in fact an anonymous alias used by the anonymous service at the site anon.penet.fi).

EXAMPLE 8.1 – TYPICAL IMAGE-SEGMENT HEADER

```
Newsgroups: alt.binaries.pictures.erotica, alt.sex.pictures
Path: provider!mainsite!uunet!mcsun!fuug!anon
From: an9999@anon.penet.fi (Fred)
Subject: som.gl 1/3 ("Both")
Message-ID: <1993Jan31.999999.9990@fuug.fi>
Sender: anon@fuug.fi (The Anon Administrator)
Organization: Anonymous contact service
X-Anonymously-To: alt.binaries.pictures.erotica
Date: Sun, 31 Jan 1993 16:19:28 GMT
Lines: 961
```

Examining the Subject: line tells us something about the image in question; here we can see that a .GL animation file has been posted – this will appear in the UU-encoded text (and may be compressed further – this will be apparent in the begin line of the UU-encoded file which itself names the resulting decoded archive). Remember that the Subject: line normally tells you what this image is, after it has been UU-decoded and/or decompressed, etc. Images can never be viewed immediately without some initial decoding (unless they are FTP'd intact). The segment number will also be included in this line, along with a descriptive image string ("Both" is used on the adult image newsgroups to denote male/female subject matter).

The 'Message-ID:' line is a message identifier, a unique code that is allocated to each posting for identification purposes. The code that is allocated to this message is normally a date, followed by a numeric code and the name of the sending site. This code will be stored by your local mailing software to determine whether or not you have already received this message. Some Unix newsreaders, such as nn, examine an ASCII file called .newsrc, and store this in the Message-Id code for this sole purpose (see Chapter 2 for more details on the .newsrc file). It would be possible, via modification to this file (the name is system specific on non-Unix machines) to control which messages you have received, thus allowing you to receive a lost or corrupted image that had previously been sent, and which you now want to get hold of again. You should also check to see if you can query your news-server directly on an interactive basis (calling it via telnet at a specific port) to scan through successive postings – see Chapter 2 for more information on NNTP news-servers.

The 'Sender:' line, as the name suggests, identifies the person who sent the message, and this may be followed by the actual person's full name if such information is available. As an extension of this name, an 'Organization:' line is sometimes included to indicate the name of the company or institution that originally sent this posting. (Anonymous postings are not uncommon – an anonymous poster can be reached using their alias.)

Anonymous messages have an additional header field called 'X-Anon-To:', or 'X-Anonymously-To:' which identifies the newsgroups to which this posting is to be sent. Anonymous postings have an additional message-body line which consists of a 'X-Anon-To:' entry to identify human recipients and/or the names of individual USENET newsgroups to which the message will be sent (X indicates that an X-Window system was used for mailing). Finally, the header contains the line 'Date:' which indicates the time and date of the posting (this will be in relation to you own time-zone), and an entry entitled 'Lines:', which indicates how many lines of UU-encoded text are contained within this posting. Around 900–1000 lines are not uncommon for a single UU-encoded image segment (approximately 50-60K of text).

ANONYMOUS POSTINGS

If you want to use an anonymous posting scheme send an email message (anything will do as a message) to the postmaster at `post-master@anon.penet.fi` (postmaster is an alias that maps your requests to the site administrator) and you will be mailed back an anonymous-id of the form `anon0000` which you use to post all your messages to, e.g. you would post your messages/images to `anon0000@anon.penet.fi` (this address is, of course, hypothetical so please don't mail to it) and the server at this site will pass on your mail to its destination, but with your anonymous name. Mail the postmaster for more help, as mentioned.

8.9   Common image problems

Problems can occur at all stages of image-processing, whether it is at the downloading, decompression or viewing stage. While the most common problems concern the actual downloading procedures, others can be caused by your decompression procedure and even your actual image-viewing software. This section will hopefully provide answers to some of your problems.

IMAGE VIEWING PROBLEMS

If you see garbage when viewing an image you may want to consider the following possibilities:

- You have downloaded the file incorrectly
- Your viewing software is incorrectly configured
- You need to update to a newer version of the utility that you are using to view a particular image
- The sender of the message has corrupted the image.

First, when downloading images from anonymous FTP sites make sure that you issue the FTP binary (or tenex on some systems). Images, compressed or otherwise, are binary files and not ASCII files. Many FTP interfaces will automatically invoke the binary mode for downloading although the vast majority do not. If you are not sure that you have downloaded a file correctly, use a disk editor such as Norton or PCTools to view the internal contents of a valid image and compare the contents–particularly around the header area. This will give you some insight into whether or not the content is corrupt (see Table 8.4). Likewise, if your image-viewing software hangs, i.e. stops while reading in an image, this points to internal file corruption, or possible memory exhaustion (the latter is more common since your utility should moan about any corruption at a much earlier stage).

If your image is not totally corrupt when viewed but instead is decreased in size (on screen) or has its colours distorted, you are probably viewing an image which is not compatible with your monitor's screen display. A common example of this problem occurs when you use a 16-colour viewing mode to show a 24 bit GIF image, the latter which has as many as 256 colours and requires your viewer to operate in Super-VGA mode. If your viewer can be configured, check to see what image-types and densities are supported. Now you know why it is so important for the original sender of an image to include a description of its dimensions and density, etc. Images such as .GIFs shouldn't give any problems, although some formats such as .GL (animation files) may require that you use a later version of a utility in order to view them successully (with .GL files many problems arise because text is inserted alongside some images and earlier versions of some .GL-viewing utilities cannot handle such textual effects).

Many utilities, such as Image Alchemy and Graphics WorkShop (GWS), allow the image headers of most static images to be examined, which, in turn, may provide some insight into the dimensions and colours of an image file. Obtaining as many versions of a viewing tool is probably the best way of overcoming version-specific images. Finally, there is the problem of system resources. Large images with high densities (such as 256 colour GIF's) require copious amounts of video memory. If your image-viewer suddenly crashes out, try removing any TSRs (under MSDOS these will reside in the files \CONFIG.SYS and \AUTOEXEC.BAT), and start afresh with a warm-reboot when re-attempting to view the image. In some cases an image may appear very large, although perfectly intact. If your viewing software does not support movement around the image you won't be able to see much, and instead you will have to rescale it to fit your screen.

A 1024 × 768 pixel image could be scaled to fit exactly on a VGA screen (with 640 × 480 pixels) using conversion tools such as ColorView and Image Alchemy (or, of course, Graphics WorkShop). Scaling down an image in this way could be the only way of viewing an image which is too large to fit in your computer's memory. Many new utilities will be available when this book is published so consult alt.graphics.pixutils on USENET for the latest gossip; more importantly subscribe to the relevant image-discussion forums for up-to-the minute news. Getting hold of the image-forum FAQs is also an invaluable source of information. You should, of course, also note that many images arrive in all manner of dimensions, especially in the SVGA modes. Be aware that some conversion packages may convert a picture using slightly different resolutions, for example 638 × 432 or 600 × 700 (these should still view satisfactorily, however, and this happens as a direct consequence of the original scanning process in many instances).

If all else fails, mail the sender of the original image and ask this person what viewer they use, and how the problem can be rectified, etc. Remember to be as specific about your problem as possible. With a bit of luck you will get a response and some insight into your problem. Alternatively mail one of the USENET discussion forums mentioned earlier, where all such problems are discussed frequently.

UU-DECODING PROBLEMS

UU-encoded files follow some basic rules. Do not include blank lines for a start. Also, when concatenating files together, you may find that a carriage-return is not inserted after each segment that you cut out of the original posting. This will lead to an extended line where one segment is joined directly on to another (yielding a line of around 122 characters in length) and your UU-decoder will respond with an error message such as 'Line too long', or words to that effect. Manual editing problems can also be the cause of your problem. You did cut out those 'CUT HERE' lines didn't you? Such comments should not be included in with your final UU-encoded file! In addition, make sure that you have not cut away the 'begin' and 'end' lines. A clue to this problem is a long wait while your UU-decoder searches through 60Kb of text for a 'begin' line, giving you an error when it finally reaches the end of the file.

All 'begin' lines should also have a name of a file which is to be used as the source file for resulting UU-decoded text. If you lose this name you may have real problems since you have lost the format of the resulting file (try looking at the original posting–if this is not available you will have to guess at the contents and add various extensions and then try viewing and/or decompressing, etc.). You may be able to instruct your UU-decoder to use an alternative name when decoding, although this will still not tell you what format the file is (a low-level file editor may allow you to see what format file a particular file is in, and you can attempt an un-formatting operation). The first few bytes of a file will often give some insight into that files internal format, so in the case that you lose track of the format of a file you may want to consider using the list of formats in Table 8.4 while browsing the file with a file viewer such as those in the Norton Utilities or PC-Tools.

Assembling your UU-encoded segments in the incorrect order will also lead to a complete, or partially corrupt image. This will probably not happen in the majority of cases since UU-encoded files have checksums which ensure that errors will result in a fatal warning. Some smarter UU-decoders can overcome this problem, since they will examine the segment order from any header information, assuming it exists. If you didn't actually download your file directly using a file-transfer protocol, but instead printed it out using your

Table 8.4 Header information of some common file-types

File format	Description and header details
.PCX image	Bytes 1 to 4 are normally the hex values 0A,05,01,01.
.GIF image	Bytes 1 to 5 normally have the string 'GIF' in them. The string 'GIF87' or hex 47,49,46,38,37 in bytes 1–5 is commonly used.
.ARJ archive	The name of the archive and compressed file(s) are normally included, around byte 30 onwards. Look for the string .ARJ in the header also.
.ZIP archive	Bytes 1 and 2 are normally 50,4B hex which in ASCII is 'PK' (for PKZIP). Other viewable information may also be available in the header.
.DL animation	These files are hard to comprehend since no viewable header is normally used. Look out for bytes 1 and 2 set to hex 02,01 (in ASCII, 2 little faces).
.GL animation	The resulting file has the names of the internal text, font, and images; look out for .CLPs, .PICs, and .TXTs.
.JPG JPEG file	These compressed images normally have the string 'JFIF' in them (around bytes 7 to 11) or hex 4A,46,49,46. Other information may include the actual JPEG version and string 'JPEG' later on in the header.
.MPG MPEG file	These animations commonly start with the ASCII values 0,0,1.
.EXE executable	Under MSDOS (not VMS) these files have bytes 1 and 2 set to hex 4D,5A or ASCII 'MZ'. .EXE files applied to an image normally means that the image must be of a 'self-displaying' nature, i.e. the image-viewing software is in-built. (Graphics Workshop can do this.)

newsreader at source and then capturing the output into a file, you may have introduced errors that are caused by line-noise from your modem device. Incorrect encoding characters can be inserted and whole lines can even be inadvertently corrupted or omitted. A file-transfer protocol such as FTP has all of the in-built mechanisms to ensure the safe transfer of your data, so such problems will almost never arise. Printing out and capturing UU-encoded files can work, however, just as long as the file is displayed at a sensible rate (in small 24-line bursts every few seconds for example), and if the newsreading software has some in-built error-detection and/or correction facilities.

A good tip to remember at this point is the use of the USENET NNTP news-servers via a reliable Telnet connection (see the A–Z resource guide for a list of servers) for people without their own USENET news-feed. You can quite easily capture the data from one of these sessions into a file and some servers allow messages to be posted to you, although this feature is sometimes denied to external users. Try accessing a server and capturing a file to see if this works. If you are accessing news-postings through an indirect connection, for example via a dial-up PAD (packet assembler disassembler) facility, you will almost certainly introduce some corruption since this part of your tele-phone-connection will have no error checking capability. Finally, there is always the possibility that the sender of a particular message corrupted the file when they originally posted it. In such a case a message should be posted telling the newsgroup of this, and the image-segments will be posted again (look out for a 'REPOST' string in the 'Subject:' field of the message concerned.

COMPRESSION PROBLEMS

A corrupt archive (a .ZIP or .ARJ, etc.) could be caused by downloading the file without binary mode being enabled. In this case you will have to download the file again. In multiple archives, for example a .ZIP with more than one file embedded within it, it is possible to retrieve those files up to the point of the interruption, e.g. a line-drop or power failure, etc. Use the archivers integrity test option (for example, the -t option for PKUNZIP) to see which parts of the file are intact and those which are not, then dearchive accord-ingly – the system should stop when it reaches a corrupted section.

Some archiving programs can hang or continue infinitely when dealing with corrupted archives, so be prepared to interrupt the session if necessary (a system reboot may also be required in some cases). For the latest archive bugs and problems make sure you get hold of the FAQ (Frequently Asked Ques-tions) document which is posted to most of the graphics forums on a regular basis, commonly every two weeks. Look for the string 'FAQ' within the 'Subject:' line of the message. The Images-FAQ is posted to the USENET group alt.binaries.pictures.* and news.answers newsgroup, and it can also be FTP'd from the site pit-manager.mit.edu. Look for the file called /pub/usenet/news.answers (in three parts).

8.10   FTP image archives

Anonymous FTP sites that contain images are scattered all over the Internet, and the ideal tool to search for such images is Archie (see Chapter 4). Image directories are frequently named after the image-format that they cater for, e.g. ~/gif for .GIF images, etc., so using a sub-case search term such as 'gif ' will produce many specially reserved directories on hosts that store .GIF files; the Archie command set search subcase should be used for this purpose (a subcase search will also locate all .GIF files themselves, of course, a useful tip to remember). GIF (graphic interchange format) files are by far the most popular image-format used on the Internet and many are left in an uncompressed form. Be sure to download all such images, compressed or otherwise, as binary files. A selection of GIF archives that you may want to examine are listed below in Table 8.5. While this list is not a complete guide, it does provide some sites with which you can start searching without any further research. Some sites mirror the larger FTP sites such as wsmr-simtel20.army.mil, and many FTP sites have a publicly writable directory (/uploads, etc.) so images may be uploaded at any time when space is available.

The names and locations of image repositories will, of course, change over time and you are advised to use the Archie service for the most up-to-date files that are available. Remember to be on the lookout for upload areas such as ~/uploads or ~/incoming, since many GIF files are uploaded on a regular basis to sites via this method.

USING ARCHIE TO SEARCH FOR FILE EXTENSIONS – HINTS AND TIPS

Using Archie you can search for individual GIF files rather than the directories that actually house them. A sub-case search for the term .gif, for example, would yield many separate files, and you can, of course, use other file-extension names, e.g. .gl, .mpg, which should all yield images, some, of course, which may be placed in a directory whose name you could never guess. Searches such as these will locate many hundreds of files, many of which are duplicates, so you may want to limit your search using the Archie command set maxhits <n>, where <n> is the number of files you want to locate. Unfortunately, Archie cannot be instructed to ignore duplicates that are found at other FTP sites, so be prepared to wade through a number of identical files.

Again, remember that searching for part of a filename (such as .gif) requires a subcase or substring search, so use the Archie command set search subcase in all such instances.

Table 8.5   GIF repositories (via anonymous FTP). Searched for using Archie with the keyword 'gif'.

FTP site name	Name of GIF directory
plaza.aarnet.edu.au	/graphics/gif
	/graphics/gif/00Catalogs/gif
	/micros/mac/info-mac/art/gif
	/micros/mac/umich/graphics/gif
	/micros/pc/garbo/pc/gif
	/micros/pc/oak/gif
	/symlinks/amiga/video/pics/gif
coombs.anu.edu.au	/pub/irc/gif
iskut.ucs.ubc.ca	/pub/info-mac/art/gif
nic.switch.ch	/mirror/info-mac/art/gif
	/mirror/msdos/gif
	/software/mac/info-mac-shadow
	/art/gif
	/software/pc/simtel20/gif
gatekeeper.dec.com	/.2/micro/msdos/simtel20/gif
m2xenix.psg.com	/pub/ms-dos/gif
quepasa.cs.tu-berlin.de	/pub/amiga/gfx/pix/fair/gif
	/pub/mac/mirrors/stanford/art
	/gif
minnie.zdv.uni-mainz.de	/pub1/images/gif
cs.bu.edu	/PC/APPLE/games/gif
barnacle.erc.clarkson.edu	/pub/simtel20-cdrom/msdos/gif
hubcap.clemson.edu	/pub/gif
csustan.csustan.edu	/pub/images/gif
solaria.cc.gatech.edu	/pub/music/gif
ftp.nau.edu	/graphics/gif
rigel.acs.oakland.edu	/pub/msdos/gif
apocalypse.engr.ucf.edu	/pub/images/gif
f.ms.uky.edu	/incoming/pictures/gif
	/pub3/pictures/gif
Host cs.utk.edu	/pub/pozo/gif
wuarchive.wustl.edu	/graphics/gif
	/graphics/gif/00Catalogs/gif
	/mirrors/msdos/gif
	/mirrors2/info-mac/Old/art/gif
	/mirrors2/info-mac/art/gif
	/mirrors3/archive.umich.edu
	/apple2/misc/gif
	/mirrors3/archive.umich.edu
	/mac/graphics/gif
	/mirrors3/archive.umich.edu
	/msdos/graphics/gif
	/mirrors4/garbo.uwasa.fi/gif
	/systems/amiga/video/pics/gif

continues overleaf

Table 8.5 – *continued*

FTP site name	Name of GIF directory
cnam.cnam.fr	/pub/Archives/comp.archives /auto/alt.skate-board/gif
dftsrv.gsfc.nasa.gov	/pub/images/gif
menora.weizmann.ac.il	/pub/gif
sabrina.dei.unipd.it	/doc/doc/ftp-sites/gif
isfs.kuis.kyoto-u.ac.jp	/Mac/info-mac/art/gif /ftpmail/ftp.tohoku.ac.jp/pub /gif /mirrors/simtel20.msdos/gif
toklab.ics.osaka-u.ac.jp	/net/misc/v13/gif
akiu.gw.tohoku.ac.jp	/pub/gif
utsun.s.u-tokyo.ac.jp	/ftpsync/info-mac/art/gif
etlport.etl.go.jp	/pub/ibmpc/distrib/gif /pub/ibmpc/local/gif
ftp.uu.net	/systems/apple2/misc/gif /systems/ibmpc/msdos/simtel20 /gif
nikhefh.nikhef.nl	/pub/atari/docs/gif
metten.fenk.wau.nl	/info-mac/art/gif
pollux.lu.se	/pub/graphics/images/gif
ftp.luth.se	/pub/OS/pc/msdos/msdos.nfs .sunet.se/graphics/gif
sics.se	/pub/info-mac/art/gif
unix.hensa.ac.uk	/pub/uunet/usenet/rec.music .gaffa/kb/pix/gif

9
Locating information from the Internet

9.1 Introduction

The Internet is ultimately about the retrieval of information, and this chapter examines the most popular tools that are currently available to help you in this task. Whether you are a student, a researcher, an educationalist or a professional computer user, this chapter will help you embark on the trail for those elusive facts. In this chapter you will learn:

- How to use the Gopher and the related veronica system for retrieving general information from the Internet
- How to use the WAIS system for browsing abstracts
- How to use the WWW (World-Wide-Web) hypertext service
- Finding out information from other sources: USENET, Archie, and email-based Internet services

9.2 The Gopher system

Apart from downloading software and technical information, users also want to use the Internet to access information on many other general subjects. The Gopher service is one of the most useful tools to achieve this. Unlike tools such as ftp and telnet, Gopher is a menu-based system which allows you to specifically state the topics that interest you. Typing in a word or phrase which describes the information you require makes Gopher search for the relevant information, and any that is found will be made available as a series of menu-options which you can then choose to examine further.

Gopher uses many tools to aid in its searching, including systems such as ftp, telnet, Archie and WAIS, and it may invoke any of these systems in order to complete its search – all without you having to issue a single cryptic command.

ACCESSING GOPHER

Like most of the interactive services on the Internet, Gopher can be installed as a client program on your own machine, or it can be accessed via telnet. A number of public-access Gopher systems exist which can be telnetted to from your host machine. Table 9.1 illustrates the most common Gopher servers that are currently in existence; many more are documented in Appendix D. As can be seen, one would log in to a public Gopher server using the name gopher (noting the differences in some machines). Gopher servers are run by a number of educational establishments all over the world, and while some of the information stored at each site will be common only to that domain, searches across all of the existing Gopher servers is possible through a new service called veronica (to be explained a little later on in this chapter).

LOGGING IN TO A GOPHER SERVER USING TELNET

To start a search using a public Gopher server we would have to choose an appropriate server machine, such as one of the server machines shown in Table 9.1. If you run a dedicated Gopher client on your machine you would simply type the command gopher and the system will start. We can call up a Gopher server via telnet in the following way (assume we have chosen the Gopher server at consultant.micro.umn.edu, a popular machine):

$ telnet consultant.micro.umn.edu↵

After a few moments the name will be resolved (an IP address will be found for the host – you could type the IP address directly in order to speed things up a bit if you like, since all textual hostnames must be resolved, i.e. an IP number must be found first) and a login: prompt will appear, to which you would most commonly type gopher (no password is required), for example:

login: gopher↵

Table 9.1   Gopher server machines accessible via telnet

Machine name	IP address	login:
consultant.micro.umn.edu	134.84.132.4	gopher
gopher.uiuc.edu	128.174.33.160	gopher
panda.uiowa.edu	128.255.40.201	panda
info.anu.edu.au	150.203.84.20	info
gopher.chalmers.se	129.16.221.40	gopher

After entering this login name, the system will present a menu. All Gopher menus are similar in structure to one another, although not similar in actual content. Here is a typical `telnet` session with the Gopher at `consultant.micro.umn.edu` which is based at the University of Michigan in the United States:

```
AIX telnet (hafnhaf)
Login as "gopher" to use the gopher system
IBM AIX Version 3 for RISC System/6000
(C) Copyrights by IBM and by others 1982, 1991.
login: gopher↵
TERM = (vt100)↵
Erase is Ctrl-H
Kill is Ctrl-U
Interrupt is Ctrl-C
I think you're on a vt100 terminal
            Internet Gopher Information Client v1.12
               Root gopher server: gopher.tc.umn.edu
 → 1.   Information About Gopher/
    2.   Computer Information/
    3.   Internet file server (ftp) sites/
    4.   Fun & Games/
    5.   Libraries/
    6.   Mailing Lists/
    7.   UofM Campus Information/
    8.   News/
    9.   Other Gopher and Information Servers/
   10.  Phone Books/
   11.  Search lots of places at the U of M <?>
```

As can be seen, this system is particularly welcoming, even asking us to log in as a 'gopher'. Not all systems will be this friendly at the log in stage, however.

Gopher terminal emulations

From the example we can see that the initial stages with this Gopher require the user to enter some configuration information, typically the name of the terminal emulation you are using. Gophers are normally run using a VT emulation, e.g. `vt100`, and this default has been shown to us by the system in our example. To accept the default terminal emulation, here vt100, simply press the carriage-return key. To specify the name of another emulation, type the name in and press the carriage-return key. Knowing which emulation you are using can be a tricky task. The vt100 emulation is very common and allows many screen effects such as the embolding and highlighting of characters, as well as the movement of the cursor. Your communications software will dictate what emulation you should use, although a dumb terminal setting may sometimes be invoked with the name 'dumb' or 'ascii', which will enable a simple textual display to be enabled. Your Gopher will tell you if the emulation you enter is valid. If you cannot find an emulation, accept the default and view the results. If this is unacceptable and you cannot obtain a response, interrupt the Gopher using [Ctrl-C] and retry your connection, this time using another emulation.

A dumb terminal emulation will not normally allow cursor movement, so you will have to navigate menus by typing in their numbers directly.

BASIC GOPHER COMMANDS

The root menu of any Gopher system contains a series of options which in turn lead to other menus in a hierarchical format. All Gopher menus respond to a number of commands, as shown in Table 9.2.

In the context of the previous example, pressing 9 would make the current item the 9th menu option (Other Gopher and Information Servers/) –note the ⟶ line selector string, which indicates which option we are currently on. Some other points should also be noted. While many terminal emulations respond to the keyboards cursor keys, some do not. You will

Table 9.2   Gopher command set

Command	Function
<Return>, <Enter>	View the current document
<Up Cursor>	Move to previous line in menu
<Down Cursor>	Move to next line in menu
<Left Cursor>, u	Move up to previous menu
>, +, <PgDn>, <Space>	View the next page
<, -, <PgUp>, b	View the previous page
0-9	Move to a specific line
m	Move back to the main menu
a	Add item to the bookmark list
A	Add directory/search to the bookmark list
v	View the current bookmark list
d	Delete a bookmark/directory entry
s	Save the current item to a file
D	Download a file
q	Quit Gopher (confirmation required)
Q	Quit without confirmation
=	Show technical information on item
o	Change options, e.g. terminal, etc.
/	Search for an item in menu
n	Find the next search item

therefore have to use a particular key to move up and down (these emulate the text editors used in the Unix environment, such as emacs and vi)-try the keys j and k to move up and down respectively.

TIPS

You can move to a particular line more quickly by entering / followed by a string to match in the Gopher menu, for example:

/Phone↵

would take you to item 10 in the context of the most previous menu shown (Phone Books/).

You cannot save a file if you are accessing a remote Gopher via telnet since you will not have the neccessary write permission. If you are going to use the Download (D command) option, be sure that your local software can deal with X/Y/ZModem or Kermit. If a file is binary be sure not to use a simple text (i.e. ASCII transfer) which some Gophers have. We discuss this later on in the chapter.

The Unix operating system has a command called script for this purpose, which saves all output to the file typescript. This file can then be printed or viewed at a later stage. Many communications programs also have log-file facilities whereby the output of a terminal session can be saved to an external file. Make sure your results are being saved prior to using the Gopher service, or your efforts may be wasted. Note the above tip regarding file downloads.

CONDUCTING A 'GOPHERSPACE' SEARCH USING veronica

It clearly makes sense to explore the widest possible area for the information you require. This is analogous to searching for a rare book in only a single library when another library down the road may have it on the shelf. Unfortunately, finding information in this way is not possible with the Internet because the network is a global resource and is too vast too search in such a casual way. As has been mentioned already, many Gopher servers exist worldwide and it is quite possible that the facts you require are stored elsewhere. Local searches, that is, local to the server you log in to, may only provide the minimal amount of information you require. Local searches can be achieved simply by browsing through the Gopher menus on the server you have connected to. You should also be aware that each Gopher administrator provides their Gopher service for a specific type of information only. General information which is specific to a single academic institution will be of no use whatsoever when you are after some rarer information. This is where a 'gopherspace' search comes in. All of your searches should be in gopherspace if you are performing the widest possible search.

All root (top level) menus in a Gopher server, such as the one shown previously, contain an option to search all the other known Gopher servers on the Internet. All of the Gophers in existence form an expanse known as 'gopherspace', and this type of search uses a service known as veronica.

The veronica service

Veronica (very easy rodent-oriented net-wide index to computerized archives) is a fairly new service to arrive on the Internet. Basically, it is an index to every gopher menu-item in the world. Using veronica it is possible to conduct a thorough search through all of the existing Gopher server menus, and then extract the required information accordingly. Without veronica it would be impossible to carry out an extensive search for any information, something the designers of Gopher realized very quickly. The Archie service operates very similarly to Gopher, in that it scans many FTP sites in its search for the information you require, and this was the model the designers of Gopher eventually used to implement veronica. Veronica maintains an index of Gopher menu-titles and allows the user to conduct a keyword search of these in the hope that the required information may be located.

Searching Gopherspace

At the time of writing there are no veronica client programs, and access to veronica is achieved by placing a call to a Gopher server via telnet, such as consultant.micro.umn.edu, etc. The veronica service is itself made available via a menu-option in the Gopher server you eventually use; this option will commonly be found in the Other Gopher and Information Servers option of your Gopher's top-level (root) menu, as was illustrated in the previous example. Once you have found the menu item mentioned, you should see a number of further options which include Search titles in gopherspace using veronica/. It is this option which will facilitate a gopherspace search (this option provides a link to the veronica directory at the University of Nevada). There are basically two searches which are currently available, and these will be shown as menu items in their own respect. They are:

- Search gopherspace using a single keyword
- Search gopherspace using a partial Boolean

Selecting either option will result in veronica asking you to provide a keyword to search for. The single keyword search allows you to search for simple expressions made up of only a single word, whereas the second uses the WAIS index with Gilbert's Boolean extensions; it is this version that can

accept limited Boolean search terms (to be examined later in the chapter). The
WAIS server's directory entry for veronica outlines the syntax of the Boolean
search patterns. The accuracy of any veronica search depends on the accuracy
of the menus used by Gopher administrators. Veronica itself does not actually
conduct a full text search of the data it finds, just as the Archie service indexes
only filenames and not their internal contents. Instead, veronica indexes the
titles of all the Gopher menus in existence, and this list is updated approximately every two weeks. By the end of 1993 nearly 400 Gophers were indexed
by veronica, with a further 200 yet to be indexed. In the context of the previous
example, choosing the Other Gopher and Information Servers
option would result in a menu similar to that shown below:

```
         Internet Gopher Information Client v1.12
            Other Gopher and Information Servers
     1.  All the Gopher Servers in the World/
 →   2.  Search titles in Gopherspace using veronica/
     3.  Europe/
     4.  Middle East/
     5.  North America/
     6.  Pacific/
     7.  South America/
     8.  Terminal Based Information/
     9.  WAIS Based Information/
```

To conduct a gopherspace search we would choose option number 2 (either
by moving to it using the cursor keys, or by typing in 2, and then pressing
[Return] –do the latter especially if you are using a dumb terminal emul-
tion. Veronica will now be invoked and in a few moments a further sub-menu
will appear, for example:

```
         Internet Gopher Information Client v1.12
         Search titles in Gopherspace using veronica
 →   1.  Search gopherspace by _SINGLE_ keyword veronica <?>
     2.  Search gopherspace by _partial Boolean_ veronica <?>
     3.  About the partial-Boolean WAIS index.
     4.  FAQ: Frequently-Asked Questions about veronica.
     5.  Proposals for veronica Development, Nov 19, 1992.
     6.  Initial veronica announcement, Nov 17, 1992.
```

The sub-menu shown above is the veronica gopherspace menu. Some
options here will lead to textual documentation from the veronica authors and
other contributors, although the searching commands themselves will nearly
always be found as the first two options in the menu. Notice the <?> which
delimits the searching options; these refer to indexed directory resources,

options which do not lead to any direct information as such, but instead a subset of the directories' contents. Choosing the first option to invoke the single word search results in a dialogue-box requesting us to enter a single keyword to search for, as illustrated below where the word quayle has been used (perhaps a reference to Dan Quayle, the former vice-president of the United States):

```
    Search gopherspace by _SINGLE_ keyword veronica
Words to search for: quayle
[Cancel ^G] [Accept -Enter]
```

Pressing [Return] commits the search pattern, and veronica searches in gopherspace for the requested menu items. In a few moments we should receive some entries similar to the following:

```
       Internet Gopher Information Client v1.12
 Search gopherspace by _SINGLE_ keyword veronica: quayle
    1.   The Bush/Quayle Campaign/
    2.   Vice-President Quayle's Acceptance Speech - 8/20/92.
    3.   Dan Quayle (fact sheet).
    4.   Dan Quayle: A Biography.
    5.   Quayle chose Guard instead.
    6.   Quayle watches "Murphy Brown".
 → 7.   We could do worse than having Dan Quayle as president.
    8.   quayle-accept.
    9.   DAN QUAYLE: Fact Sheet - 9/30/92.
    10.  BIOGRAPHY: Dan Quayle.
    11.  BUSH-QUAYLE IRAQ POLICY: Analysis.
    12.  Quayle chose Guard instead.
    13. Quayle and Murphy Brown.
```

Choosing item number 7 (by entering '7' or moving to line 7 and pressing [Return]) would make veronica pull the associated document from the Internet host that stores this information, and the document will then be shown on our screen accordingly, as shown in the hypothetical example below:

```
Headline: We could do worse than having Dan Quayle as president
Publish Date: 07/10/1991
If film director Francis Ford Coppola made a movie about a
Dan Quayle presidency, would he title it Apocalypse Now
II? During a Quayle administration, would America inex-
orably become a Third World nation - economically, geopo-
litically and militarily? In a Quayle era, would average
citizens be sapped of the courage to get up in the morning?
```

```
There is no point in arguing against the notion that Vice
President Quayle suffers from deficiencies, perceived or
otherwise. However, it is high time to rebut the irration-
ality and historical illiteracy that has always epito-
mized much of the bashing endured by Quayle, even before
the terms "irregular heartbeat" and "thyroid disorder"
were associated with George Bush.
... etc ...
```

Documents are scrolled a screenful at a time. The [spacebar] key will advance the screen, while the q command will quit you from viewing the document, and you will be returned to the previous menu of items that were located. Refer to Table 9.2 for a list of other Gopher commands which can also be used. From time to time server errors can also occur. These happen because the document you require is simply not in the place it should be. As a result, the main veronica index loses track of the document's new location and the end result will be a server error message flashed on your screen with the name of the file that couldn't be retrieved. Despite the server error, try to note the name of that file since it may still be found using a service such as Archie, which specifically works with filenames. Refer to Chapter 4 for more details on the Archie service.

Saving a file and initiating downloads

If we now wanted to save this file, we can do one of three things:

- Display the file on screen and ensure that your communications software is recording the output into a local file. On Unix you would use the script command
- Use the save (s) command – available only if you are using a local Gopher client on your machine (so that write permission is enabled)
- Use the D (download) command with a suitable protocol

Assume we pressed s to save the file that is associated with the option we have selected. We would see the dialogue:

```
Save in file: We-could-do-worse-#7
[Cancel ^G] [Accept-Enter]
```

Notice how Gopher has extracted a name for us to use (taken directly from the menu with all spaces changed to hyphens). Gopher would then save the file to disk (assuming we had permission) as soon as we press the [Return] key. Pressing [Ctrl-G] would abort the save operation. If you want to type a new name, simply go ahead and enter an alternative. Gopher's filenames are not that friendly, and many would not be acceptable under some operating systems (remember the DOS 12 character limit?). Unix systems should pose no problem because they accept horrendously long filenames. If you do save a file that has a name that is too long it will normally be truncated i.e. shortened.

Similar to the save command (s) is the download command (D). Pressing D results in the following dialogue:

```
We could do worse than having Dan Quayle as president #7
1.  Zmodem
2.  Ymodem
3.  Xmodem-1K
4.  Xmodem-CRC
5.  Kermit
6.  text
Choose a download method:
[Cancel ^G] [Choose 1-6]
```

This menu shows a number of different transfer protocols. The next important step is to find a suitable protocol that your communications software can handle. Gopher will normally allow you to start up your local transfer program before the download takes place, although such details are highly system specific. The shareware communications package Odyssey, for example, when running in the background, will wake up all of a sudden as Gopher sends it a 'get ready' message.

TIP

Apart from sz, there is also sx for XModem. Many computer systems have their equivalents. If you do not have sx or sz for downloads, try kermit. Many Unix systems have a kermit command

---

What happens when a file is missing?

Sometimes, well quite frequently actually, a file will not be found by Gopher even though it has the file's whereabouts stored in its internal index. Files come and go on an hourly basis on the network; some may be deleted by accident, or may not be available due to a system breakdown. In such cases the retrieval or selection of an item to examine may result in a gophercrash; the result of a reference to a file that no longer exists in the place it should have been. A useful command to examine a file's whereabouts is = (equals sign). Pressing this on an item will tell you its origin, i.e. the site and directory location where it resides, for example, in the context of our previous selection:

→ 7. We could do worse than having Dan Quayle as president.

pressing = would result in a display similar in content to:

```
Type=1
Name=We could do worse than having Dan Quayle as president.
Path=/facts/qov/quayle doc12
Host=site.archive.edu
Port=604
```

which basically tells us that the file we were looking at resides at the site site.archive.edu, and is located in directory /facts/gov as the file named quayle_doc12. Now if that file is moved (or deleted), or if the host goes down (crashes) for whatever reason, the Gopher will not be able to access the file. If the file has genuinely been removed due to its age or accuracy, it is up to the Gopher to rescan the necessary site to update its index (thus the file would then no longer be displayed on any menu). This takes a bit of time, so it is quite possible that you will come across the odd error now and again. Using the = command at least tells you the site where a particular file resided; you could then browse this archive with a tool such as ftp.

Boolean searches

Boolean searches are also possible with the veronica service. Rather than typing a single search keyword it is possible to supply a number of conditions to the search keyword, and, of course, provide more than one keyword, and join these together with logical expressions to match only certain articles, e.g. show all documents with 'Quayle' and 'Bush' in them:

bush and quayle

This search pattern would search for files that contain bush and quayle in the menu line (not the file contents, remember). Likewise we could use

bush or quayle

to find either name, or we could use a more complex expression using Gopher's bracket notation, such as

bush and (quayle or dukakis)

which would search for menu entries which contain bush and quayle or bush and dukakis, for example:

→ 1. Bush beats dukakis in key state
  2. Bush and quayle head for victory

The 'and' clause is the default clause used in the case that the 'and' is not mentioned. So, a Boolean search pattern of `bush quayle`

would search for articles with bush and quayle in them. Finally, there is the 'not' clause, which can be used to exclude certain words, for example:

`bush and (quayle or dukakis) not state`

would return just:

⟶ 1.   `Bush and quayle head for victory`

in the context of our previous example, since the word 'state' is excluded. Enough examples, I think you get the idea. Lastly, there is the * wildcard, which can be used to match multiple characters, for example

`qu*`

would match 'quayle' (and 'qu' by itself, coincidentally), and you can use this wildcard anywhere in a Boolean search expression, although it must come at the end of a string (or word).

UNDERSTANDING GOPHER MENUS – DELIMITER CODES

Gopher menus are delimited with a range of different codes which tell you more about a particular resource. Each delimiter code appears at the end of an item in a Gopher menu and Table 9.3 illustrates the main codes that are commonly in use. The reader should note that a menu item without a delimiter code refers to a menu item which itself is a resource, e.g. an ASCII document, whereas / at the end of a resource means that further files and possibly menus exist inside this entry (this is analogous to a 'directory' file in Unix, or DOS, etc.).

Table 9.3   Gopher menu item delimiter codes

Code	Meaning
/	A sub-menu option. Selecting this option will reveal a sub-menu of items
\<TEL\>	Telnet resource, i.e. log-in to a another machine to access information
\<BIN\>	Binary resource, i.e. a binary file, rather than an ASCII document
\<?\>	A searchable resource. Selecting this menu item will allow you to conduct a search for further information
\<CSO\>	This resource is a CSO white-pages resource server.
\<HQX\>	A compressed file in the BinHex format. Refer to Chapter 7 for compression formats
\<3270\>	Refers to an IBM mainframe emulation. Your terminal may need to emulate this in order to use it
\<Picture\>	Refers to a picture file. Use the = command to see what format the image is
\<)	Sound file (the < represents a speaker)

Images and sound files

These are delimited with the codes <Picture> for images, and <) for sounds. The ability to decode such files is system dependent. We suggest that you download the image or sound file directly, rather than playing it since the necessary software to handle the file(s) in question may not have been installed. Remember to use the − command to see the file type. Refer to Chapter 8 for details on image formats.

FINDING PEOPLE – CSO WHITE PAGES SERVERS

Some Gopher resources are delimited with the code <CSO>, which is an acronym for Computing Services Office at the University of Illinois, who originally developed this service. CSO servers are, in essence, electronic directories of Internet members which reside at various organizations (most are large academic institutions). CSO server machines are in widespread use on many Gophers in the US, and are a useful feature for locating individuals. CSO server machines can be interrogated according to each institution. The 'Phone Books/' option of many Gopher servers will allow you to browse through a list of participating organizations. When you haven chosen a particular organization, for example the Massachusetts Institute of Technology (MIT), you are provided with a minimal menu of four fields, which contain the lines entitled: Name, Phone, Email and Address. Each line is numbered, and pressing the required number will allow you to enter details into a field for that line. Building up the information allows you to pin-point the person you require.

Pressing the [Return] key at the end of the field initiates a search and if a match is found it will be shown in an expanded form for you to see. This feature is very good for finding out user-names from email addresses, and for locating the mailing address of a person.

TIP

Another 'white pages' server is the WHOIS server at nic.ddn.mil (telnet address).

One final point to note concerns the name, phone number and email address fields. These fields can only be used as the basis of a search when any of the other fields are left blank, that is to say that you could conduct a search using just the person's phone number, email address or name (given that you knew one of these items). If, however, you knew a person's address, this would not allow you to conduct a search using this information alone – you would have to fill in one of the other fields mentioned to have a chance of finding the person you require. Choosing the `Phone books/` option may lead to a menu similar to that shown below:

```
       Internet Gopher Information Client v1.1
                      Phone Books
  → 1.  University of Minnesota <CSO>
    2.  About changing information in the U of M directory.
    3.  WHOIS Searches/
    4.  Internet-wide e-mail address searches/
    5.  Phone books at other institutions/
    6.  X.500 Gateway (experimental)/
```

As can be seen, a number of other search methods have been included here, including email searches and **WHOIS** searches. Option 5 on this menu, `Phone books at other institutions/`, will allow you to conduct a much wider CSO search; its expanded menu will resemble the following:

```
       Internet Gopher Information Client v1.1
            Phone books at other institutions
  → 1.  About Phone Books.
    2.  All the directory servers in the world/
    3.  Africa/
    4.  Asia Pacific/
    5.  Europe/
    6.  North America/
    7.  X.500 Gateway (experimental)/
    8.  whois information and server list.
```

This hierarchical menu will allow you to choose a specific CSO server area, for example the European sites which run CSO servers. The second option in this menu looks particulary appealing, since we can search the entire CSO server population (useful if you do not know the country where a particular person resides – similar to a 'gopherspace search').

Wildcarded names

If you have problems with a name or email address, you can use the * wildcard to match any set of characters, in order to scale down your searches, e.g. you would enter the name `Jas*` to locate people named Jason, Jasmin, etc. Unfortunately, most CSO servers do not recognize the common ? (single character) wildcard, nor do they use the standard regular expressions (search wildcards) used on Unix. The * wildcard can be used anywhere in a line, for example `Ja* Smith`, so searches can be refined yet further. One point to note when using wildcards is the possibility of locating too many entries; in such a case the CSO server will inform you with a warning message and you should refine your search yet further.

FTP VIA GOPHER – DOWNLOADING AND VIEWING FILES

Nearly all Gopher servers have an FTP option located in their root menu. In our example the option was named `Internet file server (ftp) sites/`. Noting the delimiting / character we can see that this menu is most probably going to lead to a list of ftp sites, and you would be correct in this assumption. Ftp servers require the user to remember a series of commands, and using the ftp service through a Gopher can be much easier. When using a Gopher to conduct an ftp session, your file down loading is achieved entirely using Gopher's hierarchical menus. In essence you find yourself locating a site, and then a directory where a particular file is stored, and then the file itself that you require. This may seem the reverse of what you actually want to do, so using a tool such as Archie to locate the file you require may help you more quickly at this stage.

Of course, a Gopher may tell you about a particular site that has a file you require, so this is an additional avenue you may want to try. A typical ftp menu accessed via Gopher may resemble:

```
        Internet Gopher Information Client v1.1
           Internet file server (ftp) sites
 ──→ 1.   About FTP Searches.
     2.   Popular FTP Sites via Gopher/
     3.   Query a specific ftp host <?>
     4.   Search FTP sites (Archie)/
```

As can be seen, it is possible to run the Archie program via Gopher and even query a specific ftp host for a file (you would, of course, have to be fairly certain of the location of the file you require in order to use this option – if you don't, use Archie directly, or via Gopher itself). The `Popular FTP Sites via Gopher/` option is a good place to start searching for a file you require since many of the most common and well-established ftp sites will be available for searching directly. This option will normally break down sites alphabetically (an A–Z, e.g. `acsc.com` right through to `zebra.desy.de`). A sub-menu of such sites will commonly resemble the following:

```
        Internet Gopher Information Client v1.1
                      FTP sites
 ──→ 1.   About peruse FTP Sites.
     2.   About anonymous FTP.
     3.   a FTP sites/
     4.   b FTP sites/
     5.   c FTP sites/
     ... etc ...
    28.   z FTP sites/
```

The actual sites that can be searched can be found next to the options which have alphabetical breakdowns (a FTP sites/, for example, has a menu of anonymous ftp sites that start with the letter a, and so forth). The options at the start of the menu offer you some documentation about the ftp service in general, and you may wish to get hold of these (or, of course, read Chapter 2). In the context of the example above, choosing option 4 to select ftp sites beginning with the letter b may yield a menu consisting of the following entries, each of which is an FTP site which can be searched (this list has been shortened to conserve space):

```
          Internet Gopher Information Client v1.1
                         b FTP sites
 →  1.   bach.cs.columbia.edu 128.59.28.19 unknown/
    2.   babar.mmwb.ucsf.edu 128.218.21.42 gnu/
    . . .
   10.   bertha.pyramid.com 129.214.1.100 unknown/
```

Pressing [Return] on one of these sites would open that site and allow you to browse through a list of directories that are available. Because the file structure of ftp systems is hierarchical, Gophers are well suited to this type of menu display–bear in mind the hierarchical file system when browsing Gopher menus, since this may help you navigate more easily (substitute the Gopher u (up) for the ftp cd .. command, and the ftp cd (change directory) command for the pressing of the [Return] key on a particular line). In the context of the previous menu, pressing 2 would display the message:

```
Move to line: 2↵
```

Pressing [Return] would make then Gopher display the following sub-menu:

```
          Internet Gopher Information Client v1.1
                babar.mmwb.ucsf.edu 128.218.21.42
 →  1.   bin/
    2.   dev/
    3.   pub/
```

All of these lines are in fact directories mapped onto Gopher menu items, and you can select a directory in which to search by selecting an appropriate line (using the cursor keys, if available, or by pressing an appropriate number and pressng [Return], etc.). If you are a Unix user, you will recognize these system directories–the bin directory is a repository for binary programs, actual Unix commands such as ls and who perhaps, while dev is the Unix device directory in which all of the systems terminals and printer devices are stored. The pub (public) directory is normally put aside for anonymous ftp users and will be a good place to start searching for the file you require.

Eventually you will find the individual files themselves, and selecting the appropriate file will result in that file being displayed on your screen. Working with a Gopher in this way is very much a divide and conquer approach, breaking down the subject area into smaller pieces until you find the information you require.

Displaying non-ASCII files can be a problem, since Gopher will just display garbage on the screen. ASCII files can, of course, be viewed directly and captured into a file. Gophers are becoming ever more intelligent, and in the majority of cases you will receive an error message when trying to display a non-ASCII file. We have also assumed that you know which site(s) to choose in order to find the information that interested you. In reality you may not know where the information you require is located, so you will have to use a service such as Archie (either via `telnet` or Gopher). As mentioned, typing in a keyword on the subject matter that interests you may reveal a Gopher document that itself mentions the name of a site and file that has some relevant information. You could then use the ftp option of Gopher, as previously shown, to find the file. In some cases you may find that your Gopher doesn't know about the site you require; in such a case try a different Gopher server machine, or use the anonymous ftp service directly (see Chapter 2). You can use Archie to locate a file directly from within the Gopher system, and this is now examined in more detail.

Using Archie via Gopher

You may have noticed that one of our original menu-items allowed us to search the world's ftp sites using the Archie service (`Search FTP sites (Archie)/`). Archie is used interactively when accessed directly via `telnet`, although the Gopher interface is much more friendly. (Refer to the A–Z resource guide for more information on public Archie servers that are reachable via `telnet`.) This section concentrates on the Gopher service. Choosing the ftp-Gopher option will display a menu similar to the following:

```
         Internet Gopher Information Client v1.1
               Search FTP sites (Archie)
 ─→ 1.   Exact search of archive sites on the internet <?>
    2.   Substring search of archive sites on the internet <?>
```

An exact search, as the name suggests, allows a file to be searched for using a complete filename (note that this option will take notice of the case of any characters used in a keyword pattern – just as in the actual Archie system). A substring search is more useful when you are unsure of the name of a particular file, for example you could enter the search keyword `edi` to locate files that contain this pattern, e.g. `editor` or just `edi` itself, of course. Entering the string edi using the exact search option will result in a search for this string exactly as it appears, e.g. a file named edi (not EDI or even Edi). Choosing the substring option reveals a dialogue box requesting you to enter the name of the file you want to locate, for example:

```
Substring search of archive sites on the internet
Words to search for: guest↵
[Cancel ^G] [Accept - Enter]
```

For the purposes of this example, the word guest has been entered. Press [Return] to commit the search phrase, and commence the search; the keystroke [Ctrl-G] will interrupt the entry of the keyword and return you to the previous menu. Our search revealed the following sites that have files with the string guest in them:

```
        Internet Gopher Information Client v1.1
        Substring search of sites on the internet: guest
→ 1.    unixdl.pitt.edu:/prep/general/guest_account_policy.txt.
  2.    aun.uni.no:/ifts-data/info/stat/cap/gopher.guests.
  3.    aun.uninett.no:/drifts-data/info/stat/gopher.guests.
  4.    larry.mcrcim.mcgill.edu:/games/muck/muf/guest.asc.
  5.    dsrbg2.infor.tu-muenchen.de:/ext/Unix/sh/guestshell.
  6.    nova.cc.purdue.edu:/pub/next/guestshell.1 <BIN>
  7.    roxette.mty.itesm.mx:/next/sub/guestshell.tar.Z <BIN>
```

The salient features of this menu to note are the <BIN> delimiter codes on some files, which stand for 'Binary'. Binary files must be treated slightly differently to ASCII files. For a start, binary files cannot be viewed directly (they are either executable programs, compressed files, images, etc.). ASCII files can be recognized by the absence of any delimiter character, or by the filename itself, e.g. the filename guest.asc in line 4 – noticing the .asc extension which is commonly used to stand for ASCII, as are the extensions .DOC and .TXT. Pressing [Return] on one of the binary files in order to view it may result in error, since this would not be the appropriate option (although this is system specific); instead you may want to use the Gopher D command to download the file to your computer.

Getting hold of a file can be done in a number of ways. If the file is ASCII you can view it directly and save this into a file using the log-file feature of your communications software (Unix has the script command). The Gopher command s can also be used to save the item you have found into a file (the name will be asked for after you choose the command), although in most cases it will be best to use the D command which applies to all file types, whether they be binary or ASCII. There are no hard-and-fast rules regarding binary files. Different Gopher systems may save such files in a number of ways, e.g. a compressed file may be decompressed or it may be left intact.

Remember that the file you require could be accessed using the anonymous ftp service (after all, you now know the name and location of the file from the Gopher menu).

But a word of warning. Saving files will not be allowed if you are using a remote Gopher server. This is because the remote computer will not have granted you permission to save the file in its file system. You can only save a file to disk if you are using a Gopher client program from your own computer. The D command (download a file) will be OK, since it initiates a file transfer to your computer. Once again, be sure that your communications software can deal with a file download; many Gopher systems offer a choice of transfer protocols, e.g. XModem, ZModem (ZModem is by far the best for speedy transfers).

Using `telnet` via Gopher

Some resources shown by the Gopher system are only accessible via `telnet`. Such resources are identifiable by the delimiter code <TEL> at the end of the line. Selecting such an option will invoke the `telnet` system on the menu resource you have selected (normally another Internet site which has the information you require). Many interactive systems are available on the Internet which house a vast amount of information – refer to the A–Z resource guide in the appendices for a comprehensive list. The Gopher service can link into such services via an appropriate `telnet` connection to the service required, for example you may want to access an on-line OPAC in a library, or browse a scientific database which has some relevant information. Using Gopher to access such resources is beneficial to the user since they have been specifically grouped together when you initiated your original Gopher search.

Many Gopher menus have a specific menu option for an interactive terminal-based session. Searching gopherspace may yield an option such as `Terminal Based Information/` which will have a sub-menu of `telnet` services which you can hook into. Choosing one of these will enable you to link into another Internet site, and exiting this will return you back to your original Gopher menu from where you initiated the call. One point of warning, however: invoking a `telnet` session does have its risks – if the session breaks down, for whatever reason, you may not get back to your Gopher client. The example below illustrates a session with the Gopher client at the internet site `consultant.micro.umn.edu`. Selecting the main root-menu option `Other Gopher and Information Servers/` resulted in the following sub-menu:

```
        Internet Gopher Information Client v1.1
          Other Gopher and Information Servers
 ─→  1.   All the Gopher Servers in the World/
      2.   Search Gopherspace using veronica/
```

```
3.  Europe/
4.  Middle East/
5.  North America/
6.  Pacific/
7.  South America/
8.  Terminal Based Information/
9.  WAIS Based Information/
```

Option 8 (Terminal Based Information/) refers to a series of specific telnet sessions which this Gopher knows about. Other options to search gopherspace for telnetable services may also be an option, and your Gopher may have dedicated options to this effect – there is no substitute for a good exploration to see what is available. You may even want to conduct a search using veronica with the keyword telnet to see what all the world's Gophers have on this subject (quite a lot, I would imagine!). Returning to our previous menu, selecting option 8 resulted in the sub-menu shown below:

```
         Internet Gopher Information Client v1.1
                Terminal Based Information
 → 1.  Appalachian State University <TEL>
   2.  CUline, University of Colorado,Boulder <TEL>
   3.  Columbia University – ColumbiaNet <TEL>
   4.  Cornell CUINFO <TEL>
   5.  MIT TechInfo <TEL>
   6.  NYU ACF INFO system <TEL>
   7.  New Mexico State University NMSU/INFO <TEL>
   8.  North Carolina State University Happenings! <TEL>
   9.  Princeton News Network <TEL>
   10. U of Saskatchewan Library INFOACCESS system <TEL>
   11. University of New Hampshire's VideoTex <TEL>
   ... etc ...
```

These options are confined to services based in the US, although you will have noticed the options in the previously shown menu which refer to other countries – these will yield yet more services which you can use, for example, the European menu may yield the following options (which are specific to just the European countries):

```
   ...
 → 1.  Aston University (UK)/
   2.  BIBSYS – Library Database in Norway <3270>
   3.  CAOS/CAMM Center/
   4.  CONCISE (COSINE European Information Server) <TEL>
   5.  Centre for Sci. Computing (need account) (Finland)/
   6.  Chalmers Univ. of Technology/
```

```
7.   ComNet RWTH Aachen (Germany)/
8.   DENet Danish Academic Network/
9.   Department of Physics,University of Pisa (Pisa, Italy)/
... etc ...
```

Choosing option 1 in the above menu will result in the a dialogue similar to the following (menus differ between Gophers although the telnet interface will be much the same):

```
Warning! You are about to leave the Gopher program and
connect to another host.

If you get stuck press the Ctrl and ] key, and then type "quit".
[Cancel ^G] [OK - Enter]
Trying 128.13.43.1 ...
Connected to aston.ac.uk
Escape character is "^]"
... etc ...
```

The other options in the above menu will eventually lead to further European telnet services, each categorized under the country and service type. Once you have entered the telnet session you may be asked to provide some information regarding your terminal emulation, and even some user registration details, e.g. a username, depending on the service. Some services require you to have an account (hopefully the Gopher menu will have stated this earlier to save time, as in option 5 shown in the previous European Gopher menu). One important aspect of the dialogue above is the warning message which is shown before you press return to commence the telnet session. Once telnet has been invoked there is no guarantee that you will return safely to the Gopher that invoked it. All manner of problems could occur in the telnet phase, including the possibility that the telnet service at the site being contacted no longer exists.

If your telnet session breaks down, or locks up (i.e. freezes) you can interrupt the session using the keystroke Ctrl-]. This keystroke will return you to telnets interactive mode (identified by the telnet> prompt). To exit telnet, and close down your connection, the close command should be entered (alternatively you can use quit). Whether or not you are returned to your original Gopher session is another matter however. Refer to Chapter 5 for more information on the telnet system, including terminal emulations and telnets interactive command-mode. The Ctrl-G keystroke should be used to abort the telnet session and return to the Gopher menu.

9.3 WAIS – wide area information server

WAIS is a service that allows users to browse an extensive library of information. The WAIS service was started in 1989 and since then a whole host of WAIS servers have sprung up all over the Internet. The A–Z resource guide in Appendix D of this book lists many of the WAIS resources that are in existence. Access to the WAIS service is similar to Gopher in that you can telnet to a WAIS server, or you can get your own client and run this on your machine. The former method seems to be the most popular, simply because it requires less effort to set up. The main advantage of WAIS over a system such as Gopher is that you can search for keywords and patterns that exist in the actual text of a file (Gopher and veronica, if you will remember, only search the menu lines – if an administrator didn't name an item correctly (or sensibly) then it may not be found by your search). WAIS is essentially a database of items known as sources. Sources arrive mainly in the form of text files, e.g. ASCII documents, that are spread all over the Internet, possibly at anonymous ftp sites as well as hosts running other WAIS servers. Around 300 source databases are now maintained by WAIS on a variety of subjects. The system is menu driven and requires a terminal emulation such as a vt100 or an ANSI derivative (WAIS has cursor control and screen highlighting effects which will not work on a simple dumb terminal).

TIP

WAIS sources can be accessed through Gopher, and Gophers can work with the less 'intelligent' terminals using individual character commands. Select the WAIS Based Information/ option where relevant.

And now to the disadvantages of WAIS. The system must be told what source database it must use before you commence a search. This really takes us back to the 'Chicken and Egg' style problem, since the user is expected to know which WAIS source database has the information required.

TIP

WAIS maintains a source called directory-of-servers which outlines all the sources available. Sources are also organized into an A–Z list so you could browse all the entries in under 20 minutes to see what is available.

Finally it should be said that WAIS is not good at searching for material that is organized into separate files; searches are essentially only word and sentence-matching tasks. That is to say that a search term could be matched in many hundreds of documents even though the majority of them were totally irrelevant to what you were looking for. This couldn't happen with Gopher since all items retrieved must be given a description of what that item actually is, i.e. what its contents are actually about. WAIS does not have this refined level of file organization other than the fact that it organizes its information into separate sources.

WHAT INFORMATION IS AVAILABLE ON WAIS?

The information on WAIS is constantly updated, as with most systems on the Internet. The main subject areas contain information on science-related topics, such as microbiology, education, diseases, music, the arts, the environment, religion (full bible texts for many religions), weather information, on-line thesaurus, on-line dictionary, on-line dictionary of quotations, agricultural information, law (mainly US), the Unix manual (SunOS 4.x), sci-fi archives, USENET archives, as well as many other Internet-related documents such as on-line RFCs and FAQs. You will see many similarities in the information presented by WAIS to other systems such as Gopher, simply because different tools are essentially accessing the same information.

USING WAIS

As soon as you contact a WAIS server, the system will ask you to wait a few moments while the system is started. You will then see a list of sources, one for each line of the screen. Each source is a collection of documents that relates to the area mentioned. Sources have names ending with a `.src` suffix which stands for 'source', for example: `directory-of-servers.src`, which is a list of WAIS server machines around the world. To select a source you can use the cursor keys to move to the line required. The best way of searching multiple source files is to 'flag' them; this is performed normally by pressing the `[spacebar]` on each source. Pressing `[Return]` then allows a search pattern to be entered, and then all the documents that are relevant will be displayed on the screen for you to browse. To search a single source simple move to it and press `[Return]`. WAIS's menus are very easy to to use. Press `?` for a detailed list of commands. Here is a typical `telnet` session with WAIS, showing us how to log in (the username `wais` is typically used, and no password is required):

```
$ telnet quake.think.com↵
Trying 192.31.181.1 ...
Connected to quake.think.com
```

```
Escape character is "^]".
SunOS Unix (quake)
login: wais↵
Last login: Fri 28 12:01:56 from demon.co.uk
SunOS Release 4.1.1 (QUAKE) #3: Fri Jan 27 10:54:44 PDT 1994
Welcome to swais.
Please type user identifier (optional, i.e. user@host):↵
```

Finally WAIS asks for a user identifer, i.e. a user name. This is optional so you would simply press return, as we have done above. Now WAIS responds with a default terminal emulation. Remember that WAIS is a menu-driven system and a dumb (ASCII) terminal will not suffice. You must at least have a vt100 emulation capability, and WAIS will show this by default for your selection, for example:

```
TERM = (vt100)
```

Simply press [Return] to accept the vt100 emulation, or enter another valid emulation. WAIS is pretty fussy about the emulations you can use. If you are using a PC or Mac to access WAIS, preset the emulation before WAIS presents its main menu in order to avoid screen corruption. WAIS will then start, and shortly you will see a display similar to:

```
SWAIS                      Source Selection                     Sources 463

#      Server                   Source                          Cost
001: [archie.au]               aarnet-resources-guide           Free
002: [munin.ub2.lu.se]         academic_email_conf              Free
003: [wraith.cs.uow.edu.au]    acronyms                         Free
004: [archive.orst.edu]        aeronautics                      Free
005: [ftp.cs.colorado.edu]     aftp-cs-colorado.edu             Free
006: [nostromo.oes.orst.ed]    agricultural-market-news         Free
007: [archive.orst.edu]        alt.drugs                        Free
008: [wais.oit.unc.edu]        alt.gopher                       Free
009: [sun-wais.oit.unc.edu]    alt.sys.sun                      Free
010: [wais.oit.unc.edu]        alt.wais                         Free
011: [alfred.ccs.carleton.]    amiga-slip                       Free
012: [munin.un2.lu.se]         amiga_fish_contents              Free
013: [coombs.anu.edu.au]       ANU-Aboriginal-Studies           $0.00/minute
014: [coombs.anu.edu.au]       ANU-Asian-Computing              $0.00/minute
015: [coombs.anu.edu.au]       ANU-Asian-Religions              $0.00/minute
016: [150.203.672.2]           ANU-CAUT-Academics               $0.00/minute
017: [coombs.anu.edu.au]       ANU-CAUT-Projects                $0.00/minute
018: [coombs.anu.edu.au]       ANU-Coombspapers-Index           $0.00/minute
Keywords:
<space> selects, w for keywords, arrows move, <return> searches, q quits
```

The individual sources can be seen down the screen. Some may be immediately recognizable, for example alt.drugs is the USENET forum for drug use and this can be searched via WAIS here and now. In fact, you will see many USENET groups listed in WAIS, and searching these here can be convenient, especially if you do not have access to a newsreader (you could use an NNTP server via `telnet`, however, although no search facilities would be available).

TIP

Forget about the cost column on the right-hand side of the WAIS screen; all resources are free!

You should also recognize a few other things from this screen. The left-most column shows the various hostnames, i.e. names of Internet hosts that store the various sources shown. The sources themselves are listed in the third column, and organization of sources is done alphabetically in an A–Z fashion. You can use the the cursor keys on your keyboard to move up and down through the various screens, although if you find that your cursor keys do not work (common problem due to an emulation mismatch) try using the keys j for down (one line) and k for up (one line). Likewise, the J (upper case) key will move you down one screen, and K will move you up a screen. You can also type the number of a resource and then press [Return] to move to that item – the leading zeros on a source number can be omitted, however, e.g. 027 and 27 are the same to WAIS.

TIP

Refer to Appendix D for a list of FTP sites that are used to store articles for use in the WAIS system. Look for the entry entitled: 'WAIS Source Summary'.

Refer to Table 9.4 for a complete list of WAIS commands, or use the ? or h command for a list. WAIS will highlight the current resource (this will be the first when you start WAIS) as you move about within the system.

Selecting WAIS sources

To search a particular source simply move to it using the cursor keys (or j/k, etc.) and press [Space], i.e. the spacebar. An asterisk will then appear in the leftmost column, for example if you move to alt.drugs and pressed [Space] the screen entry for alt.drugs would look like:

```
007:    * [archive.orst.edu]        alt.drugs        Free
```

You can continue to select sources in this way; they will all be searched in succession. The [Space] key will also de-select an existing selection, and the = (equals) sign will de-select all of the sources currently selected (this is useful

Table 9.4 – WAIS command-set

Command	Function
Main commands	
?	On-line help with commands, etc.
h	Display summary of commands (as ?)
q	Quit the WAIS system
Moving around articles and sources	
[Cursor Down]	Move down one line
[Cursor Up]	Move up one line
j or [Ctrl-N]	Move down one line
k or [Ctrl-P]	Move up one line
J or [Ctrl-D]	Move up one screen
K or [Ctrl-U]	Move down one screen
<number>	Move to item numbered <number>
/<pattern>	Move to line with <pattern> in name
Selecting sources and articles	
[Return]	Ask for new keyword after selecting sources
[Space]	Select and de-select a source/article
=	De-select all sources
r	Re-display results of previous search
v	Display full entry details for source
Reading articles	
[Space]	Show next screenful of text
[Return]	Show next line of text (on some pagers)
q	Exit to the results screen
Performing a search	
[Return]	To start search after selecting keywords
[Return]	Display article from results screen
s	Re-display the source screen, i.e. start a new search
w	Ask for new keywords

in the case where you change your mind as to the current search criteria and you want to start afresh).

Starting a search

Once you have selected the source you want to search you must enter one or more keywords that you wish to find from each of the sources previously selected. The Keywords: line at the bottom of the screen will show you what is being entered. Type the keywords as you require. If you want to search for more than one keyword, simple leave at least one space between each of them in order to tell WAIS that these are separate search patterns. Some useful keystrokes to remember are: [Ctrl-W] to erase the keyword line and start afresh, and [BackSpace] or [Del] to delete the previous letter to make corrections (you may also want to try [Ctrl-H] or [Ctrl-BackSpace]

if the previous keystrokes do not work). Assume we entered the keyword
aspirin; the Keywords: line would now resemble:

Keywords: aspirin

Now press [Return] and WAIS will start searching the sources selected for
files that contain this word. The results will then be shown in a format similar
to the main menu previously seen, although this time each article found will
have a score and a line count. WAIS scores the items found in marks out of a
1000, where 1000 is an article with the most matches; all other marks will
become smaller as fewer matches within the article are found. It is also
important to note that we are no longer browsing sources, but instead actual
files. Some typical screen entries that form the result of our hypothetical search
could resemble the following:

```
SWAIS                                                        Items: 3
#       Score    Source        Title                         Lines
001:    [1000]   (alt.drugs)   Aspirin and Paracetamol       868
002:    [954]    (alt.drugs)   The aspirin miracle           432
003:    [834]    (alt.drugs)   Pain killers: side effects    190
... etc ...
```

The line count given in the rightmost column is useful when you may need
to know how extensive a particular article is. Very small articles may not be
worth looking at. Determining which articles you want to read is also made
easier by the inclusion of a small description of the article, seen above in the
fourth column. As mentioned, WAIS scores each article out a maximum of
1000, and this can be seen in column two.

At this stage you may want to select an article to read. Do this by moving to
the article and then pressing [Return]. WAIS does not have a copy of the
article in question, so it will have to connect to the server that has. A small
delay will be apparant while WAIS finds the resource you have selected. One
found, the text is displayed on your screen using a paging program of WAIS's
choice; this is commonly something similar to the Unix more command, so
you should be shown a screenful of text at a time (and pressing [Space]
should advance the text after each screen, whereas [Return] will normally
advance the screen by one line). If you have finished reading the article press q
once, and you will be returned to your original list of articles that were found.
You can now select another to read, or you can press s to redisplay the main
sources screen ready for a new search.

TIP

When conducting a new search WAIS may keep the original keywords you
have chosen. Press w to make WAIS use new keywords, and not the older ones
(assuming you want to use new keywords).

Saving articles

If you are using a remote WAIS server via `telnet`, it will not be possible to save files to disk using the S (save) command, since you will not have the necessary write permission on the remote server. Instead, use the m command to mail yourself a copy of the article in question (get into the habit of entering your full name at the WAIS log-in stage; this will save you re-entering your name). If you are using Unix, the `script` command can be used to capture all output to disk, and if you are using a PC or Mac to access WAIS, your communications software will most probably have a 'save-session-to-file' option (both of which you should invoke prior to using WAIS to ensure you capture everything – such listings will be very long because all of the WAIS menus will be captured as well!).

9.4   The World-Wide-Web

The World-Wide-Web, or WWW, is the newest information-location service to arrive on the Internet. The WWW introduces the concept of hyptertext searches which allow the user to branch off into other areas that are relevant to a particular subject area being examined. For example, you could be searching for computing-related topics, and then see a reference to another subject such as networking; this sub-topic would have its own reference number which would then allow you to explore this area, and then return to the main area after it had been examined. Searching for information in this way is similar to using a thesaurus in which you look up a word, and then find a similar word that could be used instead; looking up this new word would then lead to others, and so forth. That is all there is to say about the Web; many other hypertext-based systems exist, containing perhaps images and sounds, although the Web is really limited to textual information only at the present moment.

TIP

Use Archie to search for a Web client program using the keyword www (with the `whatis` command). This will make Archie search its Software Description Database for appropriate entries. You may also use the `prog` command to find any other files, etc. See Chapter 4 for more information on Archie.

Accessing the Web through a program such as `telnet` is the most common route used to access the service, although client programs for a wide range of machines and platforms are available (some that may support the processing of images, sounds, etc., although such client programs, or 'browsers', are rare and are very much in the experimental stage). This chapter is therefore confined to the simple texual client interface since all systems will be able to access this mode of use. Table 9.5 illustrates WWW servers reachable via the `telnet` program; others are documented in Appendix D. Note that no log-in names are normally required; If, however, a machine does ask for a username, use the name www.

For example, we could use the command:

```
$ telnet info.cern.ch↵
```

As soon as `telnet` gains access to a server, the screen will show a list of general subject areas in an A–Z fashion. You can advance the screen to show successive entries using the [spacebar] or [Return] keys. All option selection is numeric, and all hypertext links are shown in square brackets, e.g. [8]; an opening screen may resemble the following:

```
Overview of the Web

              GENERAL OVERVIEW

There is no "top" to the World-Wide-Web. You can look at it
from many points of view. If you have no other bias, here
are some places to start:
by Subject[1]     A classification by subject of inter-
                  est. Incomplete but easiest to use.
by Type[2]        Looking by type of service (access
                  protocol, etc.) may allow you to find
                  things if you know what you are looking
                  for.
About WWW[3]      About the World-Wide-Web global infor-
                  mation sharing project.
```

As can be seen from the dialogue above, the main entry screen allows searches to be carried out by subject or type. Subject searches are by far the easiest to use since you will be shown all of the subjects that the Web knows about; typing 1 would select this option, and yield a list of subjects with further links to choose, for example:

Table 9.5 WWW server machines accessible via `telnet`

Machine name	IP address	Location
info.funet.fi	128.214.6.100	Finland
eies2.njit.edu	128.235.1.43	US
info.cern.ch	128.141.201.74	Switzerland
vms.huji.ac.il	128.139.4.3	Israel

Aeronautics	Mailing list archive index [1]
Astronomy	A sample collection of astronomical images [5], also available in GIF [6] format; not yet directly browsable using W3.
Bio Sciences	See separate list [7]
Computing	Networking [8], Jargon [9], news-groups [10], Software Technology [11], Languages [12], Algorithms [13]
Geography	CIA World Fact Book [14]
...	

As you would imagine, the Web listings are quite extensive, and a wealth of information is available. When you eventually find what you are looking for, and the menus no longer can be broken down into sub-topics, the link-number will reveal the appropriate document that has been catalogued by the Web.

THE WEB VIA WAIS

The Web has access to WAIS-based documents, so it is possible to search a document internally for a particular word or pattern (use the WAIS f or find command for this). In addition to WAIS sources, the Web may use a number of other means to get at a particular file, including anonymous ftp, or even the USENET news. One annoying habit of the Web is that it will not tell you what type of resource is being accessed from its subject selection mode. Only when you select an item's link number will you find out what type of resource has been catalogued (there are no delimiter codes as in the Gopher). This is not a great problem, however, since the Web doesn't have that many commands. Use q for quit, a number for an item you want to read, b for back (to the last menu or screen), f for find, and ? or h for on-line help. Other commands may be available but these are all you need to navigate and read items. The find command (f) is particulary useful, since the Web is too tedious to search via subject – internal document searches are much better at locating those elusive facts.

After selecting a link number for an item we will be shown that item's cover-page. This is basically a description of how the article was provided, i.e. by WAIS for example. Suppose we chose item 11, Software Technology (as in the previous Web A–Z subject listing under computing), this would yield a cover-page similar to:

```
                              Software Technology Index
         SOFTWARE TECHNOLOGY
Server created with WAIS release 8 b3.0 on Jan 12 12:09:44
1992. Please send all contributions to post-
master@cc.unixa.edu. Selections from the following
subjects are available:
... list shown here ...
FIND <keywords>, 1, Back, Quit, or Help.
```

As can be seen, our selection has invoked a WAIS server which has the information (source) we require. At this stage we can quit (q), move back to the main WWW screen (b) or choose an item. Since only one WAIS source has been found that matches our requirements the number 1 is the only selection; this implies that we can only examine this source. If others were available we could select these and then conduct an appropriate search. If we now used the f (find) command to search this WAIS source database we would construct a search command using the syntax:

```
find <pattern-1, .. pattern-n>
```

The more specific a pattern, the more chances of isolating the information you have. WAIS has an in-built threshold of 40 articles which it can find in any one search so you must use as many accurate patterns as possible. For example, entering

```
find language↵
```

may result in many articles on computer languages, although a search criteria consisting of

```
find language object↵
```

will confine the search to just object-oriented languages. A list of articles would then be shown, for example:

```
             language object (in Software Technology)

                 LANGUAGE OBJECT
Index Software Technology contains the following 12 items
relevant to "language object".
obj-lang.txt      /pub/lang/c++/files/doc/[1]
                  Score: 1000, lines: 1042
intro.doc         /ftp/pub/c/docs/obj/[2]
                  Score: 868, lines: 402
... etc ...
```

WAIS has a rather strange method of telling the user which document(s) are most relevant. A 'score' system is used, the value 1000 being awarded to the document that most closely matches your requirements; all of the successive items will decrease in terms of their score value down to the least relevant items. The number of lines in the document(s) are also shown. In the context of our example above we can see the actual items and the file-system directories in which they are stored – these are most probably ftp archives indexed by the WAIS system. Choosing item [1] would result in a copy of the document being transferred from its location and on to our screen for viewing. A score of 1000 normally indicates a string that has been matched directly, so our document may literally contain the string language object side-by-side, whereas other documents lower down in the list may just have these words separately mentioned. Let's take a look:

```
...
obj-lang.txt      /pub/lang/c++/files/doc/[1]
                  Score: 1000, lines: 1042
...
...
FIND <keywords>, 1, Back, Quit, or Help: 1↵
                                              Document
...
the variable obj:c3 is a language object. This can be used
to refer to particular instances of this object.
```

10

Global chatting using Internet Relay Chat (IRC)

10.1 Introduction

You are about to enter the Twilight Zone. IRC, or Internet Relay Chat, is a new service taking the Internet by storm. Using IRC you can conduct a real-time conversation with one or more people who may be scattered anywhere in the world. If you are an established Unix user you may have already heard of utilities such as `write` and `talk` which allow two people to have a conversation with each other. Although `talk` and `write` are still widely used on the Internet, IRCs have now superseded these in terms of the range of facilities offered. For a start, IRC is a multi-user system allowing many people to simultaneously form public and private chat-groups. IRCs are constantly buzzing with activity, and the topics discussed are wide ranging. During the Gulf War, IRCs were used extensively to convey events about the conflict as they happened. In this chapter you will learn:

- How to use an IRC server via the `telnet` command
- How to become proficient with an IRC command-set
- Where to get IRC-related information and software

Many IRC systems exist, although we have concentrated on IRC II (version 2.1.x) for this chapter. The problem with IRC basically boils down to system resources; IRCs tend to slow down a system, especially when many dozens or perhaps hundreds of users are all using the same IRC server. For this reason IRC servers tend to come and go rather rapidly. The A–Z resource guide details a list of the more permament IRC servers that are used solely for chatting. Subscribe to `alt.irc` on USENET to keep up-to-date with new IRC servers that arrive on the network.

TIP

You can also `chat` to users using the `talk` and `write` commands on Unix. See Chapter 6.

As a rule of thumb, check that your terminal emulation is set to an emulation such as vt100 or ANSI, since some IRCs may require some screen drawing and cursor movement controls (Unix users will have a **TERM** variable which will hold their emulation). Also make sure that your terminal understands the delete key (this is ˆH on most systems), so you may want to issue the following commands either from the keyboard, or from an auto-login file such as `.login` (for `/bin/sh`), `.cshrc` (`/bin/csh`), etc.:

```
$ set TERM=vt100↵
$ stty erase "ˆh"↵
```

Oh, and by the way, the Twilight Zone is a discussion forum on IRC systems which is frequented by IRC system operators.

USING AN IRC SERVER WITH `telnet`

The most common way of using an IRC system is to make a `telnet` call to an IRC server. Many IRC servers exist, and more are being constantly added. Table 10.1 shows some of the existing IRC servers that were in existence at the time of writing (whether or not they are available now remains to be seen, however).

If a client system is available on your computer, the command `irc` will normally start it. The Service Provider guide in the appendices outlines those systems that have in-built IRC facilities. Also notice that some sites have a port number that must be specified (for example the site called `irc.ibmpcug.co.uk` which has port number 9999). Port numbers, if not used, will result in a login: prompt for that host being contacted (the system will not divert you through to the IRC service). In this case cancel your `telnet` session by pressing [Ctrl] and] and then type quit; you can retype the `telnet` command along with port name after the hostname, for example: `telnet irc.ibmpcug.co.uk 9999`.

10.2   Client software via FTP

You can construct your own IRC-client machine using source code that is available for a number of machine platforms. The majority of clients are built

Table 10.1   IRC server machines via TELNET

IRC server site name	Location
`aapo.it.lut.fi`	Finland
`badger.ugcs.caltech.edu`	United States
`bradenville.andrew.cmu.edu`	United States
`coombs.anu.edu.au`	Australia
`csd.bu.edu`	United States
`irc.ibmpcug.co.uk 9999`	United Kingdom
`irc.nada.kth.se`	Sweden
`ircclient.itc.univie.ac.at 6668`	Vienna
`kannel.lut.fi`	Finland
`nic.funet.fi`	Finland
`poly.polytechnique.fr`	France
`sunsystem2.informatik.tu-muenchen.de`	Germany
`suntrax1.cern.ch`	Switzerland
`ucsu.colorado.edu`	United States
`ug.cs.dal.ca`	United States
`vesuv.unisg.ch`	Switzerland

using the C language. A few IRC systems are implemented in Lisp. Table 10.2 lists a number of anonymous FTP sites that store IRC software. Instructions as to the implementation of these sources should be available along with the software, contact names, etc. These sites should also have general information about IRC systems (try Archie also).

10.3   Using an IRC system

IRC systems are interactive, and can be visually confusing to the novice user. Many commands are available, and all begin with /, for example /HELP to summon some on-line help (the case of each command is usually ignored, so /help would also be valid in this context). When you first access an IRC system a list of 'channels' will be presented. A channel can be thought of as a single discussion area, and you can switch between these just like the channels on a television set. If you type something without starting with / you are generally typing a message to be distributed to your channel. When entering messages and commands, be sure to press the [Return] key, i.e. don't wait around for a response because it won't happen without this keypress.

TIP

All IRC commands are case insensitive, so it doesn't matter if you type in UPPER or lower case when using an IRC system.

Table 10.2   IRC client software and information available via FTP

Platform	Site location/directory
EMACS (Elisp)	`cs.bu.edu` (`/irc/clients/elisp`)
	`nic.funet.fi` (`/pub/irchat`)
	`ftp.informatik.tu-muenchen.de`
	`slopoke.mlb.semi.harris.com`
	`lehtori.cc.tut.fi` (`/pub/irchat`)
MSDOS	`cs.bu.edu` (`/irc/clients/msdos`)
	`freebie.engin.umich.edu`
	(`/pub/irc/clients/MSDOS`)
Macintosh	`cs.bu.edu` (`/irc/clients/macintosh`)
	`sumex-aim.stanford.edu` (`/info-mac/comm`)
REXX client for VM	`cs.bu.edu` (`/irc/clients/rxirc`)
	`ftp.informatik.uni-oldenburg.de`
	(`pub/irc/rxirc`)
Unix	`cs.bu.edu` (`/irc/clients`)
	`plod.cbme.unsw.edu.au`
	`nic.funet.fi` (`/pub/unix/irc`)
	`ftp.informatik.tu-muenchen.de`
	(`pub/net/irc`)
	`slopoke.mlb.semi.harris.com`
VAX/VMS	`cs.bu.edu` (`/irc/clients/vms`)
	`coombs.anu.edu.au`

Commands that are not recognized will be rejected with a suitable error message. It is quite possible for one or more people to be listening on a particular channel, so a range of discussions can be in operation at any one time. You can, of course, switch to another channel, with the exception of a private channel, for which you will require permission to access (such permission is granted solely by the channel operator – the first person to open a particular channel, or the IRC systems manager in some cases). Public channels can be identified by the prefix `Pub:` (these are also known as visible channels), whereas private channels use the prefix `Prv:`. A channel name will also be allocated by the IRC system; these are simple strings, such as `#hack`. The actual people listening on a certain channel are identified by a series of nicknames (real names are hardly ever used), for example:

```
/NAMES↵
Pub: #hack      @superman spiderman iceman oldman
Pub: #hottub    wombat dingbat @koala
Pub: #USPol     @ircman
Prv: #Priv      User1 User2
```

The hash (#) is a prefix for the channel name. Older IRCs used + sign, which is now extinct in such systems. The @ (at) sign denotes the operator of a particular channel. The channel #hottub is commonly found on IRCs, and is a general discussion forum which is very popular. The system channel #Twilight_Zone is commonly frequented by IRC system operators (Sysops).

All IRC commands take the form /command, e.g. /LIST. If you forget the name of a particular command, but you know its first letter, type / followed by the first letter of the command you require, and then press the <Escape> key twice. For example, the command /W <Esc><Esc> would produce a hypothetical listing similar to:

```
Commands:
WAIT            WALLOPS         WHILE           WHO
WHOIS           WHOWAS
Aliases:
W               WA              WH              WLOFF
WLOG            WS
```

Aliases are used extensively in all IRC systems. Aliases are used for purposes such as shortening existing IRC commands (a type of short-cut command, if you like). If you are a completely new user to the world of IRCs you may want to use the commands /HELP NEWUSER and /HELP INTRO, which will give you a run-down of all the commands and facilities that exist on the IRC you are using. A discussion of some of the most fundamental IRC commands now follows.

IRC COMMANDS FOR NEWCOMERS

If you are a newcomer to the world of IRCs, be sure to learn the following subset of commands:

- /QUIT   to quit the system
- /LIST   to list what topics and subjects are being discussed
- /JOIN   to join a channel
- /NICK   to change your username to a nickname
- /MSG   to send messages
- /QUERY   to send messages to a channel

Section 10.4 discusses the USENET forums that currently deal with IRC systems.

TIP

If you are new to IRC, try joining the group #hottub, a general discussion forum that is available on nearly all IRC systems.

BASIC IRC II COMMANDS

Quitting /QUIT, /BYE, /SIGNOFF and /EXIT

The commands /QUIT, /BYE, /SIGNOFF and /EXIT can all be used to terminate your session with the IRC system.

Listing topics and channels /LIST

The /LIST command lists all of the current channels that are in use, along with the number of users in each channel and the topic being discussed. Use this command to find a topic that interests you, for example:

```
/LIST↵
Channel        Users        Topic
#hack          14           Hackers channel
#Quayle        4            Dan Quayle Fan Club Channel
```

Listing nicknames /NAMES

The /NAMES command shows you all of the nicknames that are currently in use on each the channel. The * (asterisk) denotes a user who is on-line at the time. Lines starting with Prv: indicate a private channel, for example:

```
/NAMES↵
Pub: #test        @ircman
Prv: *            superman spiderman
```

Changing your nickname /NICK

You can change your nickname using the /NICK <name> command, where the parameter <name> is the new nickname to use. Any nickname you choose will be shown by commands such as /NAMES. All nicknames are limited to nine characters. The allocation of a nickname is very important since it is the primary method by which users can identify you. By default, your nickname is set to your log-in name. The environmental variable IRCNICK can also specify your own personal nickname, for example:

```
/NICK wombat↵
jason is now known as wombat
```

Summoning on-line help /HELP

On-line help regarding a particular command can be summoned using the /HELP <command> command, where <command> is the name of a valid IRC command on your system. Using / and the first letter of the command you require and then pressing [Escape] twice will also generate a list of all the commands that begin with a certain letter, for example

```
/HELP HELP↵
Help on HELP
Usage: HELP [command]
Shows help on the given command.
... etc ...
```

and using the <Esc> key twice with a W to show all commands starting with this letter:

```
/W <Esc><Esc>
W       WA        WH          WLOFF
... etc ...
```

Identifying a user /WHOIS

The /WHOIS <nn> command identifies the real identity of a person identified with the nickname supplied as the parameter <nn>. The person's IP address and full name are normally shown, for example:

```
/WHOIS wombat
wombat is wombat@128.14.8.1 (J. Manger) on channel #hack
On irc via server somewhere.zone.edu.uk
Command last received: 4352 ...
```

If a user is on a private channel, the term *private* will be shown as the channel name. As can be seen from the example the IP and textual site address of the user are both stated, as well as the user's full name (if available). Some IRCs also show some additional information such as the idle time of a user, and the last command they issued.

Making yourself temporarily unavailable /AWAY

The /AWAY [msg] command allows you to leave a channel temporarily. Any user requesting you will be told that you are temporarily unavailable. Use the [msg] argument to include a textual string which will be shown to users that may request you. Without the [msg] argument removes the message implying you are available again.

```
/AWAY Gone for Lunch. Back at 1:00pm. ↵
You have been marked as being away
/AWAY↵
You are no longer marked as being away
```

Sending and receiving messages /MSG and /QUERY

In order to send a message to another user the /MSG <nn> <msg> is used, where <nn> is the nickname of the person you want to contact and <msg> is the message you want to send to them. For example, the command

/MSG wombat What is the weather like over there?↵

will send the message What is the weather like over there? to the person with the nickname wombat. When sending a message, the IRC system will echo the message back to you, so in the context of the previous command the sender would see

wombat What is the weather like over there?

The recipient of your message will also see a message similar to the above, although the sender's name will clearly be used. Replying to a message also makes use of the /MSG command, but with a slightly different syntax of either

/MSG <nickname of person who sent you the message>

or alternatively:

/MSG , <message>

In the second command above, the comma (,) has been used as a shorthand convention for the most recent person who sent you a message (this saves you typing in the person's whole nickname, as in the first command's syntax). Apart from the comma, a period (.) denotes: 'the last person who I (i.e you) sent a message', and can be used as another short-cut to save typing. The /MSG command can become rather tiresome to use, especially with all the punctuation commands such as , (comma) and . (period). An alternative command called /QUERY has therefore been provided to overcome this problem. The syntax of the /QUERY command is

/QUERY [nn]

where [nn] is a valid nickname of the person you are in contact with. Using /QUERY, all the text you type (without a preceding / sign) is sent as a private message to the recipient you specify in argument [nn]. Pressing the carriage-return key will send the message, so there is scope for modification using the <delete> key, etc. When the /QUERY command is used without any arguments the private conversation is ended.

To summarize, you can leave out the /MSG command completely and use just /QUERY [nn] and /QUERY to start and terminate a conversation (remembering that all text between these two last commands will be sent to the person mentioned in the [nn] argument). You can, of course, use a / command during a conversation – the results of commands are not shown on your recipient's screen, unless they are specifically designed for this purpose, such as the /MSG command.

Querying server connectivity /LINKS

You can make your IRC system show you all of the server machines that are connected to your IRC system using the /LINKS [server] command, where [server] is an optional server name which will be shown specifically, if mentioned (if omitted, /LINKS shows all servers by default). Wildcards can be used, e.g. * and ? to match multiple and single characters, respectively. All server-name arguments are assumed to be textual Internet site names, e.g. demon.co.uk. The example below uses the * to match all servers with the string .uk in them, i.e. United Kingdom servers:

```
/LINKS *.uk↵
zone.demon.co.uk: Demon Internet Systems, UK
```

Displaying administrative details /ADMIN

You can order your server to display some information regarding its administration using the /ADMIN command. Such information is usually very brief, perhaps just an email address of the IRC operator for personal help. /ADMIN takes an optional argument representing the name of an Internet host that runs an IRC system in order to display help information for this system:

```
/ADMIN↵
*** Department of Computer Science
*** XYZ University, email: fred@somewhere.com
/ADMIN somewhere.com
-somewhere.com- * The XYZ Company
-somewhere.com- * For help email: mailadmin@somewhere.com
```

Displaying the message-of-the-day (MOTD) /MOTD [host]

Similar to /ADMIN, the /MOTD displays the current machine's message-of-the-day, either for the current server, or for another. Specify an optional server name immediately after the /MOTD command to find information on that specific machine. /MOTD is named after the Unix file /etc/motd which contains an ASCII message which is displayed on all users' screens when they log in. A typical command could reveal:

```
/MOTD↵
** The server will be down from 13:30 to 14:30 for repairs
** Sorry for the inconvenience, which will be for upgrading.
/MOTD world.std.com
...etc...
```

Displaying who is on the system /USERS

The /USERS command lists the real log-in names of all the people currently connected to the IRC server machine. The username and host machine and terminal name are also shown, for example:

```
/USERS↵
UserID      Terminal      Host
wombat      ttyp10        gate.demon.co.uk
... etc ...
```

Brief user summary /LUSERS

Use the /LUSERS command to obtain a brief summary of the number of users on the current server. The number of IRC operators (#Twilight Zone channel users) will also be shown, for example:

```
/LUSERS↵
There are 55 users on 6 servers
5 users have connection to the twilight zone
```

Displaying the local time of a system /TIME

Using an IRC can be confusing because of the vastness of the network. Many countries will obviously be in different time-zones to your own. The /TIME command shows the local time of the server you specify, or of the current host. Wildcards can be used to query specific countries. The /DATE command is an equivalent command:

```
/TIME↵
world.std.com : Wed July 31 1991 -- 16:11 MET
/TIME *.jp↵
satsuma.s.u-tohoku.ac.jp : Wed July 31 1991 -- 23:12 JST
```

Joining a channel /JOIN

In order to join in a conversation on a particular channel you would use the /JOIN <channel> command, where <channel> is the channel name. Use the /LIST command to see what discussions are progressing. The /CHANNEL command is used identically. If you specify a channel name that does not exist, a new channel will be created and you will be the channel operator (what power!), for example:

```
/JOIN #hack↵
```

To un-join (or leave) a channel use the command /JOIN 0. If you are the channel operator, the whole channel will be shut down, and all users will be informed accordingly. A user who has joined an existing channel will exit temporarily, and can rejoin by issuing another /JOIN <channel> command, just as they did originally.

When you join a channel the IRC system will tell you what topic is being discussed on that channel, along with a list of users who are using that channel. Users with a '@' sign are channel operators, for example:

```
...
/join #hack
*** fred!fred@somewhere.com has joined channel #hack
*** Topic: Hacking and cracking!
= #hottub: fred jim john mary @paul
```

Other users of this channel will see just the message:

```
*** fred!fred@somewhere.com has joined channel #hack
```

By default, your username is used as an alias. You can, of course, change this via a command as we will see later. At this stage people in this group will be chatting, and you will see their messages appear on the screen one after another as they are sent to the channel, for example:

```
<jim!jim@sumara.cc.edi> What was that system you mentioned
+ earlier mary?
<mary!mary@sun1.cc.edu> It was called aix370.tt.ming.com
<jim!jim@sumara.cc.edi> Thanks!
```

This small conversation is between users jim and mary. In reality, however, you will see many other users talking away, and the pace may speed up a bit. You should also be aware that messages become irregular (out of sync), especially if a person is talking to multiple users. Get use to talking to one person at a time, and don't be afraid to join in. Remember that the ↵ ([Return] key) is used to commit a message; the ability to correct a message sometimes depends on your terminal device (ensure your Unix terminal understands the ^H key for deletions – use the command stty erase "^h" for this).

TIP

When typing in messages don't worry about the length of the typed line, since the line will be automatically wrapped for you, as in the example above, note the + sign in the leftmost column.

Inviting a user to participate in a group /INVITE

When you are using a channel you can invite another user to join it using the /INVITE <nn> [channel] command, where <nn> is the nickname of the person that you want to invite. If no channel name is specified you are implying that the user should join the channel that you are currently part of. An optional channel name can be used to invite the user to that specific channel instead, for example:

/INVITE wombat #hack↵
Inviting wombat to channel #hack

  The recipient you mention will be asked to join, and can agree or deny your request. You will be told of the user's response with an appropriate message as soon as they make up their mind. If you receive an /INVITE message you can respond with a command of the form

/JOIN -INVITE

which will allow you to join the channel which you were invited to join. Alternatively you could type

/JOIN <channel>

where <channel> is the name of the channel to which you were invited. Lastly you can issue a /JOIN command of the form

/JOIN -NICK <nn>

to join the channel that a specified nickname is on. A /JOIN command used without any parameters will tell you some information about the current channel, if it exists that is. Again, you can leave a channel using either of the commands: /LEAVE or /JOIN 0. In some cases you must be the channel operator to invite a user, although most IRC systems allow anyone to broadcast invitations to other users.

Analysing the current debate topics /TOPIC

Each channel is associated with a certain subject of discussion. You will clearly have to examine what discussion takes your interest, and this can be achieved using the /TOPIC <topic> command, where <topic> sets the title of the current channel's discussion topic. To avoid confusion, only a channel operator can change the title of the current discussion; for example:

/TOPIC IRCs on the Internet↵
wombat has changed the topic to "IRCs on the Internet"

Miscellaneous commands /!, /CLEAR and /HISTORY

Among the smaller miscellaneous commands to be included in most IRC systems are /!, /HISTORY [n] and /CLEAR. The /! command simply executes the most previous command; /HISTORY <n> is used to display all of the commands you have used in your session so far – the [n] argument is used to call back a specific command (each command in the history set is numbered). IRC screens can become cluttered, so /CLEAR has been provided to clear the IRC screen. You may want to use /CLEAR in the case of global messages which corrupt your screen, i.e. system operator messages, or messages from other Unix systems such as write, talk, etc. In addition, you may be able to use the keystroke [Ctrl-L] to 'refresh' the screen on some terminals.

Logging IRC activity /LASTLOG

/LASTLOG is a command that displays the contents of the IRC log file. The log file maintains a list of all the most recent messages that have appeared on your screen, and is useful if you were temporarily unavailable and missed such messages. The syntax of the /LASTLOG command is

/LASTLOG [number | text] [line]

The [number] argument is a numeric value representing how messages are displayed from the log file. If the command is used without the first argument the entire log file is shown. The [text] argument which can be specified instead of [number] is used to perform a specific search for a message (in other words, you enter a string to search for with the [text] argument, and the log is searched accordingly). Finally there is the [line] argument, a numeric value which specifies how many lines back into the log are displayed.

Sending private messages to a person /NOTICE

The /NOTICE command provides a way of sending private messages to a person; it has the syntax

/NOTICE <nn | channel> <msg>

where <nn> is the nickname of the person being sent the private message (a channel name can also be used here instead), and <msg> is the actual message to be sent.

Notification of users /NOTIFY

/NOTIFY is a useful command that makes the IRC system give notification of users who log in and out of the IRC system. Use the syntax

/NOTIFY [- | <nn>]

where <nn> is the nickname of the person you want to monitor. Notice the optional – (hyphen) argument which allows a previously monitored nickname to be disregarded, i.e. no longer monitored. Used without any arguments /NOTIFY tells you the state of any previous nicknames that are already added, for example:

```
/NOTIFY wombat↵
... later ...
*** Signon by wombat detected
/NOTIFY↵
*** Currently present: wombat
```

Ignoring users /IGNORE

It is possible to ignore all contact from one or more users using the /IGNORE command, which has the syntax

```
/IGNORE <nn>|<user@host> [-]<message-type>
```

The <nn> argument can be used by itself to ignore a person identified by his or her nickname (the user@host email format can also be used instead of a nickname). Specific messages can also be ignored (allowing a user to be partially ignored) using the <message-type> argument. Valid message types are: MSG, NOTICE, PUBLIC, INVITE, ALL, or NONE. Notice the optional – argument (hyphen) which allows a message type to be reinstated (the NONE keyword can also be used as well – see below). Simple wildcarded expressions can also be used, so, for example, you could ignore messages originating from people on a single Internet host, or from a specific country. Used by itself /IGNORE tells you who is being ignored. To ignore a single host, for example, we would use

```
/IGNORE *@world.std.com ALL↵
*** Ignoring ALL messages from *@world.std.com
```

while to ask who is actually being ignored we would use

```
/IGNORE↵
*** Ignorance list:
****@world.std.com ALL
```

To reinstate an ignored person (or site) you would use the similar IRC command

```
/IGNORE *@world.std.com NONE↵
****@world.std.com removed from ignorance list
```

Kicking of users /KICK

Only channel operators can use this command, which allows a user to be thrown off a channel. /KICK has the syntax

/KICK [channel] <nn>

where [channel] is an optional channel name, and <nn> is the user's nickname. Used without a [channel] argument the system attempts to locate the user using just the nickname argument; for example

/KICK #hottub wombat↵
*** wombat has been kicked off channel #hottub by Dingo

Describing your actions /ME

'Talking' over an IRC channel can be a strange experience, since no visual effects are in use. For this purpose the /ME command has been provided, which allows you to tell the current channel what you are doing! You could use a message, although this command is directed towards a complete channel. The syntax of the /ME command is simple:

/ME <my-current-action>

where <my-current-action> is a textual message telling the channel what activity you are currently engaged in, for example

/ME is feeding the cat!↵
*** Action: wombat is feeding the cat

   An equivalent method of using the /ME command is to use your own nickname as a / command, and then quote the message, for example if I were the user with the nickname WOMBAT:

/WOMBAT cannot satisfy this cat's appetite!↵
*** Action: wombat cannot satisfy this cat's appetite!

   /ME is aptly named since you must remember to think how the message will appear on the other channel-members' screens. In the first example above we can see that the /ME is substituted by your own name when it appears on the channel.

CHANNEL TYPES

Many different types of channel exist, the most common of which include:

- Limbo (or 'null') channels
- Public channels
- Private channels
- Secret channels

- Moderated channels
- Limited channels
- Topic-limited channels
- Invite-only channels
- Message-disabled channels

Channel 0 is known as the limbo channel (or null channel). The limbo channel is the default channel that you are assigned when you join an IRC. No message can be conveyed to a person using this channel, and everything will simply be seen by yourself. Public channels are those with the numeric values ranging from 1 to 999. A public channel can be seen by any user using commands such as /LIST and /NAMES, and are flagged with the string Pub:. When a channel is public, anybody can join it at will using the appropriate /JOIN command. Private channels are allocated numeric values ranging from 1000 onwards, and the prefix Prv: is shown in all user/group querying commands. A private channel has its channel name hidden, so people without the name simply cannot join. Public channels can be made private using the /MODE command (to be discussed later).

Secret channels are allocated the numeric value 0, and the channel will not be shown with querying commands such as /LIST and /NAMES. The /LUSERS command will not count secret channels. Public channels can be coerced to a private channel, again using the /MODE command. Customized channels can be constructed using the IRC's /MODE command. Clearly, only the channel operator can alter a channel's characteristics. Customized channels include moderated channels whereby only channel operators can talk. The original channel operator can make any user into a duplicate of him or herself. Non-operators can only 'listen' to messages, i.e. they cannot reply or join in. Limited channels allow only some people to use the /JOIN command, as specified by the channel operator. Topic-limited channels are users that can change the topic of a channel (using the /TOPIC command) as long as they have channel operator status.

Invite-only channels are users which can only join a channel if invited to do so by someone else on your channel. Message-disabled channels do not allow users to send messages with the /MSG command. As you can see, a combination of modes can be used, although these are the most common in use.

CHANGING CHANNEL MODES /MODE

The /MODE command allows a channel operator to change the characteristics of their channel. Typically this will define who can join and whether or not messages can be passed to the channel. The syntax of the mode /MODE command is:

```
/MODE <channel> +<channelOpts> <parameters>
/MODE <channel> -<channelOpts> <parameters>
```

where + enables a certain channel option, and − disables an option. Channel options in this context include the following, and are specified in the compulsory argument `<channelOpts>`:

i	Channel is invite only
l <n>	Make channel limited, where <n> is the maximum number of channel users
m	Make a channel moderated
n	No /MSGs to the channel are allowed
o <nn>	Makes person <nn> a channel operator
p	Make a channel private
s	Make a channel secret
t	Make a channel topic-limited

For example, to make a channel private you would issue an IRC command of the form

`/MODE #hack +p↵`

where #hack is the channel name, and +p enables the private channel status. Similarly, we can make a private channel public using the opposite command, for example:

`/MODE #hack −p↵`

Limiting the number of users that can be using a certain channel is done using the +l <n> option, where <n> is the maximum number of users to be permitted, for example

`/MODE #hack +l 20↵`

which will limit the channel #hack to a maximum of 20 people at any one time. All other options are self-explanatory.

CONFIGURING SHELL VARIABLES FOR AN IRC SYSTEM

All IRC systems depend on a series of user-defined variables to provide certain information to the IRC system. Such variables can be used to set your personal nickname, terminal emulation, and many other instances of such values. This section examines the most common variables which can be used. Depending on the system you are using, you will have to use the appropriate command to set your variables. On Unix systems the type of shell you are using will dictate the command needed to set an environmental variable. You can find out the name of your shell using the Unix command `echo $SHELL` (DOS users don't have such 'shells'). A number of standard shell-variables are used by many IRCs (these include TERM and HOME for example, and these are set up by the Unix `login` program when you gain access to your system).

For `csh` (C-Shell) users, the command set can be used to define a variable, for example:

```
set <variable-name>=<value>
```

A typical command typed under the csh shell would resemble that shown below (in this case we are setting a terminal emulation, where vt100 is a standard emulation on many Unix systems, and has controls similar to an ANSI emulator). The `irc%` is our Unix prompt throughout all examples:

```
irc% set TERM=vt100↵
```

The Unix command `setenv` can also be used under `csh` in the same way as `set`, but without the = sign. Note that quotes should be used on all character values, for example:

```
irc% setenv TERM "vt100" ↵
```

On Unix systems with the shells `sh` (Bourne Shell), or `ksh` (Korn Shell) you can set variables without a command, simply by assigning values directly, for example:

```
irc% TERM=vt100↵
```

If you make a mistake entering a value simple overwrite it by using the same command, but with the correct value. The command unset can also be used to un-set a variable, i.e. remove its existence completely. Remember also that a null (empty) value assigned to a variable does not always mean that the variable has been removed. On nearly all Unix systems a command called `export` is maintained. This is used with the name of a variable which you want to make available to all other programs on your system. For example, if you created a variable and then ran a new shell, the value you previously defined would not be available until the current shell was terminated, which may cause problems to your IRC system. Export all your variables to be on the safe side (TERM and HOME are nearly always exported by the `login` program automatically when you log in). For example you would type

```
irc% set TERM=vt100↵
irc% export TERM↵
```

DOS (PC) users set variables using their own `set` command, which has the same syntax as the Unix `set` command. The exporting of variables is required under DOS. To avoid a lot of retyping you may want to place your variable commands in a profile file. Profile files are used heavily on Unix systems, and the type of shell you are using will tell you which profile file is in use. Profile files are lists of simple Unix commands that are executed whenever a shell is created, such as when you log in. Csh shell users should alter the `.cshrc` file, whereas sh shell users should alter `.profile`. Korn shell users (ksh) normally have a `.kshrc` profile file. Use an ASCII editor to edit your profile file, and add your commands carefully so as not to disturb any existing commands. DOS users have batch files; their profile file is only executed when they first start (or reboot) their computer, and is called `AUTOEXEC.BAT`. (Alternative DOS-shells, e.g. Norton NDOS use a similar file, such as `NSTART.BTM`.) As you will come to see the IRC system also has its own profile file.

IRC variables

Now that you have some understanding of how variables are constructed, we can move on to discuss some of those which are most commonly used by IRC systems. Table 10.3 illustrates these. Those variables marked with a asterisk (*) are also standard Unix variables.

Here are some examples of all these commands in action for you to see. Shown below are some variable commands. As can be seen, we have first of all used the Unix `echo` command to show the settings for the `TERM` and `SHELL` variables; then we have set up some nicknames and usernames for yourself, and have then invoked `irc`. The sample `/WHOIS` command (used with our own nickname) shows us the output other users would see if they typed this command.

```
% echo $SHELL↵
/bin/ksh
% echo $TERM↵
ansi
% IRCNAME="The WoMbAt"↵
% export IRCNAME↵
% IRCNICK="JJ"↵
% export IRCNICK↵
% irc↵
... We are now in the IRC system ...
/WHOIS JJ↵
*** JJ is manger@128.16.4.1 (The WoMbAt), channel
   *private*
```

SETTING UP YOUR IRC PROFILE FILE (`.ircrc`)

On Unix systems, the file `.ircrc` is used as a profile file to execute any valid IRC command when you start up the system. The `.ircrc` file can be used to join or create a channel, and then configure it accordingly. Always use an ASCII editor to edit your profile file, such as `ex`, `vi`, etc. Comments can be added to your `.ircrc` file using the `/COMMENT` command, followed by the text you require. A hypothetical file could resemble:

Table 10.3   Common IRC variables

Variable name	Value
IRCNICK	Your nickname to be used, such as 'wombat'. Names can be altered using the /NICK command described earlier
IRCNAME	Specifies the name you want to be known by when other people view your entry with the /WHOIS or /WHO commands
TERM *	A standard shell variable. It is very important to get this setting correct since many IRCs need to have access to various screen controls, such as cursor positioning and even colour control. A setting of 'ansi' or 'vt100' will almost always suffice. If your display is corrupted check this variable
HOME *	Another standard shell variable. This variable tells the IRC system where your home directory is located, and is normally set by the host system
IRCPATH	This variable holds the name of the directory in which all of your IRC-related files (such as profiles) are stored. USE colons (:) to separate multiple directories

```
/COMMENT **** My .ircrc IRC profile file ****
/COMMENT Set up a nickname ...
/NICK JJ
/COMMENT Join/Create default channel:
/JOIN #JJchannel
```

Additional command files which are external to .ircrc can be called using the /LOAD <ircFile> command, e.g. /LOAD mydefs where the file mydefs contains a list of valid IRC /cmd-style commands.

FURTHER IRC CONFIGURATION /SET

The command /SET is also available. This command can be used to set the many IRC internal variables that exist. Internal variables control the behaviour of your IRC system. Table 10.4 illustrates all of the most common internal IRC variables. The syntaxes of the /SET command is simply

```
/SET <InternalVar> <value>
/SET -<InternalVar>
```

where <InternalVar> is the internal variable to be set, and <value> is the value the variable will take. In the second syntax the – sign allows IRC variables to be nullified (emptied of any value); strings therefore become " " (empty). /SET used on its own will show all of the current variable settings, while as mentioned, /SET -<InternalVar> can be used to unset an existing value. Variables come in many forms, five to be precise, and each variable can take only a certain set of values (as indicated in brackets in the following list).

Table 10.4   Common internal IRC variables

Name/function and variable type

AUTO_UNMARK_AWAY (Boolean)

When ON you will be automatically un-marked as being away whenever you send a message to a channel, or when you send a private message to a person. You can achieve the same result by using the command /AWAY. When OFF your away-status will remain the same, unless, of course, you issue an /AWAY command

AUTO_WHOWAS (Boolean)

If ON the /WHOIS <nn> will result in a null response, e.g. a 'No such nickname' will appear. In such a case a /WHOWAS <nn> will be generated. If OFF you will never be disturbed by /WHOWAS commands

BEEP (Boolean)

When ON all sound effects (beeps) will be heard. A beep is generated by inserting a <Ctrl-G> into your message. When OFF, beeps are not heard, and are replaced by a character representation instead. Note that the BEEP variable does not control effects controlled with the BEEP_ON_MSG and BEEP_WHEN_AWAY variables

BEEP_MAX (numeric: integer)

Set this variable to the number of beeps that you want to hear for any incoming message. This will override any beeps placed in the incoming message, so if set to 3 when six beeps are incoming, only the three you specify will be heard. If set to 0 ALL beeps are heard

BEEP_ON_MSG (Lvl)

Set this according to variable classes shown earlier. You can control which message types generate a beep using this variable. For example, all /MSGs could cause a beep if BEEP_ON_MSG was set to MSG

BEEP_WHEN_AWAY (numeric: integer)

If you are temporarily unavailable (using /AWAY), the number of beeps heard will be set by this variable (note: this is for /MSGs messages only). Set this variable to 0 to stop all beeps

MAIL (numeric: integer)

This variable controls the notification of new mail. The value 0 disables incoming mail notifications (like a biff n command under UNIX), while 1 will notify you with the normal message You have mail. A value of 2 will notify and show the first three lines of any mail-message

---

- BOOL   Boolean values (ON, OFF, TOGGLE)
- LVL   Level (CRAP, MSG, NOTE, NOTICE, PUBLIC, WALL and WALLOP)
- INT   Integer (0, 1, 2 ... n)
- STR   String (any textual string)
- HYBR   Hybrid (any combination of the above)

Boolean values set certain features on or off (0 and 1 can also be used on some systems, as off and on respectively). The term toggle is used to alternate the values: $0 \rightarrow 1$, and $1 \rightarrow 0$. Level variables are used to classify different kinds of IRC messages, namely:

- `MSG`   Private messages (/MSGs)
- `NOTE`   A (server) /NOTE message
- `NOTICE`   Notices operator
- `PUBLIC`   Public messages on a channel
- `WALL`   A wall message (a message sent to all IRC users)
- `WALLOP`   You get these when you are an IRC operator
- `NONE`   None of the message types mentioned here
- `CRAP`   Everything not covered (excluding NONE)

Multiple level messages are quite possible and are specified with spaces in between each level variable name. It is also quite possible to specify the name ALL which refers to all level types except NONE. Levels prefixed with a minus sign (−) will be excluded. Integer variables specify numeric limits for certain facilities, for example you can specify only to receive a certain number of beeps (tones) when receiving an incoming /MSG message, while string variables allow textual values to be incorporated into a setting.

Finally, there are hybrid variables which can contain combinations of any of the variable types already discussed.

CTCP COMMANDS

Many IRC systems support CTCP (client-to-client protocol) commands. Such commands are nearly always system specific, however, there are common CTCP commands in existence which can be tried out. All CTCP commands use the syntax

`/CTCP <nn> <ctcp-command> [arguments]`

where `<nn>` is a nickname of a person, `<ctcp-command>` is the actual CTCP command to be executed, and `[arguments]` is an optional argument allowing options to be used with the `<ctcp-command>`. All `/CTCP` commands require a nickname, even where such a name is not relevant to a command, e.g. in the case of showing IRC version information. Commands that can be used for `<ctcp-command>` vary, and may include: VERSION (which will show you IRC version information, like the `/VERSION` command); FINGER which is used analogously with the Unix `finger` command (see Chapter 6) to show idle times and other user information; and `CLIENTINFO` which will show you all of the CTCP commands available – use this command first to ascertain just what commands are available (or try `/HELP CTCP`, etc.).

`/CTCP wombat CLIENTINFO`
`*** CTCP CLIENTINFO reply from wombat:`
`SED VERSION CLIENTINFO USERINFO ERRMSG FINGER ACTION UTC`
`:Use CLIENTINFO <Command> for more specific information`

SENDING FILES TO PEOPLE /DCC

Many IRCs support a facility called DCC (direct client connections). The command /DCC exists in order for this facility to be used. A DCC request will allow a user to exchange files with another, although the method is much less responsive than systems such as FTP, and even conventional email. DCC is therefore of only any real benefit when small files are transferred. A transfer is initiated with a command of the form

/DCC SEND <nn> <filename>

where <nn> is the nickname of the person to receive the file, and <filename> is the name of the file to actually send. Fully qualified pathnames are normally acceptable, so you send a file named text.asc or /file/usr/text.asc. For example, assume user wombat wanted to send the file text.asc to user Dingo. A command of the form below would be used:

/DCC SEND Dingo text.asc

A few moments later the user with nickname Dingo would see the message:

*** DCC SEND text.asc request received from wombat

To complete the transfer, user Dingo would then have to type the command

/DCC GET wombat text.asc⏎

noting the use of the GET and SEND commands accordingly. Shortly afterwards the messages below will appear in close succession (depending on the size of the file) on both users' screens, which tell of the file-transfers progress, i.e. when it is started and completed:

*** DCC GET connection with wombat established
*** DCC GET filename connection to wombat completed

/DCC command summary

In summary here are a list of /DCC commands that can be used to transfer files and control transfers in progress. You may also want to issue a /HELP DCC command to summon additional help.

/DCC SEND <nn> <filename>

Initiates a file transfer with person called <nn>, and with the file named <filename>.

/DCC GET <nn> <filename>

Allows the recipient to accept the file transfer. A /DCC SEND command must have already been issued by the sender for this command to succeed.

`/DCC CLOSE <type> <nn> [arguments]`

Stops a file transfer, if in progress. The `<type>` argument can be ascertained from the `/DCC LIST` command (above); `<nn>` specifies the nickname of the person sending the file, while `[arguments]` allows additional options shown by `/DCC LIST` to be incorporated.

`/DCC LIST`

Shows the details of any pending or continuing file transfers that are in progress.

10.4   Further IRC information via USENET

USENET has many forums for IRC-related materials, including details of new IRC sites, as well as client program archives and up-to-date information on new releases of IRC programs. The principle discussion forums on USENET currently are:

- `alt.irc`   General discussion forum
- `alt.irc.ircii`   All about v2 IRC
- `alt.irc.corruption`   Corruption in IRC systems
- `alt.irc.sleaze`   Sleaze in IRCs discussed
- `alt.irc.recovery`   IRC recovery

  The Gopher/veronica utilities (see Chapter 9) can also be used to look up information on IRCs in general use. In addition, Archie can be used to find IRC documents and client programs.

11
Electronic mail

11.1 Introduction to electronic mail

Electronic mail (or email) accounts for the majority of the traffic that currently passes over the Internet. Email is used to send messages between users, and to post to mass-user forums such as USENET. In this chapter we examine the standard email program used on Unix, `mail`, as well as some additional tools found under Unix which are related to sending and receiving mail, such as `biff`, `vacation` and `xget`. If you are not a Unix user, you should have your own mail program. Mail programs differ between systems, although many commands have been carried over from the standard Unix `mail` program to maintain the look and feel of the original system.

Once you have learnt to use one mailing system, in theory you should be able to use any other system that exists. As with all interactive systems, you need learn only a subset of the available commands in order to get by. We start by examining how mail messages are stored, and then move on to explain some of the basic commands to read and send messages, both from the interactive mail program and Unix shell. Later sections examine how to mail to other networks such as UUCP, CompuServe, etc.

TIP

The person normally charged with the responsibility for maintaining the mail system is known as the `postmaster`. This is an email alias that can be used as a username when mailing a site to make enquiries.

The mail system is a 'store and forward', not a real-time delivery system. This means that any mail that is sent to a person will be picked up by a mailer-*daemon* (a background program) and will be sent by the Unix sendmail program on to the network for delivery. Your mail message may have to pass through several hosts (via router devices) to pass to the recipient machine, and then on to the user who you have addressed in your message. Messages that pass on to different networks, e.g. from the Internet on to a network such as JANET, will have to traverse an email-gateway machine that can process the incoming mail and then forward it on to the new network. Needless to say, all of this takes time. System load and message queues may of course affect delivery times, as may network congestion between the message sender and recipient (the latter is particularly true in the case where the sender and recipient are geographically separated).

11.2   The mail program

Mail is the standard electronic mail program found on all Unix machines. It is an interactive program whose commands and syntax mimic many of the features found in the Unix editors such as ex and vi. Starting the mail program on a Unix system requires that you type the command mail.

TIP

On a Unix system the mail program can be invoked from an auto-login file such as .login or .cshrc (Bourne Shell and C-Shell, respectively). This will invoke the system automatically to ensure you read any messages that are awaiting your attention.

The mail program cannot be invoked in its interactive mode unless some messages (one or more) await your attention, or, if any saved messages are still in the main mailbox. In the case that no new mail has arrived the mail program will simply tell you that no messages are available and you will be returned to the shell prompt. For example:

```
$ mail↵
Mail version SMI 4.2 20/1/92. Type ? for help
"/usr/spool/mail/joe": 1 message, 1 new
>N 1 fred Wed Mar 21 12:46 9/145 "Hello joe"
&
```

The above example shows the mail command in its interactive mode. The salient features of the mail interface are that the mail prompt in this example is an ampersand (&) – other systems may use a different prompt. We can also see that the file /usr/spool/mail/joe has been mentioned; this file is known as your `mailbox`. Every Unix user on the system has an entry in the `/usr/spool/mail` directory (a common directory on most Unix systems for email messages), and each person's mailbox is simply named after their own username. This file is one long collection of mail messages for this user. Assuming we were named `joe`, our mailbox would thus be named `/usr/spool/mail/joe`. `mail` also tells us the number of messages awaiting us, and the number of these that are new messages. We can also see the sender of the one message in our example, namely user `fred`.

The `mail` program can store messages that have arrived in an earlier session but which have not been read; in this case these messages will also be shown when mail is invoked. It is therefore possible to invoke `mail` in its interactive mode, even though no new messages have actually arrived. In the example we can see that there is only one message, and that it is newly arrived. Each message has its own description line in the `mail` system. Each line is broken down into a number of fields, as shown below:

```
>   N   1   fred    Wed Mar 21 12:46 9/145   "Hello joe"
                                              └→ Subject:
                                                 field of message
                            └→ Date and time that the message was sent to you
                     └→ Username of person sending you the message
            └→ Message number
        └→ Message identifier. N stands for a new message
└→ Message tag. Tells you which message you are currently on. By default this
   will be the first message when you invoke the mail program. Many
   commands act on the current message, unless specified otherwise
```

TIP

You can examine your own mailbox using an editor or other command, in order to read past messages that are no longer in your mailbox, for example:

`$ vi /usr/spool/mail/joe↵`

The most common `mail` commands that are supported are shown in Table 11.1. Each command is then examined in the context of a series of examples to clarify matters further. Figure 11.1 illustrates the `mail` system diagramatically, and shows how the various system mailboxes are read and updated.

The log-in message `You have Mail` will often be displayed when some mail is awaiting your attention. If you invoke the `mail` program when this

Table 11.1   mail commands

Command	Description
?	Show all mail commands (help command)
+	Move to next message
−	Move to previous message
[Return]	Move to next message and display it
! <cmd>	Run shell command <cmd>
!	Start a temporary shell environment and leave the mail program temporarily (see sh also)
d [msg-no]	Deletes one or more messages. If [msg-no] is omitted, the current message will be deleted
f [msg-no]	From command. Extracts all From: lines in the message numbers specified, or by default, the current message
h [msg-no]	Show header for current message, or for the messages specified in [msg-no]
lp [msg-no]	Print messages specified in [msg-no] or if not specified print the current message
m <user-1,.. n>	Mail the user specified in <user1..n>. Use full user@host convention for remote users. Multiple recipients can be specified. Refer to the r command for tips on EDITOR/VISUAL variables for message composure
n	Move to next message and display it
p [user] [msg-no]	Print command. Shows the message(s) from a particular user, if specified in [user]
r [msg-no]	Reply to current message (>) or reply to the message numbered [msg-no]. The EDITOR variable defines which editor will be used to compose the message, e.g. vi, ex, etc. If undefined the standard input is used. On some systems the VISUAL variable may also be used for an editor such as vi
s <file>	Saves current message (with header) into the external file named <file>
set <variable>	Sets a mail variable.
sh	Create a temporary shell environment (see !)
t [msg-no]	Type, or display a message. The [msg-no] allows a specific message to be typed. The current message (>) will become the message typed. [Return] will normally display the current message also
top	Shows the first few lines of a message
u [msg-no]	Undelete a deleted (d) message, or messages. The undelete command normally accepts the same message-number arguments as the d command
w <file>	Saves current message (without header). The <file> argument specifies the external file into which the message is saved
z	Show header of current message (>)

The argument [msg-no] refers to a list of separate message numbers or a range, e.g. 1–4, 1 2 3 4, etc.

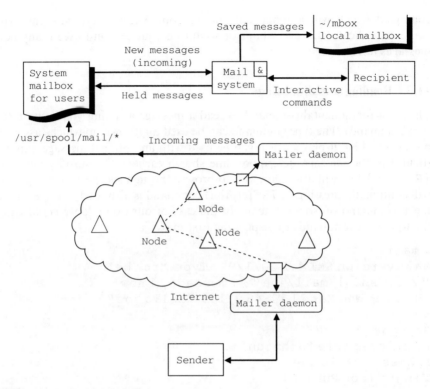

Figure 11.1   Overview of the mail program

message is not displayed, or when you have read all messages using the program, the message No mail for <person> will be displayed, where person is your username. For example,

```
login: fred↵
Password: <freds password>↵
Last Login: Wed 20 Mar 1992 16:40:12
You have new mail
$
```

indicates you should invoke the mail program, whereas

```
login: fred↵
Password: <freds password>↵
Last Login: Wed 20 Mar 1992 16:40:12
$
```

indicates that there is no new mail awaiting you. Of course, mail may arrive while you are in your Unix session. In this case you should use the biff command which will automatically notify you. Alternatively, you can type `mail` periodically, i.e. every hour or so during your session to see if any new messages have arrived.

11.3   Reading a mail-message

The most fundamental command to read a message awaiting you is the `t` (or type command). The type command can be used on its own, in which case each message will be displayed, or it can be used with an optional message number (field 3 in the message description line shown earlier). On most systems the `[Return]` key will also allow you to browse through successive messages, as will continually pressing `t`. The `p` (print) command is also used analagously to the `t` command on some systems. In the case of our example we could enter the following commands to display the first message:

```
$ mail↵
Mail version SMI 4.2 20/1/92. Type ? for help
"/usr/spool/mail/joe": 1 message, 1 new
>N 1 fred Wed Mar 21 12:46 9/145 "Hello joe"
& t1↵
Message 1:
From: fred (Fred Johnson)
Subject: Hello joe
To: joe (Joe Public)
Date: Wed Mar 21 12:46
Cc: mark (Mark Johnson)
Hi there,
Just a note to invite you down for a drink this evening.
We're all meeting up in the bar at 8.00. See you then ...
&
```

When a message is displayed in full its header is also shown. Most of the fields are self-explanatory, although the `Cc:` field may require a little explaining. The `Cc:` field, or carbon-copy field, is used to include other users who will receive this message. We can see that user `mark` is a carbon-copy recipient, so this message will also be passed to him as well. Carbon-copy messages are useful in the case where a message will be duplicated and sent to a group of users. We will return to examine some of the `mail` system's other carbon-copy commands in later sections. Once the header has been shown the actual message body follows – in this case a greeting and a request for a meeting. The `&` prompt reappears after the message note, which indicates the mail system is ready for our next command.

If you wanted to display a specific message you would use the `t` command along with the appropriate message number, e.g. `t3` for message 3 assuming it exists. Some mail systems also accept the + and − keys to move back and forth between messages, allowing you to use the t command on the appropriate message.

11.4 Replying to a message

Once you have read a message from a person you can reply to the sender of that message using the r and R commands. The r command replies to the message sender and any carbon-copy users, whereas R replies to the message sender. You can reply to specific messages using an optional message number argument in most implementations of the mail program. This saves you from moving to the message required and then typing r, R, etc. In our example we could create a reply using the following command:

```
$ mail⏎
Mail version SMI 4.2 20/1/92. Type ? for help
"/usr/spool/mail/joe": 1 message, 1 new
>N 1 fred Wed Mar 21 12:46 9/145 "Hello joe"
& t1⏎
Message 1:
From: fred (Fred Johnson)
Subject: Hello joe
To: joe (Joe Public)
Date: Wed Mar 21 12:46
Cc: mark (Mark Johnson)
Hi there,
Just a note to invite you down for a drink this evening.
We're all meeting up in the bar at 8.00. See you then ...
& R⏎
Reply to: fred
Subject: In reply to your message⏎
Thanks for your message fred, I'll be down at 8 pm sharp⏎
[Ctrl-D]
Cc:⏎
&
```

In the above example, we have used the R command to reply to a message sent by user fred, and not carbon-copy user mark. When composing a message the mail system looks at the Unix variable EDITOR to see which editor, if any, should be used for the task. If no editor is defined, the system will use the standard input, i.e. input from the keyboard directly. This can be rather a nuisance since mistakes cannot normally be corrected, especially when you have entered a line of text (there are no cursor movement commands, etc. in standard-input mode). We will examine how to interrupt the typing in of a message in one moment, but first let us return to the example. Once we have typed in our message using the standard-input mode the keystroke [Ctrl-D] should be pressed; this commits the message whereupon the mail program asks us for any carbon-copy users, i.e. other recipients for the same reply. If we have none, as in the example, simply press [Return] and the message will be sent. On some mailing systems the ending of a message is signified by a period (.) on its own line in the leftmost column (this has been carried over from the Unix line editors); mail will also ask you for a subject for your message – you can leave this blank if you wish by pressing [Return] on that field.

TIP

Refer to Section 11.13 on mail's tilde commands in order to see how to give a message a subject even when you have blanked out the line by mistake.

If your Unix EDITOR variable is set to some other text editor you will have to issue the necessary command to save the file and exit. On vi the command ZZ, is used while on ex the command is w (write) and then q (quit).

Replying to all users in a mail-message, i.e. the sender and any carbon-copy users requires the r command, for example:

```
& r↵
Reply to: fred, mark
Subject: In reply to your message
Thanks for your message fred, I'll be down at 8 pm sharp
[Ctrl-D]
Cc:↵
&
```

which sends this reply back to the users fred and mark. The final Cc: line allows us to include yet more recipients at our discretion.

INTERRUPTING MESSAGE COMPOSURE

The interrupt keystroke [Ctrl-C] should be used to kill a letter (i.e. stop it being sent). This keystroke can only be used when you are composing a message in the standard-input mode, for example we could have stopped the reply in the previous message by doing the following:

```
& r↵
Reply to: fred
Subject: In reply to your message ↵
Thanks for your message fred, I'll be down at 8 pm sharp↵
[Ctrl-C]
(interrupt - one more to kill letter)
[Ctrl-C]
&
```

Notice that mail allows us two chances at killing a message, just in case we didn't mean it the first time around. All replies (termed 'letters' in mailspeak) that are killed are saved in a 'dead-letter' file dead.letter, so all is not lost. This feature is useful if you want to postpone the sending of a message (particulary handy if the reply is very long). Note that the dead.letter file only holds the contents of the current message up to the point that you have typed and then pressed [Ctrl-C].

TIPS

When typing in messages make sure that each line is kept at around 60–70 characters in length. This should ensure that each line doesn't overrun the screen when it is being read on the recipient's screen.

Refer to Section 11.13 on mail's tilde commands in order to see how to read a message from the dead.letter file into the current mail message.

If you are using a text editor, pressing the interrupt key will not interrupt message composure; [Ctrl-C] works only in the standard-input mode. To stop a message from being sent from within a text editor simply quit without saving anything. You will get another chance to use [Ctrl-C] when the system asks you for a subject and/or carbon-copy recipients.

11.5   Sending messages to users

Rather than replying to specific users who have sent you messages, you will also want to send messages to users on an *ad hoc basis*. This is done using the m (mail) command. The m command must be followed by the name of one or more users who are the recipients of your message. In the case that users are local to your own host machine you can simply quote their user-name(s). Remote users that exist on other Internet hosts must have their full username and hostname typed in the form `user@host`, where `user` is their username and `host` is their machine name on which they reside, for example:

```
& m john@cc.vaxa.edu↵
Subject: In reply to your message↵
Thanks for your message fred, I'll be down at 8 pm sharp↵
[Ctrl-D]
&
```

Once again, after we have specified the person to mail, the `mail` program drops into compose mode (as determined by the `EDITOR` variable). In the example we have assumed standard-input mode for message composure. Again, we type a subject for the message, then type the message itself, and then we press the `[Ctrl-D]` keystroke to end the message and send it off. Notice how the recipient name has been structured. The `r` (reply) command can, of course, also reply to remote users in this way. Mailing to more than one user can be done in two ways: the first involves using the m command to specify more than one user, and the second is slightly more complex – involving the setting up of an email alias group (see Section 11.15 on the `.mailrc` file).

11.6   Deleting messages

In order to delete a message the d (delete) command should be used. The command when used by itself deletes the current message (as flagged with the > character). Optionally, you can specify one or more message numbers in order to delete specific messages. Ranges can also be specified to facilitate multiple deletions – this is done using a hyphen between the starting and ending message numbers. For example

```
& d 1 3↵
```

would delete messages 1 and 3 only, whereas

```
& d 1-3↵
```

would delete messages 1, 2 and 3 (a range – notice the hyphen). Deleting the current message could simply be done using the command

```
& d↵
```

You can undelete a message using the u command if you make a mistake. The undelete command can be used in much the same way as the d command in terms of message ranges, etc.

11.7 Quitting the `mail` program

The q (quit) command can be used for this purpose. All messages that have been read (using the t or r commands, etc.) will be saved into a local file called mbox in your home directory. Messages that are not examined will be placed back into your /usr/spool/mail mailbox. When the mail program is next invoked this mailbox will be used to extract those messages which have not been read, and so on. Your local mailbox file, mbox, holds only those messages which have been read. The only exception to this rule happens if you use the preserve (pre) command, which makes all messages (read or unread) stay in the system mailbox to be read into your session next time around.

Another command called x (exit system) also quits the mail program, but does not perform any updates on your local mbox or system mailbox files (thus leaving everything intact just as if you had not read or examined anything). So, in order to quit and update your messages use the command

  & q↵

or, use x to leave all messages unchanged (just as if you had not entered the mail program to read your messages):

  & x↵

Some systems have an exit (ex) command also. This is analagous to the x command shown above. Obtain a list of the commands on your mail system using the ? (help) command.

11.8 Viewing mail headers

A number of commands are available here, the most common of which are top, f, and h. The top command allows you to see the first few lines of a message body from a particular message. This can be useful in the case where a message is rather long and you don't want to display all of it on the screen. Alternatively, you may want to get the feel of a message from the first few lines to see if it is relevant. The f command allows you to display all of the message description lines in the current mailbox – a useful command to quickly see who has sent you some mail, for example, and to view each message's Subject: field. In our original mail session we could type the following:

  & f↵
  >N 1 fred Wed Mar 21 12:46 9/145 "Hello joe"
  &

Ranges and individual message numbers can also be specified, for example we could type the command

& f 1 3↵

to show the description lines for messages 1 and 3, whereas

& f 1-5↵

would show the desription lines for the first five messages. By default the f command shows all message lines.

The h (headers) command displays a header for a message, or range of messages, for example:

```
& h↵
From: fred (Fred Johnson)
Subject: Hello joe
To: joe (Joe Public)
Date: Wed Mar 21 12:46
Cc: mark (Mark Johnson)
&
```

As with most mail commands, the h command can be used with separate message numbers and ranges, e.g. h4 to show the header for message 4, and h1-4 to show the headers for the first four messages.

11.9   Message navigation

Moving between messages can be done using a surprisingly large number of commands, as shown in Table 11.2. In all cases the commands shown will also change the current message number, as indicated by the > character in the leftmost column.

Movement using these commands is not required in the majority of instances since many mail commands act on specific message numbers.

11.10   Mail wildcards

Commands such as p (print), d (delete), t (type) and many others, can act on specific messages if wildcards are used. A list of common wildcards used by the mail system is shown in Table 11.3

Table 11.2   Message movement commands

Command	Description
next (n)	Move to the next message (and display it)
+	Move to the next message
–	Move to the last message
–n	Move back n messages
+n	Move forward n messages

Table 11.3   Wildcards for use with the `mail` program

Wildcard	Refers to
*	All messages
.	The current message (>)
n	Message n
n–m	Range of numbers: n to m inclusive
$	The last message
^	The first message
:n	New messages
:o	Old messages
:r	Messages that have been read
:u	Messages that are as of yet unread
/pattern	Messages with pattern in them

Using these wildcards we can formulate commands such as those shown in Tables 11.4 and 11.5. These commands can be issued at any stage of the program since they do not operate on the current message.

11.11   Saving messages to a file

Saving a message into an external file will allow you to load that file into a text editor for further processing. Users that have been sent UU-encoded images via email will want to use this option to save their files. Two commands exist for this purpose, namely s and w. The s command saves a message along with its header in the file you specify, whereas the w command saves the message without the header. From within the `mail` program the command

```
& s segment1↵
Saved message in "segment1.uue"
```

Table 11.4   Example wildcarded deletion commands

Command	Meaning
d 1-3	Delete messages 1–3
d *	Delete all messages
d 1-$	Delete all messages (same as previous)
d .	Delete current message (same as d)
d :r	Delete all read messages
d :o	Delete all old messages (saved from previous session with the mail program)
d ^	Delete first message
d /usenet	Delete all messages with usenet in body

The :urno wildcards are system specific.

Table 11.5   Example wildcarded printing commands

Command	Meaning
p *	Print all messages
p 1-$	Print all messages (same as previous)
p .	Print current message (same as p)
p :r	Print all read messages
p fred	Print all messages from user fred
p :o	Print all old messages
p /usenet	Print all messages with usenet in body

The username and :urno wildcards are system specific.

would save the current message (in its entirety) into the file named segment1.uue.

11.12   Printing messages

Some older Berkeley versions of the mail program had a command called lp (line print) built in, which would allow a message, or range of messages, to be printed, for example

```
& lp 1 2↵
& lp 4-7↵
```

which prints messages 1 and 2, and then messages 4 through 7. Ranges and individual messages are supported as expected. Used by itself, lp prints the current message.

11.13   Tilde escape-commands

While composing a message or reply the mail system allows you to execute a command known as a tilde escape-command. These commands are initiated by pressing the ˜ (tilde) key on an empty line (the line must be empty). The tilde will not be inserted into the text, but instead it will make the system await another keypress, which in turn will instruct it exactly what to do. A number of tilde escape-commands are supported, as illustrated in Table 11.6. Remember to press the ˜ character and then the single character code, as required.

SHELL ESCAPE COMMANDS (˜!)

The shell commands are particulary useful, since you could perform a check to see who is on the system in order that they receive your message. For example, we could invoke the Unix who command to see who is using the system:

Table 11.6   Example tilde escape-comands

Tilde command	Description
`˜!`	Escape to a shell temporarily
`˜b <users>`	Make `<users>` blind carbon-copy recipient(s); `<users>` cannot see who `Cc:` people are
`˜c <users>`	Make `<users>` blind carbon-copy recipient(s); `<users>` can see who `Cc:` people are
`˜d`	Include `dead.letter` file into message
`˜h`	Edit header information
`˜e`	Invoke editor on current message (`ex`/`ed`, etc.)
`˜p`	View current message
`˜q`	Quit. Same as `[Ctrl-C]` twice
`˜r <file>`	Read `<file>` into current message
`˜R <username>`	Request receipt from user `<username>`
`˜s`	Edit `Subject:` field
`˜t`	Edit `To:` (recipient) field
`˜v`	Invoke visual editor on message

```
& m fred↵
Subject: In reply to your message↵
FTP to vax.ftp.com; they've got a copy of that newsreader you↵
were interested in (see /pub/msdos/xrn*).↵
˜! who↵
fred  tty08  Aug 08 16:45:12
jim   tty09  Aug 08 17:01:58
[Ctrl-D]
Cc:↵
&
```

BLIND CARBON-COPY USERS (˜b)

The `˜b` tilde-escape allows you to specify some additional carbon-copy recipients (some `mail` systems have the `bcc` command for this also). By entering a username after the `˜b` the `mail` program will include the user mentioned in the `Cc:` field (even if you blank this out after composing the message). The term `blind` arises out of the fact the recipient cannot see who any of the other carbon-copy users are, i.e. the `Cc:` line will be blanked out. In order to overcome this you may want to use `˜c` instead (the visible carbon-copy tilde-escape command). For example:

```
& m fred↵
Subject: In reply to your message↵
FTP to vax.ftp.com; they've got a copy of that newsreader you↵
```

```
were interested in (see /pub/msdos/xrn*).↵
˜b john↵
[Ctrl-D]
Cc:↵
&
```

would make user `john` a recipient of this message also, even though the final `Cc:` line is blanked out by the user. Multiple users can also be stated in the command by separating each user by a space, for example:

```
˜b john mike@uu.ftp.com↵
```

INCLUDING dead.letter FILES (˜d)

Whenever a message is being composed and is interrupted (from the standard input, or when a field such as `Cc:` or `Subject:` is being entered) the system saves the message up to that point in a file called `dead.letter`. This file can be imported into your session (in compose mode) using the `˜d` command, for example:

```
& m systen↵
Subject: /usr up yet?↵
Is the /usr file-system re-mounted yet?↵
[Ctrl-D]
& q↵
$ ... later ...
You have new mail
$ mail↵
Mail version SMI 4.2 20/1/92. Type ? for help
"/usr/spool/mail/joe": 1 message, 1 new
>N 1 mailer-daemon Wed Mar 21 13:01 9/147 "Returned mail"
& m system↵
Subject: /usr?↵
˜d
Reading contents of dead.letter into buffer
[Ctrl-D]
&
```

In the example session above we try to send some mail to user `system`, but by mistake we type `systen`. The mail is then returned by the system (the mailer daemon) since it cannot find this user. The system would also place the unsent message back in the `dead.letter` file. We then invoke `mail` again and this time correct the username. We then use the `˜d` command to read the contents of `dead.letter` into the `mail` program during message composure. We then press `[Ctrl-D]` to send the mail off to the correct user. The

~r command (import a file) is similar to ~d except that it can be used to import any ASCII file.

INVOKING EDITORS ON A MESSAGE (˜e AND ˜v)

If your systems EDITOR and VISUAL variables contain the names of the line and screen editors of your choice, e.g. ex and vi for example, you can use the ~e and ~v tilde-escapes to invoke an editor on a message. This can be useful when composing messages to load the current buffer into an editor such as vi to make searches, replacements, etc. On some systems the ~e and ~v can be used interchangeably, as can the EDITOR and VISUAL Unix variables.

VIEWING THE CURRENT MESSAGE (˜p)

The standard-input mode (default mode) of the mail system to compose messages can be a real pain, especially when the screen advances and you can't use the cursor keys to move up the screen and take a look at what you have typed. Using the ~p tilde-escape overcomes this by displaying the entire message as it currently exists in the buffer (ensure the tilde command is executed on a fresh line). If you have the PAGER variable set to a program such as more, the system will also wait after a screen of information has been shown (by default the system may just display the entire buffer without the chance to pause, although the paging functions are now pretty much standard in all mail programs by default).

EDITING THE HEADER FIELDS (˜h)

The standard header fields in a mail-message that can be modified by the user include the Subject: (topic/subject of message), To: (recipient), and Cc: (carbon-copy recipient) fields. Using the ~h tilde-command it is possible to change all of the values assigned to these fields while you are actually composing a message. When invoked the system will display each field allowing you to enter the appropriate values. If any current values are defined they will be shown next to the field; you can then delete them and provide new values as you see fit.

CHANGING THE SUBJECT: AND TO: FIELDS (˜s AND ˜t)

Similar to ~h, the ~s and ~t tilde-commands allow you to change the subject and recipient fields during message composure. The ~h command will perform the same function, although these two commands allow more specific field changes to be made, without the need to move through any other fields.

IMPORTING ASCII FILES (˜r)

The ˜r tilde-command allows an ASCII file to be imported into the current message buffer. Files can be appended to the current buffer if you wish, that is to say that any text you have typed can be added to. This command is useful in the case where you want to include some external text in with your message (rather than typing it in manually). Program output can also be captured and placed in a file, for example we could use the Unix uuencode program to convert a binary file into ASCII and then import and send it to another user:

```
& m fred@somewhere.com↵
Subject: That file you wanted (UU text)↵
˜! uuencode myfile.zip > uufile.uue↵
˜r uufile.uue↵
Reading contents of uufile.uue into buffer
[Ctrl-D]
```

The binary file to be UU-encoded in the above example is named myfile.zip; this file is converted using the uuencode program while executing the ˜! shell tilde-command feature. The ˜r tilde-command then imports the file and we press [Ctrl-D] to send it to the recipient. See Chapters 7 and 8 for more infomation on UU-encoded files.

TIP

UU-encoded files can be very large. Ensure that the file is broken up into segments if it exceeds 65K in size. Some email gateways may reject such large files. Many uuencode programs have a command-line option to specify segment sizes.

11.14   The mail program's command-line interface

The mail program's command-line interface is simple to use. The main options available to the user include: -s (include Subject: line) and -v (enable verbose mode). A -f option allows an alternative mailbox to be used (rather than the /usr/spool/mail mailbox, for example). Messages can be typed in the standard-input mode, or they can be redirected from a file; an editor of your choice can also be used via the Unix EDITOR variable. The mail program's syntax is as follows:

```
mail [-s <subject>] [-v] [-f [mbox]] [-n] <user@hostname>
mail [-s <subject>] [-v] [-f [mbox]] [-n] <user>
```

where <user@hostname> allows a remote Internet user to be contacted, whereas <user> implies a user on a local system is being contacted. The <subject> argument is a character string to be used as the Subject: line; if not used the mail program will prompt you for a subject. After you have composed your message the system will also ask you for any carbon-copy users (with a Cc: prompt). Remember also that mail's tilde-escape commands can also be used when in message-composure mode from the command-line. The simplest way of sending a message would thus require a command of the form

```
$ mail -s greeting fred@somewhere.com↵
```

which would invoke the mail system to allow us to enter our message; the subject line would be set to the word 'greeting'. If your subject line uses more than one word, make sure you enclose the string in quotes – mail will become confused about which argument is the subject argument and which is the recipient argument. Expanding upon this example, we could now enter our message and complete the mailing process:

```
$ mail -s greeting fred@somewhere.com↵
Hi fred,↵
I'm just trying out my mailer on your hostname. Just thought↵
I'd annoy you by doing that! :-)↵
[Ctrl-D]
Cc:↵
$
```

From the above example we can see that the [Ctrl-D] key is still used to terminate the standard-input session where we composed our message (if the EDITOR variable is set the system will invoke the editor you require when the mail program was started). After typing the message, the system asks for any carbon-copy recipients, and we have specified none. The mail program then terminates and we are returned to the shell prompt ($ here). Remember, subject fields with more than one word must be quoted, for example:

```
$ mail -s "Xmas greeting" fred@somewhere.com↵
Hi fred,↵
Merry Christmas!↵
[Ctrl-D]
Cc:↵
$
```

Used without the -s option, our earlier session would now resemble:

```
$ mail fred@somewhere.com↵
Subject: greeting↵
```

```
Hi fred,↵
I'm just trying out my mailer on your hostname. Just thought↵
I'd annoy you by doing that! :-)↵
[Ctrl-D]
Cc:↵
$
```

noticing here that the system asked us for the subject of the message before entering compose mode (we can assume the EDITOR variable is not set since the standard-input is being used). If your message is arriving from a file it is possible to use input redirection (a facility whereby a program takes input from source other than the keyoard). This feature requires the use of the Unix < operator in the following way:

```
$ mail fred@somewhere.com < message.txt↵
$
```

In the above example, the message to be sent arrives from the file called message.txt (a plain ASCII file). No [Ctrl-D] keystroke is required since the code is generated by the end-of-file code embedded in the last part of the file. The system ignores Subject: and Cc: fields in a command of this form and the mail is sent immediately. If you want to include a subject field, simply use the -s option, as shown already. If you require carbon-copy users, make them recipients instead. Some mail programs may ask you for a Cc: value even though input redirection is being used. Multiple users can be mailed simply by including their usernames (and hostnames, if required) on the command-line, for example

```
$ mail john fred@somewhere.com mary < message.txt↵
```

will mail local users john and mary, as well as the remote user named fred at the Internet site named somewhere.com. Again, an external file has been posted, although we could use an editor or the standard input, etc.

THE VERBOSE OPTION (-v)

The next option to be examined is -v, the verbose option. This option makes mail show you its progress as it sends your message to a recipient. Some typical output between user jim at site cc.vax.com and fred at site somewhere.com would resemble the following:

```
unixa@cc.vax.com.... Connecting to smtp.somewhere.com...
220 somewhere.com Sendmail ready at Mon, 10 Dec 93 12:01:22
>>> HELLO jim
250 somewhere.com-- Hello unixa.cc.vax.com, pleased to meet you
```

```
>>> MAIL From: <jim@unixa>
250 <jim@unixa> ... Sender ok
>>> RCPT To: <unixa@cc.vax.com>
250 <unixa@cc.vax.com> ... Recipient ok
>>> DATA
354 Enter mail, end with "." on a line by itself
>>> .
250 Mail accepted
>>> QUIT
221 smtp.somewhere.com delivering mail
fred@somehere.com ... Sent
```

All of the friendly messages shown here are system specific; many system administrators tailor their systems according to their own requirements. The >>> lines indicate our local system 'talking' to the remote sendmail program (sendmail is the program responsible for sending and receiving mail between Unix systems). The other messages starting with 250 (rather like FTP if you have seen it) are communications back to us. So, for example, we can see that tour system established a connection, and then sends across the data (the message body of our mail message), and then sends a period (.) to indicate the end of the transmission. The final QUIT message indicates the ending of the mail session.

The -v option is useful if you are experimenting with new usernames and/or hostnames since you don't want to wait hours to be told that your mailing address was incorrect (messages such as these are handled very quickly in any event although you may find out your problem only when you next invoke the mail system).

THE -f mailbox OPTION

The -f <mailbox> option allows a new mailbox file to be used for message browsing. By default the /usr/spool/mail/* files are used by the mail program although it is possible to use any valid file that maintains the same format as this file. One such mailbox file is called mbox; it is located in your home directory and is used to store messages that have been read in earlier sessions (the /usr/spool/mail files are used for messages that have not yet been read). You could read your old messages using the command

```
$ mail -f mbox↵
```

and all of your old messages will be read in to the system. When using the -f option the mailbox name is optional; this is because mail defaults to the mbox file by default in the case that a mailbox name is not specified. The command

```
$ mail -f↵
```

is therefore the same as the previous command, and will load the mbox file from your home directory. The mail command s (save messages) can be used for creating your own mailbox files since it saves the header and message body. Used with wildcarded message list you could save any messages to a file of your choosing and then read them at a later time with the -f option, for example the mail command:

```
$ mail↵
... etc ...
& s 6-$ mymail↵
& q↵
$ mail -f mymail↵
```

would save messages 6 onwards ($ is a wildcard for the last message) in your /usr/spool/mail/* file into the file called myfile. We then exit the mail program and reinvoke it with the -f option and the file we have just created. The messages saved previously will then be loaded as normal.

THE -n OPTION

The -n option makes the mail program ignore the reading of the .mailrc file (discussed next). The .mailrc file contains settings which control the behaviour of the mail program.

11.15 The .mailrc command file

The .mailrc file allows you to customize the mail program. This file is read every time the mail program is invoked and can contain a number of mail-program variable settings and username aliases. We start by explaining aliases and then move on to the mail program's internal variables which can be used to customize the mail program.

ALIASES, MAIL REFLECTORS, MAILING LISTS AND LISTSERVS

Username and group aliases are created using the alias command. This command simply defines the alias name and then is followed by a list of user-name(s) separated by spaces. The most simple form of alias is thus

```
alias fred fred@somewhere.com
```

This entry for user fred would replace fred with fred@somewhere.com every time we referred to fred in the mail system.

This type of entry allows us to make shortcuts, especially on typing. Every time we mail `fred`, we are in fact mailing `fred` at the remote site `somewhere.com`; we no longer have to type the hostname. This is the simplest form of an alias. Multiple aliases (group aliases) can be constructed by mentioning the names of each person after each other (separated by a space), for example

`alias group1 fred@somewhere.com john mark`

defines an alias called `group1` which refers to three people, namely users `john`, `mark` and `fred`. If we defined an earlier alias for these users, perhaps allowing us to refer to them using just their usernames, we could mention such aliases here (make sure if you use any aliases in an alias command, that they have been defined earlier). Every time we mail the alias `group1` we are in fact sending mail to three people; this saves using carbon-copy commands. This type of alias is also known as a 'mail reflector'. Mail reflectors can be used on both the sender's and recipient's machine in order to facilitate the distribution of messages to multiple users. The file `/etc/aliases` is normally used for such aliases of a global nature to all users. If a host called `reflect.cc.edu` were to set up a global (`/etc/aliases`) alias with the command

`alias reflect1 john@somewhere.com mark@cc.vax.edu`

anybody mailing a message to the user `reflect1@reflect.cc.edu` would have their message redirected to the users `john@somewhere.com` and `mark@cc.vax.edu`. This could, of course, be done locally with the same alias, so mail reflectors work both ways. The thing to remember is that we may not know that a mail address is in fact a reflector alias; we are assuming that the address points to a human user. Automating mail redirection in this way can be highly useful for users that have moved sites, as well as allowing a single person to maintain a central 'mailing list' of people which can be mailed without the user having to worry about who to send the message.

Mailing lists

On the subject of mailing lists you may be interested to learn how to read news from systems such as USENET and BITNET without using any newsreading software. By subscribing to a mailing list for a specific group you can arrange to be automatically sent any messages (via email) that are posted to the group(s) you specify. Mailing lists are also maintained on the BITNET network (see Appendix G for a list of BITNET newsgroups available via USENET – these are called `bit.listserv.*`).

Listserv mailing lists on BITNET

BITNET (Because It's Time Network) operates a system called listserv which is basically a software system for maintaining mailing lists. Internet users can access listserv mailing lists via the USENET network. To keep up-to-date with a particular subject area you can ask to be added to a mailing list for the group that interests you. This is done by emailing a message to the host that maintains the mailing list using the username `listserv`, for example `listserv@somewhere.edu`. The body of your message should include just three items: (i) the word `subscribe`; (ii) the group name you want to subscribe to; and (iii) your full Internet address. For example we could mail the message

`subscribe allmusic fred@somewhere.com`

which would subscribe you to the allmusic list (a group for music lovers), so that anyone mailing to this group will have their message forwarded to you, therefore keeping you up-to-date with events. You can un-subscribe from this mailing list by sending the following mail-message back to the same host:

`logout allmusic`

Refer to Appendix G for a list for the `bit.listserv.*` hierarchy on USENET which allows Internet users to browse listserv groups directly.

Mailing lists on USENET

USENET also maintains mailing lists for many of the groups shown in Appendix G. In order to subscribe to such a newsgroup you have to mail a message to a specific alias, normally by adding the string `-request` on to a USENET group and using this as the usename in the email address. Your message body can be left empty in most instances. For example you could subscribe to the `comp.risks` USENET group by sending an empty message to the username `risks-request@csl.sri.com`. Some information on how to use the service will normally be posted back to you when you subscribe (`sri.com` maintains many mailing lists coincidentally). You should also be aware that the BITNET style of subscribing to mailing lists may also be carried over to some Internet-based mailing list systems, i.e. the `subscribe <group>` style of command may be used.

TIP

Try including the single word `help` in your message body when sending a request so see if the server can send you some help information on how to use its facilities. Mailing-list servers differ from site to site and some may require specific commands to add and remove you from mailing lists.

You may have been wondering how we knew the address of the hosts to which we have sent mailing lists requests. Not all Internet hosts have mailing lists, so you will have to find such hosts before you can start mailing requests. There are many well-known list servers, such as sri.com mentioned earlier, although there are many others. Subscribe to the news.answers USENET forum. This is frequently mailed a message called 'Mailing Lists available via USENET' which you can read to get hold of mailing-list addresses. See the tip below for further information.

TIP

Mailing lists and interest groups: sources

Check out these sources:
1. news.answers: Mailing-list FAQ
2. FTP to ftp.nisc.sri.com and get hold of the file called /netinfo/interest-groups ('List of Lists')
3. FTP to lilac.berkeley.edu and look in the directory /netinfo for related BITNET/USENET lists.

MAIL PROGRAM VARIABLES

The mail program uses a series of variables which control its overall operation. The most common variables are shown in Table 11.7. Each variable is then discussed in turn. Each variable is set using the .mailrc command set and unset. Variables are all Boolean, i.e. on/off type variables where the set/unset command toggles the variable on or off as required.

A typical .mailrc file could resemble that shown below. The lines beginning with # are comment lines.

```
### Sample .mailrc file
### Set/unset commands:
unset askcc
set ask
unset autoprint
unset dot
unset ignore
unset metoo
unset nosave
unset quiet
set verbose
set toplines=5
### Aliases:
alias project fred mark bill joe
alias tony tony@cc.mona.edu
```

Table 11.7   Mail variables

Command	Description
append	When set ensures that all messages saved to your /mbox file are appended and not prepended, i.e. old → new, not new → old ordering
ask	When set causes the mail system to prompt for a Subject: line
askcc	When set causes the mail system to prompt for carbon-copy (Cc:) recipients
autoprint	Makes the d (delete) command act as a dp (delete and print next message). Deleted messages are erased from your mailbox
dot	When set the mail system expects a period (.) to be entered in order to terminate a message that is being entered. The normal [Ctrl-D] keystroke may not work when dot is set, although most systems detect both, irrespective of the setting
ignore	When set the system ignores interrrupt signals, e.g. [Ctrl-C] presses
metoo	If an email alias contains the sender of a message the metoo variable, if set, makes you receive a copy. If not set, you will not receive such a copy
nosave	When set a message aborted by pressing the [Ctrl-C] key will not save your message in a dead.letter file
replyall	When set the sense of the r and R commands is reversed, so that the r command (reply) will only reply to the sender and not any other carbon-copy recipients
toplines	A numeric value used to specify the number of lines to show when the top command is used, e.g. to show 5 lines use the command: & set toplines=5 (to show 5 lines)
quiet	When set the mail program starts up in its 'quiet mode' – no messages such as system versions will be given; the system will start with the & prompt immediately
verbose	The verbose variable works in the same way as the -v option from the command-line. If set the mail system will display a progress dialogue as message(s) are delivered

Remember that the set command enables a variable, whereas unset allows a variable to be cleared. The default settings on most systems are set to be as 'safe' as possible, although it is recommended that you set and unset all the variables in sequence to ensure that the system operates in the way you would like the most. Notice the toplines variable; this is a numeric (non-binary) option that requires a specific value to represent the number of lines displayed with the mail command top.

SHELL VARIABLES FOR USE WITH THE MAIL PROGRAM

Apart from the internal variables used by the mail program, the system also uses a number of shell variables. The EDITOR variable is used by the mail program to invoke a Unix editor when composing a message (rather than the standard-input mode) – the VISUAL variable can sometimes be used for a visual editor such as vi. The shell escape command ! can also be tailored using the SHELL variable to specify a new shell. Other variables used include MAILPATH which specifies the location of a user's mailbox: this is normally set up using a command of the form MAILPATH=/usr/spool/mail/`whoami` where whoami is a Unix command that returns your username.

11.16   Mailing to different networks

Part of the beauty of the mailing system is its ability to contact users on other networks external to the Internet. This is possible via modifying the mail address of the person(s) being contacted. When your mail is sent the remote machine receiving it will notice the change of address and will pass on the message to the appropriate gateway. Gateway machines (also known as 'routers') join together groups of networks; the Internet itself is made up of hundreds of thousands of TCP/IP routers for this task. In the case that a particular network doesn't use the Internets TCP/IP protocol, all data will be modified so that it can travel on to the network required; messages pass in both directions in this way and are converted as and when required. In this way messages can pass to networks such as CompuServe (see Figure 11.2), MCIMail, UUCP, BITNET, and FidoNet. Many other networks are supported.

   Table 11.8 illustrates the most common networks that can be accessed via outgoing Internet email. Clearly, you must substitute the username and hostnames with the required information for the site being contacted. Many of the networks shown in Table 11.8 are commercial and charge for email; as an Internet user it is quite possible to send and receive mail from such networks at no cost whatsoever.

11.17   Additional Unix mail-related commands

Unix supplies a number of other commands for use with the mail program. These include the commands:

- from   A BSD Unix program that shows mail headers
- vacation   Another BSD Unix program that allows you to tell people that you are not available to answer their mail messages
- xget   BSD command to send secret mail.
- xsend   BSD command to examine secret mail
- enroll   Sets up xget and xsend

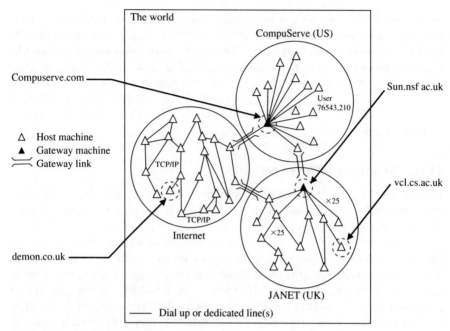

Figure 11.2 Bordering mail networks

THE from COMMAND – WHO IS MY MAIL FROM?

This Unix command works in the same way as the f (from) command in the interactive mail program. Its function is to extract the header lines from messages in your /usr/spool/mail/* mailbox and display them for viewing. Command-line options include: -s <sender> which allows messages only from specific senders to be displayed, and the [user] argument which makes the from command display the /usr/spool/mail mailbox of a particular user (since mailboxes only read and write access for the owner, you will have to be in an administrative capacity to read other users' mailboxes, i.e. a superuser such as root). Both of these command-line options and arguments are optional; by default the from command displays all messages from a mailbox, for example:

```
$ from↵
Message 1:
From: fred (Fred Johnson)
Subject: Hello joe
To: joe (Joe Public)
Date: Wed Mar 21 12:46
Cc: mark (Mark Johnson)
$
```

Table 11.8 Mailing formats for other networks

Network	What your mail address should resemble
CompuServe	nnnnn.nnn@compuserve.com The nnnnn.nnn should be replaced by the numeric address of the person required. Do not use the CompuServe comma to separate the numeric parts. For posting from CompuServe to the Internet use an address of the form: >internet:person@host for example: >internet:fred@somewhere.com
BitNet	Change an entry of the form: user@machine.bitnet to an entry of the form: user%machine@gateway.bitnet where gateway is the remote machine's Internet–BitNet gateway, e.g. wombatvm.cc.edu, thus you would use the address user%machine.@wombatvm.cc.edu substituting user%machine as required. You may also want to try simpler names of the form: user@machine.bitnet
FidoNet	FidoNet networks contain a firstname.lastname string and then a sequence of numbers in the form 1:2/3:4. If a person has the FidoNet email name 'john.williams at 2:4/6:9' use the address: john.williams@p9.f6.n4.z2.fidonet.org where p, f, n, and z are always used with the FidoNet numbers of the person's address in the reverse order (right to left, e.g. 9, 6, 2, 4) in the example above. Some systems may require you to post to the different FidoNet gateway: john.williams@p9.f6.n4.z2.fidonet .org@zeus.ieee.org Try this alternative address if the first fails
UUCP	UUCP addresses should be converted from names of the format username@host.uucp to the format: name%host for the login name portion. The final prefix will depend on the machine through which you access UUCP messages. If you receive email via UUCP from a host vax.feed.com you should use a name of the form: username%host@vax.feed.com. Bang-paths are also used extensively on UUCP. These have names similar to: ..!uunet!host!user where uunet is a common UUCP–Internet gateway. Convert such names to entries consisting of: user%host@gateway where gateway is a UUCP–Internet gateway. You can examine incoming UUCP mail to find out the name of a gateway (uunet and uupsi are common)

Table 11.8 *Contd.*

Network	What your mail address should resemble
MCIMail	You can either send mail to a numeric address or a textual address. Numeric address are of the form: `7654321@mcimail.com` whereas textual addresses are normally a person's first and last names separated by an underscore: `John_Williams@mcimail.com` `Mcimail.com` is the Internet–MCIMail gateway
AppleLink	Send messages via the Internet gateway called: `apple-link.apple.com`, for example address your mail to `username@applelink.apple.com` Mailing from an AppleLink host to an Internet host requires the format: `user@host@internet#` for example: `fred@wombat.dingo.com@internet#`

In this example the from command has been issued with no command-line options; it therefore prints out the header lines for each message in this user's `/usr/spool/mail/*` mailbox file. Only one header has been displayed so only one message can be waiting in the file. The `mail` program itself should be used to read the message body of any messages (you could use an editor to view the mailbox, of course, if you own it). If you did not own a mailbox trying to be examined, you would see the message `Access denied`, or words to that effect, for example:

```
$ from root↵
/usr/spool/mail/root: Permission denied
$
```

In this example the user has been denied access to the file. Read permission must be available to the person wanting to examine any such file, and in this case such permission was not granted.

Some `from` program implementations show shorter listings, typically only the `From:` line and the time and date that the message was received, for example:

```
$ from↵
From: fred (Fred Johnson) Wed Mar 21 12:46 1993
From: mark (Mark West) Wed Mar 21 12:59:01 1993
$
```

THE `vacation` PROGRAM

This command has its origins in version 7 Unix. TI has been carried on into many Berkeley Unix systems and is used to tell people that you are not available to answer their mail. In order to use the vacation program you must create a file in your home directory called .forward. This file must contain a single line of the form:

```
\<username>, " | <location-of-vacation-program>"
```

where <username> is your own username (or log-in name) and the argument <location-of-vacation-program> is the directory in which the vacation program is held (probably /usr/bin or /bin, or perhaps /usr/ucb for the Berkeley utilities). Note that this entry must include the name of the program also so end the line with vacation. All other characters, such as the quotes ("), pipe (|), the initial slash (\), and comma (,) must be included literally. An example entry could therefore resemble:

```
\joe, " | /usr/bin/vacation"
```

Next you must create a file called vacation.msg which stores your vacation message. This message will be mailed back to people trying to contact you so it should ideally contain a Subject: line. You may also want to get in the habit of placing a Delivered-by: The vacation program header line in your message to tell people how this message was sent back without human intervention! A typical message could be structured as

```
Subject: Sorry, I'm on holiday
Delivered-by: The vacation program
Sorry I'm not here to reply to your mail but I'm on holiday
in the Bahamas. Back on the 28th :-(
Regards,
Fred
```

When anyone mails you, the presence of the .forward file will send back your vacation.msg file (once a week) to the sender of the message. The vacation program will create the files vacation.pag and vacation.dir to hold details of the people who have tried to contact you.

TIP

When you get back from your 'vacation' don't delete the .forward file; you may want to keep it for another time – rename it to something like .forward.old with the Unix command:

```
$ mv .forward .forward.old↵
```

instead. You can rename it again later for the next time you want to use the vacation program. Renaming or deleting the file will stop the vacation program from intefering with your incoming mail.
Note: vacation will not delete any incoming messages.

The `vacation` program is started by using the `-I` option. So just before you leave issue a command of the form:

```
$ vacation -I↵
```

This initializes the `vacation` program, basically to make it start functioning from that point onwards. Messages will be sent back to people immediately and then once a week by default. The `vacation` program has a `-t<c><N>` (time) option to alter this time period. The `<c>` represents a time period which can be any of: `s` (seconds), `m` (minutes), `h` (hours), `d` (days), `w` (weeks); the `<N>` argument is a numeric value representing the physical amount of time required, e.g. 5. Thus you may want to send repeat messages back every 5 working days using the command:

```
$ vacation -I -td5↵
```

Another handy feature of the vacation program is the ability to include the `Subject:` line of a sender's message in your reply message back to them. This is done using the variable `$SUBJECT` which should be quoted and placed in your `vacation.msg` file. For example our earlier `vacation.msg` file could be altered to include this feature:

```
Subject: Sorry, I'm on holiday
Delivered-by: The vacation program
Regarding your mail on: "$SUBJECT"
Sorry I'm not here to reply to your mail but I'm on holiday
in the Bahamas. Back on the 28th :-(
Regards,
Fred
```

The `"$SUBJECT"` in the above message would be substituted with the `Subject:` line of the sender's message to make the reply a bit more friendly. Note that the `-I` and `-t` options can be specified in separate commands; the vacations control files will keep track of the options and times you specify until they are next altered.

SENDING SECRET MAIL – `xget`, `xsend` AND `enroll`

The `mail` system is not that security conscious. Messages are entered in plain text and they may pass through a number of machines that may even allow examination of the message as it passes. The Unix commands `xget` and `xsend` were specifically designed to employ encryption on messages, and therefore to provide a secure communications channel for the distribution of electronic mail messages. A password is used to encrypt outgoing messages and the recipient must know this password in order to decipher the contents. Passwords are allocated by the sender of the message prior to posting. Unfortunately, you must both agree a password to use first, and if this is sent by email someone may intercept it. Even so, the chances of this happening are pretty remote.

In order to start using the secret-mail programs, the enroll command must be invoked by both the sender and recipient to initially configure the system. The enroll program normally creates a file in the directory called /var/spool/secretmail (or /usr/spool/secretmail on some systems) to hold the encrypted key which will be derived from your password. Entering enroll therefore yields the following dialogue:

```
$ enroll↵
Gimme key: <your-secret-password>↵
```

As can be seen, enroll aks us for a key (password), which we then enter to the system. Passwords are not echoed on the screen as entered; some systems may ask you to enter the key twice to make sure it is correct and that you remember it. The enroll program then creates a file with a .key extension in the /var/spool/secretmail directory; the file prefix will be your own username, so if you were called joe, a file called joe.key would be created in order to hold your encrypted password. This file is used for deciphering purposes when you receive secret mail. If the file is deleted you must run enroll again and use the same password as previously, assuming the sender is using the same password (if you do not run enroll the system will ask you for a new key the next time you send some secret mail).

The xsend program

xsend is used to send secret mail to a single recipient, for example you could type

```
$ xsend mark@cc.fig.edu↵
```

whereupon the system will drop into standard-input mode, and you can type your letter ([Ctrl-C] interrupts this and halts the program). Use the [Ctrl-D] keystroke (on a new line) to end the message and send it to the recipient. When you have committed a message in this way, the plain text of the message is encrypted using your secret key, and is then processed by the standard mail program (sendmail) in order to send the mail to the recipient.

The xget program

When the recipient receives this mail they must use the xget program to examine the message. Using the standard mail program will be useless, and you will only see the encrypted text. Invoking xget allows you to browse through any secret messages that have arrived for you. A password will be requested when you invoke xget – this password must clearly be the same as the sender is using or deciphering will not take place. For example:

```
$ xget↵
Key: <mutual-password>↵
```

Once the mutual key (password) has been entered the system will show you the first message and will then issue a command prompt (commonly a ?). Table 11.9 illustrates the commands that can be used with the xget program.

For example, assume a person mailed a secret mail message to us. We would invoke xget and see the prompt for our password. If the password matches the sender's, the message is deciphered and displayed on the screen. A system prompt follows this, enabling us to enter a command, as shown in Table 11.9, for example:

```
$ xget↵
Key: <correct-password>↵
Hi fred,
This is an example of some text sent with the secret-mail
program xget.
? q↵
$
```

Had we entered an incorrect password we would see a load of garbage:

```
$ xget↵
Key: <wrong-password>↵
-4 dlsfkgj sfg
04398t wreW%T ˆdrg ,150y o45w059i4′ - %$Tˆ $%&$dfgdfg
    3dgrDFldfgjdfg 65tg 7@! .
? q↵
$
```

Since you must enter the password when starting the xget program, you must restart it in order to re-enter a misstyped key. If you have more than one message use the [Return] key to browse though succesive messages, or use

Table 11.9   xget **commands**

Command	Description
! <cmd>	Run a shell command <cmd> and return to xget
[Return]	Move to next message
d	Delete the current message and move to the next
n	Delete current message and read next message
q	Quit xget to shell
s <file>	Save this message as plain text in to a file named <file>

the n command. Messages are deleted if using the n command so you may want to get into the habit of saving your messages using the s command. Messages are saved by default in the `/var/spool/secretmail` directory named using your username and a numeric extension which ranges from 1 upwards, e.g. `joe.1`, `joe.2`, etc.; all such files are stored in an encrypted form.

The normal mailing system is used to tell users that secret mail has arrived; once such a message has been received the recipient can invoke `xget` and read the required message(s).

MAIL NOTIFICATION – `biff`

Checking whether or not new mail has arrived can be performed manually by simply invoking the `mail` program, for example

```
$ mail↵
No mail for fred.
```

which indicates no mail is awaiting user fred. If there were some messages we would see the message 'You have new mail'. You could then start the `mail` program to read your message(s). Alternatively you could type `mail` every hour or so to see if any messages are waiting. The only problem with this method is that it is tiresome. A much better solution involves the use of the command `biff`; this command examines your `/usr/spool/mail/*` mailbox to see if any new mail has arrived. It takes one of two command-line arguments: y for yes (show new mail messages), and n for no (do not show new mail messages).

TIP

Place `biff` in your `.login` or `.cshrc` auto-login file so that it is automatically invoked when you log in.

`biff` displays the message shown below when a new mail-message arrives:

```
New mail has arrived for joe@vax.ftp.edu:
```

where `joe@vax.ftp.edu` is the user receiving the mail in this example, followed by a short transcript of the message, for example:

```
New mail has arrived for joe@vax.ftp.edu:
----Date: Mon, 12 Jul 93 15:21:45 -0300
From: mark@cc.una.com
To: joe@vax.ftp.edu
Subject: Meeting on the 14th
```

```
Joe,
Just a reminder regarding our meeting on the 14th. Make sure
... more ...
```

Not all of the message is shown – only the first five lines are normally displayed. So, in order to enable biff messages you can use the command

```
$ biff y↵
```

whereas you can disable the program by issuing the reverse command, for example

```
$ biff n↵
```

Biff operates in the background so it may interrupt the current program you are using in order to tell you that new mail has arrived. Systems such as X-Windows have xbiff, a graphical version of biff (this displays a graphical mailbox which changes colour when new mail arrives, as well as moving a small flag upright to indicate that the mail has arrived).

Appendix A
A–Z glossary of terms, acronyms and symbols

This appendix contains a list of computing terms, acronyms and symbols which are directly relevant to the Internet. A cross-reference list has also been provided after each definition to point you in the direction of other relevant terms.

:-) *et al.* See Smiley.

@ The symbol used in mail addresses to separate a username from a hostname, for example the person `fred` who resides at the Internet host `some-site.com` would be structured as: `fred@somesite.com`. See also: email, USENET, Internet, host, `!`.

! The symbol used in UUCP mailing addresses. Also known as the bang-path symbol on the Internet. It is used to separate machine names that are connected on the network. See also: UUCP, bang-path, @, Internet, USENET, email.

* See regular expression.

<g> Stands for 'grin', i.e. someone grinning (used to a sentence in which the contents should not to be taken too seriously). A common annotation used on USENET on the Internet network. Human emotions, such as grinning, can thus be included in a message, for example: `Don't use the xyz command, since it will blow your hard disk up <g>`. See also: Smiley, USENET, RTFM, IMHO, FYI, Internet.

10BaseT 10Base-T (or 802.3i), is the standard for running 10 megabits per second Ethernet LANs over unshielded twisted-pair wiring (UTP). It is based on a star topology, where all communication goes through a central point, the LANs hub. Thus, network management tools can be used to monitor and control network resources in ways that are impossible with bus topologies. 10Base-2 refers to the IEEE standard for Thin Ethernet which is also referred to as 'thinnet'. It uses an RG58 coax cable up to 200 metres in length for a single trunk segment. 10Base-5 refers to the IEEE standard for Thick Ethernet which is also referred to as 'thicknet'. It uses an RG11 coax cable up to 500 metres in length for a single trunk segment. See also: coaxial cable, UTP, IEEE, topology, Ethernet, UTP, LAN.

AFS Andrew File System. A set of protocols that allow users to access remote files just as if they were local to the machine they are working on, i.e. transparent access. The AFS system followed on from NFS and is said to offer better performance. See also: NFS.

Anonymous FTP (AFTP) Anonymous FTP is a method of downloading public files from Internet hosts without being registered on that particular machine. The FTP protocol is used for file transfers; the user enters the name anonymous as a user-id and their email name for a password. See also: Internet, FTP, email.

ANSI An abbreviation for American National Standards Institute. A non-governmental organization that proposes, modifies, approves, and publishes data-processing standards for voluntary use in the United States. The ANSI originally specified the screen graphics standard used in many computing systems, i.e. the ubiquitious ANSI.SYS driver in DOS. See also: CCITT, ISO, IEEE, ITU, DOS.

Application A term commonly used to refer to a piece of software, such as an editor or other program. An example is the FTP program (programs and applications are pretty much the same thing). See also: FTP, program.

Application Program Interface (API) A set of calling conventions defining how a service is invoked through a software package. See also: program.

Archie Archie is a service run over the Internet network that searches anonymous FTP sites for publicly available files. Archie runs on server machines all over the world, accessed via telnet. See also: Internet, anonymous FTP, telnet.

ARCnet A token-passing LAN technology for connecting personal computers based on a star topology. The term ARCnet is an acronym for attached resource computer network. ARCnet LANs are capable of operating at speeds up to 2.5 Mb/s. IEEE 802.4 addresses the specifications for ARCnet cabling. See also: LAN, Ethernet, FDDI, token ring.

ARP Address Resolution Protocol. The Internet protocol used to dynamically map Internet addresses to physical (hardware) addresses on local area networks. Limited to networks that support hardware broadcast. See also: RARP, ARPAnet, Internet.

ARPAnet A research network built in the 1970s. Basically used as a test-bed for protocols and other communications facilities which led to the Internet network of today. See also: Internet, MILNET, NSFnet.

Article An 'article' commonly refers to a single message that is posted on an electronic mail system, e.g. the Internet's USENET system. See also: Internet, USENET, NNTP, posting.

ASCII The American Standard Code for Information Interchange is a standard 7-bit code established to achieve compatibility between various types of data-processing equipment. The Standard ASCII character set consists of 128 decimal numbers ranging from zero through 127 which are assigned to letters, numbers, punctuation marks, and the most common special characters. The Extended ASCII character set also consists of 128 decimal numbers and ranges from 128 through 255 representing additional special, mathematical, graphic, and foreign characters. See also: EBCDIC.

Asynchronous A data transmission method in which each character is sent one bit at a time. Each character is preceded by a start bit and followed by a stop bit. Asynchronous transmission allows a character to be sent at random after the preceding character has been sent, without regard to any timing device. See also: synchronous.

AUI The AUI is an IEEE 802.3 standard designation for the cable that connects workstations on a local area network often using thick Ethernet cable. See also: BNC, coaxial cable, RJ-11/RJ-45, UTP, IEEE.

Backbone The primary connectivity mechanism of a hierarchical distributed system. All systems which have connectivity to an intermediate system on the backbone are assured of connectivity to each other. This does not prevent systems from setting up private arrangements with each other to bypass the backbone for reasons of cost, performance, or security.

Bandwidth A measure of the range of frequencies within a radiation band required to transmit a particular signal. It measures, in millions of cycles per second, the difference between the lowest and highest signal frequencies. The wider the bandwidth, the more information that can be carried.

Bang-path A bang-path is a sequence of Internet hostname (machines) names joined together with exclamation marks (!), for example: `machine1!machine2`. This notation is used by the UUCP program (originally taken from Unix) to specify a remote machine when copying file(s). See also: Unix, UUCP, program.

Baud Baud is a unit of measurement that denotes the number of discrete signal elements, such as bits, that can be transmitted per second. Bits per second (bps) means the number of binary digits transmitted in one second. There is a difference between bps and baud rate, and the two are often confused. For example, a device such as a modem said to transmit at 2400 baud is not correct; it actually transmits 2400 bits per second. It is important to note that both baud rate and bps refer to the rate at which the bits within a single frame are transmitted. The gaps between the frames can be of variable length. Accordingly, neither baud rate nor bps refers to the rate at which information is actually being transferred. See also: modem.

BBS Bulletin board system. BBSs are in the main small computer systems that allow users to dial in to them and access information via a modem device. BBSs store an assortment of information, such as shareware and freeware. Most BBS systems also allow users to chat to one another via an in-built messaging system. USENET, the Internet's news network, has been compared to a BBS since it has many forums which resemble BBS systems, i.e. for software, etc. Specific BBS software is available for computers such as the PC, an example being the WildCat! application. BBSs are also run via UUCP on both Unix and non-Unix systems. See also: USENET, Internet, UUCP, PD, shareware.

Binary A numbering system that uses base 2 arithmetic, allowing numbers to be specified using just the two digits 0 and 1, for example the number 8 is 1000 in binary. It is simple to convert decimal numbers to their binary equivalent: write down all numbers from 1 increasing in size by a power of 2 in reverse order i.e: 64, 32, 16, 8, 4, 2, 1; then take your decimal number and work out which digits are required to make the number with the minimum number of powers, i.e. to make 66 we would use the 64 plus the 2; by placing a 1 under all the digits required, and zeros under the others, we are left with the binary equivalent, for example

64	32	16	8	4	2	1
1	0	0	0	0	1	0

See also: bit, byte.

BIND Berkeley Internet Name Domain. A system whereby Internet hostnames can be represented as numeric codes. Similar to the DNS system which is now more commonly used on the Internet. BIND is basically DNS, but is used on Berkeley (BSD) Unix systems. See also: DNS, Internet, BSD.

Bit Binary digit. A digit that is either 1 or 0, and is used as the basis of the binary system (base 2 numbering system, as opposed to base 10, or denary, our own common numbering system). See also: binary, byte.

BIX Acronym for Byte Information eXchange, one of many service-providers and home of *Byte* magazine on the Internet (bix.com). See also: Internet, sservice-provider, Byte.

BNC An abbreviation for Bayonet Neill-Concelman. The bayonet refers to the prong in the middle of the connector. Mr Neill-Concelman invented it. Originally designed in England for television set antennas, the BNC is a type of connector designed for use with coaxial cabling. They lock together when the male part is inserted into the female part and rotated 90 degrees. See also: AUI, coaxial cable, RJ-11/RJ-45.

Bridge In local area networks, a bridge is an interconnection device between two networks of the same type using similar or dissimilar data links such as

Ethernet, token ring, and X.25. Bridges function at the data link layer of the OSI model. Bridges can usually be made to filter packets, that is, to forward only certain traffic. Specifically, bridges operate at the media access control or MAC sublayer of the data link layer. For this reason they are often called MAC-layer bridges. A bridge monitors all traffic on the two subnets that it links. If a bridge links LANs that have dissimilar MAC layers, it does the processing necessary to change, for example, an Ethernet packet to a token ring packet. See also: gateway, repeater, router, LAN, OSI, X.25, packet, Ethernet.

Broadcast A LAN transmission technique used by Ethernet, token ring and FDDI. A node wishing to transmit information to another node broadcasts a packet that contains the MAC address of the recipient. All nodes on the network receive the packet and decide whether to act upon it by the destination address. See also: FDDI, node, LAN.

BSD Berkeley System Distribution. An acronym used in conjunction with Berkeley's Unix operating system, which originated in the academic environment and was named after the University of Berkeley, California where it originated. The BSD Unix system is oriented towards the programming and software development environment. See also: Unix, SVR4, program.

BTW Acronym used on the USENET news network standing for 'By the Way...', for example: '...BTW, have you seen that latest IRC server at somewhere.edu?'. See also: IMHO, RTFM, USENET.

Bug An error in a program or application that causes it to behave incorrectly. Some bugs are even documented as 'features' if they cause a non-dangerous outcome! See also: application, patch, program.

Byte (i) A group of 8 bits, or one character; (ii) The name of the leading-edge computing magazine. See also: bit, binary, BIX.

C A programming language that has arisen from the Unix operating system (Unix is nearly all written in C). C has low and high-level programming characteristics which make it attractive to programmers. C is also highly portable, hence the movement of Unix to other machine platforms. See also: Unix, program.

CCITT Comité Consultatif Internationale Télégraphique et Téléphonique. The CCITT is an international consultative committee, organized by the United Nations. It makes recommendations for international communications, develops interface, modem, and data network recommendations. The popular standard X.25 protocol for access to packet-switched networks was originally a recommendation of CCITT. The CCITT has now been superceded by the ITU. See also: ANSI, OSI, X.25, modem, protocol, ITU.

CIX (a) Commercial Internet Exchange. This is basically an agreement between service-providers which facilitates them to carry out accounting and audit functions on commerical network traffic; (b) The Compulink Information Exchange – a well-known Internet service-provider in the UK.

Clarinet Clarinet is part of the USENET new system that carries real-life news e.g. stockmarket news, breaking news stories. Clarinet is a subscription-based service that is not free to Internet users, although your newsreader may have access to a limited set of Clarinet forums (mainly because some sites that have paid their subscriptions propagate them to other Internet sites throughout the world, such is the operation of the USENET system). See also: NNTP, USENET, Internet.

Client A piece of software that is used to query a resource and extract some information. For example, on the Internet, an Archie client is used to extract information regarding anonymous FTP sites. See also: client-server model, Archie, Internet, anonymous FTP.

Client–server model A common way to describe network services and the model user processes (programs) of those services. Examples include the name–server/name–resolver paradigm of the DNS and file–server/file–client relationships such as NFS and diskless hosts. See also: NFS, DNS, program.

CMIP Common Management Information Protocol. The OSI network management protocol. See also: SNMP.

Coaxial cable Coaxial cable is a data transmission medium noted for its wide bandwidth and for its low susceptibility to interference. Signals are transmitted inside a fully enclosed environment, an outer conductor or screen which surrounds an inner conductor. The conductors are commonly separated by a solid insulating material. Coaxial cable has a greater transmission capacity or bandwidth than standard twisted pair wires. See also twisted pair.

Collision A situation that occurs when two devices on a network (usually an Ethernet) broadcast a packet at the same time. Both packets become corrupted and have to be retransmitted. See also: Ethernet, broadcast, packet.

Coloured Book Protocols The communication protocols used to transfer information across JANET. So called because the specifications for the different components, electronic mail, remote terminal access, etc., were published in different coloured books. See also: JANET.

Command-line The interactive session at which commands are typed to a computer system. Command-line interfaces are common to many programs, such as a Shell under Unix. A typical command line consists of: (i) the command name (e.g. `ls`); (ii) the command options (e.g. `-l`); and (iii) an optional filename (e.g. `/etc`). The command-line is commonly prefixed with a system prompt that tells the user that the system is awaiting a command. Common Unix prompts include the $ and % signs. See also: shell, Unix, program.

CompuServe A commerical information provider based in Ohio, USA. CompuServe is a large information resource, but not really a network in its own right (people dial into a central machine to access the resources of

CompuServe). The emphasis is on commerical information, and the service has on-line charges. The Internet has links to CompuServe via the gateway node `compuserve.com` allowing electronic mail to be transferred to CompuServe users, and vice versa. See also: Internet.

Cracker A person who gains unauthorized access to a computer using slightly more clever means than a computer hacker, i.e. programming a Trojan-horse style entry, or by defeating the host operating system. See also: hacker, Trojan-horse, OS, program, phreaker.

CSMA/CD Carrier sense multiple access/collision detection is a network access scheme. It is a method by which a network device obtains use of the physical network channel to send a message across the network. It allows all network devices equal access to the one set of cables that interconnect the network. No central node controls access. CSMA/CD is used predominantly with bus topologies, like Ethernet. When it detects a clear channel (carrier sense), a node transmits its message marked with the address of the receiver. All idle stations (those not transmitting) continuously monitor the channel for other messages. The receiver of a message returns an acknowledgment of receipt. Meanwhile, the sender awaits the acknowledgment. If not received after a specified amount of time, the sender assumes that a collision has occurred (a time-out) and re-sends the message after a random amount of time. Collisions occur when two or more stations attempt to transmit messages simultaneously. See also: broadcast, collision, Ethernet, time-out, node.

CSO server Computing Services Office 'white pages' service. Used in systems such as Gopher. CSO servers act as resources of information, normally about people. CSO servers can be accessed and interrogated. See also: Gopher, WHOIS.

Cursor A small character used to tell you the current position on a screen. Used in all computer systems that are character based, e.g. for option selection, typing, etc. Cursors often blink on and off to show their presence to the user. See also: VGA.

Cyberspace Coined from the Cyberpunk epic, and commonly used to refer to an imaginary universe (such as a virtual reality world), although now used to refer to the Internet as a virtual electronic world. See also: Internet.

Daemon A program (or process) that runs in the background, i.e. transparently to the user while other tasks (foreground tasks) are running. Daemons include programs that deal with electronic mail and timing events, such as the Unix `cron` (clock daemon) program. See also: Unix, process, program.

Database A store of information held on a computer. Databases are used extensively as a means of organized data storage and retrieval. Database systems include ORACLE on systems such as VAX/VMS, and dBASE on PCs. See also: PC, VAX.

Datagram See IP datagram.

Data-link layer The OSI layer that is responsible for data transfer across a single physical connection, or series of bridged connections, between two network entities. See also: OSI.

DDN Defense Data Network. This is a part of the Internet network which is used by the US military and associated bodies. Also known as MILNET (military network), although MILNET is only one part of the DDN in reality. The Internet grew out of a military experiment, hence the military's presence on the network. See also: Internet, NIC.

DECnet Digital Equipment Corporation's proprietary network architecture. DECnet is not compatible with the TCP/IP suite of protocols used on the Internet so a gateway must normally be used. See also: TCP/IP, Internet, gateway.

DES Data Encryption Standard. A complex algorithm used to encrypt files so that their contents remain secret (until decrypted). This system is used in Unix to encrypt passwords in the second field of the /etc/passwd file. See also: Unix.

DFS Analogous to the Andrew (Distributed) File System. See also: AFS, NFS.

Dial-up connection The process of making a connection with a computer via a telephone network, i.e. via a modem device. See also: asynchronous, modem.

Directory A repository for files. A term used on many systems, especially Unix, DOS, and VMS. Directories allow storage systems to be implemented hierarchically i.e. directories of directories. See also: DOS, VMS, Unix, home directory.

DNS Domain Name System. The distributed name/address mechanism used in the Internet. An Internet domain name consists of a sequence of names (or labels) separated by periods (dots), e.g. demon.co.uk. In OSI, the term 'domain' is generally used as an administrative partition of a complex distributed system, such as in the MHS Private Management Domain (PRMD), and Directory Management Domain (DMD). See also: MHS, Internet, OSI, BIND, PRMD.

DoD Acronym for the US Department of Defense. See also: ARPAnet, MILNET, Internet.

DOS Disk operating system. An operating system for microcomputers developed by Microsoft for IBM's 16-bit machine, the IBM PC and its compatibles. DOS is in fact a re-write of CP/M, an operating system for earlier 8-bit computers. DOS is a a single-user, single-tasking operating system, unlike operating systems such as Unix. MSDOS is the MicroSoft version, while PCDOS is the IBM version, both of which are identical. See also: OS/2, Unix, VMS, Windows.

Dotted decimal notation The syntactic representation for a 32-bit integer that consists of four 8-bit numbers written in base 10 with periods (dots) separating them. Used to represent IP addresses on the Internet network, for example: `138.8.8.68`. See also: DNS, Internet, TCP/IP, integer.

EBCDIC Extended Binary Coded Decimal Interchange Code. A standard 8-bit code for the representation of characters. It allows 256 possible character combinations and stores one alphanumeric character or two decimal digits within a single byte. EBCDIC is the standard code on IBM minicomputers and mainframes, but not on the IBM microcomputers, where ASCII is used. EBCDIC is an alternative to the ASCII Code. See also: ASCII, bit.

Email Electronic mail. The method of sending electronic messages between users. On the Internet, email is used principally to send messages to USENET (and, of course, between users). Different systems normally have their own email capability. See also: Internet, USENET.

Etext An 'electronic text', i.e. a book stored on-line as a file which can be accessed (downloaded) by the user. Project Gutenberg stores many such etexts, and refers to such documents as 'literary freeware'. See also: PD, shareware.

Ethernet A network access and cable protocol which breaks data into sealed and addressed packets, delivering them across the cable to the recipient device, and confirming delivery. Developed in the late 1970s at the Xerox Corporation and endorsed by the IEEE, Ethernet is one of the oldest LAN communications protocols in the personal computing industry. It is also one of the fastest, running to 10 Mb/s. However, on a network using Ethernet, if two devices attempt to transmit data at the same time a collision occurs and the data must be re-transmitted. Data transmission is supervised by a protocol known as carrier sense multiple access/collision detection (or CSMA/CD). TCP/IP is extensively used over Ethernet connections. See also: FDDI ARCnet, token ring, IEEE, CSMA/CD collision, TCP/IP.

FAQ Acronym for frequently asked questions. FAQs are documents posted to the USENET news network on the Internet. They contain tips and hints, plus details of system resources and other information useful to network users. The more complex newsgroups normally have their own FAQs. See also: Internet, RFC, USENET.

FDDI Fibre Distributed Data Interface. A standard for local area networks using fibre-optic cable. FDDI is very close to the IEEE 802.5 standard and uses an architecture similar to that of IBM's token ring. FDDI can support very large LANs, up to 500 nodes within a 100 km (62 mile) circumference, and data transfer rates up to 100 Mbit/s. See also: ARCnet, IEEE, Ethernet, token ring.

File A common term applied to an item such as a document, an image or even a computer program. Files group together information (such as sentences in a book) into individual units that can be stored on a computer. ASCII files are those which contain plain text; binary files make up files such as executable programs, non-ASCII word-processor documents (with text effects such as underlining, embolding, etc.), images and compressed files. See also: directory, ASCII, home directory, program.

Flaming A term denoting an argumentative discussion between two or more people when discussing a particular topic. Occurs frequently on the Internet network, where the term is used heavily. A special discussion forum on USENET is available called `alt.flame` for this very purpose. See also: Netiquette, RTFM, USENET.

Freenet Organizations that provide free Internet access to users. This is usually organized as a local-community project, i.e. through a local library. Refer to the resource guide for a list of freenets.

FSF The Free Software Foundation. The name says it all really. See also: GNU.

FTAM File Transfer, Access, and Management. The OSI remote file service and protocol. See also: FTP.

FTP File Transfer Protocol. A member of the Internet protocol suite used to manage the transfer of files between computers. See also: FTAM, anonymous FTP.

FYI (a) An acronym for 'For your information ...'. Used on USENET as an abbreviation. For example: 'FYI, there is a good C source at `vax.ftp.com` in `/source/c`'; (b) a document similar in content to a RFC, but not used to describe a new Internet standard. See also: RTFM, IMHO, USENET, Internet, RFC, FAQ.

Gandalf Manufacturer of data switching equipment used as the basis of the University Data Network. See also: line driver.

Gateway The original Internet term for what is now called router or more precisely, IP router. In modern usage, the terms 'gateway' and 'application gateway' refer to systems which translate from some native format to another. Examples include X.400 to/from RFC 822 electronic mail gateways. See also: bridge, repeater, router, RFC, X.400, email.

GID Group identification code. Used on operating systems such as Unix, where each user is part of a group of users (a 'user-group') to facilitate the sharing of file(s), etc. Each group has a GID, a numeric code, and each user has a UID for identification purposes. Unix uses numbers to refer to individual users and groups. See also: Unix, UID.

GIF Graphics Interchange Format. A device-independent image format, used extensively by the CompuServe system, and now widely found on the Internet in its USENET forums and FTP sites. See also: FTP, USENET.

GNU An acronym for 'GNU's Not Unix'. The Free Software Foundation established the GNU project to establish a completely new Unix that was independent of System V. See also: SVR4, Unix.

Gopher A tool used on the Internet network to locate information on a wide variety of subjects. Gophers can be accessed via `telnet`, and as dedicated client programs in their own right. See also: Archie, veronica, `telnet`, program.

GUI Graphical User Interface. A GUI is an interface in which all operation is normally controlled by a mouse device. Objects such as files (and even actual tasks) are represented by pictorial icons for ease-of-use. GUIs are in use with such systems as MicroSoft Windows, X, and the Macintosh interfaces. See also: X-Windows, Windows, WIMP.

Hacker Someone who gains unauthorized access to a computer system, normally by a determined effort, i.e. repeating various username and password combinations, etc. See also: Trojan-horse, phreaker, cracker.

HCU Acronym for home computer user – a person who connects into the Internet from home (or, of course, someone who operates a computer from home generally).

Home directory A term used on operating systems such as Unix (and VMS); it refers to a place that a user is placed when they initially log in to a computer system, and where they can store their files. See also: OS, Unix, VMS, DOS, file, login, directory.

Hop Term used to describe a one-to-one computer link. Networks, such as the Internet, are made up of computers that may be networked in a multi-hop fashion, that is to say to get from computer A to computer C would require two 'hops', i.e. 1:A → B and 2:B → C.

Host A commonly used term to represent a machine or other computer that is part of a network. The host could represent a single machine on a network, or the entire network of machines which are known under one collective name. Hence the term 'Internet hostname', 'remote hosts', etc. See also: Internet, node.

Hypertext Term referring to an application that normally has text, sound and graphics integrated within it (a multimedia application), although hypertext can also refer to a system in which information is organized in such a way as to provide multiple references to places and names embedded in some text, e.g. a paragraph of a book; these 'expand' into yet further items of information such as text, images, sounds, etc. On the Internet this level of sophistication has yet to be put into widespread use (mainly because of bandwidth allocation problems). The World-Wide-Web (also known as WWW, or W3) is a text-based hypertext system that allows multiple references to be followed from a single subject. See also: WWW, Internet, multimedia.

HYTELNET A `telnet`-based service on the Internet which offers a database of `telnet` servers which allow access to OPAC-based systems. See also: OPAC, `telnet`.

IAB Internet Architecture Board. A council of Internet elders that passes decisions about various Internet standards and issues. Nearest thing to a ruling body the Internet will probably ever get. See also: Internet, IETF.

ICMP Internet Control Message Protocol. The protocol used to handle errors and control messages at the IP layer. ICMP is part of the IP protocol. See also: TCP/IP, Internet, protocol.

IEEE Acronym for the Institute of Electrical and Electronic Engineers, a standard-setting body in the computing world. See also: ANSI, CCITT, ISO, ITU.

IETF Acronym for Internet Engineering Task Force. A group of volunteers that investigate and attempt to solve technical problems related to the Internet. The IETF work with the IAB and pass on recommendations. See also: Internet, IAB.

IMHO An acronym used on the Internet which stands for 'In my humble opinion'. Used to get over a particular point of view in a gentle, and non-offensive manner. Analogous to: 'With all due respect'. See also: RTFM, Internet, USENET, FYI, <g>, Smiley.

Integer Any whole number, that is a number without a fractional part, e.g. −1, 0, 1, 8868, etc. See also: Binary.

Internet The largest wide-area network in the world, consisting of large national backbone nets (such as NSFNET and JANET) and a myriad of regional and local campus networks spread all over the world. The Internet uses the TCP/IP protocol suite, and to actually be 'on' the Internet you must really have IP connectivity, i.e. your own IP number. Networks with only email connectivity are not really classified as actually being on the Internet (although this is not always the case since some service-providers will allocate an IP address to many HCUs). See also: HCU, IP, TCP/IP, JANET, JIPS, backbone.

Internet address A 32-bit address assigned to hosts using TCP/IP. See also: dotted decimal notation, TCP/IP.

Internetwork Two or more networks connected by a routing (router) device. See also: router.

IP Internet Protocol. The network layer protocol for the Internet protocol suite. See also: OSI, TCP/IP, IP datagram, Internet.

IP datagram The fundamental unit of information passed across the Internet. Contains source and destination addresses along with data and a number of fields which define such things as the length of the datagram, the header checksum, and flags to say whether the datagram can be (or has been) fragmented. The term is often used interchangeably with packet although they are not the same thing. A packet is a physical thing, appearing on an Ethernet or some wire. In most cases a packet simply contains a datagram, so there is very little difference. However, they can differ. When TCP/IP is used on top of a protocol such as X.25, the X.25 interface breaks the datagrams up into 128-byte packets. This is invisible to IP because the packets are put back together into a single datagram at the other end before being processed by TCP/IP again. However, with most media, there are efficiency advantages to sending one datagram per packet so the distinction tends to vanish. See also: datagram, Internet, TCP/IP, packet, X.25, byte, Ethernet.

IPC Acronym for inter-process communication. IPC describes how processes 'talk' to one another (across a network, for example). A typical IPC technique could be the TCP/IP protocol suite, or the X protocol. A common IPC technique on Unix is known as a socket. Sockets are low-level functions which are programmed in languages such as C; they allow information to be transferred between processes on local and remote systems in much the same way as the low-level file functions in C, such as open() and close(). See also: C, program, TCP/IP, X-Windows, Unix, client–server model.

IPX Internetwork Packet Exchange. A protocol, based on a Xerox's development (developed by Novell), that allows the exchange of message packets on a network running NetWare software.

IRC Internet Relay Chat. A system whereby multiple users from all over the world can chat with one another. IRCs are used on the Internet network. See also: MUD, Internet.

ISDN Integrated Services Digital Network. An emerging technology which is beginning to be offered by the telephone carriers of the world. ISDN combines voice and digital network services in a single medium making it possible to offer customers digital data services as well as voice connections through a single 'wire'. The standards that define ISDN are specified by the CCITT. See also: CCITT.

ISO The International Standards Organization, based in Paris, develops standards for international and national data communications. In the early 1970s, the ISO developed a standard model of a data-communications system and called it the Open System Interconnection model. Consisting of seven layers, it describes what happens when a terminal talks to a computer or when one computer talks to another. This model was designed to facilitate creating a system in which equipment from different vendors can communicate. See also: OSI, CCITT, IEEE, ANSI.

ISOC The Internet Society. The governing body of the IAB. See also: IAB, Internet, IETF.

ITU The new name of the CCITT body. See also: CCITT.

JANET Joint Academic NETwork; a wide area network interconnecting the majority of UK higher education and academic research establishments. Operated on behalf of the Computer Board by the Joint Network Team. Communication over JANET was originally managed by the Coloured Book Protocol suite although the Internet protocols are now widely used in addition. See also: JIPS.

JIPS Acronym for JANET Internet Protocol Service. The name used to refer to the running of the Internet protocol suite across JANET. See also: JANET, IP.

JPEG Acronym for Joint Photographic Experts Group. An image compression standard, and the name of the body which created it. JPEG images are compressed at source to allow faster file transmission and to allow greater disk storage. JEPG images commonly decompress into GIF images. See also: GIF.

K or **Kb** Abbreviation for kilobyte. A data-storage term referring to 1024 bytes of information. Thus 100K (or Kb) is 102 400 bytes, where 1 byte is a single character (or 8 bits). One megabyte (Mb) is roughly 1000K, or approximately a million bytes. See also: bit, byte, Mb.

KA9Q A system that implements TCP/IP on a personal computer, developed by Phil Karn. KA9Q is used by many dial-up Internet systems with protocols such as PPP and SLIP. See also: TCP/IP, Internet, dial-up connect on, SLIP, PPP.

Kermit Not the Frog, but instead a much-used computer protocol. Used mostly for file downloading. See also: protocol.

Knowbot Knowbots, or 'robotic librarians'. Implemented in software to seek out information on behalf of a user. Knowbots are very much in the experimental stage of the Internet. See also: Internet, Gopher, WAIS.

LAN Local area network. A network that is confined to a geographically restricted area, such as within the same building, is usually referred to as a LAN. See also: WAN.

Leased line A permanent connection from your own computer (or network) into another system. Really the opposite of a dial-up line. Many Internet service-providers are now offering leased lines, at a price. See also: dial-up connection.

Line driver A device used to boost the strength of a signal, usually from a serial port of a microcomputer, to enable it to cover greater distances than would otherwise be possible. Line drivers are used extensively with the University Data Network to connect PCs to the network. See also: Gandalf.

Log-in A log-in is the process of identifying yourself to a computer, normally by supplying a username and password. login is the name of a Unix program that does just this, although the term 'log in' is used extensively to refer to the process of identifying yourself to a secure computer system. See also: userid, UID, Unix.

Mail gateway A machine that connects two or more electronic mail systems (especially dissimilar mail systems on two different networks) and transfers messages between them. Sometimes the mapping and translation can be quite complex, and generally it requires a store-and-forward scheme whereby the message is received from one system completely before it is transmitted to the next system after suitable translations. See also: gateway, email.

MAU Medium attachment unit. A device for connecting a computer into a network, commonly an Ethernet network. See also: Ethernet.

Mb Megabyte. Term of data storage equal to one million bytes, or 1024 kilobytes (Kb). See also: K, bit, byte.

MHS Message handling system. The system of message user agents, message transfer agents, message stores, and access units which together provide OSI email. MHS is specified in the CCITT X.400 series of recommendations. See also: SMTP, CCITT.

MIB Management information base. A collection of objects that can be accessed via a network management protocol. See also: CMIP, SNMP.

MILNET Acronym for military network. See DDN, NIC, Internet.

Modem MOdulator–DEModulator. A device used in data communications, whereby the analogue tones of a telephone are converted into a digital equivalent in order to transfer data over the telephone network between geographically separated computers. See also: UUCP, dial-up connection.

Motif A presentation manager (and indeed complete environment) for the X-Windows system. Athena and 'Open-Look' are other examples of X-Window environments. Each are similar, although they present information in a slightly different way. See also: X-Windows, WIMP, GUI.

Mouse Not the rodent variety, but the electronic variety. A device used to move a screen cursor to select items from WIMP-style interfaces, such as the Windows system. See also: WIMP, Windows.

MTU Maximum transmission unit. The largest possible unit of data that can be sent on a given physical medium. Example: the MTU of Ethernet is 1500 bytes. See also: packet, Ethernet.

MUD Multi-user dungeon (and/or dimension). The name for multiple-player games that are available on the Internet. MUDs allow a user to become a character in a fictitious role-playing simulation, exploring, discovering and chatting to other players in the process (rather like 'Dungeons and Dragons'). See also: IRC, Internet.

Multimedia A branch of computing that is interested in bringing together all types of media into a single user application, although mainly concentrated around the audio and visual mediums. See also: Hypertext.

Net A term analogous to 'network', e.g. NSFnet, ARPAnet, JVNCnet, etc.

Nethack An addictive game indigenous to Unix in which the user can explore mazes and secret worlds. Similar to a 'Dungeons & Dragons' style adventure in which the user takes on a role and must collect objects and points. See also: MUD.

Netiquette The term, derived from etiquette, and applied to the correct way of behaviour over the Internet network. The Internet has created many dozens of rules which users should abide by. See also: flaming.

Netnews Analogous to USENET on the Internet, the global dicussion arena made up solely of electronic mail (email) messages. See also: Internet, USENET, email.

NetPolice An Internet term referring to the administrative controllers who police the Internet. Even though the Internet is vastly decentralized, large service and network providers do have some 'powers' to control network users. See also: Internet.

NetWare The operating system developed by Novell, Inc. The NetWare operating system is loaded on the server when it is booted; it controls all system resources and the way information is processed on the network. See also: LAN.

Network interface card (NIC) An additional piece of equipment required by most PCs to connect them to a LAN. It is usually a card that fits into an expansion slot within the PC. NICs are specific to the type of network being used, e.g. Ethernet, token ring, etc. See also: Ethernet, token ring, LAN.

NFS Network file system. A distributed file system, usually associated with Unix, developed by Sun to enable computers to share files across a network. It is a proprietary system but Sun have made the specifications widely available and versions are available for other operating systems. See also: AFS.

NIC An acronym for naming information centre. In essence, a NIC is a database of user/site details which can be interrogated by users. An example of a principal NIC is the site `nic.ddn.mil` on the Internet network. See also: WHOIS, Internet.

NNTP Network News Transfer Protcol. NNTP servers are widely available on the Internet network to facilitate the sending of messages over USENET. NNTP servers exist all over the world and can be interrogated via `telnet` as an interactive service. See also: Internet, USENET, `telnet`.

NOC Network Operations Centre. A group of people that are charged with the responsbility for the smooth-running of a computer network. Service-providers have their own NOCs which normally answer user queries. See also: service-provider.

Node When any number of devices are connected together in a network, each of them are referred to as nodes, and are assigned unique addresses within that network.

NREN National Research and Education Network. Based in the US, this group has attempted to combine networks operated by different Federal US Agencies into a single network.

NSFnet National Science Foundation Network. Like MILNET, the NSFnet makes up a large chunk of the Internet network. NSFnet was started many years ago to share scientific information between scientists for research purposes. See also: MILNET, Internet.

OPAC On-line public access catalogue. OPACs are mainly library-based systems e.g. electronic book and journal catalogue systems. OPACs can be accessed via networks such as the Internet via `telnet`. Many OPAC systems are run by academic institutions. An example is the LIBERTAS library-book system. See also: Internet, `telnet`, HYTELNET.

OS Acronym for operating system, the master program used on a computer to handle all low-level and fundamental operations such as the control of storage devices, the screen and other peripherals. See also: DOS, Unix, VMS, program.

OS/2 OS/2 is an advanced operating system for PCs and PS/2s with an 80286 processor or better. It was co-developed by Microsoft and IBM and envisioned as the successor to DOS. It was designed from the ground-up with pre-emptive multi-tasking and multi-threading in mind. It also protects applications from one another (a single misbehaved program will not disrupt the entire system), supports all addressable physical RAM, and supplies virtual memory to applications as requested, thus breaking the DOS 640K barrier. Its environment is similar to Microsoft Windows. See also: Windows, DOS, Unix, PC.

OSF Abbreviation for Open Systems Foundation, a standard-setting body in the Unix world. See also: ANSI, ISO, IEEE, CCITT.

OSI (OSI model) Open System Interconnection. A reference model defined by the International Standards Organization (ISO). It is a communications protocol consisting of seven layers intended as a standard for the development of communications systems worldwide. The seven layers of the OSI model are:
1 Physical layer: wires, plugs, and electrical signals
2 Data link layer: packaging of data for transmission
3 Network layer: connections between two separate systems
4 Transport layer: conversion for transmission over network
5 Session layer: establishes and terminates the session
6 Presentation layer: data format conversion
7 Application layer: messages between application programs
See also: ISO, IEEE, ANSI, CCITT.

Packet A packet is a group of data elements transmitted together that generally form part of a larger transmission made up of a number of packets. A packet also contains additional information such as packet number and error detecting codes. Packet switching is just a method of communication that involves splitting a transmission up into packets. Successive packets along a given channel can belong to different transmissions. A device used to create and unpack packets is called a PAD for packet assembler/disassembler. See also: IP datagram, PAD, MTU.

PAD Packet assembler/disassembler, a device for converting a data-stream to and from discrete packets for transmission over a packet switching network. Dial-up PADS allow users to log in to a remote machine via a modem and use a remote service interactively, e.g. to log in to an interactive system (e.g. a Unix system). See also: Unix, modem, packet, dial-up connection.

Patch Common term meaning to provide a fix to a bug in a program. Patches normally arrive in the form of a piece of software or a software modification which will remedy a given problem. See also: bug.

PC Acronym for personal computer. Includes the 8086/80286/80385/80486 CPUs and now the Pentium-based computers. See also: DOS.

PD Acronym for public domain. Normally refers to software and/or information that is publicly available to all users. Analogous to freeware, i.e.

software that is free, that is, requires no royalty payment to the author(s). See also: shareware, etext.

Phreaker A person who gains unauthorized access to a phone network by tricking the phone system into granting free calls. Commonly employed over tone-dialled phone networks. Phone phreakers, to use their full name, also like to employ such trickery as taking advantage of freephone numbers ('800' numbers) to gain access to secret digital switchboards which can grant access to outside phone lines. Phreakers mainly use their efforts to avoid paying phone bills, and not malicious (date corrupting) activities as widely thought. See also: hacker, cracker, Trojan-horse.

Physical layer The OSI layer that provides the means to activate and use physical connections for bit transmission. In plain terms, the physical layer provides the procedures for transferring a single bit across a physical media. See also: OSI, ISO.

Ping A Unix program used with TCP/IP-based systems to contact a host to see if it is still 'alive' (or available). Ping contacts the machine specified and makes it send back an acknowledgement. See also: Unix, TCP/IP.

Port The abstraction used by Internet transport protocols to distinguish among multiple simultaneous connections to a single destination host. Used extensively with operating systems such as Unix, and with protocols such as TCP/IP for applications such as FTP, `telnet`, `rlogin`, `rcp`, etc. See also: Unix, Internet, TCP/IP, application.

Posix The IEEE standard relating to open systems in the Unix world. See also: IEEE, ISO, ANSI, Unix, CCITT.

Posting An article sent to the USENET network on the Internet network, via email. See also: Internet, USENET, email, article.

Postmaster The person charged with the responsibility of maintaining an organization's electronic mail service (or commonly the systems manager). The name `postmaster` is in fact an email alias used on Unix systems to allow users to send messages to the person in charge of an Internet host without knowing their exact name, e.g. `postmaster@somewhere.edu`. See also: Unix, Internet, email.

PPP Point-to-Point Protocol. The successor to SLIP, PPP provides router-to-router and host-to-network connections over both synchronous and asynchronous circuits. There is currently no standard for PPP. See also: SLIP, synchronous/asynchronous.

Presentation layer The OSI layer that determines how applications information is represented (i.e. encoded) while in transit between two end systems. See also: OSI, ISO, protocol.

PRMD PRivate Management Domain. An X.400 message handling system private organization mail system. See also: MHS, X.400.

Process A word that has a wide definition in the computing world. A process commonly refers to an executing program, so let's keep it simple and stick with that since it's pretty accurate. Processes are used extensively under operating systems such as Unix. See also: daemon, OS, program.

Program A sequence of instructions that instruct a computer how to perform a task or series of operations. Programs are written in a multitude of computer languages, for example C on Unix. The most famous C program is probably 'Hello World!', so here it is in its entirety (by the way, all it does is print 'Hello World!' on the screen):

```
main()
{
printf("Hello World!\n");
}
```

Protocol A protocol is a set of rules governing the communication and the transfer of data between two or more devices. The rules define the handling of certain communication problems, such as framing, error control, sequence control, system transparency, line control, and start-up control.

r* commands The r*, or R commands, are a series of 'R'emote-based commands on the Unix operating system. Examples include: rsh (remote shell program), rlogin (remote login program), and rdist (remote software distribution program). See also: Internet, rlogin, Unix.

RARP Reverse Address Resolution Protocol. The Internet protocol a diskless host uses to find its Internet address at startup. RARP maps a physical (hardware) address to an Internet address. See also: ARP.

Reflector A reflector, or mail reflector, is an electronic mail address that allows messages to be automatically passed to other recipients. These are commonly used for mailing groups. See also: email.

Regular expression A term used in Unix to mean a wildcarded expression. Unix is rich in wildcard (or pattern-matching characters) which can be used to represent items such as filenames. Examples include: * match zero or more characters); ? (to match 1 or zero characters); and [] to match a range of characters. Many many others exist, and are used by Unix programs such as vi, ed and ex (the Unix editors). Examples: file* is a regular expression that would match the filenames: file1, file_list and file. The expression: file[12] would therefore match the filenames: file1 and file2. See also: Unix.

Repeater A device which propagates electrical signals from one cable to another without making routing decisions or providing packet filtering. In OSI terminology, a repeater is a physical layer intermediate system. See also: bridge, gateway, router.

RFC Request for comments. The document series, begun in 1969, which describes the Internet suite of protocols and related experiments. Not all (in fact very few) RFCs describe Internet standards, but all Internet standards are eventually written up as RFCs.

RIP Routing Internet Protocol. A protocol used by routers on an internetwork to forward information between networks and inform each other of changes in the state network. See also: gateway, router, protocol.

RJ-11 and **RJ-45** Designations for commonly used modular telephone line connectors. RJ is an abbreviation for registered jack. Both of these connectors serve as an interface between the telephone line and the receiving device such as the telephone or a modem. They consist of a plastic plug on the end of a wire and a jack on the phone, modem, or wall plate. The RJ-11 consists of six wires and is used for the standard telephone voice line connection. The RJ-45 consists of eight wires and is typically used for data transmission over twisted-pair wire. See also: AUI, BNC, twisted pair.

`rlogin` The remote `login` program on the Unix operating system. Allows users with the appropriate security permissions to log in on a remote Internet host (or another host on the same network portion). Part of the `r*` commands. See also: `r*` commands, `telnet`, `login`, Unix.

RPC Remote procedure call. A standard mechanism for communication between two remote programs (or applications). RPC-based services include systems such as NFS and the yellow-pages services found on Unix systems. Non-RPC based services include `telnet` and FTP. See also: telnet, FTP, application, NFS.

Router An interconnection device that links complex networks together at the network layer of the OSI model. Routers are similar to bridges between networks but generally are more active. They are capable of reading the network-addressing information and selecting an appropriate travel path. To do this it uses a routing protocol to gain information about the network, and algorithms to choose the best route based on several criteria known as 'routing metrics'. Modern routers can handle multiple protocol stacks simultaneously and move packets or frames on to the correct links to their proper destination. A brouter is a bridge-router operating at the data link layer of the OSI model. It performs the functions of a bridge between similar networks but remains independent of higher protocols. Like a router, a brouter can manage multiple lines and transmits messages accordingly. See also: bridge, gateway, repeater.

`rsh` The Unix remote-shell program. Allows a user to run a Unix command on a remote computer. See also: `r*` commands, `rlogin`.

RTFM An acronym for read the f****** manual! A commonly used acronym telling users not to ask questions which are already covered in existing system documentation. This acronym is used commonly on the Internet (and Unix based systems). See also: Internet, IMHO, Smiley.

`sendmail` The principle email delivery system used on the Unix platform. See also: email, Unix.

Server A device (usually a computer) on a network capable of recognizing and responding to client requests. The services can range from basic file and printer services, to support for complex distributed applications. For example, a distributed database management system can create a single logical database across multiple servers. See also: client–server model.

`sendmail` The principle email delivery system used on the Unix platform. See also: email, Unix.

Service-provider A company (or organization) that provides users with access to networks such as the Internet. See also: NOC, BIX. Refer to the appendices for lists of service-providers currently in existence.

Session layer The OSI layer that provides means for dialogue control between end systems. See also: OSI.

Shareware Software that can be accessed freely, i.e. via the Internet, but which requires a payment to the author if found useful. Some shareware packages are limited or 'cut-down' versions of a system to give the user a chance to see a subset of the software in action before they purchase a copy. See also: PD, etext.

Shell The term shell has its origins rooted in the Unix operating system. A shell is a program that takes input from the user and processes the output accordingly. Unix offers the user a variety of shells, such as the C-shell (`csh`), the Bourne shell (`sh`), and the Korn shell (`ksh`). The term 'shell' refers to the operating environment in which the user is encapsulated. See also: Unix.

Signature file Used in email as a means of placing a small 'signature' (some text) at the end of a mail-message automatically. Signatures are normally placed in the Unix file `.signature`; they sometimes store contact information, jokes, and even sayings or proverbs (Dan Quayle quotes are common). See also: Unix, email.

Simtel or **Simtel20** Refers to the name of the Internet (FTP) site and file archive called `wsmr-simtel20.army.mil` or the 'White Sands Missile Base'. One of the most extensive collections of publicly available files are stored here for access via anonymous FTP. See also: Internet, FTP.

SLIP Serial line IP. A protocol used to run IP over serial lines such as telephone circuits or RS-232 cables interconnecting two systems. SLIP is now gradually being replaced by PPP. See also: PPP, TCP/IP, Internet.

Smiley Smileys are used to annotate electronic mail and USENET messages on the Internet network. They consist of a series of character-made faces which denote various human emotions, e.g. :-) happy, :-(unhappy, etc. Many others are also in common use – a small selection can be seen below. Turn the page 90 degrees to see the face as it should appear. See also: USENET, Internet, <g>. Common Smileys to exhibit both emotions and human characteristics are shown here:

SMTP Simple Mail Transfer Protocol. The Internet's principle electronic mail protocol. Defined in RFC 821, with associated message format descriptions in RFC 822. See also: MHS, email, Internet.

SNA Systems Network Architecture; IBM's proprietary network architecture.

Smiley	Emotion or characteristic
:-)	Smiling–happy response, :) or for smug response
:-(	Sad face–sad response
;-)	Winking: 'nod nod, wink wink, know what I mean?!'
'-)	Left eye winking
:-D	Laughing emotion
:-I	Indifferent response
(:-...	Heart-broken response
{:-)	Smiley with a toupee
:-{)	Smiley with a moustache
:()	Person with big lips (sometimes :-O)
8-)	Person wearing sunglasses
!-)	Person with a black eye
(:-#	'I didn't mean to say that!...'
(:-&	Angry response
:-#	Kissing
:+)	A clown
=:-)	Punk rocker
[:-(	Frankenstein character
:-X	'My lips are sealed ...'
&-|	'Tired; I've been working all night ...'
:-O	Big mouth
:^)	Side angle (3D) face with protuding nose

Snail mail Term used to describe the conventional postal system (slow in comparison to electronic mail, hence the term 'snail'). See also: email.

SNMP Simple Network Management Protocol. The network management protocol of choice for TCP/IP-based internets. See also: CMIP, TCP/IP.

Socket An inter-process communication mechanism used by the TCP/IP protocol. Sockets are similar to file-opening and closing functions found in many high-level languages. A socket establishes a connection with a server entity in a asymmetric client–server relationship, e.g. the client sends some data to the server that is waiting; the server may then acknowledge the data, in which case it can transmit the next batch of data. Socket libraries are common for the Berkeley (BSD) Unix system. See also: Internet, BSD, Unix, client–server model.

SPX Sequenced Packet Exchange. A protocol by which two workstations or applications communicate across a network. SPX uses NetWare IPX to deliver the messages, but SPX guarantees delivery and maintains the order of the packet stream. See also: IPX, NetWare, TCP/IP, packet.

STP Shielded twisted pair, a type of twisted pair cabling, increasingly used for LANs, in which the cable is surrounded by a metallic layer to reduce interference from radiation emitted from the cable. See also: twisted pair, UTP.

String A term used to mean a collection of characters joined together, e.g. 'Internet'.

SunOS A Berkeley version of Unix running on Sun machines, e.g. BSD 4.1. See also: Unix, BSD, ULTRIX.

SVR4 Acronym for System V Release 4. A version of the Unix operating system that combines systems such as SunOS (Suns Berkeley BSD version of Unix) as well as System V and Xenix. SVR4 is supposed to be the 'standard' Unix system. See also: Unix, BSD.

Synchronous The term synchronous is used to designate events occurring at timed intervals regulated by pulses from the computer clock. A synchronous transmission is a communications mode in which a clock signal is transmitted with the data at precisely defined time intervals, to maintain the receiver and transmitter in synchronization. In synchronous transmissions, since events take place at fixed times, the completion of preceding events need not be acknowledged. See also: asynchronous.

Sysop System operator. Person in charge of a system. Analogous to systems manager in most cases.

TCP/IP Transmission Control Protocol/Internet Protocol. The major transport protocol in the Internet suite of protocols, providing reliable, connection-oriented, full-duplex streams. TCP breaks data transmissions up into packets, reassembles them at their destination in the correct order, and re-sends portions that do not transmit correctly. IP is responsible for the actual routing and transmission of the data (TCP/IP is in fact a suite of protocols). TCP/IP roughly equates to layer 4 of the OSI model. See also: IP, UDP, packet, protocol, OSI.

`telnet` The virtual terminal protocol in the Internet suite of protocols. This protocol allows users of one host to log in to a remote host and interact as if that user were typing commands at the keyboard of the remote machine (also known as the Internet's 'remote log-in' program). See also: Internet, `rlogin`.

Thinnet Thinnet (thin net) are the smaller portions of Ethernet networks, typically used to connect a computer or workstation into a larger backbone network. See also: Ethernet, backbone.

Time-out The event that occurs when two processes are communicating and one fails to reply. The computer that has lost contact will often try to re-establish contact until a 'time-out' occurs (a period of time after which the source computer will simply give up).

Token ring Introduced by IBM, token ring refers to the wire and the access protocol scheme whereby the workstations of a network relay packets of data, called a token, in a logical ring configuration. When a station wants to transmit, it takes possession of the token, transmits its data, then frees the token after the data has made a complete circuit of the ring. This architecture is described completely in the IEEE 802.5 set of standards, which defines the cabling, electrical and physical topology, and access scheme of network products. It connects microcomputers via a cable containing

348   THE ESSENTIAL INTERNET INFORMATION GUIDE

twisted wire pairs and transmits data at 4 or 16 Mbit/s. See also: ARCnet, Ethernet, FDDI, IEEE.

Topology The term topology can refer to either the physical or logical configuration of a local area network (LAN). Physical topologies, such as ring, star, and bus, are always associated with the layout of the workstations and the cabling that connects them. The logical topology describes the way in which the flow of data is regulated to and from the workstations on the network. ARCnet, Ethernet, and token ring are the most common logical topologies offered for todays local area networks. See also: ARCnet, Ethernet, LAN, WAN, token ring.

Transport layer The OSI layer that is responsible for reliable end-to-end data transfer between end systems.

Trojan-horse A method of gaining unauthorized access to a computer system. The 'Trojan' could be a program masquerading as something else, or it could indeed be a user with a false identity, etc. Some virus programs are Trojans in disguise. See also: virus.

Twilight Zone Not the TV series, but instead a term used to refer to a system operator channel used on IRC systems via the Internet network. See also: IRC.

Twisted pair When two small insulated copper wires are wrapped or twisted around each other to minimize interference from other wires in the cable, the result is referred to as twisted pair wiring. There are two types of twisted pair cables: unshielded and shielded. Unshielded twisted pair (UTP) wiring is commonly used in telephone cables and provides little or no protection against interference. Shielded twisted pair (STP) wiring is used in some networks for connecting workstations but the signals must be boosted periodically. Although it has limited bandwidths compared to coaxial cable or optical fibre, inexpensive twisted pair cabling is increasingly being used as an alternative to coaxial cable for Ethernet networks. See also: coaxial cable, STP, UTP.

UDP User Datagram Protocol. A transport protocol in the Internet suite of protocols. UDP, like TCP, uses IP for delivery; however, unlike TCP, UDP provides for exchange of datagrams without acknowledgements or guaranteed delivery. See also: Internet and TCP/IP.

UID User identification code. UIDs are used extensively by operating systems such as Unix, where each user has a unique UID. See also: Unix, GID, userid.

ULTRIX DECs version of the Unix operating system. Based upon the BSD Unix system, e.g. BSD 4.1. See also: DOS, OS/2, Unix, VMS, BSD.

Unix An operating system developed by AT&T. It is widely used on a variety of computers, from mainframes to micros. It is a powerful multi-tasking and multi-user system with many high-level utility programs. Unix is in fact a trademark in its own right; other manufacturers 'Unix' products have to alter their names, leading to systems such as XENIX, ULTRIX, etc. The main types of Unix are BSD (Berkeley) Unix – found mostly in academic environments, and System V – a business-oriented Unix. When 'Unix' is set in lower case, the word normally refers to the operating system and its clones; the upper-case version 'UNIX' refers to the original system as developed by AT&T (although hardly anybody uses these conventions anymore) See also: SVR4, BSD, DOS, OS/2, ULTRIX, VMS.

USENET USENET, or USErs NETwork, is the Internets news network containing many thousands of forums (at the last count, well over 5000) covering many diverse activities, hobbies and topics. USENET is made up solely of electronic mail messages. Apart from simple text messages, binary files are regularly transmitted using a scheme known as UU-encoding (a binary to ASCII file conversion). Users can subscribe to the discussion groups which interest them and up/download messages accordingly. See also: Internet, article, UU-encoding, USENET hierarchy.

USENET hierarchy Refers to a particular part of the USENET system. USENET is broken down into different newsgroup hierarchies, for example the `alt.*` hierarchy (alternative topics) or the `ieee.*` (IEEE groups hierarchy). See also: USENET, IEEE, email.

Userid A userid is a name used for identification purposes. Under Unix, a userid is the name of a user, e.g. `'jason'` (Unix also stores a numeric code known as a UID against each such name) and is used for the purpose of logging in. See also: UID, `login`, Unix.

UTP Unshielded twisted pair cabling is the wire that is often used indoors to connect telephones to outside services. It comes with two or four wires twisted inside a flexible plastic sheath or conduit. It utilizes modular plugs and phone jacks, which makes it easy to relocate the phones, modems, workstations, or other devices. UTP is an excellent choice of cable for a network installation because there are adapters for easy conversion to all other types of cabling and because UTP is used for the transmission of both voice and data. ISO 8877, RJ-45 connectors are used with UTP. See also: coaxial cable, twisted pair.

UUCP Unix to Unix copy program. A protocol used for communication between consenting Unix systems. UUCP uses dial-up lines in conjunction with a Modem device to connect to other sites. UUCP was the first real protocol used over the Internet to transfer information, and is still widely used. See also: dial-up connection, modem, Internet.

UU-encoding A process whereby binary files are converted into ASCII files, and which is used extensively over the Internet network. This process facilitates the posting of binary files, typically images, sounds, and executables, via electronic mail and USENET, which are both ASCII-based services. See also: Internet, ASCII, EBCDIC.

VAX The name of a computer produced by DEC. Many VAX machines use the operating system VMS, although the DEC version of Unix, Ultrix, could also be used. VAX is an acronym for virtual address extension, arising out of VMSs virtual memory capability. See also: VMS, Unix.

VDU Visual display unit. The screen used with a computer. Many types of VDU exist from the simplest character display to the more complex work-station displays which have Super-VGA resolutions. See also: VGA.

Veronica A service which is accessed through the Internet via the Gopher service. 'Gopherspace' is a term relating to the knowledge of all Gopher clients in existence; veronica searches Gopherspace (specifically, it searches Gopher menus) to locate information. veronica polls each Gopher server that it knows about on a regular basis and constructs a database of menu entries which can then be searched. See also: Gopher, Internet.

VGA Video graphics array. A monitor resolution that is typically capable of displaying 640×480 pixels (a pixel is the most fundamental screen unit that makes up an image on the screen). Super-VGA monitors typically support 1024×768, and higher, pixel resolutions.

Virus An executable program which replicates itself. Most viruses are harmful, that is they destroy data on computers. Others are less destructive, perhaps only annoying the user periodically, wasting system resources, etc. The best-known Internet 'virus' was termed the 'Internet Worm'. The Worm used the Unix sendmail program on the DECnet and Internet networks to repli-cate by 'posting' itself all over the network. It then tried to gain access to systems by logging in with public (or guessable) passwords taken from other usernames on the system (and variations of these); about 40 attempts succeeded. The Worm virus had anti-nuclear connotations – it would flash up anti-nuclear slogans on users' screens; the virus was not destructive to data, although it did waste an enormous amount of system resources. See also: Trojan-horse, Internet, DECnet, VAX, VMS, email.

VMS Virtual memory system. An operating system found on many DEC VAX computers. See also: ULTRIX, VAX, DOS, Unix.

W3 See WWW.

WAIS Wide area information server. A service run on the Internet which allows users to browse various sources of information. Accessible via the telnet protocol. See also: Gopher, Internet, telnet.

WAN When two or more computers are linked together for the purpose of sharing information and/or peripheral devices, a network is created. When the network is not confined to a geographically restricted area, such as within the same building, it is referred to as a wide area network (hence the Internet is a WAN). Typically, WANs serve to interconnect local area networks in different sites, cities, and countries. A global communications network of computers is referred to as a WAN. See also: Internetwork, LAN, Internet.

Waterloo TCP A library of C (programming language) routines that provide the TCP protocol for connection to the Internet (and other networks running TCP/IP). See also: KA9Q, PPP, SLIP, Internet, C, program.

Webster You may come across this term. It refers to the *Websters Word Dictionary*. Many Internet hosts offer access to this on-line dictionary. Many FTP sites also have the entire dictionary and/or software for downloading. See also: Internet, FTP.

White pages See WHOIS.

WHOIS The 'whois' database is maintained at the Internet Network Information Center (`nic.ddn.mil`) and copies of that database are maintained at many other sites. The NIC whois database keeps complete information about major US computers connected to the Internet network and can be used to find the hostname for a computer at any US educational institution connected to the Internet. This database also contains names of many individual users, but this part of the database is too small to be frequently useful. Whois databases at other sites often contain complete information about people with log-in or email accounts at those sites, but there is no mechanism to tie these databases together or even to locate active whois servers. Some Gopher servers maintain a list of known whois servers (or phonebooks). Many Unix systems provide a `whois` command which can be used to look up the details of users at other Internet sites. See also: Internet, Gopher, NIC.

Wildcard See regular expression.

WIMP An acronym for windows, icons, mouse, pointers. WIMP interfaces are made up mainly of a windowed environment with icons and an on-screen cursor to facilitate the selection of items such as commands, files, etc. The opposite of a WIMP environment is a command-line environment. WIMP interfaces are used in GUI systems such as MicroSoft Windows, X Windows, and all the Macintosh interfaces. See also: GUI, X-Windows, Windows, command-line.

Windows (MicroSoft) A popular DOS extender written by Microsoft. It provides a common graphical user interface (GUI) for all Windows applications and limited multi-tasking. Most DOS software has been, or is in the process of being, ported to Windows. See also: DOS, OS/2, GUI, WIMP.

WOMBAT Acronym for 'waste of money, brains and time!'. Used to refer to an event that was simply a waste of resources and/or time. For example: 'Making Unix user-friendly is a complete WOMBAT'.

WWW The World-Wide-Web. A hypertext-based service on the Internet that allows users to browse its vast database of information that is available on the Internet. See also: Internet, Hypertext, multimedia.

X See X-Windows.

X-Windows Refers to the X-Windows GUI. X, as it is commonly known, is a windowing system and a protocol in its own right. Used extensively on Unix machines to facilitate multi-tasking operations using multiple windows. See also: GUI, Windows, WIMP, Unix, process client-server model.

Xbase An ANSI directive used to collectively represent the dBASE-like database languages, e.g. dBASE, Clipper, FoxPro, etc. Xbase will (hopefully) be a new standard in which the language statements from many dBASE-like systems will be integrated, therefore aiding system (i.e. language) compatibility. See also: ANSI, database.

XENIX A version of the Unix operating system based upon System V Unix (a business-oriented Unix system); XENIX was really the first main Unix system for PC-based systems. See also: Unix, BSD, SVR4, PC.

X.25 X.25 is a CCITT standard communications protocol used internationally in packet switching networks. Rather than sending a stream of bits like a modem, an X.25 router sends packets of data. There are varying packet sizes and types. Each packet contains data to be transmitted as well as information about the packets origin, destination, size, and its place in the order of the packets sent. On the receiving end, the packet assembler/disassembler (PAD) in the router translates the packets back into a readable format. X.25 is used as the basis for data transmission over JANET. See also: JANET, Internet, WAN, packet, PAD, modem, CCITT.

X.400 X.400 is a term that refers to a series of OSI and CCITT standards that describe the details of encoding electronic mail messages, both textual and graphic, for transmission between unlike computers and networks. X.400 is actually a subset of the CCITT X.25 standard which governs data communication on the packet switching networks. Both of these important standards are maintained so that information can be transmitted between all types of computers and a wide variety of specialized terminal equipment from more than one manufacturer. X.500 is now well under development. See also: CCITT, X.25, OSI, email.

Zap Term used in some circles to mean 'delete' or 'destroy'. Some languages (such as some Xbase database dialects) even have a ZAP command. See also: Xbase, database.

ZEUS An on-line conferencing system found on the CompuServe network. ZEUS or 'ZiffNet' is run by *PC Magazine*, and contains information based on magazine articles, as well as general PC discussion topics. ZEUS has Internet-mail connectivity (see the resource guide). See also: PC, Internet, email, CompuServe.

ZiffNet See ZEUS.

Appendix B
A–Z Internet service-providers

Service providers offer a variety of Internet-related services, ranging from full UNIX shell access, to simple USENET feeds. The actual services offered by each provider are broken down into the following categories:

- `bbs`   Access to a providers bulletin board system.
- hytelnet   Access to telnet directory resource server.
- `irc`   System has Internet Relay Chat server.
- wais   Access to the providers wide area information server.
- `telnet`   Access to virtual terminal protocol `telnet`.
- `ftp`   Access to file transfer protocol.
- Gopher   Access to a service-providers own Gopher service.
- email   Electronic mail access (check if send and receive).
- Unix Shell   Unix shell level access (nomally `ftp`/`telnet` as well).
- uucp   Access to the uucp file-copying program.
- SLIP or PPP   Has serial line IP or point-to-point protocol running.
- FTPMail   Access to ftp via email (no direct ftp, probably).
- USENET   has USENET feeds (if it has `telnet`, you can use NNTP).

The table below illustrates which tools can be used to access the most fundamental Internet services.

Many providers now run their own Gopher and WAIS servers which can be accessed. Any user who has `telnet` can, of course, make conections with any external Gophers or WAIS servers that may exist (see the A–Z resource guide in Appendix D for listings of such servers).

Tool	What you can access with this tool
`telnet`	IRC (Internet Relay Chat)
	Archie, WAIS, Gopher, veronica, BBS, etc.
	Interactive machine (Unix) access
	USENET (via an NNTP-server)
E-mail	FTPmail (FTP via email command message)
	USENET (via listserv/USENET mailing lists)
	Archie (via email command message)
	ListServ mailing lists (BITNET)
Gopher	FTP (FTP via Gopher menus)
	Archie (via Gopher menus)
	WAIS (WAIS via Gopher menus)
WAIS	USENET (some `alt.*` forums etc. are on-line)
	FTP (FTP archives are maintained by WAIS)

WHAT SHOULD I LOOK FOR IN A SERVICE-PROVIDER?

Users should look for a minimum system that offers: USENET, `telnet` and FTP if they want to access the most basic Internet services; `telnet` offers access to systems such as Archie, Gopher, WAIS, IRC, Hytelnet and many other interactive terminal-based services. FTP by email (FTPmail) can be slow and should really be avoided if at all possible. Direct interactive FTP access is much better. Unix shell access is not always required in order to access FTP, `telnet` and email-based services. Non Unix-shell systems probably have off-line email and USENET-based services – check for the exact details. Dial-up Internet access is by far the most popular means of accessing the Internet by home-computer users. In this scenario you dial up a service-provider's machine via a modem device attached to your computer, and they provide a remote shell (such as a Unix shell) which then has access to the necessary commands to interact with the network, e.g. `ftp` and `telnet` (which are built in as actual operating system commands on Unix).

Apart from technical prerequisites, human support is also important. A freephone or 'toll-free' number is a good feature, although some companies ask you to pay a surcharge for such a service; clearly, you will want to make some further enquiries regarding this. Technical telephone support is also a feature to look out for. Many providers give free support when you subscribe, and you may want to check if they will accept facsmilies (fax) in lieu of voice contact. Also watch out for the use of mobile support lines, since these charge a much higher (premium) rate.

DIAL-UP ACCESS TO THE INTERNET

Dial-up access has advantages and disadvantages; the main advantage of dial-up access is that it is convenient, cheap and fast to set up. On the other hand, you may find that your dial-up system requires you to store files remotely, i.e. on the service-provider's machine rather than your own machine. This, in effect, means that in order to get a file to your own (local) computer you will have to engage in two download operations (known as a 'two-hop' process). This in turn means more delay and inconvenience. A system known as PPP (point-to-point protocol) allows you to communicate from your local machine with a remote service-provider's system in just one hop, that is to say that a single TCP/IP channel is set up between your machine and the service-provider's, and that all file downloading will be done to your local machine (services using the SLIP protocol share this type of access). The advantages of this system are that the service-provider does not have to provide any additional disk storage for user accounts, and that it it much quicker for you to get information to your own machine. PPP also has an added advantage since you normally get your own Internet address in the process, effectively meaning that your machine has its own IP number, e.g. 128.200.8.1 (this is commonly a sub-network of the service provider).

In most cases such an address is made up of the sub-domain name of the service-provider, so if your provider was called demon.co.uk, your site may be known as mysite.demon.co.uk. Add on to this your own username and you have a full email address, for example: fred@mysite.demon.co.uk. On a system that has a Unix account facility, your username is simply added to the Unix user database (/etc/passwd) effectively giving you permission to log in to that machine. In this instance you will also have your own username and mail address, but it will not be your own individual Internet site, rather the service-provider's machine address, i.e. if your service-provider is the site ibmpcug.co.uk your mail address could be fred@ibmpcug.co.uk, noticing the absence of the sub-domain name as in the previous example. Note the keyword PPP in the service-provider lists shown later for this service. Another system similar to PPP is called SLIP (Serial Line Internet Protocol). SLIP is another dial-up protocol used over telephone-lines, and is based around the RS-232 serial communications standard. It is equivalent to PPP in that you get your own Internet address, although it is gradually being replaced by PPP. Both PPP and SLIP access should be seriously considered when you actually come to choose a service-provider.

The disadvantage of some dial-up systems, particulary those without shell access, i.e. a Unix shell, is that tasks such as creating email and USENET messages must be done off-line, and then uploaded when you establish a connection. Constant connections and disconnections may therefore be required in order to send and read your messages if the service-provider's system does not provide you with any programs such as a newsreader (this is common in non-Unix shell systems). When choosing a provider, see how many incoming phone lines (modem lines) they have since this can speed up connection times. Waiting hours for a line on a three-line system with 500 + users all trying to gain access is not going to be much fun.

COSTS AND CHARGES

Finally, check for the existence of on-line charges, since these can build up quite rapidly. Users should choose a service that is geographically near to them in order to avoid long-distance call charges. As with all providers, costs and system facilities change on a regular basis. Please call the provider in question to get the most up-to-date details of their respective systems. Many providers now allow you unlimited dial-up access for a fixed monthly/yearly fee (Demon Systems in the UK for example), so all you pay for is your phone calls and the periodic subscription fee, plus perhaps a one-time administration charge.

Another problem with many providers is that they do not accept any payment except by credit card. This can clearly be a problem for non-plastic owners. Check with your provider to see whether or not they will accept cash, cheque or PO order payments in advance, etc.

NOTE FOR STUDENTS AND ACADEMIC INTERNET USERS

If you are a student, check with your college or university regarding Internet access, since you may not need to pay an extra penny (apart from your phone calls); many institutions have dial-up college PADs which in turn give access to services such as Guest-Telnet and FTP (see the A–Z resource guide for 'Guest Telnet'), as well as access to terminal-based services such as Archie, etc. I know, because 50 per cent of this book was written without an Internet account, by using academic connections at local colleges using an inexpensive modem and communications software (I used a freeware communications package and a cheap 2400 baud modem most of the time).

A–Z Service provider list

Each provider listed has the following details included:

- Dialup: Specifies the modem line for that system; many providers will allow payment on-line via credit card (VISA, etc.) – the login/password keywords indicate the username and password you should use to gain access to the system (either to join up, to see any introductory screens, etc.).
- Cost: Any on-line charges and subscriptions fees are shown here.
- Email: Email addresses are given for Internet contact to the provider in question.
- Voice: The provider's telephone number (for voice contact) in order to make enquiries, report problems, etc.
- Services: The level of facilities offered by each provider is shown in the Services: line; this shows all of the Internet facilities supported by the

provider in question. In all cases, the country name specified is where that host resides, not the countries that host has access to.
- Notes: Notes on each provider where research has been carried out on the system concerned.

UNITED KINGDOM

CIX: Compulink Information Exchange (cix.compulink.co.uk)
Dialup:	+44-(0)81-390-5252 (9600 baud)
	+44-(0)81-390-1255 (2400 baud).
Services:	X25 and ISDN access, telnet, FTP, USENET.
Cost:	£25 connection charge; £2.40 per minute cheap rate; £3.60 peak rate (minimum usage charge is £6.25 per month).
Email:	postmaster@cix.compulink.co.uk
Voice:	+44-(0)81-390-8446.
Notes:	CIX is a vast conferencing system with good Internet access menus; on-line charges may not appeal to the budget-conscious user.

Demon Internet Systems (demon.co.uk)
Dialup:	+44-(0)81-343-4848.
Services:	telnet, ftp, PPP/SLIP, USENET.
Cost:	£10 per month (£12.50 signon); many other options available, e.g. leased-line, etc.
Email:	internet@demon.co.uk
Voice:	+44-(0)81-349-0063.
Notes:	Uses KA9Q software (PC, TCP/IP, etc.) to gain access. No on-line charges and uses PPP for one-hop file downloads. System is slightly tricky to set up, although a joy to use when working. Good telephone support. No on-line charges; cheap access to Internet.

Exnet Systems Ltd (exnet.co.uk)
Dialup:	Contact Exnet for modem numbers.
Services:	UNIX Shell, ftp, telnet, USENET (batch).
Cost:	Various: from £5 per month upwards.
Email:	helpex@exnet.co.uk
Voice:	+44-(0)81-297-1218.
Notes:	All options including full shell access and/or just USENET feeds are available.

IBM PC Users Group (ibmpcug.co.uk)
Dialup:	+44-(0)81-863-6646.
Services:	UNIX Shell, ftp, telnet, bbs, irc, USENET.
Cost:	£15.50 per month or £160 per year (£10 signon).

Email: info@ibmpcug.co.uk
Voice: +44-(0)81-863-1191.
Notes: UNIX Shell access; appeals to the more 'UNIX-aware' user. File downloads in two-hops make this system slightly slower to use.

Infocom (infocom.com)
Dialup: +44-(0)734-340055.
Services: USENET, irc, ftp.
Cost: Free access to file downloads (locally) and email (locally). £25.00 per year for local and remote USENET (read-only), irc, etc.; £40.00 per year full access.
Email: postmaster@infocom.com
Voice: +44-(0)743-344000.
Notes: A variety of services and costs. Free limited access to local system a good feature.

UKnet (uknet.ac.uk)
Services: ftp, telnet, USENET.
Cost: Various; contact UKnet for details.
Email: postmaster@uknet.ac.uk
Voice: +44-227-475497.
Notes: Extensive facilities; range of options for Internet access are available.

a2i communications (info@rahul.net)
Dialup: 408-293-9010, 408-293-9020 (v.32, v.32 bis).
Services: UNIX Shell, ftp, telnet, USENET.
Cost: $20 per month, $45 per 3 months, $7 per 6 months.
Email: info@rahul.net
Notes: See free stock-market information in the A–Z resource guide.

Anomaly–Rhode Island's Gateway To The Internet
(anomaly.sbs.risc.net)
Dialup: 401-331-3706 (v.32), 401-455-0347 (PEP).
Services: UNIX Shell, ftp, telnet, SLIP access.
Cost: $125 for 6 months, $200 per year; Educational users: $75 per 6 months, $125 pa.
Email: info@anomaly.sbs.risc.net

ANS–Advanced Network and Services Inc (ans.net)
Dialup: Must contact ANS for modem numbers.
Services: email, USENET, ftp, etc.

Cost: Various.
Voice: 800-827-7482, 703-904-7187.

APK – Public Access UNI* Site (`wariat.org`)
Dialup: 216-481-9436 (2400),
             216-481-9425 (v.32 bis, SuperPEP).
Services: UNIX Shell, ftp, telnet, irc, gopher, USENET, bbs.
Cost: $35 per month, $200 for 6 months ($20 signon).
Email: `zbig@wariat.org`

AT&T – Data Communications Service (`ds.internic.net`)
Dialup: Must contact AT&T for modem numbers.
Services: email, USENET, ftp, etc.
Cost: TBA.
Voice/Fax: 800-247-1212 (voice)
             904-636-3078 (fax).
Email: `admin@ds.internic.net`
Note: AT&T serves the US and the rest of the world.

BARRnet – Bay Area Regional Research Network (`barrnet.net`)
Dialup: Must contact BARRnet for modem numbers.
Services: ftp, email, telnet, full service.
Cost: Various.
Email: `info@barrnet.net`
Voice: 415-725-1790.

BIX – Byte Information Exchange (`bix.com`)
Dialup: Contact BIX for modem numbers.
Services: telnet, ftp, email, Usenet, finger, whois.
Cost: Fixed monthly fee.
Email: `postmaster@bix.com`
Voice: 800-695-4775.
Notes: Home of *Byte* magazine, allowing users to post letters (and flames), etc. Has on-line registration (Modem: 1-800-695-4882; username: logon, name?: bix.byte39). Five hours of free on-line time available to new users.

CERFnet (`cerf.net`)
Dialup: Must contact them for their modem number.
Services: Unix Shell, irc, ftp, hytelnet, gopher, WAIS, WWW, SLIP.
Cost: $10 per hour ($8 per hour weekend); $20 per month surcharge.
Email: `help@cerf.net`
Voice: 800-876-2373, 619-455-3900.

Colorado SuperNet (csn.org)
      Dialup: Must contact CNET for their modem number.
      Services: UNIX Shelqrl, telnet, ftp, irc, wais, gopher, USENET feeds.
      Cost: $1 per hour (off-peak), $2 per hour peak, $250 per month
                    maximum.
      Email: info@csn.org
      Voice: 303-273-3471.

Communications Accessibles Montreal (cam.org) – Canada
      Dialup: 514-281-5601 (v.32 bis, 14.4 HST)
                    514-466-0592 (v.32)
                    514-738-3664 (PEP)
                    514-923-2103 (ZyXeL 19.2K).
      Services: UNIX Shell, ftp, telnet, USENET, SLIP, PPP, FAX gateway.
      Cost: $25 per month.
      Email: info@cam.org

Community News Service (cscns.com)
      Dialup: 719-520-1700 (Login: new, Password: newuser).
      Services: UNIX Shell, ftp, email, telnet, irc, USENET.
      Cost: $1 per hour – $10 per month min ($35 signon).
      Email: klaus@cscns.com

Cooperative Library Agency (class.org)
      Dialup: Contact CLA first for their modem number.
      Services: ftp, telnet, wais, gopher, hytelnet.
      Cost: $10.50 per hour + $150 per year for first account.
      Email: class@class.org

CR Laboratories Dialup Internet Access (crl.com)
      Dialup: 415-389-UNIX.
      Services: Shell, telnet, ftp, USENET, wais, SLIP.
      Cost: $19.50 per month ($15.00 signon).
      Email: info@crl.com

Cyberspace Station (cyber.net)
      Dialup: (619) 634-1376 (Login: guest).
      Services: UNIX Shell access, telnet, ftp, irc.
      Cost: $15 per month ($10 signon); $60 for 6 months.
      Email: help@cyber.net

DELPHI (delphi.com)
      Dialup: 800-365-4636 (JOINDELPHI Pass:INTERNETSIG).
      Services: telnet, ftp, USENET.
      Cost: $10 per month (4 h), $20 per month (20 h).
      Email: walthowe@delphi.com

Express (`digex.com`)
  Dialup: 301-220-0462, 410-766-1855 (Login: new).
  Services: UNIX Shell, telnet, irc, ftp.
  Cost: $25 per month, or $250 per year.
  Email: `info@digex.com`
  Voice: 301-220-2020.

Grebyn Corporation (`greybn.com`)
  Dialup: 703-281-7997 (Login: apply).
  Services: UNIX Shell, ftp, telnet.
  Cost: $30 per month.
  Email: `info@grebyn.com`
  Voice: 703 281 2194.

Halcyon (`halcyon.com`)
  Dialup: 206-382-6245 (Login: new).
  Services: USENET, ftp, telnet.
  Cost: $200 per year, or $60 per quarter ($10 signon).
  Email: `info@halcyon.com`
  Voice: 206 955 0160.

The IDS World Network (`ids.net`)
  Dialup: 401-884-9002, 401-785-1067.
  Services: ftp, telnet, USENET, bbs, SLIP.
  Cost: $10 per month, or $50 per 6 months, $100 12 months.
  Email: `sysadmin@ids.net`
  Voice: 401-884-7856.

JVNCnet – Global Enterprises Services Inc (`jvnc.net`)
  Dialup: Must contact JVNCnet for their modem number.
  Services: telnet, ftp, USENET, UNIX Shell, SLIP.
  Cost: $99 per month ($99 signon); UNIX Shell + $21 pcm.
                For more infomation: `market@jvnc.net`
  Voice: 800-358-4437, 609-897-7300.

Merit Network, Inc. – MichNet project (`merit.edu`)
  Dialup: Contact Merit for their modem number.
  Services: UNIX Shell, ftp, USENET.
  Cost: $35 per month ($45 signon).
  Email: `info@merit.edu`
  Voice: 313-764-9430.
  Notes: See A–Z resource guide for public-UNIX access.

MindVOX (`phantom.com`)
  Dialup: 212-988-5030 (Login: mindvox, Password: guest).
  Services: telnet, ftp, irc, gopher, hytelnet, bbs.

Cost: $15–$20 per month (no signon fee).
Email: info@phantom.com
Voice: 212 988 5987.

MSen (msen.com)

Dialup: Must contact MSen for their modem number.
Services: UNIX Shell, wais, gopher, ftp, telnet, SLIP.
Cost: $5 per month ($2 per hour, or $20 per month for a 20-hour connection).
Email: info@msen.com
Voice: 313-998-4562.

NEARnet (nic.near.net)

Dialup: Must contact NEARnet for their modem numbers.
Services: email, USENET, ftp, SLIP.
Cost: $250 per month
Email: nearnet-join@nic.near.net
Voice: 617-873-8730.

NeoSoft's Sugar Land UNIX (neosoft.com)

Dialup: 713-684-5900.
Services: UNIX Shell, ftp, telnet, irc, USENET, bbs, UUCP, etc.
Cost: $29.95 per month.
Email: info@neosoft.com
Voice: 713-438-4964.
Notes: guest access: log in with userid 'new'.

Netcom Online Communication Services (netcom.com)

Dialup: (310)-842-8835, (408)-241-9760
               (408)-459-9851, (415)-328-9940
               (415)-985-5650, (510)-426-6860
               (619)-234-0524, (916)-965-1371
               (Login: guest).
Services: UNIX Shell, telnet, ftp, irc, wais, gopher, SLIP, PPP, USENET.
Cost: $19.50 per month ($15.00 signon).
Email: info@netcom.com
Voice: 408-554-UNIX.

OARnet (oar.net)

Dialup: Contact OARnet via email/phone for numbers.
Services: ftp, telnet, USENET, email.
Cost: $4.00 per hour; $330 per month.
Email: nic@oar.net
Voice: 614-292-8100.

Old Colorado City Communications (oldcolo.com)
Dialup: 719-632-4111 (Login: newuser).
Services: UNIX Shell, ftp, telnet.
Cost: $25 per month fixed.
Email: dave@oldcolo.com
Voice: 719-632-4848, 719-593-7575/2040.

PANIX Public Access UNIX (panix.com)
Dialup: 212-787-3100 (Login: newuser).
Services: UNIX Shell, ftp, telnet, gopher, wais, irc, USENET, etc.
Cost: $19 per month; $208 per year ($40 signon).
Email: alexis@panix.com
Voice: 212-877-4854.

Portal System (portal.com)
Dialup: 408-973-8091 (9600/HST)
             408-725-0561 (2400)
             (Login: info).
Services: UNIX Shell, ftp, telnet, IRC, uucp, USENET.
Cost: $19.95 per month ($19.95 signon).
Email: info@portal.com
Voice: 408-973-9111.

PREPnet (cmu.edu)
Dialup: Must contact PREPnet for modem numbers.
Services: UNIX Shell/terminal, telnet, ftp, SLIP.
Cost: $1000 per year membership; Equipment fee: $325 (plus $40 per month).
Email: prepnet@cmu.edu
Voice: 412-268-7870.

PSIs Global Dialup Service (psi.com)
Dialup: Must contact PSI for modem numbers.
Services: telnet, rlogin.
Cost: $40 per month ($40 signon).
Email: info@psi.com
Voice: 703-620-6651.
See also: PSILink below.

PSILink – Personal Internet Access (psi.com)
Dialup: Must contact PSI for modem numbers.
Services: email, USENET, ftp.
Cost: $29 per month ($19 signon – s/ware inc.).
Voice: 703-620-6651.

Rock CONCERT Net (concert.net)
Dialup: Contact them for MODEM number.
Services: UNIX Shell, ftp, telnet, irc, gopher, wais, USENET, SLIP.
Cost: $30 per month ($50 signon).
Email: info@concert.net
Voice: 919-248-1999.

Telerama BBS (telerama.pgh.pa.us)
Dialup: 412-481-5302 (Login: new).
Services: UNIX Shell, ftp, telnet, feeds, menu, bbs.
Cost: $6 per month (10 hours), no signon.
Email: info@telerama.pgh.pa.us
Voice: 412-481-3505.

Texas Metronet (metronet.com)
Dialup: 214-705-2902 (9600 baud), 214-705-2917 (2400) (Login:
             info, Password: info).
Services: UNIX Shell, telnet, ftp, USENET, SLIP.
Cost: $10–$50 per month ($25 signon).
Email: srl@metronet.com
Voice: 214-401-2800.

The Whole Earth 'Lectronic Link (The WELL)
Dialup: 415-332-6106 (Login: newuser).
Services: UNIX Shell, ftp, telnet, bbs.
Cost: $15 per month (+$2.00 per hour afterwards).
Voice: 415-332-4335.

The World (world.std.com)
Dialup: 617-739-9753 (Login: new).
Services: UNIX Shell, ftp, telnet, irc.
Cost: $5 per month (+$2.00 per hour), or $20 per month (20
             hours usage).
Email: office@world.std.com
Voice: 617-739-0202.

AUSTRALIA

AARnet (aarnet.edu.au)–Australia
Dialup: Contact AARnet for their modem number.
Services: SLIP, PPP, TELNET, FTP, USENET.
Cost: Various; contact for exact details.
Email: aarnet@aarnet.edu.au
Voice: +61-6-2493385.

Connect Ltd (connect.com.au)–Australia
   Dialup: Contact Connect Ltd for their modem number.
   Services: ISDN, UUCP, telnet, ftp, FTPmail, SLIP, PPP.
   Cost: Aus. $2000 per year (1 hour per day limit).
   Email: connect@connect.com.au

EUROPE

EUNet (eu.net)–Europe Network
   Services: FTP, TELNET, USENET, etc.
   Email: glenn@eu.net or postmaster@eu.net
   Voice: +31-2059-25124.
   Notes: Guest access is permitted. Email: eunet@code where 'code'
              is your country code, e.g. uk, de, fr, etc., for further details.

Appendix C
Internet: questions and answers

This appendix is the question and answer section, where many of the most commonly asked questions are dealt with. Questions are broken down into separate categories, namely:

- General Internet
- FTP – file transfer
- NetNews and USENET
- `telnet`
- Locating files: Archie, etc.
- Locating people: `whois`, finger, etc.
- Unix-related
- Accessing other networks
- File compression and internal formats
- Communications related

General Internet questions

Q. How do I get connected to the Internet?

A. There are many ways of doing this. The simplest way is to approach a local service-provider (see Appendix B) and ask them; after all, they do want customers. Most connections to the Internet are 'dial-up' connections where you dial into a service-provider's machine and from thereon access the tools and protocols that are necessary to communicate with hosts on the Internet. You can get dedicated, or even leased-lines installed (if cost is not a problem). Dial-up connections are very cheap, and are very popular among casual Internet users.

Q. How can I get an up-to-date list of service-providers?

A. Register for the PDIAL document. This is mailed automatically to you (or you can FTP it) and contains an extensive list of providers along with cost and system-feature details. Read the A–Z resource guide under 'PDIAL'. The PDIAL document will be sent to you on a periodic basis every month thereafter.

Q. How can I get an up-to-date list of Internet facilities?

A. The best documents to get hold of at the current time of writing include:

- The Yanoff list, maintained by Scott Yanoff. This is a list of Internet resources available via FTP. get it from the site pit-manager.mit.edu in /pub/usenet/news.answers as the file internet-services.
- The Big Fun list, maintained by Jeremy Smith. You can FTP this from the site cerberus.cor.epa.gov in the directory /pub/bigfun as the file bigfun.txt.Z (Unix compressed file – ASCII versions may be available).
- The December list, maintained by John December. FTP this file from ftp.rpi.edu in /pub/communications as internet-cmc.
- The Porter list, maintained by Mitchell Porter. FTP this document from ftp.uu.net in the directory /doc/political/umich-poli/Resource as the file weirdness.Z (Unix compressed file).
- This book.

Q. Where can I get technical information on the Internet and its protocols, etc?

A. From an RFC document. These are the Internets self-documenting feature. They cover all of the Internets technical capabilities, such as protocol specifications, TCP/IP, etc.

Q. How can I find information on general topics?

A. Use a gopher, WAIS, or WWW service. See Chapter 9 for details on these systems. You will need access to the telnet command in most instances, in order to access these systems. The A–Z resource guide (Appendix D) contains many general topic entries; you may also want to examine Appendix G, the USENET group listings appendix, for other general topics on an A–Z basis.

FTP – File transfer

Q. I don't have FTP, so how do I download files?

A. Change to a service-provider which has FTP (the majority have), or use FTPmail. FTPmail is a service whereby you use electronic mail (we assume you have access to this, at least) to access a mail server. A good example is `ftpmail@decwrl.dec.com`. Mail this address and place the commands you require to get the files at the FTP site of your choosing. Read Chapter 3 for more details on using FTPmail.

Q.   How do I download a file from a Unix FTP site to a DOS system when the name is too long to be accepted by DOS (or other operating systems)?

A.   Simple. Use the get command with a new filename for the file to be downloaded, for example:

```
ftp> get long_filename.txt file.txt↵
```

where `file.txt` is the name you want the remote file stored as under your local system.

Q.   I logged on to an anonymous FTP site and I misspelt the username. How do I get back in to the system?

A.   Simple. Type the user command, and then supply the details again. Read Chapter 3 for more information on the ftp program.

Q.   I do not have an FTP command, but I have `telnet`. Can I access FTP in another way since I am not familiar with the FTP command-set?

A.   Yes, in a way. If you telnet to a Gopher server, you can select the 'FTP' option and access FTP using Gopher menus. File downloads may be tricky to perform, however, although ASCII files can be displayed and captured into a file. There is always FTPmail of course (see the first question in this section).

NetNews, USENET

Q.   I don't have access to a newsreader, so how do I access USENET?

A.   Use an NNTP news-server. You must have telnet access to do this. Simply telnet to a NNTP news-server of your choice (read Chapter 2 for a list, or see the A–Z resource guide) and then load the USENET group you require and read the aricles. If you want to save the articles you read make sure your software can save your session to disk: use the script command on Unix, or the 'save session to file' feature in your communications software (if it doesn't have this facility, buy one that has – its invaluable).

Q.   I don't have a USENET service or access to `telnet`. Can I access USENET news?

A.   Yes. Subscribe to a mailing list and you will be posted all articles that are forwarded to the group of your choice. You may, however, not have full access to all USENET groups, only those for which mailing lists are available. Read Chapter 2 for more details.

TELNET

Q. How can I escape from a `telnet` session that has gone wrong?

A. Press [`Ctrl`] and] together. This will take you to the `telnet>` prompt were you can type 'close' to close your connection (or `quit` on some systems).

Q. My screen display is corrupt when I try to use a `telnet` service. What is wrong?

A. It looks like the remote system is using one emulation that is not supported or configured on your own terminal display. On a Unix system you will have to play around with the `TERM` variable (there may also be some terminal emulation software you should be running beforehand). If you are accessing a remote system using a third-party communications package, i.e. from DOS, etc., you will have to ensure that the terminal emulation is the same as the remote system. Examples of `TERM` variables and emulations include: vt100/102/52 (DEC vt100/vt102/vt52 emulation); ANSI (ANSI emulation); and dumb (simple ASCII terminal). Services such as Gopher, WAIS, HYTELNET, etc. all require VT emulations, e.g. vt100 (or possibly ANSI – for cursor control, screen highlighting, etc.). Look in the index under 'terminal emulations' for specific system information.

Locating Files: Archie, etc.

Q. How can I find a file on the Internet?

A. Use Archie. You can use Archie in two ways: (i) via an Archie client program on your machine; or (ii) via an Archie server via the `telnet` program. The latter method is probably the most common in use, so read Chapter 4 for a list of Archie servers (or the A–Z resource guide in Appendix D) and the commands to find the file. Once you have found the file use FTP to download it. If you do not have FTP you must use electronic mail to access a FTPmail server (see the second quesion, above). If you have an Archie client program use this and then access FTP/FTPmail accordingly. If Archie does not find the file you require you can always email the postmaster at a well-known FTP site (such as `wuarchive.wustl.edu`) and ask them, or you can email USENET to ask (find the forum you require from Appendix G of this book).

Q. Is it possible to use Archie without typing in commands from a prompt?

A. Yes. Telnet to a Gopher server, and select its 'Archie files' option. You can then use Archie via Gophers menus, rather than typing in commands via a prompt. Ensure you save your output into a file so that you can refer back to it. Alternatively, you can mail Archie and include the necessary commands in the message. See Chapter 4 for more details on all of these solutions.

Locating people: `finger`, `whois`, etc.

Q.   How do I find a person on the Internet?

A.   Hmmm. Well, you could use the WHOIS server at `nic.ddn.mil` (via the Telnet program) and enquire there – the person must be pretty well known to get on here, however. Alternatively, you could use the fred service (see Chapter 5) to try to find the person. If you know the site where a person resides and you want to see if they are still there, you can always use the `finger` command. The USENET database server may also help you (see Chapter 1).

Unix-related

Q.   How can I access Unix from my non-Unix machine?

A.   Your service-provider may allow, or even provide shell access (see Appendix B for such a list). Alternatively, you can `telnet` to a public-access Unix machine (these are scare, although they do exist – see the A–Z resource guide under 'Public Unix machine access').

Q.   How can I get some Unix documentation on-line?

A.   If your service provider has a Unix-shell system you should have access to the man command (manual command). If you don't have shell access, or access to the man command, you can use `telnet` to access an on-line server manual. See the A–Z resource guide under 'Unix manuals'. If you do not have `telnet` you may be able to find some information via FTP (use Archie for this).

Q.   A user is trying to contact me; I see the message 'Talk Daemon' on my terminal's screen – what do I do?

A.   `talk` is a Unix program for holding a two-way conversation. Type the Unix command: `talk <username>`, where `<username>` should be replaced with the user trying to contact you. Look on the screen for the user trying to contact you; it will be be mentioned e.g. `fred@somewhere.com`, in which case you type: `talk fred@somewhere.com` for example.

Q.   How do I stop a user from sending me messages (such as with the Unix `talk` and `write` commands)?

A.   Type the Unix command: `mesg n`. To re-enable messages type `mesg y`. Note that `mesg` will not stop electronic mail messages.

Accessing other networks: via Email, `telnet`, etc.

Q. How can I send mail to the Compuserve network?

A. Address your mail-message to nnnnn.nnn@compuserve.com, for example the person 87654.456 on Compuserve would be converted to: 87654,456@compuserve.com, noting the ',' instead of a '.'. For details on other networks, i.e. UUCP, MCImail, etc., see Chapter 11.

Q. How can I send secret messages/files via mail?

A. Well, you can use the Unix `crypt` command to employ DES encryption on a file, and then send that. Your recipient must have `crypt` and the password to unencrypt it. This is not a good idea since `crypt` is not generally available outside of the US. You could use a third-party crypt utility however (i.e. for DOS, etc.). If you have access to `xget` and `xsend` you can encrypt mail-messages at source without any more fiddling about. Finally, you can use a compressor that has a password feature, e.g. PKZIP for example. Sending 'secret' information on the Internet is not encouraged since it is an open system for use by all.
    The `crypt` command is not generally available outside the US so it makes sense to employ another method if your recipient is not in the US, i.e. use `xget`/`xsend` if available, or use file compression with password security.

Q. I am an academic user – how do I communicate with the UK JANET network?

A. You need to `telnet` to sun.nsf.ac.uk, the JANET/Internet gateway machine. This will prompt you for a JANET address to call, for example uk.ac.city-poly.tvax (note that JANET hostanames are reversed). The service you require will then be called via traditional X.25 links.

Q. How can I check if my email or USENET mail is being received?

A. Post to a local newsgroup, or post to yourself (in the case of human-to-human email). The main USENET group alt.test can be used for USENET testing, i.e. posting messages to see that they arrive safely.

File compression and formats

Q. How do I uncompress a .ZIP, .Z, .tar.Z, .ARC, .UUE or other file?

A. Read Chapter 7 on file compression to obtain details of the utilities you will need to uncompress files. You will have to FTP the files from a host, or use FTPmail if you do not have access to the FTP program (assuming you have email).

Q. How do I send a binary file (i.e. an image or program) via email, or on to USENET?

A.   Get hold of the UUENCODE utility. On Unix this is standard. On other systems, such as DOS, you will have to get hold of a specific tool. Read Chapter 8 on image processing for a complete discussion on UU-encoding tools.

Communications related

Q.   My service-provider's modem won't answer. I can't get connected, so what do I do?

A.   Common problem. Some modems cycle down their mating tones so that they can deal with multiple modem speeds, i.e. if you are calling from a 2400 baud modem, the receiving modem may start at 14.4, then go to 9600, and then finally go to 2400 baud. If your modem won't wait long enough to get the correct mating tone you will have to program it to wait longer. On a Hayes modem device you will use an AT-style command. A Hayes-compatible modem has a number of registers (commonly called S) which specify various options such as waiting times. You may want to issue a command such as: ATS7=n where n is the number of seconds to wait for a carrier tone – 7 is the number of our register that deals with this – it will most probably be different on your system however, so read your Modem manual.

Bear in mind also that if you have a slow modem (2400 baud, for example), the remote system may not have many modems that answer solely on this speed; hence the wait. Eventually you will get connected, although it may depend on a line becoming free. Contact your provider and ask them about their modem setup; perhaps they don't support your modem speed (2400 baud is the bare minimum nowadays).

If your service-provider's modem does not give a mating tone you can assume it is out of order. Ring your support line to see if the system is down.

Appendix D
The A–Z Internet resource guide

This appendix summarizes a range of Internet services by the tool that is used to access them. The principle tools are:

- Email (electronic mail). These entries may consist of human contacts that can provide further information, or they may be FTPmail servers or Listservers that can send you more information by sending mail to the specified address. Example: `mail fred@somewhere.com`↵ (to mail the user `fred` at site `somewhere.com` on a Unix system). See Chapter 11 for more on the Unix `mail` program.
- Finger. The `finger` program is found on Unix and many other systems. It allows a user to call up a piece of information in real time, and display it. Example: `finger aurora@xi.uleth.ca`↵ for data on the Suns (auroral) activity. See Chapter 6 for more information on the `finger` command.
- FTP (File Transfer Protocol). FTP resources are computer sites that hold information in the form of downloadable files. An FTP entry can be accessed by FTPing to the site mentioned, and then logging in as anonymous (the password is always your email address). The directories that hold the necessary file(s) you require will also be mentioned. Example: `ftp wuarchive.wustl.edu`↵. See Chapter 3 for more information on `ftp`, specifically its directory navigation commands.
- Gopher (and veronica). This service can also be reached via telnet (see the A–Z resource guide for a list of servers). Gopher presents its information in enu form, and allows FTP, Archie and WAIS-based searches. Example: `telnet consultant.micro.unm.edu`↵ (to access the gopher system at this site). Veronica cannot be accessed by itself; you must contact a gopher server and invoke a veronica search manually.

- Listserv. These entries are mailing-list based, and are carried onto USENET in the bit.* hierarchy. You should subscribe to the mailing list shown in such instances. See Chapter 10 for more information on Listserv mailing lists.
- `telnet` (virtual terminal protocol). Whenever you see a `telnet` entry, you must use the `telnet` command with the address given, and then log in using the username and/or password mentioned. Access to the service will then be allowed. The numeric IP address of the service may also be given, where known. `telnet` gives access to: WAIS, gopher, WWW, Archie, and other interactive services. Example: `telnet archie.ans.net`↵ (for an Archie client via `telnet`). See Chapter 5 for more information on the `telnet` program.
- USENET (Internet news network). USENET can be accessed via a newsreading utility, e.g. `nn`, or a NNTP telnet-based server. Example: `telnet news.ibmpcug.co.uk 119`↵ (to access the NNTP server at the IBM PC user group). See Chapter 2 for more on USENET newsreaders and NNTP servers accessible via `telnet`.
- WAIS (wide area information server). WAIS servers are scattered about all over the world. Refer to the entry for WAIS for a list of such servers. In order to use WAIS you should `telnet` to a server machine that offers the service, and then look up the source(s) that interest you. Example: `telnet quake.think.com`↵. See Chapter 9 for more information on WAIS.
- WWW (World-Wide-Web). This service requires that you `telnet` into a WWW server (see resource guide under WWW) and then access the sources you require. Example: `telnet info.cern.ch`↵ (to access the WWW server at CERN in Switzerland). See Chapter 9 for more information.

Readers are also advised to browse Appendix G (USENET groups) for other topics that may be available. All anonymous FTP sites require a user-name of anonymous and a password which is simply your electronic-mail name, for example: `fred@somewhere.com` (you may get away with just entering a string which includes a '@' sign on some FTP systems). Read Chapter 3 for more information on browsing remote file systems and down-loading files. This resource guide will change and expand as new editions of this book are released. If you have a resource that you want included, or if you have a correction, please contact McGraw-Hill UK directly. We want to hear about all of your FTP, WAIS, gopher/veronica or telnet-based services so please contact us with all the neccessary details.

Aboriginal studies
     wais: `ANU-aboriginal-stuies.src`
     See also: Thai Yunnan Project.

Abortion-related topics
     usenet: (1) `alt.abortion.inequity`
             (2) `us.politics.abortion`
             (3) `talk.abortion`

Acronyms

The Internet is full of acronyms, and the list grows at a phenomenal rate. Check out the FTP archive shown here for an up-to-date list:

ftp: `lcs.mit.edu`

login: `anonymous`

password: `<your mail-name>`

See the files:

(1) `/telecom-archives/glossary.acronyms`
(2) `/telecom-archives/glossary.isdn.terms-kluge`
(3) `/telecom-archives/glossary.naval.telecom`
(4) `/telecom-archives/glossary.phrack.acronyms`
(5) `/telecom-archives/glossary.txt`

See also: jargon archive.

Activism

usenet: (1) `alt.activism`
        (2) `alt.activism.d`

Aeronautics archive

A number of anonymous FTP archives exist on this subject. Information such as aircraft specifications and even flight-simulation software are maintained.

ftp: `rascal.ics.utexas.edu` (see: `/misc/av`)

login: `anonymous`

password: `<your mail-name>`

See also: Aviation (DUATS).

Agricultural Information

These services have a range of information, including weather forecasts, aricultural events and information general to the farming and agricultural industries as a whole.

(1) IOWA State University – SCHOLAR system

telnet: `isn.iastate.edu`

login: `scholar`

select: `agri` for the agricultural database once a connection has been made to SCHOLAR.

(2) PEN Pages – University of Pennsylvania

A variety of information is held here, including food and nutrition data, weather statistics, newsletters, market news and much more besides.

telnet: `psupen.psu.edu` (`128.118.36.5`)

login: `PNOTPA` (or `PPREPNET`, or a two-letter id-code for your state, e.g. `NY` for New York); users outside of the US can use a fictitious code.

mail: `support@psupen.psu.edu` (for general queries).

(3) CSU Freso ATI-NET

A diverse range of agricultural information is stored here, including weather information (and imagery).

telnet: `caticsuf.csufresno.edu (129.8.100.15)`
login: `super` (or `public`).

(4) CUFAN Clemson University Forestry & Ag. Network Agricultural information, livestock reports, market prices, etc. are all available on-line from this service.
telnet: `eureka.clemson.edu (130.127.8.3)`
login: `PUBLIC`
ftp: `ftp.sura.net` (see: /pub/nic/agricultural.list)
mail: `almanac@oes.orst.edu`
message-body: `send guide` or `send mail-catalog`

(5) USDA research results
This server contains a list of recent results from the USDA's agricultural research.
wais: `usda-rrdb.src`
mail: `wais@esusda.gov`

(6) BEE biology
A server relating to the keeping of bees, with information on pollination, honey-making, etc.
ftp: `sunsite.unc.edu` (see: /pub/academic/agri-culture/sustainable_ agriculture/beekeeping/)
listserv: `bee-l@albnyvm1.bitnet`

(7) Commodity market reports
These are compiled by the US Department of Agriculture Market News Service. There are over 1000 reports concerning the US, and many are updated daily.
wais: `agricultural-market-news.src`
mail: `wais@oes.orst.edu`

(8) Not Just Cows!
An agricultural source on WAIS.
ftp: (1) `ftp:sura.net` (see: /pub/nic/agri-cultural.list)
(2) `hydra.uwo.ca` (see: /libsoft/agri-culture_internet_guide.text)
(3) `ftp.unt.edu` (see: agriculture_internet.txt)

See also: WAIS and gopher servers, which are maintained at the same hostname mentioned above for FTP.

AIDS/HIV disease and virus
usenet: (1) `bit.listserv.aidsnews`
(2) `calri.tw.health`
(3) `calri.tw.health.aids`
(4) `sci.med.aids`

See also: CHAT, epilepsy, FDA BBS, nutrition, queer resource directory.

Almanac mail servers
USDA agriculture market news; using computers in agricultural science, etc.
mail: (1) almanac@esusda.gov
      (2) almanac@silo.ucdavis.edu
      (3) almanac@ces.ncsu.edu
      (4) almanac@oes.orst.edu
      (5) almanac@ecn.purdue.edu
message-body: 'SEND GUIDE'

Amateur radio BBS
Files and general information about electronics and the world of amateur radio.
mail: info@arrl.org
message-body: (1) 'help' or 'info'
              (2) send <filename>

American Philosophical Association (APA)
BBS systems for the APA. Material is clearly biased in the area of philosophy generally.
telnet: atl.calstate.edu (130.150.102.33)
login: apa

AMIGA computers
The AMIGA computer platform is well supported on the Internet, and many hosts have amiga-related information which can be extracted from archives. Check out these archives first:
ftp: (1) a.cs.uiuc.edu
     (2) bach.berkeley.edu
     (3) cs.utah.edu
     (4) funet.fi
     (5) gtss.gatech.edu
     (6) micros.hensa.ac.uk
login: anonymous
password: <your mail-name>

Anonymous mail server
This service allows you to post articles to USENET and to individuals on the Internet anonymously.
mail: anon.penet.fi
You will be sent some information in a few days, along with your anonymous id.

Anthropology
See: Thai Yunnan project.

Archaeology
Check out WAIS with the following source for archaeology related to computing.
wais: archaeological_computing.src

Archie – file index

A wealth of information through the SURANet archie server (email: archivist@orst.edu) can be searched via the WAIS service. Many dozens of archie related WAIS sources can also be called up via WAIS.

wais: archie-orst.edu.src

Archie servers

Archie servers allow users to find files from the many thousands of anonymous-FTP sites around the world.

telnet: (1) archie.au (139.130.4.6)
        (2) archie.univie.ac.at (131.130.1.23)
        (3) archie.funet.fi (128.214.6.100)
        (4) archie.th-darmstadt.de (130.83.22.60)
        (5) archie.kuis.kyoto-u.ac.jp (130.54.20.1)
        (6) archie.sogang.ac.kr (163.239.1.11)
        (7) archie.nz (130.195.9.4)
        (8) archie.luth.se (130.240.18.4)
        (9) archie.ncu.edu.tw (140.115.19.24)
      (10) archie.doc.ic.ac.uk (146.169.11.3)
      (11) archie.sura.net (128.167.254.179)
      (12) archie.unl.edu (129.93.1.14)
      (13) archie.ans.net (147.225.1.10)
      (14) archie.rutgers.edu (128.6.18.15)
      (15) archie.edvz.uni-linz.ac.at (140.78.3.8)
      (16) archie.uqam.ca (132.208.250.10)
      (17) archie.ac.il (132.65.6.15)
      (18) archie.unipi.it (131.114.21.10)
      (19) archie.wide.ad.jp (133.4.3.6)
      (20) archie.kr (128.134.1.1)
      (21) archie.rediris.es (130.206.1.2)
      (22) archie.luth.se (130.240.18.4)
      (23) archie.switch.ch (130.59.1.40)
      (24) archie.internic.net (198.48.45.10)
      (25) archie.cs.huji.ac.il (132.65.6.15)

login: archie

mail: archie@server-name (as above)

message-body: a valid archie command (or commands). See Chapter 4 on archie for more details of the various archie commands via email

Art

(1) ASCII Cartoons

ASCII art is widely available on the Internet in a variety of forms. The FTP server below is based in Germany.

gopher: pfsparc02.phil15.uni.sb.de

select: INFO-SYSTEM BENUTZEN

(2) Arts Online

This service offers a bibliography of arts-related resources around the Internet and bordering networks (files are compressed in the Unix compress format).

ftp: `nic.funet.fi` (see:`/pub/doc/library`
    `/artbase.txt.Z`)

(3) OTIS project

OTIS (operative word is stimulate) is a project that is engaged in the distribution of art and photographs around the network. You can even submit your own work for inclusion in their `gallery`.

ftp: `sunsite.unc.edu` (see: `/pub/multimedia/pictures`
    `/OTIS`)

Astrology

usenet: `alt.astrology`

Astronomy

A number of FTP sites keep this information. NASA-related hosts may also have relevant information. You can get hold of images and texts from the following FTP hosts.

ftp: (1) `pomona.claremont.edu` (see: `/yale_bsc`)

 (2) `mandarin.mit.edu` (see: `/astro`)

 (3) `nic.funet.fi` (`/pub/astro`)

login: `anonymous`

password: `<your mail-name>`

See also: NASA – space information, auroral activity.

Auroral activity

Keep up-to-date with all the latest auroral activity from our life-giver, the Sun. This service is updated on the hour.

finger: `aurora@xi.uleth.ca (142.66.3.29)`

Automobiles

(1) USENET is the best place to look for information on cars.

usenet: `rec.autos.tech`, `rec.audio.car`, `alt.hotrod`, `rec.autos.antique`, `rec.autos`, `rec.autos.vw`, etc.

See also: Appendix G for for the `rec.*` hierarchies.

(2) Driving archives

An abundance of information regarding driving is available from the FTP site shown below (common to the US in the main).

ftp: `rtfm.mit.edu` (see: `/pub/usenet/news.answers/ca-driving-faq`)

login: `anonymous`

password: `<your mail-name>`

(3) Automative archives

Another archive, this one based at MIT again. It is a collection of articles from USENET's `rec.autos` group.

ftp: `rtfm.mt.edu` (see: `/pub/usenet/rec.autos/*`)

login: anonymous

password: `<your mail-name>`

Aviation

(1) DUATS. Information on aviation, weather, flight-planning. Caters for certified and non-certified pilots.

telnet: (1) `duat.gtefsd.com23` (pilots only)

(2) `duats.contel.com` (non-pilots)

(3) `duats.contel.com` (pilots only)

login: `<your surname>`

(2) Flight-planning archives

These FTP archives have a variety of shareware and freeware files that are related to aviation and flying generally. Source code (in C) is also available.

ftp: (1) `lifshitz.ph.utexas.edu` (see: `pub/aviation/*`)

(2) `eecs.nwu.edu` (see: `/pub/aviation/*`)

login: anonymous

password: `<your mail-name>`

(3) Slight-simulation archives

A variety of information on flight-simulation software and theory is available from these FTP archives:

ftp: (1) `ftp.iup.edu` (see: `/flight_sim/*`)

(2) `rtfm.mit.edu` (see: `/pub/usenet/news.answers/aviation/flight_simulators`)

(3) `ftp.ulowell.edu` (see: `/msdos/Games/FltSim/*`)

(4) `nic.funet.fi` (see: `/pub/X11/contrib/acm2.4.tar.Z`)

(5) `onion.rain.com` (see: `/pub/falcon3/*`)

login: anonymous

password: `<your mail-name>`

(4) Aviation gopher system

A gopher system exists at the host shown below which deals solely in aviation.

gopher: `av.eecs.nwu.edu`

(5) Aviation archives

An FTP archive that deals in the humorous side of aviation.

ftp: (1) `rascal.ics.utexas.edu` (see: `/misc/av/*`)

(3) `tfm.mit.edu` (see: `/pub/usenet/news.answers/*`)

(4) `ftp.eff.org` (see: `/pub/airliners/*`)

login: anonymous

password: `<your mail-name>`

Backgammon servers
Play some on-line backgammon in real time.
telnet: (1) `solana.mps.ohio-state.edu`
            `3200 (128.146.37.78)`
        (2) `134.130.130.46 4321`
login: `guest`

Baseball scores (US)
Baseball fans can receive the latest scores, and even subscribe to to the daily major league scores (MLB).
finger: `jtchern@ocf.berkeley.edu` (for scores) or
mail: `jtchern@ocf.berkeley.edu, subject: MLB`

BBS – Bulletin Board Systems
Bulletin board systems (BBSs) are widely available via the Internet. Here are a selection accessible via `telnet` (usernames given where applicable). A selection of USENET forums that deal in BBS systems are also given.
telnet:
(1) After Five BBS: AfterFive has many features, including a MUD and Chat system. Note the special port number on this hostname. A commercial company run this BBS, although access is free.
    telnet: `af.itd.com 9999`
(2) Auggie BBS
    Chat and talk facilities are widely used here. A real discussion BBS that never sleeps.
    telnet: `bbs.augsburg.edu`
    login: `bbs`
(3) CSB/SJU BBS
    This BBS is totally menu driven and has a variety of files and information to read and download. This BBS operates from within a university.
    telnet: `tiny.computing.csbsju.edu`
    login: `bbs`
(4) CueCosy BBS
    A BBS situated in Canada, and with full conferencing facilities. Facilities include message-areas for eductionalists.
    telnet: `cue.bc.ca`
    login: `cosy`
(5) CYBERnet
    This BBS has email and limited USENET facilities, along with standard Unix tools such as `finger`, `talk`, IRC, as well as on-line games.
    telnet: `cybernet.cse.fau.edu`
    login: `bbs`
(6) ISCA BBS
    Probably the largest BBS on the Internet, with facilities for 300+ concurrent users. Many discussion forums not found on places such as

USENET are to be discovered here.
telnet: (1) `whip.isca.uiowa.edu`
       (2) `bbs.isca.uiowa.edu`
login: `guest`

(7) **LaunchPad BBS**
Another excellent BBS with full USENET, email, WAIS and gopher facilities. What more can you want?
telnet: `launchpad.unc.edu`
login: `launch`

(8) **NSYSU BBS**
Located in Taiwan, this BBS also has gopher, USENET, and an IRC-like facility. Good for Chinese users, since a client program exists that will translate all information into this language (log in for details).
telnet: `cc.nsysu.edu.tw`
login: `bbs`

(9) **Quartz BBS**
A long-established Internet BBS. Many downloadable files to keep you occupied for many years to come.
telnet: `quartz.rutgers.edu`
login: `bbs`

(10) **Radford University BBS**
A good BBS with IRC, local email, games, plus access to many information sources such as OPACs, files, etc.
telnet: `muselab-gw.runet.edu`
login: `bbs`

(11) **SoftWords COSY BBS**
A BBS with conferencing facilities among other things. Also has an Internet email service.
telnet: `softwords.bc.ca`
login: `cosy`

(12) **SunSet BBS**
A BBS with many interesting discussion groups, along with a large selection of files to download, etc.
telnet: `paladine.hacks.arizona.edu`
login: `bbs`

(13) **UT BBS**
A BBS based in Holland. Caters for English-speaking and Dutch-speaking users alike. Large public-file areas.
telnet: `utbbs.civ.utwente.nl`
login: `bbs`

See also: Monochrome, Internet BBS lists, gopher BBS access, Appendix G – USENET lists under `alt.bbs.*` hierarchy.

Beer (the drink)
usenet: alt.beer
Billboard charts
Stores the US top pop singles for the current week.
finger: buckmr@aix.rpi.edu
Biology
(1) Biology newsletter
A selection of newsletters with biological connotations can be found at
this archive, e.g. Starnet, Flora Online, etc.
ftp: nigel.msen.com (see: /pub/newsletters/Bio/*)
(2) The biologists guide to the Internet
Many gopher services specialize in biological information. Essential for
all biologists who are connected to the Internet.
gopher: (1) finsun.csc.fi
select: 'FAQ Files – A Biologists Guide', 'Finnish EMBnet', etc.
(3) Biology sources on WAIS
WAIS has many biological sources that can be searched. Try looking at
the source below which will give you further leads to much more
information.
wais: biology-journal-contents.src
(4) Listserv lists (BITNET)
Mailing lists in the area of biology are also available. Try this FTP
source to get you started.
ftp: huh.harvard.edu (see: /pub/taxacom/taxacom.txt)
See also: molecular biology.
BITNET network
See: LISTSERV groups
BLAISE-Line (UK)
BLAISE-Line is the British Library's on-line service, which gives acccess to
13 million bibliographic records in 20 databases, covering information in all
subject areas and many languages: books, journals, miscellaneous reports,
conference proceedings, government publications, printed music, maps and
antiquarian books. Once registered, access to these services can be made
through the Internet/JANET link. For more information on BLAISE, and
to register, contact:
British Library Customer Services
Telephone: +44 937 546060
Fax: +44 937 546333.
Alternatively, telnet to sun.nsf.ac.uk and login as janet (password:
janet also). You can choose the service-names: blaise.bl.uk or
arttel.bl.uk for instructions on how to register to BLAISE.

Books

(1) Book reviews
The *Whole Earth Magazine* reviews books and publishes details on the net. Access the gopher shown here and take a browse.
gopher: `gopher.well.sf.ca.us`
select: Art and Culture – Book Reviews

(2) Bookstore reviews
An abundance of information about the operation of book shops can be found at these sources. Book reviews are also available.
ftp: `rtfm.mit.edu`   (see: `/pub/usenet/news.answers/`
     `books/stores/*`)
gopher: `consultant.micro.umn.edu`
select: Fun & Games/Games/Bookstores

(3) Computer books by O'Reilly and Associates
Information pertaining to this computer-book publisher are maintained at the FTP site below. Ordering information, book catalogues and archives are all available, as are actual book samples in text form (from the latter FTP site shown below).
gopher: `ora.com`
select: Book Descriptions and Information
ftp: (1) `ftp.ora.com` (see: `/pub`)
     (2) `ftp.uu.net` (for book samples: `/published/oreilly`)
login: `anonymous`
password: <`your mail-name`>
mail: `bookquestions@ora.com` (for any book enquiries)

(4) Book-talk mailing list
This listserv mailing-list discusses a variety of media, including books, CD and videos. Book reviews are available.
mail: `book-talk@columbia.ilc.com`

(5) The on-line book store (OBS)
The OLB is an on-line ordering system that deals solely in books, although the bias is on computing books. For more information email the alias shown below:
mail: `obs@tic.com`

(6) Unix books
Here are some of the best sources of information on Unix books, including bibiliographies and reviews from Internet users themselves.
ftp: (1) `rtfm.mit.edu` (see: `/pub/usenet/news.answers/`
         `books`)
     (2) `ucselx.sdsu.edu` (see: `/pub/doc/general/Unix-`
         `C-Booklist`)
     (3) `ftp.rahul.net` (see: `/pub/mitch/YABL/*`)

login: anonymous
password: <your mail-name>
gopher: ora.com
select: Unix Bibliography
See also: Unix manuals.

BUBL – the bulletin board for libraries

The bulletin board for libraries collects information of interest to network-using librarians and their users. A major aim is to provide librarians with information on services and resources on JANET and other networks, such as the European IXI network and the Internet. BUBL also covers items of general interest to librarians. Moreover, it is increasingly used by non-librarians – lecturers, students, and others – for the guidance it provides on finding and using networked resources and services. BUBL is run by the Universities of Strathclyde and Glasgow on behalf of JUGL, the JANET User Group for Libraries.

telnet: sun.nsf.ac.uk (128.86.8.7)
login: janet
password: janet
At the hostname prompt type: uk.ac.glasgow.bubl.
At the terminal type prompt enter vt100.

Business information

A variety of business-related information is available on the Internet, including stock-market reports and industry statistics, etc. Here are a selection of sources.

(1) Stock-market report
This site offers a daily stock-market report – a very rare service; one of the Internet's 'gold nuggets'.
telnet: a2i.rahul.net
login: guest
select: n (for new screen), 'Current System Info/Market Report'

(2) Stock-market closing quotes
This gopher server reports on closing stock-market prices.
gopher: lobo.rmhs.colorado.edu
select: Other information services/stock-market closing quotes.

(3) Economic indicators
This gopher server has a variety of economic information, including the raw data used to calculate various economic indicators in the US. Here are the main gopher menus that are of interest.
gopher: infopath.ucsd.edu
select: • News & Services/Economic information/Special Studies
         • News & Services/Economic information/Internat. market
         • News & Services/Economic information/Economic
           Indicators

- News & Services/Economic information/EBB and Agency Info.
- News & Services/Economic information/Eastern Europe trade
- News & Services/Economic information/Current Business

See also: Appendix G-biz.*, clari.* business-related newsgroups. These hierarchies carry a variety of information related to business and commerce.

CAD (Computer-aided design)
usenet: (1) alt.cad
         (2) alt.cad.autocad

Calculators
See: HP calculator BBS.
See also: Appendix G under comp.sys.hp, comp.sys.hp48, comp.sys.handhelds, comp.sys.ti, etc.

Cancer
Here are sources for coverage of the disease cancer.
(1) CancerNet
    A useful service providing cancer information between parties via email, as well as a gopher server for real-time access.
    mail: cancernet@icicb.nci.nih.gov
    message-body: help
    gopher: gopher.nih.gov
(2) National Cancer Centre Database (Japan)
    This research organization deals with cancer-related issues, and there are plans to allow direct consultation to medical experts regarding cancer-related topics. A WAIS and gopher server are also being developed.
    ftp: ftp.ncc.go.jp
    login: anonymous
    password: <your login-name>
    wais: wais.ncc.go.jp
    gopher: gopher.ncc.go.jp
    select: CancerNet service
(3) Cancer information via USENET
    usenet: alt.support.cancer

CARL bibliographic server
On-line bibliographic server, containing a fax delivery system, book reviews, etc.
telnet: pac.carl.org(192.54.81.128)
See also: fax server (FaxGate).

Cars
See: automobiles.

CD-ROM
usenet: alt.cd-rom

Chaos Corner newsletter
Keep up-to-date with Internet gossip with this electronic newsletter which is available via FTP. A number of back-issues are also available.
ftp: pelican.cit.cornell.edu (See: /pub)
login: anonymous
password: <your mail-name>
mail: chaos-request@pelican.cit.cornell.edu

CHAT
A medical service offering information on AIDS and epilepsy (see also: epilepsy).
telnet: debra.dgbt.doc.ca (142.92.36.15)

Chat servers
Offers an on-line real-time 'chat' service between users. Note the additional port numbers.
telnet: (1) ns.speedway.net 3000 (198.51.248.20 3000)
        (2) loligo.cc.fsu.edu 2010

Chemistry
This FTP site has chemistry FAQs, Internet leads, book references, and a lot more besides.
ftp: ucssun1.sdsu.edu
login: anonymous
password: <your mail-name>
See also: biology.

Chess pairing service – Chicago Chess SIG (CCSIG)
This SIG specializes in the games of chess, and offers a pairing service. CCSIG has over 200 members, and is part of FNCF, the union of Internet chess clubs. The FNCF have over 500 additional members. Contact the email address below for information via email:
mail: (1) mox@uumeme.chi.le.us
      (2) mox@vpnet.chi.le.us

Chess server
Play some real-time chess with a human opponent.
telnet: (1) valkyries.andrew.cmu.edu 5000
        (2) 128.220.55.21 5000
        (3) 130.225.16.162 5000

Child support
usenet: alt.child-support

Children
(1) Childcare newsletter
    This FTP site carries documents relating to childcare in general.
    ftp: nigel.msen.com (see: /pub/newsletters/Kids/*)

login: `anonymous`
password: `<your mail-name>`
(2) KIDS mailing list
A mailing list solely for children, allowing children to engage in email discussions around the world. To join, send an email to the following alias:
mail: `joinkids@vms.cis.pitt.edu`
message body: anything will do.
See also: Appendix G – USENET lists under `k12.*` hierarchy.

CIX (UK) – `cix.compulink.co.uk`
The Compulink Information Exchange is one of the best-known commerical BBSs in Britain. It has Internet access for users on a subscription basis, and users can subscribe and make payment on-line. They specialize in on-line conferencing, and have extensive archives for a range of machines. They offer FTP, `telnet` and USENET feeds, among other things.
telnet: `cix.compulink.co.uk` (registered users)
You can email a CIX user from the Internet using the recipient name `aperson@cix.compulink.co.uk`. If you do not have `telnet`, access CIX on one of its MODEM numbers: +44 (0)81-390-1255, or +44 (0)81-399-5252, using the `login` name of `new` to subscribe.

Coke servers
A long, long time ago a student computerized the university's coke vending machine in order that it could be queried over the network, e.g. how many bottles left, how many were cold, etc. Now isn't it really useful to be able to examine a coke machine that exists many thousands of miles away?
finger: (1) `coke@cmu.edu`
(2) `drink@drink.csh.rit.edu`
(3) `bargraph@coke.elab.cs.cmu.edu` (draws a bar-graph)
(4) `coke@cs.wisc.edu`
(5) `coke@gu.uwa.edu.au`

Compression utilities and information
Much of the information on the Internet is compressed to save storage space. This very useful FTP archive contains all of the information you will ever need to decompress files for the PC, Amiga, and Unix platforms, as well as many others.
ftp: `ftp.cso.uiuc.edu` (see: `/doc/pcnet/compression.txt`)
login: `anonymous`
password: `<your mail-name>`
See also: Chapter 7 on data compression.

Computer literature
The whole network is full of such material, so here is a guide to some of the best and most popular sources currently available:

(1) Computer underground
     This is probably the largest collection of material related to the hacker,
     cyberpunk, phreaker and anarchist genre. Many journals are available
     including *Phrack*, *Phantasy*, and the *Legion of Doom*.
     ftp: `ftp.eff.org` (see: `/pub/cud/*`)
     login: `anonymous`
     password: <`your mail-name`>

(2) Computer virus information
     Every Internet user should get hold of this since viruses are an unfor-
     tunate reality.
     ftp: `oak.oakland.edu` (see: `/pub/misc/virus`)
     login: `anonymous`
     password: <`your mail-name`>

(3) DTP – Desktop publishing
     This FTP archive has a range of material related to the DTP world,
     including Internet FAQs, and even job opportunities.
     ftp: `wuarchive.wustl.edu` (see: `/doc/misc/pagemaker/*`)
     login: `anonymous`
     password: <`your mail-name`>
     See also: desktop publishing.

(4) Hackers Dictionary – via gopher
     The famous Hackers Dictionary is available from many FTP sites,
     although this source offers a gopher server.
     gopher: `orixa.mtholyoke.edu`
     select: Document Library/The Hackers Dictionary
     See also: Hackers Dictionary, GUTENBERG project.

(5) DOS for beginners
     This document is a must for all PC novices. It contains an introduction
     to the standard operating system of every personal computer, namely
     DOS.
     ftp: `ucselx.sdsu.edu` (see: `/pub/doc/general/msdos.txt`)
     login: `anonymous`
     password: <`your mail-name`>

(6) Computer networking
     This gopher server offers information on computer networking, speci-
     fically around the PC and Unix operating systems. Also has informa-
     tion on networking in schools.
     gopher: `gopher.psg.com`
     select: Networking

(7) Networking maps
     This excellent service can show you the main computer networks that
     are currently in existence, and which exchange email. The FTP docu-
     ment version is also available.

ftp: `tic.com` (see: `/matrix/maps/*`)
login: `anonymous`
password: `<your mail-name>`
gopher: `tic.com`
select: Matrix Information/Maps of Networks

Computers

As you would imagine, an abundance of information on computers is available on the Internet. Take a glance through Appendix G to see the `comp.*` hierarchies for specific hardware and software discussion forums first, since you may see a group that deals with a specific hardware/software system that you are interested in. Here are some other leads:

ftp:

(1) `nic.funet.fi` (disk-drive technology – see: `/pub/doc/hard-disks/*`)

(2) `oak.oakland.edu` (MODEMs – see: `/pub/misc/modems`)

(3) `wuarchive.wustl.edu` (MODEM NEWS magazine – see: `/pub/modemnews/*`)

(4) `oak.oakland.edu` (EPROM Chips – see: `/pub/misc/eprom/eprom-types.list`)

gopher:

(1) RS232 – Serial port standard: `gopher.cpe.surrey.ac.uk`
(select: Misc. Technical Notes/RS232 pinouts)

(2) Supercomputers: `gopher.tamu.edu`
(select: Texas A&M gophers/Supercomputer Center gopher/)

Cooking and food

(1) Stuttgart recipe server
Various cooking and recipe information is maintained on the Internet although not in a telnetable form. Stuttgart's server can be reached as:
telnet: `rusmv1rus.uni-stuttgart.de`
login: `infoserv`
select: `cd cookbook`

(2) Recipe archives
The archives mentioned here are mainly regurgitated from the USENET forum `rec.food.cooking`.
ftp: (1) `gatekeeper.dec.com` (see: `/pub/recipes`)
        (2) `mthvax.cs.mimai.edu` (see: `/recipes`)
login: `anonymous`
password: `<your mail-name>`

(3) WAIS recipes
WAIS also maintains a source of recipes. This source also comes from USENETs `rec.food.cooking` forum.
wais: (1) `usenet-cookbook.src`
        (2) `recipes.src`

(4) Vegetarian archives
These archives deal with many vegetarian issues.
ftp:
(1) `flubber.cs.umd.edu` (see: `/other/tms/veg/*`)
(2) `rtfm.mit.edu` (see: `/pub/usenet/news.answers`
   `/vegetarian/*`)
login: `anonymous`
password: `<your mail-name>`

Culture (world)
See: Appendix G – USENET groups under `soc.culture.*` for each specific country.

Cyberpunk
Some of the most well-known cyberpunk works on the Internet are documented here.
(1) *Agrippa: A book of the dead*
The complete work of William Gibson's cyberpunk tale is available via FTP from this source.
ftp: `ftp.rahul.net`
login: `anonymous`
password: `<your mail-name>`
(2) Cyperpunk news via gopher
A collection of material related to the cyberpunk subject. They include works by Bruce Sterling, and document the whole cyberpunk language.
gopher: `gopher.well.sf.ca.us`
select: `Cyperpunk/`
(3) Bruce Sterling articles
Works by the famous cyberpunk author Bruce Sterling can be found in copious quantities at this gopher/FTP site.
gopher: `gopher.well.sf.ca.us`
select: /Cyperpunk/Essays and Articles by Bruce Sterling
ftp: `ftp.eff.org` (see: `/pub/agitprop`)
login: `anonymous`
password: `<your mail-name>`

Cyphers
See: encryption.

DANTE project
DANTE is a comedy review project.
telnet: `library.dartmouth.edu` (`129.170.16.11`)
login: `connect dante`

Demon Internet Systems (UK) – `demon.co.uk`
DIS are an Internet service-provider based in the UK, offering a dial-up Internet service to the end-user on a cheap monthly subscription. Their modem number is currently: +44 (0)81-343-4848. There is no on-line regis-

tration. For more information: phone +44 (0)81-343 3881 (voice).

mail: internet@demon.co.uk (for enquiries)

ftp: ftp.demon.co.uk (software archive)

Desktop publishing

See: computer literature.

See also: Appendix G-alt.aldus.* (for Aldus DTP products).

Dial-up Internet access

Many service-providers now offer dial-up access to the Internet. A list of these can be found at the archive below.

ftp: gvl.unisys.com (see: /pub/pubnet/pdial)

login: anonymous

password: <your mail-name>

To keep up-to-date with the latest service-providers subscribe to a service to keep you posted with the above file:

email: info-deli-server@netcom.com

Message-body: Subscribe PDIAL

See also: Appendix C.

Diplomacy

A game played entirely by email, set in pre First World War Europe. A tactical game in which your instructions are sent in via email, and results are then sent back the same way.

mail: (1) judge@morrolan.eff.org

      (2) judge@shrike.und.ac.za

      (3) judge@dipvax.dsto.gov.au

Disability software

An archive of disability-related software for handicapped people exists at this FTP site. See the /pub/index file for more details.

ftp: handicap.shed.isc.bu.com (129.189.4.184)

login: anonymous

password: <your user-name>

Earthquake information

See: geology.

ECONET

ECONET is run by IGC, the Institute for Global Communications. IGC also run PeaceNET, and ConflictNET. ECONET serves the environmental community, through a number of Internet-related services. ECONET provide a common forum for people to share and exchange information relevant to a wide range of environmental issues. ECONET is a very large and well-organized system, and has Internet, fax and telex communication to all parts of the world (a newly set-up network to reach the former Soviet Union called 'GlasNet' is also provided).

ftp: (1) cdp.igc.org

     (2) igc.org

login: anonymous
password: <your mail-name>
You can join ECONET now if you have a credit card by telnetting to igc.org and logging in as 'new', or by direct-dialling ECONET's BBS on (413) 322-0284 (set your modem to 8 data bits, no parity, 1 stop bit).
email: support2@igc.com (for all enquiries).

Education

(1) Higher education gopher
This service is run by Apple computers, and covers product information and other publications related to educational computing.
gopher: info.hed.apple.com

(2) EDUPAGE
A news-service provided by EDUCOM, a group of colleges and universities in the US who are seeking to promote the use of computing and information technology in the classroom. Send an email to the address below for more information on this service.
mail: edupage@educom.edu

(3) Health science education
This on-line service deals with the area of CBL, or computer-based learning (primarily with the PC and Macintosh platform) in health/ science education.
telnet: shrsys.hslc.org
login: cbl

(4) AAC – advanced academic computing
An on-line service promoting the use of high-end computers in education and research.
telnet: isaac.engr.washington.edu
See also: ISAAC.

(5) MicroMUSE
An on-line multi-user simulated environment designed for educationalists.
telnet: michael.ai.mit.edu
login: guest

(6) Newton BBS
A bulletin board system for people teaching maths, science or computing
telnet: newton.dep.nl.gov
login: cocotext

(7) QUERRI
An educational database service, covering information on regional universities, as well as bibiliographic data, etc.
telnet: isn.rdns.iastate.edu (129.186.99.13)
login: querri

See also: children, **FEDIX**, **MOLIS**, software for teaching mathematics.

Educational leadership

An experimental service containing information on educational leadership. Articles on this subject can be accessed via the WAIS service.

wais: `ascd-education.src`

mail: `bhughes@pc.maricopa.edu`

See also: WAIS.

Electronic Frontier Foundation (EFF)

This foundation exists to promote personal freedom in the computer world, and fights for issues such as anti-censorship and the availability of public information.

ftp: `ftp.eff.org` (see: /pub)

login: `anonymous`

password: `<your mail-name>`

wais: `eff-documents.src`

mail: `ftphelp@eff.org`

Elements – periodic table

The periodic table of elements is available electronically from the interactive systems shown below:

telnet: (1) `camms2.caos.kun.nl 2034`

　　　　(2) `kufacts.cc.ukans.edu` (login: `kufacts`, select 'Ref. Shelf')

Encryption

Data encryption FAQs, FTP sites, details on the Unix DES encryption scheme, algorithms, and much more besides, are all available from the FTP sites documented here.

ftp: (1) `nic.funet.fi` (see: /pub/doc/cypherpunks/* and /pub/crypt/*)

　　　(2) `soda.berkeley.edu` (see: /pub/cypherpunks)

login: `anonymous`

password: `<your mail-name>`

Engineering – CERCNet

A service for people interested in engineering. Contains a job area, conference system, etc.

telnet: `babcock.cerc.wvu.wvnet.edu`

login: `cercnet`

mail: `jrs@cerc.wvu.wvnet.edu`

Environment related

A number of services exist:

(1) BioSphere newsletter

An archive has issues of this newsletter for viewing. Bibilographies are also available.

ftp: `mthvax.cs.miami.edu` (see: /pub/biosph)

login: `anonymous`

password: `<your mail-name>`

(2) Carbon Dioxide Information Analysis Centre
The CDIAC provides a wealth of information to both scientists and researchers regarding climatic change, CFCs damaging the ozone layer, and many other related areas.
ftp: `cdiac.esd.ornl.gov`
login: `anonymous`
password: `<your mail-name>`

(3) EPA – Environmental Protection Agency
The EPA has much material stored about environmental issues, including: chemical pollution, lake management and protection.
telnet: `epaibm.rtpnc.epa.gov`
login: `public`

(4) ERIN – environmental resources information network
ERIN maintains an archive containing newsletters (mainly in postscript file format) regarding environmental monitoring.
ftp: `huh.harvard.edu`
login: `anonymous`
password: `<your mail-name>`

(5) UN Rio Summit agenda
The United Nations agenda on the environment can be found through the WAIS service.
wais: `unced-agenda.src`

(6) Water quality education
The WAIS service also has access to a source concerning water quality (US based).
wais: `water-quality.src`

(7) Envirogopher
A gopher service that has amassed a large amount of material from the EnviroLink network. This is as large a system as you will ever find that concentrates on all environmental issues.
gopher: `envirolink.hss.cmu.edu`
login: `gopher`
password: `envirolink`

(8) Environmental issues gopher
This gopher server indexes a variety of books, essays and stories regarding environmental issues.
gopher: `gopher.well.sf.ca.us`
select: `Environment Issues and Ideas/`

(9) Finally, a list of USENET groups that deal in environmental issues.
(1) `talk.environment`
(2) `alt.save.the.earth`

See also: ECONET.

Epilepsy
General discussion forum on epilepsy. Some HIV/AIDS information is also available.
telnet: `debra.doc.ca`
login: `chat`

ERIC digest archives
Educationalists will find this useful. A number of short reports on the topic of education are accessible by WAIS and are produced by the ERIC clearinghouses in the US.
wais: (1) `ERIC-archive.src`
        (2) `eric.digest.src`

Erotica
An abundance of erotic material is passed over the Internet in both textual and image form. Such material is nearly always X-rated. Images can be found on USENET forums such as those shown below (those with `binaries` in the name indicate forums that post UU-encoded images, although `alt.sex.pictures` is also posted using UU-encoded ASCII images – see Chapter 8).
usenet: (1) `alt.binaries.pictures.erotica`
         (2) `alt.binaries.pictures.erotica.male`
         (3) `alt.binaries.pictures.erotica.female`
         (4) `alt.binaries.pictures.erotica.blondes`
         (5) `alt.sex.pictures`
         (6) `alt.sex`
         (7) `alt.sex.stories`
         (8) `alt.sex.bondage`
         (9) `alt.sex.wanted`
         (10) `alt.sex.masturbation`
         (11) `alt.sex.movies`
         (12) `alt.sex.sounds`
See: Homosexuality.
See also: Appendix G for an up-to-date list of USENET `alt.*` groups.

ESSENCE
A new WAIS based service. Essence implements a resource discovery system which indexes both ASCII and binary files. Essence is fed a keyword and file names and the internal text of files are searched for matches, which are then shown to the user. For more information:
mail: (1) `hardy@cs.colorado.edu`
        (2) `schwartz@cs.colorado.edu`
See also: WAIS.

Ethics

Computer ethics are discussed in a wide-ranging document available via FTP, as shown below:

ftp: `ariel.unm.edu` (see: `/ethics/*`)

login: `anonymous`

password: `<your mail-name>`

usenet: (1) `bit.listserv.ethics-l` (ethics listserv)

(2) `sci.research` (scientific ethics)

Fax server (FaxGate)

Send a facsimile (fax) via the Internet! For more details on this latest service mail the aliases here. The second alias (`awa.com`) are a commercial provider, and charge fees for their email-to-fax service. Mail them for more information.

mail: (1) `faxgate@elvis.sovusa.com`

message-body: `help`

(2) `info@awa.com`

message-body: simply ask for further information.

FDA BBS

A consumer BBS offering information on consumer rights, US news releases, AIDS information, vetinary issues, congressional abstracts, etc.

telnet: `fdabbs.fda.gov` (`150.148.8.48`)

login: `bbs`

FEDIX

A BBS offering information on minority help and educational scholarships, fellowships, funding and other general information (information is biased towards the US).

telnet: `fedix.fie.com` (`192.111.228.33`)

login: `fedix`

FINGER database

This service allows the user to query an on-line database of Internet-related material via the UNIX `finger` command.

finger: `help@dir.su.oz.au`

Food

See under: cooking and food.

See also: Appendix G – USENET groups under `rec.food.*` for many food-related discussion newsgroups.

Fred

The X.500 database directory of Internet users can be interrogated via this utility.

telnet: (1) `wp.psi.com`

(2) `wp2.psi.com`

See also: whois server, KNOWBOT information servers.

Free Software Foundation (FSF)

The FSF maintains an anonymous FTP archive of software that is free from license fees or royalty payments. Some of the GNU project software is also available.

ftp: `prep.ai.mit.edu` (see: `/pub`)

FREENET

A number of 'free-nets' exist, offering a range of regional and world information. This freenet has headline news from *USA Today*, including sports reviews, etc.

telnet: (1) `freenet-in-a.cwru.edu` (login: `visitor`)
        (2) `freenet-in-b.cwru.edu` (login: `visitor`)
        (3) `freenet-in-c.cwru.edu` (login: `visitor`)
        (4) `heartland.bradley.edu` (login: `bbguest`)
        (5) `yfn.ysu.edu` (login: `visitor`)
        (6) `freenet.lorain.oberlin.edu` (login: `guest`)

FTP – guest services

See: Guest FTP.

FTPmail – FTP via electronic mail

Three major sites for FTPmail reachable via email are given below. Send an email to the site shown with the message-body 'help' (no quotes) to see what command(s) are acceptable to the FTPmail server.

email:

(1) `ftpmail@decwrl.dec.com`
    message-body: 'help' – for more information
(2) `ftpmail@doc.ic.ac.uk`
    message-body: 'help' – for more information
(3) `bitftp@pucc.princeton.edu`
    message-body: 'help' for commands, or 'ftpsites' for a list of valid FTP sites around the world (long list)

See also: Guest FTP.

FUNET – Finland

FUNET maintains a massive archive of goodies reachable via FTP. Check this one out.

ftp: `ftp.uu.net`
login: `anonymous`
password: <your `mail-name`>

Games

See under: chess, chess server, GO server, diplomacy, MUD.

See also: Appendix G – USENET groups under `rec.games.*` for many dozens of games (computer and human).

Gardening

(1) The gardener's assistant
    An archive containing some PC horticultural software. Worth down-

loading if you are a green-fingered Internet user.

ftp: wuarchive.wustl.edu (/mirrors/msdos/database)

login: anonymous

password: <your mail-name>

(2) Horticultural engineering newsletter

Copies of this newsletter are available. Subjects include: seed planting, greenhouses and technical information on horticulture. See the 'PEN Pages' entry in the agriculture section for more details.

Genealogy/ancestry

Trace your family root's using the information, software and references in this FTP archive.

ftp: hallc1.cebaf.gov (see: /genealogy)

login: anonymous

password: <your mail-name>

Genetics bank

A huge medical genetic database containing information on DNA, etc.

telnet: genbank.bio.net (134.172.1.160)

login: GENBANK

password: 4NIGMS

mail: (1) gene-server@bchs.uh.edu

　　　 (2) retrieve@ncbi.nlm.nih.gov

　　　 (3) blast@ncbi.nlm.nih.gov

subject: help

Geography

(1) Geographic server

A worldwide geographic server offering information on a country-wide basis. It has population densities and other demographic information, etc.

telnet: martini.eecs.umich.edu 3000

(2) European postal codes

This FTP archive has a list of postal codes used throughout Europe.

ftp: nic.funet.fi (see: /pub/doc/mail/stamps/*)

login: anonymous

password: <your mail-name>

(3) Global land information systems (GLIS)

A database offering land maps of the US, graphs/statistics, as well as some geological information.

telnet: glis.cr.usgs.gov (152.61.192.54)

login: guest

(4) US geographic name server

This gopher server has demographic information, such as population densities for the US, etc.

gopher: gopher.gsfc.nasa.gov

select: Other Resources/US geographic name server/

Geology
(1)   COGS – Computer Orientated Geological Society COGS is an archive
        containing much information on the general topic of geology. The files
        in this archive will point you to other resources; one file you should
        download is called `internet.resources.earth.sci`. Also
        available are: software programs, images, etc.
        ftp: `csn.org` (see: `/COGS`)
        login: `anonymous`
        password: `<your mail-name>`
        mail: `cogs@flint.mines.colorado.edu`
(2)   Earthquake information
        Brings you up-to-date with all the latest earthquake information, e.g.
        locations and times, Richter scale measurements, etc.
        finger: `quake@geophys.washington.edu`
              `(128.95.16.50)`
        telnet: `geophys.washington.edu`
        login: `quake`
(3)   Paleomagnetic archive
        This on-line database has a wealth of material on rock strata around
        the world (primarily Soviet, Europe and the US).
        telnet: `earth.eps.pitt.edu`
        login: `search`

Georgetown Medical Library
Another medical database. General discussion arena, retrievable documentation, etc.
telnet: `mars.georgetown.edu` `(141.161.40.4)`
login: `medlib`
password: `dahlgren`
last name: `netguest`

GNU software project – PC software
GNU freely distributes its own version of the Unix operating system and
encourages software without any royalty payments. The archive shown here
deals in Unix-to-PC utilities.
ftp: `wuarchive.wustl.edu` (see: `/systems/ibmpc/gnuish/*`)
login: `anonymous`
password: `<your mail-name>`
See also: Free Software Foundation.

GO Server
Play an on-line game of 'GO' with a human opponent. Help is available for
those not versed.
telnet: (1) `icsib18.icsi.berkeley.edu 6969`
              `(128.32.201.46 6969)`
         (2) `cnam.cnam.fr 6969` `(192.33.159.6 6969)`

login: `<choose your own>`
password: `<choose your own>`

Gopher BBS lists

If you are searching for BBS systems to explore, use gopher to find those elusive sites that are reachable via the Internet. Simply log in into any gopher server and invoke veronica to search gopherspace for a term such as 'bbs' or 'bulletin board', and many hundreds of sources will be returned.

See: gopher servers, BBS, Internet BBS lists.

Gopher servers

The gopher system offers an interface into many Internet services and retrieves information without the user having to use ftp or `telnet` to access the information. Gophers are an excellent way of searching the Internet for general information on nearly every subject. If a gopher server does not start with 'gopher' and the machine you want cannot be located, replace the first part of the hostname with 'gopher', e.g. `finfo.tu-graz.ac.at` becomes `gopher.tu-graz.ac.at`, and see if this works (many sites are changing their machine names to 'gopher' to use more logical names).

telnet:
 (1) `camsrv.camosun.bc.ca` (134.87.16.4)
 (2) `ecnet.ec` (157.100.45.2)
 (3) `gopher.denet.dk` (129.142.6.66)
 (4) `nstn.ns.ca` (137.186.128.11, login: `fred`)
 (5) `gopher.th-darmstadt.de` (130.83.55.75)
 (6) `finfo.tu-graz.ac.at` (129.27.2.4, login: `info`)
 (7) `gopher.chalmers.se` (129.16.221.40)
 (8) `gopher.isnet.is` (130.208.165.63)
 (9) `gopher.sunet.se` (192.36.125.2)
 (10) `tolten.puc.cl` (146.155.1.16)
 (11) `gopher.brad.ac.uk` (143.53.2.5, login: `info`)
 (12) `siam.mi.cnr.it` (155.253.1.40)
 (13) `gopher.ora.com` (140.186.65.25)
 (14) `gopher.uv.es` (147.156.1.12)
 (15) `info.anu.edu.au` (150.203.84.20, login: `info`)
 (16) `ecosys.drdr.virginia.edu` (128.143.86.233)
 (17) `gopher.ohiolink.edu` (130.108.120.25)
 (18) `scilibx.ucsc.edu` (128.114.143.4)
 (19) `wsuaix.csc.wsu.edu`   (134.121.1.40,   login: `wsuinfo`)
 (20) `twosocks.ces.ncsu.edu` (152.1.45.21)
 (21) `arx.adp.wisc.edu` (login: `wiscinfo`)
 (22) `seymour.md.gov` (128.8.10.46)
 (23) `grits.valdosta.peachnet.edu` (131.144.8.206)
 (24) `gopher.unc.edu` (152.2.22.81)
 (25) `panda.uiowa.edu` (128.255.40.201, no login)

    (26) `envirolink.hss.cmu.edu` (login: `gopher`, password: `envirolink`)

    (27) `gopher.virginia.edu` (`128.143.22.36`, login: `gwis`)

    (28) `gopher.uiuc.edu` (`128.174.33.160`)

    (29) `infopath.ucsd.edu` (`132.239.50.100`, login: `infopath`)

    (30) `gopher.msu.edu` (`35.8.2.61`)

    (31) `gopher.ibmpcug.co.uk`

    (32) `gopher.ebone.net` (European gopher)

    (33) `gopher.ncc.go.jp` (`160.190.10.1`)

    (34) `gopher.tc.umn.edu` (one of the best gophers around)

    (35) `consultant.micro.umn.edu` (`134.84.132.4`)

    (36) `pfsparc02.phil15.uni.sb.de`

login: `gopher` (unless specified otherwise)

Keep up-to-date with gopher developments in general by emailing:

`gopher-news-request@boombox.micro.umn.edu`

usenet: `comp.infosystems.gopher`

Guest FTP – NSFNET relay (UK)

This guest FTP service allows users to retrieve files from Internet hosts via the command `ftp`, and then push these to UK NRS-registered hosts. An on-line help facility can be called up for more information. File downloading from remote sites is very fast. The NRS is the naming registration scheme used to register UK computers.

telnet: `sun.nsf.ac.uk`

login: `guestftp`

password: `guestftp`

GUTENBERG project

This is a project that hopes to give away a trillion electronic texts (etexts) by the year 2001. The texts are all famous and past literary works, e.g. Shakespeare, etc. Many current books such as Brendan Kehoe's *Zen and the Art of the Internet*, and the *New Hackers Dictionary* can also be found here, along with many thousands of other works by authors for whom their copyright has expired, e.g. H.G. Wells, Mark Twain and many, many more. Full text versions of the Bible and the Koran are also available.

ftp: (1) `mrcnext.cso.uiuc.edu` (see: `/pub/etext`)

      (2) `oes.orst.edu` (see: `/pub/etext`)

      (3) `info.umd.edu` (see: `/info/ReadingRoom/Fiction`)

login: `anonymous`

password: `<your mail-name>`

email: `dircompg@ux1.cso.uiuc.edu`

telnet: `info.umd.ude`

login: `info`

See also: Poetry.
Hackers Dictionary
See: GUTENBERG Project.
Ham radio
For ham radio enthusiasts. A service offering call-sign handbooks, among other things.
telnet: (1) `callsign.cs.buffalo.edu` 2000 (128.205.32.2 2000)
      (2) `ham.njit.edu` 2000 (128.235.1.10 2000)
      (3) `ns.risc.net` (155.212.2.2) (login: hamradio)
Handicap Service/Medical Literature
An FTP site containing miscellaneous medical information (and software) for downloading.
ftp: `handicap.shel.isc-br.com` (129.189.4.184)
login: anonymous
password: <your mail-name>
History
This gopher server in the UK stores details of events that happened on the same day as you query the server.
gopher: `uts.mcc.ac.uk`
select: Today's events in history.
HOLONET
HOLONET provide a wide range of networking services for Internet users. Apart from providing Internet access on a payment-by-subscription basis, HOLONET also provides FTP, UUCP/BBS contacts, and telnet services, to mention just a few. For more information on HOLONET you will have to subscribe.
telnet: `holonet.net` (157.151.0.1)
For more help with HOLONET, email any of the aliases shown here:
mail: (1) `terms@holonet.mailer.net` (terms/conditions)
      (2) `billing@holonet.mailer.net` (billings/costs)
      (3) `support@holonet.mailer.net` (support and help)
      (4) `access@holonet.mailer.net` (accessing HOLONET)
Homosexuality
usenet: `alt.homosexual`, `alt.politics.homosexuality`, `alt.sex.motss`
See also: erotica.
Hong Kong law
An archive containing the laws of Hong Kong, including the Hong Kong Bill of Rights. Also has software for reading articles in Chinese.
ftp: `ahkcus.org` (see: /hongkong/political)
ogin: anonymous
password: <your mail-name>

HP calculator BBS

Provided by Hewlett Packard for their calculator users. A handy BBS with a chat-mode option.

telnet: `hpcvbbs.cv.hp.com` (15.255.72.16)

login: `new`

HPCWire

Good database for general information on the Internet and other network-related services.

telnet: `hpcwire.ans.net` (147.225.1.51)

login: `hpcwire`

HYTELNET server

Hytelnet is the Hypertext data retrieval system which accesses a variety of Internet-related services via `telnet`. Hytelnet is useful in the location of OPACs in academic institutions around the world. All menus are based around countries and/or specific subjects.

telnet: (1) `access.usask.ca` (128.233.3.1)

       (2) `info.anu.edu.au` (150.203.84.20)

      login: `hytelnet`

wais: `hytelnet.src`

IBM PC Users Group (UK) – `ibmpcug.co.uk`

The IBMPCUG have a wide range of Internet-related goodies which are available on a subscription basis, such as: public-access Unix accounts, USENET feed, email, IRC, gopher server (see under gopher); and more services such as a WAIS server, and even WWW are all planned. An anonymous FTP archive is also available for Internet users.

telnet: (1) `rachel.ibmpcug.co.uk` (login – registered users)

       (2) `gopher.ibmpcug.co.uk` (gopher server)

login: `gopher`

ftp: `ftp.ibmpcug.co.uk`

login: `anonymous`

password: `<your mail-name>`

Images

(1) FTP site list for images

An excellent list of FTP sites that deal solely in images, and image utility programs.

ftp: `bongo.cc.utexas.edu` (see: `/gifstuff/ftpsites`)

login: `anonymous`

password: `<your mail-name>`

(2) Satellite imagery

These are widely available, many contain images taken by the space shuttle. Most are images of the planet earth.

ftp: (1) `ames.arc.nasa.gov`

       (see: `/pub/GIF/pub/SPACE/GIF/pub/space/CDROM`)

    (2) `sseop.jsc.nasa.gov`
    (3) `sanddunes.scd.ucar.edu` (see: `/pub`)
    (4) `pioneer.unm.edu` (see: `/pub/info`)
  gopher: (1) `gopher.gsfc.nasa.gov`
  select: NASA Information/Space images and information
See also: Appendix G – `alt.binaries.pictures.*` hierarchy.

INFO – Rutgers CWIS service
Large database offering on-line quotations database, thesauraus, and dictionary. Excellent for authors without copies of these books. Select Library at start.
telnet: `info.rutgers.edu` (`128.6.26.25`)

INFOSERV – Software server
A database offering on-line access to journals on Unix and Internet material. Good source of general network information.
telnet: `rusmv1.rus.uni-stuttgart.de` (`129.69.1.12`)
login: `infoserv` (or `softserv`)

Internet BBS lists
A really good list of bulletin board systems has been put together and can be accessed via FTP/email. This file is updated periodically and so is good to download every month or so. The second reference here is for Zamfield's Internet BBS list, another well-known guide to Internet BBS and general on-line services.
ftp: (1) `aug3.augsberg.edu` (see: `/files/bbs_lists`)
    (2) `lilac.berkeley.edu`   (see: `/help/cat/network/information/zamfield/zamfield_list`)
mail: `bbslist@aug3.augsberg.edu` (send anything and the list will be returned as soon as possible by their email server)
See also: BBS, Yanoff list.

Internet Books – on-line
Some Internet books are starting to come on-line in limited FTP form, e.g. some chapters from Tracey LaQuey's Internet book and the Zen (Brendan Kehoe's book). Mostly in ASCII format, although some may be compressed.
ftp: `world.std.com` (see: `/obs`)
login: anonymous
password: <your mail-name>

Internet FTP resource guide
An FTP site with masses of Internet sites, email addresses, etc. (most are compressed).
ftp: `nnsc.nsf.net` (see: `/resource-guide.txt.tar.Z`)
login: anonymous
password: <your mail-name>

Internet-related information
(1) Domain names

This WAIS archive allows you to search for Internet domain information.
wais: `domain-organizations.src`

(2) Internet mail guide
This FTP archive contains descriptions of electronic-mail addressing techniques, and how to send mail between different networks such as Compuserve, etc. A useful guide for all email users.
ftp: `ftp.msstate.edu` (see: `/pub/docs`)
login: `anonymous`
password: `<your mail-name>`

(3) Internet Society
An international organization set up to monitor the Internet's evolution. For more information email the address below:
mail: `isoc@nri.reston.va.us`

(4) Network Information Centre – on-line aid system
This service is run by NASA, and allows users to query a service known as the Address Matrix. The Address Matrix allows a mail address to be formatted, and given a source and destination address.
telnet: `dftnic.gsfc.nasa.gov`
login: `dftnic`

(5) NorthWest Net User Services Internet Guide
A list of Internet resources are maintained on this archive (some are in postscript and some are in compressed form). A useful archive to keep abreast of Internet resources.
ftp: `ftphost.nwnet.net` (see: `/nic/nwnet/user-guide/README*`)
login: `anonymous`
password: `<your mail-name>`

(6) Internet searching – article source
Many Internet guides are available here, e.g. *Zen and the Art of the Internet, The Hitchhikers Guide (RFC)*, etc.
wais: `internet_info.src`

(7) RFC – request for comment guides
RFCs are documents that explain all the workings of the Internet. There are hundreds of RFCs each covering an Internet-related topic. Most RFCs are ASCII, although some are postscript, and some are compressed. Files take the form RFCxxxx, where xxxx is the RFC number. Many archives maintain RFCs. Here are a selection:
ftp: (1) `nisc.sri.com` (see: `/rfc`, and see `mail`)
  (2) `nis.nsf.net` (password: `guest`, see: `/rfc`)
  (3) `nisc.jvnc.net` (see: `/rfc`)
  (4) `wuarchive.wustl.edu` (see: `/doc/rfc/*.Z`)
  (5) `src.doc.ic.ac.uk` (see: `/rfc/*.Z`)

(6) `nisc.sri.com` (see: `/rfc`)

(7) `nnsc.nsf.net` (see: `/rfc`)

login: `anonymous`

password: `<your mail-name>`

wais: (1) `internet-rfcs.src`

(2) `rfc-index.src`

You can get an RFC mailed to you by mailing the address below. Include the RFC number you require in the message-body (extensions are `.txt` for ASCII versions, and `.ps` for postscript format).

mail: (1) `mail-server@nisc.sri.com` (message-body: `send rfcxxxx.txt`, e.g. `send rfc1118.txt`)

(2) `service@rs.internic.net` (same commands)

(8) Internet Resource Guide

A guide prepared by the NSF (National Science Foundation). This service is for people offering new services on the Internet to register. A good place to keep abreast of new Internet services from one of the major Internet bodies.

wais: `internet-resource-guide.src`

(9) On-line resources mailing list

A mailing list where people advertise new Internet services (both public and subscription based).

wais: `online@uunet.ca.src`

mail: `request@uunet.ca` (to join mailing list)

(10) *Zen and the Art of the Internet*

Written by Brendan Kehoe, this book is one of the most well-known guides about life on the Internet.

wais: (1) `zen-internet.src`

(2) `internet_info.src`

InterNetwork mail guide

A service offering material on Internet sites and networks around the world.

telnet: `192.134.69.8 1643`

Internet world newsletter

A new newsletter service with book reviews. Good source to keep up with Internet gossip. Daniel Dern is the current editor, and is also the author of his own Internet book published by McGraw-Hill.

mail: `ddern@world.std.com` (all enquiries)

See also: Internet books–on-line.

Iowa political/stock-market service

A service with a stock-market flavour. A non-profit service (research only) offering a stock-market simulation program.

telnet: `ipsm.biz.uiowa.edu` (`128.255.44.2`)

IP address resolver

You can resolve Internet naming problems using this service. You send this service a site name by email, and hopefully the system will help you locate its IP address.

mail: (1) resolve@cs.widener.edu
        (2) dns@grasp.insa-lyon.fr

message-body: (1) help – for general help
               (2) site <address> – mails you the IP address of the site
                   in question

IRC telnet clients (Internet Relay Chat)

A useful service offering a relay service for chatting with other users. Some require a vt100/102 emulation, or at least an ANSI screen capability. Also note that most sites answer on a specific port.

telnet: (1) bradenville.andrew.cmu.edu (128.2.54.2)
         (2) ircclient.itc.univie.ac.at 6668
         (3) ircserver.itc.univie.ac.at 6668
         (4) irc.ibmcug.co.uk 9999
         (5) loligo.cc.fsu.edu 2010

See also: Chat servers.

ISAAC

An on-line service offering information for the academic computing community (IBM users). You must have an account in order to use this facility – all details will be given upon contact.

telnet: isaac.engr.washington.edu (128.95.32.61)
mail: isaac@isaac.engr.washington.edu

Israel information archive

An archive on many topics concerning Israel, e.g. the Palestine Liberation Organisation (PLO), Israel's Declaration of Independence, etc.

ftp: pit-manager@mit.edu (see: /pub/israel)
login: anonymous
password: <your mail-name>

JANET – Joint Academic Network (UK)

JANET is a large academic network that links all of the major UK universities together. JANET has links with the Internet through a number of gateways, and through use of the new JIPS (JANET IP) service. The JANET NEWS machine will tell you much about the services offered, which are extremely diverse (see also: NISS UK)). A gopher server is now available. You can place an anonymous FTP call to JANET to download an information file, or use email to request a help document (currently this is named M124) to be mailed to you.

telnet: 192.101.5.160 (janet.news machine)
mail: infoserv@janet.news
message-body: request M214
gopher: news.janet.ac.uk

JANET UK access

Calling the National Science foundation's gateway machine is the answer. You can access various OPACs and academic bulletin boards (such as BUBL) using this gateway.

telnet: `sun.nsf.ac.uk`

login: `janet`

password: `janet`

hostname: <a janet host, e.g. `uk.ac.city-poly.jewry-vax`>

See also: BUBL.

Japanese language software

Software for handling languages such as Japanese are available from a number of FTP archives. A notable one is shown below:

ftp: `monu6.cc.monash.edu.au` (see: `/pub/nihongo`)

login: `anonymous`

password: <your `mail-name`>

Jargon archive

The computing jargon dictionary for all computer users. This service can be accessed from WAIS. Includes many thousands of 'computerese' acronyms.

wais: `jargon.src`

See also: acronyms.

Jobs (employment) – USENET forums

The Internet advertises many positions, both commerical and academic alike. In the UK the jobs forum on USENET is `uk.jobs`, although `alt.jobs.offered` covers the globe. Note that jobs offered in `uk.jobs` are always computer oriented. Businesses can also advertise here for staff, and do, of course, already. The jobs forums are convenient for users, since you can email your CV, etc. to the appropriate employer/agency immediately.

KIDSNET

An archive for the younger Internet members. Maintains lists of information regarding fostering children, and other educational information.

wais: `kidsnet.src`

mail: `request@vms.cis.pitt.edu` (for enquiries)

KNOWBOT information servers

KNOWBOT servers are 'white-page' services that offer information about users on the Internet (useful for finding people and contact details such as phone numbers, email addresses, etc.).

telnet: (1) `sol.bucknell.edu 185`

      (2) `nri.weston.va.us 185`

      (3) `cnri.reston.va.us 185`

More information on the KNOWBOT service is available from an FTP archive at MIT; this includes all the known KNOWBOT servers in existence.

ftp: `nri.reston.va.us` (see: `/rdroms`)

login: anonymous
password: `<your mail-name>`
See also: Fred.

Law-related information

(1) Law library (US)

Law library services and an FTP site for legal research. Has computer law, and state-by-state laws for the United States.
telnet: `liberty.uc.wlu.edu` (`137.113.10.35`)
login: `lawlib`
ftp: `sulaw.law.su.oz.au` (see: `/pub/law`)
login: anonymous
password: `<your mail-name>`

(2) LawNet

Another legal service, this one offering catalogue access to users. US law is covered in this service.
telnet: `sparc-1.law.columbia.edu` (`128.59.176.78`)
login: `lawnet`

(3) Project Hermes

US Supreme Court decisions all on-line.
wais: `supreme-court.src`

See also: Hong Kong law.

Library catalogues

On-line catalogues are ubiquitous. These FTP sites have documents related to retrieving such catalogues.
ftp: (1) `dla.ucop.edu` (see: `/pub/internet/libcat-guide`)
(2) `ftp.unt.edu` (see `/library/libraries.txt`)
(3) `ariel.unm.edu` (see: `/library/internet.library`)
login: anonymous
password: `<your mail-name>`

Library of Congress (US)

A large on-line service offering access to the US Library of Congress information. A VT100 terminal emulation is assumed.
telnet: `dra.com` (`192.65.218.43`)
See also: Library of Congress (US)– gopher service.

Library of Congress (US) – gopher service

A gopher with information on this subject area can be found at the address below.
telnet: `marvel.loc.gov` (`140.147.2.15`)
login: `marvel`

LIBS

A service which allows access to many Internet services, both FTP and `telnet` based. Check this service out if you want a friendly interface to the many Internet resources.

telnet: `nessie.cc.wwu.edu`
login: `LIBS`

List of lists

Many interest groups exist on the Internet. Grab the document shown below for an up-to-date list. Available via FTP and WAIS. The definitive mailing lists can be obtained from here, but be aware these are very large (over 1 Mb uncompressed; around 400K in the `.Z` format).

ftp: `ftp.nisc.sri.com` (192.33.33.22) (see: `/netinfo/ interest-groups*`)
login: anonymous
password: <your mail-name>
wais: `lists.src`

LISTSERV groups

A list of discussion groups available on the BITNET network can be found here. Information on network access is also available.

ftp: `lilac.berkeley.edu` (see: `/netinfo`)
login: anonymous
password: <your mail-name>

Literature

The best place to look for works of literature must be Project Gutenberg, which has many thousands of electronic texts (etexts) from authors past and present. See: GUTENBERG project, computer literature.

Lunar and Planet Institute information

A service containing information on astronomy, astrophysics, geophysics and geology.

telnet: `lpi.jsc.nasa.gov` (192.101.147.11)
login: `lpi`

Macintosh (Mac) related

The Macintosh (Mac) range of computers are well served on the Internet, in the form of archives and USENET forums. A gopher server is also available at one site. Primary sites include:

ftp: (1) `mac.archive.umich.edu` (see: `/micros/mac`)
　　 (2) `wuarchive.wustl.edu` (see: `/micros/mac`)
　　 (3) `src.doc.ic.ac.uk` (see: `/packages/mac/umich`)
login: anonymous
password: <your mail-name>

Miscellaneous Mac software can also be found at FTP sites (anonymous) including:

ftp: (1) `f.ms.uky.edu`
　　 (2) `emily.rice.edu`
　　 (3) `cadre.dsl.pittsburgh.edu`
　　 (4) `brownvm.brown.edu`
　　 (5) `arisia.xerox.com`

login: anonymous
password: <your mail-name>
telnet: gopher.uis.itd.umich.edu (gopher server)
login: gopher (if required)
USENET forums include:
  (1) comp.binaries.mac
  (2) comp.sys.mac.announce
  (3) comp.sys.mac.hardware

Magazines
  (1) *UnixWorld* open computing magazine
      UUNET archives the listings from the Hands-On Help section in
      UnixWorld magazine. For instructions on how to get them, retrieve the
      file /published/unix-world/downloading via anonymous
      FTP.
      ftp: ftp.uu.net (192.48.96.1)
      login: anonymous
      password: <your mail-name>
  (2) *Byte*
      Back issues from this leading-edge computer magazine are available
      from the following archive. Most issues are compresed into the .ARC
      format.
      ftp: oak.oakland.edu (see: /pub/misc/byte)
      login: anonymous
      password: <your mail-name>
  (3) *PC Magazine*
      Back issues from the popular Ziff–Davis magazine are available here.
      ftp: ftp.cco.caltech.edu
      login: anonymous
      password: <your mail-name>

Mail fileservers
email: smiley@uiuc.edu
message-body: Filesend: help, or Filesend: list for FTP server
             lists.
See also: FTPmail.

Mailing lists
A number of mailing lists exist to which you can be added in order to receive
network information. Some of the largest mailing lists available are shown below:
ftp: (1) ftp.nisc.sri.com (see: /groups/email)
     (2) sri.com (see: /netinfo/interest-groups)
login: anonymous
password: <your mail-name>

Matchmaker service

A matchmaker service for people is now available on the network. All correspondence is conducted via email initially. You may be surprised to know that 20 couples have now tied the knot after initially corresponding over the net, so go on, give it a try!

mail: `perfect@match.com`

Message-body: `SEND FORM` (for information and questionnaire)

Mathematics – E-MATH service

Mathematics BBS offering maths software reviews and general discussion forum.

telnet: `e-math.ams.com` (130.44.1.100)

login: `e-math`

password: `e-math`

Medicine educational technology network

Forums on medical technology and education can be found on this service.

telnet: `etnet.nlm.nih.gov`

login: `etnet`

MEDLINE – medical database

MEDLINE contains citations from medical articles and abstracts. Over 4000 journals were used to compile the bulk of the information found here.

telnet: (1) `melvyl.ucop.edu`

(2) `lib.dartmouth.edu`

(3) `library.umdnj.edu` (login: `LIBRARY`)

(4) `utmem1.utmem.edu` (login: `HARVEY`)

Meteorology

See under: weather.

Microsoft Windows

Software for MS Windows is abundant on the Internet. Here are some of the main FTP sites for such material, including bitmaps and other wall-papers, utilities and games.

ftp: (1) `wuarchive.wustl.edu` (see: `/systems/ibmpc/win3/*`)

(2) `ftp.cica.indiana.edu` (see: `/pub/pc/win3`)

login: `anonymous`

password: `<your mail-name>`

Molecular biology – WAIS/USENET services

WAIS has many sources for biology-related forums. See also: 'genetics bank' entry. Examples on WAIS include:

wais: (1) `bionic-directory-of-servers.src` (main list)

(2) `bionic-sequence-bibiliography.src`

(3) `bionic-arabidopis.src`

(4) `bionic-biosci.src`

(5) `biosci.src`

(6) `biology-compunds.src`

(7) `EC-enzyme.src`
(8) `bionic-ai-research.src`

usenet: see Appendix G – USENET lists for the `bionet.*` biological forums.

MOLIS

The minority on-line information service.
telnet: `fedix.fie.com` (192.111.228.33)
login: `molis`

Monochrome

Monochrome BBS/Chat service. This service is run by City University UK, although others are in existence. It has on-line chat facilities, games, discussion forums and Internet-related information. Sixty users are currently supported at any one time. Recommended. Make sure you have an ANSI or VT100 screen emulation running.
telnet: `mono.city.ac.uk` (138.40.17.1)
login: `mono`
password: `mono`

Other `telnet` servers at City UK include:
telnet: (1) `138.40.11.1`
         (2) `138.40.21.1`
         (3) `138.40.31.1`
         (4) `138.40.41.1`

Movie database service

A service run from the IBM PC users group in the UK allows you to interrogate a database of movie-related information, e.g. actor/credit information, movie facts, etc.
mail: `movie@ibmpcug.co.uk`
message-body: `HELP` (for more information)

MUD – Multi-user dimension games

MUD is an acronym for multiple user dialogue (dungeon or dimension). MUDs are multi-user games (accessed via `telnet` to facilitate multiple players) which allow you to meet and chat with other users, explore a maze-like environment, fight with monsters, solve puzzles, etc. When you join, you become a character who is actually a character in the game.
telnet: (1) `actlab.rtf.utexas.edu` 4000
         (2) `benford.cc.umanitoba.ca` 9165
         (3) `cix.compulink.co.uk` 4242
         (4) `copper.denver.colorado.edu` 4000
         (5) `dszenger9.informatik.yu-muenchen.de` 4242
         (6) `hobbes.linfield.edu` 7777
         (7) `marcel.stracken.kth.se` 4000
         (8) `mccool.cbi.msstate.edu` 4000
         (9) `mud.stracken.kth.se` 4000

```
(10) next5.cas.muohio.edu 4000
(11) nova.tat.physik.uni-tuebingen 4242
(12) peabrain.humgen.upenn.edu 4000
(13) sun1.cstore.ucf.edu 4000
(14) seismo.soar.cs.smu.edu 9393
```

gopher: (1) `actlab.rtf.utexas.edu 3452`

(2) `cix.compulink.co.uk 3450`

(3) `castor.tat.physik.uni-stuttgart.de`
select: Fun & Games/GameServer in Tuebingen, login: as GAMES

(4) `consultant.micro.umn.edu`

(5) `dszenger9.informatik.yu-muenchen.de 7000`
select: Fun & Games/Games/MUDs

(6) `nova.tat.physik.uni-tuebingen 4242`
select: Enter Nightfall

usenet: (1) `rec.games.mud.misc` (MUD miscellany)

(2) `rec.games.mud.announce` (announcements)

(3) `rec.games.mud.admin` (administrative news)

email: `mudlist@glia.biostr.washington.edu` (info)

ftp: `caisr2.caisr.cwro.edu` (see: /pub/mud)

login: anonymous

password: `<your mail-name>`

MUD documentation via gopher

A good gopher server at the University of Tuebingen in Germany, has all the documentation you will ever need on the MUD world.

gopher: (1) `nova.tat.physik.uni-tuebingen.de 4242`
select: Documents and Papers about MUDs\

(2) `actlab.rtf.utexas.edu`
select: Virtual Spaces: MUD\

MUD gopher server

This gopher server will locate all the available MUDs and will then initiate a `telnet` call to the one of your choice.

gopher: `solaris.rz.tu-clausthal.de`

select: Studenten/Mud-Servers/

MUDWHO user server

MUDWHO servers are scattered all over the place. They keep track of users who are using MUD systems all over the Internet.

telnet: (1) `actlab.rtf.utexas.edu 6889`

(2) `af.itd.com 6889`

(3) `amber.ecst.csuchico.edu 6889`

(4) `nova.tat.physik.uni-tuebingen.de 6889`

(5) `riemann.math.okstate.edu 6889`

Music

(1) Guitar chords

An FTP site for guitar players (see: /pub/guitar). Contains a variety of information on chords, music, etc.

ftp: ftp.nevada.edu (131.216.1.11)

login: anonymous

password: <your mail-name>

(2) Acoustic guitar digest

Another archive for guitar players.

ftp: casbah.acns.nwu.edu (see: /pub/acoustic-guitar)

login: anonymous

password: <your mail-name>

(3) Indian classical music

An archive available through WAIS; contains a database of Indian compact disks. Music includes: Shankar, Hindustani and Karnatic.

wais: indian-classical-music.src

(4) MIDI information

An archive on Musical Instrument Digital Interface (MIDI) is available on WAIS for computer-generated music.

wais: midi.src

(5) The music of Bob Dylan

This FTP server has a massive archive on Bob Dylan, along with CD and book lists.

ftp: ftp.cs.pdx.edu

login: anonymous

password: <your mail-name>

(6) Folk music

A selection of information relating to folk music, including lyrics, publications, folk music societies and much more besides. All available via gopher.

gopher: gopher.uwp.edu

select: Music Archives/Folk Music Files and pointers/

(7) Lyrics archives and servers

The largest archives that deal with song lyrics from many thousands of singers and groups can be found here.

gopher: (1) gopher.uwp.edu

select: Music Archives/Lyrics Archives/

(2) consultant.micro.umn.edu

select: Fun & Games/Music/Music Archives/Lyrics

ftp: (1) ocf.berkeley.edu (see: /pub/Library/Lyrics/*)

(2) ftp.uwp.edu (see: /pub/music/lyrics/*)

login: anonymous

password: <your mail-name>

(8) Music for sale
CDs, records, and other recordings for open sale and swapping.
mail: (1) mwilken@silver.ucs.indicana.edu
subject: BOOTHELP
(2) used-music-server@cs.ucsb.edu
subject: help
See also: Appendix G – USENET groups under rec.music.* for many different musical tastes from Afro-Latin to synthesizers.

NASA – space information
A number of NASA services exist on the Internet. Here are a selection.
(1) NASA/IPAC extragalactic database (NED)
Information on over 200 000 astronomical objects are held here. Bibliographic information is also available.
telnet: denver.ipac.caltech.edu
login: ned
(2) NASA Headline News
Daily press-releases from NASA, updated continually.
finger: nasanews@space.mit.edu
(3) NASA SpaceLink
See the latest NASA news, including launch dates for the shuttle. Also has satellite news.
telnet: spacelink.msfc.nasa.gov (192.149.89.61)

NASDA
The National Space Development Agency of Japan offers space-related information via telnet.
telnet: nsaeoc.eoc.nasda.go.jp (133.56.72.1)
login: nasdadir

National Education BBS
A general educationalists forum.
telnet: nebbs.nersc.gov (128.55.160.162)
login: guest

NETFIND – user lookup service
Finds names and organizations from just a username and some domain hints. An excellent program which will tell you the hosts on a given network. It will also attempt to contact mail and finger servers running on host machines to find out user information. A typical search pattern may be: 'root kent uk', to find user 'root' (superuser) at Kent University, UK. A lot of (useful) output can be generated.
telnet:
(1) redmont.cis.uab.edu (138.26.64.4)
(2) mudhoney.micro.umn.edu (134.84.132.7)
(3) bruno.cs.colorado.edu (128.138.243.151)

```
(4)  ds.internic.net (198.49.45.10)
(5)  archie.au (139.130.4.6)
(6)  netfind.oc.com (192.82.215.92)
(7)  macs.ee.mcgill.ca (132.206.61.15)
(8)  malloco.ing.puc.cl (146.155.1.43)
(9)  netfind.vslib.cz (147.230.16.1)
```
(10) nic.uakom.cs (192.108.131.12)
(11) nic.nm.kr (143.248.1.100)
(12) nic.uakom.sk (192.108.131.12)
(13) lincoln.technet.sg (192.169.33.6)
(14) dino.conicit.ve (150.188.1.10)
(15) monolith.cc.ic.ac.uk (155.198.5.3)
(16) sun.uakom.cs (192.108.131.11)
login: netfind

NetLib

A software-via-email service, i.e. like FTPmail.
email: netlib@uunet.uu.net or netlib@ornl.gov
message-body: 'send index' – for more information
See also: FTPmail.

News

(1) Clarinet
     Clarinet is the Internet's business and news-related hierachy. See:
     Appendix G – USENET listings under clari.*.
(2) French language press review and French news
     A selection of news summaries in the French press are available on
     this gopher server. Updated daily. Many other news stories are avail-
     able through the gopher menus available here. The second gopher
     server also publishes many stories from the French press on a daily
     basis.
     gopher: (1) gopher.msu.edu
                 select: News & Weather/Electronic Newspapers/
                          General Newspapers/French Language
                          Press Review/
             (2) yaleinfo.yale.edu
                 select: Internet Resources/News & Weather/France/
(3) Russian news
     Moscow news articles in English are available from this gopher server.
     gopher: gopher.msu.edu
     select: News & Weather/Electronic Newspapers/Sample Newspapers/
             Moscow News/
     See also: RUSSIA
(4) US newspaper articles
     Articles from the *USA Today* paper are available via the same gopher

service as previously mentioned. Articles from the *Washington Post* are also available.

gopher: `gopher.msu.edu`

select: News & Weather/Electronic Newspapers/Sample Newspapers/ [*USA Today/* or *Washington Post/*]

NewsMail servers (USENET posting service)

You can post messages to USENET forums using this service. Good for people without direct USENET transmission facility, but who have email access.

mail: `[group]@cs.utexas.edu`

For example you could mail `rec.pets.cats` using the mail name: `rec.pets.cats@cs.utexas.edu` etc.

See also: NNTP news servers.

NeXT computers – FAQs

A set of FAQs are maintained about NeXT computers on this service. The service can only currently be accessed via WAIS.

wais: `NeXT.FAQ.src`

mail: `akers@next2.oit.unc.edu`

NICOL

Access to a collection of Internet resources through a single menu system.

telnet: `nisc.jvnc.net` (`128.121.50.7`)

login: `nicol`

NICOLAS

Network information server. Also has an on-line aid system for Internet users.

telnet: `dftnic.gsfc.nasa.gov` (`128.183.10.3`)

login: `dftnic`

NISS (UK)

NISS UK (National Information on Software and Services) offer many Internet related services, and have guest `telnet` facilities, not to mention to a wide range of academic information and services such as WAIS and Archie, to name but a few. Also has access to BUBL, the network bulletin board database.

telnet: `niss.ac.uk`

See also: BUBL, WAIS, Archie servers.

NNI bulletin board system

The NII, or National Information Infastructure bulletin board system (BBS) is run to provide the public with documentation, schedules, committee reports and even the minutes of meetings about setting up the 'information superhighway' of the future, a vast US project promoted by the Clinton and Gore political campaign. It is accessible via gopher or via `telnet`.

gopher: `iitf.doc.gov`

telnet: `iitf.doc.gov` (login: `gopher`)

See also: President of the USA, Whitehouse press releases.

NNTP news servers

These servers allow users with `telnet` to read messages from all the USENET forums. Some also allow users to post to USENET groups while on-line. Useful if you do not have a USENET feed or the necessary news-reading software. The prefix 'news' on the site name can be tried (along with port 119) with other hosts to see if they have a NNTP server (most of these were found this way). You can also sometimes leave off the `news` prefix just as long as the port number 119 is still included.

telnet: (1) `quip.eecs.umich.edu` 119 (141.212.99.8 119)
      (2) `vaxc.cc.monash.edu.au` 119 (130.194.1.23 119)
      (3) `suntan.ec.usf.edu` 119 (131.247.10.40 119)
      (4) `munnari.oz.au` 119 (128.250.1.21 119)
      (5) `etl.go.jp` 119 (192.31.197.33 119)
      (6) `news.fu-berlin.de` 119
      (7) `news.demon.co.uk` 119
      (8) `news.ibmpcug.co.uk` 119

NOAA

The National Oceanic and Atmospheric Administration. A large on-line database of relevant material.

telnet: `nodc.nodc.noaa.gov` (140.90.235.10)
     `esdinl.nodc.noaa.gov` (140.90.235.168)
login: `NOAADIR`

NODIS

A server with menu-driven access to the National Space Science Data Center. A wealth of data and scientific material can be found here.

telnet: (1) `nssdc.gsfc.nasa.gov` (128.183.36.25)
     (2) `nssdca.gsfc.nasa.gov` (128.183.36.23)
login: `nodis`

Nuclear Data Center (NDS)

Data on all things nuclear. A government-to-public service based in the US.
telnet: `bnlnd2.dne.bnl.gov` (130.199.112.132)
login: nndc

Nutrition

International food and nutrition database. A database of articles concerning nutrition in food. Has some HIV and AIDS-related nutrition information.
telnet: `psupen.psu.edu` (128.118.36.5)
login: PNOTPA (or PPREPNET)
mail: `support@psupen.psu.edu` (for all queries)

Oceanic Information Center (OIC)

An on-line database to the world's oceans.
telnet: `delocn.udel.edu` (128.175.24.1)
login: `info`
See also: NOAA.

Oceanography
  See: NOAA, Oceanic Information Center (OIC).
OPACs (on-line public access catalogues)
  See: library catalogues.
Oracle (USENET)
  The USENET oracle deals with all user problems related to the use of the
  USENET service. The Oracle will attempt to answer all those tricky Internet
  questions.
  mail: `oracle@cs.indiana.edu`
  subject: `help`
O'Reilly and Associates, Inc. (publishers)
  See: books.
OSS-IS
  A useful FTP service, containing files dealing with Internet sites, FAQs,
  FTP lists and the like.
  ftp: `soafl.ssa.gov`
  mail: `info@soafl.ssa.gov`
  message-body: `send index` (for an index)
Oxford Dictionary (concise version)
  The 8th edition of the Oxford Dictionary can be searched on-line to look up
  word meanings, derivations, etc.
  telnet: `info.rutgers.edu`
  select: `library`, then `reference`
Oxford Dictionary of Familiar Quotations
  Another useful service, especially for authors, writers, etc. Feed it keywords
  to find that quote.
  telnet: `info.rutgers.edu`
  select: `library`, then `reference`
Oxford Thesaurus
  Use this service to look up equivalent meanings for words. See also: Roget's
  Thesaurus.
  telnet: `info.rutgers.edu`
  select: `library`, then `reference`
PC Magazine – executable DOS utilities
  A 'mirror' of disk utilities release with *PC Magazine* are stored for downloading. All software is for the PC/DOS platform.
  ftp: `oak.oakland.edu` (see: `/pub/msdos/pcmag`)
  login: `anonymous`
  password: `<your mail-name>`
PC Magazine – text material
  On-line versions of *PC Magazine* are available to users via anonymous FTP.
  ftp: `wuarchive.wustl.edu`

login: anonymous
password: <your mail-name>

PDIAL document (dial-up access)

See: dial-up Internet access.

Personal advertisements (worldwide)

Since the forums are global, you may search the headers of articles for specific country codes, e.g. .uk, etc. in order to see articles for sale in your own country.

usenet: (1) alt.personals
        (2) alt.personals.ads
        (3) alt.personals.misc

Pets

The USENET forum rec.pets covers this area. Extensions of this forum are rec.pets.cats, rec.pets.dogs, etc. Some other references are available, however:

(1) Aquaria

Fish-keeping information including plant and water information, feeding instructions, buyer guides, etc.

ftp: caldera.usc.edu (see: /pub/aquaria/*)
login: anonymous
password: <your mail-name>

(2) Birds and bird-keeping

A variety of information relating to bird-keeping, including book and magazine reviews, terminology and feeding information.

ftp: rtfm.mit.edu (see: /pub/usenet/news.answers/
    pets-birds-faq/*)
login: anonymous
password: <your mail-name>

(3) Cats

Another FAQ, this one for our feline friends.

ftp: rtfm.mit.edu (see: /pub/usenet/news.answers/
    cats-faq/*)
login: anonymous
password: <your mail-name>

(4) Dogs

Another FAQ, this one for our canine friends.

ftp: rtfm.mit.edu (see: /pub/usenet/news.answers/
    dogs-faq/*)
login: anonymous
password: <your mail-name>

(5) Reptiles

The USENET group rec.pets.herp deals with reptile pets.

THE A–Z INTERNET RESOURCE GUIDE

Physics
The HEPNet facility is a special resource for physicists, and is available via the World-Wide-Web (WWW) service at CERN, the famous Particle Physics Laboratory.
telnet: `info.cern.ch`
See also: World-Wide-Web servers

Pictures
See: images

Pirate radio
usenet: `alt.radio.pirate`

Poetry
A collection of poems are available through WAIS. Poets include: Yeats, Eliot and Byron. Project Gutenberg also has on-line literature via FTP and WAIS.
(1) WAIS
    wais: `poetry.src`
(2) Project Gutenberg
    ftp: (1) `mrcnext.cso.uiuc.edu` (see: `/etext`)
         (2) `quake.think.com` (see: `/pub/etext`)
    login: `anonymous`
    password: `<your mail-name>`
    wais: `proj-gutenberg.src`
    mail: `hart@vmd.cso.uiuc.edu`
See also: GUTENBERG Project.

Poland
'PigKuli' is a collection of documents concerning Poland. A variety of material exists about Poland in the form of press reviews and the like.
ftp: `mthvax.cs.miami.edu` (see: `/pub/poland`)
login: `anonymous`
password: `<your mail-name>`

Politics
(1) CNI–Coalition for Networked Information Political events in the US Congress can be accessed here.
    telnet: `a.cni.org`
    login: `brsuser`
(2) Politics and the network community
    A gopher server specializing in information regarding politics with a bias on computing and networking.
    gopher: `gopher.well.sf.ca.us`
    select: `Politics/`
(3) USENET Archives
    usenet: (1) `alt.politics.british`
            (2) `alt.politics.clinton`
            (3) `alt.politics.correct`

    (4) `alt.politics.democrat`
    (5) `alt.politics.elections`
    (6) `alt.politics.homosexuality`
See also: Presidential information, US., Appendix G – USENET lists under
`alt.politics.*`

Pop music
See: Billboard charts, Appendix G – the A–Z USENET guide, under
`rec.music.*`.

President of the USA
You can now email the President directly using the email address below.
Don't expect an immediate reply, however.
mail: `president@whitehouse.gov`
See also: NNI bulletin board system, presidential information, Whitehouse
        press releases.

Presidential information, US
You can use WAIS to obtain speeches of former Presidents, such as Mr
Bush, and of course more up-to-date data. Quayle quotes are available at
`princeton.edu` via FTP (always good for a laugh).
wais: `bush-speechs.src`
wais: `clinton-speeches.src`
See also: President of the USA, NNI bulletin board system, Whitehouse
        press releases.

Public domain (PD) software sources
PD software is diverse on the Internet. Use Archie to find potential
programs, although the novice may want to examine the UK PDSOFT
centre at Lancaster University, which has many thousands of PD programs
for the PC and other platforms.
See also: UK Software Archive (Lancaster).

Public UNIX machine access
Some universities are opening up public-access machines to allow users
access to FTP, `telnet`, etc. Some systems will require registration before
Unix shell access, although some are less stringent and you can be up-and-
running immediately.
telnet:
(1) `nyx.cs.du.edu` (130.253.192.68)
    login: `new`
(2) `hermes.merit.edu` (35.1.48.150)
    login: `newuser`
(3) `m-net.ann-arbor.mi.us` (35.208.17.4)
    login: `newuser`
(4) `halcyon.com`
(5) `panix.com`
See also: BBS – bulletin board systems.

Queer resource directory

A service offering information on Gay rights. Also has information on HIV/ AIDS, etc.

ftp: `nifty.andrew.cmu.edu` (see: `/pub/QRD/README`)

Religion

Religous sources and archives are listed here.

(1) ANU – Asian religions bibiliography. A collection of bibilographic material pertaining to the Asian and Buddhist religions.

wais: `ANU-Asian-Religions.src`

mail: `wais@coombs.anu.edu.au`

(2) King James Bible

A complete Kings James Bible is available on-line for searching off-line as an FTP archive, or on-line via gopher or WAIS. The second FTP archive shown lists some statistics for the KJ Bible, including phrase and word counts, etc.

ftp: (1) `wuarchive.wustl.edu` (see: `/pub/bible/README`)

(2) `oak.oakland.edu` (see: `/pub/bible/kjvcount.txt`)

login: `anonymous`

password: `<your mail-name>`

gopher: (1) `joeboy.micro.umn.edu`

select: `/Ebooks/By Title/King James Bible`

(2) `consultant.micro.umn.edu`

select: Libraries/Electronic Books/By Title/King James Bible/

wais: `Bible.src`

(3) The Koran (Quran)

A translation by M.H. Shakir is available from an FTP archive and via WAIS. A separate file contains each chapter. The text in the first archive was originally scanned in, so expect some minor text errors.

ftp: (1) `quake.think.com` (see: `/pub/etext/koran`)

(2) `oes.orst.edu` (see: `/pub/data/etext/koran/koran`)

(3) `ocf.berkeley.edu` (see: `/pub/Library/Religion/ Koran`)

login: `anonymous`

password: `<your mail-name>`

wais: `Quran.src`

(4) The Book of Morman

A WAIS version of this entire source is available for searching on-line, and there are numerous FTP archives.

wais: `Book_of_Morman.src`

ftp: (1) `gatekeeper.dec.com` (see: `/.2/micro/msdos/ simtel20/books/mormon12.zip`)

        (2) `ocf.berkeley.edu` (see: `/pub/Library/Religion/`
           `Book_of_Morman`)

(5) The Torah

An archive of the Tanach in Hebrew can be found on this FTP archive
for downloading.

ftp: `nic.funet.fi` (see: `/pub/doc/bible/hebrew`)

login: anonymous

password: `<your mail-name>`

(6) Bible quiz

A program that asks over a thousand different biblical questions can be
found at this FTP archive.

ftp: `oak.oakland.edu` (see: `/pub/bible/bible.arc`)

login: anonymous

password: `<your mail-name>`

(7) Biblical texts

Here are some other FTP sites that keep complete text listings of the Bible.

ftp: (1) `oak.oakland.edu` (see: `/doc/bible/journey.arc`)

      (2) `ocf.berkeley.edu` (see: `/pub/Library/Religion/*`)

(8) Pagan religion

You can join a mailing list on this subject by mailing the alias below.

mail: `pagan-request@drycas.club.cc.cmu.edu`

message-body: `SUBSCRIBE <your mail-name>`

Roget's Thesaurus

Another on-line thesaurus, this one is part of project Gutenberg.

wais: `roget-thesaurus.src`

See also: GUTENBERG project.

RUSSIA

See: Soviet archives.

San Diego supercomputer information

A wealth of information pertaining to supercomputers can be found here,
e.g. the CRAY XMP/YMP, etc.

wais: `San_Diego_Super_Computer_Center_Docs.src`

Science

Many science-related archives and facilities exist on the Internet. Here are a
selection.

(1) History of science server

A catalogue of many well-known scientific papers all gathered together
in a single archive.

ftp: `fatman.hs.jhu.edu`

login: anonymous

password: `<your mail-name>`

(2) Scientific database BBS

A scientific BBS for social and natural scientists alike. Various discussion groups exist, including: database technology, earth sciences, astronomy, and much more besides. Upon logging in you will have to create your own log-in name.

telnet: `scid3b.eid.anl.gov`
login: `cocotext`
password: `WISDM`

(3) Scientific articles – general

Book reviews and other scientific articles can be found in this gopher server, among other things.

gopher: `gopher.well.sf.ca.us`
select: Science/

(4) Science and technology information system (STIS)

STIS has a range of scientific material, with a technological bias to its information. STIS is an interactive system run by the US Government, and is accessed via `telnet`. A gopher interface is also available.

telnet: `stis.nsf.gov`
login: `public`
gopher: `stis.nsf.gov`
select: Science/

Science fiction (SF)

A variety of archives exist for SF material. Here are a selection:

(1) Science fiction reviews

An archive of discussions on SF book reviews, mainly through email.

ftp: `brolga.cc.uq.oz.au` (see: `/pub/sfguide6.tar.Z`)
login: `anonymous`
password: `<your mail-name>`
wais: `Science-Fiction-Series-Guide.src`
mail: `farrell@coral.cs.jcu.edu.au`

(2) Science fiction newsgroup

Archives of the USENET science fiction group `rec.arts.sf.reviews` can be found here. Get the README file to see how the archive is organized, or search it through WAIS.

ftp: `turbo.bio.net` (see: `/sf-reviews`)
login: `anonymous`
password: `<your mail-name>`
wais: `sf-reviews.src`

(3) Star Trek archive

An archive for all trekkies. You will find images (X11 format), games (X-based), and an abundance of discussion material on the past and present Star Trek series (can't beat the old series, though). The `telnet` resource has many reviews and synopses of this cult series.

ftp: (1) `coe.montana.edu` (see: `/pub/STARTREK`)

(2) `mac.archive.umich.edu` (has some Star Trek)
login: anonymous
password: `<your mail-name>`
finger: `franklin@ug.cs.dal.ca` (for random Star Trek quotes!)
telnet: `panda.uiowa.edu`
select: 'General Information' and then 'Star Trek Reviews'

SDDAS
A software research service. Data display and analysis seems to the flavour of this interactive service.
telnet: (1) `espsun.space.swri.edu 540`
              (`129.162.150.99 540`)
          (2) `espsun.space.swri.edu 1000`
              (`129.162.150.99 1000`)

Sex
See: erotica.

Shakespeare's written works
Here are a selection of the great bard's work:
(1) The complete works of Shakespeare, all on-line. telnet: `lib.dartmouth.edu`
(2) Dartmouth College (plays and sonnets) telnet: `library.dartmouth.edu` (`129.170.16.11`)

Simpsons' archive
I don't know anyone who would want to access this, although information on credits, bibliographies and episode summaries are available to fans of this animated series (personally, it drives me mad).
ftp: `ftp.cs.widener.edu` (see: `/pub/simpsons`)
login: anonymous
password: `<your mail-name>`
wais: `simpsons.src`

Skiing FAQs
A series of FAQs regarding skiing information are available from the FTP site below.
ftp: `ski.utah.edu`
login: anonymous
password: `<your mail-name>`

Smileys
Smileys are small character annotations which accompany mail and news messages on the Internet. They are used nearly everywhere, and are widely accepted. Created and catalogued by David Sanderson (O'Reilly books), Smileys can be used to express your feelings in textual messages, for example: sad `:-(`, happy `:-)`, etc. A list of smileys are available from the FTP archive shown here, and a selection can be found in Appendix A. The gopher resource has a massive list of smileys.

ftp: `ftp.uu.net` (see: `/usenet/comp.sources.misc/`
`volume23/smiley`)
login: `anonymous`
password: `<your mail-name>`
gopher: `pfsparc02.phil15.uni-sb.de`
select: INFO-SYSTEM BENUTZEN/Fun/Cartoons/Smilies :-)/
See also: Appendix A – under 'Smiley'.

Software archives – various platforms
(1) Commodore Amiga – games, tools, source code and much more.
  ftp: `wuarchive.wustl.edu` (see: `/systems/amiga/*`)
  login: `anonymous`
  password: `<your mail-name>`
(2) Apple II – games, demos, source-code, documentation, etc.
  ftp: `ccosun.caltech.edu` (see: `/pub/apple2/*`)
  login: `anonymous`
  password: `<your mail-name>`
(3) CPM – for users of the CP/M OS
  ftp: `oak.oakland.edu` (see: `/pub/cpm/*`)
  login: `anonymous`
  password: `<your mail-name>`
(4) Commodore 64 and 128 – games and other utilities en masse
  ftp: `ccosun.caltech.edu` (see: `/pub/rknop/*`)
  login: `anonymous`
  password: `<your mail-name>`
(5) Macintosh – games, utilities, source-code and more
  ftp: `oak.oakland.edu` (see: `/pub2/macintosh`)
  login: `anonymous`
  password: `<your mail-name>`
(6) PC (DOS/Windows, etc.) archives
  There are only two places to really look.
  ftp: (1) `wsmr-simtel20.army.mil` (see: various places)
       (2) `wuarchive.wustl.edu` (see: `/systems/ibmpc/*`)
  login: `anonymous`
  password: `<your mail-name>`

Software server
You can carry out on-line software searches using this service.
telnet: `askhp.ask.uni-karlsruhe.de` (`192.67.194.33`)
login: `ask`

Software for teaching mathematics
An archive of software to help in the teaching of mathematics. Software
supplied is mostly for IBM PCs and compatible machines.
ftp: `wuarchive.wustl.edu` (see: `/etc/math`)

login: anonymous
password: <your mail-name>

Sounds

Sound files in a variety of formats (e.g. WAV and VOC) are available via ftp and email. The principle ftp site for sound files is sounds.sdsu.edu (as well as the larger FTP sites – see Chapter 3). USENET forums for sounds include:

usenet:
(1) alt.binaries.sounds.misc (miscellaneous sounds)
(2) alt.binaries.sounds.erotica (erotic sounds)

Soviet archives and information

An archive containing a variety of information on Russia in the past, including the Chernobyl disaster, The Cold War Era, the Cuban Missile Crisis, etc.

ftp: seq1.loc.gov (see: /pub/soviet.archive)
login: anonymous
password: <your mail-name>

People interested in Soviet news and history may want to subscribe to the USENET forum soc.culture.soviet. Many commercial services allow the user to read Soviet news, such as TASS and EPIC via the site oclc.org (a commerical site – $75 per year, $3 a search). The SOVSET' network at sovset.org is a massive on-line database of Soviet and Eastern European information. It is a commercial service, and average costs are $15 per hour. The information available is diverse and includes: macro-economic data, E. Europe Newsletter, The Express Chronicle, Moscow phone directory, and over 30 conference areas. The service is heavily used by governmental users in a wide range of countries.

Space

(1) Space Telescope Science Institute (STSI)
    An archive containing information about the Hubble Telescope. Also has software, FAQs, and space data, as well as some space images.
    ftp: stsci.edu
    login: anonymous
    password: <your mail-name>

(2) European Space Agency (ESA)
    ESA offers a variety of space-related services, including information retrieval from its extensive file area, plus details of the Arianne rocket/satellite program, etc.
    telnet: esrin.esa.it

(3) FIFE information system
    This is a good service to get hold of raw data from satellites, shuttle flights, etc. FIFE has many other searchable databases and archives.
    telnet: pldsg3.gsfc.nasa.gov

login: FIFEUSER

See also: NASA – space information; astronomy.

Spacemet

Another galactic BBS, with information and discussion on space-related topics.

telnet: `spacemet.phast.umass.edu` (`128.119.50.48`)

Space-shuttle images

A selection of space-shuttle images are available via anonymous FTP from these sites:

ftp: (1) `sseop.jsc.nasa.gov`

(2) `ames.arc.nasa.gov`

login: `anonymous`

password: `<your mail-name>`

SPAN

You can access the Space Physics Analysis Network from here. The host machine is a DEC/VAX.

telnet: `nssdca.gsfc.nasa.gov` (`128.183.36.23`)

login: `SPAN_NIC`

Sport – general

Sport schedules (US NBA)

On-line sports schedules. Details of games playing today are available (relevant to the US only). Once in, type 'help' or simply press <Return> for game details.

telnet: (1) `culine.colorado.edu 859` (NBA)

(2) `culine.colorado.edu 860` (NHL)

(3) `culine.colorado.edu 862` (MLB)

(4) `telnet: culine.colorado.edu 863` (NFL)

See also: Appendix G – USENET groups under `soc.sport.*` for all of the most popular sports.

Star Trek

The cult science fiction series has its place on the Internet in various FTP archives. You can beam up all manner of information.

See: science fiction – Star Trek; television – Star Trek.

STIS

A scientific-flavoured BBS.

telnet: `stis.nsf.gov` (`128.150.195.40`)

login: `public`

Stock-market information

See: business information.

SuperNET

A BBS for supercomputing people. See the 'San Diego' service on supercomputing also. This BBS has mail, a journal review, and some good software for downloading.

telnet: `supernet.ans.net`
login: `supernet`

Television

(1) Television shows archive
An archive containing material on many past and present TV series, such as *The Prisoner, Lost in Space*, etc. Most of the material is based upon situation comedy.
ftp: `coe.montana.edu`
login: `anonymous`
password: `<your mail-name>`

(2) Nielsen TV ratings
This finger server allows you to see various TV ratings. These are updated weekly.
finger: `normg@halcyon.halcyon.com`

(3) Situation comedies and series scripts
The actual scripts from a wide variety of TV shows and series are available from this FTP archive, e.g. *Star Trek, Monty Python, Twin Peaks, Cheers*, etc.
ftp: `nic.funet.fi` (see: `/pub/culture/tv+film/*`)
login: `anonymous`
password: `<your mail-name>`
See also: Simpsons archive.

(4) UK sitcom lists
This gopher resource maintains a list of every situation comedy shown in the UK.
gopher: `info.mcc.ac.uk`
select: Miscellaneous/The definitive list of UK sitcoms/

TeX – Unix typesetting software

TeX is used widely in the Unix world as a typesetting package for documents. A number of FTP archives support TeX material. Check these out first:
ftp: (1) `hcfdemo.hcf.jhu.edu`
      (2) `gpu.utcs.toronto.edu`
      (3) `gatech.edu`
      (5) `ctrsci.utah.edu`
      (6) `cs.washington.edu`
      (9) `a.cs.uiuc.edu`
login: `anonymous`
password: `<your mail-name>`
gopher: `niord.shsu.edu`
select: TeX related materials

Thai Yunnan project

Research notes on the collection of the Thai Yunnan anthropology project.

Data on ethnic groupings in SE Asia, religion and language.

wais: ANU-Thai-Yunnan.src

Trade Wars – multi-user game

Play this new multi-player game on Trade Wars BBS system based in Switzerland.

telnet: nelsons.cern.ch 2002 (128.141.8.248 2002)

See also: MUD.

Travel

The main FTP sites for travel information (and leads to other network resources) are:

ftp: (1) ftp.cc.umanitoba.ca (see: /pub/rec-travel/*)

(2) rtfm.mit.edu (see: /pub/usenet/rec.answers/travel/*)

usenet: (1) rec.travel (general travel and tourism)

(2) rec.travel.air (air travel discussed)

(3) bit.listserv.travel-l (listserv mailing list)

Tropical storm forecast

Storm forecasts for the Atlantic ocean can be called up here.

finger: (1) forecast@typhoon.atmos.colostate.edu

(2) forecast@129.82.107.24

UFOs – unidentified flying objects

Keep up-to-date with all the UFO sightings around the world using this interactive service and FTP resource.

telnet: grind.isca.uiowa.edu

login: iscabbs

ftp: grind.isca.uiowa.edu (see: /info/paranet/*)

login: anonymous

password: <your mail-name>

usenet: alt.alien.visitors, alt.paranormal, alt.out-of-body, etc.

See also: NASA, Appendix G – USENET listings.

UK Net – Kent University

Kent University have recently set up UK Net to access the Internet. The network primarily advertises its links to USENET, although other Internet-based services are also in use. For more information on how to subscribe to UK Net, email the alias shown below.

mail: uknet@ukc.ac.uk

UK Software Archive – Lancaster University

One very useful archive which has many shareware and freeware programs for the AMIGA, BBC, PC, UNIX and ATARI platforms is based at Lancaster University. Each machine type has its own directory in the / micros subdirectory.

ftp: micros.hensa.ac.uk (see: /micros)

login: `ftp`

password: `hensa`

UKUUG archive – Imperial College London

The UKUUG has an extensive FTP archive and UNIX shell access for users (with access to uuencoding, UNIX compress, etc.). All files can be accessed via FTP or from a UNIX shell, so you can encode and compress files before FTPing them afterwards (you can store files in the `/tmp` directory for this purpose).

ftp: `src.doc.ic.ac.uk` (`146.169.2.1`)

login: `anonymous`

password: `<your mail-name>`

telnet: `src.doc.ic.ac.uk` (limited shell-access)

login: `sources`

UMD information database

A general purpose information server, although offering specific information on US Supreme Court decisions.

telnet: `info.umd.edu` (`128.8.10.29`)

login: `info`

UNC BBS

Another legal database, this one offers US Library of Congress facts.

telnet: `launchpad.unc.edu` (`152.2.22.80`)

login: `launchpad`

United Nations (UN) gopher

This gopher server carries press releases, conference news, and a wealth of information about the UN and how it operates.

gopher: `nyworkl.undp.org`

University College London – Computer Centre (ULCC)

Guest FTP service. I thought I'd include my old college, since it has a good Guest FTP facility. Once you have got the file you want, you can 'push' it to a NRS-registered host in the UK to retrieve it. Make sure you note the JANET-like addresses.

See also: Guest FTP.

UCL also have an FTPable machine with some very good public software collections:

ftp: `bells.cs.ucl.ac.uk`

login: `ftp`

password: `<your mail-name>`

See also: UKUUG service.

Unix booklist

A list of books that are currently available. This seems to be applicable to the US only, but is still useful for US books that are distributed overseas. Contains publisher details, ISBN numbers and all the normal information. Contributions are welcome.

ftp: `ftp.rahul.net` (see: `/pub/mitch/YABL/yabl.Z`)

login: anonymous

password: `<your mail-name>`

See also: books.

Unix manuals

You can view any page of the SunOS 4.1 Unix manual using this service on WAIS. Useful for those without direct Unix access to the man (manual) utility.

wais: `unix-manual.src`

Unix reference card

Another source of the standard Unix commands.

ftp: `uscelx.sdsu.edu` (see: `/pub/doc/general`)

login: anonymous

password: `<your mail-name>`

See also: `vi` reference card.

USENET – general information sources

The main USENET forums available on WAIS are:

`comp.*` – Computing subjects

`rec.*` – Recreation related

`alt.*` – Alternative subjects

Other USENET-related information on the Internet:

(1) USENET software – history and sources

A list of USENET-reading software. This list is updated regularly, and is a useful archive to keep abreast of newsreading software.

ftp: `pit-manager.mit.edu` (see: `/pub/usenet` `/news.answers/usenet-software`)

login: anonymous

password: `<your mail-name>`

(2) USENET FAQs

A selection of frequently asked questions (FAQs) on USENET are available on WAIS. Look here first if you are a novice USENET user.

wais: `usenet-FAQ.src`

(3) USENET periodic posting archives (PPA)

This archive contains information on USENET forums and discussion groups.

ftp: `pit-manager.mit.edu` (see: `/pub/usenet`)

login: anonymous

password: `<your mail-name>`

wais: `jik-usenet.src`

(4) What is USENET?

Another USENET archive, this one containing background information on USENET (from a historical viewpoint).

ftp: `pit-manager.mit.edu` (see: `/pub/usenet/news/announce/newusers`)

login: anonymous
password: <your mail-name>
(5) USENET via gopher
Access USENET via gopher.
gopher: gopher.msu.edu
select: News & Weather/USENET News
See also: oracle (USENET).

UUNET FTP archives

UUNET maintain one of the largest FTP archives on the Internet. The file
ls-lR.Z is a compressed list of all that is available. The WAIS service also
has sources for UUNET. UUNET has much to offer – beware of doing a
dir command in the /usenet directory since it is very long.
ftp: ftp.uu.net
login: anonymous
password: <your mail-name>
wais: (1) uunet.src
       (2) wuarchive.src (Washington archive)

veronica

Veronica (very easy rodent-orientated net-wide index to computerized
archives) is a newish Internet service which offers a keyword search of
most of the gopher server menus from the majority of gophers in existence.
Veronica is similar to Archie in many respects, except that it searches
gopher servers rather than anonymous FTP sites. The veronica system
cannot be accessed through a direct telnet call; instead you must use an
existing gopher client (by telnetting to that instead), such as consul-
tant.micro.umn.edu and accessing the veronica service situated
there.
telnet: consultant.micro.umn.edu (or others)
login: gopher
select: veronica from the main-menu
It is important to note that veronica does not index the actual core material of files, rather it indexes the menu-titles of existing gopher systems. At
the the time of writing over 250 gopher servers are now indexed, and over
500 gopher servers exist worldwide.
See also: gopher servers.

vi reference card

The Unix screen editor vi is documented on this gopher server.
gopher: uts.mcc.ac.uk
select: Experimental and New Services/VI Reference card/
See also: Unix manuals.

VMS – machine access

VMS (virtual memory system) is an operating system found on the VAX
(Virtual Address eXtension) range of machines. Not many on-line VMS

services exist (or are documented) although this one is. It is operated on a payment-by-subscription (credit card). Features: GNU C++ compiler, VAX BASIC, FORTRAN, PASCAL, COBOL, `telnet`, FTP, `mail`, `finger`, `talk`, IRC, USENET, and a public BBS.

telnet: `ids.net` (`155.212.1.2`)

login: GUEST

mail: `info@ids.net` (for more information)

WAIS

(1) WAIS servers

The wide area information server is one of the best information retrieval tools on the Internet, allowing users to access a variety of documents and services through FTP and `telnet`. Some USENET forums can also be retrieved. Good for non-FTP people, although you must really have `telnet` to access WAIS. A VT100 terminal emulation (or ANSI) must really be used. To access WAIS issue a `telnet` call to one of the following WAIS servers:

telnet: (1) `quake.think.com` (`192.31.181.1`)

(2) `nnsc.nsf.net` (`128.89.1.178`)

(3) `wais.funet.fi` (`128.214.6.100`)

(4) `sunsite.unc.edu` (`152.2.22.81`)

(5) `swais.cwis.uci.edu` (`128.200.15.2`)

(6) `info.funet.fi` (`128.214.6.100`)

(7) `kudzu.cnidr.org` (`128.109.130.57`)

login: `wais` (or sometimes `swais`)

(2) WAIS FTP server

A prototype FTP server for WAIS is up-and-running for file location and examination. Similar to the Archie service with an immediate file download capability.

wais: `quake.think.com-ftp.src`

(3) WAIS directory of servers

A list of the most well-known WAIS servers are available as a WAIS source. Additional information on the WAIS service is also available in numerous other sources.

wais: (1) `directory-of-servers`

(2) `au-directory-of-servers`

(4) WAIS search

See: Essence protocol.

(5) WAIS source summary

A list of FTP archives that contribute facts to the WAIS sources can be found at this site. This can help speed up your searches.

ftp: (1) `kirk.bond.edu.au` (see: `/pub/Bond_Uni/doc/wais/*`)

(2) `archive.orst.edu` (see: `/pub/doc/wais/*`)

login: anonymous
password: <your mail-name>
Weather
(1) US weather
Also has earthquake and ski-forecast information. A menu-driven service.
telnet: downwind.sprl.umich.edu
          3000 (141.212.196.177 3000)
wais: weather.src
(2) Weather – NCAR data support section server
The National Centre for Atmospheric Research has a wealth of data
and software to aid meteorological research. Read the README file
first, since there is just so much material.
ftp: ncardata.ucar.edu
login: anonymous
password: <your mail-name>
(3) Weather maps – images
Actual maps can be FTP'd anonymously – the file format is GIF
(Graphics Interchange Format). Other information such as raw
weather-data is nearly always available. The quake.think.com
FTP site has dozens of such images. You will, of course, need an image-
viewer to see such images on your computer – see Chapter 8 for details
on these.
ftp: (1) vmd.cso.uiuc.edu (see: /wx for GOES-7 data)
      (2) unidata.ucar.edu (see: /images)
      (3) auriele.soest.hawaii.edu (see: /pub/avhrr/
          images)
      (4) quake.think.com (see: /proj/wais/db/weather/
          weather/*.GIF)
      (5) snow.nohrsc.nws.gov (snow images in: /pub/snow)
      (6) vmd.cso.uiuc.edu (infra-red imagery in: /wx)
login: anonymous
password: <your mail-name>
(4) Weather – network sources for meteorology and weather
An excellent archive for meteorologists. This archive contains the
sources for software, images, data, and climatical studies.
ftp: bears.ucsb.edu (see: /pub/windsurf/netweather)
login: anonymous
password: <your mail-name>
(5) Australian weather reports
Weather reports, forecasts, river conditions, etc.
telnet: vicbeta.vic.bom.gov.au 55555

Webster's Dictionary

Access the popular dictionary to search for word definitions, etc. (be sure to use capital letters for all searches).

telnet: `cs.indiana.edu 2627 (129.79.254.191 2627)`

Whitehouse press releases

Access press information, speeches, and general news from the US administration. Subscribe using the email address given below, and press releases will be sent on to you periodically.

email: `almanac.esusda.gov`

message-body: `subscribe wh-summary`

Whois server list

Whois servers help locate people on Internet sites. Many servers exist, and are documented in a number of files available from anonymous-FTP. Type 'whois' when using telnet-based access to access.

ftp: `sipb.mit.edu` (see: `/pub/whois/whois-servers.list`)

telnet: `rs.internic.net (198.41.0.5)`

See also: whois server, knowbot information servers, NETFIND.

Whois server

Using this WHOIS server machine you can find out a complete user-entry, given a single username. A number of other services on this machine exist; use the command 'whois' to initiate a person search.

telnet: `nic.ddn.mil (192.112.36.5)`

mail: `service@nic.ddn.mil`

Subject: `help`

World news

See: Appendix G – clarinet USENET groups (`clari.*`).

World-Wide-Web servers

The WWW offers a 'hyper-text' search of many people, topics, and places. A very good service to locate information on a wide range of general topics.

telnet: (1) `info.cern.ch (128.141.201.74)`

       (2) `www.njit.edu (128.235.163.2)`

       (3) `vms.huji.ac.il (128.139.4.3)`

       (4) `info.funet.fi (128.214.6.100)`

       (5) `fatty.law.cornell.edu (132.236.108.5)`

       (6) `ukanaix.cc.ukans.edu (129.237.1.30)`

       (7) `sun.uakom.cs (192.108.131.11)`

       (8) `www.bradley.edu (136.176.5.252)`

login: www (this may not be required)

Yanoff list – Internet services guide

An up-to-date guide of Intenet services via `telnet`, `ftp`, and email, get hold of the Yanoff list via FTP.

ftp: `csd4.csd.uwm.edu` (see: `/inet_services`)

login: `anonymous`

password: <your mail-name>

mail, finger: yanoff@csd4.csd.uwm.edu

Yellow Pages server

This server offers an interface into the abundance of Internet resources and services (a *Yellow Pages* style guide to services).

telnet: wugate.wustl.edu (128.252.120.1)

login: services

Zen and the Art of the Internet

See: Internet related.

ZIB Electronic Library

A German interactive software library. Networked to other libraries around the Internet.

telnet: elib.zib-berlin.de (130.73.108.11)

login: elib

ZModem protocol

This protocol for file transfer can be implemented in languages such as C, and the source code for ZModem is available along with details of similar protocols, e.g. X and YModem from the FTP archive shown below.

ftp: oak.oakland.edu (see: /pub/misc/zmodem)

login: anonymous

password: <your mail-name>

Appendix E
A–Z anonymous FTP listings

This small appendix contains listings of many popular FTP sites around the world along with a list of interesting files and/or software utilities that can be downloaded from that site. The Archie program can be used with the site command to list such FTP hosts also, and this is the best way of keeping up-to-date with new FTP hosts. Lists of FTP hosts for specific machine platforms can be found at the end of the list (sites marked with an asterisk (*) are the major repositories for the software sites listed later). As well as the software shown, these FTP sites may also house other files and applications. It is best to choose a site and have a browse yourself (see Chapter 3 on FTP for more details).

If you find that a site no longer exists, it is probably the machine that no longer exists, not the site's network. In such a case try cutting off the machine name from the leftmost part of the hostname, and try again, e.g. zug.ai.mit.edu becomes ai.mit.edu. If no such name is found by FTP, try cutting the name again to leave the bare hostname—in our context we would be left with mit.edu. If this is not found then you can be sure that the site in question has gone. This method may not give rise to the file(s) you were looking for since they were originally stored on a different machine; however, you could always try posting an email to the postmaster of the site to ask where the old machine now resides.

FTP site	IP number	Files and utilities
a.cs.uiuc.edu	128.174.252.1	TeX, dvi2ps, gif, texx2.7, Amiga, gnu-make, GNU stuff
a.isi.edu	26.3.0.103	info-ibmpc (Tenex)
accuvax.nwu.edu	129.105.49.1	PibTerm 4.1.3
ads.com	128.229.30.16	Mailing lists, GNU, etc.
aeneas.mit.edu	18.71.0.38	GNU, emacs, kerberos
aerial.unm.edu	192.31.154.1	Bibliographic data-bases (/library)
ahwahnee.stanford.edu	36.56.0.208	PC-IP interface specs
ai.toronto.edu	128.100.1.65	SunSpots, Sunpatches
ajpo.sei.cmu.edu	128.237.2.253	ADA in abundance
albanycs.albany.edu	128.204.1.4	Usenet: comp.graphics
allspice.lcs.mit.edu	18.26.0.115	RFC1056 (PCMAIL), MIT SNMP
ames.arc.nasa.gov	128.102.18.3	pcrrn, GNU grep, conf, grep, xfer, zmo-dem protocol
apple.com	130.43.2.2	WORM papers, Mac stuff
aramis.rutgers.edu	128.6.4.2	RFCs, etc.
arisia.xerox.com	13.1.100.206	Sunfixes, Mac, Lisp, TCP/IP
arizona.edu	128.196.128.118	Icons, Prolog
b.scs.uiuc.edu	128.174.90.2	LaTex
bach.berkeley.edu	128.32.135.1	Amiga related
bbn.com	128.89.0.122	UUmap program
berlin.acss.umn.edu	128.101.193.1	NeXT stuff, antiVirus
bitsy.mit.edu	18.72.0.3	WORM papers
bmc1.bmc.uu.se	130.238.96.1	VMS news, drivers over Decnet, X.25 and SLIP for CMU TCP/IP v6.3
boulder.colorado.edu	128.138.238.18	Sun, Esperanto, Ghostscript PS
brownvm.brown.edu	128.148.128.40	Mac stuff
bu-it.bu.edu	128.197.2.40	Sun386i, Unix games
bugs.nosc.mil	128.49.16.1	Minix (Unix clone) for PC
cadre.dsl.pittsburgh.edu	130.49.128.1	Jove editor for the Mac
cayuga.cs.rochester.edu	192.5.53.209	Xfig, LaTeX styles, Jove
ccvax1.ncsu.edu	128.109.153.4	Vax, Unix ARC com-pressor (login: public)

FTP site	IP number	Files and utilities
celray.cs.yale.edu	128.36.0.25	Ispell, word dictionary
chalmers.se	129.16.1.1	RFCs, whois server
charon.mit.edu	18.80.0.13	Perl stuff, xdvi
cheddar.cs.wisc.edu	128.105.2.113	Lisp stuff, X11 courier fonts
cheops.cis.ohio-state.edu	128.146.8.62	Usenet: comp.sources, alt.sources, Unix-PC stuff
citi.umich.edu	35.1.128.16	Webster dictionary
clutx.clarkson.edu	128.153.4.3	Turbo C stuff
cmns.think.com	131.239.2.100	StarLisp simulator
cod.nosc.mil	128.49.16.5	PC stuff, military phonelist
crocus.waterloo.edu	129.97.128.6	STEVIE (vi-clone)
cs.bu.edu	128.197.2.1	Telecom archives
cs.cmu.edu	128.2.222.173	MS-DOS interrupt list, zoo archive
cs.orst.edu	128.193.32.1	X-Lisp
cs.utah.edu	128.110.4.21	WORMs, Amiga, Forth, UtahRaster graphics system
cs.washington.edu	128.95.1.4	TEX, netinfo
cs.yale.edu	128.36.0.3	UUCP paths
csli.stanford.edu	36.9.0.46	Gandalf stuff
ctrsci.utah.edu	128.110.192.4	Tex fonts, GNU make
cunixc.cc.columbia.edu	128.59.40.130	MM mailer, Kermit
cygnusx1.cs.utk.edu	128.169.201.12	GCC debugger
dartvax.dartmouth.edu	129.170.16.4	rn newsreader, mail, etc.
devvax.tn.cornell.edu	192.35.82.200	tn3270 (telnet for IBM370)
dinorah.wustl.edu	128.252.118.101	X11R3 stuff
dla.ucop.edu		Library OPACs (/pub/internet)
dorm.rutgers.edu	128.6.4.7	NCSA telnet, Waterloo TCP/IP
dsl.cis.upenn.edu	130.91.6.12	GIFs, IBM
elbereth.rutgers.edu	128.6.4.61	Sci-Fi works, Star-Trek guides
emil.csd.uu.se	130.238.64.4	Old GNU, X v10
emily.rice.edu	128.42.10.2	Mac
eng.clemson.edu	130.127.8.11	Sendmail source
eru.mt.luth.se	130.240.0.9	Gnews 19, plp, gcc
expo.lcs.mit.edu	18.30.0.212	X Windows, portable bitmaps

FTP site	IP number	Files and utilities
f.ms.uky.edu	128.163.128.6	Mac archive, IBM, Unix-PC, etc.
freja.diku.dk	129.142.96.1	GNU, X11R3, TeX 2.9, nn, RFCs
ftp.demon.co.uk		KA9Q, PKZIP, MS-DOS/UNIX, etc.
ftp.iastate.edu		Music lyrics (/pub/lyrics)
ftp.ibmpcug.co.uk		386i BSD software repository
ftp.nevada.edu	131.216.1.11	Guitar chords (/pub/guitar)
ftp.nisc.sri.com	192.33.22.22	Email lists (/netinfo)
ftp.sura.net		Internet: 'How to...' guides
ftp.uwp.edu		Music lyrics
funet.fi	128.214.1.1	MS-DOS PD archive, Minix PD, NFS, RFCs, Amiga stuff BSD-sources, NeWS-software
gaak.lcs.mit.edu	18.26.0.33	Ethernet codes
gang-of-four.stanford.edu	36.8.0.118	gcc, Usenet: rec.humor.funny
gatech.edu	128.61.1.1	GNU, RFCs, TeX
gatekeeper.dec.com	16.1.0.2	X11, recipes, cron, C sources
giza.cis.ohio-state.edu	128.146.8.61	X11R3, PEX
gpu.utcs.toronto.edu	128.100.100.1	TeX, C++, Ksh, Unix games
grape.ecs.clarkson.edu	128.153.13.196	Opus BBS, MS-DOS, graphics (lots)
gregorio.stanford.edu	36.8.0.11	Vmtp-ip, IP-multicast
gtss.gatech.edu	128.61.4.1	Amiga rexx stuff
gw.ccie.utoronto.ca	128.100.63.2	Cold fusion papers (pub/cld.fsn)
hamlet.caltech.edu	192.12.19.3	Nansi (for VMS)
handicap.shel.isc-br.com	129.189.4.184	Handicap information, software and medical information
hcfdemo.hcf.jhu.edu	128.220.2.15	Unix-PC related
hemuli.atk.vtt.fi	130.188.52.2	HP-UX stuff, BSD ported programs HP-UX (finger, gcc, rdist, etc.) TPS (TeX to postscript)
hipl.psych.nyu.edu	128.122.132.2	Jove in /pub (v4.9)

FTP site	IP number	Files and utilities
hotel.cis.ksu.edu	129.130.10.12	XBBS, MS-DOS, Unix-PC stuff
hubcap.clemson.edu	130.127.8.1	GIF images, RFCs
hurratio.tde.lth.se	192.36.121.22	GNU stuff, Elisp stuff
husc6.harvard.edu	128.103.1.56	PC IP, Apple II, uumap
hydra.helsinki.fi	128.214.4.29	TeX, X, Usenet: archives for: comp.sources.[misc,sun, unix], comp.binaries.ibm.pc
ibm1.cc.lehigh.edu	128.180.2.1	Virus-L programs/archives
icarus.riacs.edu	128.102.16.8	SLIP, macdump, Xpostit
interviews.stanford.edu	36.22.0.175	InterViews X toolkit
isi.edu	128.9.0.32	Lisp
isy.liu.se	130.236.1.3	GNU stuff, screen v2.0, ftpd, TIFF image library.
iuvax.cs.indiana.edu	129.79.254.192	Unix ARC decompressor, etc.
ix1.cc.utexas.edu	128.83.1.21	Amiga related
ix2.cc.utexas.edu	128.83.1.29	Amiga related
j.cc.purdue.edu	128.210.9.2	Usenet: comp.sources.[unix,x, Amiga] Elm mailer, uupc
jpl-devvax.jpl.nasa.gov	128.149.8.43	Perl sources
jpl-mil.jpl.nasa.gov	128.149.1.101	Tex, Mac, GNU, X11
june.cs.washington.edu	128.95.1.4	TeXhax, SmallTalk
jyu.fi	128.214.7.5	Unix, Atari, Amiga, Mac, MUD, Nethack v3.x game
kampi.hut.fi	128.214.3.9	DES routines (unrestricted), GNU Pascal stuff
kolvi.hut.fi	128.214.3.7	KA9Q, Kermit, radio amateurs
kth.se	130.237.72.201	Sendmail v5.x
kuhub.cc.ukans.edu	129.237.1.10	VMS news
labrea.stanford.edu	36.8.0.47	X-Windows stuff
lambda.lanl.gov	128.165.4.10	Internet tools (/pub/inet)

FTP site	IP number	Files and utilities
lancaster.andrew.cmu.edu	128.2.13.21	CMU PCIP, RFC1073 telnetd
linc.cis.upenn.edu	130.91.6.8	TeX, Unix-PC related
lll-lcc.llnl.gov	128.115.1.1	SUN Local Users Group archive
loke.idt.unit.no	129.241.1.103	Amiga archive, news, rrn, NNTP
louie.udel.edu	128.175.1.3	Minix, Amiga
lurch.stanford.edu	36.22.0.14	InterViews
lut.fi	128.214.25.8	GIF images, HP-UX sources
m9-520-1.mit.edu	18.80.0.45	Xim (X image viewer)
marvin.cs.buffalo.edu	128.205.32.4	RFCs, Sun
maxwell.physics.purdue.edu	128.46.135.3	Bible (/pub/bible.tar.Z)
merit.edu	35.1.1.42	RFCs, etc.
merlin.cs.purdue.edu	128.10.2.3	Concurrent C, Xinu, Mac, GIF
mimsy.umd.edu	128.8.128.8	SLIP
monk.proteon.com	128.185.123.16	cc:mail to SMTP gateway
mthvax.cs.miami.edu	129.171.32.5	WORM, Elm mailer
nic.ddn.mil	26.2.0.74	MS-DOS, Unix, CP/M, Mac archive
nic.mr.net	192.12.250.5	Minnesota regional traffic data
nifty.andrew.cmu.edu		AIDS/HIV and Gay rights (/pub/QRD)
nisc.nyser.net	192.33.4.10	GNU Emacs, Nysernet, IETF, GOSIP
nnsc.nsf.net	192.31.103.6	Internet resource guide (/res*)
nyu.edu	128.125.1.1	GIFs and games
oak.oakland.edu		Huge archive of DOS/ UNIX, graphics plus CRYNWR packet drivers, KA9Q
ocf.berkeley.edu	128.32.184.254	Bible, song lyrics (/pub)
oddjob.uchicago.edu	128.135.4.2	NNTP, Sendmail
oddput.efd.lth.se	130.235.48.4	xps – postscript previewer
omnigate.clarkson.edu	128.153.4.2	PS maps of the DNS
otax.tky.hut.fi	128.214.8.1	Mikkar accounting program

FTP site	IP number	Files and utilities
p6xje.ldc.lu.se	130.235.133.7	NCSA telnet 2.2ds, PC networking
pawl.rpi.edu	128.113.10.2	Sun raster images
pprg.unm.edu	192.31.154.1	Sun bitmaps
prep.ai.mit.edu	18.71.0.38	GNU, MIT C Scheme, gnu *grep
radio.astro.utoronto.ca	128.100.75.4	MS-DOS Sun User Group
relgyro.stanford.edu	36.64.0.50	Sunrast-to-pc, VGA pictures
research.att.com	192.20.225.1	TEX, gcc, Ghostscript PS viewer
riacs.edu	128.102.16.8	SLIP
safe.stanford.edu	36.44.0.193	3COM/Interlan 4.X BSD UNIX
santra.hut.fi	128.214.3.1	Pax (pascal compiler)
sauna.hut.fi	128.214.3.119	Gnu, Unix, Amiga, FTP directories, Elm mailer, NNTP, X-Windows, jove
sbcs.sunysb.edu	129.49.2.3	Sun raster tools
scam.berkeley.edu	128.32.138.1	X sources
science.utah.edu	128.110.192.2	TeX related
score.stanford.edu	36.8.0.46	TexHax, Atari stuff
sh.cs.net	192.31.103.3	NetLists, NetMaps
shambhala.berkeley.edu	128.32.132.54	xrn (X rn newsreader)
sirius.nada.kth.se	130.237.222.29	Mac stuff
skagul.dna.lth.se	130.235.16.28	Sendmail, DNS
spam.istc.sri.com	128.18.4.3	Gnu, X stuff
spot.colorado.edu	128.138.238.1	RFCs, netinfo
squid.cs.ucla.edu	131.179.96.44	Usenet: soc.med.aids
ssyx.ucsc.edu	128.114.133.1	Atari, Amiga, GIF images
sulaw.law.su.oz.au		Law information (/pub/law)
sumex-aim.stanford.edu	36.44.0.6	Mac archives
sun.cnuce.cnr.it	192.12.192.4	KA9Q for PC
sun.soe.clarkson.edu	128.153.12.3	X11 fonts, TeX, PCIP
surya.waterloo.edu	129.97.129.72	GIFs, TIFFs, gif2SunRas
sutcase.case.syr.edu	128.230.32.2	Zoo archiver, TCP/IP stuff
svax.cs.cornell.edu	128.84.254.2	NetHack game
terminator.cc.umich.edu	35.1.33.8	MS-DOS, Atari
titan.rice.edu	128.42.1.30	Sun-spots, Amiga ispell

FTP site	IP number	Files and utilities
tmc.edu	128.249.1.1	FUBBS BBS list
tolsun.oulu.fi	128.214.5.6	Amiga/Atari, c64, IBM PC, Mac, IRC
topaz.rutgers.edu	128.6.4.194	Amiga (big archive)
trantor.umd.edu	128.8.10.14	Network Time Protocol (NTP), Amiga
trwind.ind.trw.com	129.4.16.70	Turbo C stuff
tumtum.cs.umd.edu	128.8.128.49	NeWS, PD software
tut.cis.ohio-state.edu	128.146.8.60	GNU
tut.fi	128.214.1.2	Images, Unix
ucbarpa.berkeley.edu	128.32.130.11	tn3270
ucbvax.berkeley.edu	128.32.133.1	NNTP, gnews
ucdavis.ucdavis.edu	128.120.2.1	Elm 1.7
ucsd.edu	128.54.16.1	KA9Q archives
uicbert.eecs.uic.edu	128.248.166.25	AT&T, Unix-PC
uihub.cs.uiuc.edu	128.174.252.27	Amiga
ummts.cc.umich.edu	35.1.1.43	Atari ST
umn-cs.cs.umn.edu	128.101.224.1	Sendmail, Mac, Unix-PC, Atari, Apple II, GIF images, etc.
unh.cs.cmu.edu	128.2.254.150	cold-fusion (/afs/cs/user/vac/ftp)
unix2.macc.wisc.edu	128.104.30.1	hosts.txt Internet host lists
unocss.unl.edu	129.93.1.11	Usenet: alt.sex, alt.*, etc.
unsvax.nevada.edu	131.216.1.11	FTP lists
urth.cc.buffalo.edu	128.205.3.48	Ksh source
usc.edu	128.125.1.45	Emacs
utadnx.cc.utexas.edu	128.83.1.26	VMS sources
uunet.uu.net	192.48.96.2	Usenet: many miscellaneous
uwasa.fi	128.214.12.3	Mac, PC, Suntools, Unix, VMS
ux.acss.umn.edu	128.101.63.2	Usenix 87 archives
uxa.cso.uiuc.edu	128.174.2.1	Mac
uxc.cso.uiuc.edu	128.174.5.50	Games, HitchHiker's (hgi.txt), food recipes, GIF images
uxe.cso.uiuc.edu	128.174.5.54	Amiga/Fish disks
vax.ftp.com	128.127.25.100	FTP software
vaxa.isi.edu	128.9.0.33	X stuff
vega.hut.fi	128.214.3.82	MS-DOS, Mac, Kermit, fusion docs, sci-fi author lists
venera.isi.edu	128.9.0.32	NNstat, GNU chess

FTP site	IP number	Files and utilities
venus.ycc.yale.edu	192.26.88.4	SBTeX
vgr.brl.mil	128.63.4.4	BSD ping/record route, images
vm1.nodak.edu	134.129.111.1	Minix
vx2.gba.nyu.edu	128.122.130.85	PC telnet
watsun.cc.columbia.edu	128.59.39.2	Kermit, etc.
winie.princeton.edu	128.112.128.180	Music software (Unix/NeXT)
wpi.wpi.edu	230.215.24.1	Anime art, Mac, GNU, X
wsmr-simtel20.army.mil	26.0.0.74	DOS, UNIX, Mac, everything!
wuarchive.wustl.edu	128.252.135.4	Another massive DOS/ UNIX archive
xanth.cs.odu.edu	128.82.8.1	Usenet: comp.sources.[x,unix, misc, games, amiga], X, Amiga stuff
xx.lcs.mit.edu	18.26.0.36	RFC documents
yahi.stanford.edu	36.83.0.92	g++, Unix stuff
yale-bulldog.arpa.edu	128.36.0.3	UUCP paths, tar, ispell
zaphod.ncsa.uiuc.edu	128.174.20.50	NCSA Telnet source, Mathematica
zeus.mgmt.purdue.edu	128.210.1.3	MicroEmacs
zip.eecs.umich.edu	35.3.64.8	Esperanto sentence analyser
zug.ai.mit.edu	18.26.0.247	Scheme software

A–Z archive/platform breakdown

MS-DOS archives

FTP site	IP number	Details
cs.cmu.edu	128.2.222.173	MS-DOS
ftp.demon.co.uk		MS-DOS
funet.fi	128.214.1.1	MS-DOS *
garbo.uwasa.edu		MS-DOS *
grape.ecs.clarkson.edu	128.153.13.196	MS-DOS
hotel.cis.ksu.edu	129.130.10.12	MS-DOS
nic.ddn.mil	26.2.0.74	MS-DOS
terminator.cc.umich.edu	35.1.33.8	MS-DOS

Amiga archives

FTP site	IP number	Details
vega.hut.fi	128.214.3.82	MS-DOS
wsmr-simtel20.army.mil		MS-DOS *
wuarchive.wustl.edu		MS-DOS *
a.cs.uiuc.edu	128.174.252.1	Amiga
amiga.physik.unizh.ch		Amiga *
bach.berkeley.edu	128.32.135.1	Amiga
bongo.cc.utexas.edu		Amiga *
cs.utah.edu	128.110.4.21	Amiga
funet.fi	128.214.1.1	Amiga *
funic.funet.fi		Amiga
gtss.gatech.edu	128.61.4.1	Amiga
ix1.cc.utexas.edu	128.83.1.21	Amiga
ix2.cc.utexas.edu	128.83.1.29	Amiga
j.cc.purdue.edu	128.210.9.2	Amiga, Usenet:comp.sources.amiga
jyu.fi	128.214.7.5	Amiga
loke.idt.unit.no	129.241.1.103	Amiga
sauna.hut.fi	128.214.3.119	Amiga
ssyx.ucsc.edu	128.114.133.1	Amiga
tolsun.oulu.fi	128.214.5.6	Amiga
topaz.rutgers.edu	128.6.4.194	Amiga
uihub.cs.uiuc.edu	128.174.252.27	Amiga
uxe.cso.uiuc.edu	128.174.5.54	Amiga (Fish disks)
wuarchive.wustl.edu		Amiga *
xanth.cs.odu.edu	128.82.8.1	Amiga

Atari archives

FTP site	IP number	Details
atari.archive.umich.edu		Atari *
jyu.fi	128.214.7.5	Atari
score.stanford.edu	36.8.0.46	Atari
ssyx.ucsc.edu	128.114.133.1	Atari
terminator.cc.umich.edu	35.1.33.8	Atari
tolsun.oulu.fi	128.214.5.6	Atari
ummts.cc.umich.edu	35.1.1.43	Atari ST
umn-cs.cs.umn.edu	128.101.224.1	Atari

Apple / Macintosh archives

FTP site	IP number	Details
apple.com	130.43.2.2	Apple/Mac related
arisia.xerox.com	13.1.100.206	Mac
bongo.cc.utexas.edu		Mac *
brownvm.brown.edu	128.148.128.40	Mac
cadre.dsl.pittsburgh.edu	130.49.128.1	Mac
emily.rice.edu	128.42.10.2	Mac
f.ms.uky.edu	128.163.128.6	Mac
husc6.harvard.edu	128.103.1.56	Apple II
jpl-mil.jpl.nasa.gov	128.149.1.101	Mac
jyu.fi	128.214.7.5	Mac
mac.archive.umich.edu		Mac *
merlin.cs.purdue.edu	128.10.2.3	Mac
nic.ddn.mil	26.2.0.74	Mac
sirius.nada.kth.se	130.237.222.29	Mac
sumex-aim.stanford.edu	36.44.0.6	Mac *
tolsun.oulu.fi	128.214.5.6	Mac
umn-cs.cs.umn.edu	128.101.224.1	Apple II, and Mac
uwasa.fi	128.214.12.3	Mac
uxa.cso.uiuc.edu	128.174.2.1	Mac
vega.hut.fi	128.214.3.82	Mac

Notes: UNIX archives are the most abundant, and Unix-related documentation can be found on the majority of FTP sites, especially larger sites such as wuarchive.wustl.edu and the 'White Sands' anonymous FTP site wsmr-simtel20.army.mil.

Appendix F

Internet domains: country codes and hostname details

This appendix details the Internet top-level domain names that are used for Internet hostnames, as well as defining the individual country code suffixes that are in use. Details of Internet hostnames and how they are constructed is also provided in this appendix.

Internet hostnames

Internet hostnames are made up of one or more strings separated by periods (`.`), for example: `demon.co.uk`. Hostnames are broken down into separate domains. Hosts must have a minimum of two domain portions in a name, so `sony.com` is valid, as is `demon.co.uk` as is `ames.arc.nasa.gov`. Hostnames contain commonly less than five domain portions. The domain name system (DNS) is now used to convert such names to IP (numeric) addresses, that is to say that all Internet hosts have a numeric IP address, e.g. `128.16.32.1` that identifies them. The character names are used to make hosts easier to refer to, since numbers are rather hard to remember. For example, the name `demon.co.uk` would be broken down as follows:

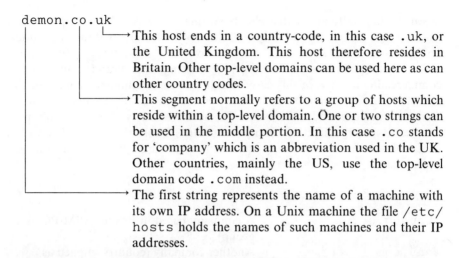

demon.co.uk

→ This host ends in a country-code, in this case .uk, or the United Kingdom. This host therefore resides in Britain. Other top-level domains can be used here as can other country codes.

→ This segment normally refers to a group of hosts which reside within a top-level domain. One or two strings can be used in the middle portion. In this case .co stands for 'company' which is an abbreviation used in the UK. Other countries, mainly the US, use the top-level domain code .com instead.

→ The first string represents the name of a machine with its own IP address. On a Unix machine the file /etc/ hosts holds the names of such machines and their IP addresses.

You should be aware that hostnames can be organized in many different ways. Domains are organized so that machines run by certain organizations can control their expansion and configuration. For example, the .EDU top-level domain is used to refer to all the academic or EDUcational Internet hosts. A host with a suffix mit.edu therefore has its own domain or 'zone' within the educational world in which it can operate. Mit.edu can reference computers using names such as machine1.mit.edu, etc. Likewise, mit.edu can also create a new sub-domain (perhaps a new computer network) within the mit.edu domain, for example 'sun'. It could then reference machines using the names sun1.sun.mit.edu. In this way domains are broken up into a series of sub-domains. Of course, some organizations may only have the most minimal of hostnames, e.g. sony.com, which in this case refers to the company Sony which is located in the top-level domain of commercial companies (.COM).

Not all hostnames immediately tell you in which country they are located, for example sony.com. However, the top-level domains such as .COM always refer to the United States. Country codes may also be valid in other portions of a hostname, so a host called sun1.ca.com may not be located in Canada, although biome.bio.na.ca most definitely is. As a rule of thumb, all European and non-US countries commonly use their top-level country domain codes at the end of their hostnames. American hosts have followed a path whereby their country code (.US) is hardly ever used; instead US sites end in top-level domains such as .EDU e.g. harvard.edu for Harvard University, .COM for commercial companies, etc.

Finally, a hint about machine names and organizational departments. As well as a top-level domain such as .EDU, the first couple of portions of a hostname normally give you a clue regarding that host. For example, a host called `ftp.ug.unig.edu` looks like an FTP host within the under-graduate department of a university, whereas the host `apache.telebit.com` is assembled using the brand names of a commercial company, in this case Telebit modem's. Similary, names such as `cs`, and `uni` are common hostname-parlance in the educational arena for 'computer science' and 'university'. The acronym `cc` is also commonly used to refer to an organizations 'computer centre'. Table F.1 below illustrates a series of the most commonly used acronyms that are used in Internet hostnames.

EXAMPLE HOSTNAMES IN USE

`ibmpcug.co.uk`	A company based in Britain (IBM PC user group).
`sony.com`	Another company (country implied as United States).
`archive.umich.edu`	Educational establishment in the US (University of Michigan).
`alw.nih.gov`	A governmental user based in the US.
`etl.go.jp`	An Internet host based in Japan.
`ajk.tele.fi`	An Internet host based in Finland.
`adder.maths.su.oz.au`	The maths department of Sydney University, Australia.
`vax.ftp.com`	A DEC/VAX host running FTP services in the US.

Table F.1   **Common acronyms used within Internet hostnames**

Acronym	Meaning
`ai`	Artificial intelligence (department, etc.)
`cc`	Computer/computing centre
`cs`	Computer/computing science (department, etc.)
`econ`	Economics (department, etc.)
`ftp`	File transfer protocol site (an archive, etc.)
`it`	Information technology (department, etc.)
`math`	Mathematics (department, etc.)
`nic`	Network information centre (directory services)
`sun`	Sun machine host
`tn370`	An IBM 370 mainframe host
`ug`	Undergraduate (department of a university, etc.)
`uni`	University
`uu`	USENET university
`vax`	DEC/VAX machine host

Top-level domain suffix codes

The top-level domain codes are used as suffixes on the end of hostnames. As well as those codes shown in Table F.2, which are used mainly in the United States, individual country codes are also used as suffixes on hostnames, e.g. for European hosts, etc. (see Table F.3).

International top-level domain codes

International top-level domain codes indicate the country in which a specific host resides (Table F.3).

Table F.2   Top-level domain suffix codes

Domain	Organization/company	Example
com	Commercial Internet user	sony.com – US implied
edu	Educational Internet user	princeton.edu – US implied
gov	Government user	ames.arc.nasa.gov – US implied
mil	Military organization	wsmr-simtel20.army.mil – US implied
net	Network provider	rahul.net – International
org	Non-commercial organization	zeus.ieee.org – International

Note: There is also a top-level domain called 'int' for international organizations, although it is rarely used.

Table F.3   International top-level domain codes

Suffix	Country
aq	Antartica
ar	Argentina
at	Austria
au	Australia
be	Belgium
br	Brazil
ca	Canada
ch	Switzerland (Cantons of Helvetia)
cl	Chile
de	Germany (Deutschland)
dk	Denmark
ec	Ecuador
ee	Estonia
es	Spain (España)
fi	Finland
fr	France
gr	Greece
hk	Hong Kong
hu	Hungary
ie	Ireland
il	Israel
in	India
is	Iceland
it	Italy
jp	Japan
kr	Korea (South)
mx	Mexico
nl	Netherlands
no	Norway
nz	New Zealand
pl	Poland
pt	Portugal
re	Reunion (French)
se	Sweden
sg	Singapore
su	Former Soviet Union (now CIS)
th	Thailand
tn	Tunisia
tw	Taiwan
uk	United Kingdom (Great Britain)
us	United States
yu	Yugoslavia
za	South Africa

Appendix G
A–Z USENET group listings

This appendix contains an A–Z listing of the newsgroups carried over the USENET network. This is by no means a complete list, however; USENET currently has over 7000 newsgroups and those not specified here are mainly USENET hierarchies specific to particular countries, e.g. `de.` for Germany. As well as the name of each group, a short description of the forum's main discussion topic is also given. A dagger (†) in front of a newsgroup indicates a group that receives binary postings, i.e. UU-encoded ASCII files such as images or executable applications. Other hierarchies specific to certain Internet service-providers are also widely available. For a full list of groups please refer to the group `news.lists`. The USENET hierarchies detailed in this section are shown below:

`alt.*`	Alternative subject newsgroups
`bionet.*`	Biology-related newsgroups
`bit.*`	BITNET network newsgroups
`biz.*`	Business, marketing and adverts newsgroups
`clari.*`	CLARINET network: world news
`comp.*`	Computer-related newsgroups
`eunet.*`	European network newsgroups
`misc.*`	Miscellaneous subject newsgroups
`news.*`	Newsgroups for the USENET system itself
`rec.*`	Recreational newsgroups
`sci.*`	Science-related newsgroups
`soc.*`	Social-issues newsgroups
`talk.*`	Talk newsgroups: controversial debates
`uk.*`	Newsgroups in the United Kingdom
`us.*`	Newsgroups in the United States
`k12.*`	Newsgroups for educationalists and teachers

Alternative hierarchies (`alt.*`)

Miscellaneous topics. Groups come and go regularly here, although the majority shown will probably be around for a long time to come, and may even be promoted to other more permanent hierarchies, i.e. in the `misc.*` USENET hierarchy.

Group name	Description
`alt.1d`	Images: one-dimensional imaging
`alt.3d`	Images: three-dimensional imaging
`alt.abortion.inequity`	Abortion issues
`alt.abuse-recovery`	Abuse recovery (sexual, physical, etc.)
`alt.abuse.offender.recovery`	Helping past offenders
`alt.activism`	Activities for today's activists
`alt.activism.d`	Discussion group for above
`alt.adoption`	Child adoption
`alt.aeffle.und.pferdle`	The two German cartoon characters
`alt.agriculture.fruit`	Fruit in agriculture
`alt.agriculture.misc`	Miscellaneous agriculture discussion forum
`alt.aldus.freehand`	Aldus Freehand software forum
`alt.aldus.misc`	Aldus software: miscellaneous discussion
`alt.aldus.pagemaker`	Aldus software: PageMaker DTP system forum
`alt.alien.visitors`	Extra-terrestrial (alien) experiences
`alt.allsysop`	System operators' discussions
`alt.amateur-comp`	Amateur computer users
`alt.amiga.demos`	Demonstration programs for the Amiga computer
`alt.angst`	Anxiety in today's society
`alt.answers`	FAQs in the `alt.*` hierarchy
`alt.appalachian`	Appalachian regional discussion group
`alt.aquaria`	Collecting fishes, basically
`alt.archery`	Sport: archery
`alt.architecture`	Architecture discussion group
`alt.artcom`	The artistic communities discussion group
`alt.astrology`	You will meet a tall dark stranger...
`alt.atheism`	For the non-believers
`alt.atheism.moderated`	A moderated group for the above
`alt.autos.rod-n-custom`	Customized automobiles
`alt.authorware`	Software for authors
`alt.autos.antique`	Classic and vintage cars discussed
`alt.autos.rod-n-custom`	Custom cars and 'hot-rods'
`alt.bacchus`	The non-profit BACCHUS organization's group

Group name	Description
alt.backrubs	Massage and backrubs discussed
alt.baldspot	Hair related?
alt.bbs	Bulletin board systems to access
alt.bbs.ads	Adverts for various BBSs
alt.bbs.allsysop	BBS system operators group
alt.bbs.internet	BBS systems accessible via the Internet
alt.bbs.lists	Lists of BBS systems around the world
alt.bbs.lists.d	Discussion of various BBS listings
alt.bbs.metal	Metal telecommunications environment
alt.bbs.pcbuucp	UUCP for DOS (PC) computers
alt.bbs.searchlight	SearchLight BBS systems discussed
alt.bbs.unixbbs	Unix BBS systems
alt.bbs.unixbbs.uniboard	Unix Uniboard BBS system
alt.bbs.waffle	BBS acess via the well-known 'Waffle' program
alt.beer	Ales and various other brews discussed
alt.best.of.internet	The best things happening on the Internet
alt.binaries.multimedia	† Sound, graphics and text applications
alt.binaries.pictures	† Miscellaneous pictures
alt.binaries.pictures.d	Discussions about picture postings
alt.binaries.pictures.erotica	† Erotic pictures (and text posts)
alt.binaries.pictures.erotica. blondes	† Erotic pictures (blonde women)
alt.binaries.pictures.erotica.d	Discussion group for abpe
alt.binaries.pictures.erotica. female	† Female erotic pictures
alt.binaries.pictures.erotica. male	† Male erotic pictures
alt.binaries.pictures.fine- art.d	† Fine-art pictures
alt.binaries.pictures.fine-art. digitized	† Digitized pictures
alt.binaries.pictures.fine-art. graphics	† Fine-art and computer graphics
alt.binaries.pictures.fractals	† Fractal (chaos) pictures
alt.binaries.pictures.misc	† Miscellaneous pictures
alt.binaries.pictures. supermodels	† Pictures of supermodels
alt.binaries.pictures.tasteless	† Tasteless pictures (really!)
alt.binaries.pictures.utilities	† Programs for picture processing
alt.binaries.sounds	† Miscellaneous sounds and utilities
alt.binaries.sounds.d	† Discussion group for sounds
alt.binaries.sounds.misc	† More miscellaneous sounds
alt.binaries.sounds.erotica	† Erotic sounds
alt.birthright	Birthright parties discussion group
alt.bitterness	For people who are bitter

Group name	Description
alt.bonsai	Bonsai (or the art of miniature trees)
alt.books.deryni	Katherine Kurtz's books (Deryni series)
alt.books.reviews	Book reviews (various subjects)
alt.books.technical	Technical book reviews and discussion
alt.boomerang	Those things that you can't get rid of!
alt.buddha.short.fat.guy	Religious discussion area for Buddhists
alt.business.multi-level	Business discussion group: marketing related
alt.cable-tv.re-regulate	Regulatory areas of cable TV
alt.cad	Computer-aided design (CAD)
alt.cad.autocad	Computer-aided design: the AutoCad system
alt.california	Discussions about this state of the US
alt.callahans	Callahan's bar (puns and fellowship)
alt.cascade	Everyday objects as art
alt.cd-rom	CD-ROM optical storage newsgroup
alt.cellular	Cellular phones, etc.
alt.censorship	Censorship: speech, press, and computing
alt.cesium	The radioactive substance discussion group
alt.chess.ics	Internet chess server
alt.child-support	Child support for parents
alt.chinchilla	Chinchilla farming, etc.
alt.chinese.text	Chinese postings and chinese text software
alt.chinese.text.big5	Posting in Chinese (BIG 5)
alt.clearing.technology	Clearer and healthier skin
alt.clubs.compsci	Computer science clubs
alt.co-evolution	Whole earth review
alt.co-ops	Co-operatives discussion group
alt.cobol	The ancient programming language lives on...
alt.collecting.autographs	Autograph collectors forum
alt.colorguard	Marching bands, etc.
alt.comedy.british	Best of British comedy. What a carry on
alt.comics.buffalo-roam	Postscript comic strip
alt.comics.superman	Superman comics forum
alt.comp.acad-freedom.talk	Academic freedom in relation to computing
alt.comp.compression	Data compression discussion group
akt.comp.fsp	The FSP file transport protocol
alt.config	Alternative subnet: creating new alt.* groups
alt.consciousness	Is this a dream or is it reality?
alt.conspiracy	Conspiracies in today's world
alt.conspiracy.jfk	The Kennedy assassination discussed
alt.cosuard	Council of Sysops and users against discrimination

Group name	Description
alt.cult-movies	Cult movies discussed
alt.cult-movies.rocky-horror	The Rocky Horror Picture Show
alt.culture.alaska	Alaskan culture
alt.culture.argentina	Argentinian culture
alt.culture.austrian	Austrian culture
alt.culture.indonesia	Indonesian culture
alt.culture.karnataka	Indian Karnatic culture
alt.culture.kerala	Malayalam language and culture
alt.culture.ny-upstate	The Big Apple's culture (New York, that is)
alt.culture.oregon	Culture of Oregon, US
alt.culture.theory	Cultural theory
alt.culture.tamil	Tamil culture
alt.culture.tuva	Culture of the Tannu Tuva Republic
alt.culture.us.asian-indian	Asian/Indian culture
alt.culture.usenet	The USENET culture
alt.current-events.inet92	Events at the Inet '92 meeting
alt.current-events.somalia	Events in the Somalia famine region
alt.cyb-sys	Cybernetics and systems
alt.cyberpunk	You've read the book now read the group...
alt.cyberpunk.chatsubo	Virtual reality in cyberspace
alt.cyberpunk.movement	How to cybernize the universe
alt.cyberpunk.tech	Cyber* technology
alt.cyberspace	Cyberspace discussion group
alt.cybertoon	Cyberspace cartoon epic
alt.dads-rights	Rights of fathers to win custody control
alt.dcom.catv	Telecomunications related
alt.dcom.telecom	Telecomunications related
alt.decathena	DEC Athena system discussed
alt.desert-shield	The Gulf war – phase 1
alt.desert-storm	The Gulf war – phase 2
alt.desert-storm.facts	Facts about the Gulf war
alt.desert-thekurds	The impact of the Gulf war on the Kurds
alt.destroy.the.earth	We're going this way gradually...
alt.discordia	Disagreement in today's society
alt.discrimination	Discrimination in society: sexual, racial, etc.
alt.divination	Divination techniques e.g. Tarot, I Ching
alt.dreams	Our subconscious lives are examined here
alt.drugs	Discussion group about drugs (Q and A)
alt.drugs.caffeine	The drug caffeine discussed
alt.drumcorps	Drum and Bugle Corps group
alt.earth_summit	Past Earth Summit at Rio
alt.education.bangkok	Education in Bangkok

Group name	Description
`alt.education.disabled`	Education for the disabled
`alt.education.distance`	Education over the network
`alt.elvis.sighting`	Sightings of the king (and others)
`alt.emulators.ibmpc.apple2`	Emulating a PC on an Apple II
`alt.emusic`	E* music: Ethnic, electronic, elaborate *et al.*
`alt.etext`	Electronic texts, e.g. Project Gutenberg *et al.*
`alt.evil`	Evil experiences and tales
`alt.exotic-music`	Exotic music discussed
`alt.exploding.kibo`	For people who like to blow things up!
`alt.fan.amy-fisher`	Fans of Amy Fisher and the famous AF trial
`alt.fan.anne-rice`	Fans of writer Anne Rice
`alt.fan.asprin`	Fans of the most deadly drug in the world
`alt.fan.brother-jed`	Born-again minister touring American campuses
`alt.fan.dan-quayle`	Fans of Mr Quayle, former US Vice President
`alt.fan.dave_barry`	Electronic fan club for humourist Dave Barry
`alt.fan.disney.afternoon`	Disney afternoon characters and shows
`alt.fan.don.no-soul.simmons`	From: *Amazon Women On The Moon* film fame
`alt.fan.douglas-adams`	*The Meaning of Life* and *Hitch-hikers...*
`alt.fan.elvis-presley`	Fans of the king of rock and roll
`alt.fan.enya`	Fans of the singer Enya
`alt.fan.frank-zappa`	Fans of Frank Zappa
`alt.fan.furry`	Fans of Steve Gallacci's furry animals book
`alt.fan.goons`	Fans of the Goons
`alt.fan.itchy-n-scratchy`	Bart Simpson's favourite cartoon
`alt.fan.james-bond`	My name's Bond, James Bond...
`alt.fan.letterman`	Fans of David Letterman (the US chat-show host)
`alt.fan.madonna`	Fans of the pop singer Madonna
`alt.fan.monty-python`	Monty Python fan club forum
`alt.fan.q`	Fans of the new Star Treks 'Q'
`alt.fan.run-dmc`	Fans of the band 'Run DMC'
`alt.fan.shostakovich`	Fans of this classical music composer
`alt.fan.spinal-tap`	Fans of the group Spinal Tap
`alt.fan.tolkien`	Fans of the writer J.R.R. Tolkien
`alt.fan.vic-reeves`	Fans of Vic Reeves (of 'Big Night Out' fame)
`alt.fan.wodehouse`	Fans of P.G. Woodhouse
`alt.fan.woody-allen`	Fans of Woody Allen
`alt.fashion`	Fashion discussion group (clothes)

Group name	Description
alt.fax	Facsimile discussion group (Q and A)
alt.feminism	The feminism movement
alt.finals.suicide	Got the exam blues? Then read this group
alt.fishing	Fishing (game, sea, etc.)
alt.flame	Have a good moan at someone for no reason
alt.flame.gigantic.sigs	Moans about large .signature files!
alt.flame.spelling	Moans about bad speling
alt.folklore.college	College humour and everyday life
alt.folklore.computers	Computer stories and anecdotes
alt.folklore.ghost-stories	Ghost stories. Good bed-time reading
alt.folklore.science	Traditional science beliefs discussed
alt.folklore.urban	Urban folklore discussed
alt.food	Food-related newsgroup
alt.food.cocacola	Coca-Cola discussion group
alt.forgery	Forgery related group
alt.forsale	Items for sale (miscellaneous)
alt.fractals	Fractal pictures discussed
alt.fractals.pictures	† Fractal pictures (posted, some binaries)
alt.freedom.of.information.act	Discussing this important US act
alt.galactic-guide	Entries for the real Hitch Hikers guide
alt.games.gb	The Galactic Bloodshed game
alt.games.lynx	Atari Lynx games
alt.games.omega	Omega games
alt.games.mornington.cresent	The Mornington Cresent game
alt.games.sf2	Street Fighter 2
alt.games.torg	Gateway to TORG mailing list
alt.games.xtrek	Star Trek for X-Windows
alt.gathering.rainbow	Annual Rainbow discussion group
alt.geek	Group for Geeks!
alt.good.morning	Group for morning greeting messages?
alt.good.news	And now the good news...
alt.gopher	Gopher service discussions and developments
alt.gothic	The Gothic movement discussed
alt.gourmand	Recipes and other cooking information
alt.graffiti	Discussions about graffiti
alt.graphics.pixutils	Graphics utilities (discussion group)
alt.great-lakes	The Great Lakes of America
alt.guitar	For guitar players everywhere
alt.guitar.bass	Bass guitarists forum
alt.hackers	Group for hackers and crackers
alt.hackers.malicious	Group for malicious hackers
alt.heraldry.sca	Heraldry in the Society of Creative Anachronism
alt.hindu	Hindu religion: discussion group

Group name	Description
alt.homosexual	Homosexual and Gay discussion group
alt.horror	Horror discussion group
alt.horror.werewolves	For those only when a full moon is out!
alt.hotrod	High speed cars and hot rods
alt.hurricane.andrew	Discussion about hurricane Andrew in the US
alt.hypertext	Hypertext (sound, graphics and text)
alt.hypnosis	You are feeling sleepy...
alt.individualism	Individual rights, etc.
alt.industrial	Industrial Computing Society
alt.industrial.computing	Industrial computing
alt.inet92	Inet '92 forum: discussion group
alt.info-science	Science information
alt.info-theory	Information theory
alt.internet.access.wanted	Internet access wanted by users
alt.internet.services	Internet services (lists, etc.)
alt.internet.talk-radio	The Internet Talk Radio program
alt.irc	Internet Relay Chat
alt.irc.corruption	Corruption in IRCs
alt.irc.ircii	IRC v2 system discussed
alt.irc.recovery	Recovering from the effects of IRCs
alt.irc.sleaze	Sleaze in the world of IRCs (what?)
alt.journalism	Jouralists column
alt.journalism.criticism	Criticism of journalists and the media
alt.journalism.music	Music journalism and media
alt.ketchup	Lovely stuff, especially with fish 'n chips
alt.kids-talk	Group for pre-college children
alt.lang.asm	Assembly language group
alt.lang.awk	The awk language group
alt.lang.basic	BASIC (bloody awful system is continuing)
alt.lang.cfutures	Future of the C programming langugage
alt.lang.intercal	The joke language and compiler
alt.lang.ml	ML and SML symbolic languages
alt.lang.teco	The TECO editor language
alt.locksmithing	Locksmiths forum
alt.lycra	The clothing material Lycra discussed
alt.magic	Stage magic, etc.
alt.magick	Supernatural arts
alt.manga	Non-western comics; comic art, etc.
alt.materials.simulation	Computer modelling of materials
alt.mcdonalds	I'll have a Big Mac please
alt.mcdonalds.cheese	...What about a cheese-burger?
alt.mcdonalds.gripes	Moaning forum for McDonald's food
alt.mcdonalds.ketchup	Discussion of McDonald's ketchup
alt.mcdonalds.vegemite	Discussion of McDonald's vegetarian vegemite
alt.med.cfs	Chronique Fatigue Syndrome forum

Group name	Description
`alt.meditation.transcendental`	Transcendental meditation group
`alt.mensa.boston`	Mensa members in Boston, US
`alt.messianic`	Messiniac traditions and life
`alt.mindcontrol`	Control your mind
`alt.misanthropy`	For people who do not like anybody
`alt.missing-kids`	Locating missing children
`alt.models`	Model design and building, etc.
`alt.motorcycles.harley`	Harley motorcycles discussion group
`alt.msdos.programmer`	MS-DOS programmers group
`alt.mud`	Multi-user dungeon/dimension group
`alt.mud.bsx`	Mud systems on BSX VR
`alt.mud.german`	German MUD systems
`alt.mud.lp`	The LP MUD system
`alt.mud.tiny`	TinyMUD systems
`alt.music.alternative`	Alternative music
`alt.music.canada`	Canadian music discussed
`alt.music.enya`	The music of pop-star Enya
`alt.music.filk`	Sci-fi related music
`alt.music.hardcore`	Hard core music
`alt.music.karaoke`	Sing at your hearts content. No one's listening!
`alt.music.marillion`	Music by the group Marillion
`alt.music.progressive`	Asia, Marillion, King Crimson, etc.
`alt.music.queen`	Freddy Mercury fan group
`alt.music.rush`	Music by the rockers RUSH
`alt.music.ska`	SKA music
`alt.music.the.police`	Sting *et al.* (formerly of rock band, The Police)
`alt.mythology`	Mythology discussion forum
`alt.national.enquirer`	The National Enquirer newspaper
`alt.native`	Indiginous people's countries discussion group
`alt.necromicon`	Bizarre political talk
`alt.net.personalities`	Personalities on the network
`alt.newbie`	For new users of the `alt.*` USENET hierarchy
`alt.newbies`	Ditto
`alt.news-media`	Discussion group for the news media
`alt.org.food-not-bombs`	Means what it says, really
`alt.org.pugwash`	Technological/social implications
`alt.os.bsdi`	BSD Unix forum
`alt.os.linux`	The Linux UNIX clone operating system
`alt.os.multics`	The Multics OS (Unix's daddy)
`alt.out-of-body`	Out of body experiences, e.g. near-death, etc.
`alt.pagan`	Paganism discussion group
`alt.paranormal`	Paranormal experiences

Group name	Description
alt.parents-teens	Parent–teenager relationships
alt.party	Parties and celebratory activities
alt.pcnews	PCnews software forum
alt.personals	Personal advertisements
alt.personals.ads	More personal advertisements
alt.personals.bondage	Adverts: bondage
alt.personals.misc	Adverts: miscellaneous
alt.personals.poly	Adverts: multiple people
alt.planning.urban	Adverts: urban planning
alt.politics.british	British politics
alt.politics.bush	George Bush related news
alt.politics.clinton	Bill Clinton related news
alt.politics.correct	Politically Correct party
alt.politics.democrats	Politics: US Democrats
alt.politics.democrats.clinton	Politics: US Democrats, Bill Clinton
alt.politics.democrats.d	Politics: US Democrats (discussion group)
alt.politics.democrats.house	Politics: US House of Representatives
alt.politics.democrats.senate	Politics: US Senate
alt.politics.ec	European community politics
alt.politics.economics	Economics in politics
alt.politics.elections	Politics: elections
alt.politics.europe.misc	Politics: European (miscellaneous)
alt.politics.homosexuality	Homosexuality in politics
alt.politics.italy	Italian politics
alt.politics.reform	Reform in politics
alt.politics.sex	Sex in politics
alt.politics.usa.constitution	Politics: US constitution
alt.politics.usa.misc	Miscellaneous US politics
alt.polyamory	For people with multiple love relationships
alt.postmodern	Postmodernism in society
alt.president.clinton	Mr Clinton being discussed yet again
alt.privacy	Privacy issues
alt.prose	Stories, poetry and other writings
alt.prose.d	Discussion group for the above
alt.psychoactives	Better living via chemistry
alt.pub.dragons-inn	A computer fantasy scenario
alt.pulp	Paperback fiction
alt.radio.pirate	Pirate radio discussion group
alt.radio.scanner	Radio scanner devices
alt.rap	Rap music related
alt.rap-gdead	Grateful Dead and rap fans
alt.rave	Rave culture: drugs, dancing, music, etc.
alt.recovery	Recovery programs, e.g. Alcoholics Anonymous
alt.religion.computers	Computing is the way of the Lord...
alt.religion.emacs	For those who just love emacs

Group name	Description
alt.religion.satanism	Satanism as a religion
alt.restaurants	Restaurants and good eating discussion area
alt.revisionism	Come to a new conclusion; the facts are here
alt.rock-n-roll	Rock and roll music discussion group
alt.rock-n-roll.acdc	ACDC rock and roll group discussion
alt.rock-n-roll.hard	Hard rock
alt.rock-n-roll.metal	Heavy metal music
alt.rock-n-roll.metal.heavy	Ditto
alt.rock-n-roll.metal.metallica	The Metallica group
alt.rodney-king	The Rodney King/Police case
alt.rodney.dangerfield	More on Rodney King: the dangers
alt.rodney.king	Yet more on Rodney King
alt.romance	Romance and love
alt.romance.chat	Romantic chatting between users
alt.satanism	Satanism and a general discussion of 'Old Nick'
alt.save.the.earth	Save the earth: environmental discussions
alt.sb.programmer	Sound Blaster programming (for the PC user)
alt.sci.astro.aips	The astronomical image processing system
alt.sci.physics.acoustics	Sounds and acoustics in physics
alt.sci.physics.new-theories	New theories in physics
alt.sci.planetary	Planetary activity
alt.security	Security related discussion forum
alt.security.index	An index to USENET's alt.misc.security
alt.self-improve	Self-improvment for beginners
alt.sewing	Sewing, knitting, etc.
alt.sex	Sexual matters discussed
alt.sex.bestiality	Sex: bestiality
alt.sex.bondage	Sex: bondage
alt.sex.fetish.feet	Sex: feet fetishes!
alt.sex.masturbation	Sex: masturbation
alt.sex.motss	Sex: members of the same sex
alt.sex.movies	Sex: sex in the movies
alt.sex.pictures	† Binary erotic pictures (alternative to abpe)
alt.sex.pictures.d	Discussion group for the above
alt.sex.pictures.female	Alternative to abpef
alt.sex.pictures.male	† Alternative to abpem
alt.sex.sounds	† Erotic sounds (alternative to abse)
alt.sex.stories	Stories about sex from various people
alt.sex.stories.d	Discussion group for the above...
alt.sex.trans	Group for transexuals

Group name	Description
alt.sex.wanted	Sex: wanted in written form, or in the flesh
alt.sex.wizards	Experts at sex (questions and answers)
alt.sexual.abuse.recovery	Discussion of sexual abuse
alt.sexual.abuse.recovery.d	Discussion group for the above
alt.shenanigans	Practical jokers forum
alt.showbiz.gossip	Gossip in the showbusiness world
alt.silly.group.names.d	Discussion group for groups with silly names!
alt.skate	Ice/skateboarding
alt.skate-board	Skateboards
alt.skinheads	Skinhead movement and culture
alt.snowmobiles	All about snowmobiles
alt.society.anarchy	Anarchy in society
alt.society.ati	Activist Times Digest
alt.society.civil-disob	Civil disobediance in society
alt.society.civil-liberties	Individuals rights
alt.society.civil-liberty	Civil liberties
alt.society.foia	The Freedom of Information Act in the US
alt.society.futures	The future of society discussed
alt.society.revolution	Revolution in society
alt.sources	Source code for computers
alt.sources.amiga	Amiga source code
alt.sources.d	Discussion group for the alt.sources
alt.sources.index	Index to source code in alt.sources
alt.sources.patches	Source-code patches for software problems
alt.sources.wanted	Source code wanted by users
alt.sport.bowling	Sport: bowling
alt.sport.bungee	Sport: bungee jumping
alt.sport.darts	Sport: darts
alt.sport.lasertag	Sport: the new laser fight simulations
alt.sport.paintball	Sport: paintball guns in fight simulations
alt.sports.darts	Sport: darts (again)
alt.stagecraft	Technical theatre issues
alt.startrek.creative	Star Trek stories and parodies
alt.stupidity	Discussion about stupidity
alt.suburbs	Local suburbs being discussed
alt.suicide.finals	Suicides during final exams: discussion
alt.suicide.holiday	Why suicides happen more during holidays
alt.superman.dead	Is Superman really dead?
alt.supermodels	Supermodels discussion forum
alt.support	Dealing with emotional problems
alt.support.cancer	Cancer support
alt.support.diet	Diet support

Group name	Description
alt.support.mult-sclerosis	Multiple Sclerosis support
alt.surfing	Surfing the waves
alt.sustainable.agriculture	Sustainable agriculture
alt.sys.amiga.demos	Demo programs for the Amiga computer
alt.sys.amiga.uucp	UUCP-related programs for the Amiga
alt.sys.amiga.uucp.patches	Patches for UUCP programs (Amiga)
alt.sys.intergraph	Support for Intergraph machines
alt.sys.sun	Sun systems
alt.sys.unisys	UniSys systems
alt.tasteless	Disgusting topics discussed (very popular)
alt.tasteless.jokes	Tasteless (and mostly offensive) jokes
alt.tasteless.pictures	† Tasteless pictures (see also: abpt)
alt.tennis	Sport: tennis
alt.test	Test forum only
alt.text.dwb	AT&Ts Documenter's Workbench system
alt.thrash	Thrashlife
alt.timewasters	Time wasters discussion forum
alt.toolkits.xview	Xview toolkit forum
alt.toon-pics	† Cartoon pictures
alt.true-crime	True-life crime discussed
alt.tv.90210	Discussion of BH 90210 TV show
alt.tv.90210.sucks.sucks.sucks	People who hate Beverley Hills 90210 TV show!
alt.tv.antagonists	Antagonists on television
alt.tv.dinosaurs	Dinosaurs and television
alt.tv.la-law	LA-Law TV programme discussed
alt.tv.mash	The M*A*S*H TV series discussed
alt.tv.muppets	The Muppet puppets discussed
alt.tv.northern-exp	Northern Exposure TV show discussed
alt.tv.prisoner	The cult show The Prisoner is discussed
alt.tv.red-dwarf	For all Smeg Heads everywhere!
alt.tv.simpsons	The Simpsons TV show
alt.tv.twin-peaks	Twin Peaks cult TV series
alt.unix.wizards	UNIX experts group
alt.usage.english	English grammar discussed in detail
alt.usenet.recovery	Discusses new USENET programs/ newsreaders, etc.
alt.uu.announce	Announcements of the USENET University
alt.uu.comp.misc	Computer department of USNET University
alt.uu.future	The future of the USENET University
alt.uu.lang.esperanto.misc	Esperanto language study at USENET University
alt.uu.lang.misc	Language Department of USENET University

Group name
Description

alt.uu.math.misc	Maths Department of USENET University
alt.uu.misc.misc	Miscellaneous events at the USENET University
alt.uu.tools	Tools for USENET University in education
alt.uu.virtual-worlds.misc	Study of virtual worlds at USENET University
alt.vampyres	Vampire hangout
alt.wais	The WAIS service discussed
alt.wanted.mars.women	Wanted: women from Mars
alt.wanted.moslem.men	Wanted: Moslem men
alt.wanted.moslem.women	Wanted: Moslem women
alt.war	War and its impact on the world
alt.war.civil.usa	The USA's civil war
alt.war.vietnam	The Vietnam war
alt.whine	Complain and moan at your heart's content...
alt.wolves	Forum for wolves (how do they type?)
alt.zines	Small magazines (non-commerical)
alt.znet.aeo	Z*NET: Atari computer enthusiasts forum
alt.znet.pc	Z*NET: International PC, electronic magazine

Bionet hierarcyies (bionet.*)

Biology-related topics

Group name	Description
bionet.agroforestry	Discussion on agroforestry
bionet.announce	Announcements in the biology world
bionet.biology.computational	Computational biology
bionet.biology.tropical	Tropical biology
bionet.general	General interest area to biologists
bionet.genome.arabidopsis	Information about the Arabidopsis project
bionet.genome.chrom22	Chromosome 22 discussed
bionet.immunology	Immunology in biology
bionet.info-theory	Biological information theory
bionet.jobs	Jobs in biology
bionet.journals.contents	Contents of biological journals
bionet.molbio.ageing	Cellular and organismal ageing
bionet.molbio.bio-matrix	Computer appications in biology
bionet.molbio.embldatabank	Information about EMBL nucleic acid database

Group name	Description
bionet.molbio.evolution	How genes and proteins have evolved
bionet.molbio.gdb	Messages to and from the GDB database staff
bionet.molbio.genbank	Information about the GenBank nucleic acid DB
bionet.molbio.genbank.updates	Updates on the above
bionet.molbio.gene-linkage	Genetic gene linkage information
bionet.molbio.gene-org	Gene organization information
bionet.molbio.genome-program	The Human Genome Project: issues, etc.
bionet.molbio.hiv	Discussions about the HIV virus
bionet.molbio.methds-reagnts	Request for information and lab reagents
bionet.molbio.news	News service for molecular biologists
bionet.molbio.proteins	Research information on protein databases, etc.
bionet.neuroscience	Neurosciences related
bionet.plants	Plant biology
bionet.population-bio	Population biology
bionet.sci-resources	Funding agencies and scientific resources, etc.
bionet.software	Computer software for biologists
bionet.software.sources	Sources for biology-related software
bionet.users.addresses	Names and addresses of important biologists
bionet.virology	Virus-based biology
bionet.women-in-bio	Women in biology: general discussion forum
bionet.xtallography	Protein crystallography information

BITNET hierarchies (bit.*)

Discussion groups from the BITNET network: miscellaneous topics

Group name	Description
bit.admin	BITNET newsgroups discussion list
bit.general	General BITNET/USENET list
bit.listserv.3com-l	3COM products
bit.listserv.9370-l	IBM 9370 and VM topics
bit.listserv.advanc-l	GEAC Advanced Integrated Library System Users
bit.listserv.advise-l	User services list
bit.listserv.aidsnews	Information on AIDS
bit.listserv.aix-l	IBM AIX discussion list
bit.listserv.allmusic	Music-related lists
bit.listserv.appc-l	APPC discussion list
bit.listserv.apple2-l	Apple II list

Group name	Description
bit.listserv.applicat	Applications available under BITNET
bit.listserv.ashe-1	Higher education: policy and research
bit.listserv.asm370	IBM 370 Assembler language discussions
bit.listserv.autism	Autism and disability list
bit.listserv.banyan-1	Banyan Vines network software discussions
bit.listserv.big-lan	Large LAN systems discussions
bit.listserv.biosph-1	BioSphere, ecology discussion list
bit.listserv.bitnews	BITNET news service
bit.listserv.buslib-1	Business libraries list
bit.listserv.c+health	Computers and health discussion list
bit.listserv.c18-1	18th century interdisciplinary discussion
bit.listserv.c370-1	C/370 discussion list
bit.listserv.candle-1	Candle products discussion list
bit.listserv.catholic	Free Catholics
bit.listserv.cdromlan	CD ROM on LAN systems
bit.listserv.christia	Practical Christian life
bit.listserv.cics-1	CICS discussion list
bit.listserv.cinema-1	Discussions on cinema
bit.listserv.cmspip-1	VM/SP CMS pipelines discussion list
bit.listserv.commed	Communications educations
bit.listserv.contacts	Contacts on BITNET
bit.listserv.csg-1	Control System Group network
bit.listserv.cumrec-1	CUMREC-L administrative computer use
bit.listserv.cw-email	Campus-wide email discussion list
bit.listserv.cwis-1	Campus-wide information systems (CWIS)
bit.listserv.cyber-1	CDC computer discussions
bit.listserv.dasig	Database administration
bit.listserv.db2-1	DB2 database discussion list
bit.listserv.dbase-1	dBASE IV discussion list
bit.listserv.deaf-1	Deaf list
bit.listserv.decnews	Digital Equipment Corporation news list
bit.listserv.dectei-1	DECUS education sofware library discussions
bit.listserv.dipl-1	Diplomacy game discussions list
bit.listserv.disarm-1	Disarmament discussions list
bit.listserv.domain-1	Domains discussion group
bit.listserv.earntech	EARN technical group
bit.listserv.edi-1	Electronic data interchange issues
bit.listserv.edpolyan	Professionals and students discuss education
bit.listserv.edstat-1	Statistics education discussion list
bit.listserv.edtech	EDTECH: educational technology
bit.listserv.emusic-1	Electronic music discussion list

Group name	Description
bit.listserv.envbeh-l	Forum on environmental behaviour
bit.listserv.erl-l	Education research list
bit.listserv.ethics-l	Computer ethics discussions
bit.listserv.ethology	Ethology list
bit.listserv.euearn-l	Eastern Europe list
bit.listserv.film-l	Film making and reviews list
bit.listserv.fnord-l	News ways of thinking list
bit.listserv.frac-l	Fractal discussion list
bit.listserv.games-l	Computer games list
bit.listserv.gaynet	Gay people discussion list
bit.listserv.gddm-l	The GDDM discussion list
bit.listserv.gguide	BITNET GGUIDE list
bit.listserv.govdoc-l	Discussion of government document issues
bit.listserv.gutnberg	Project GUTENBERG discussion list
bit.listserv.hellas	The Hellenic discussion list
bit.listserv.history	History list
bit.listserv.i-amiga	Info-Amiga list
bit.listserv.ibm-hesc	IBM Higher Education Consortium
bit.listserv.ibm-main	IBM mainframe discussion list
bit.listserv.ibm-nets	BITNIC IBM-nets list
bit.listserv.ibm7171	Protocol convertor list
bit.listserv.ibmtcp-l	IBM TCP/IP list
bit.listserv.info-gcg	INFO GCG: genetics software discussion
bit.listserv.infonets	Infonets redistribution list
bit.listserv.ingrafx	Information graphics
bit.listserv.innopac	Innovative interfaces online public access
bit.listserv.ioob-l	Industrial psychology
bit.listserv.isn	ISN data-switch technical discussion list
bit.listserv.jes2-l	JES2 discussion group
bit.listserv.jnet-l	BITNIC JNET-L list
bit.listserv.l-hcap	Handicap list
bit.listserv.l-vmctr	VM CENTER components discussion list
bit.listserv.lawsch-l	Law school discussion list
bit.listserv.liaison	BITNIC liaison
bit.listserv.libref-l	Library reference issues
bit.listserv.libres	Library and information science research
bit.listserv.license	Software licensing list
bit.listserv.linkfail	BITNET link failure announcements
bit.listserv.literary	Discussions about literature in general
bit.listserv.lstsrv-l	Forum on BITNETs listserv system
bit.listserv.mail-l	BITNIC Mail-L list
bit.listserv.mailbook	MAIL/MAILBOOK subscription list
bit.listserv.mba-l	MBA student curriculum discussion

Group name	Description
bit.listserv.mbu-l	MegaByte University: computers and writing
bit.listserv.medlib-l	Medical libraries discussion list
bit.listserv.mednews	Medical news: InfoCom newsletter
bit.listserv.mideur-l	Middle Europe discussion list
bit.listserv.netnws-l	NETNWS-L Usenet list
bit.listserv.nettrain	Network trainers
bit.listserv.new-list	New list announcements
bit.listserv.next-l	NeXT computers list
bit.listserv.notabene	Nota Bene WP system list
bit.listserv.notis-l	NOTIS/DOBIS discussion group list
bit.listserv.novell	Novell LAN interest group
bit.listserv.omrscan	OMR scanner discussion list
bit.listserv.ozone	Ozone discussion list
bit.listserv.pacs-l	Public-access computer system forum
bit.listserv.page-l	IBM 3812/3820 tips and problems list
bit.listserv.pagemakr	PageMaker DTP system
bit.listserv.politics	Political discussions forum
bit.listserv.power-l	IBM RS/6000 Power family
bit.listserv.procom-l	Procomm communications software list
bit.listserv.psycgrad	Psychology graduate student discussions
bit.listserv.qualrs-l	Qualitative research of the human sciences
bit.listserv.relusr-l	Relay users forum
bit.listserv.rexxlist	REXX programming
bit.listserv.rhetoric	Social movements, etc.
bit.listserv.rscs-l	VM/RSCS mailing list
bit.listserv.rscsmods	RSCS modifications list for the above
bit.listserv.s-comput	Supercomputers list
bit.listserv.sas-l	SAS database discussion
bit.listserv.scuba-l	Scuba diving discussion list
bit.listserv.seasia-l	Southeast Asia discussion list
bit.listserv.security	Security related discussion list
bit.listserv.sfs-l	VM shared file system discussion list
bit.listserv.sganet	Student–government: global mail network
bit.listserv.simula	The SIMULA language list
bit.listserv.slart-l	SLA research discussion list
bit.listserv.slovak-l	Slovak discussion list
bit.listserv.snamgt-l	SNA network discussion list
bit.listserv.sos-data	Social science data list
bit.listserv.spires-l	SPIRES conference list
bit.listserv.sportpsy	Exercise and sports psychology
bit.listserv.spssx-l	SPSSX statistics system discussion list
bit.listserv.sqlinfo	SQL database language discussion list
bit.listserv.stat-l	Statistical consulting discussion list
bit.listserv.tech-l	BITNIC TECH-L list
bit.listserv.test	Test newsgroup only

Group name	Description
bit.listserv.tex-l	The TeXnical topics list
bit.listserv.tn3270-l	IBM tn3270 protocol discussion list
bit.listserv.trans-l	BITNIC TRANS-L list
bit.listserv.travel-l	Tourism discussion list
bit.listserv.ucp-l	University Computing Project mailing list
bit.listserv.ug-l	Usage guidelines
bit.listserv.uigis-l	User interface for geographical information system
bit.listserv.urep-l	UREP-L mailing list
bit.listserv.usrdir-l	User directory list
bit.listserv.valert-l	Virus alert list
bit.listserv.vfort-l	VS-Fortran discussion list
bit.listserv.virus-l	General virus discussion list
bit.listserv.vm-util	VM utilities discussion list
bit.listserv.vmesa-l	VM/ESA mailing list
bit.listserv.vmslsv-l	VAX/VMS listserv discussion list
bit.listserv.vmxa-l	VM/XA discussion list
bit.listserv.vnews-l	VNEWS discussion list
bit.listserv.vpiej-l	Electronic publishing discussion list
bit.listserv.win3-l	Windows 3 forum (PC)
bit.listserv.word-pc	MicroSoft Word for the PC discussion list
bit.listserv.words-l	English lanuage discussion list
bit.listserv.wp50-l	WordPerfect 5.0 forum
bit.listserv.wpcorp-l	WordPerfect corporation products discussion
bit.listserv.wpwin-l	WordPerfect for Windows forum (PC)
bit.listserv.x400-l	X.400 protocol list
bit.listserv.xcult-l	International intercultural newsletter
bit.listserv.xedit-l	VM system editor list
bit.listserv.xerox-l	The Xerox discussion list
bit.listserv.xmailer	The CrossWell mailer system
bit.listserv.xtropy-l	Extopian discussion list
bit.mailserv.word-mac	Word-processing on the Macintosh platform
bit.mailserv.word-pc	Word-processing on the IBM PC and clones

BIZ hierarchies (biz.*)

Business, marketing and advertisements, etc.

Group name	Description
biz.books.technical	Booksellers and buyers forum
biz.clarinet	Announcements regarding Clarinet

Group name	Description
biz.clarinet.sample	Samples of Clarinet postings
biz.comp.hardware	Hardware information postings
biz.comp.services	Commerical service postings
biz.comp.software	† Commercial software postings
biz.comp.telebit	Telebit modem support
biz.comp.telebit.netblazer	Netblazer modem support
biz.config	Biz USENET configuration and administration
biz.control	Control information and messages
biz.dec	Digital Equipment Corporation (hardware/software)
biz.dec.decathena	DEC Athena OS environment
biz.dec.decnews	DEC Newsletter
biz.dec.ip	IP networking on DEC workstations
biz.dec.workstations	DEC workstations discussion group
biz.jobs.offered	Employment positions
biz.misc	Miscellaneous commercial postings
biz.next.newprod	New products for NeXT computers
biz.sco.announce	Santa Cruz operation: product announcements
biz.sco.binaries	† Binary programs for the SCO Unix/Xenix/ODT
biz.sco.general	General information on SCO (Q and A)
biz.sco.opendesktop	ODT environment: Q&A and technical information
biz.sco.sources	Source code for (and ported to) SCO environment
biz.stolen	Postings regarding stolen merchandise
biz.tadpole.sparcbook	Discussion group for the Sparcbook portable
biz.test	Biz newsgroup test postings group

Clarinet hierarchies (clari.*)

Clarinet newsgroups deal solely with news and business information. There are many more local Clarinet groups for the United States which take the form clari.local.<place>, e.g. clari.local.florida which contain local news for that specific area. Although Clarinet is not free, some newsgroups still propagate to public sites and NNTP news servers.

Group name	Description
clari.biz.commodity	Commodity news and price reports
clari.biz.courts	Lawsuits and legal matters
clari.biz.economy	Economic news (local to US)

Group name	*Description*
clari.biz.economy.world	Economic news (non-US countries)
clari.biz.features	Business feature stories
clari.biz.finance	Financial information, corporate finance
clari.biz.finance.earnings	Earnings and dividend reports
clari.biz.finance.personal	Personal investing and finance
clari.biz.finance.services	Banks and other financial organizations
clari.biz.invest	News for investors
clari.biz.labor	Union, strike and labour relations information
clari.biz.market	Stock-market news
clari.biz.market.amex	American Stock Exchange reports and news
clari.biz.market.dow	Dow Jones NYSE reports
clari.biz.market.ny	NYSE reports
clari.biz.market.otc	NASDAQ reports
clari.biz.market.report	General market reports
clari.biz.mergers	Mergers, company acquisitions and takeovers
clari.biz.misc	Miscellaneous business news
clari.biz.products	Important new products and services
clari.biz.top	Top business news
clari.biz.urgent	News that is just breaking to the markets
clari.canada	Canadian news
clari.canada.biz	Business summaries for Canada
clari.canada.briefs	Information briefs on the Canadian market
clari.canada.briefs.ont	Canada (Ontario) market news
clari.canada.briefs.west	Canada (Western) market news
clari.canada.features	Ottawa Special; Almanac, etc.
clari.canada.general	Canadian news stories from the local press
clari.canada.gov	Government-related news stories
clari.canada.law	Law-related news stories
clari.canada.newscast	Newscasts for Canada
clari.canada.politics	Political and election news from Canada
clari.canada.trouble	Accidents and other problems related to Canada
clari.feature	Feature columns: general information
clari.feature.dave_barry	Feature column of humorist Dave Barry
clari.feature.kinsey	Q&A on sex from the Kinsey Institute
clari.feature.mike_royko	Chicago's opinion columnist Mike Royko
clari.feature.miss_manners	The Judith Martin column: humorous etiquette
clari.feature.movies	Movies/film details
clari.nb	NewsBytes (Nb) section:

Group name	Description
clari.nb.apple	Nb: Apple Macintosh news
clari.nb.business	Nb: business related news
clari.nb.general	Nb: general computer news
clari.nb.govt	Nb: government news
clari.nb.ibm	Nb: information on PC/IBM computing
clari.nb.index	Nb: index to the 'nb' series of groups
clari.nb.telecom	Nb: telecommunications news
clari.nb.trends	Nb: trends and new developments in business
clari.nb.unix	Nb: Unix news
clari.net	Information on the Clarinet network
clari.net.admin	Administrative information for Clarinet Sysops
clari.net.announce	Announcements for all Clarinet readers
clari.net.newusers	Information for new Clarinet readers
clari.net.products	Product information for Clarinet users
clari.net.talk	Discussion of Clarinet system (unmoderated)
clari.news.almanac	Daily Almanac: today's news
clari.news.arts	Arts news
clari.news.aviation	Aviation/plane news
clari.news.books	Books and publications news
clari.news.briefs	Regular news summaries
clari.news.bulletin	Breaking stories of the week
clari.news.canada	Canadian news stories
clari.news.cast	US news summary (newscast)
clari.news.children	Children in the news (parenting, etc.)
clari.news.consumer	Consumer news: reviews of products, etc.
clari.news.demonstration	Demonstrations around the world
clari.news.disaster	Disasters around the world: earthquakes, etc.
clari.news.economy	Economic news/world markets, etc.
clari.news.election	US and international election news
clari.news.entertain	Entertainment industry news
clari.news.europe	News in Europe and the EC
clari.news.features	Unclassified feature stories
clari.news.fighting	Wars/clashes around the world
clari.news.flash	Once-a-year news flashes
clari.news.goodnews	Stories of success in the world, e.g. peace
clari.news.gov	Central government related news stories
clari.news.gov.agency	US government agencies in the news, e.g. FBI
clari.news.gov.budget	Budget news
clari.news.gov.corrupt	Government corruption, etc.
clari.news.gov.international	International news (government/party related)
clari.news.gov.officials	Government officials and their problems

Group name	Description
clari.news.gov.state	State governments news (international)
clari.news.gov.taxes	Tax-related news
clari.news.gov.usa	US Federal Government news
clari.news.group	SIGS: special interest groups
clari.news.group.blacks	Black people in the news
clari.news.group.gays	Homosexuals in the news
clari.news.group.jews	The Jewish community in the news
clari.news.group.women	Women in the news
clari.news.headlines	Main news headlines
clari.news.hot	'Hot' News
clari.news.hot.east_europe	Eastern Europe, e.g. former USSR's break-up
clari.news.hot.iraq	Iraq, e.g. post Gulf-War news
clari.news.hot.panama	US Panama invasion
clari.news.hot.rodney_king	Rodney King police violence/LA riots, etc.
clari.news.hot.somalia	Events in Somalia
clari.news.hot.ussr	USSR: the former USSR's break-up
clari.news.interest	Human interest stories
clari.news.interest.animals	Animal stories
clari.news.interest.history	History in the making type news
clari.news.interest.people	People in the news
clari.news.interest.people.column	Famous people in the news
clari.news.interest.quirks	Unusual and bizarre news, e.g. Elvis sightings
clari.news.issues	Stories regarding major issues
clari.news.issues.civil_rights	Civil-rights news
clari.news.issues.conflict	News about countries, e.g. wars, etc.
clari.news.issues.family	Family issues, e.g. abuse, divorce, etc.
clari.news.labor	Unions, strikes, etc.
clari.news.labor.strike	Strike-specific news
clari.news.law	Law-related news
clari.news.law.civil	Civil trials and litigations, etc.
clari.news.law.crime	Major crimes in the news
clari.news.law.crime.sex	Sex crimes
clari.news.law.crime.trial	Trials before the courts (criminal)
clari.news.law.crime.violent	Violent crime in the news
clari.news.law.drugs	Drug-related crimes in the news
clari.news.law.investigation	Criminal investigations in the news
clari.news.law.police	The police in the news
clari.news.law.prison	Prison information; escapes, etc.
clari.news.law.profession	News for lawyers and judges, etc.
clari.news.law.supreme	US Supreme Court news
clari.news.lifestyle	Fashion and leisure-related news, etc.
clari.news.military	Military news, e.g. people and new equipment
clari.news.movies	Movie reviews

Group name	Description
clari.news.music	Music reviews
clari.news.politics	Politics and politicians in the news
clari.news.politics.people	Political personalities in the news
clari.news.religion	Religion-related stories in the news
clari.news.sex	Sex in the news (politics, etc.)
clari.news.terrorism	Terrorist outrages in the news
clari.news.top	Top US news stories of the week
clari.news.top.world	Top world news stories of the week
clari.news.trends	Surveys and trend information, polls, etc.
clari.news.trouble	Minor accidents and mishaps in the news
clari.news.tv	Television in the news, schedules, reviews, etc.
clari.news.urgent	Major breaking stories of the day
clari.news.weather	Weather news and reports (many)
clari.sports	Sports-related news, results, etc.
clari.sports.baseball	Sports: baseball
clari.sports.basketball	Sports: basketball
clari.sports.features	Sports features
clari.sports.football	Sports: football
clari.sports.hockey	Sports: hockey
clari.sports.misc	Sports: miscellanous roundups of sports news
clari.sports.motor	Sports: motor racing, etc.
clari.sports.olympic	Sports: Olympic events
clari.sports.tennis	Sports: tennis
clari.sports.top	Top sports news of the day/week
clari.streetprice	Prices for computer equipment
clari.tw.aerospace	Aerospace news: aerospace company news
clari.tw.computers	Computer news: news/views from industry
clari.tw.defense	Defense news: defense industry, etc.
clari.tw.education	Educational news: college and university news
clari.tw.electronics	Electronics in the news
clari.tw.environment	Environmental news
clari.tw.health	Health issues: AIDS/HIV, political news
clari.tw.health.aids	AIDS news, specifically. Also political news
clari.tw.misc	General technical news
clari.tw.nuclear	Nuclear power related, e.g. waste, pollution
clari.tw.science	Science stories in the news
clari.tw.space	Space news: NASA, astronomy, spaceflight, etc.
clari.tw.stocks	Computer technology: stock/share prices
clari.tw.telecom	Communications: satellites, phones, etc.

Computing hierarchies (comp.*)

Computer-related topics.

Group name	Description
comp.admin.policy	Adminsitration policy for comp.* hierarchy
comp.ai	Artificial intelligence
comp.ai.edu	AI: artificial intelligence in Education
comp.ai.fuzzy	AI: fuzzy logic and set theory
comp.ai.genetic	AI: AI used in genetic research
comp.ai.nat-lang	AI: AI used in natural language processing
comp.ai.neural-nets	AI: neural networks
comp.ai.nlang-know-rep	AI: knowledge representation in language
comp.ai.philosophy	AI: computing philosophy
comp.ai.shells	AI: shell environments for AI
comp.ai.vision	AI: visual research
comp.answers	A place for periodic USENET articles; FAQs, etc.
comp.apps.spreadsheets	Spreadsheet applications, e.g. 123, etc.
comp.arch	Computer architecture
comp.arch.bus.vmebus	Hard/software for the VMEbus system
comp.arch.storage	Storage issues in hardware and software
comp.archives	Archives for computer-related information
comp.archives.admin	Administration details for the above
comp.archives.msdos.announce	Announcements about MSDOS archives
comp.archives.msdos.d	Discussion about DOS archives
comp.bbs.misc	Bulletin board systems: miscellaneous
comp.bbs.waffle	The Waffle BBS programs discussion forum
comp.benchmarks	Benchmarks and testing information/data
comp.binaries.acorn	† Binary programs for the Acorn platform
comp.binaries.amiga	† Binary programs for the Amiga platform
comp.binaries.apple2	† Binary programs for the Apple II platform
comp.binaries.atari.st	† Binary programs for the Atari ST platform
comp.binaries.ibm.pc	† Binary programs for the IBM PC and clones
comp.binaries.ibm.pc.d	Discussion group for the above
comp.binaries.ibm.pc.wanted	Binary programs wanted by users
comp.binaries.mac	† Binary programs for the Macintosh platform

Group name	Description
`comp.binaries.ms-windows`	† Binary programs for the Windows OS
`comp.binaries.os2`	† Binary programs for the OS/2 operating system
`comp.bugs.2bsd`	Bugs (errors) in version 2 BSD
`comp.bugs.4bsd`	Bugs (errors) in version 4 BSD
`comp.bugs.4bsd.ucb-fixes`	Bug fixes for BSD version 4
`comp.bugs.misc`	Miscellaneous bugs/errors discussed
`comp.bugs.sys5`	Bugs in System V Unix
`comp.cad.cadence`	For the users of Cadence Systems products
`comp.client-server`	Client–server discussion group
`comp.cog-eng`	Cognitive engineering/human factors group
`comp.compilers`	Compilers and linkers discussion group
`comp.compression`	Data-compression discussion group
`comp.compression.research`	Research in data compression
`comp.databases`	Databases: all platforms; general discussion
`comp.databases.informix`	Databases: Informix
`comp.databases.ingres`	Databases: Ingres
`comp.database.object`	Object orientation in databases
`comp.databases.oracle`	Databases: Oracle/SQL
`comp.databases.sybase`	Databases: Sybase
`comp.databases.theory`	Datbase theory; algorithms, etc.
`comp.dcom.cell-relay`	Data Comms: cell relay-based systems
`comp.dcom.fax`	Data comms: facsimile
`comp.dcom.isdn`	Data comms: Integrated Serial Digital Network
`comp.dcom.lans`	Data comms: local area networks
`comp.dcom.lans.ethernet`	Data comms: Ethernet-based networks
`comp.dcom.lans.fddi`	Data comms: fibre optics
`comp.dcom.lans.hyperchannel`	Data comms: Hyperchannel
`comp.dcom.lans.misc`	Data comms: local area networks: miscellaneous
`comp.dcom.modems`	Data comms: MODEM devices
`comp.dcom.servers`	Data comms: server machines
`comp.dcom.sys.cisco`	Data comms: Cisco TCP routers and hardware, etc.
`comp.dcom.sys.wellfleet`	Data comms: the Wellfleet bridge/router systems
`comp.dcom.telecom`	Data comms: general telecommunications
`comp.doc`	Documentation newsgroup
`comp.doc.techreports`	Technical reports
`comp.dsp`	Digital signal processing
`comp.editors`	Text editors newsgroup
`comp.edu`	Educational newsgroup (colleges/universities)

Group name	Description
comp.edu.composition	Writing instructions in computer-based classrooms
comp.emacs	Emacs editor newsgroup
comp.fonts	Newsgroup for discussing fonts, etc.
comp.graphics	Graphics newsgroup
comp.graphics.animation	Animation in graphics
comp.graphics.avs	Audio-visual simulations
comp.graphics.explorer	Explorer Modular Visualization Environment (MVE)
comp.graphics.gnuplot	The Gnuplot function plotting system
comp.graphics.opengl	The OpenGL 3D API
comp.graphics.research	Research in computer graphics
comp.graphics.visualization	Scientific visualization
comp.groupware	Groupware for computers discussed
comp.human-factors	Human factors in computing, e.g. ergonomics
comp.infosystems	Information systems
comp.infosystems.gis	Geographic information systems (GIS)
comp.infosystems.gopher	Information systems: Gopher/veronica
comp.infosystems.wais	Information systems: WAIS databases
comp.internet.library	Electronic libraries, OPACs, etc.
comp.ivideodisc	Interactive Video: CDi, etc.
comp.lang.ada	Languages: ADA
comp.lang.apl	Languages: the APL programming language
comp.lang.asm370	Languages: assembly language for IBM370
comp.lang.c	Languages: C
comp.lang.c++	Languages: C++
comp.lang.clos	The Common Lisp Object System
comp.lang.clu	Languages: CLU language
comp.lang.dylan	Languages: the Dylan language
comp.lang.eiffel	Languages: the object-orientated Eiffel language
comp.lang.forth	Languages: Forth
comp.lang.forth.mac	Languages: Forth for the Macintosh
comp.lang.fortran	Languages: Fortran
comp.lang.functional	Languages: functional languages
comp.lang.hermes	Languages: Hermes language for Dist. Environments
comp.lang.icon	Languages: the ICON programming language
comp.lang.idl	Languages: Interface Description Language
comp.lang.idl-pvwave	Languages: Interface Description Language
comp.lang.lisp	Languages: Lisp
comp.lang.lisp.franz	Languages: Lisp (Franz Lisp)

Group name	Description
comp.lang.lisp.x	Languages: Lisp (X Lisp)
comp.lang.lisp.mcl	Languages: Apple Mac's Common Lisp language
comp.lang.logo	Languages: Logo teaching and learning language
comp.lang.misc	Miscellaneous language discussion group
comp.lang.ml	Languages: ML languages, e.g. ML, Lazy ML, CAML, etc.
comp.lang.modula2	Languages: Modula 2
comp.lang.modula3	Languages: Modula 3
comp.lang.oberon	Languages: the Oberon language and system
comp.lang.objective-c	Languages: C (OOP)
comp.lang.pascal	Languages: Pascal
comp.lang.perl	Languages: Perl
comp.lang.pop	Languages: Pop
comp.lang.postscript	Languages: Postscript (Adobe, etc.)
comp.lang.prolog	Languages: Prolog
comp.lang.rexx	Languages: REXX command language (for IBM VM)
comp.lang.scheme	Languages: Scheme language environment
comp.lang.scheme.c	Languages: Scheme/C languages
comp.lang.sigplan	Information and announcements: ACM SIGPLAN
comp.lang.smalltalk	Languages: SmallTalk
comp.lang.tcl	Languages: TCL and tools, etc.
comp.lang.verilog	Languages: the PLI and Verilog languages
comp.lang.vhdl	Languages: the VHSIC hardware description language
comp.lang.visual	Languages: visual programming languages
comp.laser-printers	Laser printer newsgroup
comp.lsi	Large scale integration (CAD/Chip design, etc.)
comp.lsi.cad	CAD applications of LSI
comp.lsi.testing	Testing environment for LSI
comp.mail.elm	The Elm mailing system
comp.mail.headers	Elm: header information
comp.mail.maps	Elm: maps (locations) of other email systems
comp.mail.mh	Elm: MH-MAIL related applications
comp.mail.mime	Internet mail extensions (RFC 1341)
comp.mail.misc	Miscellaneous electronic mail discussion area
comp.mail.multi-media	Multimedia email systems
comp.mail.mush	MUSH (MUD) systems on email

Group name	Description
comp.mail.sendmail	The Unix sendmail program
comp.mail.uucp	Electronic mail via the UUCP network
comp.misc	An overspill for other topics not in comp.*
comp.multimedia	Main multimedia discussion group
comp.music	Music newsgroup (all tastes)
comp.newprod	New computer products on the market
comp.object	Object-based systems
comp.org.acm	Association for Computing Machinery (ACM)
comp.org.decus	Digital Equipment Corporation: user's society
comp.org.eff.news	Electronic Frontiers Foundation: user's society
comp.org.eff.talk	EFF strategies and goals discussed, etc.
comp.org.fidonet	Official forum of the FidoNet association
comp.org.ieee	The IEEE forum
comp.org.issnnet	International Student Society for Neural networks
comp.org.sug	Sun User's Group
comp.org.usenix	USENIX associations events and announcements
comp.org.usenix.roomshare	How to find accommodation during USENIX events
comp.os.386bsd.announce	Announcements about 386 BSD Unix
comp.os.386bsd.apps	BSD 386 Unix applications discussed
comp.os.386bsd.bugs	Bugs in BSD 386 Unix discussed
comp.os.386bsd.development	Development on the 386 BSD Unix platform
comp.os.386bsd.misc	Miscellaneous postings regarding 386 BSD
comp.os.386bsd..questions	Q & A regarding 386 BSD
comp.os.aos	AOS operating system
comp.os.coherent	Coherent operating system
comp.os.cpm	CP/M operating system
comp.os.cpm.amethyst	CP/M (Amethyst operating system)
comp.os.eunice	Eunice operating system
comp.os.linux	All about Linux, the Unix clone for PCs
comp.os.linux.announce	Announcements in the Linux world
comp.os.mach	Mach operating system
comp.os.minix	Minix (UNIX clone for PC) operating system
comp.os.misc	Miscellaneous operating system discussion area
comp.os.ms-windows.advocacy	MS-Windows: general debate
comp.os.ms-windows.announce	MS-Windows: new announcements

Group name	Description
comp.os.ms-windows.apps	MS-Windows: applications
comp.os.ms-windows.misc	MS-Windows: programmers miscellany
comp.os.ms-windows. programmer.misc	MS-Windows: miscellaneous prog. notes
comp.os.ms-windows. programmer.tools	MS-Windows: miscellaneous prog. tools
comp.os.ms-windows. programmer.win32	MS-Windows: 32 bit Windows
comp.os.ms-windows.setup	MS-Windows: setup discussion area
comp.os.msdos.4dos	The 4DOS system for MS-DOS (PCs)
comp.os.msdos.apps	MS-DOS applications
comp.os.msdos.desqview	Desqview (Windows clone) for MS-DOS
comp.os.msdos.misc	Miscellaneous MS-DOS discussion forum
comp.os.msdos.pcgeos	PC-GEOS system for MS-DOS
comp.os.msdos.programmer	Programmer area for MS-DOS (assembly)
comp.os.os2.advocacy	General debate about OS/2
comp.os.os2.announce	Announcements in the OS/2 world
comp.os.os2.apps	OS/2 applications discussed
comp.os.os2.beta	OS/2 beta applications discussed
comp.os.os2.bugs	OS/2 software bugs discussed
comp.os.os2.misc	Miscellaneous forum for OS/2
comp.os.os2.multimedia	Multimedia products and implementations
comp.os.os2.networking	Networking forum for OS/2
comp.os.os2.programmer	Programmer notes for OS/2 (assembly)
comp.os.os2.programmer.misc	Miscellaneous programmer notes for OS/2
comp.os.os2.programmer.porting	All about porting software to OS/2
comp.os.os2.setup	All about installing OS/2
comp.os.os2.ver1x	All about OS/2 versions 1 to 1.3
comp.os.os9	The OS9 OS discussed
comp.os.research	Research notes for miscellaneous OSs
comp.os.rsts	The DEC PDP-11 RSTS/E OS
comp.os.v	The V distributed OS from Stanford
comp.os.vms	The VMS operating system (DEC/VAX etc.)
comp.os.vxworks	The VxWorks real-time OS discussed
comp.os.xinu	The Xinu operating system
comp.parallel	Parallel systems forum
comp.parallel.pvm	The PVM system of multi-computer parallelization
comp.patents	Patents and copyright discussion forum
comp.periphs	Peripherals: miscellaneous forum
comp.periphs.printers	Peripherals: printers (all types)
comp.periphs.scsi	Peripherals: SCSI devices, e.g. disks
comp.privacy	Privacy in computing forum

Group name	Description
comp.programming	For programming issues that transcend OSs
comp.programming	Miscellaneous programming discussion forum
comp.protocols.appletalk	AppleTalk protocol forum
comp.protocols.ibm	IBM-based protocols
comp.protocols.iso	ISO protocols, e.g. OSI model, etc.
comp.protocols.iso.dev-environ	The ISO development environment
comp.protocols.iso.x400	X.400 protocol (see also: .iso.x400.gateway)
comp.protocols.kerberos	The Kerberos protocol
comp.protocols.kermit	The Kermit protocol
comp.protocols.misc	Miscellaneous protocols
comp.protocols.nfs	The Network File System protocol
comp.protocols.pcnet	The PCNET PC network discussed
comp.protocols.ppp	The Point-to-Point protocol
comp.protocols.snmp	The SNMP mail protocol
comp.protocols.tcp-ip	The TCP/IP protocol suite
comp.protocols.tcp-ip.domains	Domains for TCP/IP networks
comp.protocols.tcp-ip.ibmpc	TCP/IP for the IBM/PC
comp.protocols.time.ntp	Network Time protocol
comp.realtime	Real-time applications discussion forum
comp.research.japan	Japanese computing research forum
comp.risks	Risks in computing discussed
comp.robotics	Robotics in computing
comp.security.announce	Security announcements forum
comp.security.misc	Miscellaneous security discussion forum
comp.simulation	Computer simulations
comp.society	Computers in society
comp.society.cu-digest	The Computer Underground Digest
comp.society.development	Development of computers in society
comp.society.folklore	Computer folklore
comp.society.futures	The future of computing in society
comp.society.privacy	Privacy in society (computer related)
comp.society.women	Women in society (computer related)
comp.soft-sys.andrew	The Andrew File System from CMU
comp.soft-sys.khoros	The Khoros X11 visualization system
comp.soft-sys.matlab	The MathWorks calculation system
comp.soft-sys.nextstep	The NeXTstep computing environment
comp.soft-sys.shazam	Shazam software discussed
comp.software-eng	Software engineering in computing
comp.software.licensing	Software licensing
comp.sources.3b1	Source code postings (only): AT&T 3b1
comp.sources.acorn	Source code for Acorn machines
comp.sources.amiga	Source code for Amiga machines
comp.sources.apple2	Source code for Apple II machines
comp.sources.atari.st	Source code for Atari ST machines
comp.sources.bugs	Bugs/errors in source code listings

Group name	Description
comp.sources.d	Discussion area for source code postings
comp.sources.games	Source code for computer games
comp.sources.games.bugs	Bugs/errors in games source code
comp.sources.hp48	Programs for HP48/28 calculators
comp.sources.mac	Source code for Macintosh machines
comp.sources.misc	Miscellaneous source code listings/postings
comp.sources.postscript	Source code for postscript programs
comp.sources.reviewed	Source code reviewed
comp.sources.sun	Source code for Sun machines
comp.sources.testers	Testers wanted for source code programs
comp.sources.unix	Source code for UNIX machines
comp.sources.wanted	Source code wanted by readers
comp.sources.x	Source code for X-Windows environment
comp.specification	Computer specifications forum
comp.specification.z	For the formal specification language Z
comp.speech	Speech recognition and processing
comp.std.announce	Announcements about standards, e.g. ANSI, etc.
comp.std.c	C language standards announcements
comp.std.c++	C++ language standards announcements
comp.std.internat	International standards announcements
comp.std.misc	Miscellaneous standards announcements
comp.std.mumps	Standards for the MUMPS OS
comp.std.unix	Standards for the UNIX OS
comp.sw.components	Software components and related areas
comp.sys.3b1	AT&T 7300 3B1 UnixPC system
comp.sys.acorn	The Acorn computer discussion forum
comp.sys.acorn.advocacy	Debate about Acorn computers
comp.sys.acorn.announce	Announcements regarding Acorn machines
comp.sys.acorn.tech	Technical notes on Acorn machines
comp.sys.alliant	Alliant computers discussed
comp.sys.amiga.advocacy	Amiga computers discussed
comp.sys.amiga.announce	Announcements regarding Amiga machines
comp.sys.amiga.applications	Amiga computer applications
comp.sys.amiga.audio	Audio processing on Amiga machines
comp.sys.amiga.datacomm	Data communications on Amiga machines
comp.sys.amiga.emulations	Emulation systems on the Amiga platform
comp.sys.amiga.games	Amiga games
comp.sys.amiga.graphics	Amiga graphics

Group name	Description
comp.sys.amiga.hardware	Amiga hardware
comp.sys.amiga.introduction	Introduction to the Amiga
comp.sys.amiga.marketplace	Amiga in the marketplace: prices, model, etc.
comp.sys.amiga.misc	Miscellaneous Amiga discussion forum
comp.sys.amiga.multimedia	Multimedia applications for the Amiga
comp.sys.amiga.programmer	Programmer notes for the Amiga
comp.sys.amiga.reviews	Amiga reviews in the press and from readers
comp.sys.amiga.tech	Technical notes for Amiga users/ programmers
comp.sys.apollo	The Apollo system discussion forum
comp.sys.apple2	The Apple II system discussion forum
comp.sys.apple2.gno	The Apple IIgs GNO multitasking environment
comp.sys.atari.8bit	The Atari (8 bit) system discussion forum
comp.sys.atari.advocacy	The Atari computer discussed
comp.sys.atari.st	The Atari ST system discussion forum
comp.sys.atari.st.tech	Technical notes for Atari ST users/ programmers
comp.sys.att	AT&T systems discussion forum
comp.sys.cbm	CBM (Commodore Business Machines) discussion forum
comp.sys.cdc	Control Data Computers (CDC)
comp.sys.concurrent	Concurrent/Masscomp computers
comp.sys.dec	DEC discussion forum
comp.sys.dec.micro	Microcomputing on DEC platform
comp.sys.encore	The Encore computer systems discussion forum
comp.sys.handhelds	Hand-held computer systems forum
comp.sys.hp	Hewlett-Packard computer systems forum
comp.sys.hp48	HP48 systems forum
comp.sys.ibm.pc.demos	Demo programs for the IBM PC and clones
comp.sys.ibm.pc.digest	IBM-PC digest
comp.sys.ibm.pc.games	Games on the IBM-PC
comp.sys.ibm.pc.games.action	Action games on the IBM-PC
comp.sys.ibm.pc.games.adventure	Adventure games on the IBM-PC
comp.sys.ibm.pc.games.announce	Announcements in the PC games world
comp.sys.ibm.pc.games. flight-sim	PC flight simulators, e.g. MicroSoft
comp.sys.ibm.pc.games.misc	Games miscellany
comp.sys.ibm.pc.games.rpg	Role-playing games (RPGs)
comp.sys.ibm.pc.games.strategic	Strategy games
comp.sys.ibm.pc.hardware	Hardware for the IBM-PC
comp.sys.ibm.pc.misc	Miscellaneous postings on the IBM-PC
comp.sys.ibm.pc.rt	Real-time processing on the IBM-PC

Group name	Description
comp.sys.ibm.pc.soundcard	SoundCard forum for IBM-PC, e.g. AudioBlaster
comp.sys.ibm.ps2	PS2 (IBM) forum for the IBM-PC
comp.sys.ibm.ps2.hardware	Hardware for the IBM PS2 PC
comp.sys.intel	Intel discussion forum, e.g. chips development
comp.sys.intel.ipsc310	The Intel 310 discussed
comp.sys.isis	The ISIS discussion forum
comp.sys.laptops	Laptop computers discussion forum
comp.sys.m6809	6809-based processors
comp.sys.m68K	68000-based processors
comp.sys.m68K.pc	68000-based computers
comp.sys.m88k	88000-based computers
comp.sys.mac.advocacy	Macintosh computers discussion forum
comp.sys.mac.announce	Announcements in the Macintosh world
comp.sys.mac.apps	Applications for the Macintosh
comp.sys.mac.comm	Communications hw/sw for the Macintosh
comp.sys.mac.databases	Databases for the Macintosh computer range
comp.sys.mac.digest	News and reviews on the Mac scene
comp.sys.mac.games	Games for the Macintosh
comp.sys.mac.hardware	Hardware for the Macintosh
comp.sys.mac.hypercard	HyperCard/Mac discussion forum
comp.sys.mac.misc	Miscellaneous Macintosh discussion forum
comp.sys.mac.oop.macapp3	Object-based systems for Mac (v3)
comp.sys.mac.oop.misc	Object-based systems for Mac: miscellaneous
comp.sys.mac.oop.tcl	The Think Class libraries for the Mac
comp.sys.mac.programmer	Programmer notes for the Mac (assembly)
comp.sys.mac.system	Macintosh system software discussed
comp.sys.mac.wanted	Macintosh information, etc.: wanted by readers
comp.sys.mentor	Mentor graphics products
comp.sys.mips	The MIPS range of computer systems
comp.sys.misc	Miscellaneous system discussion forum
comp.sys.ncr	NCR computer systems forum
comp.sys.next.advocacy	The NeXT computer systems discussion forum
comp.sys.next.announce	Announcements in the NeXT computing world
comp.sys.next.bugs	NeXT: bug reports, etc.
comp.sys.next.hardware	Hardware for the NeXT platform
comp.sys.next.marketplace	The NeXT marketplace
comp.sys.next.misc	Miscellaneous NexT information

Group name	Description
comp.sys.next.programmer	Programmers forum for the NeXT platform
comp.sys.next.software	Software forum for the NeXT platform
comp.sys.next.sysadmin	Systems administrators: notes on NeXT systems
comp.sys.northstar	Northstar systems forum
comp.sys.novell	Novell networks forum
comp.sys.nsc.32k	National Semiconductor 32000 chip series
comp.sys.palmtops	High-powered palm-held calculator thingies
comp.sys.pen	Pen-based computer interaction
comp.sys.prime	Prime computer systems forum
comp.sys.proteon	Proteon gateway products
comp.sys.pyramid	Pyramid computer systems forum
comp.sys.ridge	Ridge 32 computers and ROS
comp.sys.sequent	Sequent Systems (balance and symmetry)
comp.sys.sgi.admin	Silicon Graphics Irises SysAdmin group
comp.sys.sgi.announce	Silicon Graphics: announcements forum
comp.sys.sgi.apps	Silicon Graphics: applications on SGI machines
comp.sys.sgi.bugs	Silicon Graphics: software bugs, etc.
comp.sys.sgi.graphics	Silicon Graphics: graphics packages on SGI machines
comp.sys.sgi.hardware	Silicon Graphics: hardware discussion forum
comp.sys.sgi.misc	Silicon Graphics: all other related topics
comp.sys.stratus	Stratus Products, e.g. System/88, CPS-32, FTX etc.
comp.sys.sun.admin	Sun: postings for administrators
comp.sys.sun.announce	Sun: announcements to users
comp.sys.sun.apps	Sun: computer applications forum
comp.sys.sun.hardware	Sun. hardware discussion forum
comp.sys.sun.misc	Sun: miscellaneous postings
comp.sys.sun.wanted	Sun: information wanted by readers
comp.sys.super	Supercomputers
comp.sys.tahoe	CCI 6/32, Harris HCX/7 and Sperry 7000 computers
comp.sys.tandy	Tandy computer systems forum
comp.sys.ti	Texas Instruments products forum
comp.sys.ti.explorer	Texas Instruments: Explorer systems
comp.sys.transputer	Transputer systems
comp.sys.unisys	UniSys computer systems forum
comp.sys.workstations	Workstations discussion forum (all makes)
comp.sys.xerox	Xerox systems discussion forum

Group name	Description
comp.sys.zenith	Zenith systems discussion forum
comp.sys.zenith.z100	Zenith Z100 family of computers
comp.terminals	Computer terminals discussion forum
comp.terminals.bitgraph	The BB&N BitGraph terminal forum
comp.terminals.tty5620	The AT&T dot-mapped terminals (5620/BLIT)
comp.text	Text processing forum
comp.text.desktop	Desktop publishing
comp.text.frame	FrameMaker *et al.*
comp.text.interleaf	Interleaf software forum
comp.text.sgml	The ISO 8879 SGML language
comp.text.tex	TeX related
comp.theory	Theoretical computing forum
comp.theory.cell-automata	Discussion of cellular automata
comp.theory.dynamic-sys	Discussion of ergodic theory
comp.theory.info-retrieval	Information retrieval
comp.theory.self-org-sys	Self-organization topics
comp.unix.admin	UNIX: administrators forum
comp.unix.aix	UNIX: IBM's AIX Unix system
comp.unix.amiga	Amiga Unix
comp.unix.aux	Apples Unix discussed
comp.unix.bsd	BSD Berkeley-based Unix
comp.unix.cray	Unix on Cray supercomputers
comp.unix.dos-under-unix	MS-DOS running under UNIX
comp.unix.internals	Hacking about with Unix internals!
comp.unix.large	Large UNIX-based systems
comp.unix.misc	Miscellaneous notes on UNIX systems
comp.unix.osf.misc	The Open System Foundations (OSF) UNIX forum
comp.unix.osf.osf1	The OSF/1 Unix operating system
comp.unix.pc-clone.16bit	16-bit PC UNIX
comp.unix.pc-clone.32bit	32-bit PC UNIX
comp.unix.programmer	UNIX Programming (nearly all in C)
comp.unix.questions	UNIX Questions and Answers forum
comp.unix.shell	UNIX shells: discussion forum
comp.unix.solaris	Sun's Solaris OS forum
comp.unix.sys3.misc	System III Unix
comp.unix.sys5.misc	System V: miscellaneous discussion forum
comp.unix.sys5.r3	System V release 3: discussion forum
comp.unix.sys5.r4	System V release 4: discussion forum
comp.unix.ultrix	The Ultrix (DEC) UNIX system
comp.unix.wizards	Unix experts forum
comp.unix.xenix.misc	Xenix (MiroSoft) UNIX system
comp.unix.xenix.sco	SCO Xenix system (Santa Cruz Operation)
comp.virus	Computer viruses forum

Group name	Description
comp.windows.interviews	InterViews object-orientated windowing system
comp.windows.misc	MS-Windows: miscellaneous discussion forum
comp.windows.ms	MS Windows: specific discussion forum
comp.windows.ms.programmer	MS-Windows: programmers forum
comp.windows.news	MS-Windows: new news
comp.windows.open-look	The 'Open Look' X-Windows environment
comp.windows.x	X-Windows discussion forum
comp.windows.x.announce	X-Windows user announcements
comp.windows.x.apps	X-Windows: applications
comp.windows.x.i386unix	XFree86 Window system et al.
comp.windows.x.intrinsics	X-Windows: the Xt Intrinsics system
comp.windows.x.motif	X-Windows: the X-Motif environment
comp.windows.x.pex	X-Windows: PeX

European network hierarchies (eunet.*)

European network (EUNET): miscellaneous topics.

Group name	Description
eunet.aviation	Aviation-related forum
eunet.bugs.4bsd	Bugs and fixes for BSD version 4 UNIX
eunet.bugs.uucp	UUCP bugs and fixes
eunet.esprit	The European ESPRIT project forum
eunet.europen	European news and views from EUNET
eunet.euug	The European User Group
eunet.jokes	Jokes forum
eunet.micro.acorn	Computer systems: Acorn
eunet.misc	Miscellaneous notes on EUNET
eunet.newprod	New product information
eunet.news	EUNET News discussion forum
eunet.politics	Political discussion forum
eunet.sources	Computer source code
eunet.test	Test forum only

Miscellaneous network hierarchies (misc.*)

The miscellaneous groups contain information on a wide variety of subject areas.

Group name	Description
misc.activism.progressive	Forum for the progresssive activist
misc.answers	FAQs and other goodies

Group name	Description
misc.books.technical	Technical books: reviews and news
misc.consumers	Consumer information: product reviews, etc.
misc.consumers.house	Consumer information: houses, ownership, etc.
misc.education	The education system discussed
misc.emerg-services	The emergency services: for paramedics, etc.
misc.entrepreneurs	Miscellaneous notes on running a business
misc.fitness	Fitness information: diet, exercise, etc.
misc.forsale	Miscellaneous items for sale (large group)
misc.forsale.comp	For sale: computers
misc.forsale.computers	For sale: computers
misc.forsale.computers.d	Discussion group for the above
misc.forsale.computers.mac	For sale: Mac computers
misc.forsale.computers.other	For sale: other computers
misc.forsale.computers.pc-clone	For sale: PCs and clones, etc.
misc.forsale.computers. workstation	For sale: workstation computers
misc.handicap	Items of interest for the handicapped
misc.headlines	Current interest: e.g. news
misc.health.alternative	Alternative health care and medicines, etc.
misc.health.diabetes	Diabetes discussed
misc.int-property	Intellectual property rights
misc.invest	Discussion forum on investment
misc.invest.real-estate	Investment in real estate (land, etc.)
misc.jobs.contract	Discussions about contract labour
misc.jobs.misc	Miscellaneous employment discussion forum
misc.jobs.offered	Miscellaneous jobs offered
misc.jobs.offered.entry	Job listings for entry-only positions
misc.jobs.resumes	Postings of résumés and situations wanted
misc.kids	Childrens behavioural patterns, etc.
misc.kids.computer	The use of computers by children
misc.legal	Legal issues and the law in general
misc.legal.computing	Computing and the law
misc.misc	Overspill for all other miscellaneous areas
misc.news.east-europe.rferl	Radio Free Europe/Radio Liberty
misc.news.southasia	News and discussion about South Asia
misc.rural	Rural living discussed
misc.security	Security discussion forum
misc.taxes	Tax laws; Questions and Answers, etc.
misc.test	Test forum only

Group name	Description
misc.wanted	Requests for items wanted (no computers)
misc.writing	Discussion forum for the writer

News (USENET) hierarchies (news.*)

The news hierarchy contains postings which are relevant to the USENET system itself only.

Group name	Description
news.admin	News administrators forums
news.admin.misc	General topics of interest to administrators
news.admin.policy	Policy issues for the USENET system
news.admin.technical	Technical aspects of maintaining USENET
news.announce.conferences	Conference announcements
news.announce.important	Important news
news.announce.newgroups	News on newsgroups
news.announce.newusers	Forum for new USENET users
news.answers	Period USENET articles: FAQs, etc.
news.config	System down-times and interruptions, etc.
news.future	The future of the USENET system
news.groups	Lists of newsgroups and discussion area
news.lists	Main list of USENET newsgroups/statistics
news.lists.ps-maps	USENET traffic-flows/statistics
news.misc	Discussions about USENET itself
news.newsites	New site announcements
news.newusers.questions	New users Question and Answer forum
news.software.anu-news	VMS B-News software and compatibles
news.software.b	Discussion about B-news compatible s/ware
news.software.nn	Discussion about the nn newsreader
news.software.nntp	Discussion about the NNTP news protocol
news.software.notes	Notefile software from Illinois University
news.software.readers	Discussion about newsreading packages
news.sysadmin	Postings directed to USENET administrators

Recreational hierarchies (rec.*)

Topics on recreational activities can be found in this newsgroup.

Group name	Description
rec.answers	FAQs and other periodical postings
rec.antiques	Antiques and other old items discussed (QA)
rec.aquaria	Keeping fish as a hobby
rec.arts.animation	Animation in the arts
rec.arts.anime	Japanese animation and drawings
rec.arts.anime.info	The art of animation
rec.arts.bodyart	Tattoos and other decorative body-art
rec.arts.books	Books and the publishing industry forum
rec.arts.books.tolkien	Books by the author J.R.R. Tolkien
rec.arts.cinema	Cinema and discussion of art in the cinema
rec.arts.comics.info	Information on comics; news and views, etc.
rec.arts.comics.marketplace	Comics in the marketplace; exchanges, etc.
rec.arts.comics.misc	Miscellaneous forum on comics
rec.arts.comics.strips	Short-form comic discussion forum
rec.arts.comics.xbooks	The mutuant universe of Marvel comics
rec.arts.dance	Dance in the arts
rec.arts.disney	Walt Disney related subject area, e.g. film
rec.arts.drwho	The 'Dr Who' sci-fi series forum
rec.arts.erotica	Erotic films and other written works
rec.arts.fine	Fine arts forum
rec.arts.int-fiction	Interactive fiction forum
rec.arts.manga	Japanese story-telling through comic art
rec.arts.misc	General arts discussion forum; events, etc.
rec.arts.movies	Movie discussion and movie making, etc.
rec.arts.movies.reviews	Reviews of the latest movie reviews
rec.arts.poems	Postings of poems
rec.arts.sf.announce	Sci-fi: announcements in the SF world
rec.arts.sf.fandom	Sci-fi: activites in the SF world
rec.arts.sf.marketplace	Sci-fi: for sale forum; mags, films, etc.
rec.arts.sf.misc	Sci-fi: general discussion forum
rec.arts.sf.movies	Sci-fi: SF movies discussed, etc.
rec.arts.sf.reviews	Sci-fi: reviews of SF movie and other works
rec.arts.sf.science	Sci-fi: real-life aspects of SF
rec.arts.sf.starwars	Sci-fi: 'Star Wars' fan forum
rec.arts.sf.tv	Sci-fi: SF on television forum

Group name	Description
rec.arts.sf.written	Sci-fi: written SF; discussion forum
rec.arts.startrek	It's life, but not as we know it Jim
rec.arts.startrek.current	Discussion of 'new-generation' Star Trek
rec.arts.startrek.fandom	Star Trek conventions and meetings, etc.
rec.arts.startrek.info	Information about the Star Trek series
rec.arts.startrek.misc	General discussion of Star Trek (Q&A)
rec.arts.startrek.reviews	Reviews of all things Trekkie
rec.arts.startrek.tech	Star Trek's depiction of future technology
rec.arts.theatre	The theatre and stagework forum
rec.arts.tv	Television – its history and future
rec.arts.tv.soaps	Soap operas on TV
rec.arts.tv.uk	TV in the United Kingdom
rec.arts.wobegon	Literature and music
rec.audio	High fidelity audio forum
rec.audio.car	In-car audio and hi-fi systems
rec.audio.high-end	High-end audio systems forum
rec.audio.pro	Profesional audio recording equipment, etc.
rec.autos	Cars and their laws, etc.
rec.autos.antique	Antique (vintage) cars
rec.autos.driving	Car drivers forum
rec.autos.sport	Racing and general car-sport forum
rec.autos.tech	Technical aspects of cars
rec.autos.vw	The Volkswagen car enthusiasts forum
rec.aviation	Aviation communities forum
rec.aviation.announce	Announcements in the world of aviation
rec.aviation.answers	Questions and answers about aviation
rec.aviation.homebuilt	Restoring and building aircraft
rec.aviation.ifr	Flying under Instrument Flight Rules (IFR)
rec.aviation.military	Military aircraft: past and present
rec.aviation.misc	Miscellaneous topics in aviation
rec.aviation.owning	Information related to ownership of planes
rec.aviation.piloting	Information on piloting an aircraft
rec.aviation.products	Aviation products for pilots, etc.
rec.aviation.simulators	Flight simulation systems forum
rec.aviation.soaring	Sail-planes and gliders
rec.aviation.stories	Aviation stories from readers
rec.aviation.student	Student aviators forum
rec.backcountry	Outdoor activities
rec.bicycles.marketplace	Bicycles on the market
rec.bicycles.misc	Miscellaneous forum on cycling
rec.bicycles.racing	Racing bikes forum
rec.bicycles.rides	Discussions on tours and commuting routes

Group name	Description
rec.bicycles.soc	Bicycles impact on society
rec.bicycles.tech	Technical bicycles notes; construction, etc.
rec.birds	Bird watching (Ornithology, that is)
rec.boats	Boats and boating forum
rec.boats.paddle	Boats that require human power
rec.climbing	Mountain climbing, etc. and techniques
rec.collecting	Collectors forum (all objects)
rec.crafts.brewing	Brewing as a hobby; beer, etc.
rec.crafts.metalworking	Working with metal
rec.crafts.misc	Miscellaneous crafts (overspill subjects)
rec.crafts.textiles	Textile crafts, e.g. sewing, weaving, etc.
rec.equestrian	Horse riding, etc.
rec.folk-dancing	Folk dancers forum
rec.food.cooking	Cooking and recipes, etc.
rec.food.drink	Drinking; wines and spirits, etc.
rec.food.historic	The history of food-making arts
rec.food.recipes	Recipes for a wide variety of dishes
rec.food.restaurants	Dining out forum
rec.food.sourdough	Baking with sourdough
rec.food.veg	Vegetarians forum
rec.gambling	Gamblers forum
rec.games.abstract	Pure strategy games, etc.
rec.games.backgammon	The game of backgammon
rec.games.board	Board games: general discussion forum
rec.games.board.ce	The 'Cosmic Encounter' board game
rec.games.bridge	The game of bridge
rec.games.chess	The game of chess
rec.games.corewar	The core ware computer game discussed
rec.games.cyber	CyberPunk-related games
rec.games.design	Designing games
rec.games.diplomacy	The diplomacy conquest game
rec.games.frp.advocacy	Flames and rebuttals about games
rec.games.frp.announce	Role-playing announcements
rec.games.frp.archives	Archived fantasy stories and projects
rec.games.frp.cyber	Cyperpunk role-playing games
rec.games.frp.dnd	TSR's Dungeons 'n Dragons game
rec.games.frp.marketplace	Role-playing games: for sale and wanted
rec.games.frp.misc	General discussion of role-playing games
rec.games.go	The game of Go!
rec.games.hack	The hack and nethack games discussed
rec.games.int-fiction	Interactive fiction games
rec.games.misc	Games and computer games forum
rec.games.moria	The Moria game discussed
rec.games.mud	Multi-user dimension/dungeon games
rec.games.mud.admin	Administrator notes for MUD games
rec.games.mud.announce	Announcements in the MUD world

Group name	Description
rec.games.mud.diku	DikuMUD games forum
rec.games.mud.lp	LpMUD games forum
rec.games.mud.misc	Miscellaneous MUD forum
rec.games.mud.tiny	TinyMUD games forum
rec.games.netrek	The Netrek and XtrekII games
rec.games.pbm	Forum for play-by-mail games
rec.games.pinball	Pinball machines and issues
rec.games.programmer	Adventure-game programmers forum
rec.games.rogue	The Rogue game discussed
rec.games.trivia	Discussion forum about Trivia
rec.games.vectrex	The Vectrex game system
rec.games.video	Video games forum
rec.games.video.arcade	Video arcade games forum
rec.games.video.classic	Classic video games of the past
rec.games.video.marketplace	Video games for sale/swapping
rec.games.video.misc	Miscellaneous video game discussion forum
rec.games.video.nintendo	Nintendo video games discussed
rec.games.video.sega	Sega video games discussed
rec.games.xtank.play	Notes for the game of Xtank
rec.games.xtank.programmer	Programmer notes for the game of Xtank
rec.gardens	Gardeners forum
rec.guns	Firearms forum
rec.golf	Games: golf
rec.ham-radio	Ham radio enthusiasts forum
rec.ham-radio.packet	Packet radio forum
rec.heraldry	Coats of arms and all things heraldic
rec.humor	Jokes newsgroup (all tastes!)
rec.humor.d	Discussion about the jokes in rec.humor
rec.humor.funny	Jokes the moderator thinks are funny
rec.humor.oracle	Advice from the USENET Oracle
rec.humor.oracle.d	Comments about the USENET Oracle service
rec.hunting	For the indescribable after the inedible
rec.juggling	Jugglers forum; events and techniques, etc.
rec.kites	Kites and kiting, etc.
rec.mag	Magazine summaries, etc.
rec.mag.fsfnet	Science fiction fanzine
rec.martial-arts	Martial arts magazines
rec.misc	Recreational activities in general
rec.models.railroad	Model railroads/railways
rec.models.rc	Radio control forum
rec.models.rockets	Model rockets for hobbyists
rec.models.scale	Scale modelling
rec.motorcycles	Motorcycling, etc.

Group name	Description
rec.motorcycles.dirt	Off-road motorcycling
rec.motorcycles.harley	Harley Davidson riders forum
rec.motorcycles.racing	Racing motorcyclists forum
rec.music.afro-latin	Music: Afro-Latin music
rec.music.beatles	Music: The Beatles and their music
rec.music.bluenote	Music: Jazz, blues, etc.
rec.music.cd	Music: compact disk (CD) music
rec.music.christian	Music: Christian music: contemporary/ traditional
rec.music.classical	Music: classical music
rec.music.classical.guitar	Music: classical guitar music
rec.music.compose	Music: creating music and lyrical works
rec.music.country.western	Music: country and western music
rec.music.dementia	Music: comedy music forum
rec.music.dylan	Music: the music of Bob Dylan
rec.music.early	Music: pre-classical music
rec.music.folk	Music: folk music
rec.music.funky	Music: funk, jazz-funk, etc.
rec.music.gaffa	Music: alternative music
rec.music.gdead	Music: music of the 'Grateful Dead'
rec.music.indian.classical	Music: Indian classical music: Hindustani, etc.
rec.music.indian.misc	Music: miscellaneous Indian music discussed
rec.music.industrial	Music: industrial-related music
rec.music.info	Music: information on all musical topics
rec.music.makers	Music: information for musical performers
rec.music.makers.bass	Music: information for bass guitarists
rec.music.makers.guitar	Music: information for guitarists
rec.music.makers.guitar. tablature	Music: guitar tablature, chords, etc.
rec.music.makers.percussion	Music: information for percussionists/ drummers
rec.music.makers.synth	Music: information for synthesizer operators
rec.music.marketplace	Music: for sale and wanted in the marketplace
rec.music.misc	Music: miscellaneous music forum
rec.music.newage	Music: 'new age' music
rec.music.phish	Music: the Music of Phish
rec.music.reggae	Music: Reggae music
rec.music.reviews	Music: music reviews
rec.music.synth	Music: synthesizer music/electronic/ computer music
rec.music.video	Music: music videos/MTV, etc.
rec.nude	Naturist activites; nudists, etc.
rec.org.mensa	Mensa forum (high-IQ people)

Group name	Description
rec.org.sca	Create Anarchism forum
rec.outdoors.fishing	Fishing in the wilds
rec.pets	Pet keepers forum
rec.pets.birds	Pets: birds
rec.pets.cats	Pets: cats
rec.pets.dogs	Pets: dogs
rec.pets.herp	Pets: reptiles and other exotic pets
rec.photo	Photography forum
rec.puzzles	Puzzles and quizzes enthusiasts forum
rec.puzzles.crosswords	Crossword puzzles; making and playing
rec.pyrotechnics	Fire, fireworks, rockets and other topics
rec.radio.amateur.misc	Amateur radio enthusiasts forum
rec.radio.amateur.packet	Packet radio enthusiasts forum
rec.radio.amateur.policy	Radio enthusiasts regulations, etc.
rec.radio.broadcasting	Local area broadcast radio forum
rec.radio.cb	CB radio enthusiasts forum
rec.radio.noncomm	Non-commerical radio forum
rec.radio.shortwave	Shortwave radio forum
rec.radio.swap	Swap and trade equipment between people
rec.railroad	Real and model trains forum
rec.roller-coaster	Roller-coaster and other similar rides
rec.running	Running for sport and fitness
rec.scouting	Youth scouting organizations forum
rec.scuba	Scuba diving
rec.skate	Skating (ice/roller)
rec.skiing	Skiing; snow skiing, etc.
rec.skydiving	Sky diving forum
rec.sport.baseball	Sport: baseball
rec.sport.cricket	Sport: cricket
rec.sport.cricket.scores	Cricket scores
rec.sport.disc	Flying disc-based sports
rec.sport.fencing	Sport: fencing
rec.sport.football	Sport: football
rec.sport.golf	Sport: golf
rec.sport.hockey	Sport: hockey
rec.sport.misc	Miscellaneous sport discussions
rec.sport.olympics	Olympic sports news
rec.sport.paintball	The paintball survival game
rec.sport.pro-wrestling	Professional wrestling
rec.sport.rugby	Sport: rugby
rec.sport.soccer	Sport: soccer
rec.sport.swimming	Sport: swimming
rec.sport.table-tennis	Sport: table-tennis
rec.sport.tennis	Sport: tennis
rec.sport.triathlon	Sport: the triathalon event
rec.sport.volleyball	Sport: volleyball
rec.travel	Travel forum

Group name	Description
rec.travel.air	Travelling by air
rec.video	Video and video components
rec.video.cable-tv	Video and cable-TV
rec.video.production	Video production methods
rec.video.releases	New releases on video discussed
rec.video.satellite	Satellite TV, etc.
rec.windsurfing	Windsurfers group
rec.woodworking	Woodworkers group

Scientific hierarchies (sci.*)

Scientific information is maintained in this hierarchy.

Group name	Description
sci.aeronautics	Aeronautics and related technologies
sci.aeronautics.airliners	Airliner technology
sci.answers	FAQs and other periodicals
sci.anthropology	Mankind and origins
sci.aquaria	Collecting fish and other aquatic life
sci.archaeology	Archaelogy forum
sci.astro	Astronomers forum
sci.astro.fits	Flexible image transport system
sci.astro.hubble	The Hubble telescope system
sci.bio	Biology and related sciences
sci.bio.technology	Technology in the biological sciences
sci.chem	Chemistry and related sciences forum
sci.chem.organomet	Organometallic chemistry
sci.classics	Studying classical history
sci.cognitive	Cognitive science: human factors, etc.
sci.comp-aided	Computers as tools in scientific research
sci.cryonics	Suspended animation, biostatis, etc.
sci.crypt	Data encryptiona and decryption, etc.
sci.econ	The science of economics
sci.edu	The science of education
sci.electronics	Electronic theory
sci.energy	Energy in science and technology
sci.engr	Technical discussions regarding Engineering tasks
sci.engr.biomed	Biomedical engineering
sci.engr.chem	Chemical engineering
sci.engr.civil	Civil engineering
sci.engr.control	The engineering of control systems
sci.engr.mech	Mechanical engineering
sci.environment	The environment and ecology
sci.fractals	Chaos-related information
sci.geo.fluids	Geophysical fluid dynamics

Group name	Description
sci.geo.geology	The solid-earth sciences
sci.geo.meteorology	Weather-related sciences
sci.image.processing	Image processing and analysis in science
sci.lang	Language and communication in science
sci.lang.japan	Japanese science forum
sci.life-extension	Forum discussing age prolongment (see: .cryonics)
sci.logic	Logic, philosophy and computational science
sci.materials	Aspects of material engineering
sci.math	Mathematical discussions and pursuits
sci.math.num-analysis	Numeric analysis
sci.math.research	Current research in mathematical science
sci.math.stat	Statistical branch of mathematics
sci.math.symbolic	Symbolic algebra discussion
sci.med	Medicine and related topics
sci.med.aids	AIDS/HIV discussion forum
sci.med.dentistry	Dentistry forum
sci.med.nutrition	Dietary topics forum
sci.med.occupational	Treating and preventing occupational injury
sci.med.physics	Issues of physics in medical care
sci.med.telemedicine	Clinical consulting through computer networks
sci.military	Science and the military
sci.misc	General interest topics
sci.nanotech	Molecular-scale, self-reproducing machines
sci.optics	Optical science, e.g. lasers, etc.
sci.philosophy.meta	Metaphilosophy forum
sci.philosophy.tech	Technical philosophy: logic, maths, etc.
sci.physics	Physics laws and properties, etc.
sci.physics.fusion	The study of fusion as a new power source
sci.physics.research	Current research in the physics world
sci.psychology	Psychology-related discussion forum
sci.psychology.digest	The Psychology Journal
sci.research	Research methods: funding and ethics, etc.
sci.research.careers	Careers in science: general information
sci.skeptic	Science skeptics: pseudo-science, etc.
sci.space	Space-related science
sci.space.news	Space-related news
sci.space.shuttle	News regarding the NASA space shuttle
sci.systems	Theory and application of systems science
sci.virtual-worlds	The modelling of fictitious universes
sci.virtual-worlds.apps	Applications for modelling virtual worlds

Social hierarchies (soc.*)

The social hierarchy contains newsgroups that pertain solely to social issues affecting people and their countries.

Group name	Description
soc.answers	Periodic USENET mailings, e.g. FAQs, etc.
soc.bi	Bisexuality discussion forum
soc.college	Collge and campus life
soc.college.grad	Graduate schools
soc.college.gradinfo	Information about graduate schools
soc.couples	Discussions for couples
soc.culture.afghanistan	The culture of Afghanistan
soc.culture.african	The culture of Africa
soc.culture.african.american	The culture of African-Americans
soc.culture.arabic	The culture of Arabia
soc.culture.asean	The culture of the SE Asian nations
soc.culture.asian.american	The culture of Asian-Americans
soc.culture.australian	The culture of Australia
soc.culture.baltics	The culture of the Baltic states
soc.culture.bangladesh	The culture of Bangladesh
soc.culture.bosnia-herzgvna	The culture of Bosnia
soc.culture.brazil	The culture of Brazil
soc.culture.british	The culture of the British
soc.culture.bulgaria	The culture of Bulgaria
soc.culture.canada	The culture of Canada
soc.culture.caribbean	The culture of the Caribbean
soc.culture.celtic	The culture of the Irish, Scottish, Welsh
soc.culture.china	The culture of China
soc.culture.czecho-slovak	The culture of Bohemia, Slovak and Silesia
soc.culture.esperanto	The international language
soc.culture.europe	The culture of Europe
soc.culture.filipino	The culture of the Philippines
soc.culture.french	The culture of France
soc.culture.german	The culture of Germany
soc.culture.greek	The culture of Greece
soc.culture.hongkong	The culture of Hong Kong
soc.culture.indian	The culture of India
soc.culture.indian.telugu	The culture of the Telugu people of India
soc.culture.iranian	The culture of Iran
soc.culture.italian	The culture of Italy
soc.culture.japan	The culture of Japan
soc.culture.jewish	The Jewish religion and culture
soc.culture.korean	The culture of Korea
soc.culture.latin-america	The culture of Latin America
soc.culture.lebanon	The culture of the Lebanese
soc.culture.magyar	The culture of Hungary
soc.culture.malaysia	The culture of Malaysia

Group name	Description
soc.culture.mexican	The culture of Mexico
soc.culture.misc	Miscellaneous culture discussion forum
soc.culture.nepal	The culture of Nepal
soc.culture.netherlands	The culture of the Netherlands and Belgium
soc.culture.new-zealand	The culture of New Zealand
soc.culture.nordic	The culture of the Nordics
soc.culture.pakistan	The culture of Pakistan
soc.culture.polish	The culture of Poland
soc.culture.portuguese	The culture of Portugal
soc.culture.romanian	The culture of the Romanians and Moldavians
soc.culture.soviet	The culture of the former Soviet Union
soc.culture.spain	The culture of Spain
soc.culture.sri-lanka	The culture of Sri Lanka
soc.culture.taiwan	The culture of the Taiwanese
soc.culture.tamil	The culture of the Tamil people
soc.culture.thai	The culture of Thailand
soc.culture.turkish	The culture of Turkey
soc.culture.usa	The culture of United States of America
soc.culture.vietnamese	The culture of the Vietnamese
soc.culture.yugoslavia	The culture of Yugoslavia
soc.feminism	Feminists forum
soc.history	Discussion of general history/social issues
soc.libraries.talk	Libraries discussion forum
soc.men	Male issues
soc.misc	Miscellaneous social issues discussed
soc.motss	Social contacts: homosexuality/lesbianism
soc.net-people	Announcements and requests about net people
soc.penpals	Pen-pals forum
soc.politics	Politics in society
soc.politics.arms-d	Arms discussion digest (ADD)
soc.religion.bahai	Discussion of Baha'i faith
soc.religion.christian	Christianity related topics
soc.religion.christian.bible-study	Biblical studies
soc.religion.eastern	Eastern religions discussed
soc.religion.islam	The Islam religion
soc.religion.quaker	The Quaker way of life
soc.rights.human	Human rights, e.g. Amnesty International, etc.
soc.roots	Family origins; genealogical matters, etc.
soc.singles	Newsgroup for single people and activities
soc.veterans	Military veterans from wars past
soc.women	Issues relating to woman

Talk hierarchies (talk.*)

The talk hierarchy is a place where general chatting on controversial topics can take place. A good argumentative series of forums.

Group name	Description
talk.abortion	Arguments and discussion regarding abortion
talk.answers	Periodic postings: FAQs, etc.
talk.bizarre	Bizarre and curious discussions
talk.environment	Discussing the environment
talk.origins	Darwinism vs creation; many arguments!
talk.philosophy.misc	Philosophical discussion forum
talk.politics.animals	Abuse of animals by humans
talk.politics.china	Chinese politics forum
talk.politics.drugs	Drugs and poltical issues relating to them
talk.politics.guns	Guns and their political impact
talk.politics.medicine	Medicine and politics
talk.politics.mideast	Middle-East politics
talk.politics.misc	Miscellaneous politics
talk.politics.soviet	Politics of the former Soviet Union
talk.politics.space	Space politics, e.g. 'Star Wars', spying, etc.
talk.politics.theory	Theory behind political systems
talk.rape	Rape and its effects
talk.religion.misc	Religious chit-chat forum
talk.religion.newage	Esoteric religions and ways-of-life
talk.rumors	Rumours about future events

United Kingdom hierarchies (uk.*)

Newsgroups specific to the United Kingdom have been included for UK USENET users.

Group name	Description
uk.announce	UK announcements for USENET users
uk.bcs.announce	British Computer Society announcements
uk.bcs.misc	British Computer Society news forum
uk.events	Events around the UK (computing, etc.)
uk.jips	The JANET/IP project forum
uk.jobs	Computing jobs in the UK (offered/wanted)
uk.lisp	LISP language forum
uk.misc	Miscellaneous UK-related news
uk.net	UK-NETs news forum
uk.net.maps	UK-NET connectivity, etc.

Group name	Description
uk.net.news	UK-NET miscellaneous news
uk.politics	UK politics; party talk, etc.
uk.sources	Sources of information on UK systems
uk.sun	Sun Microsystems UK forum
uk.telecom	UK telecommunications forum
uk.test	Test forum only
uk.tex	UK TeX users forum
uk.transport	Discussion about the UK transport system
uk.ukuug	UK Unix users group

United States hierarchies (us.*)

Newsgroups specific to the United States are given here.

Group name	Description
us.arts.tv.soaps	Soap operas on US TV
us.forsale.computers	Computer equipment for sale
us.forsale.d	Discussion group for the above
us.forsale.misc	Items for sale (not computers)
us.jobs.contract	Contractual employment news
us.jobs.misc	Miscellaneous employment news
us.jobs.offered	Jobs offered
us.jobs.resumes	Job résumés
us.legal	US Legal information
us.misc	Miscellaneous US-related discussions
us.politics.abortion	Abortion-related newsgroup
us.sport.baseball	US sport: baseball
us.sport.football.misc	US sport: football
us.sport.misc	Miscellaenous US sports
us.taxes	US tax information
us.test	Test forum only
us.usenet	United States USENET forum
us.wanted.misc	Items wanted (miscellaneous)

K12 school hierarchies (k12.*)

The k12.* hierarchy is of interest to teachers and educationalists whose schools are connected to the Internet. Mainly biased towards the US, although the information can be useful to all people with an interest in teaching and education generally.

Group name	Description
k12.chat.elementary	Elementary students: grades K–5
k12.chat.junior	Elementary students: grades 6–8
k12.chat.senior	High-school students forum
k12.chat.teacher	Teachers forum
k12.ed.art	Art curriculum forum
k12.ed.business	Business education curriculum
k12.ed.comp.literacy	Computer literacy forum
k12.ed.health-pe	Physical education (PE), etc.
k12.ed.life-skills	Home economics and career related
k12.ed.math	Mathematics
k12.ed.music	Music and the performimg arts, e.g. drama
k12.ed.science	The sciences: biology, chemistry, etc.
k12.ed.soc-studies	Social studies forum
k12.ed.special	Students with special needs/handicaps, etc.
k12.ed.tag	For talented and gifted students
k12.ed.tech	Industrial arts and vocational education
k12.lang.art	Language arts
k12.lang.deutsch-eng	German/English practice with native speakers
k12.lang.francais	French/English practice with native speakers
k12.lang.russian	Russian/English practice with native speakers
k12.library	For libraries and librarians
k12.sys.channel0	Teachers forum 0
k12.sys.channel1	Teachers forum 1
k12.sys.channel2	Teachers forum 2
k12.sys.channel3	Teachers forum 3
k12.sys.channel4	Teachers forum 4
k12.sys.channel5	Teachers forum 5
k12.sys.channel6	Teachers forum 6
k12.sys.channel7	Teachers forum 7
k12.sys.channel8	Teachers forum 8
k12.sys.channel9	Teachers forum 9
k12.sys.channel10	Teachers forum 10
k12.sys.channel11	Teachers forum 11
k12.sys.channel12	Teachers forum 12
k12.sys.projects	Teaching projects

Index